MAGIC LANTERN ART

Magic Lantern Art: The American Screen's First Great Narrative Artist, Joseph Boggs Beale

TERRY BORTON

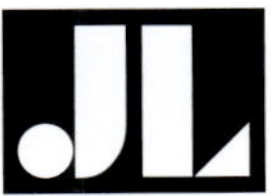

British Library Cataloguing in Publication Data

Magic Lantern Art:
The American Screen's
First Great Narrative Artist,
Joseph Boggs Beale

Borton, Terry

A catalogue entry for this book is available from the British Library

Hardback ISBN: 9780 86196 758 2
Paperback ISBN: 9780 86196 759 9
EPUB: 9780 86196 997 5
EPDF: 9780 86196 998 2

Published by
John Libbey Publishing, 205 Crescent Road, New Barnet, Herts EN4 8SB, United Kingdom
e-mail: johnlibbeypublishing@gmail.com; web site: www.johnlibbey.com

Distributed Worldwide by
Indiana University Press, Herman B Wells Library – 350, 1320 E. 10th St.,
Bloomington, IN 47405, USA. www.iupress.indiana.edu

Printed and bound in China by 1010 Printing.

Contents

Pre-Publication Reviews of *Magic Lantern Art*

A groundbreaking book ... As fascinating as it is convincing ... Restores a lost chapter to the history of narrative art.
– Shalyn Claggett, Ph. D., Professor of Victorian Studies, author, *Equal Natures*

One of America's foremost magic lanternists shares his knowledge and reflections on the exceptional artistry of slide designer Joseph Boggs Beale.
– Jeremy Brooker, Ph. D., author, Past President, The Magic Lantern Society

Reviews of The American Magic Lantern Theater

(The American Magic Lantern Theater, directed by Terry Borton, toured nationally for 25 years, re-creating magic-lantern shows using Beale's slides.)

"An incredible experience ... If they come to your town, don't miss them. They're a living national treasure."
National Public Radio

"One of the nation's most remarkable theater productions. You'll be enthralled, enchanted, and totally engaged in this captivating performance."
The Family Adventure Guide to Connecticut

"The ideal way to enjoy the show (*you'll cry as well as laugh*) is to sit between one of your own parents and a child."
Middlesex Magazine

"The audience for this show was the most enthusiastic crowd I've witnessed in my 20 years of presenting at the National Gallery".
Peggy Parsons, National Gallery of Art

Acknowledgements

Above all I'd like to thank my wife, Deborah Borton, for her willingness to read and re-read this book in many versions over many years. Her comments have been invaluable. I'd also like to thank those who have read the current or previous drafts and offered very helpful suggestions, or contributed substantially in other ways: Dick Balzer, Lady Borton, Lynn Borton, Mark Borton, Jeremy Brooker, Shayln Claggett, Erkki Huhtamo, Jack Judson, Charles Long, Dick Moore, Charles Musser, Gary Rhodes, George Caughey, Paul Schweizer, David Shipman, Artemis Willis, the staff of the George Eastman Museum, the staff of the Lucas Museum of Narrative Art, and John Libbey Publishing.

Picture Credits

All pictures are from the author's collection unless otherwise indicated. Except for family photos, the artifacts from which the photos were made are now in the collection of the Lucas Museum of Narrative Art in Los Angeles. Some pictures have been digitally enhanced to increase clarity.

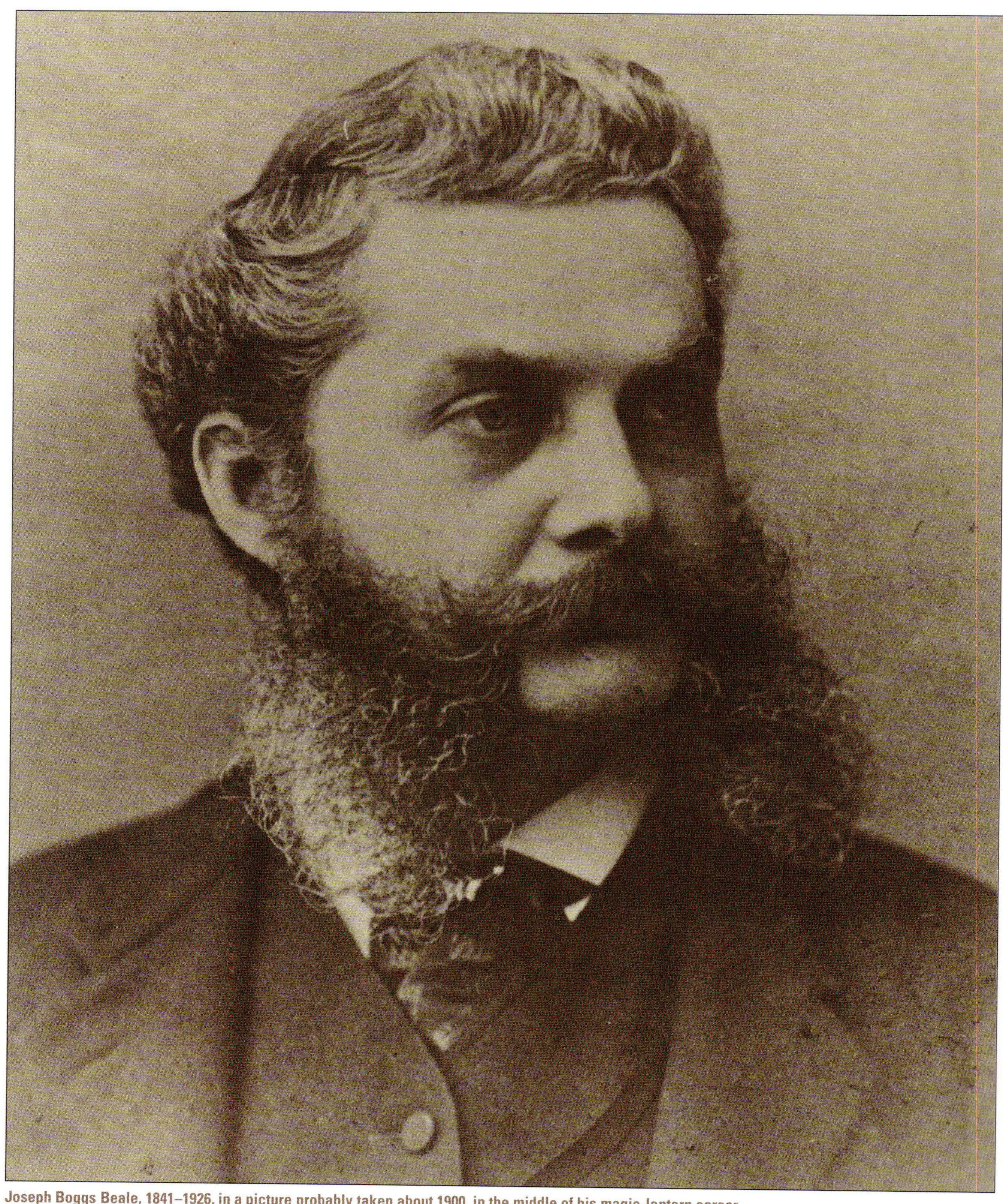

Joseph Boggs Beale, 1841–1926, in a picture probably taken about 1900, in the middle of his magic-lantern career.

Chapter One

End of an Era – Start of a Passion

Fig. 1.3 Slide 12 from Beale's set of *Hiawatha*. Description on p. 3.

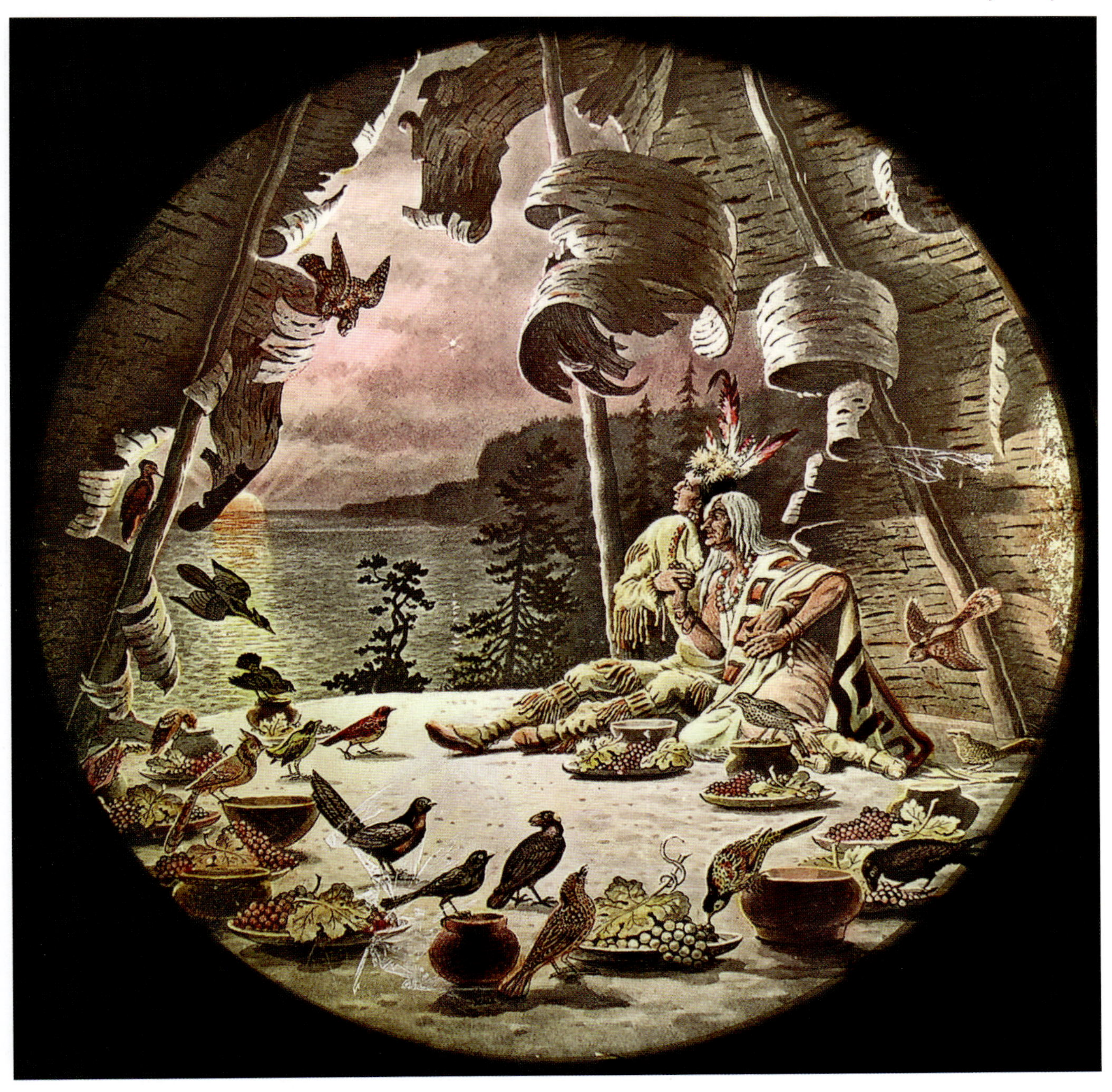

1909 – Philadelphia, Pennsylvania

Two unrelated events that will reconnect about a hundred years later:

That fall, Joseph Boggs Beale, America's leading artist for the magic lantern projector, received a devastating letter.[1] It marked the ending of his magic lantern career, and the ending of an era. Magic lantern shows had been one of the most significant educational and entertainment media of its time. Suddenly, 250 years of magic lantern art were drawing to a close. Within 10 or 15 years, magic lantern entertainment would have largely disappeared.

And by pure happenstance, at just about this time, and just down the street, my great grandfather gave a magic lantern show for his grandchildren. His show delighted the little boy who would later become my father. Such shows became a seminal experience in my family – the excitement passed down through four generations. Eventually it led to my career researching Beale's life and paintings, performing his magic lantern slides on the nation's stages, and writing this book on magic lantern art.

Joseph Boggs Beale

By the end of his career, Beale had painted 2,085 master designs for lantern projection. Because the same image was often sold under different names, Beale actually produced 2,621 different slides – illustrating literature, history, current events, the Bible, and comedy (Fig. 1.1). He was the largest single creator of slide imagery for the American lantern medium, producing nine-to-ten percent of *all* the 20,000 to 25,000 slides commonly offered for sale in the lantern catalogs at the end of the lantern era. Millions of people saw and admired his work every year.[2] His magic lantern narrative art, his visual storytelling skills, were unmatched in the industry at the time, and they continued to be recognized after his death. In 1940, for instance, *Life* magazine, the leading illustrated journal of the 20th century, devoted a four-page spread to his work, calling him, "A Great Magic Lantern Artist".[3] Yet despite Beale's success, that 1909 letter from Beale's employer, Casper W. Briggs, said that he was laid off. His magic lantern career was ending because of the explosive growth of the lantern's new competitor, the movies.

From 1881 to 1909, Beale had worked as the Briggs Company's primary artist, producing what Briggs and Beale called the master "designs" – the paintings or "wash drawings" from which the company made glass lantern slides.[4] The Briggs factory manufactured slides renowned for their quality and brilliant color, which could then be projected on a screen by magic lanterns – large mahogany-and-brass (or black-metal) machines that were the ancestors of today's slide and movie projectors.

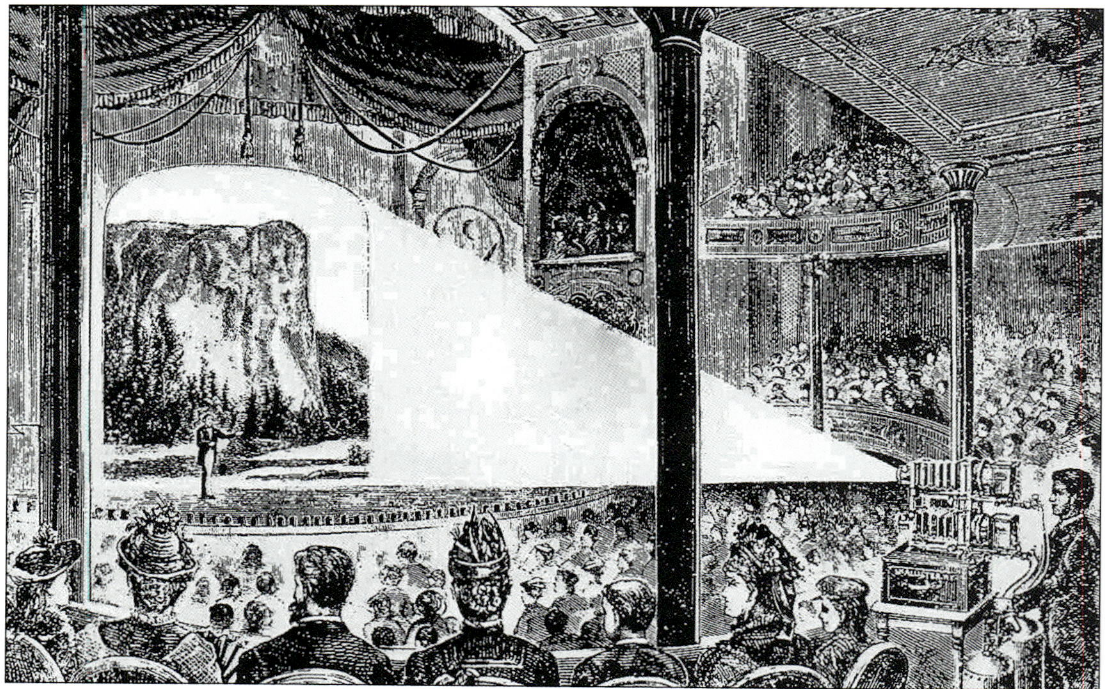

Fig. 1.1 A magic lantern show, in a picture by the McAllister lantern slide company. Lantern shows in large halls like this were common. The magic lantern projector and its operator are at right, the showman on stage.

As we will see in the next two chapters, Beale had come to his job at the Briggs company with a rich artistic background – a childhood filled with art, and 15 years working as a commercial illustrator for some of the nation's leading companies. The Briggs company had an outstanding reputation and was an ideal fit for Beale, although the artistic procedures of the magic lantern medium were mostly new to him. Early in his work at the company Beale learned the techniques of sequential narrative art and became very sophisticated in their use, which added significantly to the appeal of his slides. Although Beale's name was largely unknown because it was rarely promoted to slide audiences, his art was probably as familiar to his generation as Norman Rockwell's would be to a new generation 50 years later.

Briggs had hired Beale to help fulfill his vision of bringing great secular and religious literature to the screen. The slide production procedure for achieving that vision was complicated and unique. Nowhere else in America was art being created as it was in the Briggs company. The process began when Briggs selected a subject for a set of magic lantern illustrations, perhaps the poem, *The Night Before Christmas*, or the novel, *Ben Hur*. Then Beale illustrated the work by creating a set of six to 24 black-and-white designs on paper. The Briggs company photographed Beale's designs, printed them to emulsion-covered glass slides, and then meticulously hand-colored them (Fig. 1.2). One Beale design might result in a hundred slide copies, or a thousand, or for some images, perhaps ten thousand. Over the years Briggs probably sold between 1,300,000 and 2,200,000 Beale slides.[5] But audiences never saw the original paintings or the slides; they saw the projected image made from them.

Lanternists used Beale's lantern slides to produce shows of all sorts. Story-telling shows and their more sedate (but still very popular) cousins, the "illustrated lecture", could be seen everywhere. Huge audiences watched them every year – in schools, churches, fraternal or secret societies, homes, and theaters. Audiences certainly knew Beale's images by their distinctive style, but they did not know his name as did the showmen who purchased them from the lantern-slide catalogs where "By Beale" was touted. That lack of name recognition by mass audiences is one of the reasons that Beale's work is not better known today.

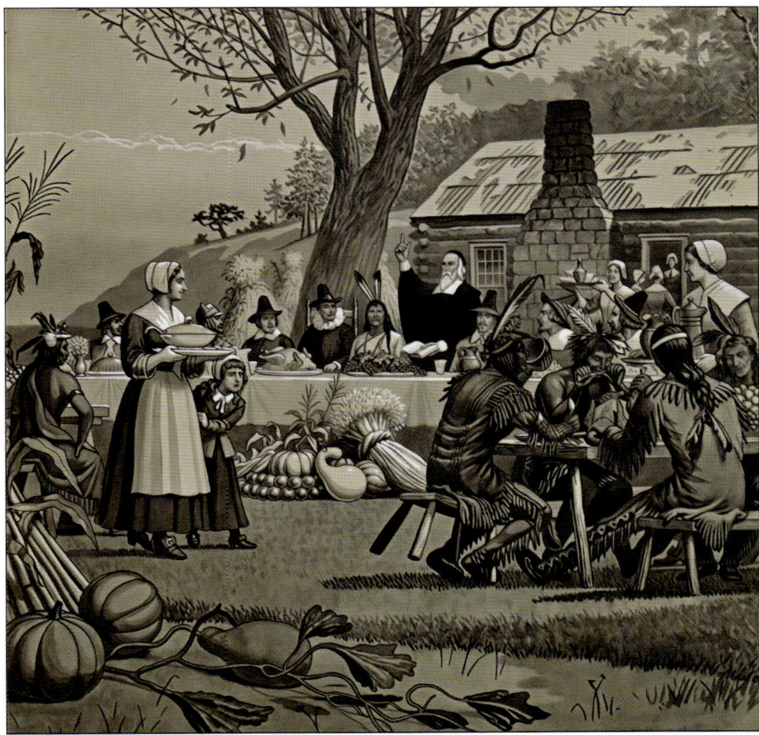

Whether recognized by name or not, Beale was a master of narrative art, of using sequential still images to make the drama flow on screen. The introductory image for this chapter, Fig. 1.3, is a good example. Within the story of *Hiawatha*, Beale illustrates an Indian storyteller's "wondrous tale" about an old man miraculously turned into a young man. He uses a *framing device* in the form of curling birchbark to separate the storyteller's tale from the larger story

Fig. 1.2 Beale's master design (top) for "The First Thanksgiving". It is painted on paper, in monochrome, about 13" x 13". The hand-colored glass slide Briggs made from it (bottom), is a 3" image.

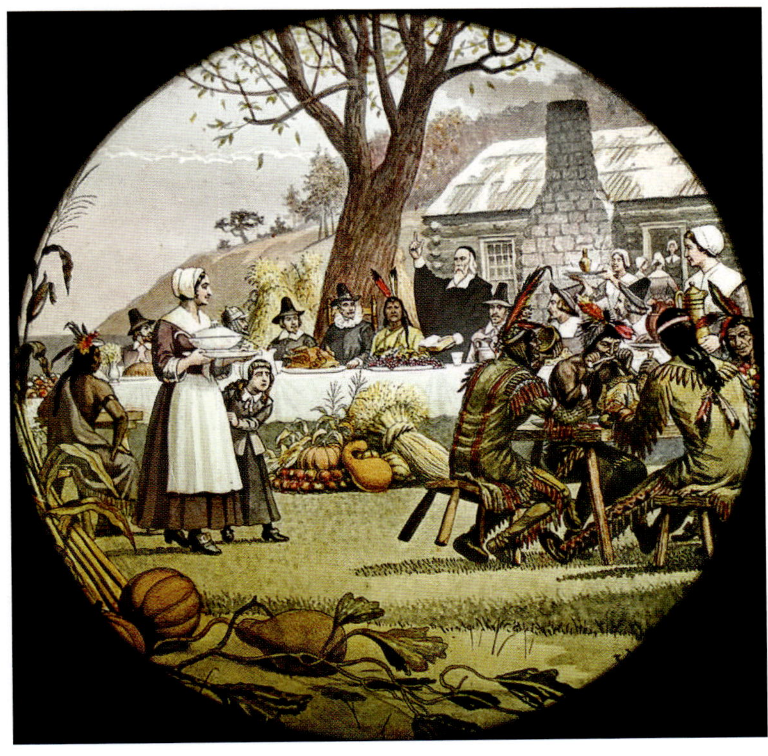

about Hiawatha himself. The birchbark also gives a greater sense of depth, and locates the audience inside the wigwam, inside the storyteller's mythic world. It's a complex example of narrative art, a story within a story, visually dramatized in a stunning composition.

I use the term "narrative art" to distinguish art that "tells a story" from that which usually does not, like abstract art, portraits, and landscapes. Narrative art can be a single picture – think Norman Rockwell again – or a series of pictures, like a set of Beale lantern slides. It is an art tradition that can be seen 20,000 years ago in the cave paintings of France, in the carvings of the late-dynasty pyramids, in the Sistine Chapel, in the "history painting" of the fine-arts movement of the 1700s and 1800s, and in the story-telling painting so popular in the 19th century. In the last half of the 19th century, when Beale was studying art and working for Briggs, it was the predominate fine-arts tradition in America. It avoided the romanticism of earlier styles, and – responding to the rapid spread of photography – it stressed realism anchored by accurate detail. Beale's magic lantern art clearly falls within this tradition, but by the end of the century the tradition itself was declining. In the fine arts, the rise of modernists and abstract art at the beginning of the 20th century pushed it aside for a time. In the 21st century it is attracting attention once again in several different genres: in the fine arts, in graphic novels, in comics, in interactive video games, and of course, in the movies.[6]

What is Magic Lantern Art?

In this book I'll be investigating a specific genre of narrative art, one that was very widely seen in the 19th and early 20th centuries, but is little known today: magic lantern art. I won't be dealing much with the photographic "illustrated lectures" that also used the lantern, but will concentrate instead on hand-drawn storytelling images such as Beale's. Until the movies arrived in America in 1896, and except for the moving panorama (a giant painted scroll), there was almost no other visual art experience like it – not in galleries, not in books, not in the great museums, not in sculpture gardens, not on the walls of private homes. Today we are so used to watching movies that it is hard for us to understand what watching lantern shows was like for these early audiences. For them, magic lantern art was radically different from their experience with almost any other form of the visual arts:

> They never saw physical "magic lantern" art objects – lantern paintings or slides. These were simply production materials. For us today to think that they are "magic lantern art" is like thinking a strip of film is a movie. They experienced magic lantern art as a *show*.
>
> The show's pictures were not episodic, as in book illustration, but sequential images, specifically designed to tell a story. Except for the moving panorama and a small number of story-telling stereo cards, that concept was rare in the American mass market until the first comics appeared in 1895.
>
> The show was not viewed by a single person or in small groups, but in a large audience. It was a live, communal experience, but the audience did not make the decisions. The showman controlled the content, the pace, the audience behavior.
>
> Audiences did not view the pictures in a lighted gallery or beneath an armchair lamp, but in the dark. Audience members were hidden, sitting among many other people, but not easily seen. Anonymity increased communal involvement.
>
> Most of Beale's magic lantern slides were in color. Color art was scarce at the time. The well-off enjoyed color paintings and picture books, but other than Currier and Ives prints, most people saw only black and white images. Beale's color slides were showstoppers.
>
> The color images were projected with a powerful light onto a screen. That gave them a brilliance that no painting could hope to achieve. The lighted screen in the dark became the only world the audience could see; the *story-world* was the only world that existed.
>
> The pictures were huge – 8, 12, sometimes 20 feet in diameter – much larger than most gallery art, and much, much larger than book illustrations. Life-size or more, they offered an immersive experience, a colorful, spotlit world to enter, explore, and enjoy.
>
> The lantern illustrations did not compete for attention with writing, as pictures did in children's books. The illustrations had the audience's total visual attention. The words were spoken – dramatized by the showman – a primal story-telling voice in the dark.
>
> The lantern illustrations and the narration did not exist by themselves. They were often

> supported by music and sound effects. The audience participated, singing along with the songs, chanting, interacting with the showman.
>
> The lantern images were not static as in a book or a gallery. Special lantern manipulations like "dissolves" and "superimpositions" increased the drama. Sophisticated techniques of visual narrative held audience attention and immersed them in the story.
>
> Serious literature, such as that often illustrated by Beale, might well be mixed with animated cartoons, created with moving pieces of glass. The cartoons delighted all elements of the audience, but especially the children. Magic lantern art was fun.
>
> The illustrations were ephemeral. There was no returning to a painting to look again, no way to turn back the page of a picture book. Magic lantern art was seen on screen, then lost to the dark. It was elusive, mysterious, an art of the moment.

In the following pages I'll be digging into the nuances of this magic lantern art – and in particular the techniques that Beale used to bring his screen world to life. In doing so I'll draw on authors who have defined the techniques of other genres of narrative art.[7] Most especially – because of the close links between the magic lantern and the movies – I'll draw on the many books about the techniques of cinema. In fact, almost all introductory college books on the movies define "the art of film" in terms of the techniques used – *flashbacks, storyboards, close ups* and the like.[8]

A review of the techniques listed in such books demonstrates that Beale was using about 100 of these "cinema techniques". He used them well before the movies, and he used them in a consistent, self-aware fashion. I refer to them here as "cinematic" techniques – "like cinema" – since their magic lantern use came before film. I've found such cinematic terms very useful in understanding the nature of magic lantern art. They appear in *italics* when they are first used in the text, and explained in context if necessary. I don't mean to suggest, however, that the cinema copied these techniques from Beale or other lantern artists. It's certainly likely that some techniques came from lantern practice – the *dissolve*, the *superimposition*, the *wipe* for instance. But early movie makers could also find their techniques in sources such as classical art, literature, theater, and popular culture, just as lantern artists did. Or they could discover them on their own, playing with their cameras.

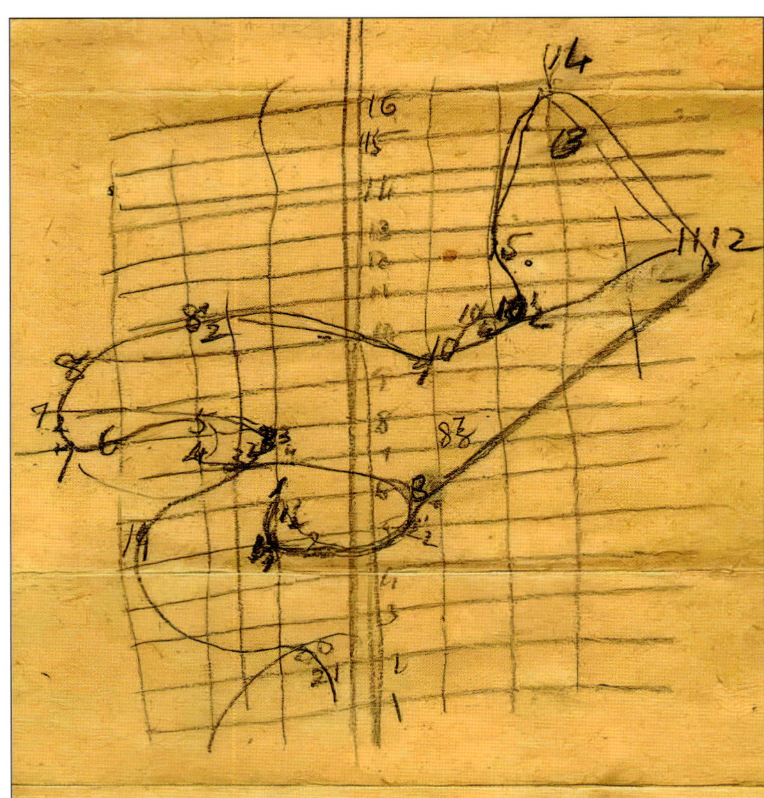

Fig. 1.4 Beale's job-hunting sketch of Philadelphia's streets. When he went looking for work after being laid off, he planned sixteen stops on this little map of downtown Philadelphia.

Separate from these cinematic techniques, I'll also describe about 100 traditional lanternist's techniques that were used to tell stories, and that are not used in film – like the ***flicker***, the ***flash***, the ***phantasmagoria***. They appear in ***bold-italic*** when first used.[9] (See all terms in the Index.)

To explore Beale's magic lantern art then, I'll be using lantern terms, cinematic terms, concepts drawn from other genres of narrative art, and my own personal experience. I hope that the combination will give you a rich understanding of the sophisticated techniques that Beale employed to draw his audience into his stories.

Beale's early mastery of the techniques of magic lantern art made him pre-eminent in the field, but he certainly wasn't famous like his school mate Thomas Eakins, the great American naturalist painter who Beale had once beaten in an artistic competition for his first job. When Beale was laid off in 1909 no reporters came to interview him about the end of the magic lantern era. Fame wouldn't come for another 25 years, in the 1930s, ten years after his death. Then the discovery of his art created a sensation, with extensive coverage in the national media,

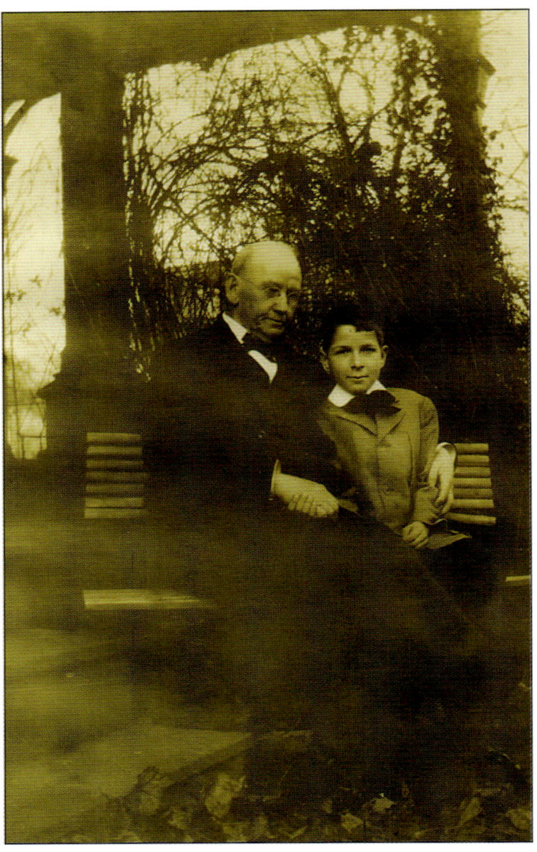

Fig. 1.5 My Great Grandfather Carter and my father, Johnny, on the porch of the Carter house in Germantown, PA, about 1909. Johnny inherited the magic lantern and slides and passed them on to me.

and an exhibit at a leading art museum in New York. But, as we will see, that sensational media attention and the museum exhibit itself were the result of a promotional sham that hid the magic lantern nature of his art. It wasn't until the 1940's that Beale's lantern art was exhibited and praised for what it was. Further exhibits were launched in the 1950's and 70's. In the 21st century his narrative art spread to 25 museums around the country,[10] and re-created lantern shows featuring his art toured major theaters.

But in 1909 all that was in the future, a future unknown to Beale. Suddenly without a job he had to make some money. He pulled a sheet of paper from his desk and made a list of more than a hundred Philadelphia businesses that might be able to use an artist. Then he sketched the street grid of center-city Philadelphia, and numerically keyed the most likely companies to his map so that he could plot out the most efficient walking route (Fig. 1.4). He was about to go job hunting.

The age of lantern entertainment was drawing to a close. It had been mortally wounded by its child, the movies. Soon, few would remember it had ever existed, to say nothing of remembering its leading artist, or the techniques we will explore in this book – the techniques Beale used to give life to a narrative art that enthralled millions.

Great Grandfather's Show – Start of a Passion

At almost the same place and time that Beale's magic lantern career was ending, my own magic lantern journey was just beginning – a journey that would eventually involve 40 years of collecting Beale material, researching his techniques, and performing his art.

A few blocks from Beale's studio in the Germantown section of Philadelphia, and at about the same year Beale was studying his layoff letter from Briggs, my great grandfather, John E. Carter (Fig. 1.5), was preparing a magic lantern show for his grandchildren. Despite the proximity of Great Grandfather Carter and Beale, no evidence exists that they knew each other. Great Grandfather didn't even use any of Beale's slides, probably because he had purchased his lantern and slides before Beale began work. Nor was Great Grandfather Carter one of those famous magic lantern showmen, touring nationally and performing before millions. He was an amateur who gave shows only for family and friends.

> Around 1909, my father, Johnny, pressed against his grandfather's windowpane, watching as the lamplighter outside made his way up the street – the signal for the start of his Grandpa's magic lantern show:
>
> "He's coming! He's coming, Grandpa! Will thee start the show now?" Johnny cried, using the Quaker plain speech of his family and time.
>
> Grandfather Carter would explain, once again, that under no circumstances could he start a show for the grandchildren until the lamplighter lit the lamp in front of the house. Only then would he know it was dark enough for the slides to look their best and brightest on the sheet Grandma had stretched across the mantle.
>
> The slow tease continued. The lantern lenses had to be warmed so they wouldn't crack in the heat. The kerosene lamp inside the lantern had to be lit with a long straw, pulled from Grandma's broom. The sheet had to be re-adjusted, so creases didn't distort the images.
>
> Then, finally, the show started. The Nose Man appeared on the sheet (Fig. 1.6).

> "Oh, please, children", the Nose Man cried, "Don't start the show with that magic word. Please, please, children, no, no, no … ."
>
> "ABRACADABRA!" the children screamed altogether. The Nose Man wailed, and his nose started to grow. Longer and longer it grew while the kids howled with delight, until at last it hit the edge of the sheet, distorted, and jerked to the side. The children howled again.

The show continued. The children sang *The Muffin Man.* They chanted the words for *This is the House That Jack Built* – faster and faster, so fast they became tongue-tied trying to keep up with the flying pictures. They marveled at the moving astronomy slides, especially one that showed a growing eclipse of the moon. And most of all, they waited for the most exciting, the most disgusting slide of all – the slide of the snoring man who swallowed a rat. (You'll see it yourself shortly.[11])Family shows such as Great Grandfather Carter's, were common, but lantern shows came in a remarkable array of other

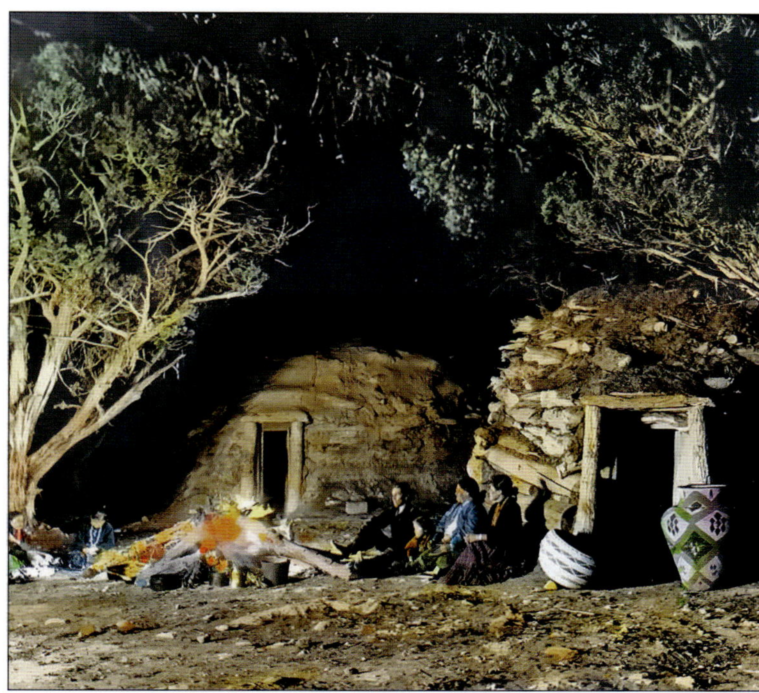

Fig. 1.7 A hand-colored lantern slide prepared by the Santa Fe Railroad for illustrated lectures promoting travel on its rail lines. Most lantern slides were photographs like this, rather than the illustrations Beale made.

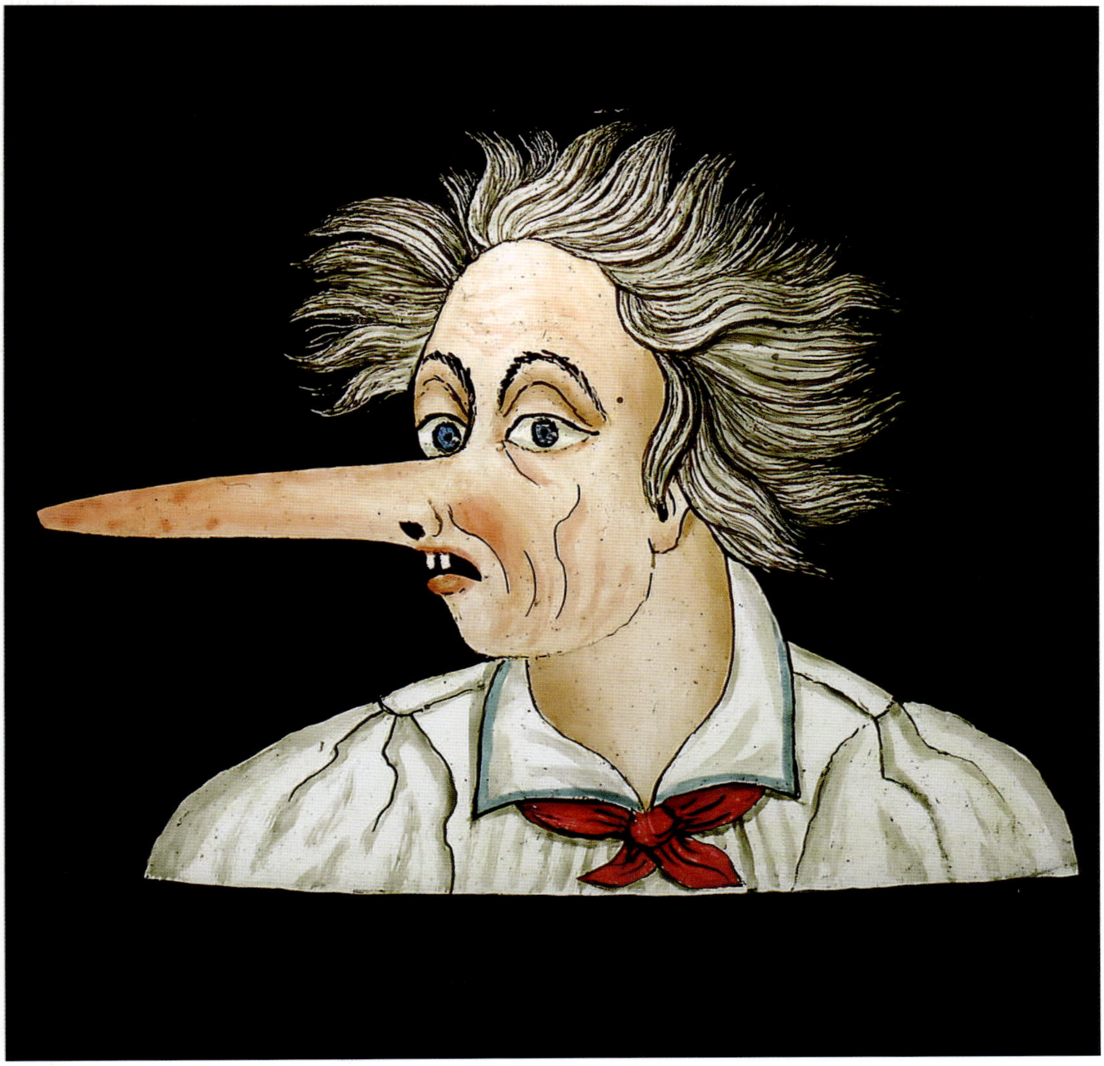

Fig. 1.6 When the Nose Man had a normal nose a black mask on a separate piece of glass covered its full length. To make the nose grow, the showman drew the mask to the left.

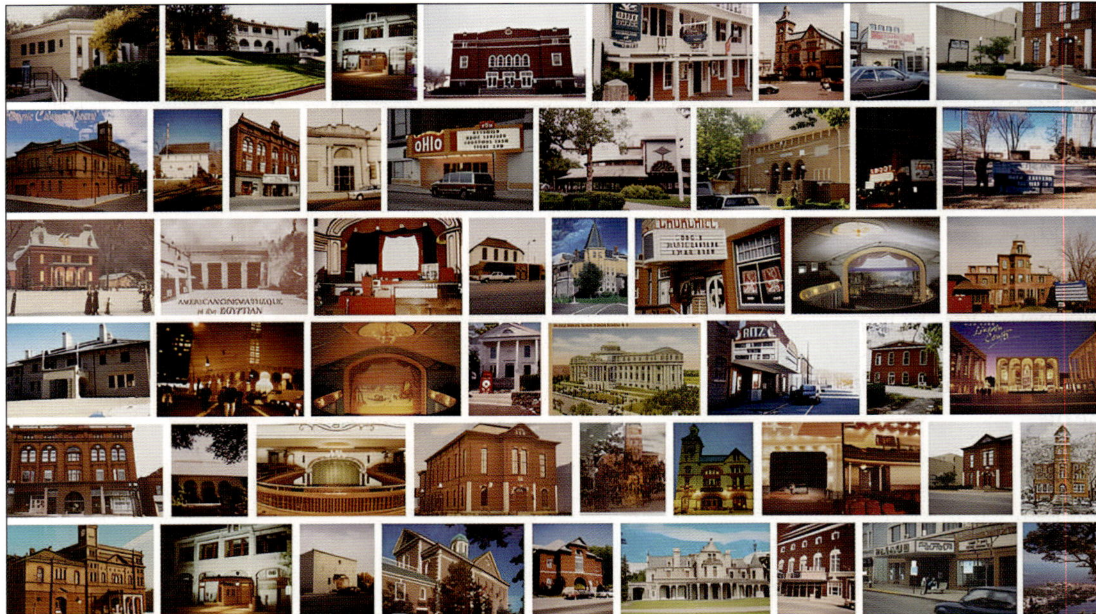

Fig. 1.8 Some of the theaters in which The American Magic Lantern Theater performed. They range in size from 100 seats to 3,000.

sizes and degrees of sophistication. By the 1890s, all these different uses of the magic lantern had created a pervasive form of entertainment and education. Here's just one indication: If you go on eBay right now, and search for "magic lantern slides" you'll find about *60,000* slides for sale more than a hundred years after the medium collapsed. Just imagine how many were around back then! Most of the slides you'll find today are black and white photographs, especially travel views, but Beale's distinctive images also have a substantial presence.[12]

Lantern shows themselves went under many names – "magic lantern shows", "illustrated lectures", "stereopticon shows". ("Stereopticon" was a common American term that connoted a fancier type of two-lens lantern, but stereopticons did not produce a 3-D image.) Whatever the name, Americans were fascinated, even in the pre-movie period, by screen entertainment. The lantern business, if not the corporate juggernaut of today's cinema, was still a good-sized industry, with stars, tie-ins, and multimedia merchandising (Fig. 1.7). Great Grandfather Carter's show entranced his grandchildren, but shows like his made up only a part of the sprawling lantern industry.

From Lantern Show to Lantern Book

Great Grandfather Carter's lantern and slides passed down to my father, who gave us shows when I was a kid, and then to me, who also gave shows for friends and family. Word got out. Then, in about 1981, the local historical society asked me to do a show, my first "public" appearance. Two months later, the society was gathered at 8:00 on a Wednesday night, sitting in the basement of the local library, waiting patiently. Twenty of them. Quite intimidating.

Using Grandfather Carter's magic lantern and slides I performed our usual family show – the show Grandfather Carter had given my father in 1909, that he had given us when I was a child in the 1940's, and that I had given for my own kids in the 1960s. I was so nervous the slides shook in my hand, so the images shook on the screen. Nonetheless, the audience liked the show.

Afterwards those amateur historians asked questions. I was embarrassed. I knew nothing about the lantern or slides, or how they were ordinarily used. Though they were obviously manufactured, I had always thought of the lantern as just another family artifact in our somewhat quirky family – simply part of the mythic world of my childhood.

Those questions from the historical society led me to a serious interest in the subject of the magic lantern. I started reading. I discovered that the world of the lantern was much larger than our family's one lantern. I became hooked, badly bitten by the collecting bug. Much to my own surprise, I was bitten by the performing bug as well. Despite my nervous nature, I started doing more little shows in libraries and historical societies. Then, still very much a newbie, I came upon a remarkable opportunity – the chance to obtain a large collection of Beale's slides. These were the very same slides Beale himself had purchased from the Briggs Company, one by one, as they were produced from his designs. The scope, the artistic beauty, and the narrative sophistication of Beale's work staggered me. I bought the collection and began hunting for information about Beale.

My wife and I found – amazingly enough – a treasure trove of sketches, letters and paintings that had been left in Beale's attic studio when he died, then put in trash bags by a house cleaner and given to an artist friend of his. In museums, private collections, and art galleries around the country we located Beale's boyhood diary, almost all his design paintings for slides, and related material from the Briggs company. Again – amazingly enough – a portfolio of his etchings turned up on eBay. Eventually we put together a very large collection of Beale-related material, on which I have drawn heavily for this book. The collection has been very little used by scholars because it was a private collection – open to anyone who asked, as some did, but not promoted publicly. That is a second reason, in addition to Beale's anonymity during his lifetime, that he is not better known today.

About the same time as we were searching for material on Beale, I began giving magic lantern shows at larger libraries and at museums, billing myself as something of a fourth-generation lanternist. Using Beale's slides, the shows grew in sophistication.

In 1992 I left my job in publishing to form the American Magic Lantern Theater, a two-person professional troupe – myself and a singer/pianist. We re-created lantern shows in theaters, museums, and cultural centers around the nation and the world (Fig. 1.8). I loved the travel, and the interaction with audiences – like riding the surf. It felt like a calling. Gradually the business built. We eventually developed a repertoire of ten different 1–1/2-hour shows, most with seasonal themes such as *Halloween, Christmas*, or *Spring*. We toured the East Coast and the American heartland, and then some major venues like Lincoln Center in New York, and festivals in Poland, Mexico, Singapore and Taiwan. Over the years we performed more than a thousand shows.

As I tried to juggle my performing schedule with my research on Beale's life and on his art, I realized that the performing and the research fit together. I was in a truly unique position – the only American in almost 100 years whose full-time profession was creating magic lantern shows. I knew about them not only from studying source documents, drawings, and artifacts, but also from the inside – I felt them in my bones and in my fingers – the muscle memory of a professional showman. I became, to borrow a term from the field of archeology, an "experiential archeologist" – one who does research on the past not only by studying artifacts in a museum or manuscripts in a library, but also by trying to *use* those artifacts as they were actually used in a bygone era.

It's an area of research that the Chairman of the British Magic Lantern Society suggested back in 1990 in his Preface to the Society's fist publication, a book on magic lantern art:

> Further investigation ... might explore the showmanship of the magic lanternist – detailing the procedures used to bring the slides to life in performance – that twin art which

Fig. 1.9 One of our publicity photos from about 2000. I developed an exuberant performing style that helped Beale's slides come alive for modern audiences.

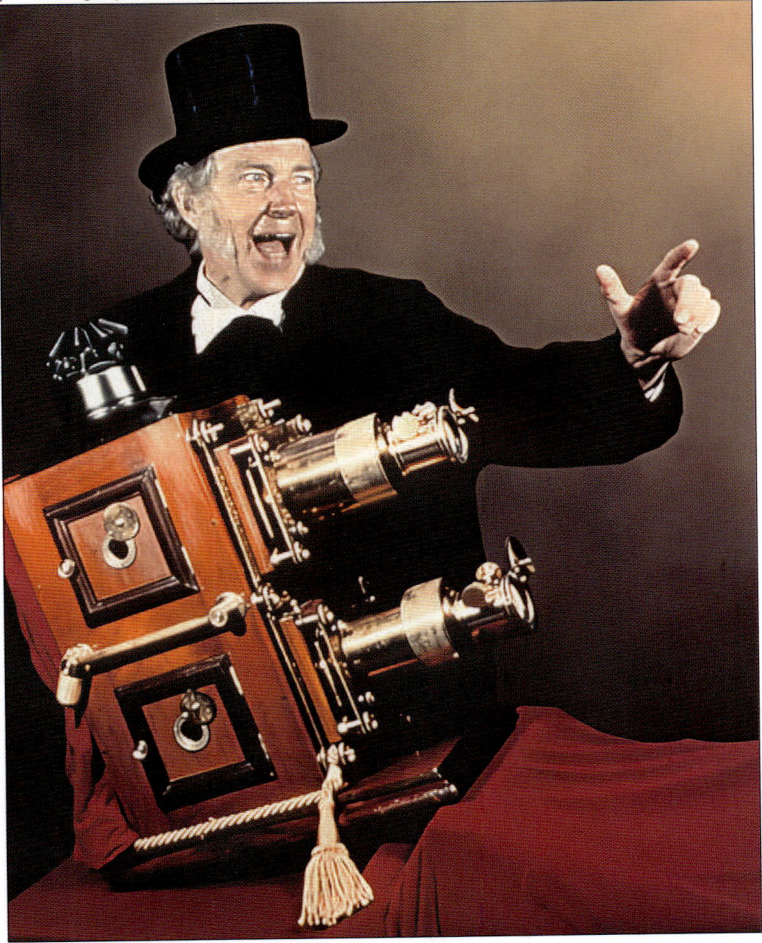

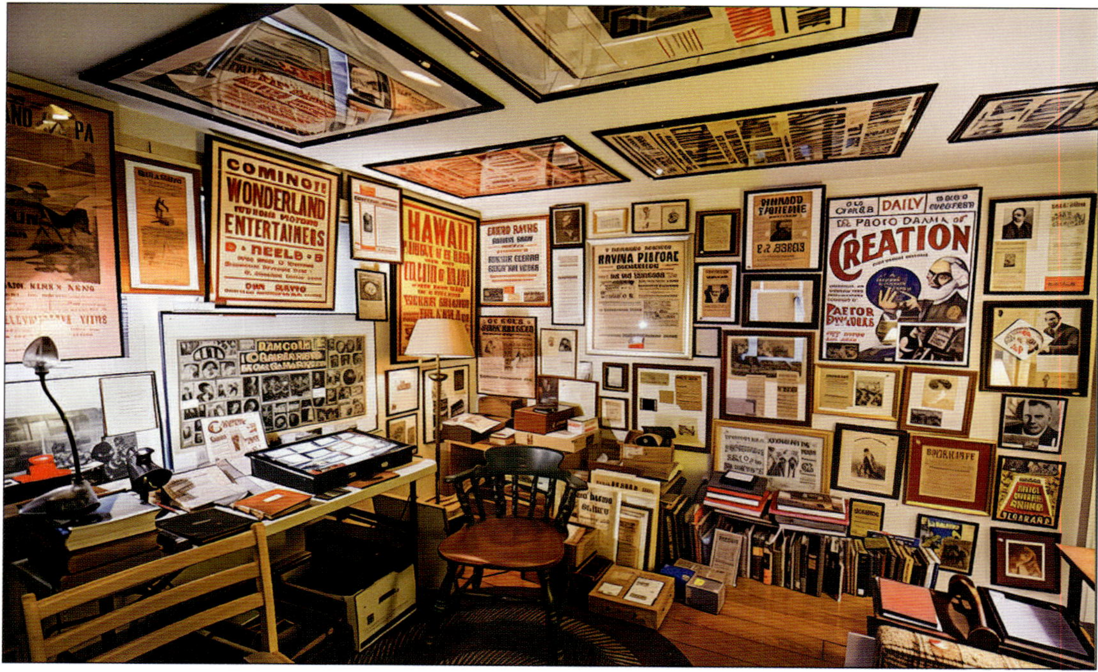

Fig. 1.10 The "Broadside Collection" gradually overtook our house. Finally, I resorted to putting broadsides on the ceiling.

> exactly complements that of the slide-maker in his creation of images, and whose absence can so easily undermine all his efforts".[13]

After being on the road for 30 years, making a living of sorts with the magic lantern and competing with thousands of other professional performers for a spot on the nation's stages, I had certainly learned what it took to bring those slides to life. I had mastered dozens of techniques for managing lantern slides that helped turn what might seem like a crude lantern technology into a vibrant and enthralling art form (Fig. 1.9). I realized I could use that knowledge to help explain what professional lantern shows were like 100^+ years ago, and will share that "showman's art" with you here as I discuss Beale's images.

Performing for so long, I saw how Beale's art affected hundreds of thousands of people from all walks of life, all over the world. Those people did not see Beale's working materials – his master design paintings, or his lantern slides. In fact, as one scholar has pointed out, it is only in performance that slides become meaningful objects.[14] In our shows audiences saw Beale's magic lantern art as it was meant to be seen: projected and enlarged on screen, in the dark, in color, experienced together as a group, manipulated by a skilled lanternist, melded with music, and dramatized by the power of the story-teller's voice – a Magic Lantern Show. I can't recreate such a show for you in a book, but I'll come as close as I can by describing how I managed Beale's slides for maximum effect, and how audiences reacted.

While I projected Beale's slides and was experiencing them this way myself, again and again, I saw how those huge images led modern audiences to laugh or cry or sit mesmerized, and I could make more informed hypotheses about how Beale's work affected his audiences. Putting these modern responses together with 19th century reports allows me to give you a reasonably good sense of Beale's impact on his audience. (When I've found modern reactions to be quite different from the way his audiences seem to have responded – and I certainly have in some cases – I'll point that out.)

While giving shows, I was also researching Beale. In 2014, my wife, Deborah, and I published a book for scholars and museum curators, *Before the Movies: American Magic Lantern Entertainment and the Nation's First Great Screen Artist, Joseph Boggs Beale.*[15] The book documents the attribution, provenance, and dating of *each* of Beale's lantern images, and compares his work with the very limited output of other American artists creating lantern slides in the same period. It demonstrates that Beale – almost single handedly – created American screen entertainment before the movies, and establishes his primacy in the field. The detailed "who, what, where, when" information about Beale's work described in *Before the Movies* underlies this present volume, providing a carefully documented database for this more general discussion of his artistic style and technique.

After writing *Before the Movies*, my interests broadened to the larger world of the magic lantern. Gradually I came to understand and write about its pervasive influence in America.[16] In the 19th and early 20th century thousands of men and women were giving lantern "illustrated lectures" about almost any subject you could imagine. As a way of documenting who was giving such lantern shows, when, why and to whom, I began collecting their broadsides, programs, advertisements, and slides. After years of such collecting, thousands of items jammed our house (Fig. 1.10). This collection, and the Beale collection, are now at the Lucas Museum of Narrative Art in Los Angeles. I have drawn upon both to create the present volume.

This book then draws upon 40 years of personal experiences in collecting, researching and performing Beale's work. *Magic Lantern Art* weaves together four strands: It explores Beale's life, especially his artistic childhood and early years as a commercial illustrator, during which he had a series of experiences that turned out to be an ideal preparation for his later magic lantern profession. It puts Beale's art in context by reviewing the power of traditional lantern story-telling techniques, and surveying a wide range of American lantern shows. It explains the many ways that the showman manipulates slide images to create the audience experience – knowledge I gained by performing all those lantern shows featuring Beale's slides. And most especially, it concentrates on the magic lantern art of the man who mastered the techniques of cinematic storytelling before the cinema even existed – Joseph Boggs Beale – the first great narrative artist of the American screen (Fig. 1.11).

It's time then for me to introduce you to Beale. We'll start when he was a precocious 15-year-old, embarking on his first great artistic project, one that probably had a profound impact on the magic lantern art he developed 25 years later.

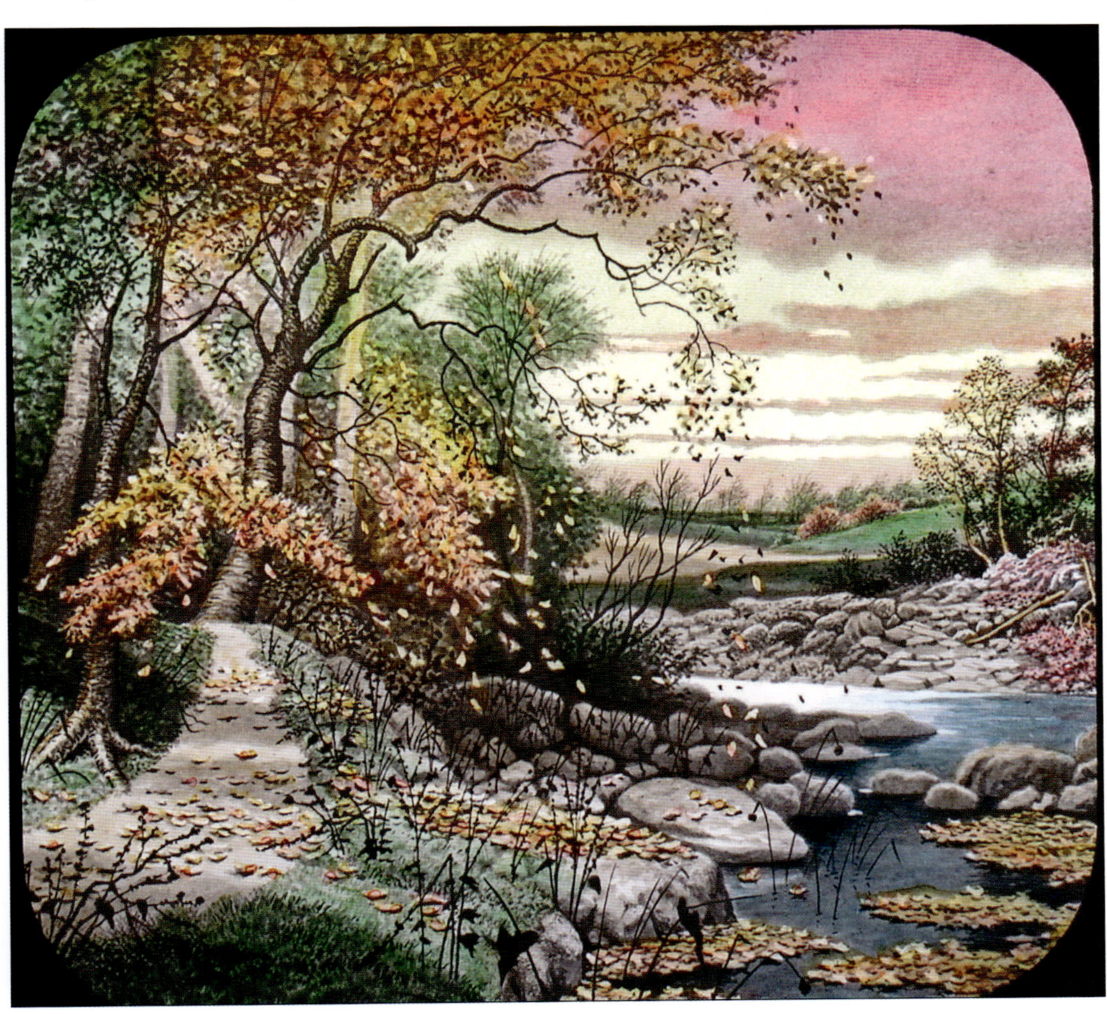

Fig. 1.11 A Beale image illustrating slide 14 of a set for the *Oddfellows*, a Secret Society. Such societies were major venues for Beale's images, as they used his slides in monthly rituals seen by millions.

Chapter Two

Beale's Early Years – A Life of Imagery

Fig. 2.8 Beale's slide of "The Destruction (Burning) of Washington by British 1814" in the *American History* group. To create this scene, Beale no doubt drew on fires he saw as a child. Discussion on p. 18.

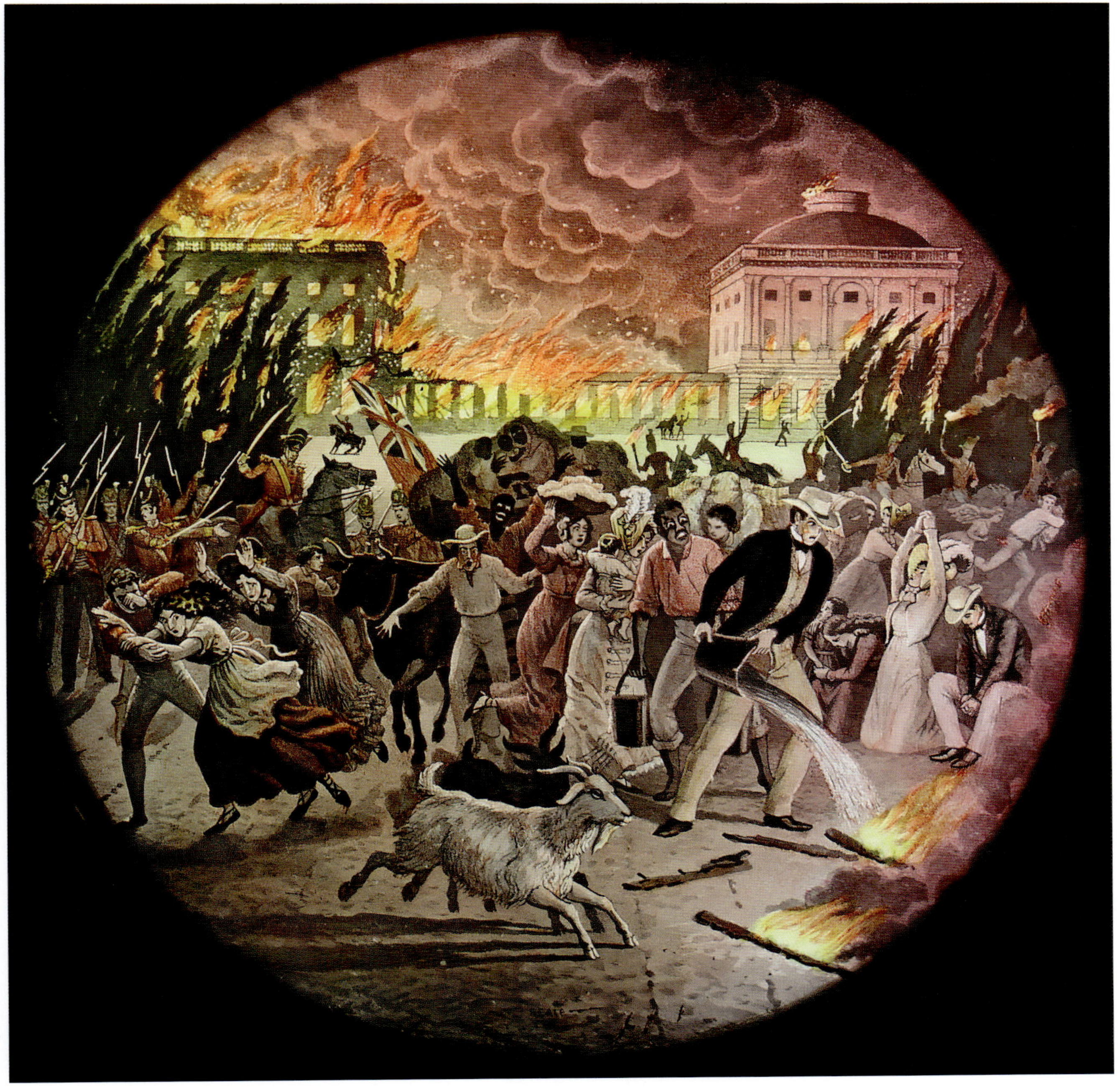

Beale's Moving Panorama

It was January 1856 in the attic of the Beale family home, in Center City Philadelphia. Seated beside a giant rocking horse, fifteen-year-old Joseph Boggs Beale was painting a model panorama, a much more elaborate device than the toy panoramas commercially available at the time (Fig. 2.1).[1]

His model copied one of the most popular forms of entertainment of his time, a giant painting that unrolled to tell a story. Professional moving panoramas were much larger than young Joseph's, with 50–300 scenes, each 8–12 feet high. The scenes were not projected on the screen; they were painted on long scrolls. The entire painting, often 1,000 feet long, sometimes 3,000, was wound on huge spools hidden on each side of the stage, so that scene after scene rolled before the viewer, creating a performance that could last two hours. Usually the panoramas were travelogues, accompanied by sound (a lecturer), music (such as a piano), and sound effects such as thunder and lightning. The best estimate is that over 100 million people worldwide saw a panorama between 1850–1900.[2] (The term "panorama" was created in the nineteenth century to describe this new art form. From it derives the concept and the term *panoramic shot* or (*pan shot*) in the movies, and *panoramic* lantern slides.)

Fig. 2.1 A manufactured toy panorama with a moving picture. The wheels that turn the picture scroll are hidden at the sides.
Courtesy of The Bill Douglas Cinema Museum, University of Exeter.

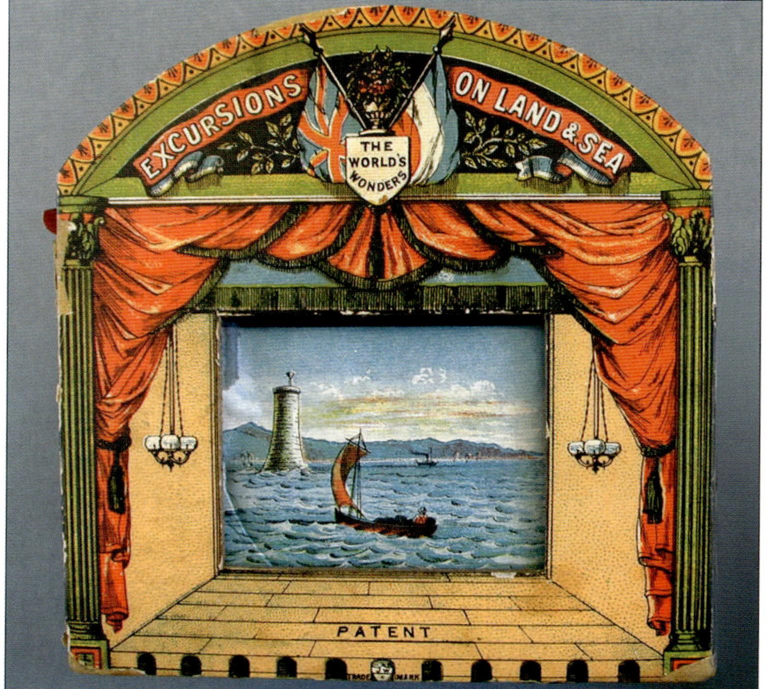

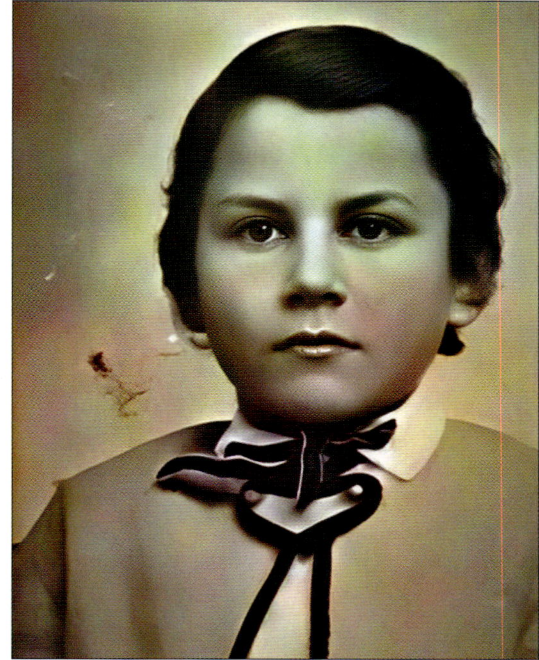

Fig. 2.2 Beale as a young boy, probably about seven or eight, well before the panorama project.

Beale's model panorama consisted of a painting on muslin, two feet high by 150 feet long, containing about 70 dramatic scenes. He added some puppet action, sound effects, and magic tricks – a multi-media show! – all woven together in what was apparently not a travelogue, but, intriguingly enough, an on-screen story, something that was unusual in the professional panorama. Beale's project went on for months, and likely had a profound effect on his development as a magic lantern artist

All through the winter and spring he progressed steadily on his project, foot-by-foot and day-by-day, with a persistence that would characterize his later magic lantern work (Fig. 2.2). He documented his endeavors in his diary. On January 22 he "worked on panorama and got 1½ pictures drawn". On February 16 he "fixed the lightning, stars & reflection in the water". On March 11 he gave some cousins a preview of the "panorama and poppets [puppets] & 3 or 4 tricks up in the garret". But it was not until August 29 that the whole project was completed. He showed it off to family and friends in his father's dental office on the first floor. A few technical difficulties surfaced – he and Pa stayed up till 1:30 one night fixing them – but the new show was a resounding neighborhood success.

Years later, Beale's sister, Clara, remembered the excitement of the panorama performances in the garret given by young Joe:

> The acme was reached, to the 'fearful delight' of the children, in the "Storm at Sea" with its natural accompaniments – lightning flashes and reverberating thunder (the product of ... rolling ... short logs of wood upon boards laid across the rafters in the loft overhead).[3]

(Note here that, like a modern movie-goer, Clara remembers the special effects of Beale's production, both the on-screen lighting flashes, and the effects created backstage by a young *foley artist*, the sound effects man.)

Beale's interest in the panorama, a good deal of his visual skill, and perhaps the "Storm at Sea" scene itself, came from his Uncle Edmund Beale, who was one of the country's leading professional panorama showmen.[4] Edmund traveled extensively, both in the United States and abroad, and even gave a command performance for Queen Victoria. Joseph, understandably enough, was star-struck with his famous uncle, and tracked Edmund's travels in his diary as Edmund exhibited for several months in one city and then moved on to another, selling one show when he was ready to launch another. Edmund, and his panorama artist, George Heilge, were young Joe's first art teachers (Fig. 2.3). From them he probably learned the basics of sequential narrative illustration – how to tell a story by depicting the action in a series of pictures, integrated for maximum effect. Twenty years later that skill would help make Beale the preeminent artist of the American magic lantern.

Heilge was a well-known Philadelphia theatrical artist who once visited Joseph's family, and did the actual painting of Edmund's panoramas. His dramatic scenes of icebergs, polar bears, sunsets, and ship disasters (Fig. 2.4) "added the brightest star to the firmament of fine arts" – or so the *Washington Post* thought. Presumably, Edmund himself was responsible for the overall concept and the sequencing of the images. Reviewers commented upon his pacing, the special effects such as the lightning and the burning of a ship at sea, and the rising of the moon – a new effect probably created with a magic lantern. Edmund also continually re-worked his canvas, adding scenes to create new attractions and topical information, subtracting scenes to avoid repetition, and arranging for "visual punctuation marks" and "dramatic turns".[5]

During much of the time Joseph was painting his model-panorama in the garret, Uncle

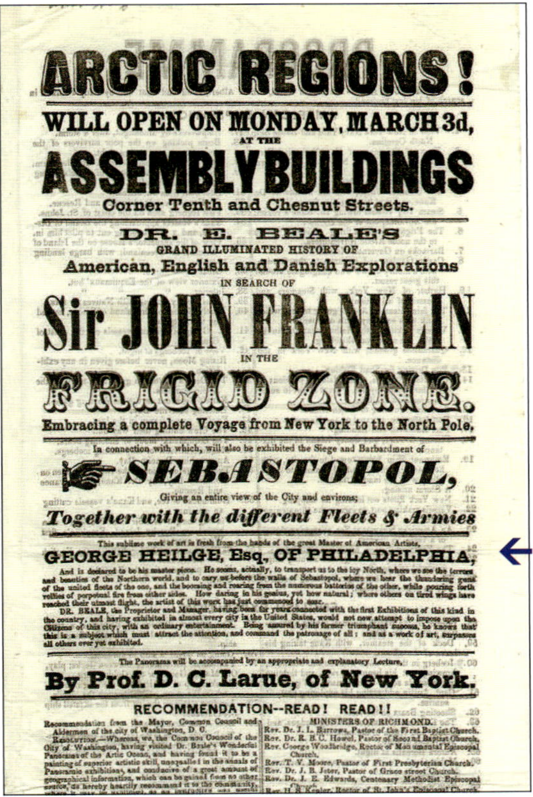

Fig. 2.3 A broadside advertising Edmund Beale's "Arctic Regions" panorama. George Heilge, the panorama artist, receives prominent billing as "the great Master of American Artists".
Courtesy of The Library Company of Philadelphia.

Edmund's Arctic Show was playing in Philadelphia. Joseph was fascinated, visiting it 20 times in its first two months. We cannot know for certain how he felt about these experiences – at this stage of his diary writing he simply recounts the facts, like a boy writing home from camp.

Fig. 2.4 Hand-painted British slide. Panoramas and magic lantern shows about the Artic explorations shared much of the same spectacular imagery.

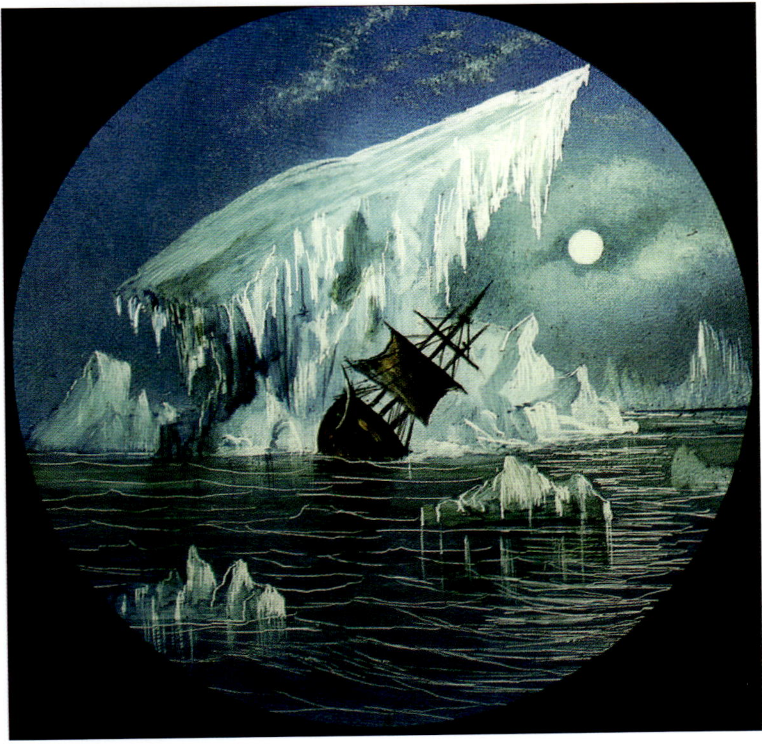

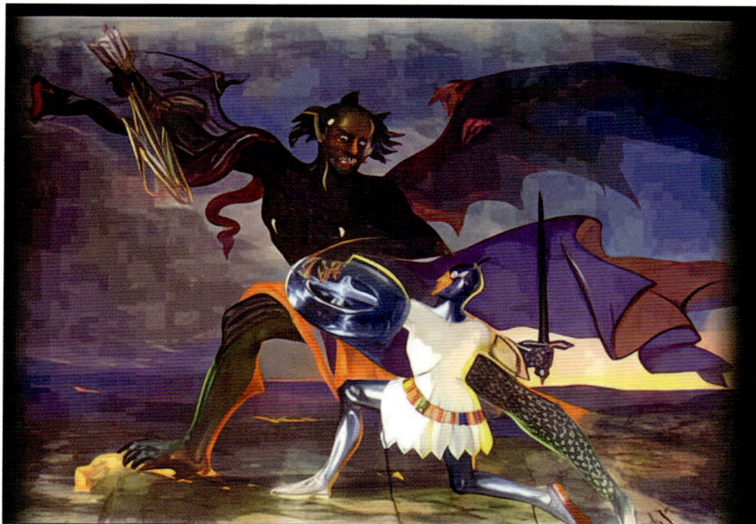

Fig. 2.5 "Fight with Apollyon", an image from *The Pilgrim's Progress Panorama*. Image enhanced. Courtesy Saco Museum, Saco, ME.

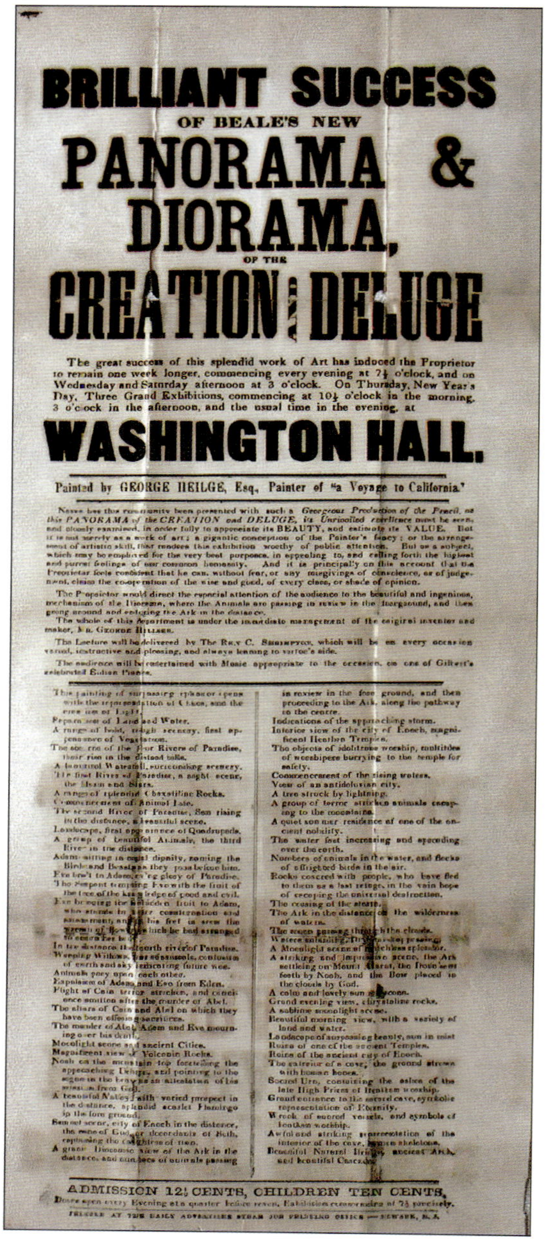

BRILLIANT SUCCESS
OF BEALE'S NEW
PANORAMA & DIORAMA,
OF THE
CREATION AND DELUGE

The great success of this splendid work of Art has induced the Proprietor to remain one week longer, commencing every evening at 7½ o'clock, and on Wednesday and Saturday afternoon at 3 o'clock. On Thursday, New Year's Day, Three Grand Exhibitions, commencing at 10½ o'clock in the morning, 3 o'clock in the afternoon, and the usual time in the evening, at

WASHINGTON HALL.

Painted by GEORGE HEILGE, Esq., Painter of "a Voyage to California."

ADMISSION 12½ CENTS, CHILDREN TEN CENTS.

Fig. 2.6 Edmund Beale's broadside for his 1851 *Creation and Deluge* panorama. Every scene is described. Young Joe Beale would probably have noticed, and copied this approach.

But Edmund loved children – he had twelve of his own – and was Joseph's favorite uncle, so we can imagine the excitement and the barrage of questions when, in October, the world-famous panorama showman himself came to see Joseph's show in the attic theater.

As a privileged member of Uncle Edmund's panorama audience, a backstage regular, a promising nephew, and a panorama artist himself, young Joseph Beale was in an ideal position to learn the on-screen narrative art that would later become his major work. At his uncle's shows he watched the same performance given again and again before different groups, soaking up those sequences that consistently moved an audience, and those that did not, studying the mechanics of the art form. Then he went home and created panorama scenes of his own. He watched his own little audience react; he revised; he performed again.

As a showman myself, I know that artists have a lot to learn about the response of audiences – the kind of knowledge that cannot be developed working alone in a studio. There is a pattern of audience response to a given slide, to a given show, and most importantly, a pattern of response to the medium itself. When I first began writing lantern show scripts, I put them together as best I could, drawing on what I knew about 19th century programs, and on my own previous writing experience. But the shows never functioned on screen as I had imagined they would. One scene would not merge with another, or transitions were unclear, or the pacing was off. Gradually, by watching the reactions of hundreds of different audiences, I built up an understanding of the pattern of responses to the magic lantern medium, and it became much easier to write new scripts.

I believe that while young Joseph Beale was working on his panorama, he experienced first-hand this process of "see what works, see what flops", and that this experience was critical for his later success in creating an effective magic lantern art. The importance of audience "feedback" for narrative artistic development is evident in the fact that even the most prestigious of American panorama artists, the creators of the famous *Panorama of Pilgrim's Progress* (Fig. 2.5) – artists who were associated with the National Academy of Design – made some serious mistakes when they had to adapt their "single-frame" artistic training to a "multi-frame" moving panorama. They were criticized and had to revise their work substantially. In a similar fashion the modern movie industry gets feedback before a movie's release through focus groups and previews, and often changes the movie's format or content as a result.

Because Beale is so laconic in the early stages of his diary, we cannot know precisely what he learned about sequential narrative art, but if he was as aware as he was just a little later in life when he was writing more expansively, four features of panorama art were likely to have impressed him.

First, since his project was not a continuous landscape, but a "scene panorama" – broken up into scenes like Uncle Edmund's *Creation* (Fig. 2.6) – he needed to think very carefully about what would later be called *storyboarding*. This is the technique of sketching out the scenes ahead of production to ensure *continuity*, and is one that we know he later used to create his magic lantern stories. To make his panorama, he had to divide the story action into a series of *scenes* with logical transitions, hopefully pacing the action toward that "fearfully delightful" dramatic climax of the "Ship at Sea", with all its lightning and special effects. (The creators of *Pilgrim's Progress* faced the same issues, and rethought their "storyboarding" in their revision, removing some scenes and adding others to increase the dramatic effect.)[6]

The second feature of the panorama's art – one of the secrets of panorama success, commented upon again and again in newspaper reviews – was that the painting contain a wealth of detail. The specifics gave a sense that the artist himself had seen the event, and so contributed to its authenticity and believability. Edmund Beale's promotion for his shows highlighted the talents of his artist – the "celebrated Heilge", proclaiming his work a "masterpiece" – a point surely not lost on the young artist Joseph, who would have wanted to copy that style.[7] As you may have already noticed, and as we shall certainly see later, abundant detail became characteristic of Beale's magic lantern slides, a conscious and conspicuous part of his narrative art.

The third feature is that the panorama was, like the magic lantern show, an art form that merged image and *voice over* to tell a story on screen (Fig. 2.7). In this sense it was a more "modern" form of on-screen entertainment than many

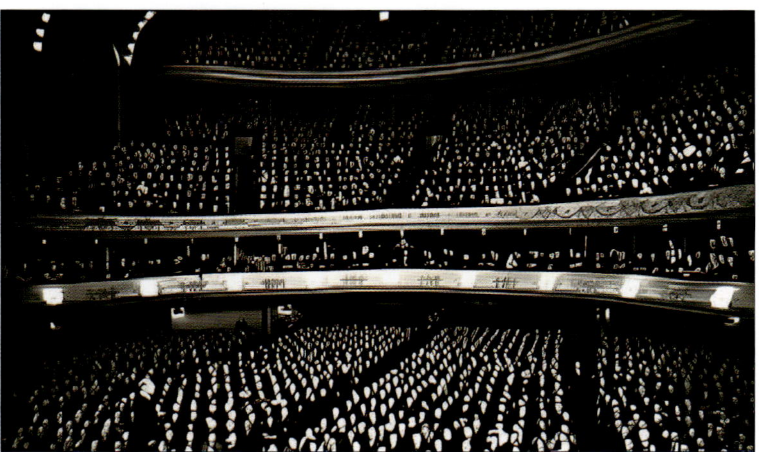

Fig. 2.7 Burton Holmes, one of America's most famous lantern showmen, performs before a large audience, typical for him. He invented the term "travelogue".
Courtesy Burton Holmes Archive.

silent movies. Young Joseph would have been faced at an early age with all the modern questions of balancing word and picture: Which story elements should be carried by one, which by the other? When should the two supplement each other? Later, in Beale's magic lantern slide work, he became a master at integrating his images and the words of America's greatest writers, supplementing their text with a visual drama that today holds audiences enchanted in ways that 19th century literature alone can no longer do.

The fourth feature of the panorama is that it was not a still image like one of the huge landscapes of Albert Bierstadt. In fact, it did move. The creators of *Pilgrim's Progress* apparently saw this movement as a necessary evil in their first conception of it. For them the moving scroll was simply a way to get from one still picture to another. As the images scrolled across the screen, occasionally they even had the same characters visible at the same time in two different scenes. In their second version they fixed this problem by adding material (usually landscapes) between the scenes. But in some sequences, they went much further. They used the fact that the image was moving to add to its dramatic effect. Because the image was only gradually revealed, part-by-part, they could use the techniques of *continuity editing* to build suspense, pointing with devices of lighting and imagery to the revelation that was to come – for instance a giant foot that only slowly becomes an entire threatening giant. Beale must have seen some of the same possibilities while studying his own and Uncle Edmund's panorama. Certainly, he was aware of them by the time he came to the magic lantern.

I am almost certain that when Beale began producing lantern designs, he created for himself a feedback opportunity like that he had experienced years earlier with those 20 visits to his uncle's panorama. In 1890 he purchased a magic lantern from Briggs, and then purchased slide copies of his own work, one by one, as they were produced – more than 2,000 slides over the years.[8] Briggs sold them to him at half price, $.75 apiece, for a total of $1,500, which comes to about $52,000 in 2025. Why would Beale lay out such a sum? Pride in his work, of course, but also having these slides would allow him to test out his work on a live audience – his ever-present, very artistic, and very lively family. During his magic lantern years, Beale lived with his extended family, and it had a tradition of its members providing entertainment on Friday nights. Though no direct evidence exists, "Uncle Joe" would certainly have been likely to give Friday magic lantern shows for the family. As I have already emphasized, it is in a "show" – the melding in the dark of large projected images with music and the narrative voice – that magic lantern art is best experienced. Surely there were comments after these family shows, and surely the feedback Beale received helped him form and polish his story-telling art.

(Feedback has also been essential in forming the showmanship that I use to complement Beale's art. After every show in my early years of performing, my wife would drive us home while I held a flashlight over the script book and went through it line by line, discussing the performance with her. Of course, every audience is different, so I couldn't draw a conclusion from any one performance. But if, on the third try, no one was laughing at a slip-slide comic, I'd try a different framing, or a different build, or a different punch line. If I couldn't make the slide work after a few more tries, I'd drop it. How about complaints? In general, I listened very carefully. But once a woman came up and complained that The Nose Man was too suggestive. I didn't change a thing. Her problem, not mine.)

A Life of Imagery

The panorama, its associated narrative techniques, and feedback were only some of many aspects of Beale's early life that influenced his development as a narrative artist.

Born on December 10, 1841, Beale was the eldest child of a large and active clan – eleven children in all. The older children regularly put on those Friday night entertainments for the family. Young Joe's panorama was a special treat, but he was often busy supporting the efforts of the younger children – carving heads for marionette shows, training a family of white mice to perform tricks, and, during the Civil War years, creating a "vast army of Lincoln's Soldiers", correctly dressed in their myriad uniforms, who paraded with gusto, accompanied by music and singing.

After August of 1857, the Beale family's entertainments were at their new home at 1223 Chestnut Street in the center of the bustling city of Philadelphia.[9] The Chestnut Street house was within a few blocks of all the major theaters and the magic lantern and photography district – perhaps the most important lantern district in the world. There Beale could see all the newest visual technology of the age. Yet the countryside was also within a few minutes walking distance, and a bed at Uncle Edmund's farm outside the city was within easy reach. Unlike today's children who spend much of their time in supervised "activities" or watching manufactured images on TV or their cell phones, Beale, by age 15, had the run of the city and the countryside, and experienced first-hand the full range of mid-nineteenth century life. This daily interaction embedded in his consciousness the sense of particulars that would later allow him to create those thousands of remarkably detailed and vividly real images of the life that surrounded him.

For instance, in the course of the first year of the diary (1856), Beale has a tooth pulled under ether; sketches regularly; visits innumerable fires – four in a glorious two-day period (Fig. 2.8; this is the illustration on the title page of this chapter); endures mustard-plaster home remedies; attends a hanging; is photographed at several of the newly-opened photo studios; watches a dozen parades; sees a ship afire; attends church three times on Sundays and often twice during the week; rakes hay; goes boating; drags a cow and calf to market; goes fishing and leaves 14 of his catch for a sick man; catches a snapping turtle and keeps it in a barrel; winnows oats; hunts rabbits in the fields and birds in the marshes; "whips" a yellow jacket's nest (drives a stick into the nest and flings it into the sky – a little excitement there!); goes to stare at a

Dutchman who was killed by lightning; descends 300 feet into a chrome mine; sings regularly in the family chorus; fastens his sister's window against a Peeping Tom; attends school; plays cricket; watches a balloon ascension; hears an Indian Chief preach; carves and bakes porcelain teeth for his father's dental practice; visits almost daily with a vast network of relatives; catches the dreaded influenza – all the while working away on that panorama.

It was busy, varied young life. And a productive one, for many of these experiences – transmuted by the creative process and the demands of specific illustration assignments – appear among the images Beale painted later for the magic lantern, and help make his art a rich source of documentation for nineteenth-century life.

Beale's large family was the center of all this activity, and most of what he did was in the company of one or more of them. He was intensely interested in family history, and the spirits of relatives past were palpable in the family consciousness. His mother was Louise Boggs McCord, and, on her side, he could trace his ancestry back to Andrew Griscom who sired a family that helped build Independence Hall and barricaded the Hudson River against the British during the Revolutionary War. Beale's great aunt, Elizabeth Griscom, better known to us as Betsy Ross, was part of this line (Figs. 2.8/9). (Toward the later part of his life, Beale became involved in a controversy about whether Betsy Ross did in fact sew the first American flag. In 1909, in company with his brothers and sisters, he signed a notarized deposition on the subject. Modern scholarship has tended to back up the family's claim.)[10] The flag-waving sense of patriotism that infused many of Beale's 300 historical designs for the magic lantern was, quite literally, in his blood.

Through his father, Stephen Thomas Beale, Joseph could trace his family history back nineteen generations to Lincolnshire, England in the 1300s. Joseph's father migrated with his parents to America from England in 1831. As a young man he studied dentistry while supporting himself by teaching singing. When Joseph was born, Dr. Beale was in the process of helping to found the Pennsylvania Association of Dental Surgeons.[11] His practice was a successful one, though it was limited by an eye disease (probably glaucoma) which required that he spend a day every few weeks with a pin in his eye to relieve

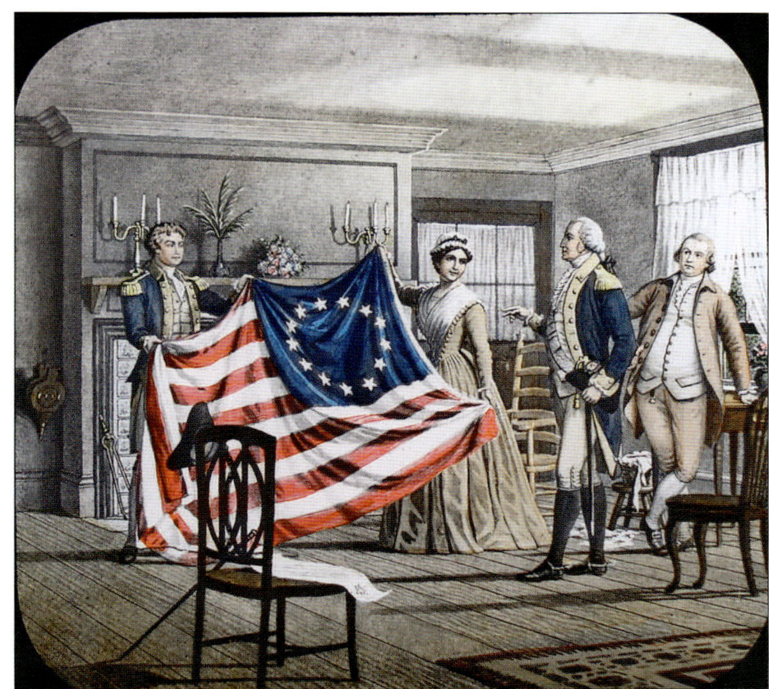

Figs. 2.8/9 Two slide images of "Betsy Ross Showing the Flag", from the *American History* group. The one above is certainly by Beale, the one below probably is also.

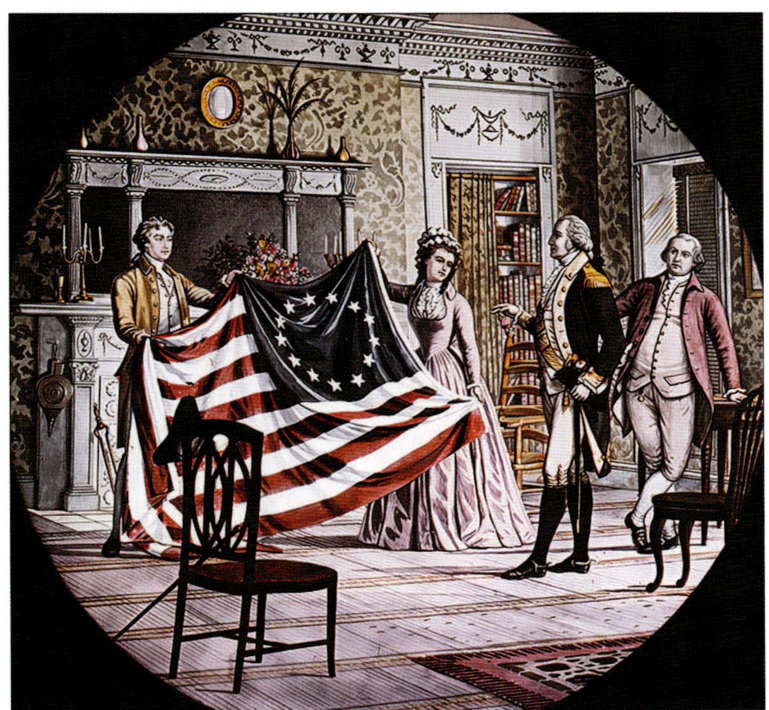

the pressure. The family was prosperous but not wealthy. Money was a constant cause for concern. A weekly chore of Joseph's was to collect the bills still outstanding from his father's dental practice. Often, he returned empty-handed from a full day's collecting. On a good day he would note with pride the collection of ten dollars – about $400 in 2025. But money issues did not stand in the way of a good time for young Joesph – visiting with relatives, attending church functions, and participating in the

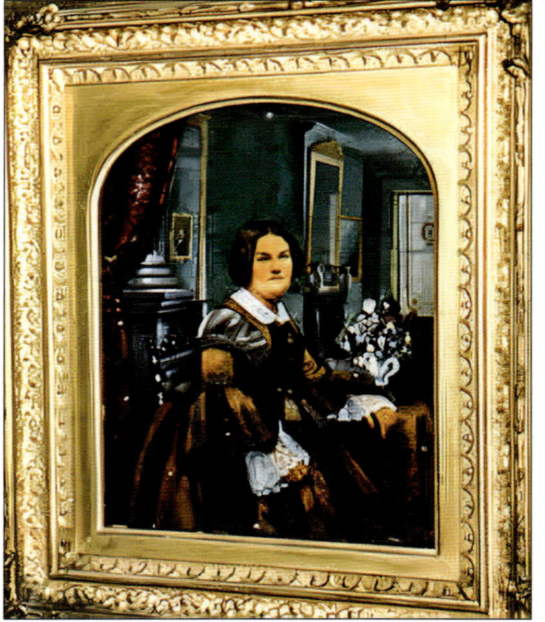

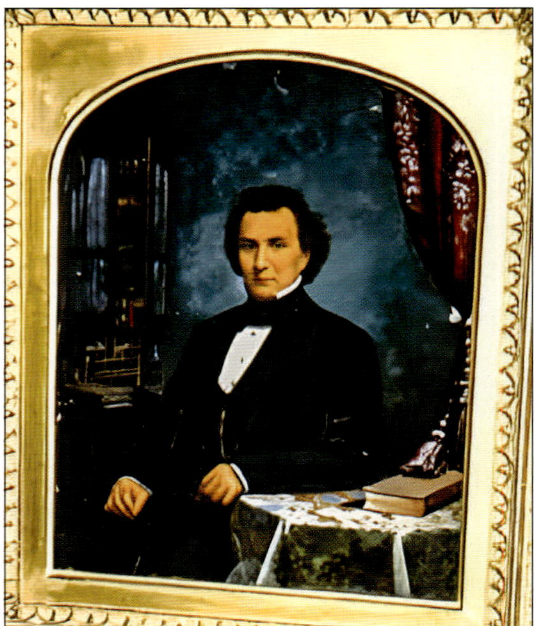

Fig. 2.10 Ivorytypes by Beale of his mother and father. Author's snapshots, with permission of Katherine Barclay.

scientific and artistic life of the city – including making ivorytypes of his parents (Fig. 2.10). Creating the ivorytypes was a complicated business. Beale used two salt prints of each photograph; coloring one lightly, the second heavily. He then sealed the lightly-colored photograph to glass, which made it translucent. Then he placed the second photograph behind it, carefully aligned, giving the whole a richly colored, almost 3-D appearance. With these ivorytypes, young Joseph used his developing artistic skills to celebrate his heritage, his parents, and their standing in the city.

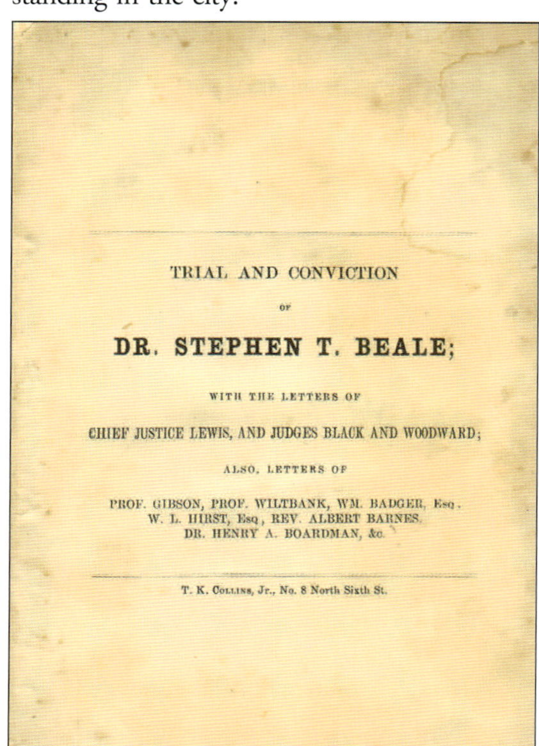

TRIAL AND CONVICTION

OF

DR. STEPHEN T. BEALE;

WITH THE LETTERS OF

CHIEF JUSTICE LEWIS, AND JUDGES BLACK AND WOODWARD;

ALSO, LETTERS OF

PROF. GIBSON, PROF. WILTBANK, WM. BADGER, Esq.
W. L. HIRST, Esq., REV. ALBERT BARNES.
DR. HENRY A. BOARDMAN, &c.

T. K. Collins, Jr., No. 8 North Sixth St.

Fig. 2.11 "Trial and Conviction of Dr. Stephen T Beale", a thirty-two-page pamphlet circulated in Dr. Beale's defense.

Accusations of Rape

This bustling, tight-knit home received a terrible blow in August 1854, when Joseph was thirteen – just coming into puberty. A young woman patient of his father's, Miss Narcissa Mudge, accused the doctor of raping her while she was in his dentist's chair under ether. Dr. Beale's sensational trial was front-page news, not only in the Philadelphia papers, but also in the *New York Times* and across the country. The testimony was detailed and scandalous, as this sample suggests:

> [He] put his hand on my arm under the sleeve up my arm. I had a loose sleeve; he did it once; he put his hand on my breast under my dress on the bosom, he put his hand on my person under my dress ... He went round before me and raised my clothes. I am perfectly distinct in my memory of that ... .[12]

Though a physician had never examined Miss Mudge to confirm the rape, and no witnesses ever came forth, a jury convicted Dr. Beale with a recommendation for clemency, which was rejected. It was a classic "he said, she said" situation, and as nasty a business as any we have seen in our modern times, with legal grandstanding, accusations of a prejudiced and drunken jury, political cowardice, melodramatic spin doctors, and sinister hangers-on. Dr. Beale began serving a four-and-a-half-year prison sentence.

His wife and colleagues refused to accept the verdict, mounting attempt after attempt to have

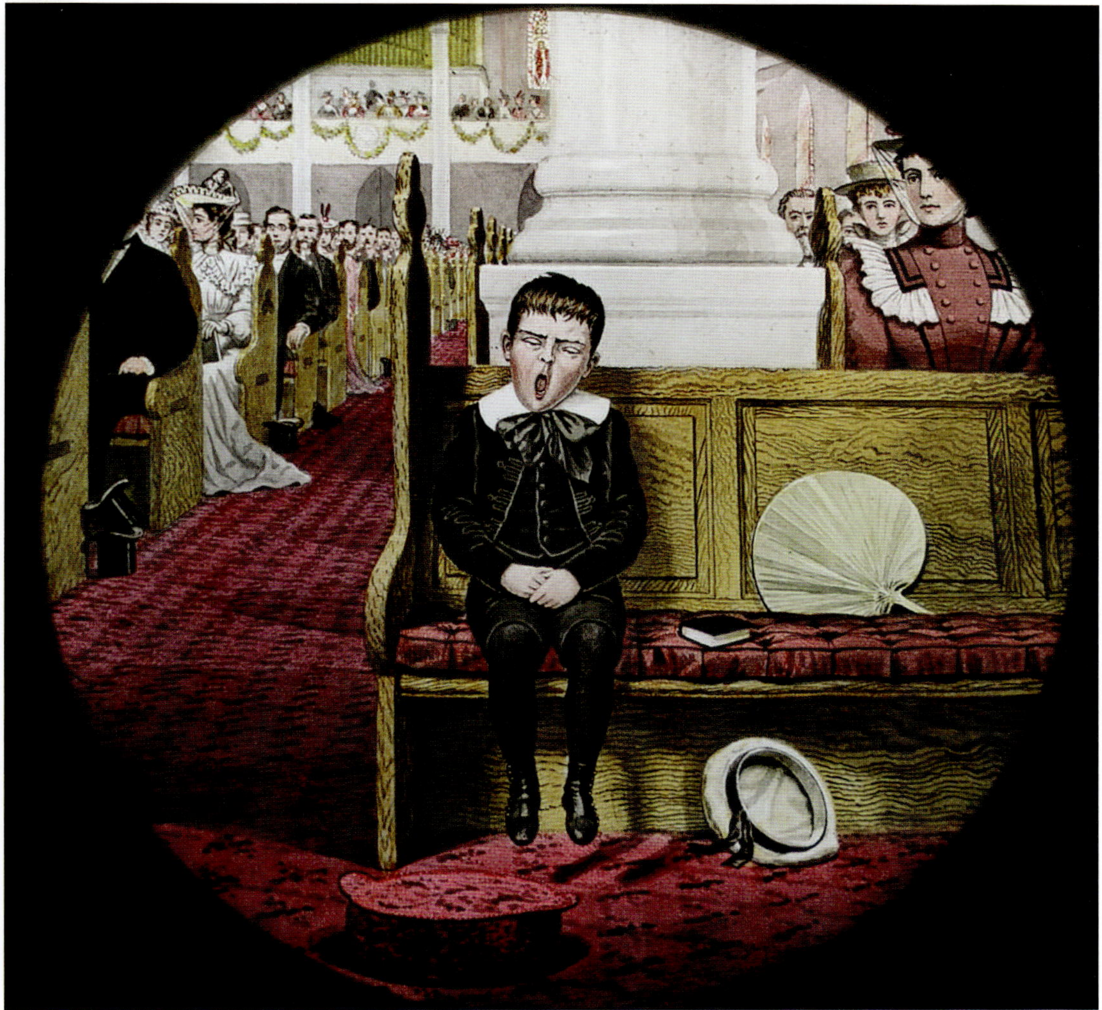

Fig. 2.12 Beale's slide of "Jack in Church" from the *Artistic Gems* group. Perhaps young Joe sometimes felt like the boy pictured here.

him pardoned. Governor Pollock received letters from 63 dentists and doctors saying that, "testimony as to matters transpiring under the influence of ether is unsafe and unreliable", and a booklet of similar import was printed and distributed by Dr. Beale's friends to rouse the public (Fig. 2.11). He received character testimonials from Philadelphia's mayor and fifty members of the city council, from five thousand citizens, and from five members of the jury. Eventually the appeals worked. After Dr. Beale had served a year in prison, Governor Pollock decreed, according to newspaper accounts:

> *I am now satisfied* that the defendant, Dr. Stephen T. Beale, is not guilty of the crime whereof he stands charged, and was convicted upon evidence unreliable in its character and insufficient in amount.[13]

Dr. Beale returned home and resumed his practice. Though Joseph never once mentions the trial in his diary (which began two months after his father's return), the experience must have been a searing one for a 13-year-old boy, especially since the trial was so public and Joseph's mother took such an active part in the efforts to have her husband released from prison. Surely, it drew the family more tightly together – facing shame and financial ruin, yet supported by so many friends. It may also have contributed to Joseph's choice to avoid a career as a dentist, though his father had trained him as his apprentice, and he was a good enough practitioner to take care of his father's patients when his father was ill. If the rape trial caused him to question a dentistry career, perhaps some good came out of this incident. For at the first public recognition of his artistic talent, Joe moved rapidly away from dentistry, and toward a career as an artist.

Religious Education

Beale's family was intensely religious, attending services frequently (Fig. 2.12). Often these services were those of denominations other than their own Presbyterian faith – a rather unusual ecumenical approach:

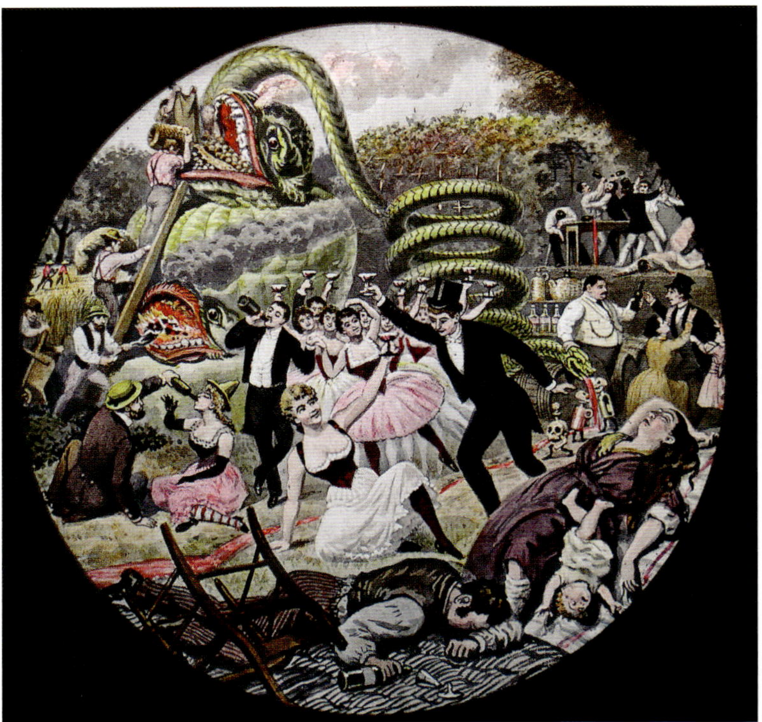

Fig. 2.13 Beale's slide of "The Whiskey Demon" in the *Intemperance Subjects* group. Extravagant images were common in the fight against alcohol.

> Sunday is pleasant. This morning Aunty went to Dr. Boardman's church & heard a stranger preach, & Pa, Ma, Steve, Clara, Emily & I went to Mr. Chamber's Church & the Rev. Mr. Neill preached & Pa & Ma lead the singing. This afternoon Steven & I went up to Mr. Breed's Church & found there was no service there this afternoon. Tonight Aunty, Steve & I went to Concert Hall & heard a stranger [preach].[14]

Usually, this frantic church going was within white Protestant traditions, but it also included a Black church and a Catholic Mass.

The vast fund of biblical lore that Beale learned during these hundreds of church visits was to become invaluable to him once he began painting religious pictures for magic lantern slides. (He eventually painted about 700 religious subjects.) His knowledge of the Bible was so thorough that he could combine details from different biblical sources to provide a rich visual texture for each scene.

The ecumenical nature of Beale's early religious education had another benefit as well. It helped him avoid references or images that might offend important religious denominations, and hence cut into the market for his slides – a danger of which Briggs and his distributors were well aware.

Connected with the Beale family's religion was its awareness of the dangers of alcohol, and the importance of temperance (Fig. 2.13). By the 1860s the temperance movement had grown to significant proportions. Temperance parades passed the Beale home on a regular basis, and the family attended temperance meetings regularly.

> This evening Pa, Ma, Steve & I went to hear Mr. Gough lecture on "temperance" at the Academy of Music ... The place was jammed, & it is pretty certain more tried to get in & had to go away than did get in. I had to stand up all the time, but had a very good position. The lecture lasted about 2 hours long, but did not seem so.[15]

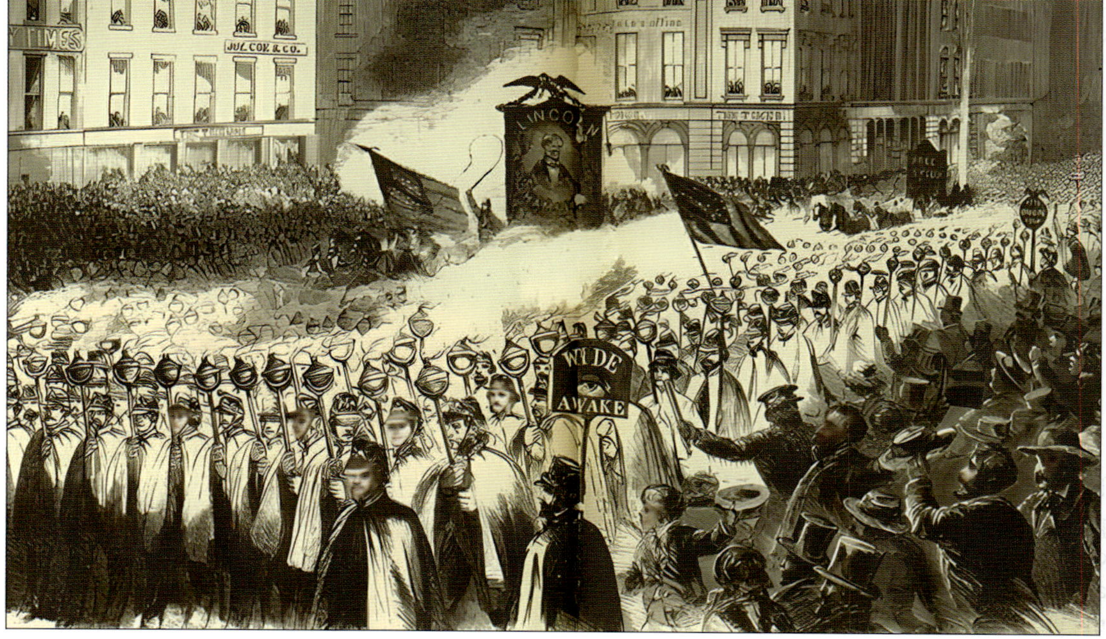

Fig. 2.14 *Harper's Weekly*, October 13, 1860 depicts a political parade of the sort that Beale described. Note the torches, the costuming, the sequencing of different kinds of imagery.
Library of Congress.

Beale's belief in temperance allowed him to sympathetically interpret the lantern slides used in temperance lectures and to create some remarkable images of the horrors of liquor.

Pictures on Parade

Once things settled down in the Beale home, its central location in Philadelphia made it easy for young Joseph to indulge in one of his favorite pastimes – parade watching. In the 1850s and '60s parades were a common expression of a wide range of social sentiment (Fig. 2.14). Besides the yearly Fourth of July and Washington's Birthday celebrations, Beale witnessed parades by the Oddfellows Fraternal Order, The Independent Order of Temperance Cadets, The Colored Free Masons, The Firemen, a French company in Zouave uniform, a Dutch company in Turkish uniform, and – once the Civil War began to brew – scores of parades for Abraham Lincoln and the soldiers of the Army of the Potomac.[16]

Parades were not exactly a form of cinema since they did not appear on screen, but, like panoramas, they did consist of a series of visual images, passing before an audience, and those images were designed to stir the emotions and to convey a message. Beale was fascinated, and because of his constant exposure to the efforts of so many different parading groups, he became an expert critic of the art of the parade. He commented regularly in his diary about the effectiveness of different parade presentations, and gradually built his own sense of visual spectacle, attending particularly to matters of light and color.

> The Republican Invincibles [alone] had over 800 in line, with their 4 flags, 1st an American, then a Red, a White & a blue. They also had some drummers in the middle of their line to make it more lively or to serve as a connecting link. The clubs all wear the uniform of hat, & cape, & each carries a lantern. There is variety of color of the uniforms, but they are all alike in all other respects. As "Abe Lincoln" is called a "Rail Splitter" there were some axes & mauls in the line. One axe of blue glass had some lights in it & looked very well.[17]

Notice that while Beale is thinking about artistic patterns here, he is not thinking of patterns of color and form in a fixed space, as the usual artist of his time would. Instead, he was studying the effect of moving images passing by the spectator's view – the ***sequence*** of flag colors, the drummers "to serve as a connecting link", the variety of color for the same type of uniform. He was studying something analogous to what the showmen of the time called "the continuous plan" of lantern lecturing, where thought was given to the relationship of the parts, avoiding the "spasmodic, hitchy way" of stringing together pictures. This was similar to the approach that the movies would come to call *continuity editing*, linking together a sequence of images so that they made sense and had dramatic impact.

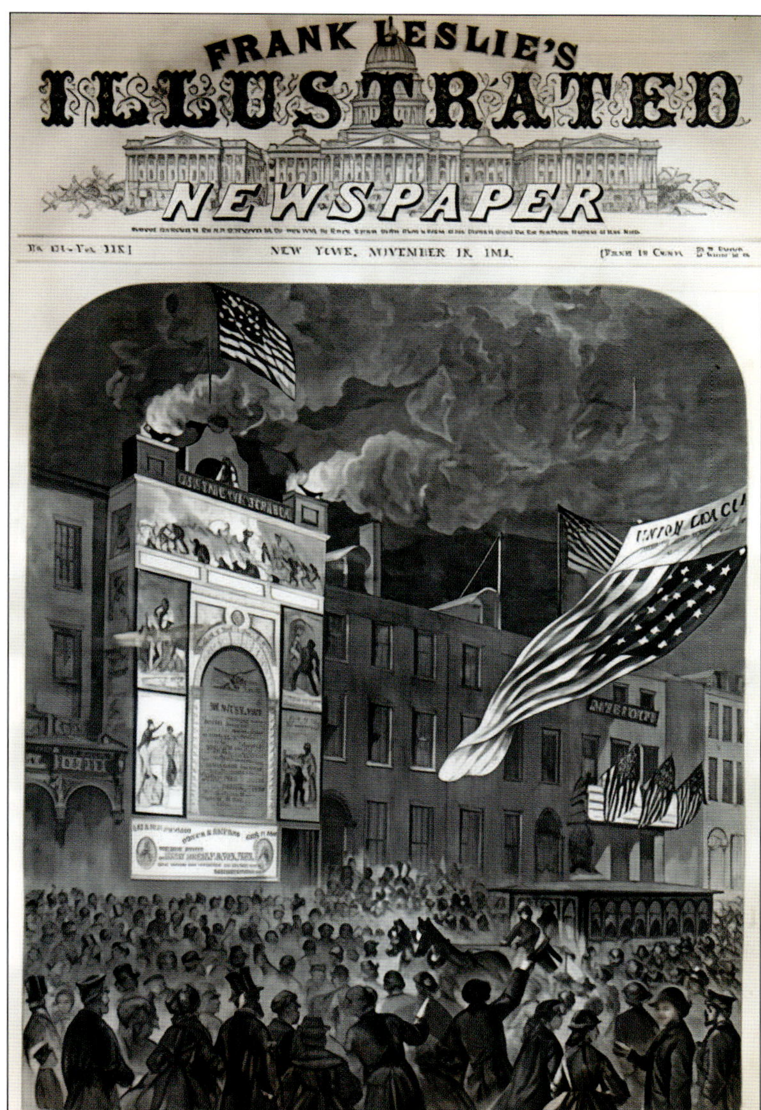
FRANK LESLIE'S ILLUSTRATED NEWSPAPER

Fig. 2.15 ***Frank Leslie's Illustrated Newspaper*****, page 1, September 18, 1864 featured the transparency Beale had worked on.**

The second thing that Beale often comments on concerning parades and other public celebrations is their use of light, as in the lighted blue axe mentioned above. Here is his description of the Washington's Birthday display in

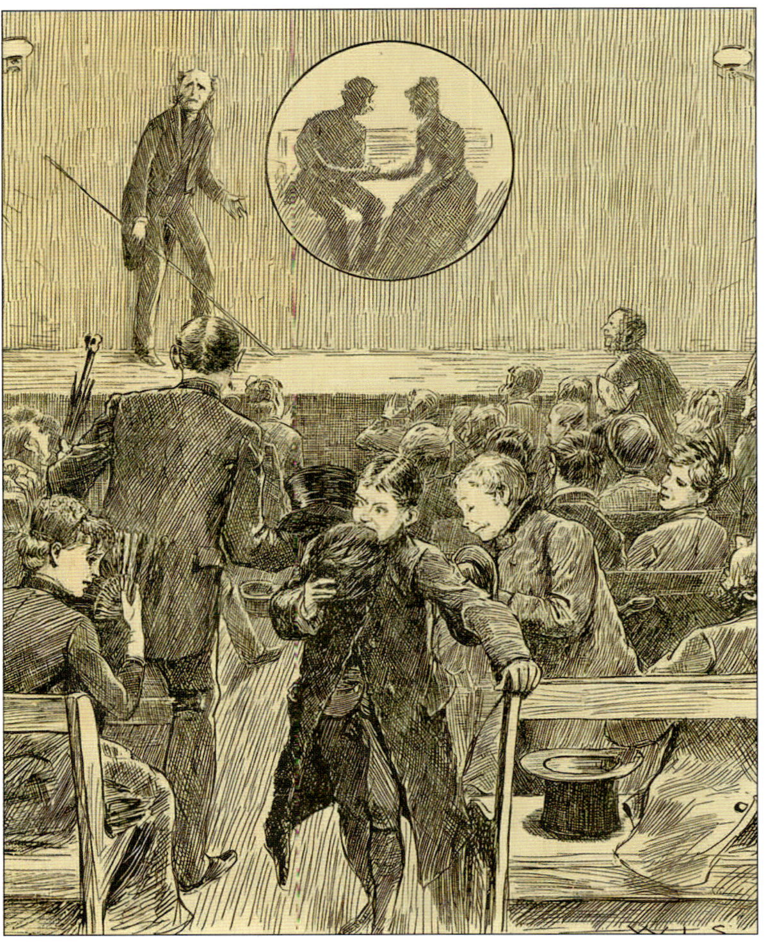

Fig. 2.16 Boring lantern showmen could expect to lose their audiences ... or worse.

1862, in the evening, after the ritual reading of Washington's *Farewell Address.*

> All the way down Chestnut street there were beautiful transparencies both sides, & the street was jammed with people on the pavements, & in the middle of the street too, & we, of course, got our share of rough treatment and mud ... .
>
> The club house, 13th & Walnut, was illuminated with candles at every pane of glass, & had a beautiful American flag hanging so that the light on it showed several squares away. In one of the windows, they had a pure white marble head & bust of Washington & the American flag. (silk) covering the pedestal & this was set off with a dark red background & brilliantly lighted from above ... About 10 o'clock the rain began to descend & drove the people home, & thus ended the illumination, which was beautiful while it lasted.[18]

The streets of Philadelphia were giving the young artist not only a "hands-on" education in sequential staging and visual storytelling, but in the effects produced by combining color and light, and in the drama that could be achieved with techniques like the *top lighting* used to emphasize Washington's bust. Even more important was his experience with *back lighting* that he gained by working on a major city project, a huge transparency. When the state of Maryland freed the slaves in 1864, Philadelphia celebrated with a painted color transparency, about 100 feet high, backlit with 154 gas lights – "one of the most imposing ever displayed to public view". Beale drew some of the elaborate lettering on it, so he tried to obtain the issue of *Leslie's* that featured it on its front page (Fig. 2.15). Unfortunately, all copies were sold out.[19]

Later he employed his understanding of light to the fullest when creating the art of the magic lantern. There he could use the lantern light reflected back from the screen to give his images a luminosity that no canvas painting could hope to achieve. Magic lantern art was, quite literally, painting with light, and once he had the chance to move from the black and white engravings on which he spent the first 15 years of his professional life, he must have reached back into this well of early artistic analysis. His spectacular use of dramatic lighting and light-infused color became one of the most distinctive qualities of his magic lantern art.

Young Joseph's family supported his interest in art and parades, but they also attended a wide range of amusements that give a good sense of the entertainment with which the magic lantern show was competing. As a musical family, they often went to concerts, but Beale also enjoyed the more popular entertainments – dwarfs like Little Fairy ("smaller than Tom Thumb!"), the black-faced Campbell's Minstrels, watching a high-wire act over the Schuylkill River, watching laughing gas administered "to about a dozen gentlemen and 6 ladies", getting shocked at an Electrical Show, and going to the circus. "The lepards got up on The Professor's shoulders & sat on his knees."

As this little sampling suggests, it was a varied and boisterous period of American entertainment, where "the people" and their champions in the press quite consciously formed public taste. Shakespeare was popular in the theaters because he appealed to the high brows and to the pits; all classes frequented music halls in this period; everybody loved the melodramas. Theaters were raucous, noisy, and participatory – more like one of today's sports events than one of today's plays.[20]

In our recreated magic lantern shows, we do

our best to ease the modern audience back into this participatory mode – so different from most modern theater. But for the young Beale, immersive theatrical interaction was a natural form of entertainment. Growing up in this environment, the nephew of an internationally known entertainer, a bit of a panoramacist himself, Beale must have absorbed the importance of holding audience attention. Back then, "audience feedback" was often frequent and direct. Audiences felt free to get up and leave (Fig. 2.16). Boos and hisses were not simply for melodramatic villains, and the tomatoes not simply for salad.

Magic Lantern Shows

Of course, Beale's most direct training for the magic lantern medium must have been his experience of magic lantern shows themselves. Beale's diary records several times during his teenage years when the family went to see such shows. Once Beale took his little brothers and sisters to see an Exhibition in the lecture room of Calvary Presbyterian Church. The show was probably a series of illustrated Bible stories, perhaps mixed with a few comic slides to amuse the children. Beale reports that the "room was crowded" and that "it was very interesting & the children behaved very well". A second time, five of the children went to see a show the day after Christmas, 1859, no doubt featuring some Christmas stories. Both of these shows probably used hand-painted slides and an oil lantern that produced a relatively weak projected image.

The next year, also at Christmas, an advertisement for a much more expansive magic lantern show caught the collective eye of the Beale family. The ad promised "An Entertainment of INTELLECTUAL GRANDEUR" with "GIGANTIC STEREOSCOPIC PICTURES", and included "an accomplished artist [presiding] at the Piano". The family passed up a chance to see Tom Thumb at the Assembly Building and chose instead this "ENTERTAINMENT WITHOUT AN EQUAL" at the classically sedate Concert Hall (Fig. 2.17).

The press was ecstatic about this "stereoscopic" performance, produced by P. E. Abel and T. Leyland, using slides produced by the Langenheim Brothers. Despite its name, the show did not create a 3-D images, but it was one of the first in the city to project photographic images with a powerful illuminant (limelight) in a large hall.[21] The *Philadelphia Bulletin* critic predicted (quite accurately, as it turned out) that the "wonderful combination of chemical and optical apparatus ... promises an exhaustless fund of intellectual amusement for the future. Pictures start forth in living clearness, so life-like and distinct that ... a very little force of imagination would form you a component of the scene."

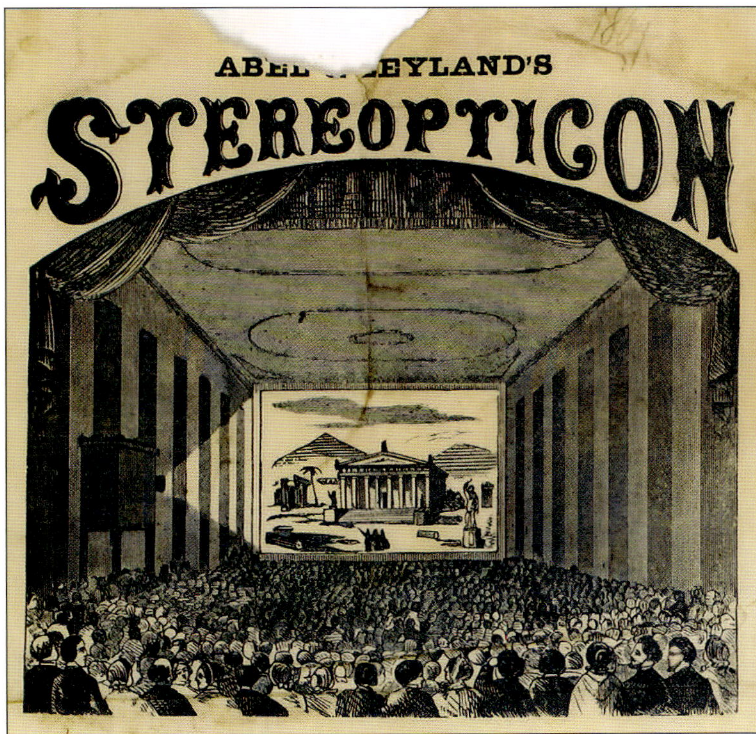

Fig. 2.17 Portion of a broadside for Abel and Leyland's *Stereopticon*, 1860–61. This broadside for a later run of the *Stereopticon* captures the "Big-Screen" excitement. Courtesy, Library Company of Philadelphia.

Beale was also enthusiastic, though he kept his critic's hat on:

> This evening Pa, Ma, Aunt Harriet Cox, Aunty Boggs, Steve, Louey, & I went to Concert Hall to the "Stereopticon", a new exhibition, a little like a magic lantern but much more powerfully lighted. The pictures are all taken from nature & are transparent photographs on glass, & are pictures for the stereoscope. By this new instrument they are thrown on a large canvas containing 600 square feet. The pictures are from all parts of the world, especially Europe, & some are shown much larger than reality; so that they appear on most too grand a scale; such as ladies & gentlemen, 10 feet high, looking at Niagara falls. The Hall was crowded, & the audience seemed to be very much pleased, & gave extra applause when familiar places were shown.[22]

Obviously, the new medium impressed Beale. He saw immediately its ability to hold the attention of a large audience, and, as usual when reporting on spectacles, noted those aspects that

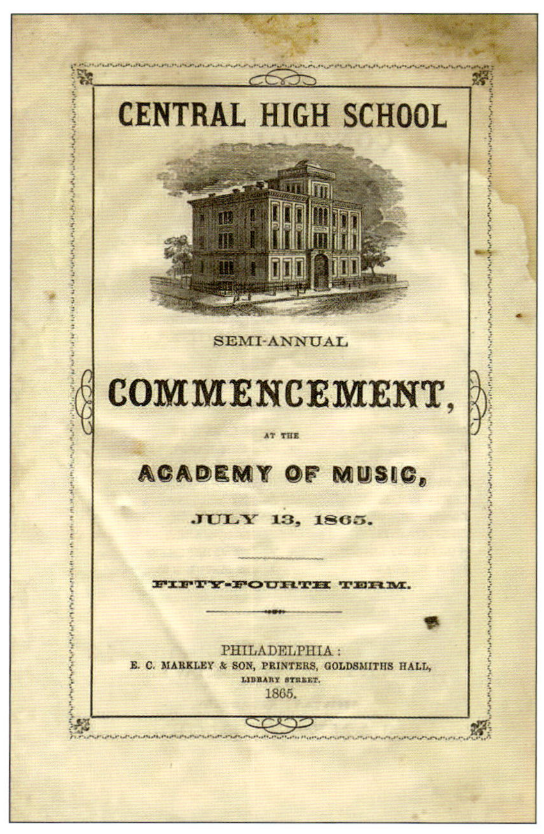
CENTRAL HIGH SCHOOL

SEMI-ANNUAL

COMMENCEMENT,

AT THE

ACADEMY OF MUSIC,

JULY 13, 1865.

FIFTY-FOURTH TERM.

PHILADELPHIA:
E. C. MARKLEY & SON, PRINTERS, GOLDSMITHS HALL,
LIBRARY STREET.
1865.

Fig. 2.18 Central High School Commencement program, July 13, 1865. It shows Central as it appeared in the first graduation Beale attended as a Professor at the school.

were appealing, especially those fitting the old showman's maxim, "they like what they know".

Beale's comment that some of the pictures were "shown much larger than reality; so that they appear on most too grand a scale" is significant in part because it is one of the very few times he comments negatively about any public presentation. But even more important, when Beale himself became a magic lantern artist, he and Briggs decided to avoid the *close-up* that could be achieved by using a short *distance of framing* – the apparent distance between the *frame* of the picture and the scene within. With very few exceptions his images for the magic lantern use *medium long shots* or *medium shots,* and only occasionally, *medium close-ups* or *long shots*. That is, he generally places the action in the middle distance, so that even when the actors are projected on a large screen they do not appear "too grand" or, for that matter, "too small". Beale's approach was consistent with the generally accepted lantern practice of his time. It also fit with his overall attempt to create "reality" on the screen by placing the actors in a stage setting and then supporting their action with rich contextual detail – detail that could only be seen if the actors were of medium size.

Learning To Create Space for the Screen

Beale's comments on the distance of framing in the Stereopticon Exhibition probably grew out of the more formal art training he was now receiving. He was attending Central High School (Fig. 2.18), where he received an excellent and unusual grounding in the skills that would later be necessary to create three-dimensional *space* on a two-dimensional screen.

Central was the elite public boys' high school of Philadelphia – the pride of the city. Admission was by examination and open to all classes of society. Competition for entry was keen. Beale took the examination in February 1857, and at first failed with a 58.8 mark. But during the following summer and fall he prepared for another attempt, all the while sketching steadily. This time he was accepted with a score of 77.4, about the middle of his class.

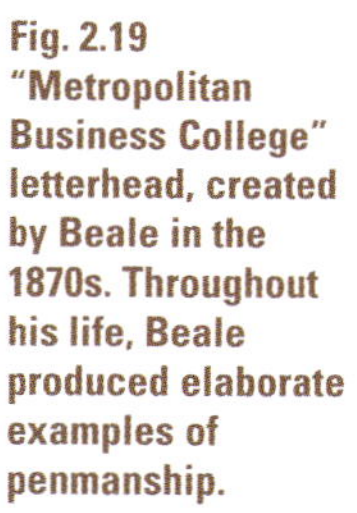
Fig. 2.19 "Metropolitan Business College" letterhead, created by Beale in the 1870s. Throughout his life, Beale produced elaborate examples of penmanship.

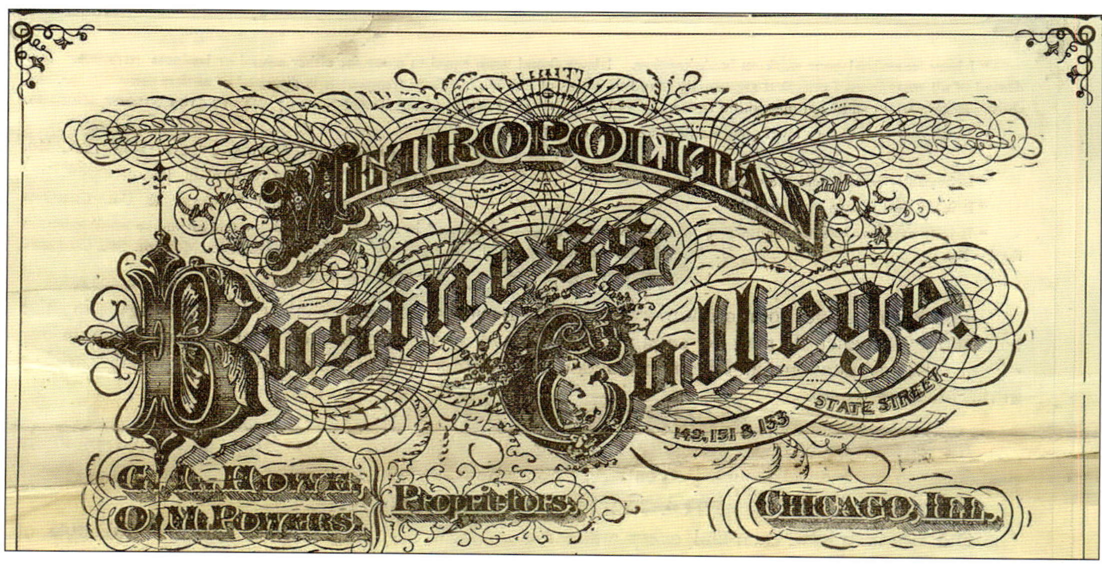

The course of study at Central was as rigorous as admission.[23] Of the 120 admitted with Beale, only 24 would graduate four years later. Students studied Greek and Latin, French and English, classical and modern history, literature, mathematics, penmanship, moral philosophy, botany and biology, physics and chemistry. All students at Central were required to take drawing, since it was assumed that if a student could draw clearly, he could think clearly. Much of the drawing instruction had a practical bent, designed to help future artisans and mechanics, which may be one reason Beale later fit so easily into a production environment, drawing for illustration jobbers, and a manufacturer of lantern slides.

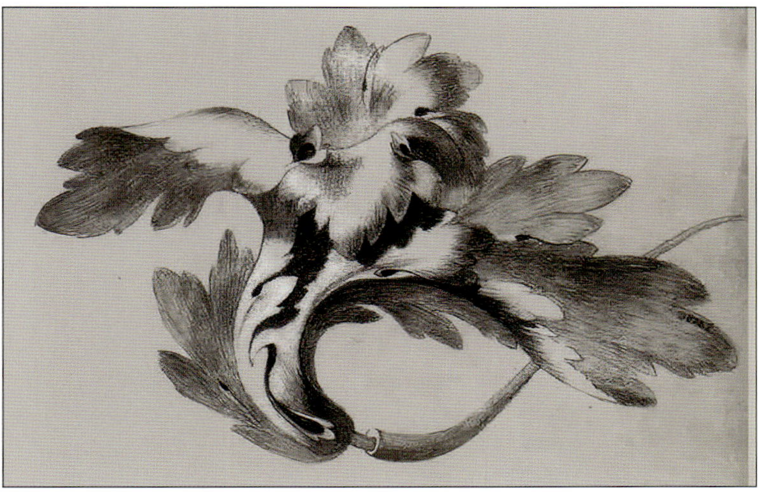

Fig. 2.20 School sketch by Beale, shows him learning to create perspective and form with shadow. Courtesy Beale Family Collection.

Fig. 2.21 Beale's "The Hanging Gardens of Babylon" from the slide set of *The Seven Wonders of the Ancient World*.

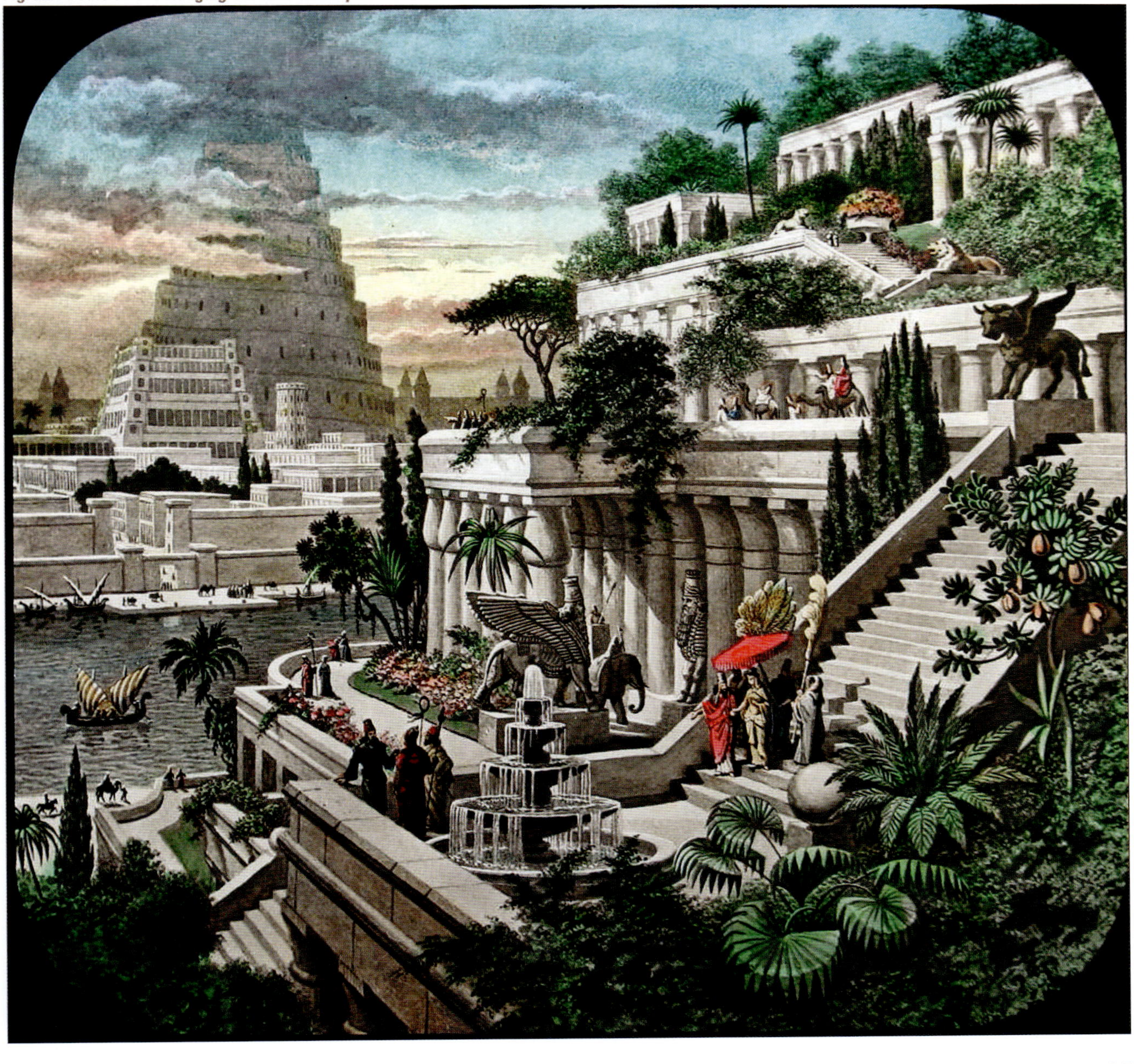

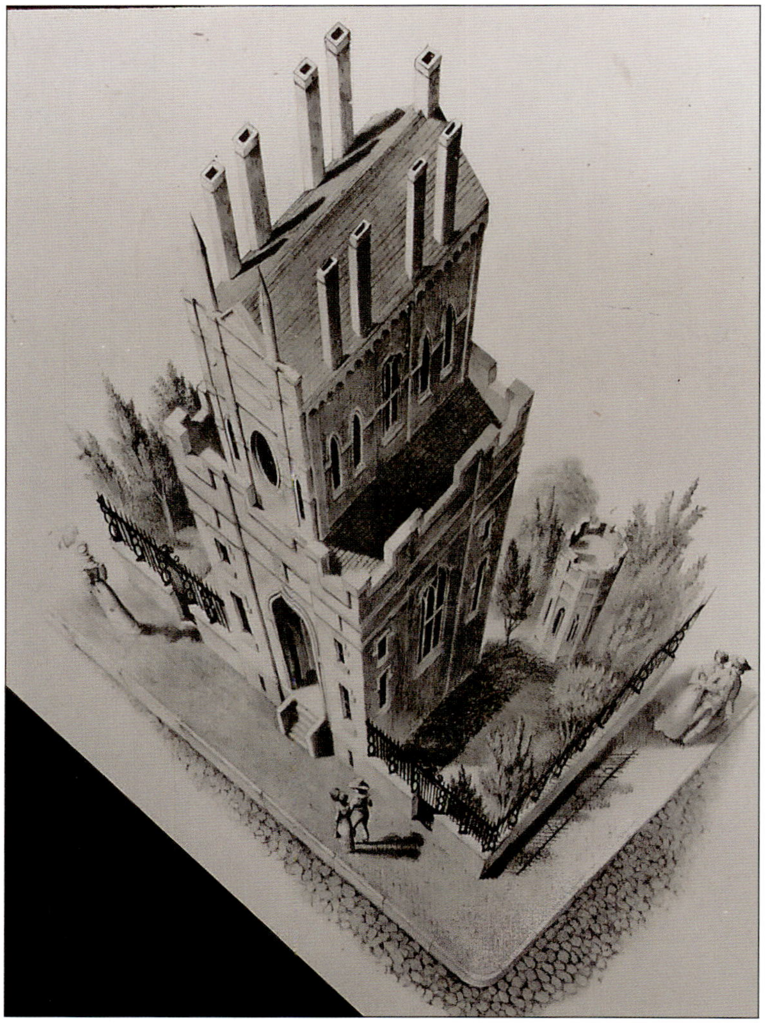

Fig. 2.22 Lantern slide of a horizontorium. Beale drew a "horizontorium" like this to demonstrate his mastery of perspective. Image from a lantern slide.

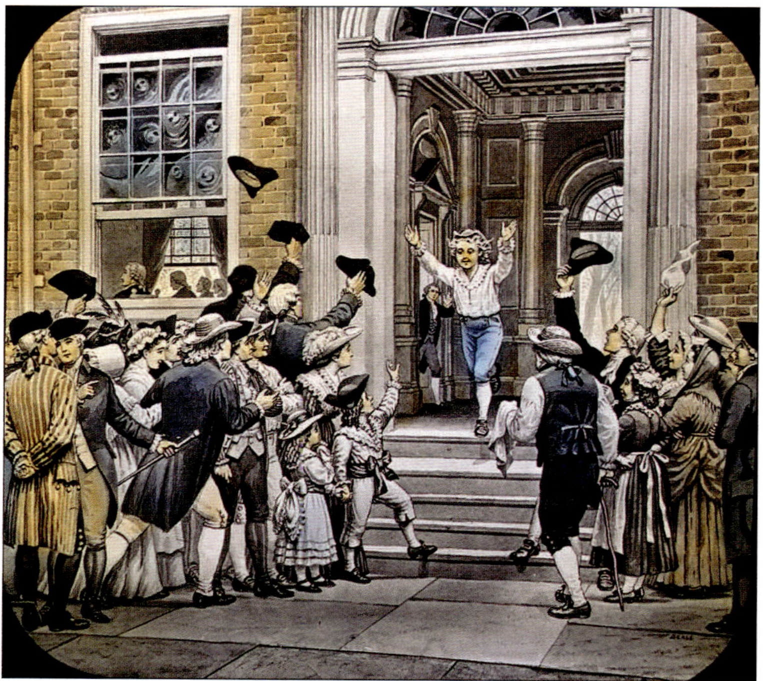

Fig. 2.23 Beale's slide 5 of *Independence Bell*. Even in a scene like this one in which the depth of field is relatively shallow, Beale could find many ways to create a sense of deep space.

Beale got off to a good start in his art class, receiving a "100" on his first project. He continued to progress well, and in the spring of the next year was chosen for a project that would launch his artistic career. It was a presentation piece, inscribed in ornamental penmanship of various styles (Fig. 2.19). It contained half a dozen portraits, each the size "to be covered by a three cent piece". Written up in the *Public Ledger*, which mentioned (as Beale notes proudly) his "name in full", the piece was carried around to show local artists, and was exhibited in the window of Bailey's store on Chestnut Street. The success of this project was an important milestone in Beale's career, for it clearly established him in his own mind and in the minds of his teachers and family as an artist with potential that should be cultivated.

The next steps in Beale's art education at Central followed the progression that had been laid out in 1840 by Central's first Professor of Drawing, the noted artist, Rembrandt Peale (son of Charles Wilson Peale), and approved as the official curriculum in 1843.[24] The heart of the Peale *Graphics* system was "accurate delineation", "practice of the hand", and "analyzing geometrical axioms". These were not so much mathematical methods of perspective as free-form "geometric eye measures" that were designed to train students to draw perspective using careful observation and a few simple tools such as reducing a scene to its component triangles, and "copying by squares". This free-hand approach was supplemented by the study of mathematical models of perspective, and by a rigorous, mathematical course in mechanical drawing. For instance, Beale's junior-year term project was "four or five mechanical figures drawn in perspective in india ink"; the next was "perspective shadows" bending over a variety of objects (Fig. 2.20).

This combination of "eye measures" and "perspective" led to a remarkable mastery, as seen in the carefully-worked-out perspective paintings of Beale's famous school-mate Thomas Eakins. But it is equally evident in the thousands of complex scenes that Beale himself rendered with such astonishing speed and realism, like this image of "The Hanging Gardens of Babylon" (Fig. 2.21). Beale used many different perspective techniques here to create a remarkable sense of grandeur and space. The image was printed in a number of magic lantern catalogs to promote the set, and was part of a series of "Seven Wonders" stamps issued by Cuba.

One of Beale's final perspective projects in school was a "horizontorium" (Fig. 2.22) – a drawing meant to be viewed with the picture placed flat on the table ("horizontally"), and the viewer looking *across* it, with the eyes almost level with the picture.[25] To see the 3-D, effect, hold this book almost level before your eyes and close to them. Look across the flat of the page. Alternately shut one eye and then the other, while twisting the page back and forth sideways, and then tipping it up and down. You'll see the building rise up off the page, and then bob and weave as the perspective changes.

Just imagine the mental gymnastics that creating such an image takes! If Beale could draw something like this, he could easily produce the on-screen equivalent of any normal *camera angle.* And he did, sometimes creating an extraordinary fluidity in his slide stories, shifting his angle with almost every slide, following the drama of the action.

The mastery of perspective that Beale gained from his Central training was strengthened later when he developed a specialty in architectural renderings, which was to become one of the most critical aspects of his success with the magic lantern. It gave him control of space and allowed him to create, without photography, a three-dimensional universe on a flat screen. Elaborate "stage sets" became characteristic of his work. He knew from his experience with the panorama that these sets were important. They created a convincing alternate universe that the viewer could enter to experience an imagined reality – the emotional life of the story or poem Beale was illustrating.

Exactly how did Beale give such dimensionality to his magic lantern art? He used the full repertoire of techniques that he had learned at Central, techniques that had long been familiar to realistic artists, photographers and the lantern community,[26] and that the movies themselves were eventually to employ.

Typically, he created the illusion of *deep space* (the distance between the plane closest to the viewer and the one furthest away) by using stage-like floors with patterned boards, flagstones, or rocks that drove the eye into the distance, and by drawing linear buildings (Fig. 2.23). Since he was ***drawing*** the different picture planes, not ***photographing*** them, it was easier for him to create sharp *focus* throughout the *depth of field* than it was for the early movies, and he used this ability to great effect. He anchored foregrounds with casually placed *props*, and used "coulisse" framing like trees along the edges of the picture to give a sense of depth to the scene beyond. He employed *size-diminution*, making objects in the distance smaller. He *overlapped* light and dark areas, objects, and figures to create different planes of space, receding into the distance. He used *sidelights* to wrap shadows around objects in order to give them depth. He used *aerial* or atmospheric techniques, putting distant details in a monochromatic haze, so that they seemed far away.[27] And he used the design elements of shape and line not only to direct the eye over the surface of the image, but also to lead it in circular patterns ever deeper into the distance.

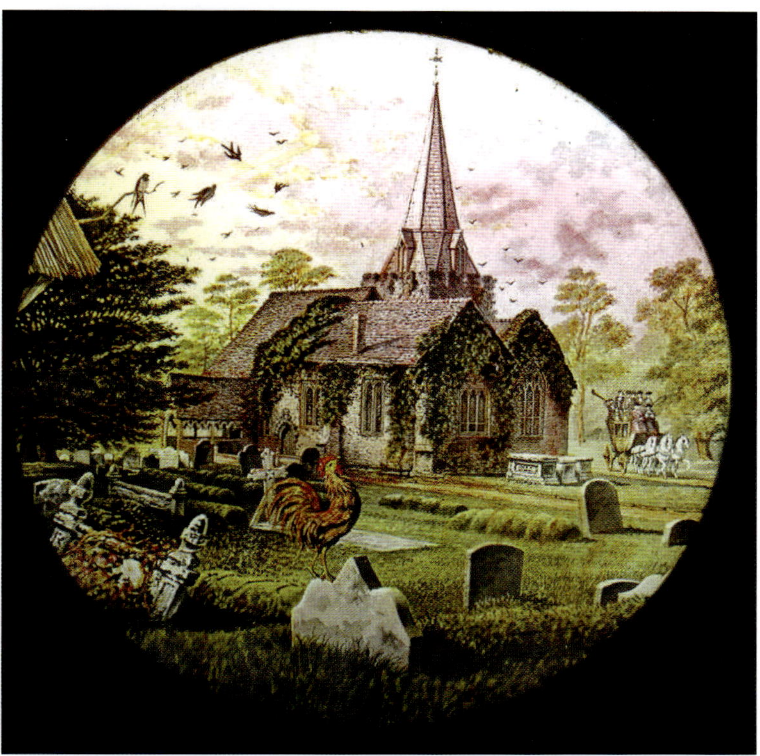

Fig. 2.24 Beale's slide 25 from *Elegy in a Country Churchyard* by Thomas Gray. Beale's design for this scene was in black and white, but he also had to be thinking ahead to color slides.

When I project one of the slides in which Beale uses his full array of perspective techniques, the "3-D" effect is stunning if you are sitting near the lantern, in the center of the hall, directly perpendicular to the screen. That is Beale's ***point of station***, the imaginary point from which he himself created the perspective drawing, so that is where the perspective effect is most powerful. If you get up and walk to the

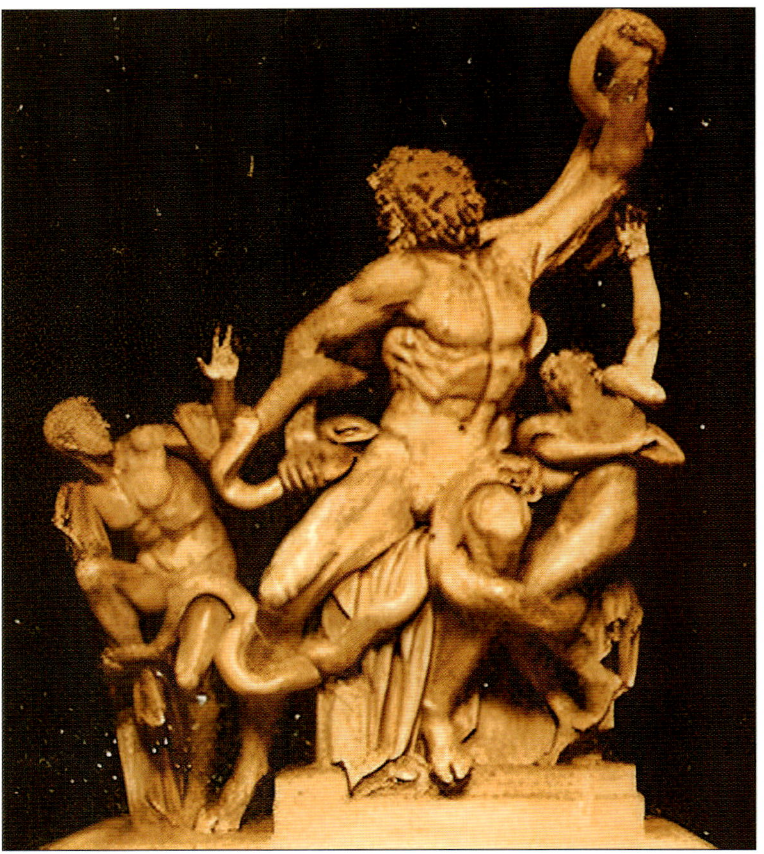

Fig. 2.25 Lantern slide of The Laocoön Group, a Roman statue that Beale studied in his drawing class.

side, you will still be able see the picture, but the "3-D" effect will diminish as you move.

Likewise, to get the full impact of the lantern images printed in this book, you need to view them as Beale intended them to be seen on screen. If you are reading with this book flat on a desk or on your lap, you are missing the full impact of Beale's art. Try holding the book up directly in front of your eyes at ninety degrees to get a sense of how Beale's perspective techniques create depth when his scenes are projected.[28]

Perspective devices were the stock-in-trade of an academic artist of Beale's time, and Beale was especially skillful in their use. But Beale turned these artistic techniques for working on a single canvas into an art form of sequential images, creating the illusion that the darkened two-dimensional screen contained a living, 3-D world of ever-changing light and space. When the movies themselves first arrived, most designers and cinematographers were satisfied with shallow space sets, like the theater, created, appropriately enough, by stage "flats". But they too would eventually seek greater depth of field, and the perspective repertoire that Beale was using for lantern slides would also become part of the art of film.

Learning to Bring Color to the Screen

Photography, newly popular in the 1850s, was another aspect of Beale's childhood that had a profound influence on his art for the magic lantern. After the success of Beale's ornamental penmanship, Professor MacNeill, Beale's art professor, introduced him to the art of photo coloring – providing flesh tones or the color of a favorite dress to black-and-white photographs. Beale was soon busy coloring photographs for family and friends, and, later, for the professional photographic studios of Philadelphia. As we've seen, he also mastered the art of ivorytype, a process that required the artist think through several overlapping steps to get from the black and white image to the final colors.[29]

These skills contributed to Beale's later proficiency as a magic lantern artist. First, his work emphasized the sense that photography was art and art was photography – that the artist's role was to do photography one better, and capture those facets of nature and life that the camera could not document, like color. It was a kind of thinking that reinforced Beale's commitment to the *realism* so typical of his work.

Second, the coloring of photographs trained Beale to think of a black-and-white medium's potential for color (Fig. 2.24). Every one of the pictures that he painted for the magic lantern was painted without color, in shades of gray. But as he painted in monochrome, Beale had to conceive of each picture as a full-color screen image, illuminated with the lantern's light. At a time when most illustrators, including Beale for many years, were limited to black and white engraving, and never worried about color, Beale in his earliest training was shifting frequently between monochromatic and color images. This facility would serve him well later, for the on-screen color of magic lantern shows continued to be one their advantages in competition with the mostly black-and-white (or only single-tint) movies.

Learning to Bring Figures to the Screen

While studying art at Central, Beale was also admitted to the Academy of the Fine Arts in Philadelphia, and began taking the Antiques Class, in which students drew from plaster casts of famous sculptures. This was the typical beginning training for art students, because, as one of the instructors at the Academy commented, the uniform color of a cast showed "form more clearly and truly than in life where the various tints of the flesh often bewilder the young and inexperienced student". The students' drawings were expected to be accurate and reportorial. Beale spent almost a month correcting one drawing, The Laocoön Group (Fig. 2.25), once again reinforcing a commitment to precision.[30]

While Beale was drawing from antique casts, he was also studying anatomy in a series of lectures, first in the Academy, and then at Jefferson Medical College. The "Program of Anatomical Studies" was taught by Dr. A. R. Thomas, and covered human skin, muscles, bones, joints, comparative anatomy, sexual and national characteristics, and finally, the "Passions and Emotions" and their impact on the "Anatomy and Expression of the Face".

For a while Dr. Thomas had experimented with using mannequins for his lectures, since female students found the cadavers "too repugnant", but the mannequins were prohibitively expensive. Beale did not object to the cadavers:

> We are now on the muscles, & the lecturer is using a "recent subject", which we believe to have been a colored man.

The knowledge of anatomy that Beale derived from these courses, and from books he studied were essential to him later as a magic lantern artist, when he did not have the luxury of models. He had to construct whatever action and expression was required by the demands of the stories he illustrated from his knowledge of the basic structure of the human body. This knowledge was a significant advantage over his coworker at the Briggs company, Herman Tholey, whose figures were often faulty. Briggs complained that Tholey had "not the ability to correct or improve drawings", and sometimes sent Tholey's work to Beale to "make the figures anatomically correct".[31]

While Beale's work was definitely better than Tholey's, it was not consistent. Usually, Beale's slide figures are well proportioned and have a natural, though nineteenth-century, sense of energy and action. Sometimes, however, the action does not flow from the subject's center, as Beale had been taught to do in Peale's *Graphics*, but seems imposed by a concept of what the movement should look like, and as a consequence appear stiff and formal, like the poses struck by actors and politicians.

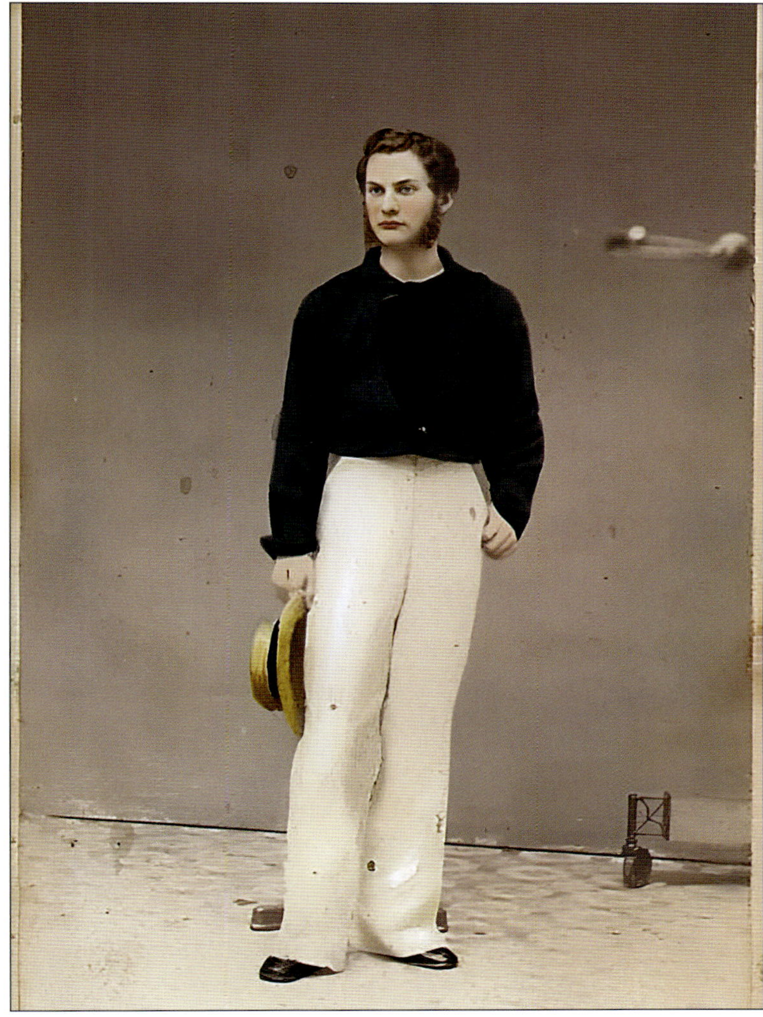

Fig. 2.26 Beale in his Undine Rowing Uniform, a picture taken May 23,1863. He has sprouted new "sideburns", a hair style named after Union general Ambrose Burnside.

Once Beale graduated from Central in February of 1862, the intensity of his outside art activities at the Academy increased. He drew steadily from the antique casts; he frequented photography establishments, increasing his coloring business; he made those ivorytypes of Pa and Ma; he began doing serious watercolors; he exhibited at the Philadelphia Sketch Club; and he met with other artists around the city. Then on June 21st, Professor MacNeill, the long-time art professor at Central, resigned to go into the navy.

The Student Becomes the Teacher

Beale wanted the job. Almost immediately he started preparing for the competition to determine the successor to MacNeill's position as Professor of Drawing and Writing (Penman-

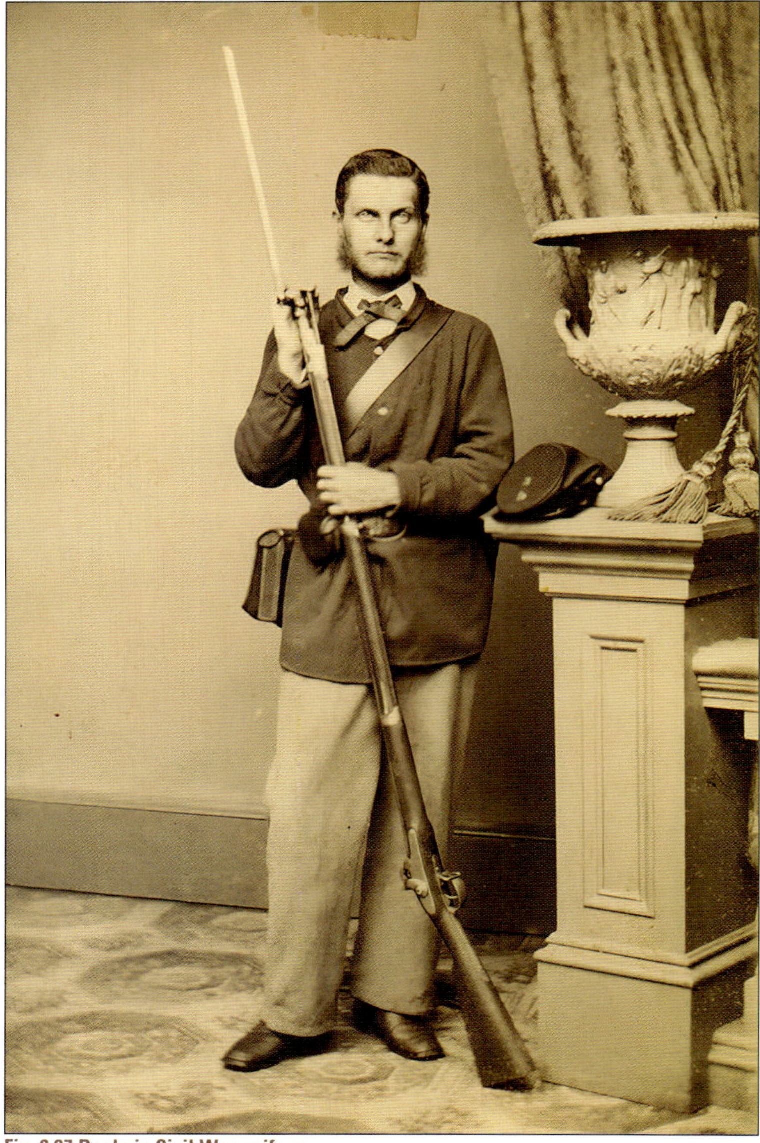

Fig. 2.27 Beale in Civil War uniform.
Collection of the Historical Society of Pennsylvania.

ship). He began working in new media – sketching outdoors in oils for the first time, and modeling a head in clay. He created another horizontorium, and met personally with almost all 25 School-Board members.

Four applicants began the examination process, among them Beale's schoolmate at Central, Thomas Eakins who was two years his junior. Eakins would later become Director of the Pennsylvania Academy of the Fine Arts, and one of America's most outstanding painters, known especially for his mastery of perspective and naturalistic style. The examination was extremely arduous for them both, requiring personal interviews, a large portfolio of work (Beale sent his up in a cart), and answers to 40 written questions, including items such as:

> 11. Show by an example how to find the shadow cast by a horizontal straight line situated in the angle formed by two vertical planes perpendicular to each other when the shadow falls upon the angle.
>
> 15. Show by example how circular steps are drawn in perspective.

Two of the competitors quit before the examination was completed. Beale and Eakins worked until midnight. Both finished, but Beale won the appointment, and the day after receiving his notification, set off for work:

> I went to the High School, not as a pupil, as I was a year ago, but as professor. Each division, every boy in the school, comes to me.[32]

He had five classes a day, 52 seats to a class, for which he was paid $1,200 a year (about $38,000 in 2025).[33] When you think about it, this was quite an extraordinary situation. Imagine young Joe, just a year or so older than his students, training 250 of them a day in the Rembrandt Peale art curriculum. The pressure must have been intense. What better environment for mastering that curriculum, which, years later, was to give him the freedom to move his magic lantern settings so freely?

Apparently, he was a good teacher, and had little trouble with discipline, except with two students, one "Graham", whom he expelled for throwing an inkwell across the room; and with the wonderfully-named trio of "Little, DeHaven, and Grim", to whom he assigned 50 notes each for making rude "noises with india rubber".[34]

Beale continued his lessons in penmanship (at which he became quite expert); he continued the Antiques Classes; and he was elected an active member of the Undine Barge Club, the same rowing club to which Eakins belonged (Fig. 2.26). The city was full of Union soldiers from the Civil War then raging in the south, and although Beale had discussed enlisting with his family, the battles seemed very far away amidst the pleasures of his new-found status as Professor – a title he continued to use throughout his life.

Training by War

Then it was June 16, 1863. Suddenly, unexpectedly, the rebels were in Pennsylvania. Philadelphia itself was threatened. The city was in an uproar.

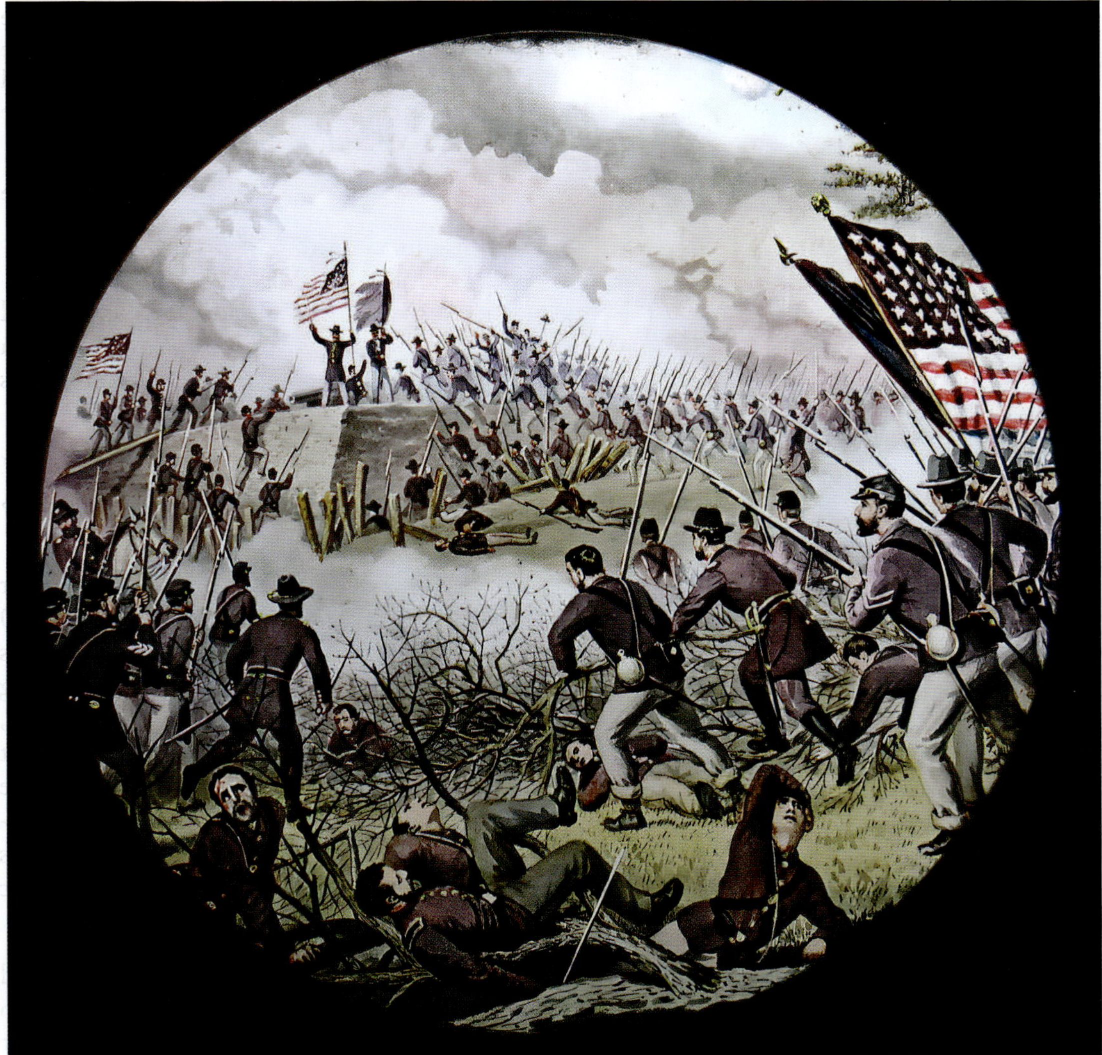

Fig. 2.28 Beale's "Battle of St. Petersburg" from the *American* History group. Beale's Civil War images are similar to those of the "artist correspondents" for the national magazines.

The next day, June 17, Beale and his brother Steve enlisted in the 33rd Pennsylvania Volunteers, Blue Reserves. On June 18th he had his hair cut a quarter inch long all over – "sandpapered style" – the full extent of his military training. On the 19th he found himself in Company D, sleeping in his overcoat on the floor of a boxcar ... headed for the front (Fig. 2.27).

He was encamped at what would become Fort Washington, just outside of Harrisburg. Under the command of one of his former students, he set to work building defenses for the city. His artistic talents were quickly recognized however, and he was appointed regimental artist, giving him a chance to sketch some of the scenes around him.

Twelve thousand men were in the camp, the air was hot and steamy with rain, mud was everywhere, food was scarce. White soldiers worked side by side with Black laborers, day and night, feverishly clearing trees and digging rifle pits. The enemy was expected to attack momentarily.

Beale's regiment was sent out to harass the rebels in the mountains. His unit met Union soldiers who had been captured by the rebels, stripped of their guns and shoes, and set free to wander barefoot, famished, and desolate. The regiment camped in fields that reeked of rotting flesh because the rebels had slaughtered horses and cattle at all the strategic locations in order to infect the water and air. As a result, Beale's unit not only became sick, they starved. They went so long without food that their general refused an order to march until his men had been fed.

Twice they saw action:

> We were so near the Rebels that the bullets went through those who were shot. I was at the same stack of wheat with a Cavalry man when he was hit; the bullet passed through the wheat stack & then struck him. He said he was shot & carried his carbine away with him toward his

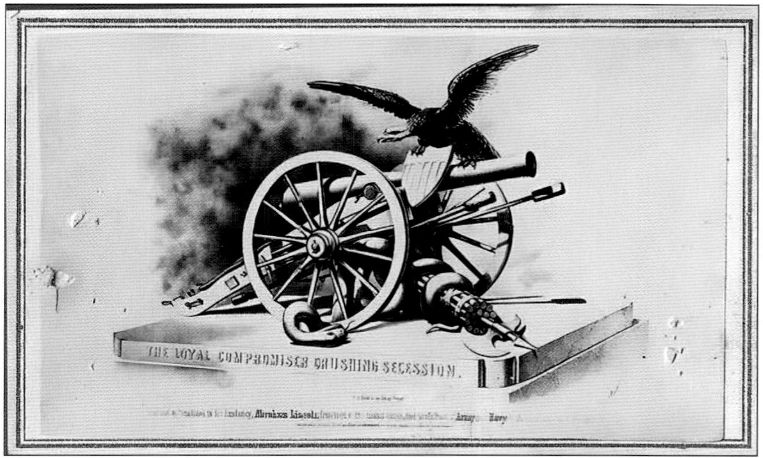

Fig. 2.29 Beale's "The Loyal Compromiser Crushing Succession". He drew this image to be sold at the 1864 Great Central Fair for the Sanitary Commission.

> horse. I then ran one stack ahead & saw an infantry man shot through his left hand. He dropped his musket & left it, & wrapped his handkerchief around his hand as he went out. I fired about fifteen rounds of ball cartridges & only one cap missed fire.[35]

This passage of Beale's diary, typical of the way he reports war scenes, suggests the strength of his reportorial nature – his cinema verité style. He does not embellish the horrors of war, nor even express the emotions he must have felt under conditions of severe stress. Instead, he piles fact upon fact, until the reader sees the scene precisely. The same reportorial technique gives Beale's slide images much of their power. The visual facts anchor the action in time and space, until the viewer feels exactly what it must have been like to be there (Fig. 2.28).

Beale was sketching the war as well as writing about it. He sent some of his sketches to *Frank Leslie's Illustrated News*, but they were not published, probably because *Leslie's* already had a "special artist", George Law, providing pictures from the same area. Unfortunately, the rest of Beale's drawings were lost. To facilitate a rapid march after the enemy, Beale's regiment was ordered to leave their knapsacks on the courthouse steps in Carlisle. When the knapsacks were returned to the regiment outside of Harrisburg after the engagement, Beale's was not among them.[36]

However, Beale's mental images of the War remained, and years later he drew upon many of his own experiences to create about 130 magic lantern slides on the Civil War and other conflicts. Some of the most memorable of those on the Civil War echo directly scenes he described in his diary, "the farmers 'skedadeling' along the road", the lights in tents making a field "look like a good sized city lighted up", "much singing and other fun" at victory, "50 ambulances passing", "sisters waving their handkerchiefs at us" upon their return from the front.

Beale came back from the war on August 3, 1863, after the Rebel defeat at Gettysburg. He took a week's vacation hunting and fishing in New Jersey, and then settled into his former life of teaching and being a young man about town. He rowed with Undine Club several times a week, went to some parties, and hung out with other young artists including Eakins. Once a week he taught free art classes at the Spring Garden Night School to the "mechanics" of the Young Men's Institute. Becoming more active in politics (Fig. 2.29), he joined the "Republican Invincibles" – a pro-Lincoln group of sometimes rowdy young men who were given cheap uniforms and trained in elaborate marches. As Emancipation approached, Beale participated in the parades he had once watched, and got into several fights. In one, he was hit with a torch handle and thrown across the street. Unrelated to these incidents, he also spent several days at home in bed with what sounds like migraine headaches. If so, such headaches probably continued to plague him for the rest of his life. He continued his extra money-making activities – coloring photos, making ivorytypes, creating signs and ornately penned certificates and transparencies – and juggled them with his day-time teaching and regular night classes in figure drawing.

> Monday very cold. We went to school. This evening I painted a little on the background of the photograph of Thomas W. Ayer's niece or nephew. This evening I commenced a drawing of a new female model at the Academy of the Fine Arts.[37]

On-Screen Magic

The magic lantern continued to fascinate Beale. During 1863–64 he went to no less than *five* lantern shows, including church shows, ***stereopticon lectures***, and a ***phantasmagoria*** or ghost show.[38] In addition, he also began to probe how unusual lantern effects were achieved. His brother had gone to see "The 'Ghost', a stereopticon exhibition" that was one of the classic forms of lantern *special effects* called *Pepper's* Ghost (Fig. 2.30).

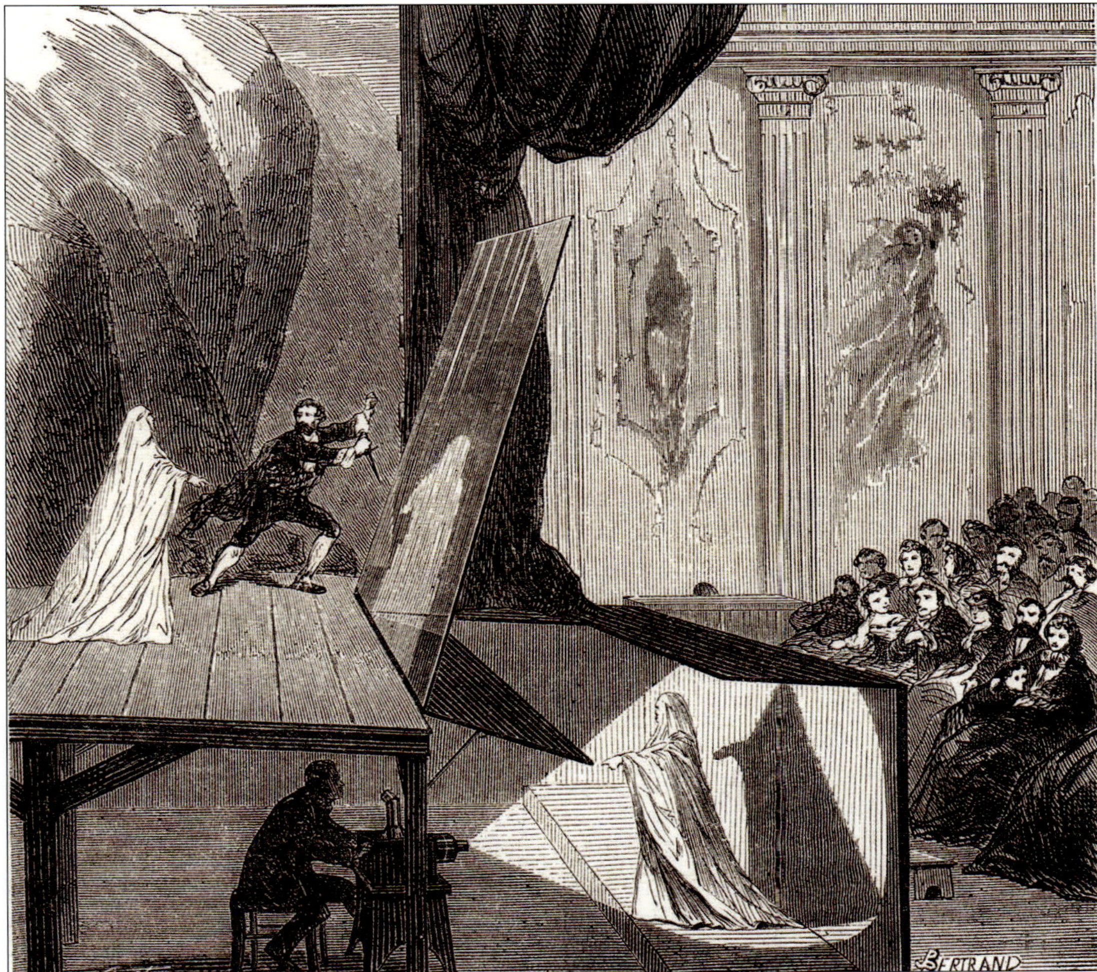

Fig. 2.30 Picture of "Audience watching Pepper's Ghost effect, with cutaway of stage to show method" by J. Bertrand, c. 1880. *Wikimedia Commons.*

To create the "Ghost", a lanternist used a magic lantern as a light source, projected on a live actor below stage. A large piece of glass at the front of the stage reflected the high-lighted actor as he moved. To the audience it looked as if the ghost were walking up to the man at the table, and perhaps through the table, to touch the man. Beale followed up his brother's enthusiastic report on Pepper's Ghost with a visit to the Franklin Institute, a leading scientific research center, to see how the ghost was created and to have several related patents explained.[39] (A version of Pepper's Ghost is still in use at a number of attractions around the country, and is even promoted by that name.)

Beale also attended lectures on projected light effects by "Prof. Morton", the Prof. Henry Morton who would later write regularly for the industry trade publication, *The Magic Lantern.* Beale did not use any of these elaborate techniques in creating his own magic lantern slides – he made ghosts or angels appear with ***dissolving effects***, which we will examine later. But he was being grounded in the technical aspects of early projected art, just as he had been grounded in the artistic elements by his childhood experiences. Of course, at the time, he could not have anticipated it, but the combination probably contributed to the ease with which he mastered the magic lantern art twenty-five years later.[40]

What else contributed to Beale's dexterity and skill? How did he hone the techniques he first learned in the streets and schools of Philadelphia? Where did his huge supply of mental images come from? His speed? His dramatic use of light? His grasp of architecture, costuming, political events, cartooning?

These abilities were the result of a varied career in the top echelons of 19th century commercial illustration – a career that took him from Philadelphia, to New York, then to Chicago, and then back home again to Philadelphia – back home to what had become the center of the American magic lantern industry.

Chapter Three

Training for Narrative Art

Fig. 3.8 Beale slide 3 from *The Village Blacksmith* by Henry Wadsworth Longfellow. Discussed on p. 43.

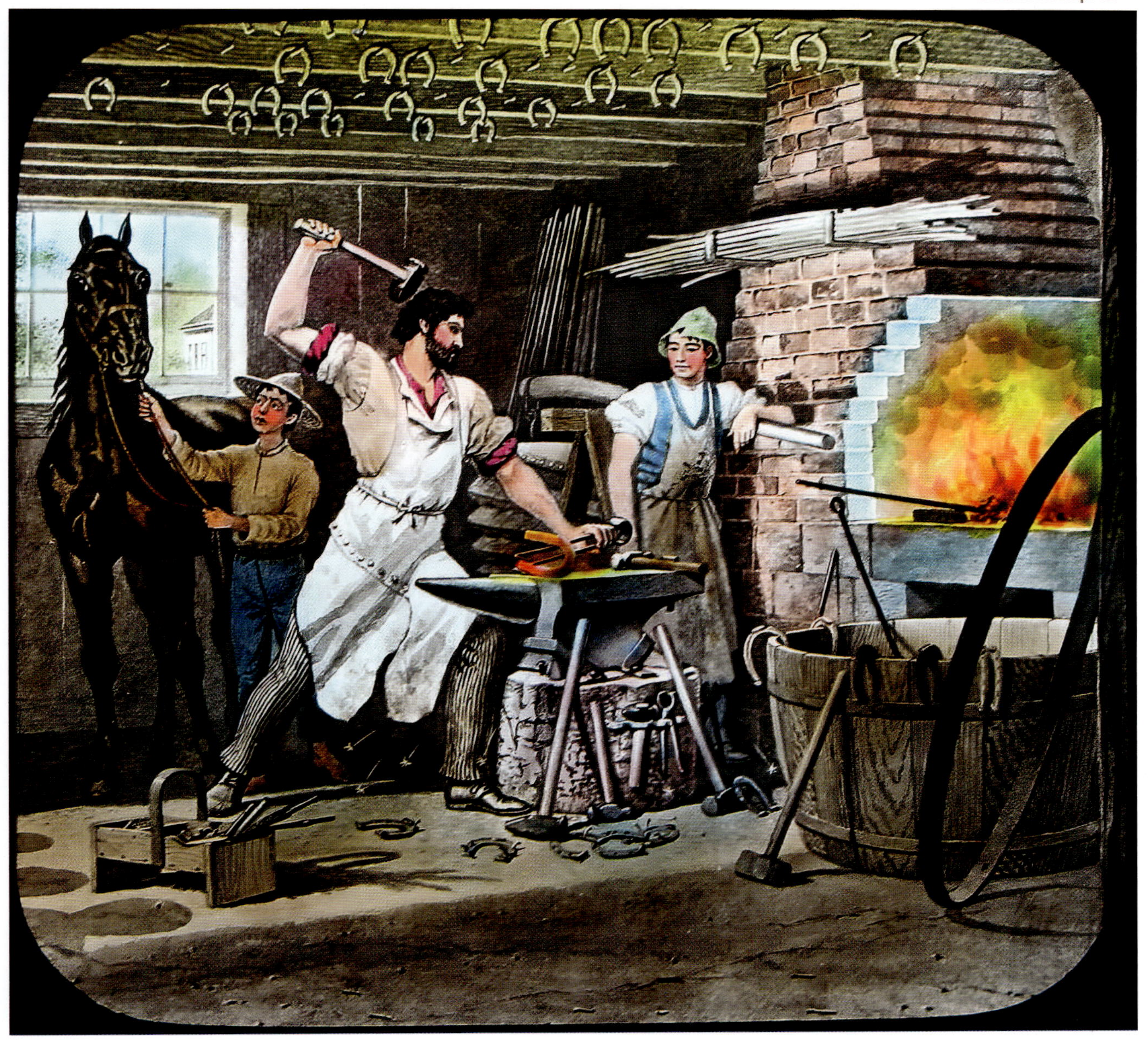

National Success

On October 30, 1865, Beale's classes at Central High School were dismissed at noon. He went to sketch a baseball game between the Philadelphia Athletics and the perennial champions of early baseball, the Atlantics of Brooklyn. Baseball was a sport that was enjoying a tremendous upsurge of post-war popularity, with nation-wide interest in the champion Atlantics. Beale sent his sketch to the country's leading illustrated newspaper, *Harper's Weekly*. *Harper's* printed it on a half-page in the November 18, 1865 issue, the first time a picture of Beale's had been published nationally with his name under it (Fig. 3.1). In September of 1866 he also sent in a sketch of the "Burning of the Union League" in Philadelphia, and that was also published on a half-page.[1]

Also, at about the same time, Beale created for a local Masonic lodge a large testimonial scroll to honor Col. John K. Murphy, who had commanded a Pennsylvania Volunteers unit in the Civil War (Fig. 3.2). (In August of 1864 Beale had created a similar testimonial for which he was paid $35.00 – about $680 in 2025. Such work was becoming a significant addition to his income.) A newspaper reporter saw the new testimonial and commented:

> We have not for a long time seen anything in the way of artistic skill and genius more remarkable or more beautiful, than [this] testimonial ... The gift consists of a set of resolutions complimentary to the veteran ... embellished with a most striking and excellent full-length portrait ... surrounded by the American flag and eagle and various other appropriate emblems ... The whole is executed in exquisite style in India ink drawing and entirely by hand. The chirography [penmanship] ... is very beautiful ... The whole is the work of Mr. Joseph B. Beale ... a young gentleman, who, for one of his age, has exhibited, we think, as high an order of talent in this line as can be found in our country.[2]

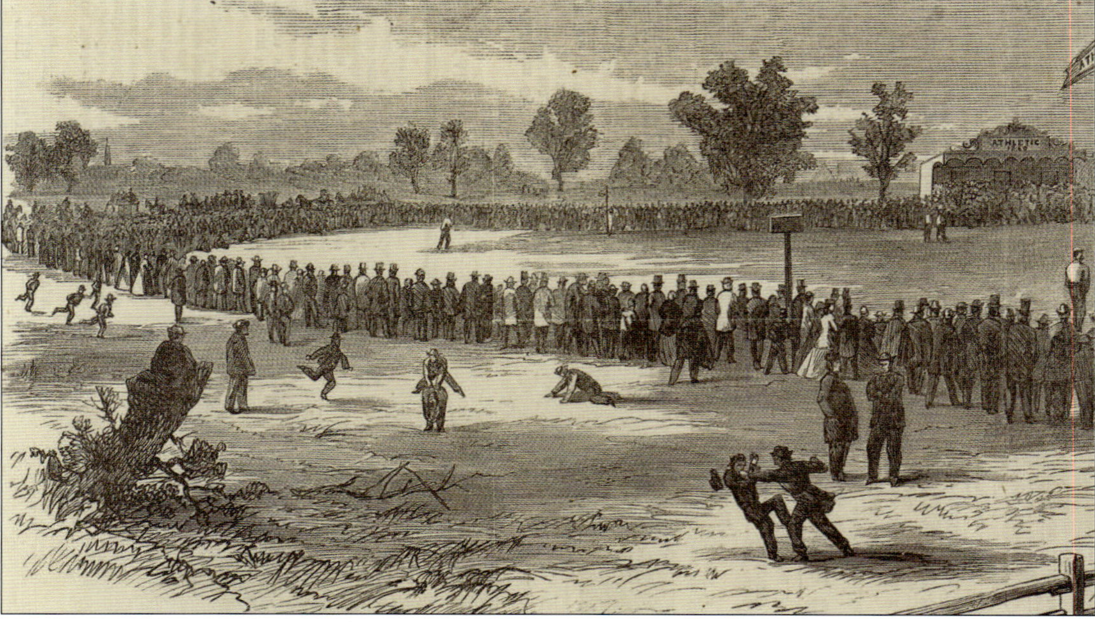

Fig. 3.1 Beale's "Baseball Match", *Harper's Weekly*, November 18, 1865, Image cropped.

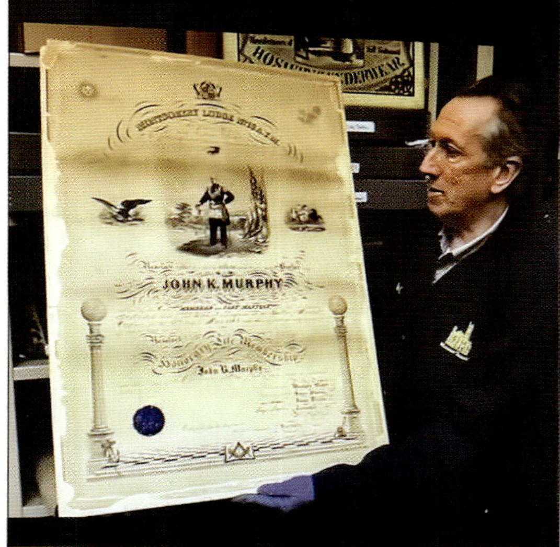

Fig. 3.2 A YouTube screen shot showing Michael Comfort, Director of the Masonic Library and Museum of Pennsylvania, admiring the detail in Beale's testimonial for Col. John K. Murphy.

Publication of two drawings in the nation's leading illustrated newspaper, and fulsome praise in the local press – that must surely have impressed Beale's family, friends, and the "young gentleman" himself. If he were dreaming of heading to the big time, to New York, to join one of the illustrated newspapers headquartered there, this combination of events would certainly have encouraged him to think more seriously about it.[3]

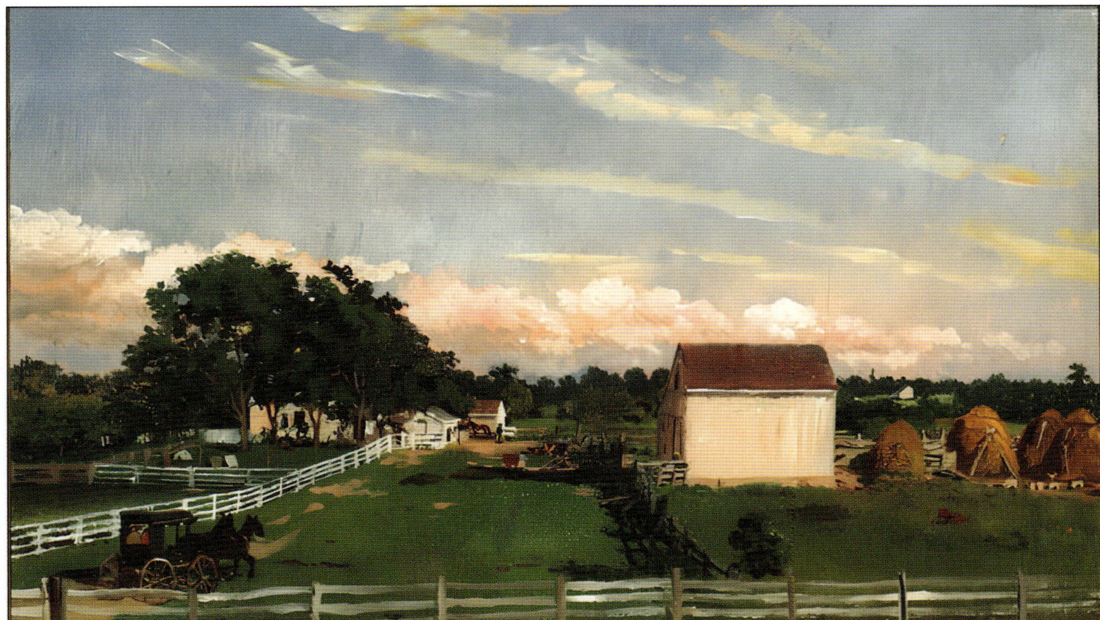

Fig. 3.3 Beale's oil painting of "The Farm of Dr. Stephen Thomas Beale", Joseph's father. Biggs Museum of American Art, Dover, DE.

The other alternative that he almost certainly considered – though no explicit evidence exists – was to go to Paris and become a "fine artist", producing paintings to be sold in galleries. In the years after the Civil War, hundreds of young American painters flocked to France for just this purpose – to soak up the atmosphere, to see the famous art in the museums, and to be trained by the great French masters. For an aspiring artist, it was the thing to do. Beale's friend, Thomas Eakins, himself made this choice. Eight of Beale's other artistic friends from the "bohemian" Philadelphia Sketch Club, including the already well-respected Thomas Moran, would soon be in Paris or at the new French art colony of Pont-Aven.[4]

The last two months of Beale's diary, June and July of 1865, show him heavily involved with the "fine arts" in a way that might well have led to Paris. Though he documents a productive share of illustrative work – ornate penmanship, ivorytypes, etc. – he was also painting portraits for pay, taking advanced classes drawing from male and female models at the Pennsylvania Academy of the Fine Arts, visiting galleries, meeting famous artists, taking private lessons in painting, and creating some very handsome "fine art" (Fig. 3.3). He was elected to the Philadelphia Sketch Club, and became an active member, sketching with them weekly. And he continued to pursue his interest in anatomy, attending the lectures of Dr. Thomas, and the clinical operations of Dr. Gross at Jefferson Medical College – a form of study that Eakins was to immortalize in his painting, "The Gross Clinic". His high-school training (and teaching) had had a decided commercial objective, but now, clearly, he was also part of the Philadelphia fine-arts scene. He was young, talented, promising. What might have induced him to forego the allures of the artist's life in Paris, and stay in America?

Perhaps it was money, specifically a steady salary. He always meticulously documented the dollars he earned from his major illustrative work. He was making steady money as a teacher; he might well expect to make the same as a commercial artist. And he might well have felt that fine art did not pay. While Beale was a member of The Philadelphia Sketch Club it organized a very elaborate Grand National Exhibition of American Art at the Pennsylvania Academy. A handsome catalog was printed. Three hundred and fifty paintings were put up for sale, and extraordinary prizes of $2,000 (about $40,000 in 2025), made it an exciting competition. Beale submitted three pictures, no doubt with great hopes. But the Exhibition was, in the words of the Sketch Club's biographer, a "flat failure". The Club made nothing, and the Exhibition's chief financial sponsor, the Club's president, lost a lot of money. The experience, organized by all the high-powered artists that Beale knew, would hardly have encouraged him to think that an artist could make a living from the fine arts.[5]

Other factors may also have entered into Beale's decision not to go to Paris. The last sentence of Beale's Diary – the last sentence of the last entry in a diary he had kept faithfully for 3,439 days

– introduces a totally new subject, one he has never mentioned before. You know where this is going. In that entry for July 26, 1865, he for the first time mentions a woman he seems attracted to (Fig. 3.4):

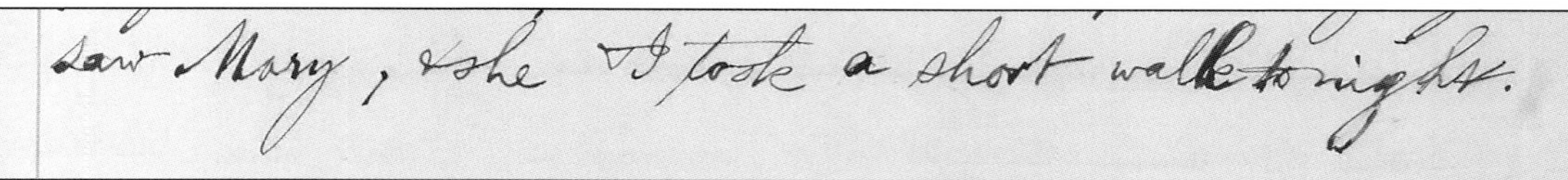

Fig. 3.4 Beale's *Diary*, July 26, 1865, the very last sentence of the very last page. Why the Diary stops here is a mystery. Collection of the Historical Society of Pennsylvania.

We do not know who "Mary" was, but on that day, something happened that made Beale abruptly end a diary he had kept for seven years, reporting faithfully what he did and who he did it with. Detailed though it is, the whole thousand-page manuscript never mentions any relationship with a young lady and contains barely a hint of Beale's personal emotions and inner life. Perhaps on July 26 (or the day after) he met up with a force so deeply important that his usual "just the facts" diary was no longer adequate to describe it, and so he simply stopped writing. Perhaps, to speculate even further, his feelings about a woman were strong enough not only to stop the diary, but also to anchor Beale home in America, when other artists around him were sailing abroad. What we do know for sure is that Beale moved not to Paris, but to New York, an hour and a half by train from Philadelphia.

We also know that three years later, in December of 1868, Beale forsook the charms of the New York ladies and reached back to Philadelphia in order to marry a home-town girl, Maria Louise Taffard. Very little is known about her other than that her father had immigrated from Paris and was a painter-glazier, and that she had two brothers, who, like Beale himself, were involved in the Civil War. It at least seems possible that "Maria" Taffard was the "Mary" that Beale had taken walking three years earlier. In formal public records she was often listed as "Mary" or "Maria", though in later life Beale called her "Louise".[6]

Eakins, in Paris, and those who joined him there, were profoundly affected by their foreign experience. Not only did they learn a great deal about their craft, but they learned a very French conception of what it meant to be an artist. Whether they became bohemians or fashionable flaneur, (the "strollers"), they tended to distain the illustrative path that Beale was to follow. And, no matter how they touted their ideals of "American" painting, they could not help becoming a little Frenchified in their choice of subject matter, composition, and style.[7]

Not so with Beale. His subject matter was largely American, his composition was American, and his style was American. That "American" quality was in large part a result of his early training in Philadelphia, and then his later experience in New York, for the New York illustrated newspapers were the best place in the world to learn American narrative art – how to tell visual stories to a home-grown audience in a style that communicated to them powerfully and directly. In particular, a series of specialty jobs in commercial illustration and his own study would prepare Beale with almost uncanny precision to handle the creation of realistic detail, varied settings, authentic costumes, dramatic action, and theatrical lighting that would one day make his narrative screen art so powerful. Unfortunately, since he wasn't keeping a diary anymore, we can no longer follow his growth day by day. Rather, we'll look at some of the general artistic experiences that built the repertoire he would later use in his magic lantern slides.

Anchoring Reality with Detail

In New York, Beale began illustrating for Frank Leslie's publications, probably *Frank Leslie's Gazette of Fashion*, drawing "women's fashion ... every month". No doubt he also helped out on the other *Leslie's* magazines, and also worked freelance for various publications like *Harper's*. After Beale was married it certainly seems likely that the young couple became part of the artistic community that was helping to build New York into the greatest publishing center in the world. Though Beale enrolled at the New York Academy of Design in 1868–69, his primary training probably came from the loose fraternity of artists working at *Leslie's* and the other illustrated publications of the period. In a caricature of the

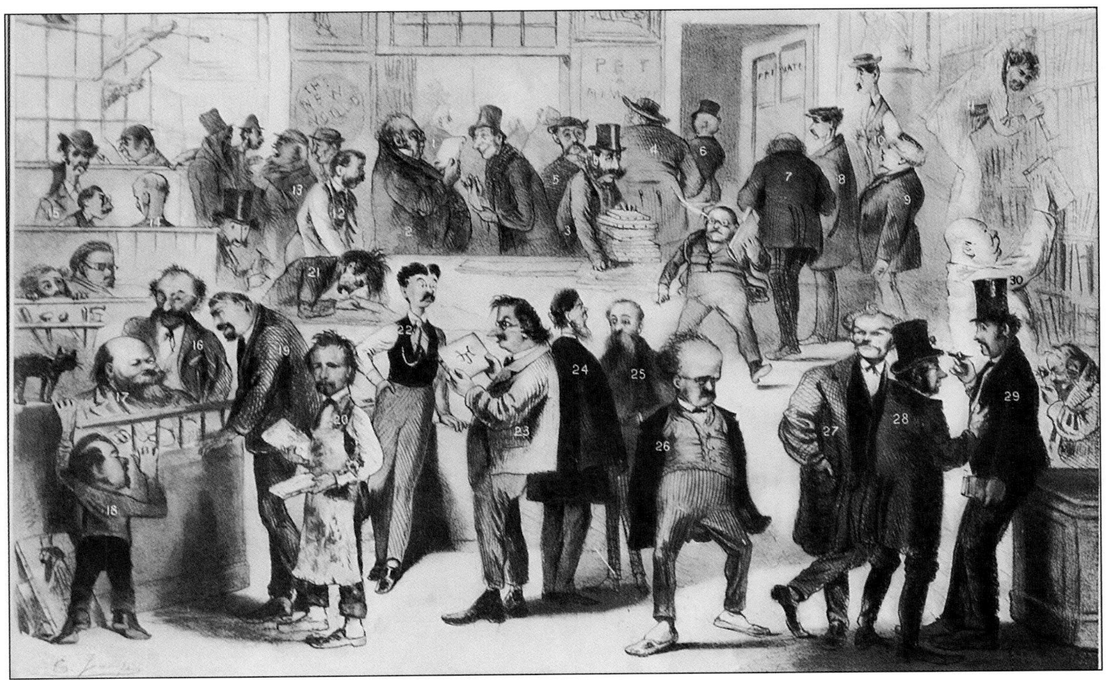

Fig. 3.5 "Frank Leslie's Staff Caricatured in Its Palmiest Days", *Leslie's Illustrated Weekly Newspaper*, December 16, 1915 (Sixtieth Anniversary Edition).

Leslie's staff made the year after Beale arrived, we can get some sense of what the fraternity was like, and of Beale's role in it when he first started (Fig. 3.5). He's the newbie fashion illustrator on the far left, behind and above the cat, peering timidly over the counter at the raucous newsroom full of famous artists.[8]

What did Beale learn at *Leslie's*? Accuracy and speed.

The *Leslie's* publishing empire had been started in 1854 by a young English immigrant, Henry Carter. Carter took the "Frank Leslie" name to hide his artistic activities from his father, who wanted him to be a glove-maker. Leslie was trained as an engraver at the *Illustrated London News*, and then trained as a promoter by none other than the best of the best, P. T. Barnum. *Frank Leslie's Illustrated Newspaper* was the first American illustrated news periodical and, over the years, its emphasis on copious illustration and fast-breaking news defined the very nature of the genre. Unlike *Harper's*, it did not aim to be "A Journal of Civilization" for an elite audience, but attempted to reach the full spectrum of the American public with a combination of moralizing text and sensationalized "PICTORIAL NEWS". By the time Beale worked at *Leslie's*, the firm was headquartered at 537 Pearl St., within a few blocks of the Brooklyn Bridge, just then being constructed. The company employed 300–400 people, ran a dozen periodicals (most containing the *Leslie* name), and boasted a combined circulation of about a half-million copies a week.[9]

Because of the wide appeal of *Leslie's* and *Harper's*, such weekly periodicals were the showplaces of American illustrative art. They attracted some of the best talents of the day – Winslow Homer, Felix O. C. Darley, Thomas Nast. These "artist correspondents" or "special artists" had celebrity status. During the Civil War many had been in the midst of the bloody action; several were wounded. Their gripping written dispatches and dramatic pictures added to their cachet, and their reports provided practically the only way that the people at the time could know what the war *looked* like. The range of their coverage was extraordinary. *Leslie's* alone produced over 6,000 images of the war. The special artists who created these images were akin to the ubiquitous television reporters today, stars bringing the world's events to those at home.

Accuracy of detail was essential, for the war artists were reporting on actions that had been witnessed by thousands of participants, each of whom was writing home and could nit-pick about minor illustration mistakes. One of the artists who later worked with Beale at *Harper's* went so far as to make careful graphic notes during the war about the different saddle harnesses used by General Grant and each of the other Union commanders. Leslie himself was a notorious stickler for accuracy. After the war,

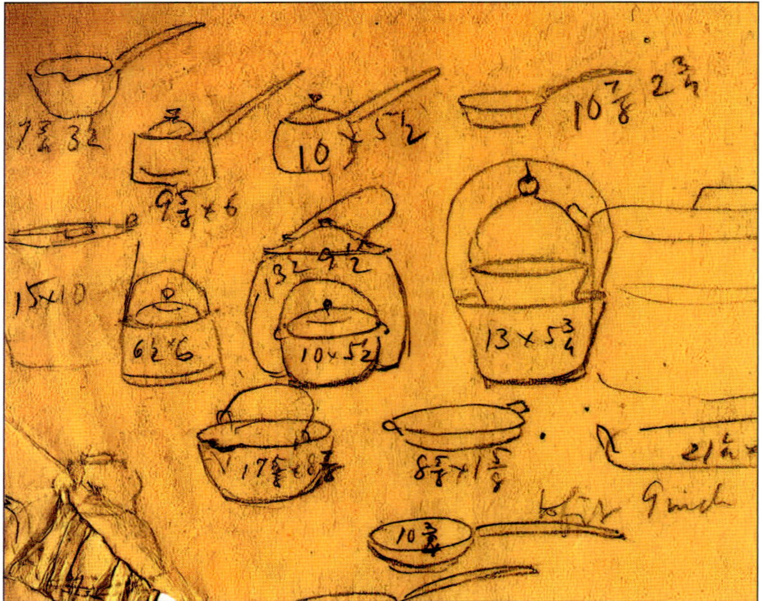

Fig. 3.6 Beale's preliminary sketch for illustrations of the wedding of President Grant's son, to be published in *Leslie's*.

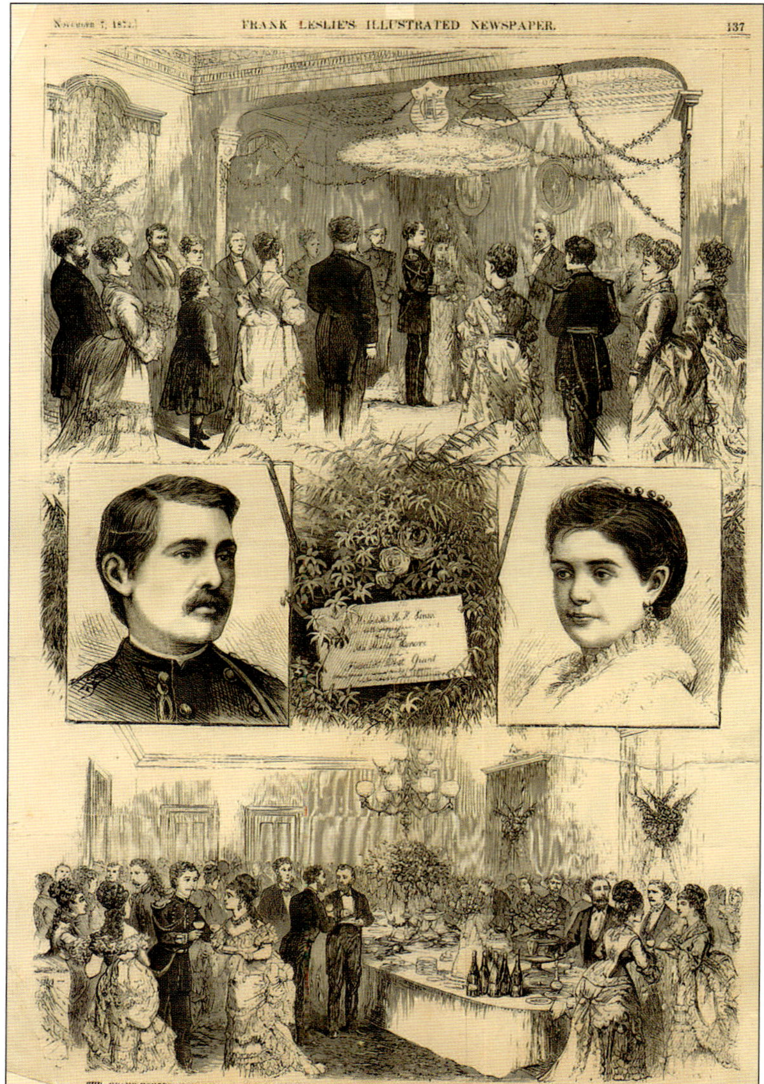

November 7, 1874.] FRANK LESLIE'S ILLUSTRATED NEWSPAPER. 137

Fig. 3.7 Beale's full-page display on the Grant-Honore wedding, as it appeared in *Leslie's*, November 7, 1874.

he once delayed printing a picture while he cabled to San Francisco to find out which direction the wind was blowing aboard the ship carrying President Grant back from his world tour. He wanted to be sure the flags flew in the right direction.[10] The importance of accurate detail must have been pounded into Beale on a daily basis, reinforcing what he had learned from his experience with panorama painting. We can see the result in his sketch of the kitchen preparations for President Grant's son's wedding (Fig. 3.6). Every pot in precisely measured, down the last eighth of an inch.

Speed of execution was another essential of the complex *Leslie's* production process. Since photography could not yet be reproduced in print, all pictures in the *Leslie's* publications were wood engravings made from drawings. After the field artists submitted their sketches, in-house artists drew them in detail on the dense end grain of wooden blocks. (Artists working entirely in-house often drew or painted – in reverse – directly on the block.) Then the engravers took over. They reproduced the pictures by cutting lines of various lengths and thickness into the blocks. Then the pictures were printed using these blocks. One of the innovations that Leslie took credit for was breaking the large wooden block up into as many at 18 small two-inch square blocks that were then clamped together to make one large surface to print from. (If you look closely at large *Leslie's* engravings, you can often see thin white lines left by the joints between the blocks.) Dividing the block allowed the reporter's image to be parceled out to different engravers, so that it could be reproduced more quickly – essential for rapid reporting on breaking news. A double-page spread could be engraved in only eight hours. Very tight deadlines might require that the artist himself work "block by block", sending each section off to the engraver as it was completed, or even that the field artist's rough sketch was re-drawn block-by-block by the in-house staff artists. Illustrating for an engraver demanded that the artist provide clear outlines for him to follow, and use a range of tonalities in order to get as much texture as possible into the black and white illustrations. And do it now!

Working in a news environment – covering a national story like the Grant wedding for instance – put a premium on being fast and accurate. The pots and pans that Beale had sketched did not make it into his final display spread for *Leslie's*. On the other hand, we can be sure that the shape and dimension of the vases on the table shown at bottom were exactly right (Fig. 3.7).

Beale would later need both traits of accuracy and speed when he turned to magic lantern production, for he would be, in effect, a one-man studio, creating thousands of different productions by himself. He *had* to get the details right, and work rapidly. There was no backup.

Detail itself was an important characteristic of Beale's magic lantern work. A good example is the image from *The Village Blacksmith*, a Henry Wadsworth Longfellow poem praising the virtues of a disciplined tradesman, seen in Fig. 3.8 at the start of this chapter. Most of the details in the picture are not described in the poem itself: the shadows of the children at left, come to admire the blacksmith's strength; the horseshoe in the center of the image – a glowing symbol of good fortune; the 32 spare horseshoes arrayed on the ceiling and floor; and the 13 blacksmith's tools, each meticulously documented. All these *subsidiary contrasts* help convey a sense of the smith's disciplined and "worthy" life, and help support the *dominate contrast*, the powerful central figure of the blacksmith himself. Such abundance of specificity creates a powerful sense that Beale's imagined screen world really exists, and anchors the poem's lofty moral coda in concrete reality.

> Thanks, thanks to thee, my worthy friend,
> For the lesson thou hast taught!
> Thus at the flaming forge of life
> Our fortunes must be wrought;
> Thus on its sounding anvil shaped
> Each burning deed and thought.

One of the most common reactions to Beale's slides is to life-like illusions such as those created in *The Village Blacksmith*. The slides are so detailed and "realistic" that people in antique stores or on eBay often mistake them for photographs. In a sense, this is just what Beale intended. Remember that he was producing illustrated slides at a time when most slides on the market were photographic. He had to be better than the photographers. As one lanternist commented about hand-drawn lantern slides:

> To put the thing in a nutshell, photography with its precision has accustomed the eye to detect irregularities or seeming coarseness in hand-painted work, whereas in reality it is probably the work of infinite merit.[11]

Beale certainly wanted his work to be seen as of "infinite merit". His academic style avoided the "irregularities" and "coarseness" that had indeed been characteristic of many earlier illustrated slides. But he went further. His meticulous detail provided a sense of photographic realism that photography at that time could often not attain if movement was in the scene. Certainly, that realism is one of the things that impresses the people who come up to chat with me after our shows. Probably they are not aware of the skill with which Beale uses detail to give a feeling of reality to a place and time and personality – though I have no doubt that they respond unconsciously. Their conscious fascination is more voyeuristic. The specificity of Beale's screen worlds gives them the feeling that for two hours they had been, as they often say, "really there", living in a time of long ago.

I have been particularly struck by the response of modern children to our shows. Children today spend 30–60 hours a week watching TV and other screen entertainment such as videos and cell-phone games. These moving images shift about every two seconds, so kids are bombarded with sounds and special effects. You might well imagine that lantern shows, in which the images are static and change at a much slower rate, would bore modern children beyond endurance. Yet, time and time again, we've given shows – in the dark no less – for hundreds of kids at a time. If they were bored, we would certainly know about it. They're not shy on that score. But most do not fidget or make rude comments. They laugh at the comic stories and are awe-struck by the sad ones – captivated by Beale's slides, by those detailed images of a strange world, by the showman's drama. Most magic lantern art seems to communicate to today's children as well as it did to those in Queen Victoria's day. In Fig. 3.9, for instance, fifth graders watch our *Patriotic History Show*. At top, they laugh at an animated cartoon slide, like the Nose Man. At bottom, they react to a scene in which the American flag is desecrated in the story of *Barbara Fritchie*. They react because the magic lantern art used to tell stories on screen is so similar to the art that modern children know from watching TV and movies. Children are captivated by cinema – today's, and yesterday's.

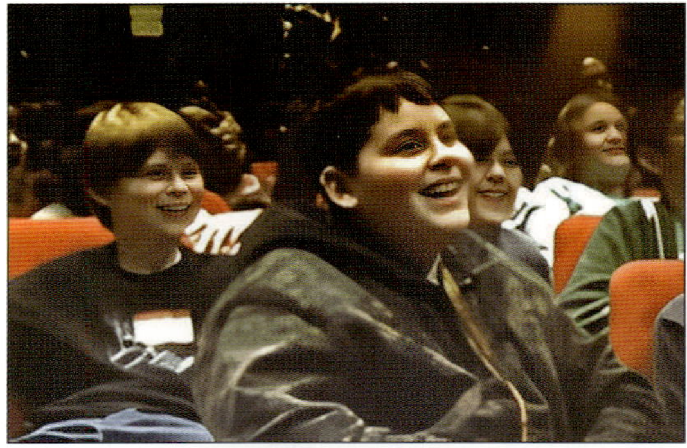

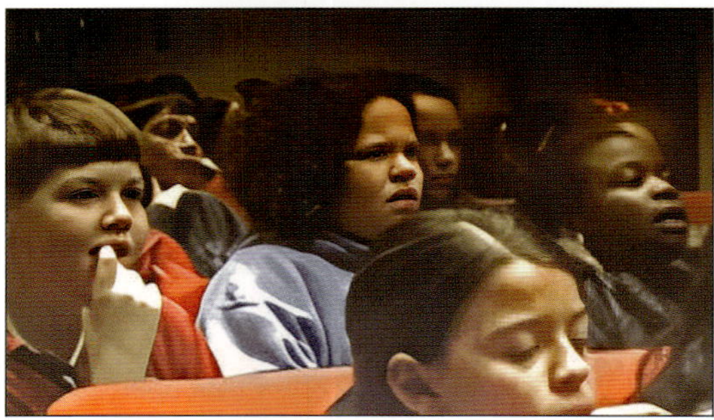

Fig. 3.9 Two screen shots from a video of fifth graders watching our *Patriotic History Show.*

Learning to Make the Set Tell the Story

In a letter to *Harper's Weekly,* Beale wrote that in the summer of 1870 he brought to their offices a sketch showing a Society Parade of "young ladies representing the States of the Union with our flag above all".[12] Charles Parsons, the art director, made some minor changes, had Beale draw the image on the wooden block, and ran it as the front page of *Harper's.* Then he offered Beale a job at $30 a week. But despite what must have been the temptations of working for such a prestigious publication, Beale turned him down because he had already accepted a job in Chicago at $50 a week, about $1,200 in 2025. And Chicago, as it turned out, would add important new experiences in his unknowing preparation for a career as magic lantern artist, building new abilities in set design and casting.

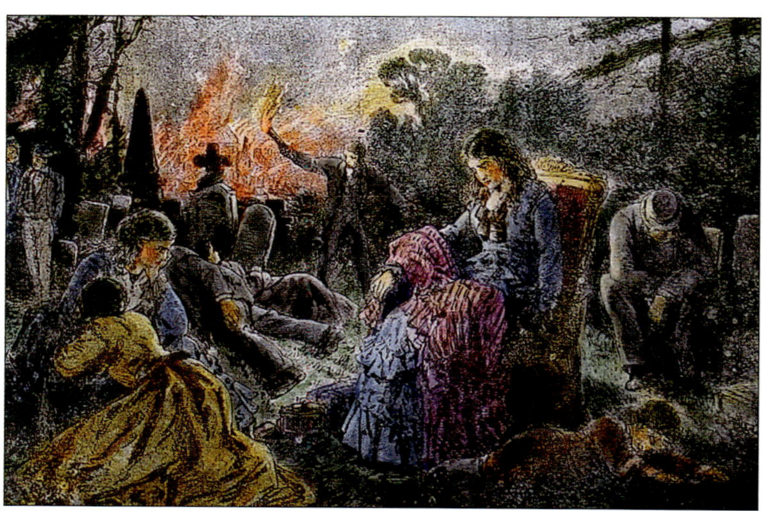

Fig. 3.10 The Chicago fire, in a lantern slide created from an engraving.

In Chicago, Beale began working for Baker and Company, a firm that billed itself as the "largest and oldest wood engraving establishment in the West". It was a major source for documenting the emerging new "set design" that was the City of Chicago. The company occupied the top floor of an imposing new office building at the bustling corner of Clark and Monroe Streets, which caught the "peculiar northern light required by their artists". The firm provided a full range of engraving services, employed 25 "hands", and grossed about $25,000 a year, roughly $625,000 in 2025.[13]

The Chicago of 1870 that Baker and Co. served with its engravings throbbed with commercial activity. In the forty years since its incorporation in 1830, Chicago had grown to a population of 340,000 people, the largest city in the Mid-West. By the time Beale arrived there, ten railroads converged at the city; and the port was equally busy. Beale's work took him throughout the area, capturing images of stockyards and stock markets, of marble quarries and brick factories, of stables and carriage houses, of churches and train stations, and of the ornate banks where the new-found wealth was kept.

Then, in 1871, the great fire swept Chicago (Fig. 3.10). About 300 people were killed, property damage was nearly $200 million (about a half billion in 2025 dollars), and 90,000 were homeless. Beale rushed to his lodgings when the fire struck, threw his clothes into one trunk and his drawings into another, dragged both trunks into the street and flagged down a passing wagon. The driver already had such a heavy load that he would only take one trunk. Beale chose the trunk of drawings. When he reached safety, he opened the trunk, only to find that in his haste he had chosen the wrong one.[14]

(This wonderful story may well be apocryphal. What is more certain is that Beale did lose his drawings from this period in the fire, just as he lost his Civil War sketches in Carlisle.)

After the fire, in May of 1872, Beale rented an apartment on LaSalle St., "the Wall Street of Chicago". The building was an impressive new five-story structure of Philadelphia pressed-brick. Above the roof flew the Union flag, as the building also housed the British Vice Consulate. A picture of Beale and his wife taken in

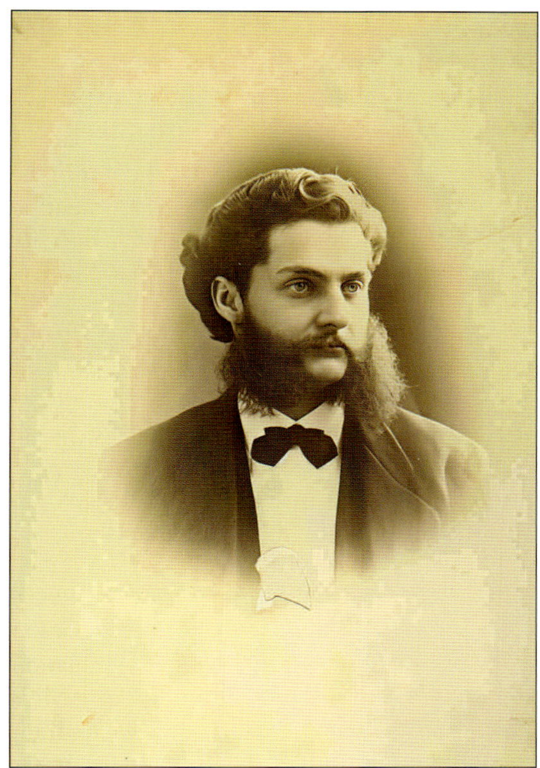

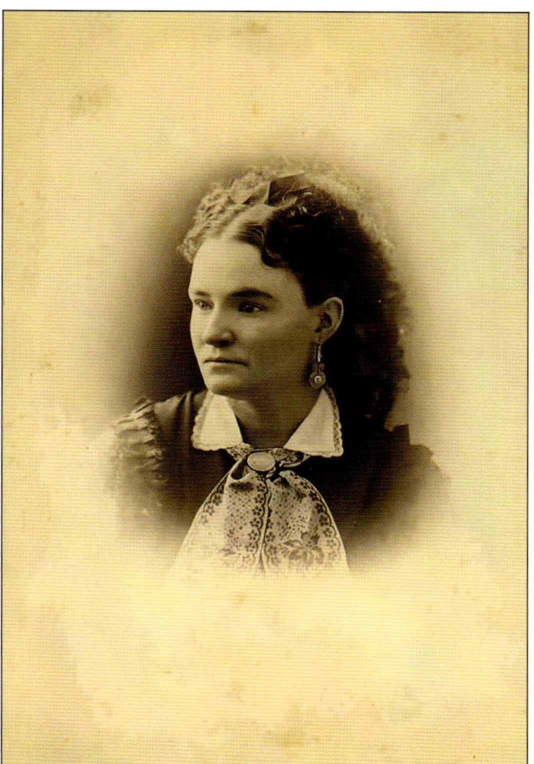

Fig. 3.11 Beale and his wife, Louise, in Chicago, 1873.

January of 1873, while they were living in these quarters, shows an intense young couple. Louise is attractive, but looks rather stern. Beale, dashingly decked out in the muttonchops that he kept throughout his life, nonetheless looks a little timid (Fig. 3.11).[15]

Immediately after the fire, and for several years thereafter, Chicago concentrated on building a larger, grander city (Fig. 3.12). Suddenly more clients appreciated Beale's skill with architectural perspective, and gave him many opportunities to perfect it. A presentation book of Beale's art from this period, which appears to have been sent home to his parents, gives a good sense of his work, It contains a dozen copies of *The Land Owner* from January, 1872 to March, 1874, plus an 1873 copy of *Leslie's,* and a few other publications, many with Beale's handwritten comments beside his pictures. *The Land Owner* was a large-format monthly periodical, a "Journal of Real Estate Building and Improvement". It was a publication with a national scope, but at this period the biggest real-estate story in the country was the rebuilding of Chicago, where *The Land Owner* was based. The paper was lavishly illustrated with many illustrations attributed to Baker and Co. Beale seems to have been Baker's lead illustrator. Hand-written comments to Beale's parents about the prints cite several cases where he had been asked to "fix up" the work of other artists. The visual

Fig. 3.12 Engraving based on a Beale drawing, "Rebuilding Chicago", cover illustration, *The Land Owner*, May, 1873.

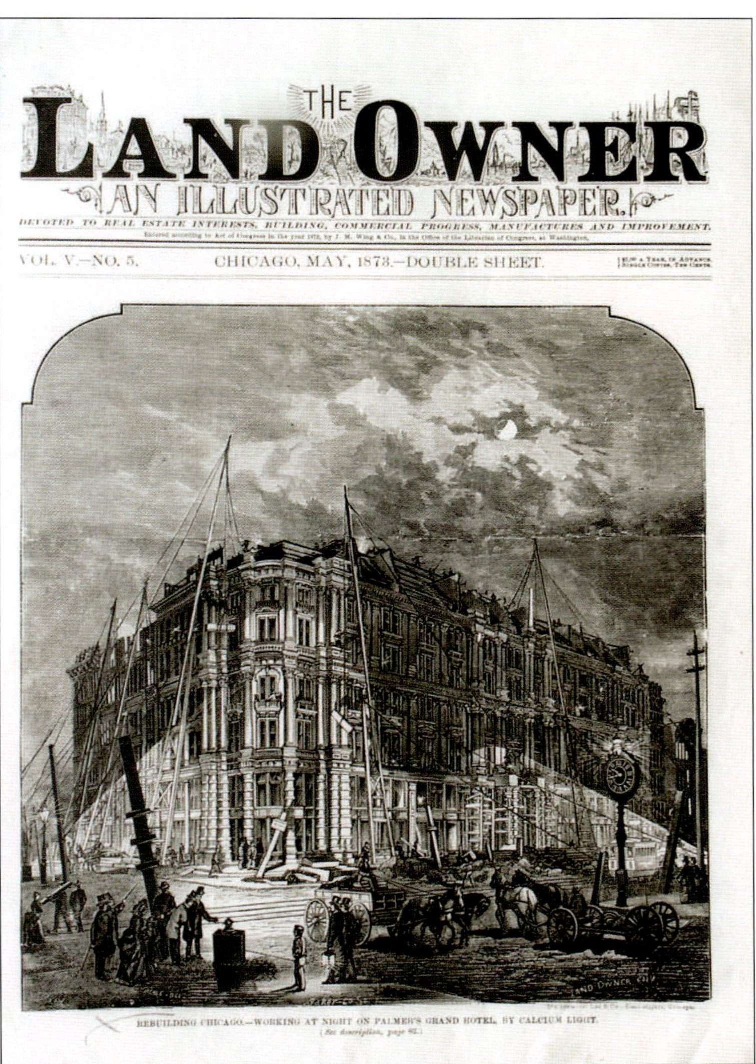

THE LAND OWNER

AN ILLUSTRATED NEWSPAPER.

DEVOTED TO REAL ESTATE INTERESTS, BUILDING, COMMERCIAL PROGRESS, MANUFACTURES AND IMPROVEMENT.

VOL. V.—NO. 5. CHICAGO, MAY, 1873.—DOUBLE SHEET.

REBUILDING CHICAGO.—WORKING AT NIGHT ON PALMER'S GRAND HOTEL, BY CALCIUM LIGHT.

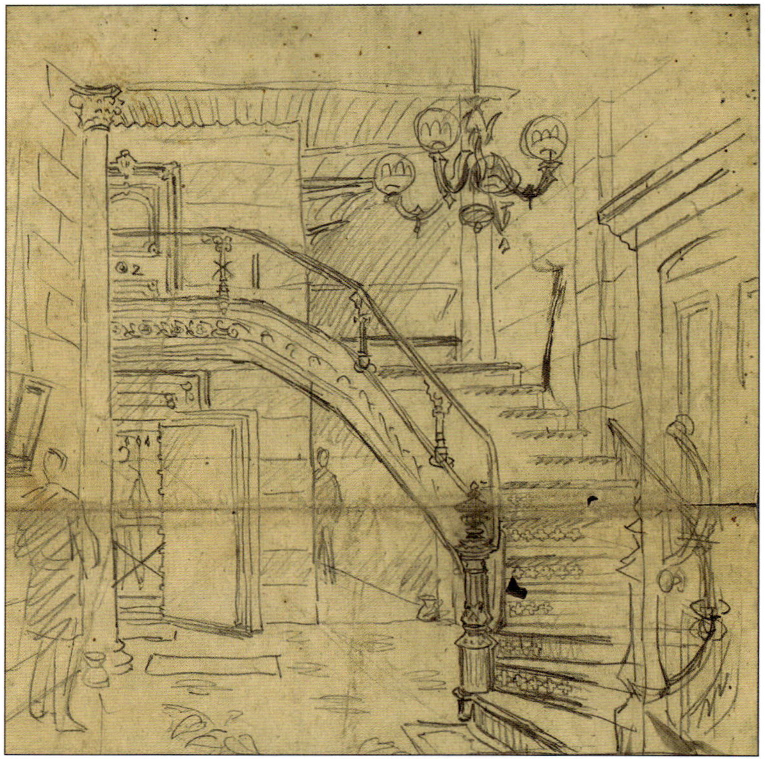

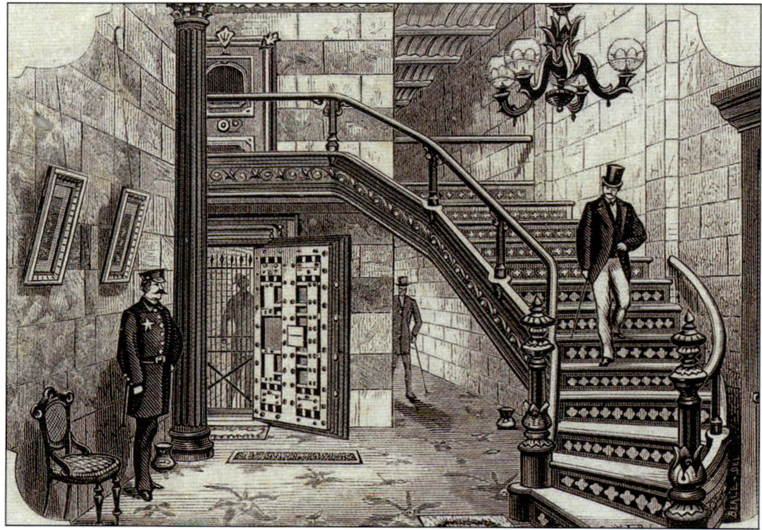

Fig. 3.13 Beale's preliminary sketch and the final etching of a Chicago bank interior.

complexity of the architectural style was a challenge for any artist, and the demand of the new buildings' proud owners for handsome and accurate renderings must have done much to hone Beale's talents in perspective drawing. *The Land Owner* offered reprints of the engravings for sale, and several of Beale's drawings were designed as fold-out supplements, becoming very impressive 24" x 31" display pieces.[16]

Working for Baker & Co. in Chicago meant that Beale was involved first-hand with a broad range of city life, just as he had been as a young man in Philadelphia, but this time he was often viewing the business and industrial life of the city, rather than its street life. And this time he surely had his sketchbook in hand, building the storehouse of images that would one day feed the imaginative creation of hundreds of magic lantern designs. "On location", he learned to sketch in a scene quickly, to establish perspective and ambiance and design with swift strokes, and to define those key details that would give the scene a sense of place when he came to draw it later on the engraver's block. In his on-site sketch of a bank for instance (Fig. 3.13), he concentrates on the *general layout* and tricky *perspective* of the stairs, as well as a few *emblematic details* like the precise shapes of the newel post and the chandelier – all typical of how he worked. (Note that the final engraving has been compressed vertically to fit the space limits.)[17]

Once Beale began producing magic lantern slides for Briggs, he no longer had the luxury of going on location. Working in his studio, and always on deadline, painting one picture after another, he had to create hundreds of different physical worlds, in detail, out of his imagination. He used "scrap" (other illustrations or photos) for reference whenever he could – some of it survives in his papers. But he had no "research department". If he wanted to create a certain set design, he would have to make do, and make it look real. Because of his facility in handling perspective and architecture, he was able to create hundreds and hundreds of such sets – the counting houses of Scrooge's London, the farms of Little Breeches' Mid-West, the plantations of Uncle Tom's south, the castles of the Pied Piper's medieval Europe, the hovels of Bethlehem, and the great temple of Jerusalem. And his facility with perspective, in turn, allowed him to handle sets so that his *mise-en-scène* – the composition of his scenes and the materials in them – helped to tell the story.

Beale's mastery of sets when creating magic lantern designs is exemplified by his illustrations for *The Little Match Girl* by Hans Christian Andersen.[18] In the story, a homeless little girl who has been unsuccessfully trying to sell matches, retreats to a corner and sees a series of visions, culminating in her grandmother, who takes her to Heaven. In Beale's version of the story, he often uses ***effect dissolves*** – dissolving from one scene to another with the slides perfectly registered so that the background does not change but the visions do. Using this device, he drives the story forward by employing contrasting *mise-en-scènes*.

In the first slide (Fig. 3.14, upper) Beale places the little beggar girl on the snow-filled corner of a fancy street that recedes into distant perspective, lit by a series of windows draped in rich red curtains. This world of wealth, to which the little girl can never belong, seems to extend back toward infinity. The children of this rich world, loaded down with their dolls, stand beside the little match girl in her rags. They ignore her begging, intent on a magnificent store window – a wealthy world framed within a wealthy world – one within their reach but beyond that of the little match girl.

In the next slide (Fig. 3.14, lower) Beale uses a standard dissolve and creates a stark contrast in mise-en-scène. The little girl has sought shelter from the wind behind a wall. It is the back alley of the glorious window-filled street we saw before. She sits against bare, snow-covered stones. A huge, barred grate locks her away from the world of the wealthy. Her misery is emphasized by a single lighted window, again draped in rich red, a repetitive pattern of *abstract form* from the street scene. Like the street window, this one is unobtainable, high above her and dripping with icicles. Into this bleak world her imagination brings a large glowing stove.

Other visions (not shown) create her own world of imaginary warmth and comfort below the "real world" window in a series of five sequential effect dissolves. The first two dissolves use exactly the same set.

But on the third dissolve (Fig. 3.15, upper) when the little girl's vision of a glorious Christmas tree appears, the mise-en-scène changes subtly. The window has become dark, and hardly visible. Beale has all but removed it, defining it only with vestigial icicles, and a new dusting of snow on the windowpanes. The intensity of the little girl's imagination is remaking the real word into her own.

In the next effect dissolve (Fig. 3.15, lower) when the lights of the tree slowly change into stars, the window totally disappears, leaving nothing to distract the girl, or us, from her starry destiny in heaven.

In the final scene of the "real world" (Fig. 3.16) the discovery of the girl's dead body, the window re-emerges, darkened now like the little girl herself. The bright red drape, no longer *backlit*, has taken on a somber maroon reality, as the people cluster around the little match girl, totally unaware of the transforming power of the "beautiful things she had seen".[19]

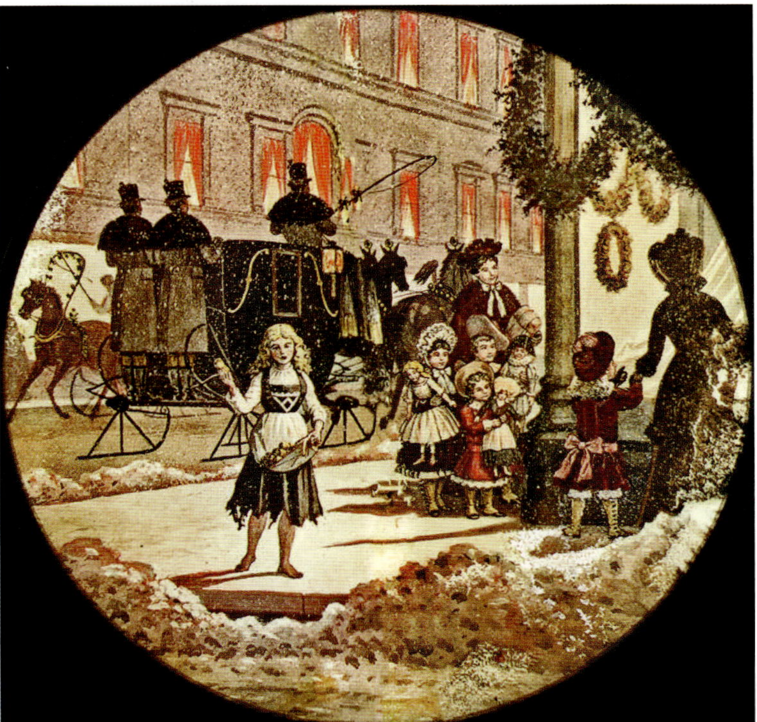

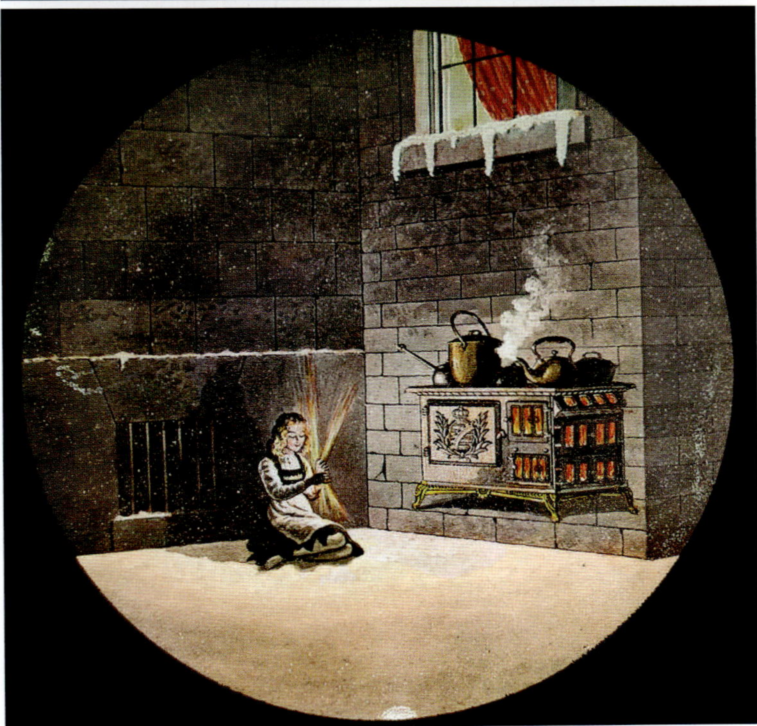

Fig. 3.14 Beale's slides 1 and 2 illustrating Hans Christian Andersen's *The Little Match Girl*.

The Little Match Girl is one of the highlights of our *Christmas Show*. As Hans Christian Andersen's words and Beale's spectacular images carry the audience through the story, the architectural setting and mise-en-scène play a subtle but important role in controlling the mood and emotion. The contrast of light and dark, of sweeping distance and cramped corner, of

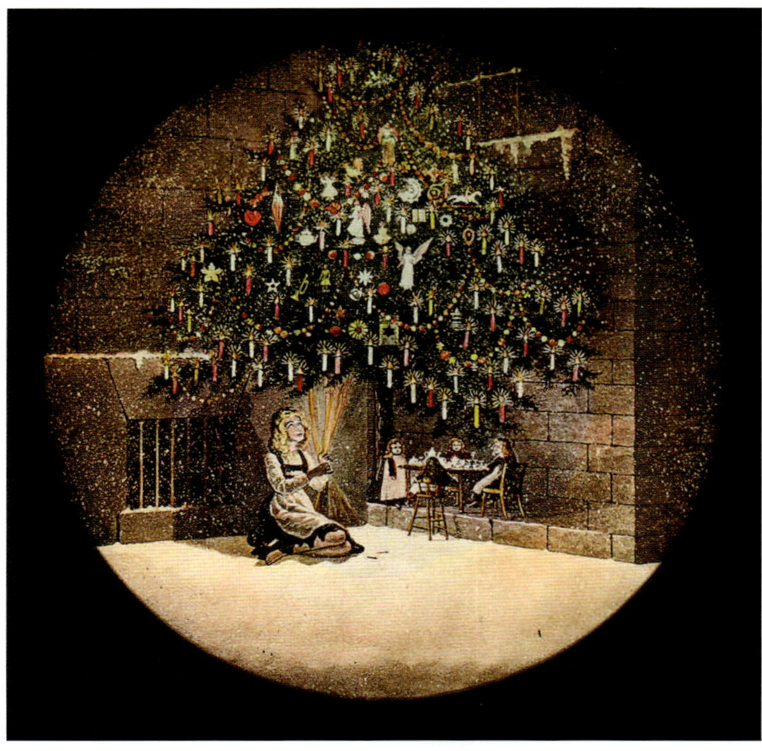

multiple lighted windows and the one darkened one – all these contribute to the effect. Beale's management of the set's window is radical. Imagine, actually removing a portion of a building because it no longer supports the artistic intent! But the change is made with great subtlety, gradually, over a series of slides. Despite having projected this story hundreds of times, I never consciously realized that the window was disappearing until I studied the slides in preparation for writing this description. Likewise, the audience is probably not consciously aware of Beale's changes, but at an unconscious level I'm sure they *feel* them.

Fig. 3.15 Beale's slides 4 and 5, *The Little Match Girl.*

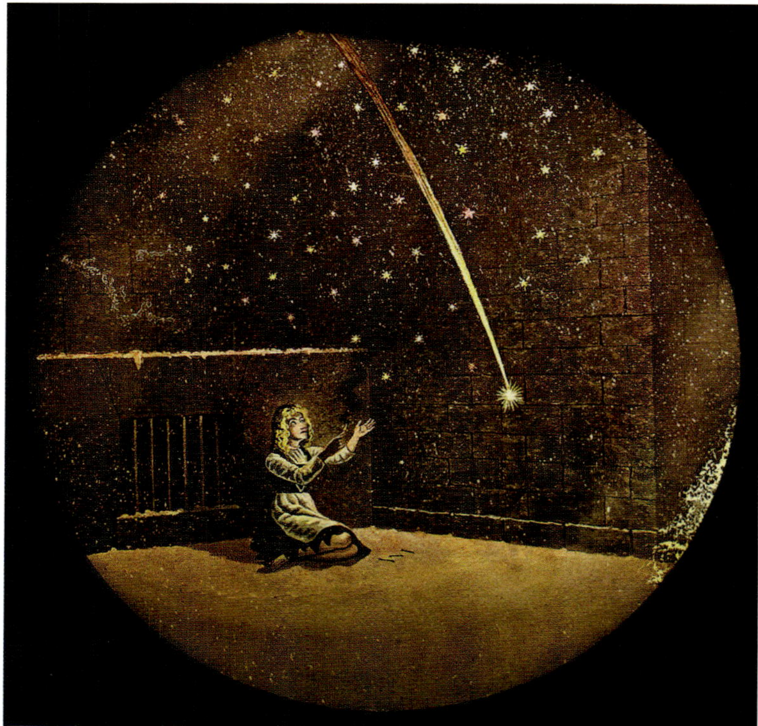

The Little Match Girl is a powerful piece because it connects with audiences at this feeling level. In our shows I can often sense the viewers dropping down into the story, captured by the changing imagery, by the words and tone of voice, by musical accompaniment and other sound effects.[20] Slowly, the small noises an audience makes – the shuffles, the coughs, the creaking chairs – all fade away. Finally, it becomes so quiet that hundreds of people seem to breathe as one. The hard-bitten eyes of the twenty-first century mist over, a tribute to the literary and visual mastery of a century ago.

Casting For Impact

While Beale worked for Baker and Co. in Chicago, creating architectural drawings and honing what would become his mise-en-scène skills, he also did free-lance work for *Leslie's* that helped build his mental images of a huge cast of characters. His assignments for *Leslie's* not only allowed for tête-à-têtes with presidents, and a chance to visit and record their life-space. They also brought him face-to-face with the Chicago masses. The entire world had come to Chicago, eager to work in its many industries. Representatives of many nations, many of them still in portions of their native dress, jammed the city's streets. To someone like Beale who had been trained to study and reproduce differences in "national characteristics", the faces hurrying along the streets must have been fascinating. With so many examples of any one "type" it would not have taken him very long to begin to see the many different individuals within the stereotyped groups presented at the Academy. Surely, he was sketching what he saw.

Unfortunately, no "character scrapbook" or portfolio, like the ones that help us understand other aspects of Beale's art, has survived to let us watch him learn. But his daily exposure over a twelve-year period to such a range of human diversity must have helped build his own central casting bureau, one he used in his later work. Though Beale has a recognizable way of presenting people in lantern slides, he did not use a "stable" of twenty faces that he repeated over and over in different guises. In his role as his

Sound in Magic Lantern Shows

The Little Mitch Girl

One of the appeals of the magic-lantern stories like *The Little Match Girl* was that they had sound. The narrator's voice could be enormously expressive, creating a whole host of different characters to populate the screen, and of emotions to fill the heart.

In addition, music was key – sometimes mechanical music like that provided by a "Cabinetto", occasionally a band or orchestra played. Often the show featured a piano and a singer, which is what we use in our shows.

Our version of *The Little Match Girl* starts in the dark with a melancholy piano carol, "What Child is This". The piano continues as the bleak street scene fades slowly up to low light. After that opening scene, I fade to dark again, and, without piano, stay in the dark as I describe the little girl hunting for a place to hide from the cold. Then, when she is in her corner and the first of her visions appear, the piano begins again with "A Great and Mighty Wonder", which is used each time a new vision appears. At the start of the final scene, when the people discover the little girl lying dead, no music plays at all. We let the silence speak. Then the piano comes in again softly with "Silent Night" under the final lines:

> No one even imagined what beautiful things she had seen, and how happily
> she had gone with her old grandmother into the star-studded Christmas night.

No applause follows this story, it is too somber, so "Silent Night" continues in the dark after the fade out as a bridge to images of the Nativity, where the soprano sings "Silent Night", and the audience joins in, singing goodbye to the little match girl.

> Sleep in heavenly peace. Sleep in heavenly peace.

Nancy Stewart, the singer/pianist that I worked with the longest, had a lyrical voice, and superb piano improvisational ability. She was not simply playing these carols during *The Little Match Girl*, she was composing off of them to complement and support my narration. At our best, we were integrated down to the syllable level.

The magic-lantern manuals of the period, as well as the scripts, indicate that often their music was carefully integrated into the show, just as we did with *The Little Match Girl*. Modern cinema terminology for the management of sound is unfamiliar jargon to many non-specialists, so I'll leave the terms themselves to note 20. But the terms do describe a whole range of techniques that lanternists could and did employ to strengthen the impact of their shows, so here's a description without the jargon.

Of course they used sound coming from the world of the story, like the conversation of characters, created by the narrator's voice. They used sounds coming from the story's environment (like the wind); internal sound, coming from the mind of one of the characters; and off-screen sound, like that of an approaching crowd. They also used mood music, like our piano Christmas carols-sound that was audible to the audience, but not to the characters in the story, and not directly related to the action on screen.

They sometimes used the reverse, simultaneous sound matched with what was seen on screen, though not, lip synched, except with certain "moving mouth" lever slides. They used mickey mousing, sound imitating the effects of cartoon characters. Finally, they used dialogue overlap—sound from one scene spilling into the next; and sound perspective – for example a fading shout – that could be used to suggest distance or movement.

In short, magic-lantern art in its full form as a Magic Lantern Show used most of the "modern" techniques of cinema sound management, without, of course, any of the fancy electronic enhancements. Most of this sound was created by the showman and the piano and the singer, but even relatively modest shows such as ours could and did go much further. We start the show with the "Boom!" of a huge gong; we sometimes use a thunder sheet, or a duck call, or a whistle.

And we always end the show with a "clacker", an old-time noise maker that makes a very loud continuous firecracker noise to accompany the flashing lights of the final image.

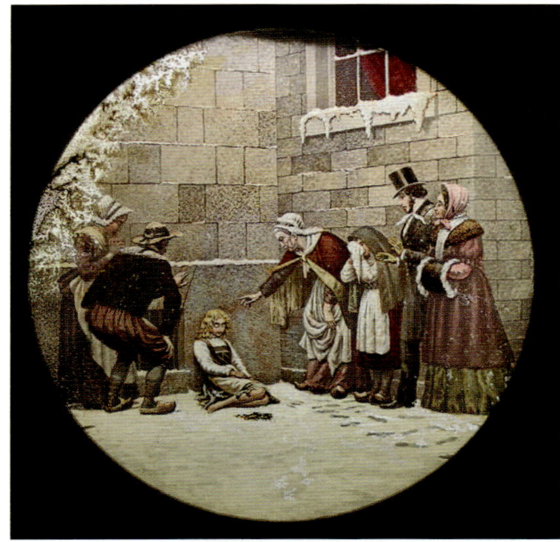

Fig. 3.16 Beale's slide 8, *The Little Match Girl.*

own casting director, he populated his screen worlds with the individual faces and body types of a "cast of thousands" – all created from memory. Their variety helps keep his work as distinct and invigorating as the Chicago streets that were his school.

The Pied Piper, by Robert Browning, is a good example of Beale's ability to create different, individual depictions of people (Fig. 3.17). In this story of eight slides Beale presents 83 different characters, each separately realized. As we have seen in other aspects of Beale's work, his casting is not diverse for its own sake; he uses it to tell the story on screen. The two leads, the Piper and the Mayor, are as different physically as they are in personality – the Piper tall, willowy and flamboyant; the Mayor stout, florid, plain and pompous. It is their contrast of temperament that drives the plot. Each of the counselors has a distinct presence, and is recognizable in each of the three scenes in which he appears, serving as the chorus for this drama. While you can spot the "Beale" style – the women full-faced, the children even more so – no two women, and no two children in the crowd scenes look exactly alike, a stark contrast to the *Pied Piper* illustrations of Kate Greenway. Even the rats, the villains, are individually cast – an additional 25 characters. The "grave old plodders, gay young friskers/ Fathers, mothers, uncles, cousins/ cocking tails and pricking whiskers" are all there, each distinct, each portraying its part in the story.

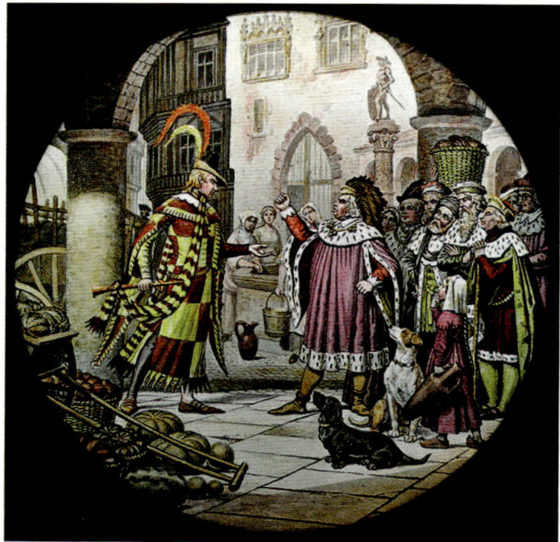

Fig. 3.17 Beale's slide 3 of *The Pied Piper* by Robert Browning.

Creating Action on Screen

When Beale was reporting for *Leslie's* from Chicago, whether covering the great events of the day or local news, Leslie insisted that dramatic events be rendered dramatically. Joseph Becker, who was Art Director at *Leslie's* during the later years that Beale worked there, liked to recall that Frank Leslie's motto was "Never shoot over the heads of the people". From Becker and from the legendary "artist correspondent" superstars of *Harper's* like Winslow Homer and Thomas Nast, Beale would have learned – directly or indirectly – how to create illustrations that were accurate renderings of "reality", and yet captured the imagination of the masses with drama and action.

Beale worked on dramatic composition by keeping a pictorial reference book of images by other artists that appealed to him.[21] It was a project which he may well have started when he was still in high-school – a collection of melodramatic illustrations from dime novel fiction. Though not directly related to much of his Chicago reportorial work, these pictures were suggestive of the future style he would develop for the magic lantern, for they contained techniques that would help him create storytelling drama on screen.

Of the 197 images in Beale's scrapbook, at least 44 are by F. O. C. Darley, an artist whose masterful narrative art for James Fenimore Cooper's books helped make them famous. Beale selected Darley images that represent the full range of his presentations – from a detailed steel engraving of "Emigrants Crossing the Plains", to an "outline drawing" of *The Spy*, to scenes like that on the cover of *Confession*, which typify the dramatic poses, complex composition, and exaggerated expressions that gave Darley's early work its excitement (Fig. 3.18).

As Beale began to illustrate fictional literature

for the magic lantern, these images of Darley provided a ready museum of techniques for adapting his earlier style to the needs of a story. As the director of magic lantern art, he was responsible for *blocking*, for putting his characters into motion in order to bring screen action to literary *narration*.[22]

And while he was doing that, he would have to convey the emotions that motivated action, or were revealed by it. Darley was a master at both, with a story-telling style that was well suited to lantern slides. (In fact, Beale was later to adapt two of Darley's illustrated stories – *Rip Van Winkle* and *The Legend of Sleepy Hollow* – to create slide sets, making only minor changes in the images.)

In his study of Darley, Beale was once again broadening his range, building the repertoire of skills that would make the magic lantern capable of projecting the full scope of American history, and the excitement of the great literature of the age. The dramatic flair of that on-screen storytelling style would, in turn, foreshadow the melodramatic visual style of the early cinema.

The Pied Piper illustrates not only how Beale individualized characters, but how skillfully he put those characters into motion. The first scene of the story for instance (Fig. 3.19), suggests bedlam, but the *proxemic patterns* – the relations between elements – is carefully planned. Rats race down the stairs in a massed charge from the left, pummel dogs and gloat over dead cats in the lower center, and sweep on to a howling baby on the right. The human figures, in contrast, are all going in different directions, screaming in terror, with hands raised. A mother reaches for her baby and the baby reaches back for its mother in an arc that parallels the rats' advance. Another woman runs terrified out the door, her flailing hands contrasting with the quiet church towers in the distance.

The raised-hands *motif* continues in subsequent slides – raised in desperation in the council chamber, and then with cheers as the rats fall into the river (Fig. 3.20). (Note, by the way, Beale's management of the figures of the rats themselves in the river scene. Again, they pour down in a mass from the left. Their forepaws – mirror images of the jubilant spectators uplifted hand – are spread downwards in terror.)

The Pied Piper is a strange combination of horror and humor, with its gory story, bouncing rhythm, triple rhymes, and swirling rats and hands. When we perform it in our *Halloween Show*, I can often hear people reacting to the humor of Beale's images, especially pointing out the antics of the different rats. It's a wonderful story for audience participation – one of the keys to success of magic lantern shows a hundred years ago, and today. We get the audience making the "rumbling and grumbling" of the rats by pounding their feet on the floor, followed,

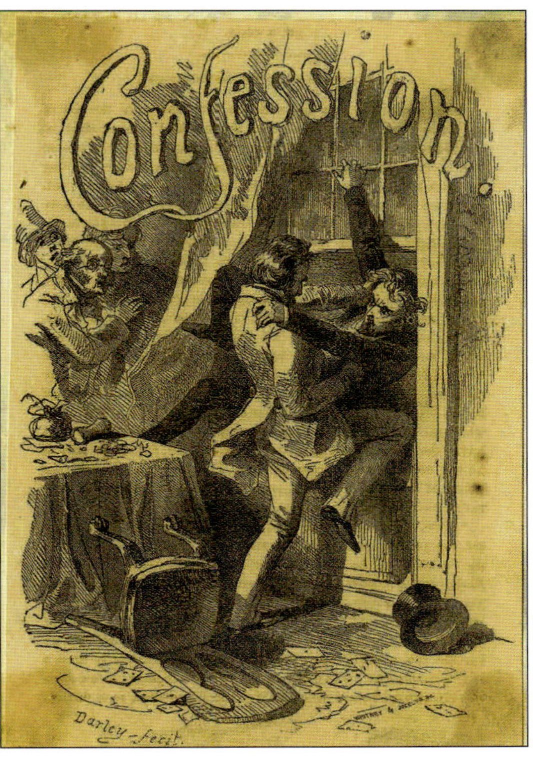

Fig. 3.18 F. O. C. Darley's cover illustration for *The Confession*, a promotion for a dime novel pasted in Beale's scrapbook.

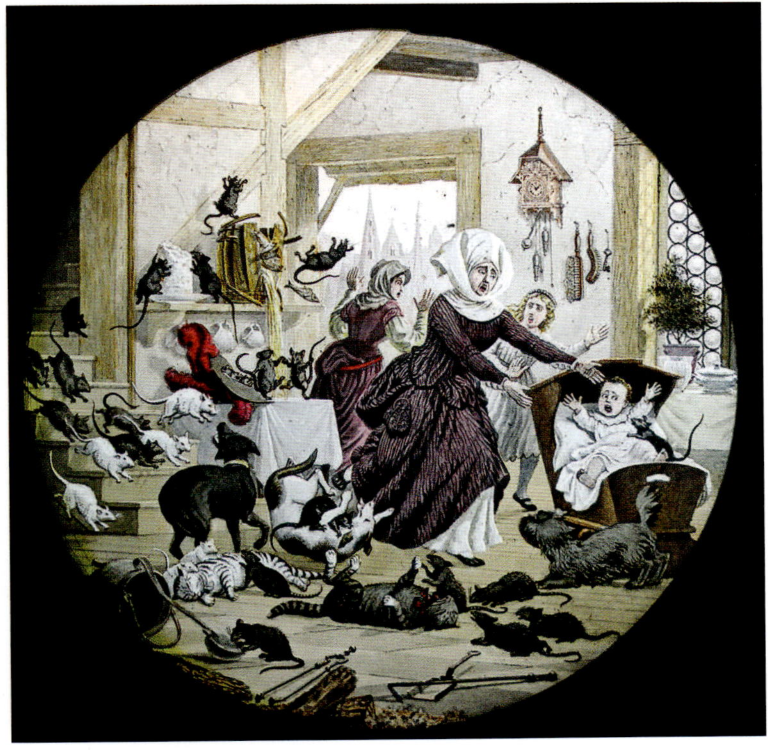

Fig. 3.19 Beale's slide 1, for Robert Browning's *The Pied Piper*.

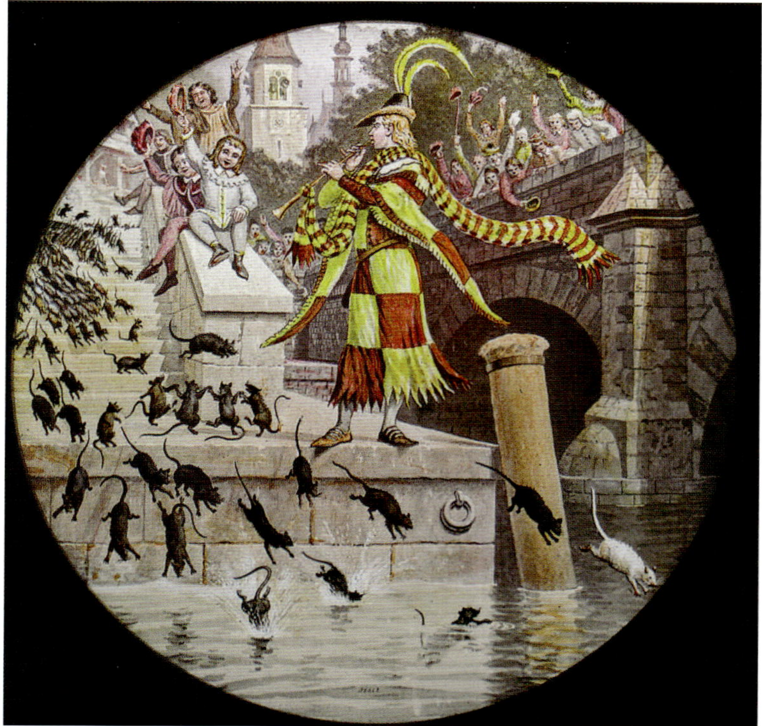

Fig. 3.20 Beale's slide 5 for *The Pied Piper*.

by the "little hands clapping", as the music bounces merrily along and the children follow the Piper. Suddenly, the lively music and clapping cease. Both the Hamelin folk *and the audience* realize what will happen to the children as they are led into the mountain cavern (Fig. 3.21). And when "the door in the mountain side" shuts fast with a great rumble from the piano, when the screen goes dark and the little children are seen no more, an awed hush falls upon the audience. It is only the coda recited in the dark – an extravagant rhyme, supported by a lively piano "button" – that brings the story back to comedy, that releases the tension:

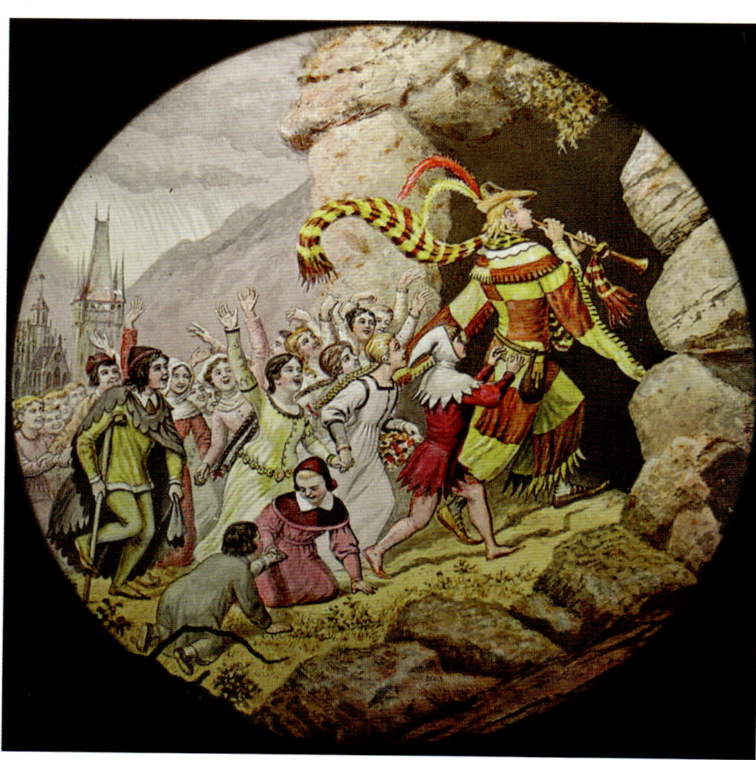

Fig. 3.21 Beale's slide 8 for *The Pied Piper*.

> So children, let you and me by wipers
> Of scores out with all men, especially pipers.
> And whether they pipe us free from rats or from mice,
> If we've promised them aught, let us keep our promise! [Pronounced "pro-mice!"]

That rhyme, indeed the whole text of the poem, was completely lost on the children of Singapore when we performed there. We had been assured that "they all speak English", which, it turned out meant they all knew how to say, "Hello". We were there for a week, two shows a day, with an audience that was polite, of course, but clearly didn't understand the performance at all. It was time for a drastic overhaul. On the fly we developed what we later called out "International Format" – a combination of native-language introductions, simplified English, and over-the-top dramatics. For *The Pied Piper* the key was dropping the original poem entirely. Instead, I started by pointing at that first slide (Fig. 3.19), and yelling, "RATS"! Again, I yelled "RATS"! – this time motioning for the audience to join in. "RATS! RATS! RATS"! They were into it by that fifth "RATS"! – yelling their new-found English at the top of their lungs. We continued with this extremely simplified format, teaching key words with lots of drama, but mostly relying on Beale's action images to tell the story. The first time through the show was a bit bumpy, but by the second day we were in the zone. The kids loved it. The applause was no longer polite; it was enthusiastic. Lesson? Do whatever it takes to reach your audience.

Lighting for Drama

In Beale's scrapbook, another major artist besides Darley accounts for about 90 of the images, and probably affected Beale's dramatic treatment of light in his lantern slides. Certainly, they indicate Beale's early fascination with the potential of dramatic back lighting. These unsigned pictures are taken from dime novels and periodicals (Fig. 3.22). At least some were published by Beadle and Adams, who produced thousands of dime novel images. Their leading artist was George G. White, a Philadelphian just 12 years older than Beale, who went to work at *Leslie's* in 1863, three years before Beale arrived there. He stayed until 1870, so he and Beale overlapped for three years, at which point White moved over to illustrate Beadle's *Saturday Journal* and his dime novels, just about the time that Beale himself left *Leslie's* to go to Chicago. Beale was almost certainly collecting his work as a young artist, and certainly knew him at *Leslie's*. Given all these connections, it is natural that Beale would have been interested in White's work, and not surprising that White's dramatic use of light and dark would make its way into Beale's magic lantern art.[23]

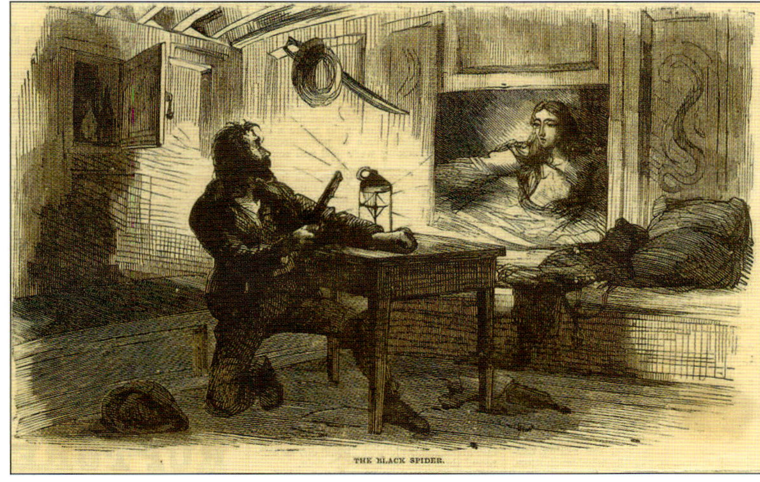

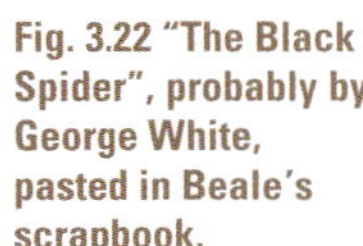
Fig. 3.22 "The Black Spider", probably by George White, pasted in Beale's scrapbook.

White often worked with heavy lines and areas of almost pure black or dark shadows, using *low-key lighting* (also called *high contrast* or *hard lighting*). Dramatic streaks of *side light* created by artificial sources like a lamp or fire were common in White's work. Contrasting light and dark gave his scenes the melodramatic feeling that Darley achieved with contorted body lines and facial expressions. Such high-contrast lighting was to become a favorite artistic device of early film storytellers, who, like White, were trying to achieve their visual effects using only black and white images – especially, of course, in *film noir*.

Beale had studied the use of light and dark – Samuel Prout's *Hints on Light and Shadow* was one of the books Beale read in school – but few of Beale's reportorial or commercial engravings use dramatic contrast. He seems more comfortable with *soft lighting* – a gradual transition of light and dark.[24] Or perhaps that is simply what his customers (or bosses) wanted. For at about the same time that he was producing these sedate images, Beale began illustrating more than 50 books, especially those of Allan Pinkerton, the founder of the famous Pinkerton Detective Agency. Pinkerton's "true-life" detective stories were full of melodramatic situations and violent action – a perfect place for Beale to use what he learned by studying White's dime-novel technique (Fig. 3.23).[25]

Pinkerton gave Beale plenty of practice, since Beale illustrated about a dozen of his books. For just one book, Pinkerton's best-selling *The Mollie Maguires and the Detectives*, Beale created 48 illustrations. This "true-life" story is about one of Pinkerton's detectives who spent three years undercover in "The Mollies", an Irish labor organization that was a leader of the strife in the Pennsylvania coal mines during the 1870s. Dark, brooding, images appear about every ten pages.[26] Many of the scenes are of mid-night violence, using *key lights* of torches and fires that throw threatening shadows across the scene. The

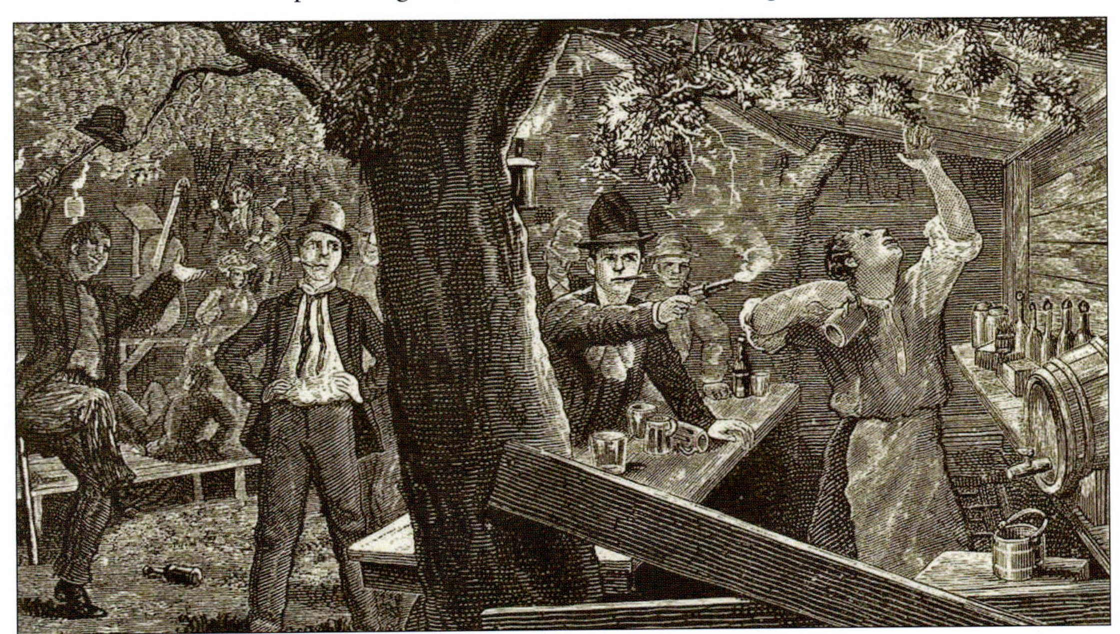
Fig. 3.23 A Beale illustration from the book, *The Molly Maguires* by Allan Pinkerton.

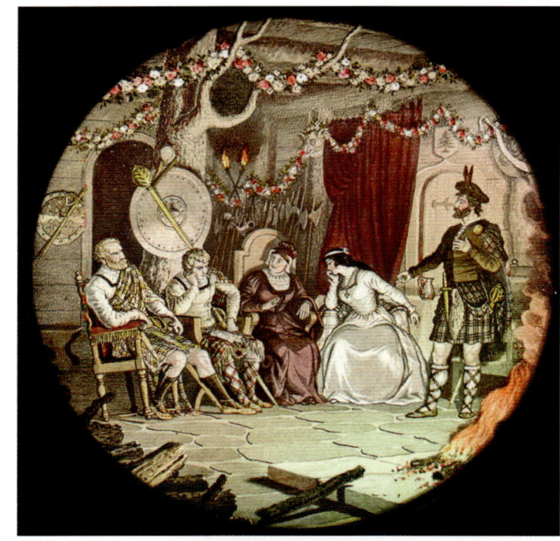

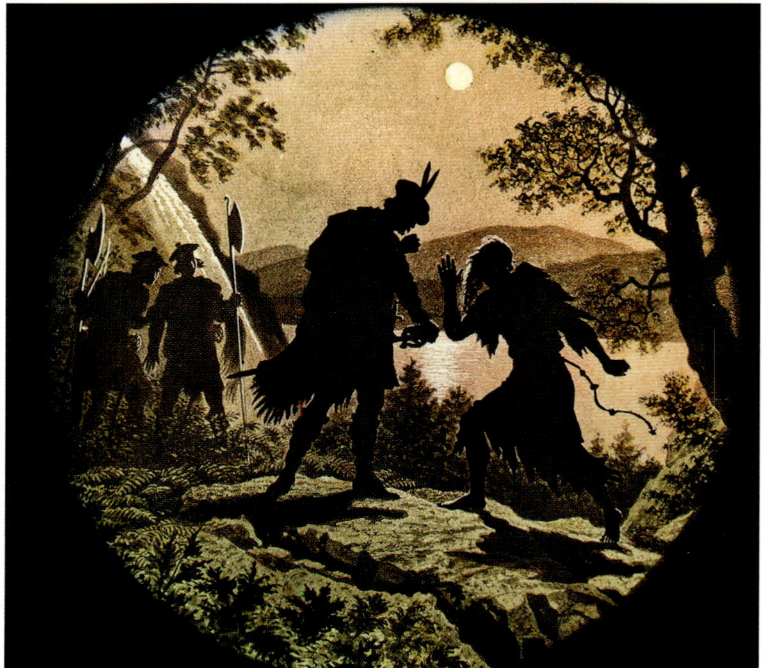

Fig. 3.24 Beale's slide 6 and 11 for Sir Walter Scott's poem, *The Lady of the Lake*.

strong light draws attention to small details of *intrinsic interest* – the terrified whites in the eyes of a killer's victim, the smoke curling from a pistol. The picture in Fig. 3.23 combines the theatrical composition and contorted figures characteristic of Darley, with the dramatic lighting characteristic of White. The dark form of the tree, dividing most of the drunken Mollies from their victim, is a compositional device that Beale never used in lantern slides because it would divide the big screen so sharply. (Beale's stark illustrations probably influenced a 1970's movie of *The Molly Maguires*, starring Sean Connery and Richard Harris.)

When a few years after Beale had illustrated the *Mollies*, he began to work on lantern slides, such *high-contrast* images soon became a major part of his repertoire – and not just in monochrome. Unlike White, and unlike the early movies, Beale also had color at his disposal, thanks to the lantern-slide colorists. He reached back to his fascination with light and color in the parades and illuminations of his youth, and to his Academy studies of the flamboyant 17th century chiaroscuro techniques that Caravaggio used for contrasting light and shadow. He combined this high-contrast style with dramatic color, melding them with the luminosity of the projected lantern light itself.

Beale clearly had audience appeal in mind when he used these techniques. *Soft lit* slides were fashionable among elite photographic lanternists, but, one photographer ruefully admitted, *hard* slides were admired by the general public:

> Plenty of sparkling light combined with deep shadows [produces] an effect similar to limelight scenery on stage, [and] will often call forth rounds of applause, while a softer, more natural slide will be allowed to pass away from the sheet without eliciting any marks of approbation.[27]

"Limelight" was very bright and used both on stage, and to light lanterns as well. But Beale did not use this theatrical hard lighting for most slides. He rationed them out, making them all the more effective by contrasting them with a softer approach in most of a story. Here are some examples from his version of *The Lady of the Lake*, a tale of Scottish magic, love, and warfare.

Beale's slide in Fig. 3.24, top, uses a *two-point lighting* system, an unseen *front light* that illuminates the entire scene evenly, and then the *key light* of the fire to help define the forms of the characters. This two- or three-point lighting is typical of Beale's usual *soft-lit* scenes, when he is not striving for dramatic lighting effects.

In another scene (Fig. 3.24, bottom), the moon provides a *backlight* that creates a dramatic black *silhouette* of the figures. The moonlight also illuminates the lake between them, increasing the contrast. The *rim lights* around the old man's face gives him a ghostly appearance, and the darkly shadowed crack in the rock adds to the sense of mystery and danger.

In the third scene (Fig. 3.25), the moon continues to provide backlight, silhouetting the horse in the background, while the two central figures are dramatically *underlit* by a fire that semi-silhouettes one, and front-lights the other. The fire also reflects off the vines on the crag, providing a gentle sprinkle of greenery that frames and contrast with the violence of the scene below. Thus, in a few stunning images of light and dark, Beale carries his audience from his world (or the world of today), into an exotic landscape of danger, suffused with mystery. Geroge White would have been proud.

Lighting – Fade for Effect

The presentation of lantern shows involves not only Beale's artistic use of light, but the showman's handling of it in the lantern, and in special effect slides. These techniques manipulate the *amount* and *quality* of light on the screen. They were a common part of lantern practice, frequently discussed in trade journals like *The Magic Lantern* and *The Optical Magic Lantern Journal,* and in the many manuals for showmen. These discussions covered a variety of ways for controlling the lantern's light, but a consistent refrain was the great care that had to be taken with its manipulation. *Modern Magic Lanterns and Their Management*, for instance, carries this cautionary tale of a lantern presentation ruined by poorly manipulated light in a two-lens lantern:

> The writer remembers seeing a lantern display in which a poor waif, seated on a doorstep, was exposed to what was intended to be a shower of rain. Owing to the operator having, if anything, a brighter light in the "rain" lantern than in the other, the shower suggested nothing so much as one of white-hot knitting needles, and the effect on the audience was anything but what was intended.[28]

In our re-created lantern shows, we also use the "techniques of light" in every performance – carefully, I hope. In our *Little Match Girl,* for instance, we begin the story, as we do all stories, by *fading in* – starting in the dark and gradually increasing the illumination of the picture. Each of the little girl's visions is a different scene, created when she lights a match, so we *fade-out* between them. The little girl, and the audience, are left in the dark, waiting for a vision to appear. The effect on the audience is like that which we all experience when wait in the dark for the lights to come up as a play begins, except here the anticipation is more intense, for we are already involved in the story.

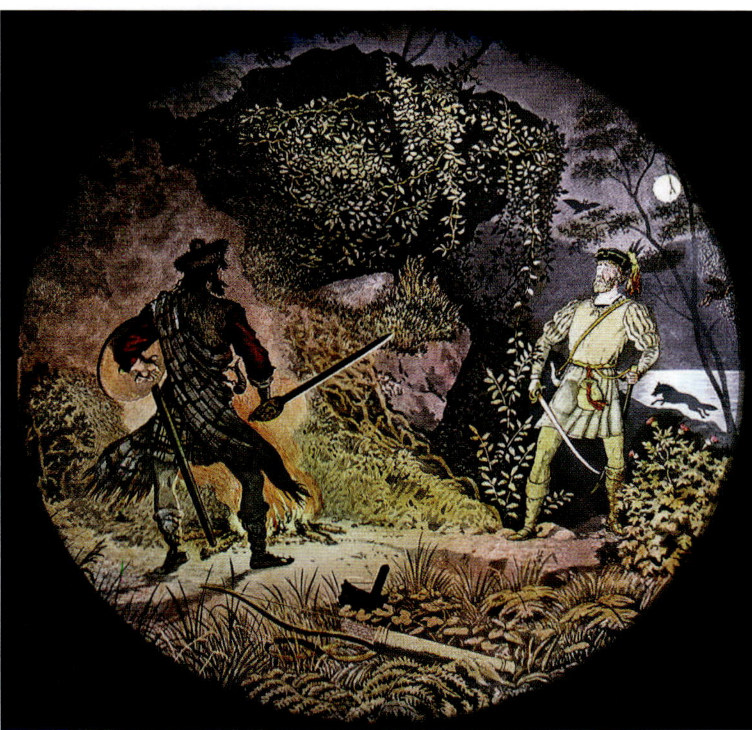

Fig. 3.25 Beale's slide 16 for *The Lady of the Lake*.

Fades can be a slow or fast. The old magic lantern manuals also make clear that it is not only the *intensity* of the illumination that is important. The *rhythm*, the *timing* of illumination, like the timing of jokes, can be critical. The showman who handles his timing crudely, said one lantern manual, will "spoil the illusion" and "is likely to be laughed at".[29] A magic lantern show, after all, is essentially painting with light. The light itself is the show's most powerful element, and its manipulation for artistic purposes is a significant part of the showman's skill. A fade-out must be timed so that it enhances the tone and pace of the narration, the tempo and quality of the musical underscoring, the depth of feeling in the story. A slow fade-out as the little match girl rises to Heaven with her grandmother will swell a lump in the throat. A fast fade on the same slide could make the scene seem ridiculous.

Beale was no doubt aware that fading-out an image does not just darken it; it changes the tonal values between the colors. He probably intended this change to be used. In a fade, the lighter sections of the slide become indistinct, as do the darkest; finally, only the clearest part "reads". This highlights that portion of the slide, which often creates a powerful effect. In the *Hiawatha* story, for instance, as I fade-out the final scene of Hiawatha going to the "Islands of the Blessed", the sunset gradually darkens, just as it does in real life. At the end, as the scene "fades to dark", all we can see are the

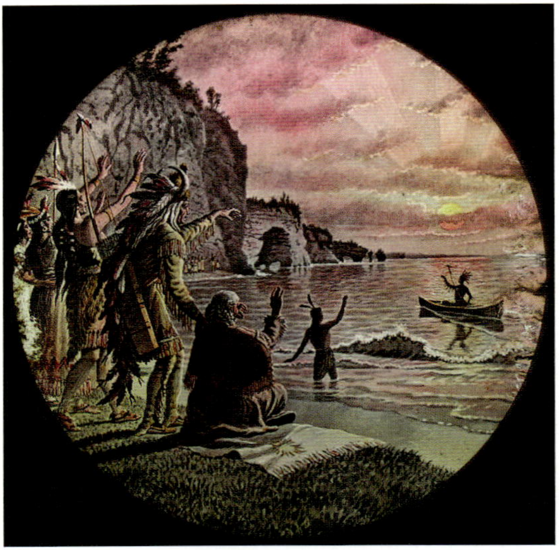

Fig. 3.26 Beale's slide 22 from *Hiawatha* by Henry Wadsworth Longfellow.

silhouettes of the waving figures, and the indistinct image of Hiawatha in his canoe. Fading such a picture to dark, changes both tonal range, and emotional impact (Fig. 3.26).

Fade-ins can be used for similar artistic effect. In the song, *We Are Climbing Jacob's Ladder*, I start the slide for the chorus at a very low light. Gradually I fade-in, increasing the light as the audience sings the refrain,

> "Every step goes higher, higher."

Finally the image seems to dazzle the eyes with the brilliance of Heaven. Elaborate forms of the *fade* like this were frequently used and discussed in the 19th century, because each gave a characteristic and prized quality.[30]

Masks could also be used to black out a portion of the image until needed. This was done by using a moveable *mask* called a *dodger*, held before the lens. In *Marley's Ghost,* for instance, I use the dodger to cover the grave at first. Then I slowly remove it so Scrooge (and the audience) can see Scrooge's name on the stone, and realize its significance. Other forms of a mask could not only indicate transitions, but heighten the artistic effect of the image, and create action itself.[31]

Another way of creating a magical effect is to superimpose a gauze screen, or a color *filter*, or *tinter* as they were often called. Many lanterns, like Marcy's, came with built-in red and blue filters. The red filter could be slowly raised into the light, creating the effect of a gradually increasing sunset glow. The blue filter could be used for turning a daylight scene into night – a technique the movies still use in *day-for-night* shooting. Colored filters of all hues were also used to make classical nude statues emerge from a background with a type of vertical *wipe*, created by a *curtain slide* that was slowly drawn up, gradually revealing a figure standing on the pedestal.[32]

Light – its presence or absence, its intensity, its hue, its pattern, its movement – was a critical part of early magic lantern shows, just as it is in today's movies. Whether the lanternist controlled the light, or the slide artist controlled it, or a combination of the two, its artistic treatment was essential for the success of the show. Beale's early sensitivity to light and dark is obvious from his boyhood diary. It is also evident in Beale's black and white illustrations for Pinkerton. Once Beale began to work in the magic lantern medium – to paint what were to become color slides, and to paint with light itself – he blossomed. In a tender story like *The Little Match Girl* his lighting effects were restrained. In other situations, when the story called for it, he could employ very dramatic chiaroscuro effects. The results were some of Beale's most beautiful slides – showstoppers in which the action is highlighted by the rich shimmering colors of various artificial lights, and the action's significance is heightened by the dark shadows beyond. So stunning are these scenes that you can often hear a sudden intake of breath from the audience when they are projected on screen.

Cartoon Animator

In Beale's scrapbook some surprising images differ from White's melodramatic lights and darks, and Darley's action-packed compositions. Four cartoons by an unknown artist are simply drawn, with exaggerated gestures and visual/verbal puns. They foreshadow a side of Beale's artistic talent that had not emerged in his earlier work, but which was to make up about 60 of his slides, and, of course, was to become a mainstay of the movies.

Beale's cartooning abilities were exercised in the fall of 1880, perhaps for the first time, when he created a series of biting political cartoons as the covers and centerfolds for the *Vampiretcher*, a new journal supporting the short-lived Greenback-Labor Party (Fig. 3.27). The Greenback movement grew from the pain of the 1873 Panic and the subsequent depression. It advocated the flexible use of paper money ("greenbacks"), rather than gold-backed currency, and garnered a million votes at its height in the 1878 congressional elections. The *Vampiretcher* matched Beale's acid brush with an acid pen, describing its editorial purpose and its extensive use of graphics with (coincidentally) a metaphor that foreshadowed Beale's future career.

> The Vampiretcher ... is of the opinion that the people are not kept posted in regard to the ill-smelling attics, sub-cellars and closet traps in the political edifice they inhabit, and he proposes to turn the rays of the magic lantern full upon these national sink holes.[33]

Beale may have been a little uneasy about being associated with such a populist platform. He signed the first cover only as "JOSH", a mode of signature he never used elsewhere, and limited his other signatures to "J.B.B.". He seems to have dropped his association after the first six issues. Perhaps payment was an issue; the magazine seems to have ceased publication after nine issues. Beale's illustration style in the magazine is similar to other political cartoons of the period, except that he refuses to relinquish his passion for detail, and includes more than is typical.

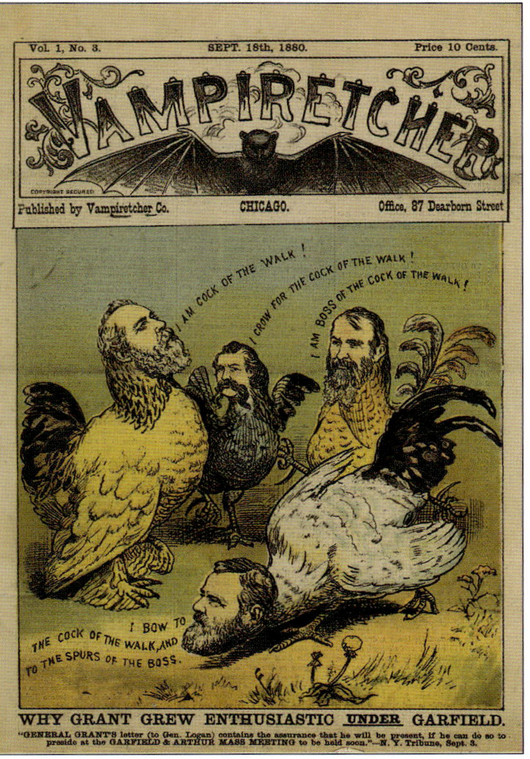

Fig. 3.27 Beale cover for *The Vampiretcher*, September 18, 1880.

Years later, when he came to producing comic lantern slides, Beale kept the same predilection for detail. For instance, Briggs asked Beale to draw a "before and after" set of animated comic slides that mimicked the movement seen in slip slides. Most of these slides (perhaps all) were based on pre-existing sets. Beale took the simple comic images he had been given to copy, and made them much more complex (Fig. 3.28). In one about a boy smoking his first cigar, Beale added a more realistic setting, and then a whole other level to the joke by introducing the reactions of a stern cigar store Indian. Briggs did not approve of this approach.

> Some years ago you will remember that you redrew a number of our comic designs – and as there was supposed to be less detail &c you made them for $5.00 each. I thought at the time you put too much work in them because those comic subjects [are most effective] if the main thought is brought out forcibly. [T]he accessories and surroundings would better be kept back and not too distinct – quite different from a Bible subject.[34]

Whether he altogether approved or not, Briggs accepted the comic scenes Beale produced. From a sales point of view, he may or may not have been right to do so. Beale's comic slides do not show up frequently on eBay. And they were certainly nowhere nearly as popular as slip-slides for presenting comic action.

While Beale's smoking set and the other ten comic sets are technically effect dissolves, they are not meant to change slowly, as such dissolves usually were. They are instead *jump cuts*, achieved by the lanternist shifting the light quickly from one slide to another, which shifts the scene abruptly (Fig. 3.29). The limelight lanterns could not create the jump cut by simply dissolving quickly from one lantern to the next, because the limes cooled gradually, which, by their nature, created a gradual transition. Instead, lanternists achieved the jump cut either

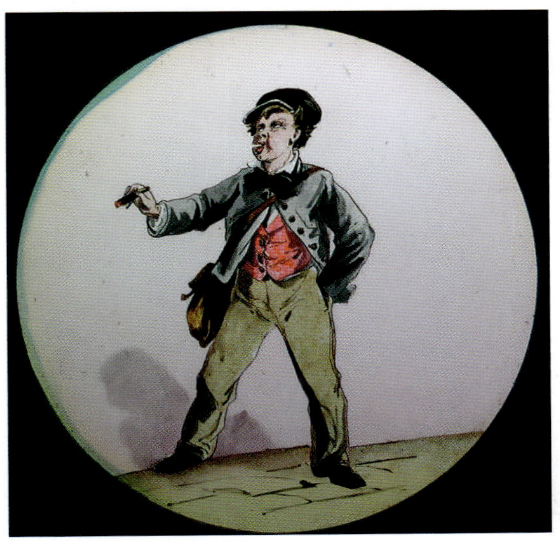

Fig. 3.28 The slide in the "First Cigar" set that Beale was given to re-draw.

with mechanical dissolving "fans", or with the *flashed effect*:

> The best way of representing such effects is to have [two] slides and "flash" them on ... The [first slide] is shown first. [The second slide] is to be put into the darkened lantern, and the objective [lens] covered with one hand and the lantern lighted up; at the decisive moment the hand that covers this second picture is to be removed and the other hand at the same instant placed over the objective of the lantern containing the first picture. The change is instantaneous ... .[35]

Fig. 3.29 Beale's "First Cigar" slides 1 and 2, in the Comic Children Dissolving group.

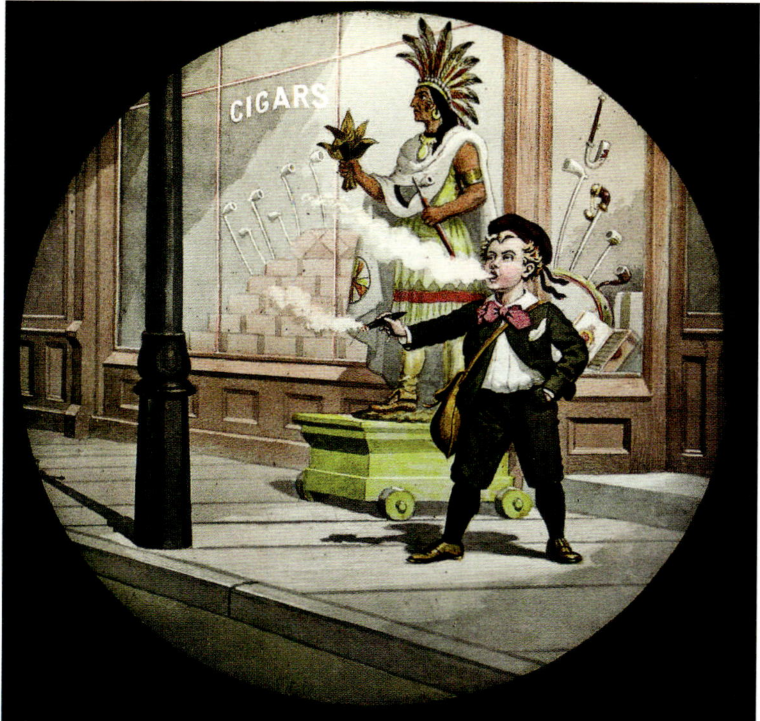

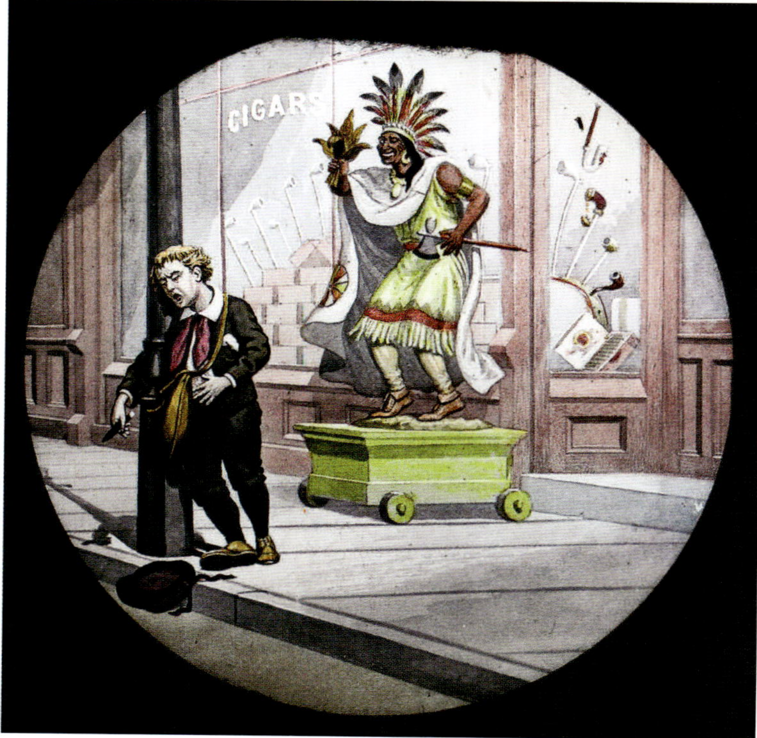

When this ***flashed effect*** or "jump cut" is used with the smoking set, it makes the boy and Indian the equivalent of *animated cells* like the Nose Man slip slide. But while the slip slides usually move just a portion of the image on each piece of glass, and so provide *limited animation*, the use of the jump cut allows Beale to show movement within a complete scene. The background remains stationery, while multiple figures can become *fully animated* – often moving in different directions, though of course only once. For instance, in the *First Cigar* set, the store and lamp post remain a carefully rendered and constant world of concrete reality, contrasting with the zany comic action. When the slide changes, the proud little cigar-smoker suddenly doubles over in nausea. As a double joke, the stern "wooden" Indian doubles over too – in laughter. And so does the audience.

Modern audiences love Beale's comic slides. After all, they are used to his approach to comic animation. Beale was foreshadowing the future, the type of detailed animation modern audiences have grown up on – classic Disney. Disney's realistic and meticulous "full animation" set the standard for years, and overwhelmed all attempts to create limited animation. (Appropriately enough, Disney himself first learned his cartoon skills in 1920, working on advertising lantern slides and animated film commercials for the Kansas City Slide Company, later called the Kansas City Film Ad Company. Many Disney cartoons like Mickey's adventures were subsequently produced for toy lanterns.)[36]

A Last Hurrah in Chicago

Beale continued to work at Baker in Chicago, and to act as the mid-western stringer for *Leslie's*. In the summer of 1880 came an assignment he must have relished – covering the Democratic Convention to be held June 22 to 24, at the Music Hall in Cincinnati (Fig. 3.30).

The Convention choose Winfield S. Hancock as their standard bearer. Never heard of him? That's because he lost to Republican, James A. Garfield. But Beale's drawing makes clear that his nomination generated plenty of excitement. The double-page spread documenting the event is probably the last picture Beale created for *Leslie's* (Fig. 3.31).

Louise, Beale's wife, died in Chicago on April 23, 1881. She wanted to be buried beside her parents in Philadelphia, so Beale brought her body back home. Other factors were making Chicago less appealing. Frank Leslie had also died recently. Leslie's flamboyant widow now controlled the firm and was downsizing it to bring it back to profitability. It was surely a stressful period, and Beale probably felt it was time for a change.[37]

A New Life in Philadelphia

Beale decided to stay on in Philadelphia (Fig. 3.32). His father and mother were still alive and his brothers and sisters were busy building families and careers. (Steve and Alonzo would become dentists like their father; Emily a public-school teacher; Albert the Superintendent of the Philadelphia Board of Education; Eddy would achieve local fame as organizer of the Municipal Band of Philadelphia.) Joseph settled down with a changing assortment of relatives in the Germantown suburb of Philadelphia, and became part of the bustling family life again. He was known as a "staunch Republican" and though an active member of the Second Presbyterian Church in Germantown, may well have continued the ecumenical attitudes of his early years, as his funeral was conducted by an Episcopalian minister.[38]

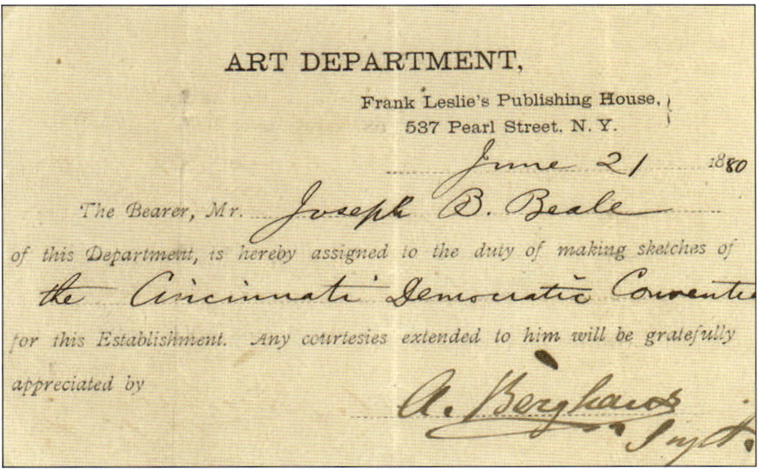

ART DEPARTMENT,
Frank Leslie's Publishing House,
537 Pearl Street, N. Y.
June 21 1880
The Bearer, Mr. Joseph B. Beale
of this Department, is hereby assigned to the duty of making sketches of the Cincinnati Democratic Convention
for this Establishment. Any courtesies extended to him will be gratefully appreciated by
A. Berghaus Supt.

Fig. 3.30 Beale's Press Pass for the 1880 Democratic Convention.

Though Beale did not pick up his Diary again, he did take and develop hundreds of photos. These were found in his studio when the Beale family home was sold, and from them we can infer something of the family's life.

Joseph and the family used several houses in the same Germantown neighborhood at different times (Fig. 3.33).[39] It is impossible to tell from the pictures exactly which is which, and who is where, but a pattern certainly emerges. The houses are uniformly large and comfortable, full of good-quality furniture, cluttered with plants and knick-knacks. A Black servant, well-dressed and holding a chicken, stands before an arbor in one photo; in another she is in maid's uniform, attending dinner. An up-to-date dentist

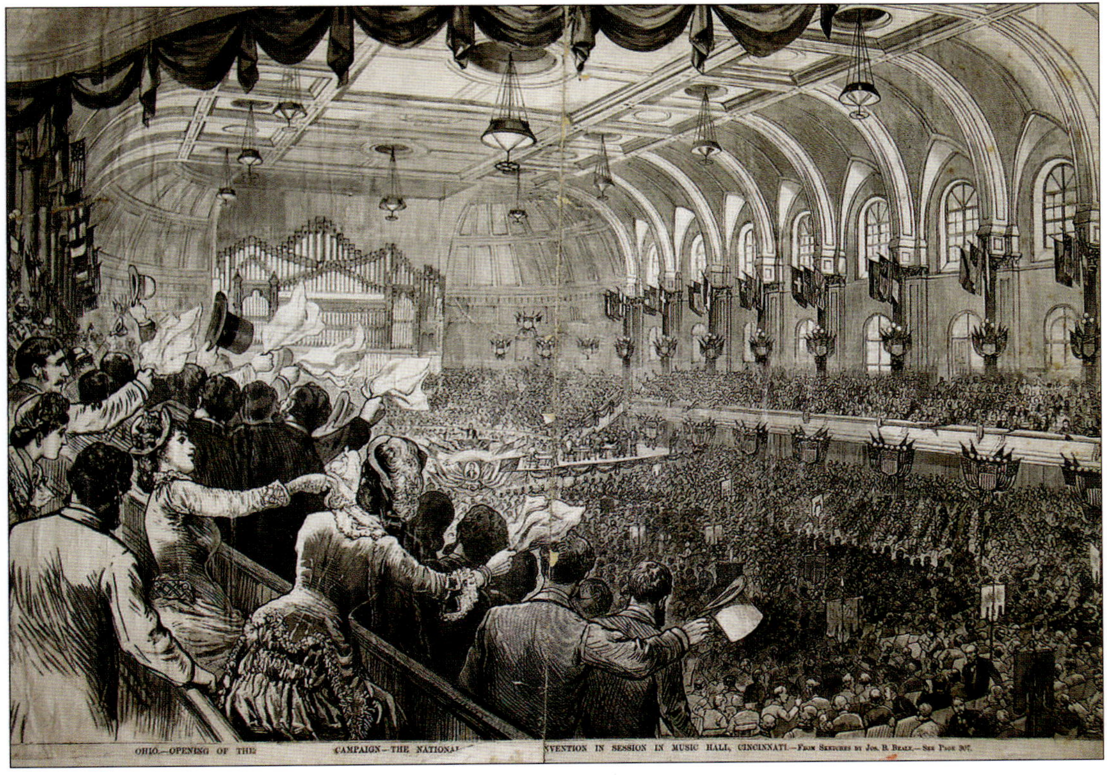

Fig. 3.31 Beale's double-page, center-spread engraving, "Opening of the Democratic Convention", *Frank Leslie's Illustrated Newspaper*, July 3, 1880.

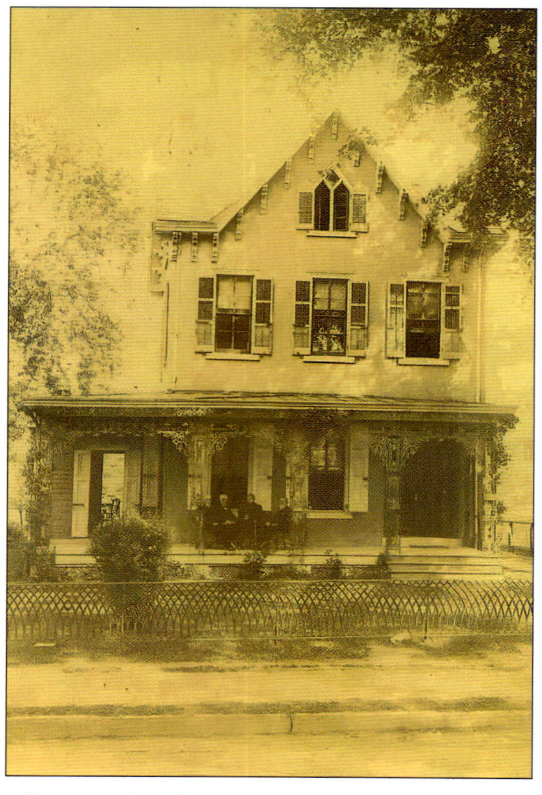

Fig. 3.32 The Beale family home in the Germantown section of Philadelphia, where Beale's effects were found when the house was sold in mid-20th century.

office in the front room has a comfortable homey look. A piano in the next room is a testament to the continuing Beale family passion for music. One photo shows the family in action – an eight-person ensemble!

The Beales were not a stay-at-home bunch. Photos often show them hiking and fishing at the nearby Wissahickon Park, or visiting Stephen's farm near Media, and posing there under Emily's "trysting tree". Other pictures capture them further afield – paying homage at Mt. Vernon, home of the man who they believed approved the flag of Beale's great aunt, Betsy Ross; moose hunting in Maine; shopping in Bermuda; girl-watching at the Ocean City beaches; horseback riding in the Wild West; and taking the grand tour of Europe. (The European trip was probably in 1889, as Beale's effects contained copies of *Illustrated London News* and *Figaro Illustré* from that year, presumably brought home so that he could study foreign illustration styles. All travel was to become useful to Beale, for he would have to create scenes from all over the world in his lantern slides.)

The photos also show a fun-loving family, despite the shadow of the rape trial which still hung over them.[40] Beale captures the antics of a New Year's celebration, with the teetotaling family "popping" each other with bananas rather than champagne corks (Fig. 3.34). Come summertime, he snaps a picture of one of his brothers with his feet up – the feet filling half the picture. (In this shot we see Beale playing with *close-ups*, a technique he avoided in his slides, where he wanted to give a sense of the whole scene.) Beale also arranges the family hiding like so many fairies amid three-foot leaves of Elephant-Ears in the back yard; or, more elfin yet, smiling cheek-to-cheek beside the head of a plaster leprechaun.

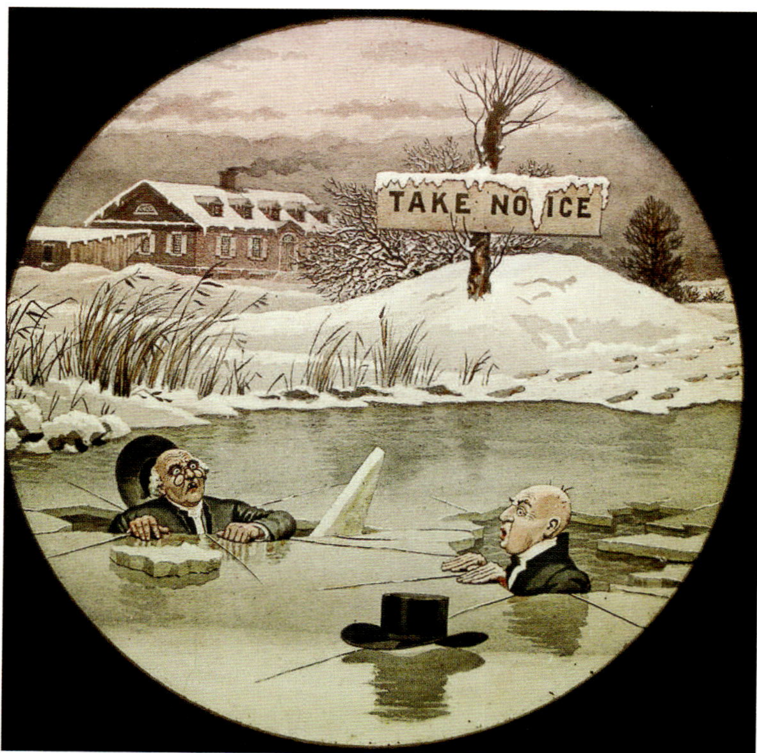

Fig. 3.33 Beale's "Coolness Between Friends", from the Comic, Ethnic group, pokes fun at the Quaker neighbors who surrounded him in Germantown.

Though no snapshots exist of Beale in this general time period, a professional portrait of him was taken, probably in April 1886, when Beale was 45. I use it in the cover of this book.[41] The photograph shows a face that has filled out somewhat; a man with an open, confident, but gentle air. That fits with the recollection of one of his nephews, who remembered him as a man of "quiet demeanor, modest, retiring" with a "charm consist[ing] in spontaneity". The nephew also called Beale a "brilliant conversationalist".[42] (Perhaps he meant "voluble", as he substantiates his characterization by citing a boyhood incident in which young Beale was sent home from school with a note to his father asking, "What would you do with a boy who talks too much"?)[43] The nephew also commented on Beale's ability to give an "accurate and detailed description of events" – a trait that certainly rings true, as that ability is abundantly evident in his art.

Costumes To Drive a Story

When Beale first returned to live in Philadelphia with his family in 1881, he began working for Frank Harris and Company, the largest engraving firm in the country, where he received fifty dollars for 47 hours work a week – equivalent to about $81,000 a year in 2025. His main work was illustrating clothing, particularly women's fashions.

Beale had a studio on the 4th or 5th floor of the company's office, at 712 Arch St., just a few blocks from where he had grown up. But the city had changed dramatically since his boyhood. Though still compact – most people lived within two miles of Beale's old house – it had grown from a population of about 500,000 people in 1860 to 850,000 by1880, *half* of them immigrants and their children (Fig. 3.35). The old central area was becoming much less residential, replaced by department stores and other commercial interests.

As is obvious from the sylvan nature of the family snapshots, Beale did not live in the midst of all this commercial activity, as he had when he was a young man. The busy central core of Philadelphia had become surrounded by block after block of the row houses where the immigrant factory workers lived.[44]

The Beales, like many prominent families, had moved out to Germantown to escape the babble of downtown, with its strange costumes, languages, and smells. Nor did Beale's new job take him out of his office into this hurly-burly of the city, as his Chicago assignments had. *The Graphic*, a competitor to *Leslie's* did hire him as a stringer for "all important transactions in and around Philadelphia ... on telegraph from us".[45] But for Beale's full-time job illustrating clothing he worked in a studio (Fig. 3.36). For eight of the ten years that he was employed at Harris and Company he illustrated fashions for *Godey's Lady's Book*, the *Vogue* magazine of the day. During the same period, he also created advertising pictures for various clothing manufacturers, with the dresses "always on a saleswoman to fill out the figure and sleeves". For other clients Beale prepared large "theatrical posters ... and portraits of actors and actresses".[46]

This experience in the fashion and theater industries, supplementing the years he spent working in fashion at *Leslie's*, added another area to Beale's skills as a magic lantern artist – that of costume designer. The illustrated stories, songs, and historical episodes that Beale would create for the magic lantern would require thousands of characters, of difference classes, different countries, different periods of history. Beale would have to clothe each of these in a manner that would convince the audience that what they were seeing was genuine. It was a mammoth undertaking. Altogether, I estimate that Beale designed more than ten thousand individual costumes that were appropriate to the character's place in history and station in life.

But beyond the sheer quantity of output, Beale

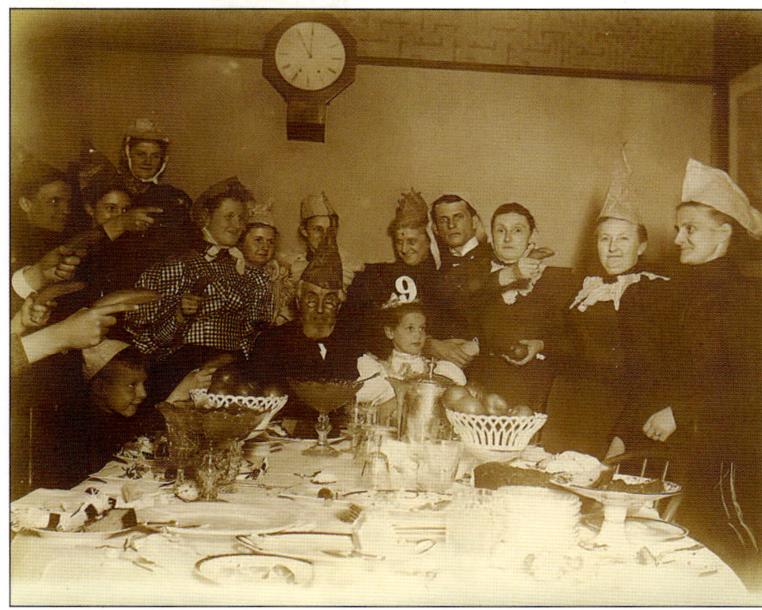

Fig. 3.34 Photo of the Beale family. gathered for the New Year's celebration of 1896, probably taken by Joseph Beale.

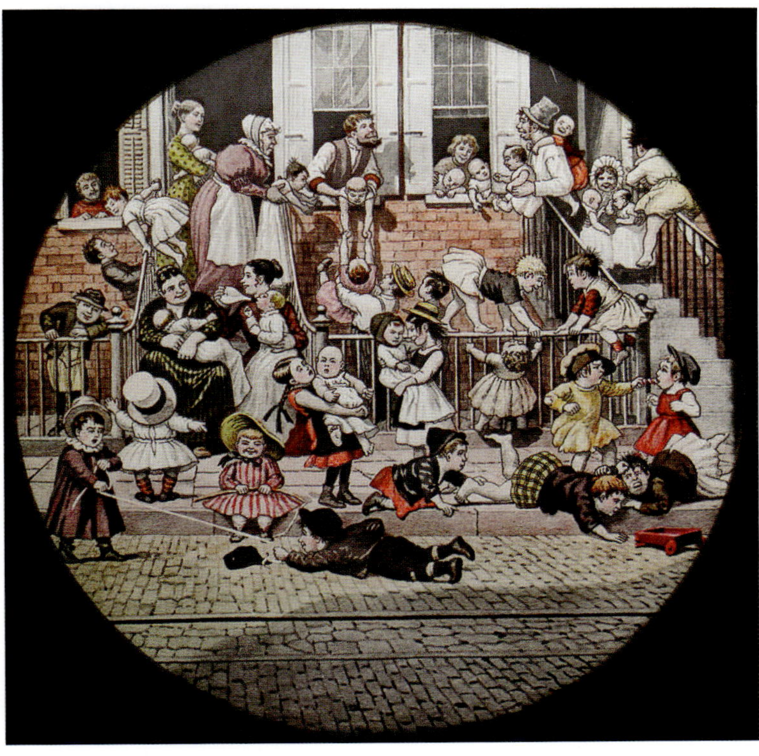

Fig. 3.35 Beale's "Babies on Our Block" from the Comic Songs group, a humorous take on the immigration issue.

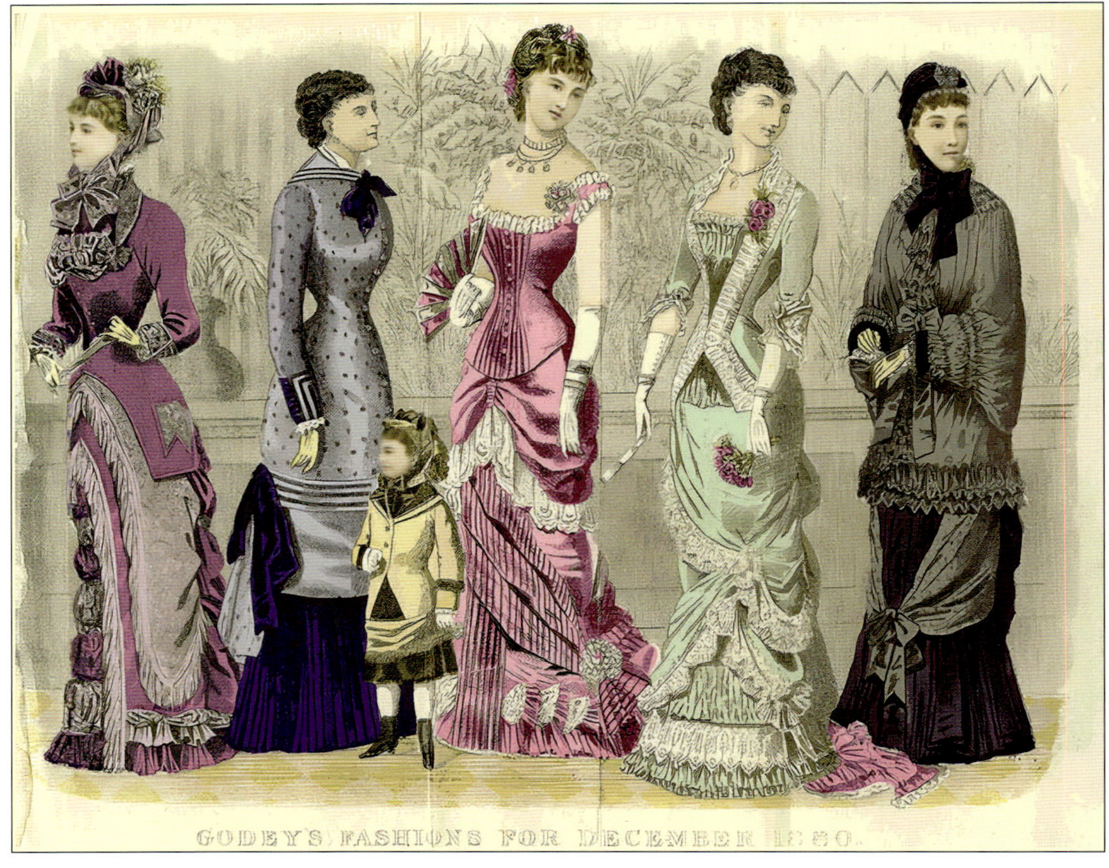

Fig. 3.36 For Harris and Co, Beale illustrated fashions like these for *Godey's Lady's Book*. Each issue of the magazine had one hand-colored plate.

used costuming as part of his narrative approach, making the costumes add their part to the power of the story, specifically by defining character, and change in character over time. We've seen how, in *The Pied Piper*, the theatrical personality of the Piper is suggested by his sweeping red and yellow cape, which contrasts with the ermine robes of the rich burgers who cheat him, and the simple white or earth-colored smocks of the children he eventually leads to their doom.

Evangeline, a long poem by Henry Wadsworth Longfellow, gives Longfellow even more scope to develop the heroine's character over time. Evangeline is a young French Acadian woman whose community is driven from their homes by the British. She spends her life searching across America for her fiancé. Beale's illustrations follow that character arc. It's a narrative approach that uses costumes to add their part to the story text, specifically by defining changes in character over time. In fact, Beale emphasizes the tragic arc of Evangeline's story with the details of her hats alone. They provide a *motif*, a recurring theme, tracking the changes in her life. As a little girl she wears a perky crown; when betrothed, a floating dove; as a young care-free dancer, a whirling train; when her people are driven from their homes, a drooping skullcap; as she searches for her lover, a bedraggled coif; in middle age, a cap still lifted with hope; when she misses her betrothed in the wilderness, a weeping train of sorrow; and – when she finally finds her long-lost sweetheart on his deathbed – a soaring swan of hope fulfilled (Fig. 3.37).

Beale Finds His Life's Work

A substantial part of the commercial activity around the center-city location of Beale's employer, Frank Harris and Company, was the magic lantern business. Philadelphia had become the national retail and mail-order center of the industry, with eight different national companies located in what was probably thought of as the Magic Lantern District, focused around Chestnut and Seventh Streets. It is no wonder that Beale soon found himself in the magic lantern business. It is probable that as soon as he returned to Philadelphia in 1881, Beale began working for C. W. Briggs, making his first lantern-slide designs on a free-lance basis. It was a job in which he had no previous experience, but for which he was ideally suited, and which would command his energies for the next 36 years.

Beale must have been confident in his ability

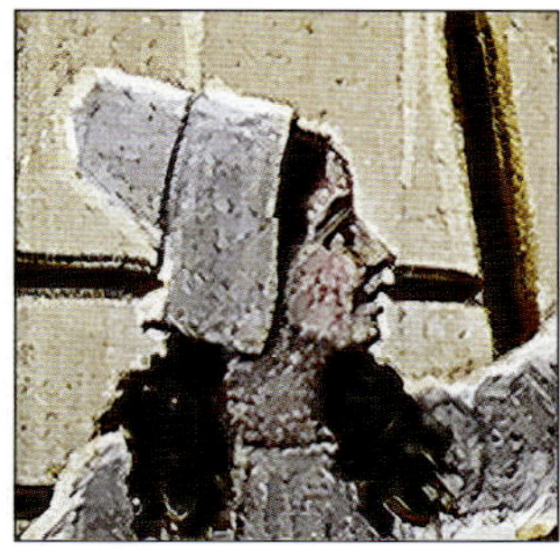
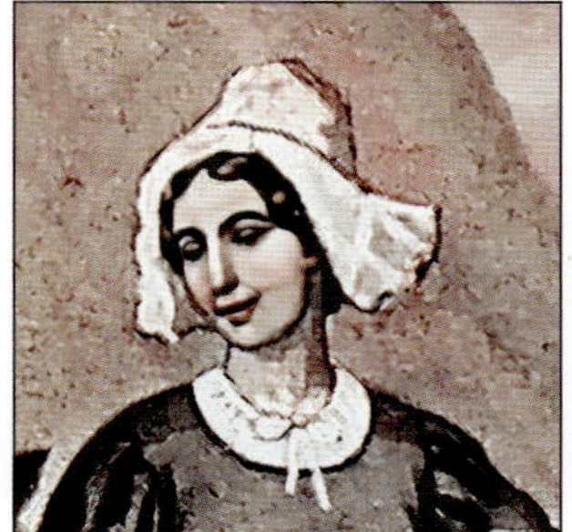
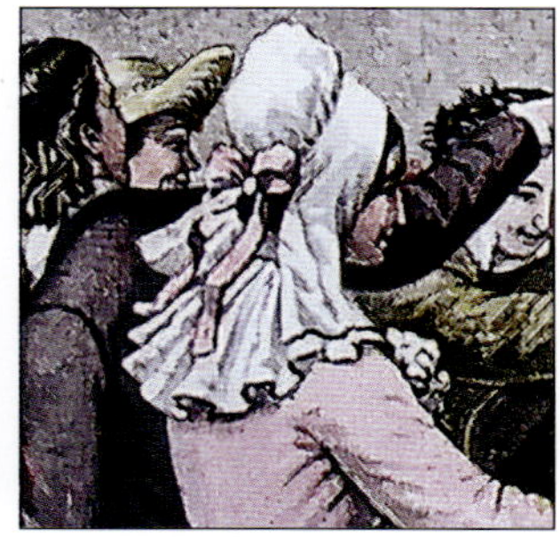
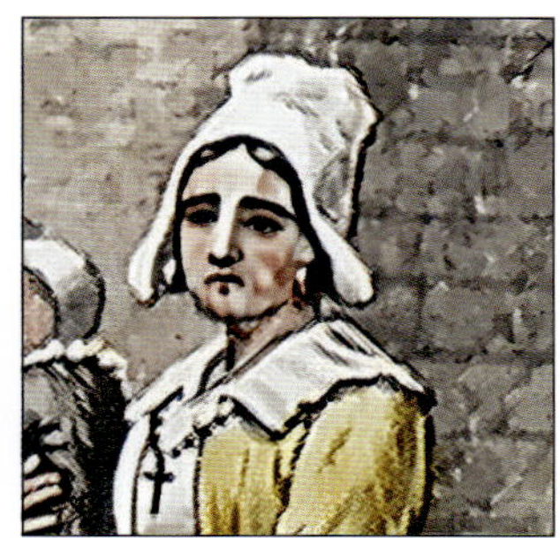
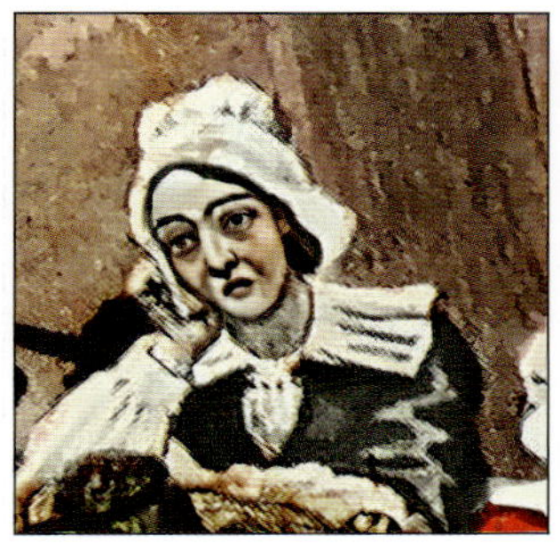
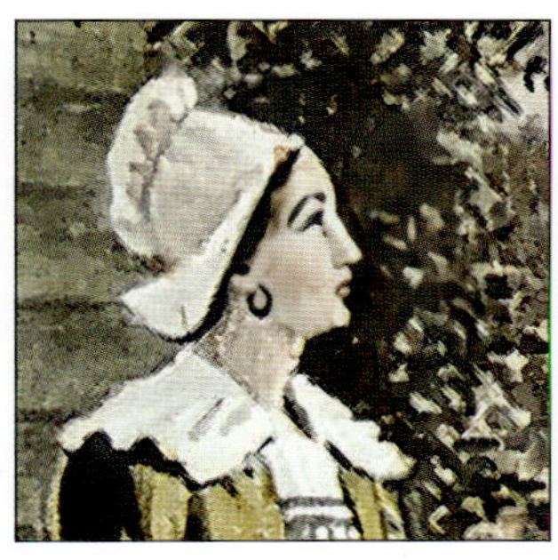
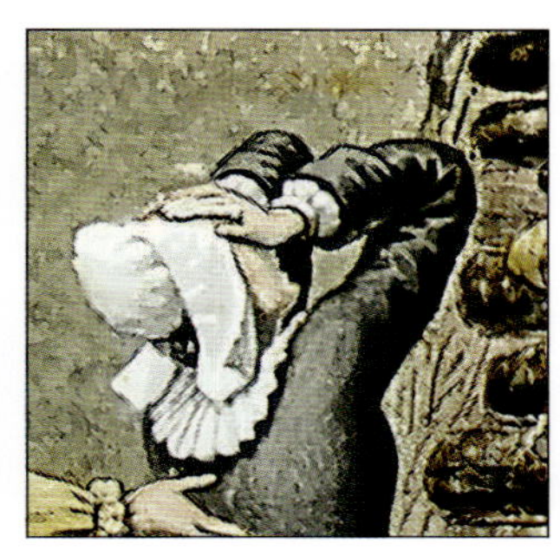
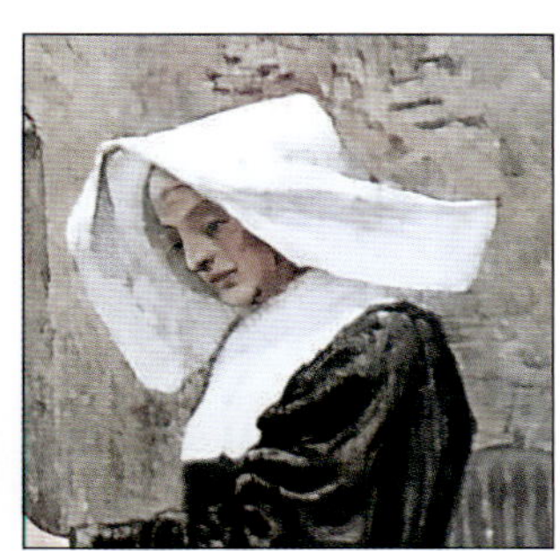

Fig. 3.37 Details from Beale illustrations for *Evangeline*, slides 4, 5, 8, 9, 16, 17, 21, 22.
Beale emphasizes visually the tragic arc of Evangeline's story in the details of her hats.

to create *individual* pictures on almost any subject; he had done it thousands of times. But now he faced a new problem – how to hold an audience in their seats for two hours by telling stories with a *series* of pictures. As Damion Macdonald has pointed out in describing the narrative art of those who create comics, a much wider range of skills is needed to succeed in sequential art than in painting single pictures.[47] Luckily for Beale, and for us, the breadth of his career had given him many of those skills. In his childhood days as a panorama artist; in his professional training in art at Central and the Pennsylvania Academy; in the tinting of photographs and in fine lettering – in all of these activities he was building skills. His work as a free-lance artist, artist-correspondent, fashion illustrator, and creator of architectural renderings gave him years of practice in applying those skills. Gradually he built up a range of abilities which seem ideally suited for his new career in sequential narrative art. For instance, as we have just seen, it was his work as a fashion illustrator that gave him the skills to dramatize Evangeline's long sad story through the changes in her hats, and to create those thousands of costumes that helped tell many other stories.

Before we turn to the fascinating illustrations Beale's created in his new career, and the techniques he used to create them, it will be helpful to look at how magic lantern slides, and magic lantern performances themselves, developed in the 200 years before Beale, first, primarily in Europe, and then in the United States. Beale drew upon that rich heritage, and it is in that context that he pursued a unique, large, and important niche – illustrating narrative art for the American screen.

Chapter Four

The Power of Early Lantern Techniques

Fig. 4.25 Great Grandfather Carter's animated slide of "The Tiger". Discussed on pp. 81–82.

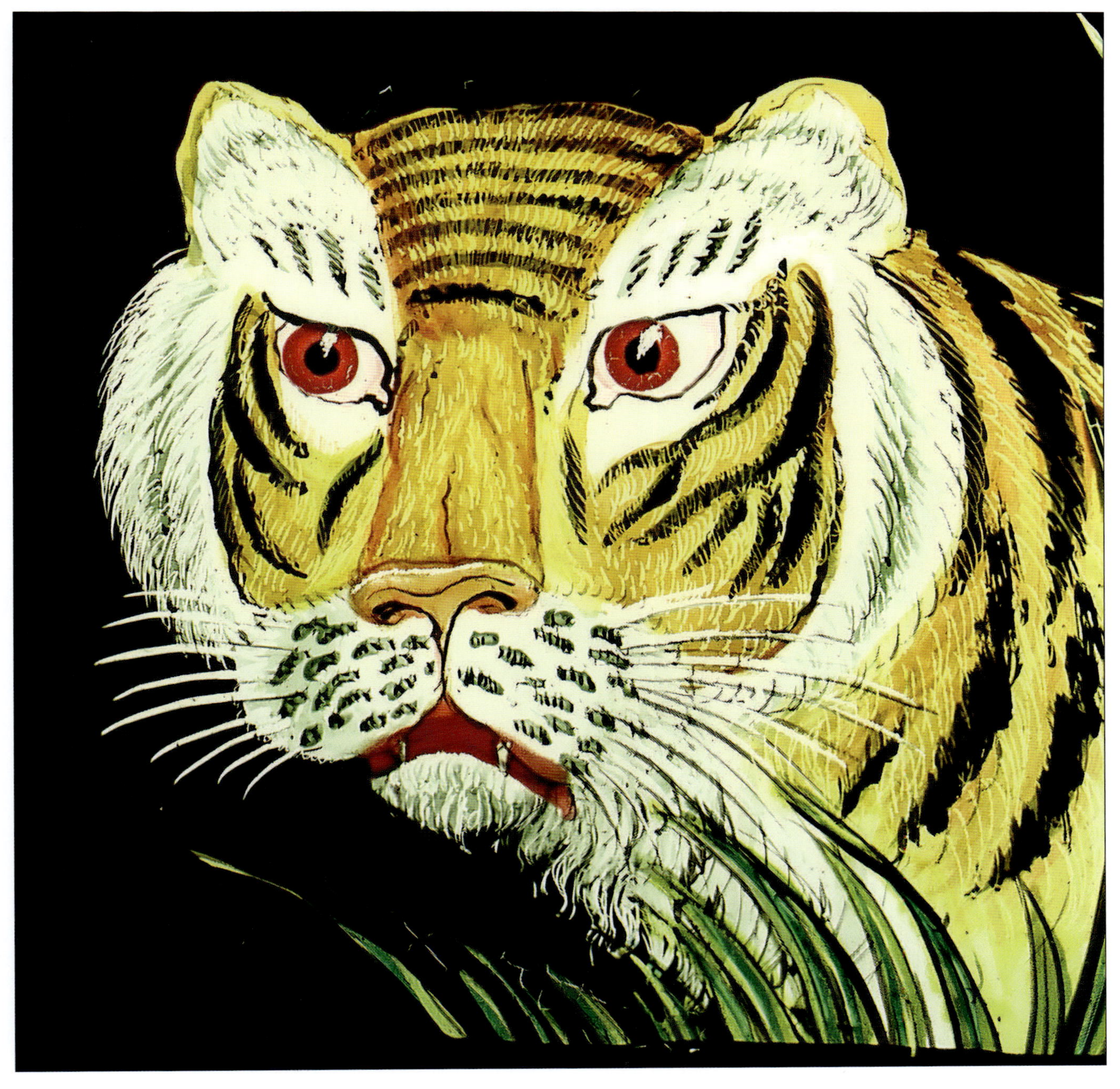

Before we concentrate on Beale's magic lantern art, let's back up a few centuries to put his work in the context of the larger and longer lantern tradition. Where, for instance, did the early lantern screen techniques come from? How were they first used, how did they work, how did they change over time? And to what degree did Beale himself use such early techniques as *animation, panoramas, dissolves, close-ups, fades, and zooms*?

Though Beale was a talented, and uniquely American practitioner of the magic lantern art, he was only part of a long history of on-screen entertainment. The generally accepted history I present here draws upon much more detailed works[1] and so is not documented item by item. But if you understand the basics of the magic lantern tradition, you will not only be able to better appreciate Beale's contribution. You will also have a much richer perspective on the movies and TV you see today.

First Magic

When Beale was a teenager in the 1860s, the lantern was well known, but still seemed magical. As we've seen, Beale himself marveled at the projected images of the stereopticon, and sought to understand how some of the Pepper's Ghost effects were produced. Two hundred years earlier, at the time the magic lantern was invented, people did not understand *lenses* and *projection*, even if the lantern was right beside them. They were focused on the screen, and what they saw were skeletons and devils and angels appearing and disappearing on command. The "magic lantern" seemed well named.

Fig. 4.1 Projecting lantern, by Athanasius Kircher in the second edition of *Ars Magna Lucis et Umbrae* in 1671, the first printed image of a magic lantern.

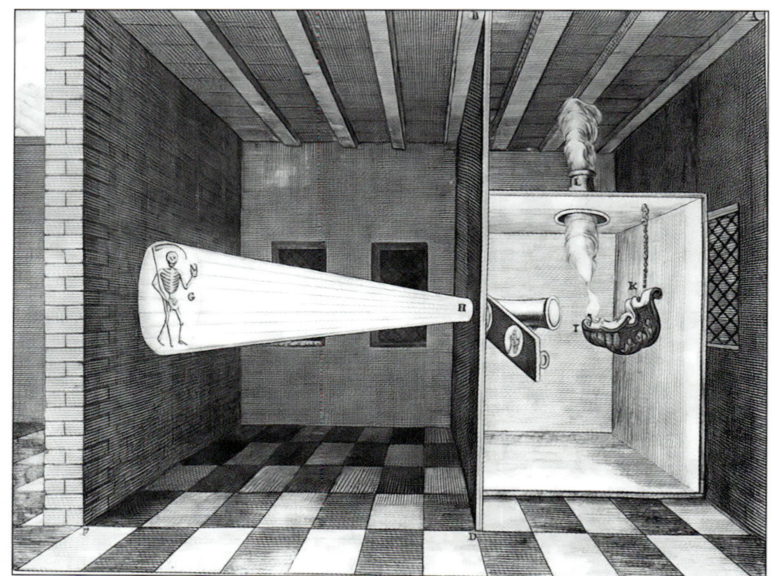

The roots of lantern history reach well back in time, but true magic lantern shows that could produce identical images at any time and place emerged about the middle of the 17th century out of a complex range of efforts to project images with mirrors, lenses, and light. Credit for the invention of the lantern was for generations given to an erudite German Jesuit, Athanasius Kircher, who described many optical devices in his 1646 book, *Ars Magna Lucis et Umbrae* (*The Great Art of Light and Shadow*). One of Kircher's illustrations was for a "magic mirror" that projected images painted on a mirror through a lens – certainly similar to a magic lantern, but not quite the same thing, as a magic lantern projects transparent slides. The second 1671 edition of Kircher's book contained an illustration of a projecting lantern that was in fact a "magic lantern", which Kircher claimed to have invented (Fig. 4.1). This was the first printed image of a magic lantern – a room-sized contraption, with a separate compartment for the lantern's smoke. Kricher's lantern used multiple images in a frame to facilitate quick changes from one to the next. The images on the slide are depicted right-side up, not upside down as they need to be because of lantern optics. That may suggest that Kircher knew less about the lantern than he claimed, or that he was using less-than-optimal projection techniques. Or the oddity may simply have been an artist's mistake.

However, recent scholars believe that a leading Dutch scientist, Christiaan Huygens, probably invented the first workable magic lantern – and hence the prototype of the movie projector (Fig. 4.2). Huygens had read Kircher's first edition work, but his circle of Enlightenment scientists (which included Newton) did not take Kircher seriously, since they saw him as a defender of knowledge gained through tradition and the church, rather than through science. As part of Huygens' independent experimentation on optics, he created a workable magic lantern, probably as early as 1659, certainly by 1662 – well before Kircher's 1671 illustration. To amuse his family and friends, he projected animated lantern images of skeletons on a screen (Fig. 4.3). However, Huygens did not want the lantern, which he apparently saw as a frivolous toy, to detract from the seriousness of his scientific reputation. Though lanterns quickly appeared among his associates around Europe, Huygens put away his own lantern in a cabinet. He effectively hid his involvement from the reading public, and hence opened the way for Kircher's claims to be accepted for 300 years.[2]

Early Showmen

By the end of the 17th century the lantern had been improved optically, had spread to scientists and wealthy collectors throughout Europe, and had been carried by Jesuit priests as far away as China and Japan. Then it took on a more popular form. In the early days of the 18th century, and perhaps earlier, traveling Savoyards from the Savoy region between Italy and France began wandering across Europe with inexpensive lanterns and slides on their backs, providing entertainment at fairs, taverns, and mansions. The slides were usually crudely painted stories and history. Because the Savoyards often spoke only a few words of the language of the country they were visiting, and had very few slides with them, they may have developed a raucous, gushing style of delivery that depended on pidgin exhortation to create excitement, and on pointing out slide details to hold attention (Fig. 4.4).

> Ah! That is a touching scene, dear one! Give attention to the cat, to the lady, to the clock, what she sees! To her fun, what he bakes – to the funny Savoyard![3]

The Savoyards' performance was understood because of the narrative slide images and the enthusiasm of the Savoyard's patter. Even an illiterate audience could grasp the action, no matter how deficient the language skills of the Savoyard, just as those non-English-speaking audiences in Singapore could follow our pidgin version of Beale's *Pied Piper*.

Fig. 4.3 Huygens's sketch of skeleton slides, which – even at this early stage – were animated. *Wikimedia Commons.*

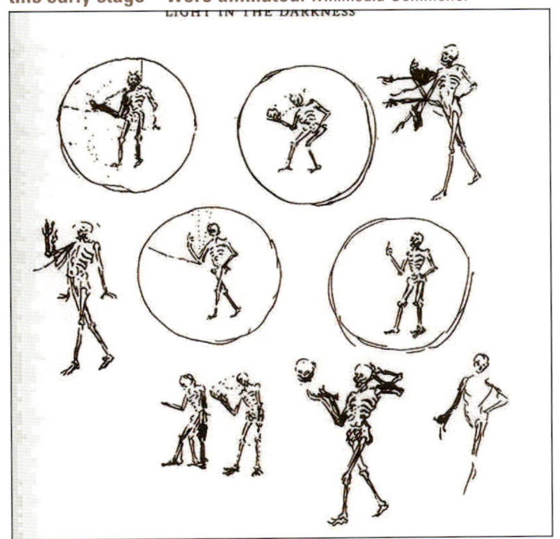

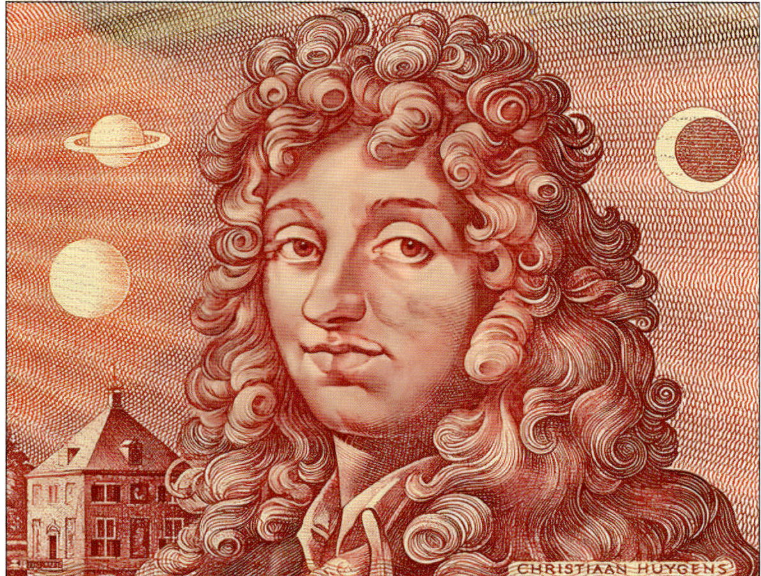

Fig. 4.2 Christiaan Huygens, inventor of the magic lantern, was honored for his scientific achievements with this portrait on a 1955 Dutch bank note.

The Savoyards did not make it to America, but magic lantern shows appeared in the country well before independence. It is possible that the first lanterns came to the United States with the Jesuit missionaries; certainly, they were in Mexico by 1692. The first well-documented performance in the U.S. was held in Boston on December 3, 1743. The "Magick Lanthorn" show, promoted in the *Boston Evening Post*, was produced by John Dabney, a mathematical instrument maker, "for the Entertainment of the Curious". It exhibited a "great Number of wonderful and surprising Figures, prodigious large; and vivid".[4] Since Dabney was an instrument maker, he may well have made his own lantern,

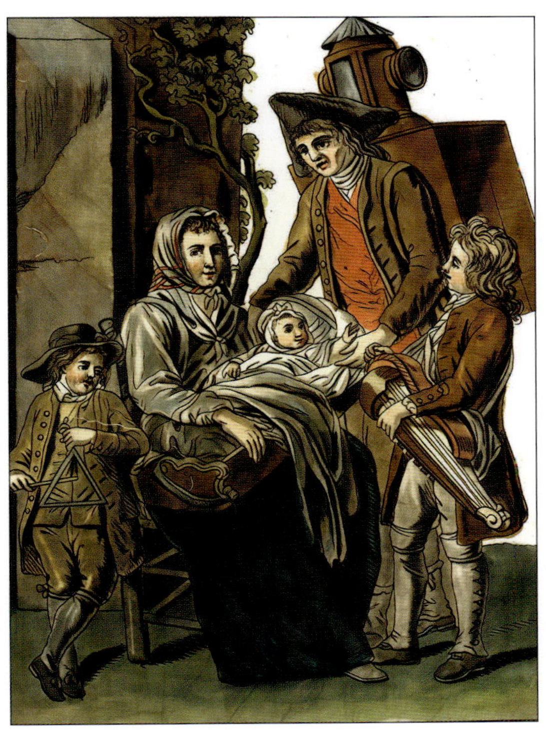

Fig. 4.4 Engraving of a 1790s Savoyard with lantern and slides on his back, traveling with his family. His lantern serves as a walking billboard. *Wikimedia Commons.*

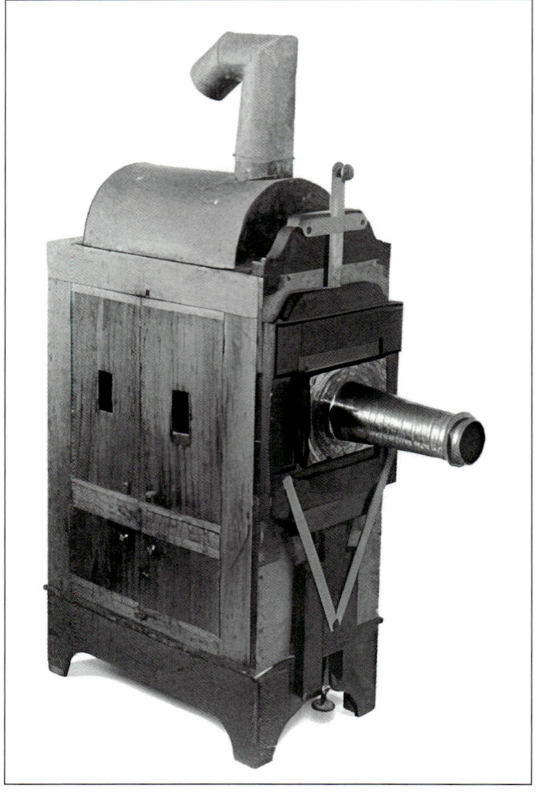

Fig. 4.5 The earliest known American magic lantern still in existence was created before 1776. Courtesy, Harvard Scientific Instrument Archives.

rather than importing one. By the 1770s, lanterns were being used at Harvard to project complex mechanical slides that demonstrated the movements of the heavens (Fig. 4.5).

Animated Cartoons

Significant advances in moving lantern slides were made by a variety of ingenious 17th and 18th century craftsmen. Chief among the inventors and popularizers of these more sophisticated slides was a Dutch instrument-making family, the van Musschenbroeks. Various members of this family worked with Huygens, invented several moving slides or simplified previous designs, manufactured them, and – beginning in the 1730s, sold them in the catalogs of the family firm. The basic technical designs of these slides remained unchanged for 200 years, but the permutations – more than 70 in all – proliferated across the world to animate thousands of different subjects.[5]

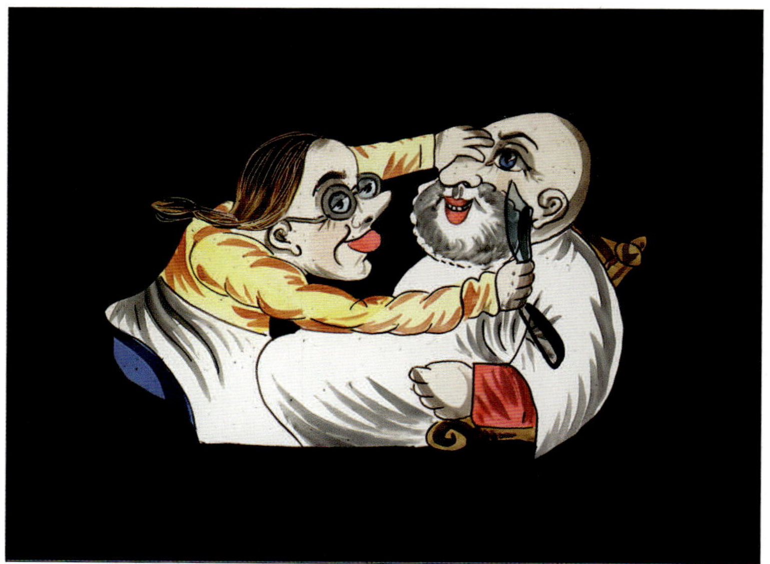

Fig. 4.6 Slip slide of a man being shaved. The arm and razor move back and forth.

By the mid-19th century, the vast majority of ***mechanical slides*** were *animated cartoons*, like the "Nose Man" that Great Grandfather Carter used. Every lanternist since the von Musschenbroeks owes them a debt of gratitude, for these comics were truly funny, and so were often mixed in with other subject matter to lighten the discourse. It was common for magic lantern advertisements to ballyhoo the inclusion of ***comic views*** or *animated pictures* in their shows, even if the main subjects were serious. The animated comedy was often aimed especially at the children, and their delight continues. Our own recreated magic lantern shows would not be nearly as appealing to modern audiences if it were not for this "comic relief" from the more dramatic or sentimental Victorian stories.

The simplest form of the mechanical slides, called a ***slipping slide***, uses two pieces of glass in a wooden frame, one with the image fixed in the frame, and the other with a black mask placed directly over it in a groove so that it can slip back and forth, like the Nose Man we saw earlier (Fig. 1.6). When I use this slip slide in our *Spring Show*, I employ a different bit of stage business than did Great Grandfather Carter. (The slide only performs its designated movement, but the showman can create all sorts of jokes or stories to go with the action.) In this case, as I jiggle the slide itself to make the Man appear agitated, I lead the audience in a Spring hay-fever sneeze, "Ah, ah, ah, AH, AH, **AH ...** ". The audience tries to keep up, wondering when and how it will all end. **"CHOOO!"** The nose leaps out a foot from the man's face. The audience is convulsed just as my father was by this slide, just as I was when I was a child, just as my children were, just as my grandchildren were. The techniques of *masking* and *limited animation* in the slip slide are fine examples of cinematic art that has maintained its power to delight from the Victorian era to the present.

In a similar version of the slip slide (Fig. 4.6), one part of the picture is on one glass, another on a different, moving glass slipper that moves

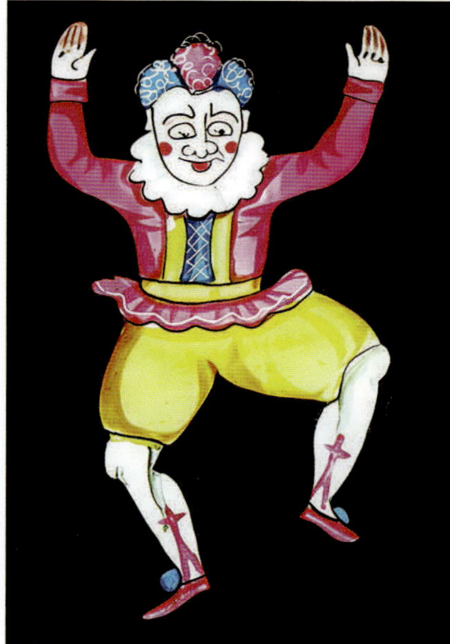

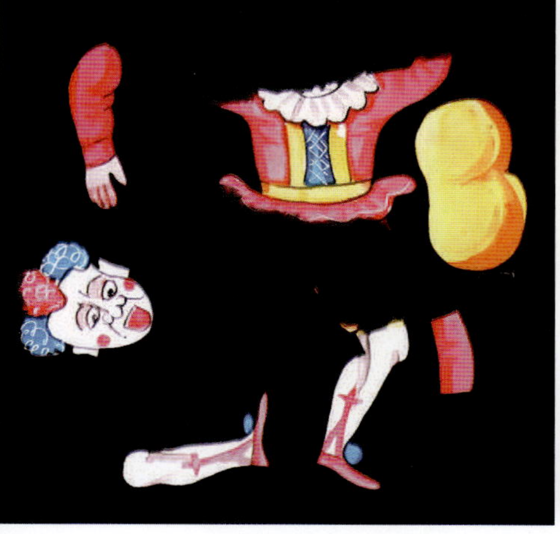

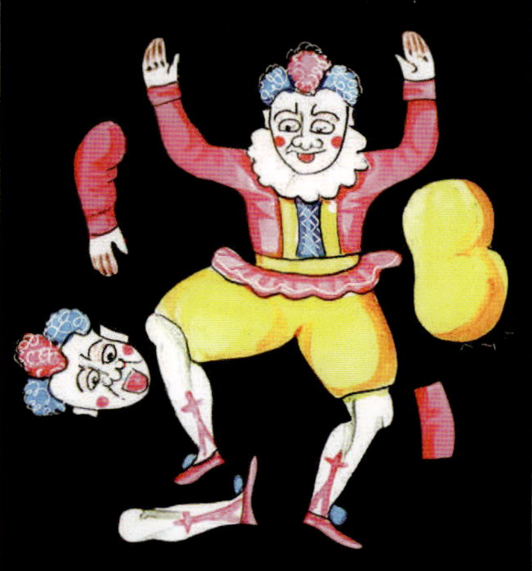

Fig. 4.7 Slip slide of an exploding clown. At top left, the clown as he first appears; at middle, after he explodes; at right, all the clown's parts painted on the stationary slide. At bottom left, the moving mask that creates the exploding body by covering some body parts and revealing others.

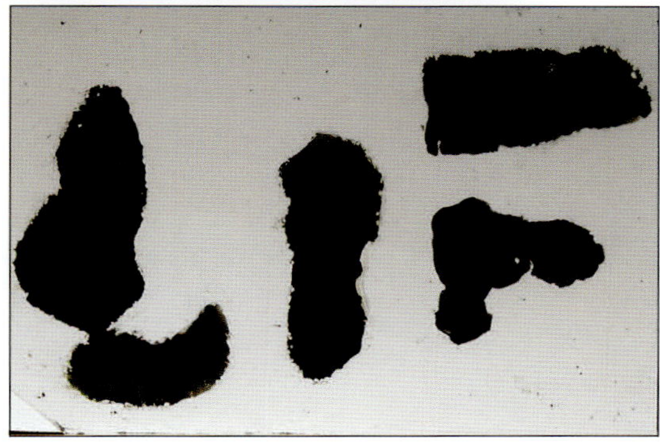

back and forth. For instance, the arm of a barber can be made to wield a giant straight razor, creating another kind of limited but repeating animation. The difference between the magic lantern and the movies is in the amount of animation used. Two or three slipping glass images are common in lantern slides; I have one that has four. By putting together several slides I might create a sequence of a dozen rapidly changing moving images. The movies simply extend this technique further, with first hundreds, and later thousands of images put together to make more and more extended animated sequences.

(The fact that some magic lantern slides are so animated is a surprise and a delight to modern audiences, who perhaps grew up with a less-than-favorite-uncle's 35mm "slide shows" which did not have this capacity. The animated slides are usually painted directly on the glass in a distinctive cartoon style that is immediately understood as funny, especially by kids. In our school shows, the kids laugh as soon as one of these slides goes up on screen, even before the image performs its slapstick comedy.)

Variations on the basic slip slide enable the lanternist to introduce other motions. A slip side with a pair of legs painted in different positions can create a limited form of continuous motion, such as walking. A clown can be made

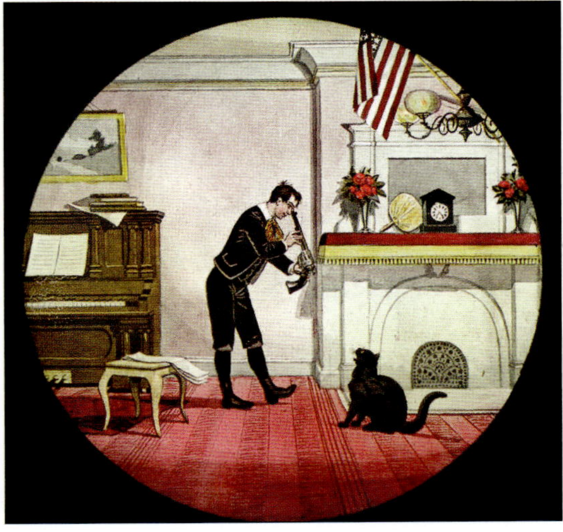

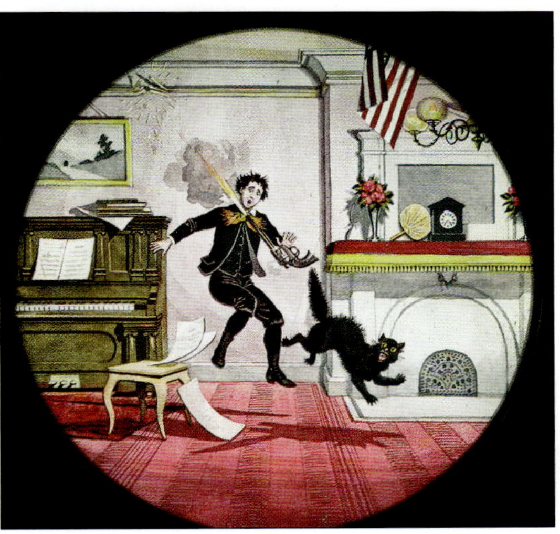

Fig. 4.8 Two Beale slides, "I Wonder If It's Loaded?" and "It Was Loaded", from the Comic Dissolves – Children group.

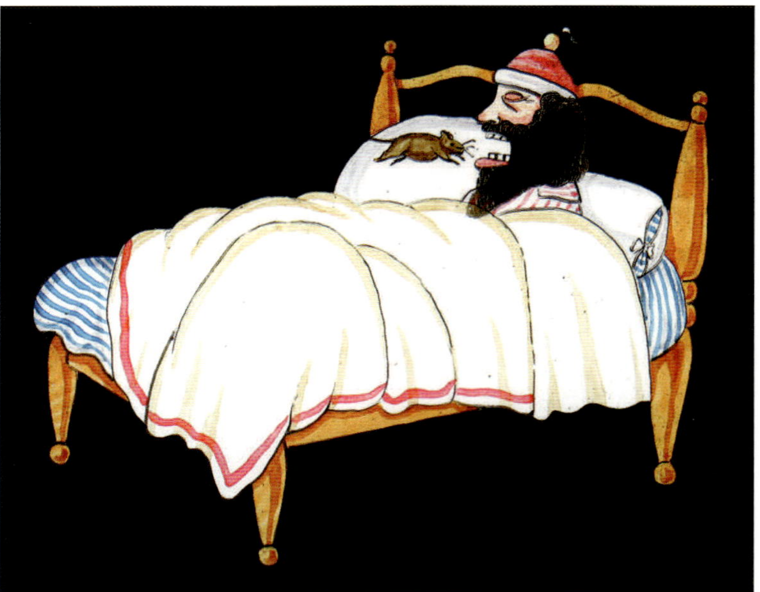

Fig. 4.9 The "Ratcatcher", a double slip slide, with a moving jaw and rat.

to explode (Fig. 4.7); a woman with eyes painted on the slipper creates a character that can search the audience for a particular child; a pirate with a moving jaw can bark orders; a pompous butler can suddenly find himself with a pig's head on his shoulders. Double slipping slides can create more complex action, like a gentleman being squirted with a hose, and then turning his head in a *reaction shot.* Angled slip slides, like a toboggan run, could create a *canted* or *tilt shot.* Hundreds and hundreds of different slip slides brought comic animation to the screen.

Early showmen provided additional movement by ***jiggling*** a slip slide up and down while simultaneously moving it sidewise to make a "seem to prance" across the screen as it carries a young boy, and then culminating with the "slipping" comic action of the boy flying into the air.[6]

Beale did not paint slip slides, but, as we have already seen, he did create similar ***animation*** – movement on screen – by using two slides with the figures in slightly different positions, seen against a background that did not change (Fig. 4.8). These comic effect dissolves prefigured what would later be the basic form of movie animation – a series of rapidly changing scenes or *cells*, almost identical except for the comic action.

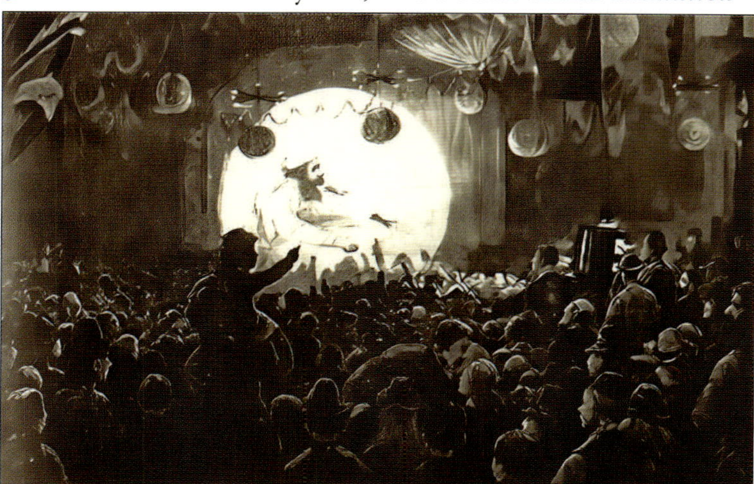

Fig. 4.10 "Magic Lantern Show Given to Poor and Destitute Children", Engraving from *The Graphic*, February 23, 1889. Today, we often see the same pointed fingers and excited gestures.

A Cinematic Example – Animation

Let's look now at an example of how a showman can use the relatively simple and early lantern technology of the animated slip slide for maximum cinematic effect on the screen, and maximum impact on the audience. We'll begin with a case in which the lantern does create actual movement on screen, the double slip slide.

While most slip slides change the scene with a simple motion – the nose grows, the audience laughs, and that's that, it is possible, indeed common, to ***milk a slide*** over an extended period of time, or to use a number of the slip slides to create continuous narrative motion of fairly long *duration.*

My favorite example – everyone's favorite example – of a magic lantern slip slide that can be milked over an extended time is "The Ratcatcher" (Fig. 4.9). It's the delightfully repulsive slide I mentioned when describing Great Grandfather Carter's show. In this animated sequence, probably first created by the English artist, C. Constant, a man asleep in a bed swallows a rat, or, in some versions, many rats moving on a wheel. During the Victorian period, this was in fact the most popular, the most famous, of all moving magic lantern slides, and it remains so to this day (Fig. 4.10). Here are two examples of 19th century audience reactions. One lanternist, remembering his maiden performance at a local village hall, described its dramatic opening this way:

> All being in place the first picture was projected on the screen. This was *a man swallowing rats* [and] caused a stamping and shouting, such as would eclipse a more civilized audience, and made the beams of the floor to spring … .[7]

Unfortunately, the lanternist's screen was braced by poles that ran from the floor to the ceiling. The bouncing floor shook the poles loose. The screen fell down and hit the lantern table. The lantern table fell down and landed on the floor.

The lantern broke. The "Ratcatcher" provided the show's dramatic opening, and almost instantaneously ... its grand finale.

A second lanternist, in fact the vice chairman of the British Magic Lantern Society in 1891, describes a more successful show that he saw in his boyhood, where the lanternist wisely left the "Ratcatcher" for the end. The lanternist used a complicated form of the Ratcatcher slide, in which the rats were on a turning disk of glass, so one rat after another could dive down the man's throat:

> All [these earlier slides] paled before the climax – the man eating the rats. With the other boys I began counting, but I shall never muster up the courage to tell your readers how many rats that man ate. It was very wonderful.[8]

When lantern lectures began to become an "elevated" form of "moral entertainment" after the introduction of photographic lectures, the "Ratcatcher" became controversial. Said one commentator, vainly trying to deny human nature:

> Such slides as a man eating rats are now out of date, and are accountable in a great measure for much of the unpopularity of the lantern with persons possessing the slightest artistic taste.[9]

"Tasteful" the "Ratcatcher" was not, but it continued to be so popular that it remained a staple of nineteenth century shows. It is still so irresistible that I have found a way to work it into all ten of our modern magic lantern productions (Fig. 4.11). In each of these shows the "Ratcatcher" slide becomes a different character, though of course he always performs the same tasteless movement.

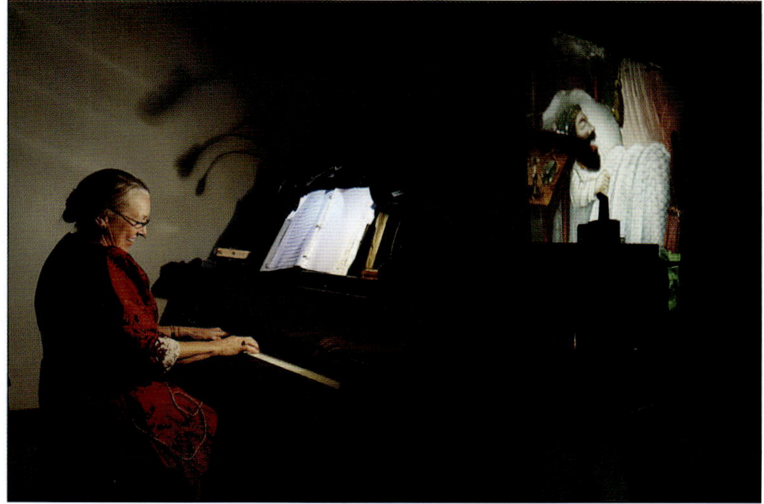

Fig. 4.11. Nancy Stewart, my long-time accompanist and singer, cracks up as she creates the suspenseful music of the rat's approach, even though she has seen the Ratcatcher hundreds of times.

Here's how the slide works physically, described in more detail than our showmen provide, so that you can understand the technology that creates the movement. I'll also describe how a skilled showman can manipulate the slide for maximum screen effect – an art that goes well beyond simply moving the pieces of glass. By extension, I hope this description will help you better understand the nature of animated magic lantern art.

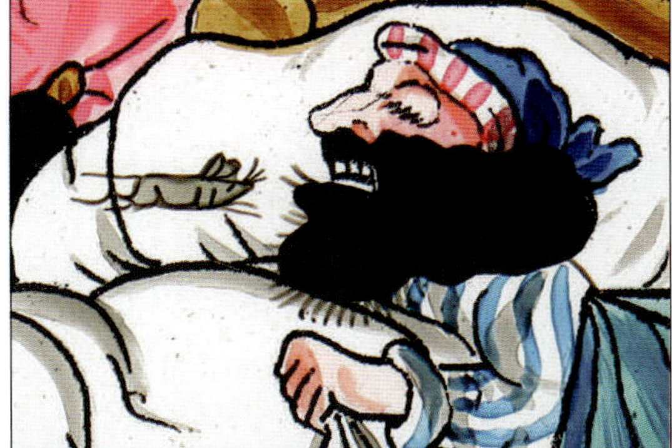

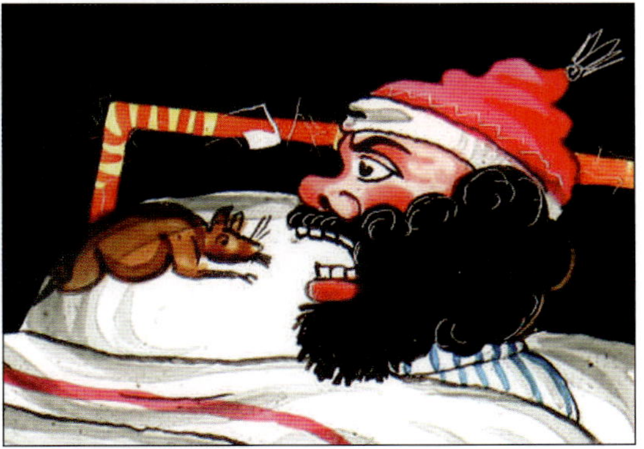

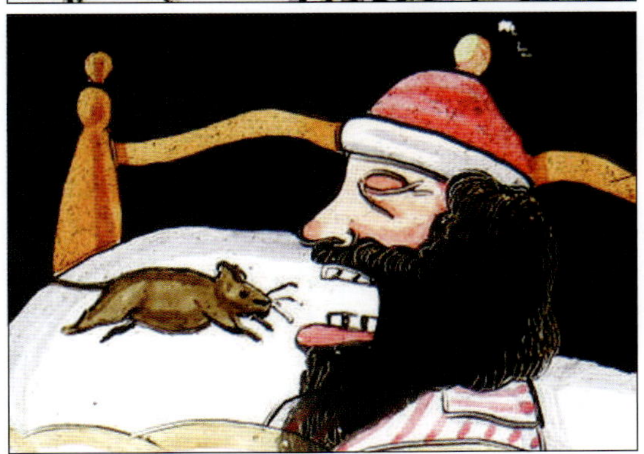

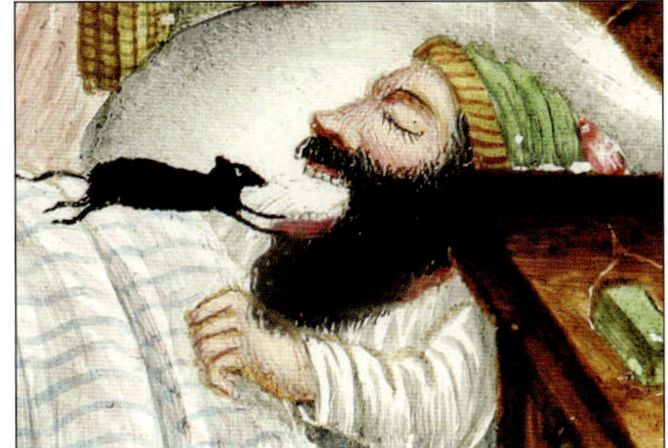

Fig. 4.12 Detail of four different versions of "The Ratcatcher" slip slide. Mechanical slides like this were produced by many companies, so variation exists in the images.

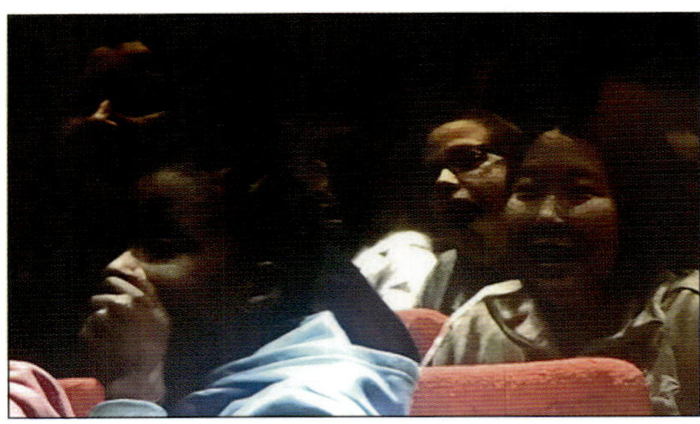
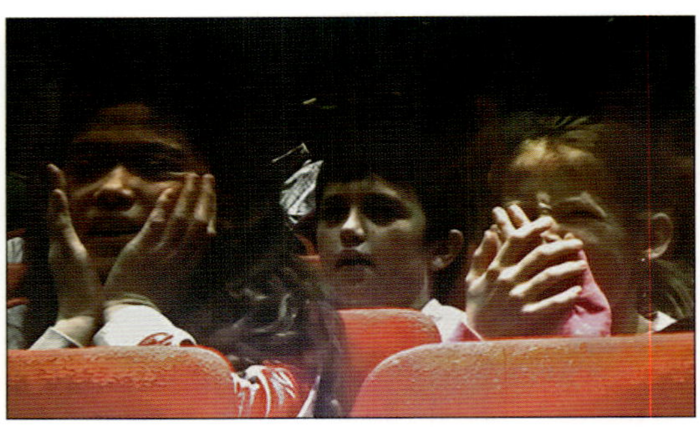

Fig. 4.13 Modern fifth graders react to the "Ratcatcher". At left, the rat first appears. At right ... Oh My God!

The audience first sees the man asleep on a bed, the rat hidden. I ask them to make the man snore, and as they begin to make snoring noises, the man does indeed begin to snore, his jaw moving slowly up and down (Fig. 4.12).

The audience laughs at the moving jaw, but (led by me) gets into the snoring rhythm, following the up-and-down movement in an exaggerated series of snorks, physically and imaginatively becoming the sleeper themselves. Suddenly a large rat peeks over the foot of the bed. The audience gasps. The rat "hears" the noise, and retreats to safety. The audience picks up the rhythm of snoring again. The rat peeks out once more, and crawls over the covers, the music building the tension, the rat sniffing at the man's quivering jaw. The snoring of the audience collapses in a nervous titter, but then I make the man give a tremendous snork. The rat runs away again. The snoring picks up, raggedly. The rat reappears, hesitates a second, and then, with an accompanying crescendo from the piano, makes a mad dash across the covers and dives down the man's throat. The audience erupts in gags and groans and laughter (Fig. 4.13).

(Occasionally, if I'm in the right mood and I think the audience is, I may continue the *kinetic* action a bit longer, or use the following bit of business as an encore: The man chews the rat slowly, the tail sticking out of his mouth and flailing frantically. The audience laughs, but nervously. Then the man swallows, gags, and, with a tremendous retching heave and a piano crescendo, vomits the rat out across the bed. Mothers blanche. Small boys howl with glee.)

How is all this motion accomplished? The "Ratcatcher" slide is a combination ***pivoting*** and ***slipping*** slide that consists of one wooden frame containing three separate images on three separate pieces of glass – the stationary man on the bed, the moving jaw, and the moving rat. Movement is in two directions, the jaw going up and down (a ***pivot***), and the rat side to side (a ***slipper***). Movement is continuous – something is always happening on screen – and usually simultaneously in two directions. The whole continuous movement sequence lasts about 50 seconds, just about the same amount of time as the first movies on film.

To create the impression that a whole series of rats is being swallowed several rats are painted on a circular glass disk that fits into the slide frame. The rats can reappear, so that any number can run down the man's throat. This movement on screen can go on indefinitely, and a favorite sport of Victorian children was to chant out the number of rats the "Ratcatcher" swallowed.

As a modern-day showman, I am much too refined and tasteful to use such a disgusting slide as the repeating rackwork "Ratcatcher". But in my role as a media archeologist, I have tried it experimentally on audiences of modern school children. Sure enough, the children counted out the rats with great glee. The "Ratcatcher" groaned and gasped with the ordeal. He swallowed a dozen rats before enthusiasm began to wane, adding an extra 40 seconds to the sequence.

Then, of course, came the 12-rat barf, pushing the sequence well past two minutes.

The Magic Lantern Show and The Movies

The "Ratcatcher" serves to point out three important distinctions between the magic lantern show and the movies – between what Lenny Lipton calls the "glass cinema" and the "celluloid cinema".[10] First, as the movement potential of the "Ratcatcher" slip slide makes clear, the technology of flexible film did not so much create new on-screen continuous movement, or even (at first) greater duration of movement. It created a greater *subtlety* of movement, a result of more frames per second. A good example of this is how a Disney animated film is developed. An early step presents the basic movement of the scene in a series of still sketches on screen. The sketches change every few seconds like the slides of a magic lantern show, only a bit faster. The last step is the finished film, running at 24 frames a second. The movement at that point is much more subtle of course, but everything else is the same. Subtle movement in the subsidiary details is what often impressed the first viewers of film who had grown up on lantern shows. For instance, in Lumiere's early film, *Feeding the Baby*, the audience was not primarily focused on the operation of feeding the baby, a "gross muscle" movement similar to the animated lantern slides they already knew. What intrigued them was the subtle movement of the tree leaves in the background.[11]

A second difference between the lantern and the movies is that after the first few years the movies were able to produce a *duration* of continuous motion that was not available in lantern shows. This combination of subtlety and duration opened up wondrous new possibilities for screen entertainment. It became possible to tell fully-developed stories with the subtle movement of film, just as had been done for centuries with the slowly-changing lantern slides. Yet, as we will see, most of the cinematic techniques used to create the art of this more subtle movement were basically the same as in lantern shows.

A third difference between the magic lantern and the movies is also highlighted by the "Ratcatcher." In a magic lantern show the movement is clearly at the instigation of the showman, while in the movies it seems to occur "by itself." When the movies first appeared, this autonomous motion was a novelty that added to the movies' appeal. But that fact should not obscure the point that 100 years ago, and today as well, the ***showman's*** presence and interaction with his audience is a major part of the lantern show's appeal – much more so than in the movies. This ***audience interaction*** in magic lantern shows takes a number of different forms. The showman often ***directly addresses*** the audience, encouraging them, for instance, to snore with the "Ratcatcher". The ***audience participates*** with the show, snoring, and providing other sound effects like the "stamping and shouting" that our intrepid lanternist described. The showman ***reacts to the audience***, adding (or omitting) something like the barfing of the rat, making rejoinders to audience remarks like "My Dad snores like that!" – responding to audience feelings, and pacing, and energy level.

The showman shapes the response of the spectators. But he also feeds from their energy, rides the waves of their emotion, shares their pleasures, plays with their playfulness. The magic lantern show, in short, is live entertainment, an art form highly responsive to its audience. As a result, the show's success is heavily dependent on the ***showman's skills***. Though the early movies often had a showman (or "explainer") to help make clear what was happening and create audience interaction, the movies soon lost this element as they became more and more pre-packaged, which allowed cheaper and wider distribution. Bit by bit the movies became, quite literally, canned entertainment. For better or worse, magic lantern shows were never canned, and are not today.

The First Pans

Animated slip slides like the "Ratcatcher" were not the only widely-available ways that the lantern created movement on screen. The history of the lantern provides examples of many cinematic slides that made their way directly to the movies – ***pans, zooms, close-ups, and dissolves***.

We'll begin with the "pans" or ***panorama*** slides, though Beale did not create any of these. Pans created motion by using a long strip of glass containing a panoramic view. They were developed very early, and came in several forms. One form is the direct ancestor of the *pan shot* in the movies. As the panorama slide is pulled before the lens, the audience sees different portions of the image appearing on the screen, just as if a camera had panned across a scene. You can experience the effect yourself by making a small circle with your thumb and forefinger, holding it close to your eye, and then, while viewing the image in Fig. 4.14 through the circle, moving your hand very slowly from right to left. The early lanternists warned that great care had to be taken in controlling the pan, as "an irregular motion" could be "very detrimental to the general effect". The editor of the *Optical Magic Lantern Journal*, in praising a type of panoramic slider that provided greater control, gives a sense of the power of this cinematic technique when it was well handled:

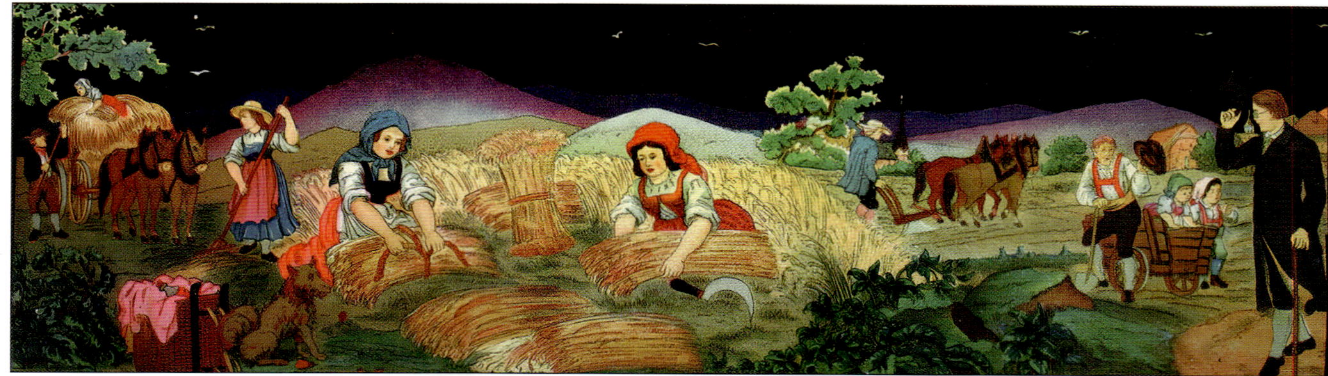

Fig. 4.14 A continuous image panorama slide, a very fine example of a children's lantern slide using a chromolithographic image.

> The effect of such a panoramic view, when passed through the lantern with a slow uniform motion, is truly astonishing to those who are unaware of its real length, for it seems as if it never was to come to an end.[12]

Another type of pan slide, the ***panoramic slipping slide*** has a fixed image (of a lighthouse, for instance) in a slotted frame, before which a series of action scenes pass on a long glass slipper. (While the audience blows gently a ship sails slowly by. Then the "wind" picks up and the passing ships toss. Finally, with shrieks of terror provided by the audience, a ship plunges beneath the waves of a howling gale.)

Pan slides like this also provide an ideal mechanism for ***reverse motion***, another technique also seen in the early movies. Running entire films backwards was a favorite gambit of the first projectionists, intent on getting the most play from their little snippets of film. Likewise, early lanternists ran their pan slides in the wrong direction. When the pan slide of a train or fire engine, or Noah's animals is run backwards, the effect on screen changes from the dramatic to the comic, just as in the movies.[13]

A different type of pan slide, the ***discrete images pan*** has a series of images in a long frame (Fig. 4.15). This type was also used from as early as Kircher's days, and allowed the showman to present a story in a sequence of separate pictures that was easily and quickly changed. This is the technique that Great Grandfather Carter used to speed up his telling of "The House That Jack Built". I use these "Jack Built" slides in our shows, first changing the pictures slowly and reciting slowly. But by the end, once the audience knows the sequence, I am changing the pictures about every two seconds – just about the same time as a fast movie *shot* today. Much of the fun of the slide comes as the audience races through the poem, trying to keep up with the flashing images.

Horror Shows

Let's now pick up some other lantern techniques that were later used by the movies. They emerged as part of a popular early magic lantern show, the "***Phantasmagoria***", a form of ghost or horror show (Fig. 4.16).

As early as 1768 the first lantern showmen brought forth ghosts amid a tremendous commotion of wind and noise. The ghosts were ***projected on smoke***, which made the images seem to writhe in the air. Then, in the 1780s, Paul de Philipsthal (often called Philidor) developed a similar ghost show called the *Phantasmagorie*. Like the earlier showmen, he began his show with a storm, but he added ghostly portraits (including turning Ben Franklin's head into a skull), and an important new feature, the ghost that seemed to approach the audience on screen:

> Rain, hail, and winds form simultaneously the overture and the symphony for the scene which will unfold. There rises, from the very floor, a white figure, which grows by degrees to human size.[14]

Audiences all over Europe loved Philidor's ghosts and skeletons that seemed to grow from nothing – except for Germany where the show was banned as too extreme. His productions contained many of the elements of the later *Phantasmagoria*, made famous in 1798 by a Belgian performer, Etienne-Gaspard Robert, who called himself Robertson. He copied the elements of these earlier shows, and expanded them – firmly establishing the phantasmagoric tradition in magic lantern practice, and in the horror-show tradition.[15] Robertson's show underwent several evolutions, but the culmination was held in the remains of an old Paris convent, surrounded by tombs and gravestones, which may have been props rather than the real thing. Dark passages decorated with mysterious pic-

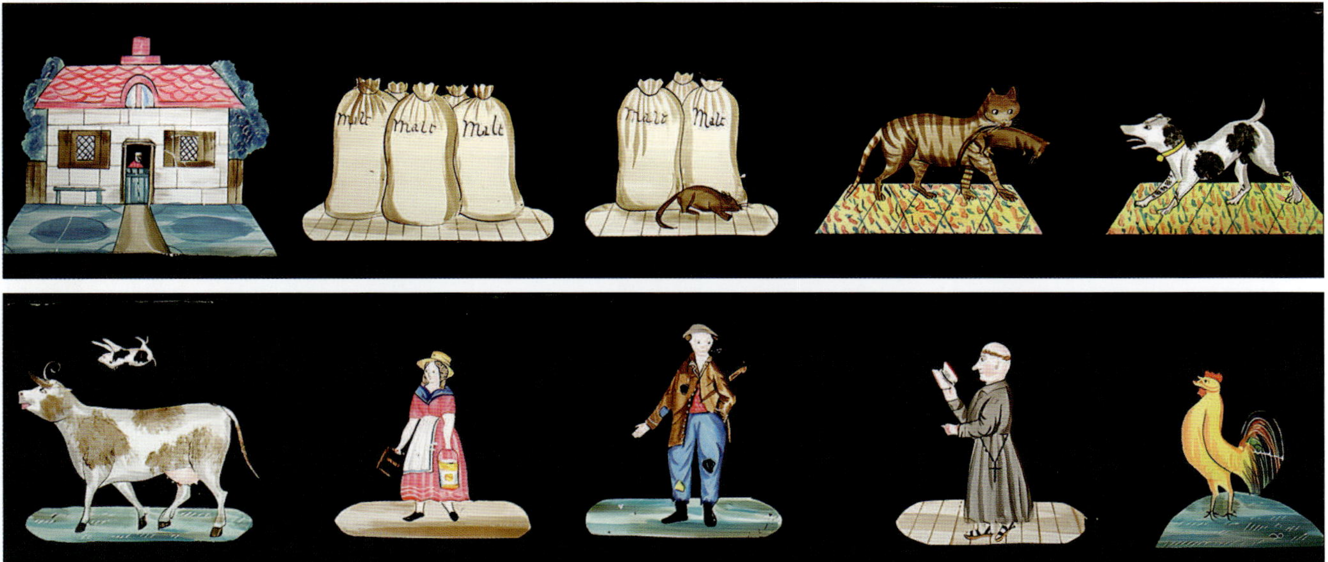

Fig. 4.15 A pair of panorama slides illustrating the nursery rhyme of "The House That Jack Built".

tures and the bones of the dead led to a chamber hung with black velvet and lighted by a single lamp.

Robertson began by discussing in "scientific terms" the sensations created by thoughts of phantoms and witches. Suddenly the lamp went out. Thunder roared and lightning flashed. Weird music, produced by the glass harmonica, sent shivers down the spine. Bats fluttered, ghosts and goblins groaned, strange figures seemed to stalk the room. This elaborate *production* was staged with the help of several magic lanterns and six assistants. Most of this activity was hidden from the audience by using ***rear projection***, behind the screen, which was wet with water or coated with wax to let the light shine through. Many of the images were quite elaborate. For instance, mechanical moving effects created those bats and devils with beating wings. The images were usually painted on the glass against a black background, to make them emerge from the darkness more dramatically – later called the ***phantasmagoria slide*** technique. Robertson also used a ***phantascope*** – much like what we now call an "opaque projector" – to create an ***episcopic projection***, a 3-D effect achieved by projecting solid objects like the ***model*** of a skeleton rising from a casket. He made the phantasmagoric bats and devils dart around the room in a *zip pan* or *swish pan* by projecting them with small, hand-held lanterns that were moved quickly.

When Robertson's show in Paris closed, he took his production elsewhere. Imitators were soon performing all over the continent, and throughout the coastal United States as well. Jack Bologna gave the first well-documented Phantasmagoria show in America in New York in 1803.[16]

Robertson's *special effects* (or *F/X*) previewed many cinematic techniques. His *rear projection*

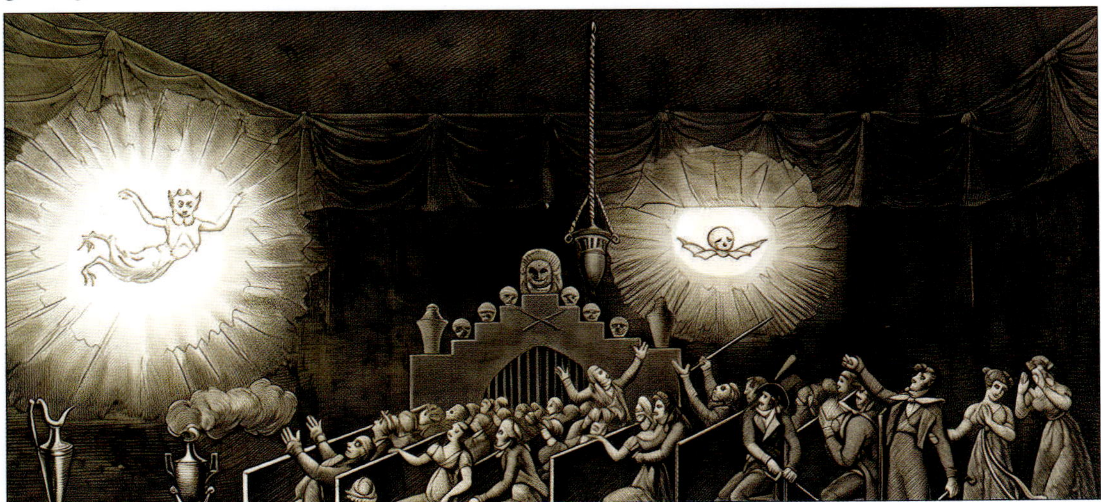

Fig. 4.16 "Fantasmagorie de Robertson dans la Cour des Capucines en 1797". *Wikimedia Commons.*

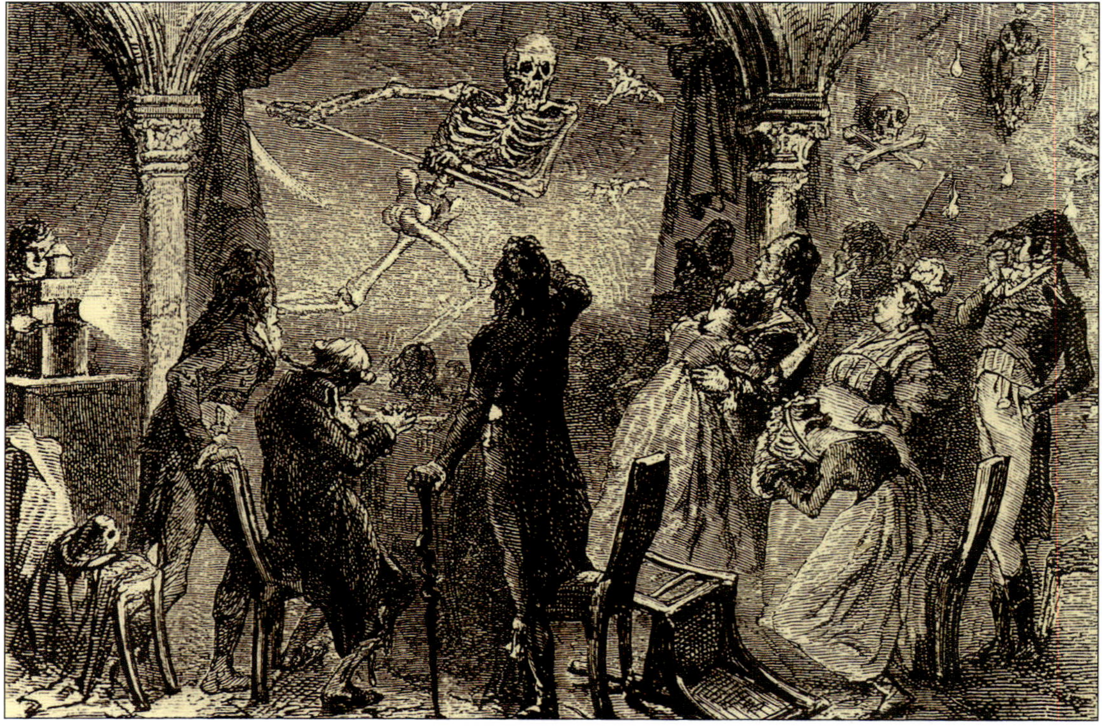

Fig. 4.17 "Robertson's Phantasmagoria in the Capucine Convent, 1797", from Marion, *L'Optique*. The wheeled lantern, at the far left, was hidden behind the screen.

would later be applied in the movies, projecting a background in front of which live actors performed. The *hand-held* lantern, or what the 19th century lanternists called a ***phantasmagoria lantern*** or a ***breast lantern*** because it could be held to the chest, was used to produce the same life-like, naturalistic on-screen movement that the hand-held camera would create later – a type of *cinema verité*, if you will.[17]

The most important aspect of Robertson's show, picked up from those earlier productions and perfected to a remarkble degree, was the ***zoom***.

The Continuous Zoom

An analog to what we now call the *zoom shot* was a lantern technique that might be called the ***continuous zoom***, popularized by Robertson. Speaking of one of today's movies we might say, "As the camera zoomed in on the skeleton, the figure exploded before the audience." Robertson did not take a "camera" and *zoom in* on his figure so that it grew larger; he did exactly the opposite to achieve the same effect on screen. Robertson took his projector and pulled backwards from behind the screen, making the skeleton grow continuously larger as he did so. (His lantern was mounted on a wheeled platform, so that it moved smoothly. The lens was constructed so that it could be easily ***rack focused*** to keep the image sharp on screen as it grew, while an ***iris*** kept the light at the same brightness.) On screen, a tiny half-human figure appeared in the air, shimmering and ghostly. The figure loomed closer to the audience, growing larger and larger, until suddenly it disappeared with a wail. Women in the audience fainted and bold men hid their eyes (Fig. 4.17).[18]

Some think the reactions in the etchings of Robertson's shows are exaggerated, but I don't think so. I think they leave little doubt that Robertson used this zoom technique with great skill, so that his looming figure of Death created an emotional response of fear and terror in the audience. Contemporary reports confirm the reaction to Robertson's phantasmagoria that is depicted in these pictures. Even the French sophisticates at Robertson's show, who understood that it was a carefully constructed optical or "catoptric" illusion, commented on, "the astonishing magic of the [ghosts] truly terrifying growth", and the general power of the new cinematic techniques:

> Reason has told you well that these are mere phantoms, catoptric tricks devised with artistry, carried out with skill, presented with intelligence, [but] your weakened brain can only believe what it is made to see, and we believe ourselves transported into another world and into other centuries.[19]

Whether the technology was "zooming back",

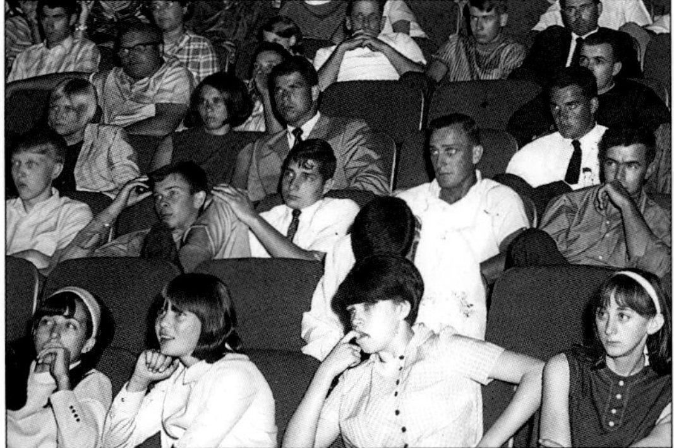

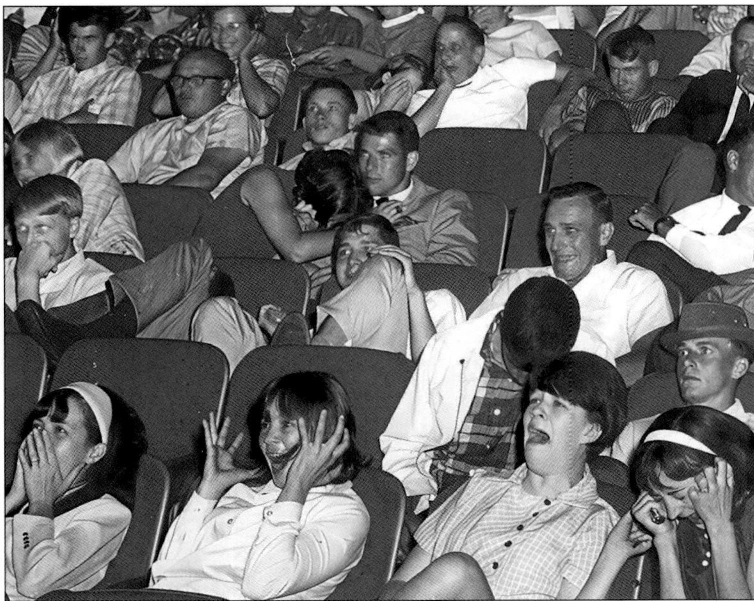

Fig. 4.18 Audience reactions to the movie *Wait Until Dark*, 1967.
Photos courtesy of the Pal Theatre and photographers Barron Godbee and Billy Yarbrough.

with a magic lantern, or "zooming in" with a movie camera, the on-screen artistic effect was the same – a sudden continuous increase in the size of the image, so that it seemed to be steadily (and usually rapidly) advancing toward the viewer, often in a threatening manner. It was scary in the 1700s, and can still be so in the modern period.

I found these two extraordinary pictures demonstrating that point in the lobby of the Pal MovieTheatre in Vidalia, Georgia when we were there to perform a magic lantern show (Fig. 4.18). They were taken in the Theatre just before and after the climactic scene of Audrey Hepburn's 1967 thriller, *Wait Until Dark*. In that scene, the villain makes a sideways leap across the screen at the heroine, and then, with a quick mid-air change of camera angle, the lunge seems to continue, coming straight at her and at us, the audience – just as in the Phantasmagoria. (Note, in addition to the general reactions of fright, that the young man in the second seat of the third row has retreated entirely, hiding behind the seat.) An ancient magic lantern technique still has the power to terrify modern-era audiences. The similarity of audience experience from lantern show to movies is an excellent example of Musser's point about the continuity of "screen practice" over the centuries.

The zoom tradition continued into the Victorian era and beyond, and though the phantasmagoric form of magic lantern performance was not a common occurrence at public shows, a standard feature of lantern manuals aimed at amateurs was instruction on how to give a "phantasmagoria" family show with a moving lantern. These instructions contained an explicit recognition of the difference between what audience perceived on screen, and the technology that produced the zoom effect:

> It will be understood that the object of the Phantasmagoria is to produce the idea of *approaching* and *retiring* by means of images which really only *contract* and *expand* [on screen.] (Emphasis in original.)[20]

The Step Zoom

The moving "phantasmagoria" lantern was not the only way of creating this *zoom* experience of "retiring" and "approaching." It could also be done in a step-by-step fashion, with a series of dissolving slides, Each slide contained almost the same image, but of different sizes, so that the picture on screen appeared to be slowly getting larger or smaller. Beale used this technique several times in sets of two dissolving slides.[21] It was also done with multiple slides. Here is Edward Wilson – editor of *The Magic Lantern* – on the use of what might be thought of as the ***step-zoom*** technique to make the image of Mercury gradually appear larger and larger (Fig. 4.19).

> The crowning effect of all the things we saw [was] the "Flight of Mercury". Mercury appears of diminutive size in the far distance, coming down from the blue heavens, gradually sinking towards the earth, when suddenly the sky becomes clouded and then dark as night. Now the clouds break, and Mercury appears nearer and larger. Again, the clouds thicken, and his image seems out of sight; flashes of lightning spring out from different directions, and here and there the clouds are broken by the forked

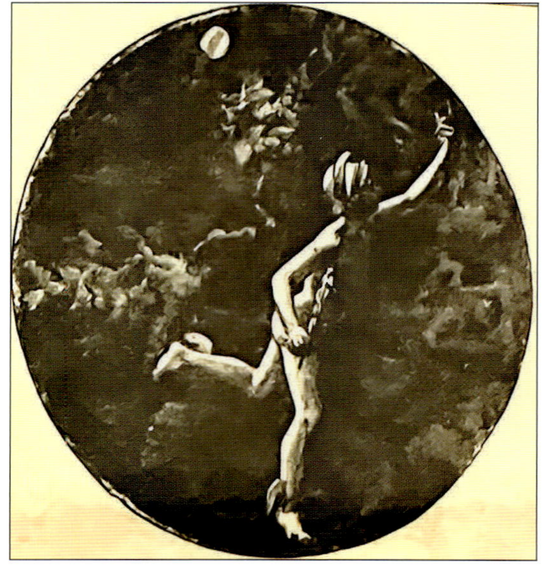
Fig. 4.19 *The Flight of Mercury*, pictured in a broadside for B. A. Bamber's *Dime Show*, 1880s.

> chain lightning, and with the piano the thunder is made to roll, until the sky is clear again, and Mercury is nearer still, bright and beautiful and triumphant. The effect is decidedly the most wonderful we ever saw produced with the lantern.[22]

The Flight of Mercury was the featured set in Wilson's catalog for several years. In 1882, Wilson offered a new dissolving set called *The Flight of the Soul* (Fig. 4.20). This was a set of seven dissolving slides that presented a series of ever-smaller images of the departing soul, alternating with clouds to smooth the transitions. It created a diminishing zoom effect, as the soul "melt[ed] away into a cloud of the brightest ruby tints" and, as the soul neared Heaven, angels appeared to guide it. Wilson describes *The Flight of the Soul* as a set "of the utmost brilliancy". It became very popular, and was used by itself with musical accompaniment, in conjunction with various hymns like *Abide With Me*, and as part of the Masonic and other Secret Society rituals.[23]

Was it just 18th and 19th and 20th century audiences who were affected by the effects of close-ups, and zooms – who could lose their sense of the *aesthetic distance* between art and reality, or be awe-struck by the power of such techniques? Not at all. Even audiences of the 21st century who know how the technology works, are affected by such early cinematic experiences, as our own re-created shows attest.

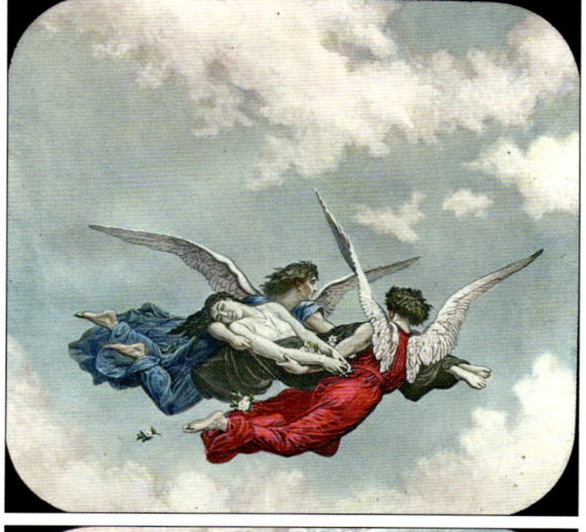
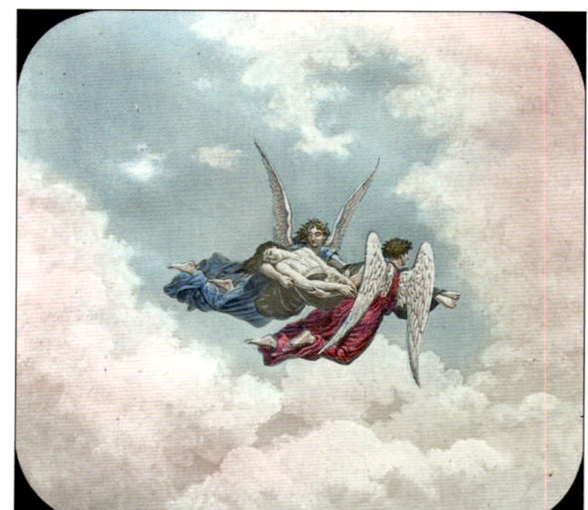
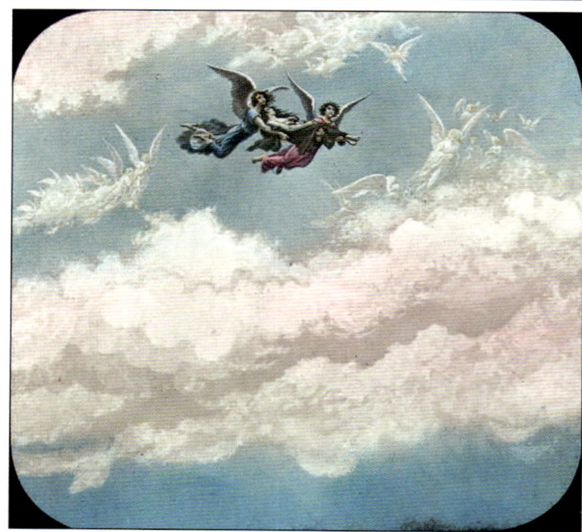
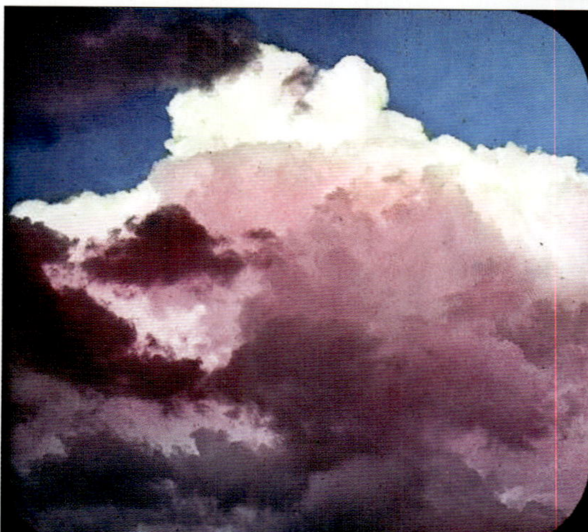
Fig. 4.20 Portion of a set of slides, not by Beale, for *Flight of the Soul.*

The "Phantasmagoria" has become such a popular part of our shows that I work in into almost every performance. Robertson's lantern on wheels is too heavy and complicated for us to use in a touring show, but I try to give a sense of what his show was like by doing a comic version, using a small hand-carried "breast lantern". As I carry the lantern up to the screen, I explain that fearsome things are about to unfold. To lessen the fear I will explain exactly what I'm going to do, including the fact that I have a slide of a terrifying lion in the lantern.

> "Are you going to be brave"? I call. "Yes"! the audiences hollers.
>
> "How about you kids? Are you going to be brave"? **"YES"!** they scream.
>
> "All right then, here we go. All together, One, two three"! The lantern is two feet from the screen; the terrifying lion is nothing but a tiny kitten. "Meow"! I say. Everyone laughs.
>
> "So that lion is not very scary. But what happens if I move further away? He'll be bigger, and really scary this time. Are you going to be BRAVE"?
>
> On it goes, as I work my way off the stage, back into the middle of the theater. The lion gets bigger and bigger, roaring louder and louder. In the final sequence, the huge lion suddenly leaps off the screen, up onto the ceiling, over to the walls, and then down into the audience as I charge about, pretending to terrify the four-year-olds.
>
> It's all very funny, and (purposely) not terrifying at all, as I want to be sure not to scare the even the youngest children. But as I explain about Robertson's show, I work my way to stand about six feet in front of the first row, and, picking a solid adult citizen, suddenly charge with arms out and lungs at full tilt. I seem to get bigger and bigger. Even the bravest flinch. Zoom!

I suspect that you too, gentle reader, would feel a clutch of the stomach and a tightening of the sphincters when I charge, just as you would if you saw Robertson's skeleton screaming toward you out of the dark catacomb, just as you would when a modern camera's zoom shot brings some howling alien apparition charging toward you on an IMAX screen. The technology of the Phantasmagoria and the IMAX is different. But the cinematic art – and hence the response – is the same.

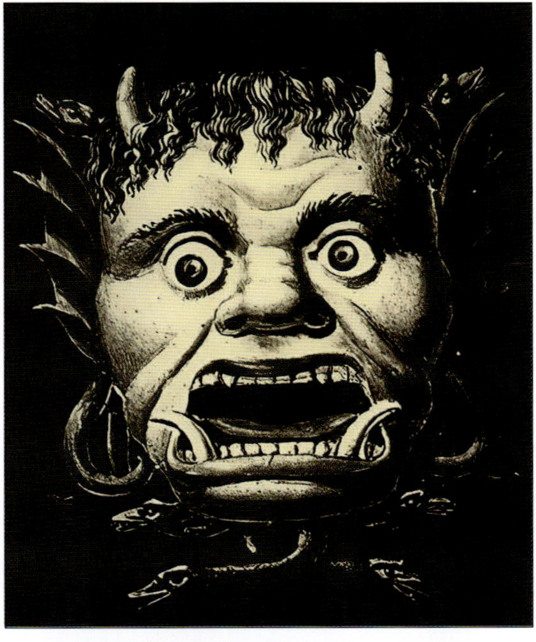

Fig. 4.21 A phantasmagoria goblin slide, and Edwin S. Porter's pistol-firing cowboy from *The Great Train Robbery*. Both from *Wikimedia Commons*.

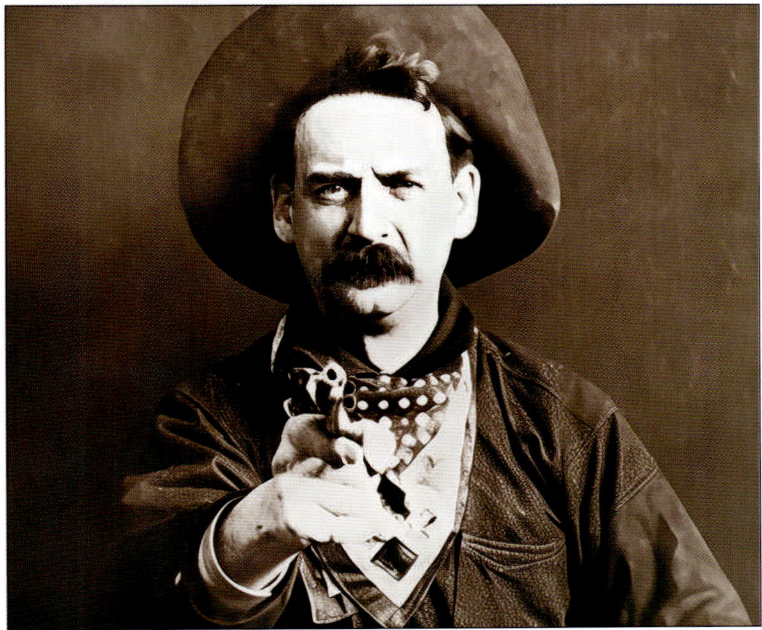

To be effective, these early techniques for creating motion on screen had to be used with restraint, carefully, and skillfully. If expertly handled the same technique could be integrated into shows for all sorts of different dramatic purposes, just as I used the breast phantasmagoria lantern for comic effect. As a 19th century lantern manual, emphasized, finding unique ways to use the basic lantern techniques was up to the showman:

> All of these effects may, with the exercise of a little ingenuity, be varied and extended in dozens of ways. I have not space to do more than explain how the principal effects are produced, and must leave the reader to adapt them.[24]

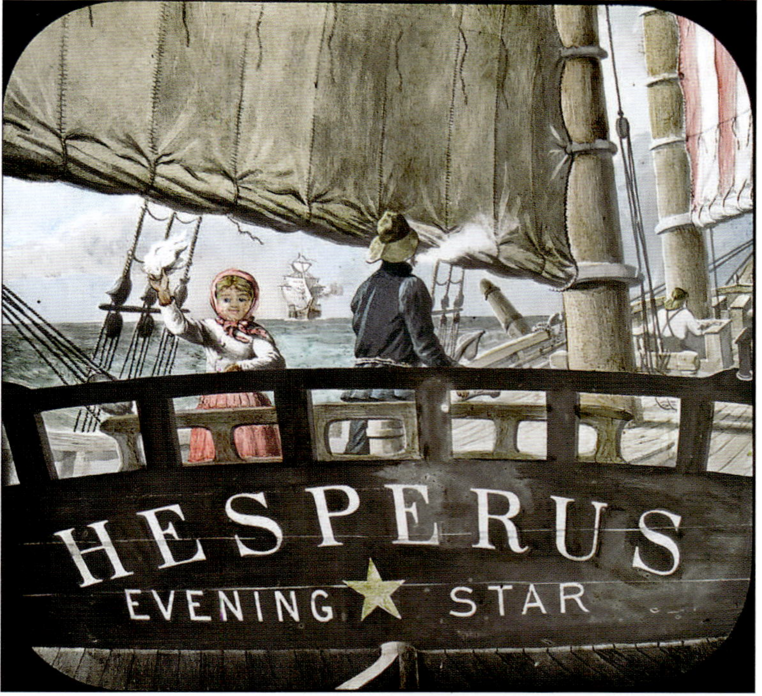

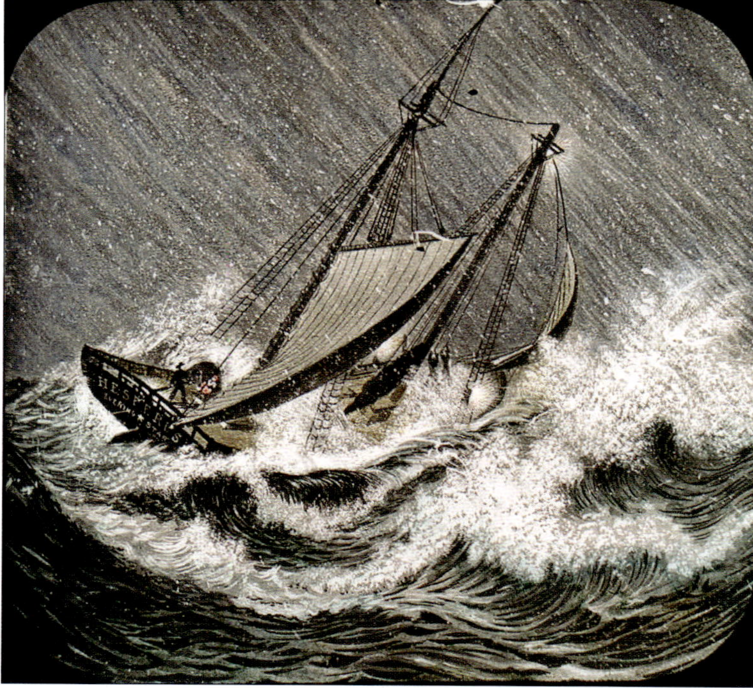

Fig. 4.22 Beale's slides 1 and 5 for Henry Wadsworth Longfellow's, *The Wreck of the Hesperus*.

Close-ups

A second aspect of the phantasmagoria shows that became a standard part of the lantern repertoire, and of the movies, was the close-up.

In the history of the movies, much has been made of Edwin S. Porter's innovative use of the *close-up* for dramatic effect in the 1903 film, *The Great Train Robbery* (Fig. 4.21). At the end (or sometimes at the beginning) of the movie, one of the robbers, in close-up, fires his gun directly at the audience. Robertson's show used a similar close-up effect on screen for the same reasons, the only difference being that instead of bringing the camera up close to the subject, Robertson painted some of his images – both portraits and goblins – on the slides as large "face only" or "head and shoulders" images rather than as full figures. Robertson did not, so far as is known, go from a *medium shot* to a *close-up* of the same figure, but he certainly varied from medium shots to close-ups within the show, and surely those huge and fantastic heads appearing on screen, decorated with horns and glaring directly at the audience, must have been every bit as menacing to Robertson's audiences as Porter's famous close-up of a gun-toting cowboy were to his.

Beale did not create close-ups, nor were they much used as a storytelling technique within other artist's lantern stories. The general attitude seemed to be, as one Victorian lanternist put it in an article called "Size or Realism", that pictures exhibited above their normal size were not "realistic" and had "a more or less grotesque appearance, *especially* if containing figures".[25]

However, Beale certainly knew how to use the narrative power of contrasting size. For instance, the poem of *The Wreck of the Hesperus* (Fig. 4.22), which is based on an actual incident, tells the story of a little girl who goes off for a sailing jaunt on her father's boat, is caught in a winter hurricane, and is drowned. The opening slide shows a "medium shot" of the little girl in her bright red dress, waving gaily. She dominates the scene, and Beale's composition makes us, in effect, part of her family, giving her a happy send-off. In slide 5 the hurricane hits her father's boat. The little girl is almost totally lost amid the welter of snow, waves and wind. Beale tears her from our friendly circle, her red dress now only a tiny dot, lost in the roaring confusion of the hurricane. The contrasting size of these two images of the captain's daughter is effective storytelling indeed. When we come to the storm slide in our performances the audience often gasps with the realization of what is likely to happen to their little girl.

Even if audiences of Beale's period did not often see close-ups within a story, they certainly did see them, and in almost every show. Close-up portraits of literary or historical figures were commonly used to begin show segments – McAllister's catalog offered more than 200 choices. Close-ups of cartoon figures – clowns, witches, pirates, and other outlandish types – sometimes with moving eyes or mouths, were often used to begin the show itself. The huge heads of these ***introductory figures*** dominated the screen so that the show started with a dramatic, and often humorous punch. *The Magic Lantern*, the showman's trade journal in America, even offered its readers pre-printed broadsides showing a full-screen head of a crying baby (Fig. 4.23). In the accompanying article on "How to Start a Show" the editors suggested that a comic close-up like this would, "interest the people and make them laugh beforehand".[26]

We've taken *The Magic Lantern's* advice for our own modern re-creations, and open our shows with a close-up of the outlandish face of a famous Victorian character, Ally Sloper. Ally was perhaps the first cartoon *star*, who appeared 20 years before the advent of *The Yellow Kid* in American comics (Fig. 4.24). He made his way from cartoons into comic strips, magazines, books, music halls, magic lantern shows, and – within two years after the birth of film – into the movies themselves.[27]

When Ally Sloper comes on screen with his red nose and fizzy hair, audiences laugh immediately. When his moving eyes dance in response, the audience laughs again, and we're off, with the audience hooked.

That lantern trade journal gave very good advice on how to start a show.

In addition to closeups of people, close-ups of animated animals, like a lion or tiger, were painted naturalistically rather than in the cartoon style that signaled humor. (See Fig. 4.25, the opening picture of this chapter.) When such images appeared on the screen after a story set that had been presented in *long shots* (the view we see in live theater), the sudden change to these huge "in-your-face" realistic images was dramatic and often frightening. Among the most disturbing were those lions and tigers with moving eyes and mouths. They were presented ***frontally***, searching with their great gleaming eyes for victims in the audience. Often the showman would add to the effect, making the animals roar with their red mouths, and threaten to eat small children – just as I did with my comic phantasmagoria, just as Porter's cowboy threatened his audience with his exploding pistol. The effect of such a "close-up confrontation" was powerful.

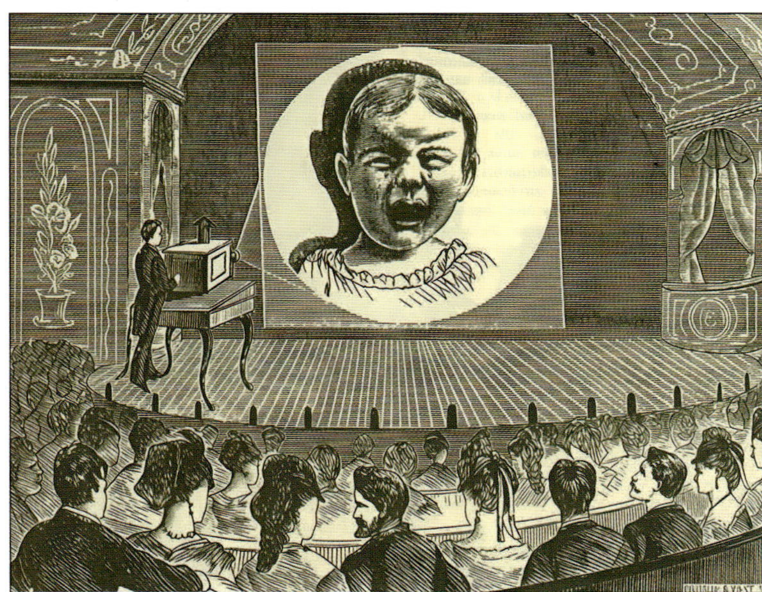

Fig. 4.23 Close-up of a crying baby from a Liesegang projection manual. The image dominates the screen and starts the performance with a laugh.

Figure 4.26 demonstrates the point. The photo is of our family watching a lantern show when I was a boy – that's me on the right. We're watching "The Tiger" slide, while my father makes him roar. We're all laughing because we had seen this slide many times, so it had lost its terror. We had my sister take the photo because we all knew how our dog Lassie would react to "The Tiger". She did it every time. She'd put her muzzle in the air and give a low, long moan. Magic lantern technology is so powerful it even affects dogs.[28]

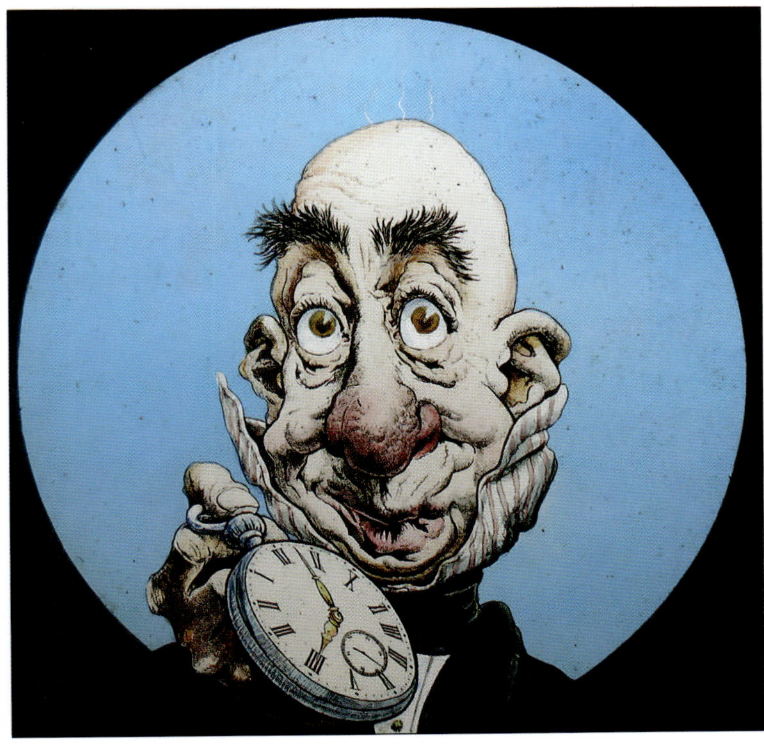

Fig. 4.24 Ally Sloper, a well-known cartoon character, gets ready to start one of our shows.

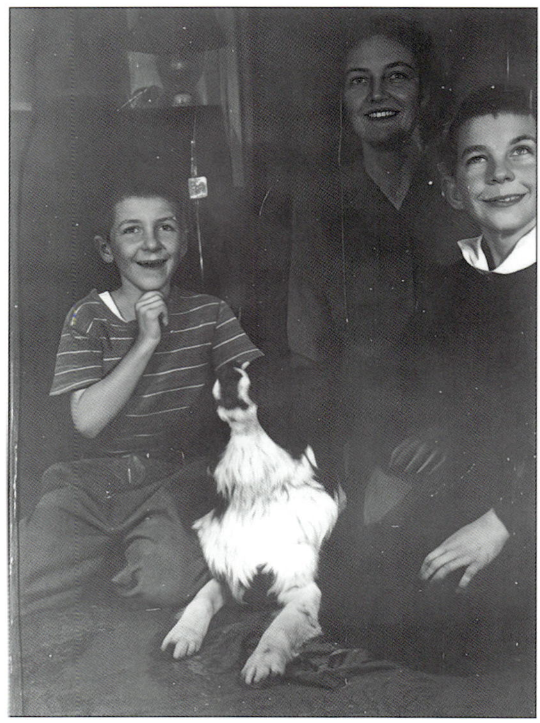

Fig. 4.26 My brother, mother, and I, along with our dog Lassie, watch The Tiger slide in a family show about 1946.

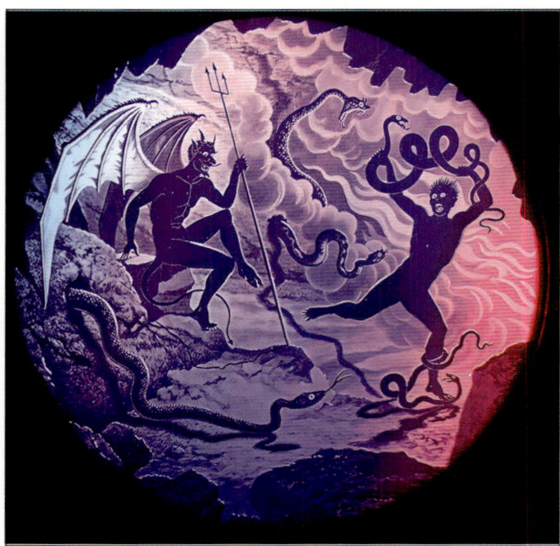

Fig. 4.27 Beale's "Delirium Tremens" from the *Intemperance Subjects* group.

One more personal story about the power of the magic lantern close up: About 45 years ago my Dad asked me to do a show at his Quaker retirement community. After the show a little old lady – 80 or so – came up to me and said,

> "I'm so glad to have seen thy show. I redeemed myself".
>
> I didn't understand. "Redeemed yourself? What do you mean"?
>
> "Well, when I was three, I lived up the street from thy great grandfather, and one night I was taken to see his show. There was a giant tiger on the screen. I was so scared I started to scream, and had to be taken from the room. Thee showed that same tiger tonight, didn't thee"?
>
> "Yes", I said, "I did. The very same".
>
> "It scared me this time too, but I didn't scream. So, I've redeemed myself".

I have learned to be careful about showing "The Tiger" slide if small children are in the audience. The black phantasmagoric background blends with the dark room, so that the tiger seems to charge up out of the shadows in 3-D when it is flashed on the screen, even though it isn't actually getting closer. Both the eyes and the mouth seem directed right at the audience, and both move, so that the tiger can actively threaten those he sees, dogs and children alike. Remembering a little girl in Quaker garb, I restrain myself.

Whether or not close up or zooms were involved, ghosts and goblins remained a feature of lantern shows for the rest of magic lantern history. The fact that the lantern shows were in the dark, the strange effects that could be created, and the very name, "magic lantern" – all made it natural that images of death and horror would remain part of the tradition. You may remember that in the 1860's, when Beale was a young man, he saw a Phantasmagoria, and a different kind of ghost show, "Pepper's Ghost".[29] Later, as a magic lantern artist, he contributed his fair share to the tradition with temperance images (Fig. 4.27), and stories such as *The Raven*, *The Spectre Pig*, and *Bridget's Dream*, stories which form the core of our *Halloween Show*.

Expanding Lantern Technology

Each new generation of magic lantern showmen did exercise their ingenuity and extend the magic-lantern art. Magic lantern technology itself also continued to improve, creating more effects, and more opportunities for artful manipulation (Fig. 4.28).

The illuminating source of the lantern in the early days was various forms of oil. The intensity of the lantern's projection light increased in the 1780s with new illuminants such as Argand lamps, which burned oil with a wick through which air flowed, and gave 12 times the light of earlier systems. (Great Grandfather Carter's Marcy Sciopticon, invented in 1869, used kerosene, which eventually supplanted the Argand lamps.) For professional shows limelight was adapted to the lantern in the 1840s. The light was made by heating a piece of limestone (calcium oxide) to incandescence in a mixture of burning oxygen and hydrogen. (The same device was also used for spotlights. That's where the theatrical expression "in the limelight" comes from.)

The limelight was brilliant, making it possible to give magic lantern shows to a much larger audience, even to thousands. The brighter light made the pictures more life-like – a major advance for magic lantern art. (Remember how Beale was delighted when he saw his first limelight "stereopticon" show in 1860.) But the mixture of hydrogen and oxygen was difficult to control and not suitable for anything but professionally managed productions. The hydrogen was also extremely dangerous, as a newspaper account of 1870 indicates:

> SAD ACCIDENT: On the evening of February 4th while Mr. J. W. Black of Boston, and his worthy assistant, Mr. J. L. Dunmore, were about to commence a lantern exhibition in Lowell, one of the gas bags exploded with tremendous force, threw Mr. Dunmore high in the air and burned him sadly about the face and eyes, knocked Mr. Black senseless, drove a stick through the nose of the organist, and damaged the organ-loft, organ, and church considerably.[30]

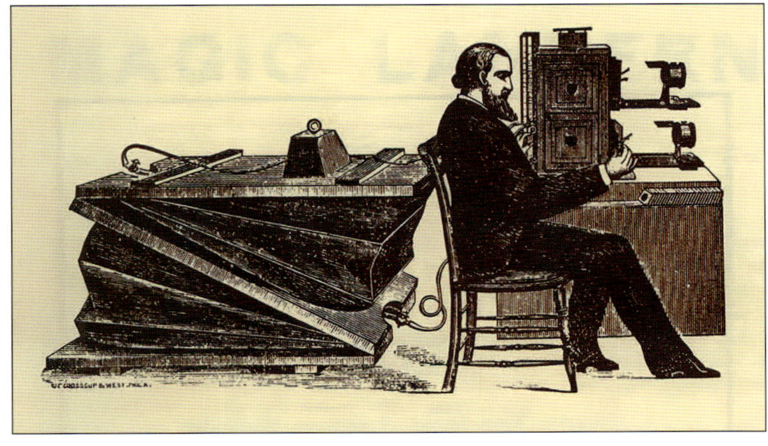

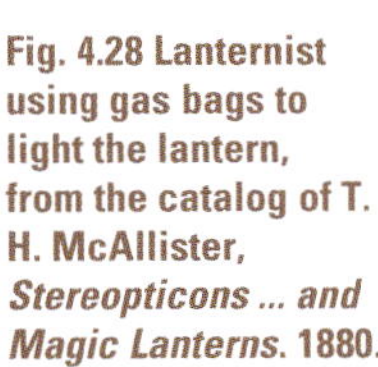

Fig. 4.28 Lanternist using gas bags to light the lantern, from the catalog of T. H. McAllister, *Stereopticons ... and Magic Lanterns.* 1880.

At the same period that the light for the lantern became brighter, the cost of slides decreased,

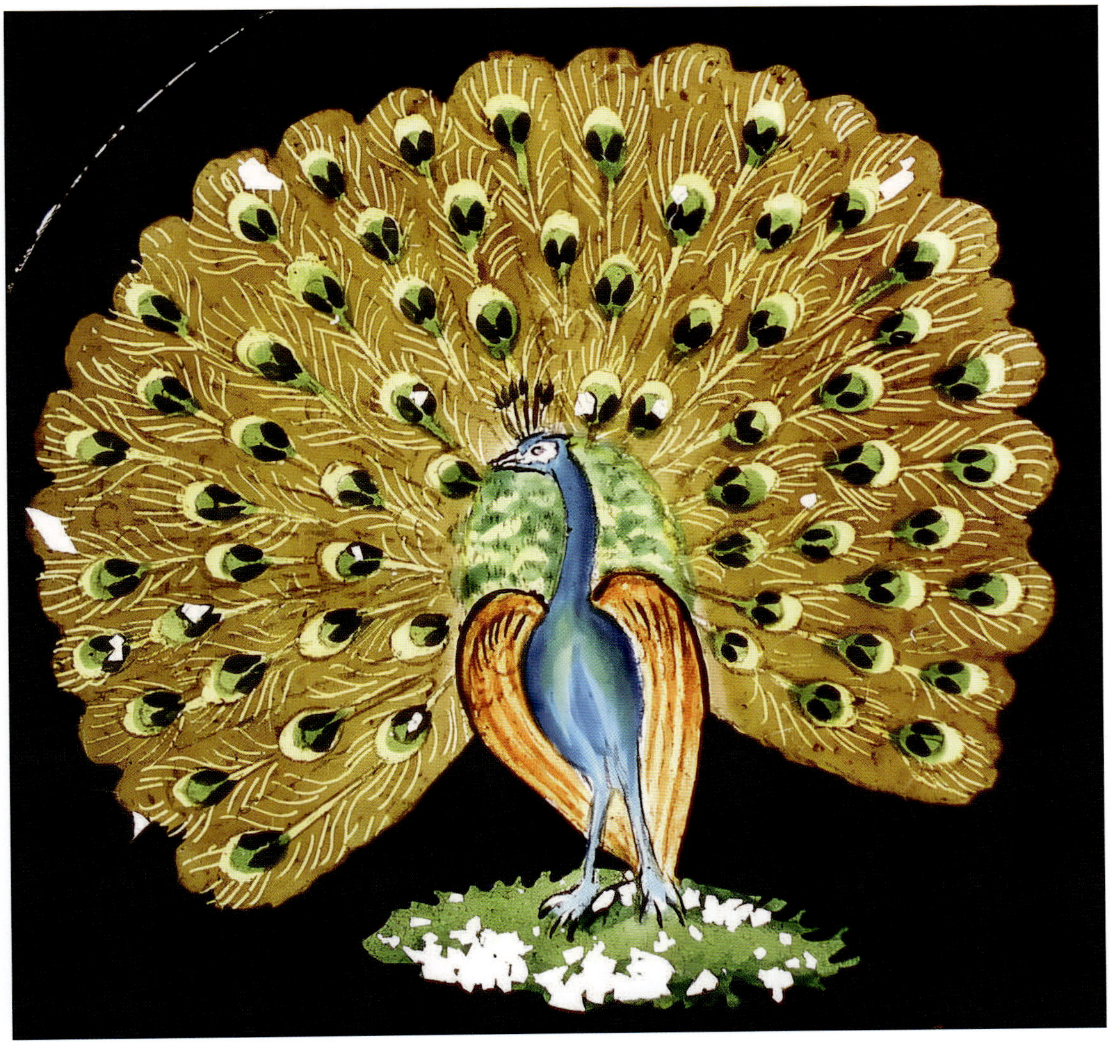

Fig. 4.29 Copper-plate slider by Carpenter and Wesley, 1850s. Sliders combined standardized production and beautifully colored hand-painted images.

while standards of quality improved. Prior to the 1820s, all the slides were individually painted by hand, an expensive process that limited distribution. Some slides were exceedingly well executed, but many were not, and the unsophisticated nature of many slides had made magic lantern shows seem a rather crude form of entertainment. In 1823 an Englishman, Philip Carpenter, changed this when he began mass-producing ***copper-plate sliders*** (Fig. 4.29). Carpenter made these slides by having an artist first engrave images on copper plates, and then print them on thin sheets of glue which were pasted to the glasses and fired in a kiln. This process produced detailed, identical outlines on glass that could then be colored. Because of the quality of Carpenter's slides, the copper-plate process became the standard way of mass-producing slides before photography, and substantially improved the quality of many shows.

Mass-produced images also brought the cost down enough so that lantern shows could become more widely available, making on-screen entertainment a lively competitor to the stage melodramas, magicians, lecturers, and other "genial showmen" of the day. A low price also brought the lantern show within the financial resources of churches, and Sunday School instruction became one of the leading uses of the lantern in this period.[31]

The copper plate process established the concept of standardized lantern images that Briggs was later to employ when he mass-produced Beale's designs photographically. Thus, the plate sliders were an important first step toward the mass production of screen images that would later become a hallmark of the movies, and allow them to spread rapidly once a successful storytelling formula was developed for film.

The Dissolve

As standardization began to take hold and illuminants improved, effects that had at first been used on a very limited basis became more common. Philidor and Henry Childe were probably the first to use dissolving views in 1820s. The dissolve, which we discussed briefly earlier in the context of "flashing" comic slides, required two lanterns, with the light shifting from one to the other so that one projected image changes (dissolves) into another – rapidly in the case of comics, slowly in other cases. This provided a more subtle way to shift from one slide scene to another than simply shoving one slide after another through the lantern.

But what fascinated lanternists, and their audiences, was that this slow dissolve could also be used not just for comic effect, but to create beautiful changes within an image, or to create a subtle sense of movement. This development required both a dissolving set of two or more lantern lenses, and a set of dissolving slides. One of the slides pictured a scene, perhaps a cottage in sunshine. The other slide pictured the identical scene, except in a violent rainstorm. By ***registering*** the two slides, aligning the images exactly, and shifting the light from one lantern to the other, the lanternist could create a transformation of the image from sunny, to storm, to sunny again. When the transformation was done slowly, it produced, as one 1870s broadside boasts, "a magical effect that never fails to please".[32] Dissolving Views became a popular part of magic lantern shows from the 1850s on, and, before the novelty wore off in the 1880s, were often advertised as the chief attraction of a show.

The advertising broadsides often called this type of slides ***dissolve effects***, and we will adopt the term ***effect dissolve*** to distinguish this approach from the simple scene-to-scene "dissolve" described earlier.

The "effects" listed in the catalogs also contained another type of dissolve, in which a portion of one image is projected over another. For instance, Beale created fantasy scenes to appear and disappear over Scrooge's head. For purposes of clarity, I will use the more modern term for this dissolve technique, *superimposition*.[33]

In our *Halloween Show* we use a striking effect dissolve that was originally part of a temperance set (Fig. 4.30). A beautiful woman, loose robe draped revealingly around her breasts, holds a wine glass in one hand and jangles a tambourine with the other. It isn't hard to get the audience singing with her. But then, as they sing and gaze and imagine, the dissolving effect begins. Her flesh slowly seems to disintegrate. Soon, only the shadows of her lush form are visible as her bones emerge. Finally, the last of the flesh disappears and only the skeleton remains, holding aloft a bloody dagger instead of tambourine, while a serpent slithers from the wine glass.

Sobering!

Beale painted a number of spectacular effect dissolves, though the dissolving woman is not his. Few of these dissolves are simply stand-alone effects of the "summer to winter" variety. Except for comic sets, Beale usually employed effect dissolves as part of his narrative art – to heighten a moment in the drama, or to advance a story. A similar evolution was to appear later in the development of the cinema – from the simple display of the "effects" of the new medium's movement (in "actualities" like shots of feeding a baby, a kiss, the arrival of a train), to the later integration of movement into the storyteller's art.

Beale's six-slide set of *Pygmalion and Galatea*, based on a play of that name, is an excellent example of his approach. The story is about a famous Greek artist who is so bedazzled by his own statue of Galatea that he falls in love with it and asks the gods to bring it to life. The gods comply, and, as you might expect, unexpected consequences ensue. The script accompanying the set is the Briggs' original. It summarizes the story and also provides some key dialogue – a common magic lantern *convention* between artist and audience that compresses a full-length play into a brief span while still giving it life.

To produce a series of dissolving effects such as those in the *Pygmalion* set, Beale would sometimes first paint the scene set and then paint cutouts of the different actors (Fig. 4.31). The "actors" were then moved about the set, and photographed, creating a series of slides. The technique was essentially the same as the *matte shot* later used in the movies. (Beale only used this technique a few times. Usually, to create greater interest, he varied the background as well as the blocking of the characters' actions.)[34]

The impact of the *Pygmalion* set on an audience is not simply the art of Beale's effect dissolves, but is a combination of Beale's artistic skill and the dissolving skill of the lanternist.

Look first at Beale's narrative art in the first side (Fig. 4.32) – the way he sets things up to make the most of the dissolve technique. He begins by creating an enormously elaborate scene set. The room is given a sense of *deep space*, using the perspective techniques at which Beale was a master. The set is also rich with *production values*. Each detail is designed to both enhance the sense of perspective, and to dramatize the story: The masks and shield establish the foreground and create *overlapping* forms that give a sense of depth; but they also set up the idea of a Greek drama. The burning torch gives a sense of perspective by providing a *contrast* of light against dark; but it also creates the sense that Pygmalion is worshiping his own creation. The proscenium arch and drapes above Galatea and above the hallway behind Pygmalion provide *linear* perspective cues; but they also frame the

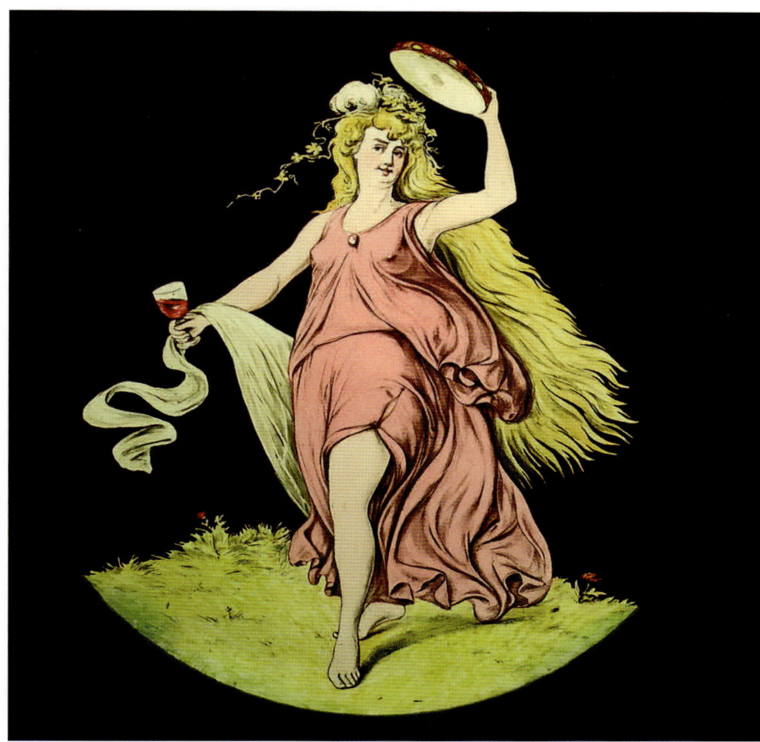

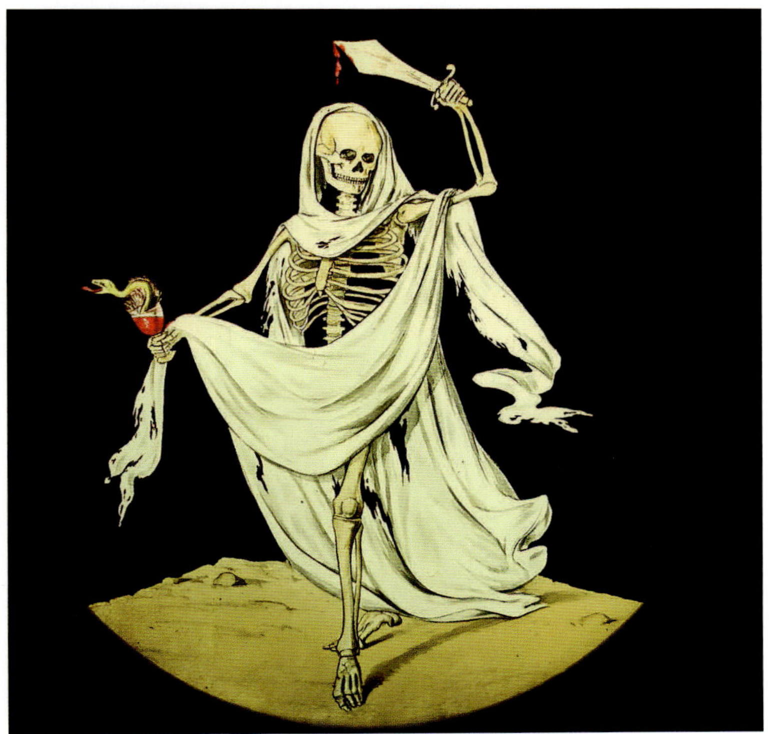

Fig. 4.30 Dissolving views of Woman and Skeleton. Though not by Beale, these temperance slides are extremely effective.

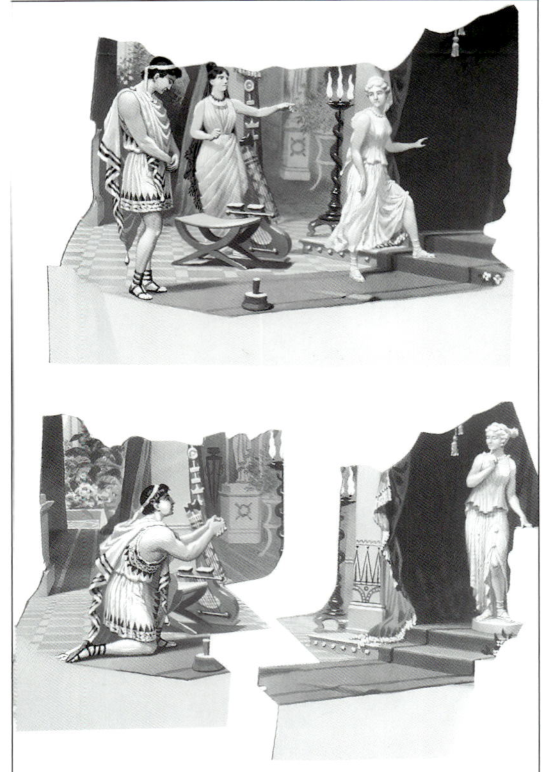

Fig. 4.31 Beale's cutout images for the dissolving slide set of *Pygmalion and Galatea*.

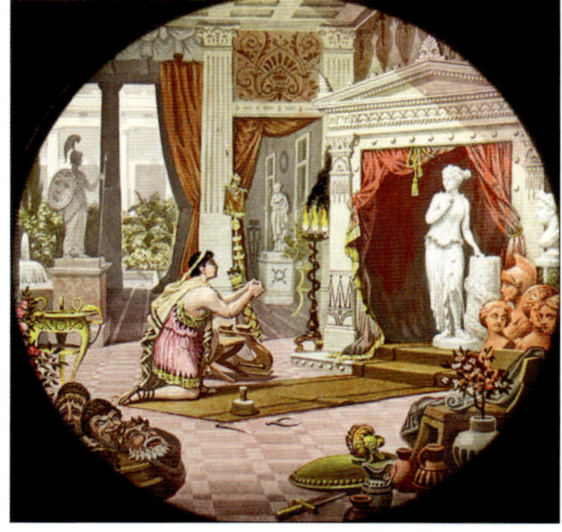

Fig. 4.32 Beale's slide 1 from *Pygmalion and Galatea*, a story based on the play by William S. Gilbert of Gilbert and Sullivan fame.

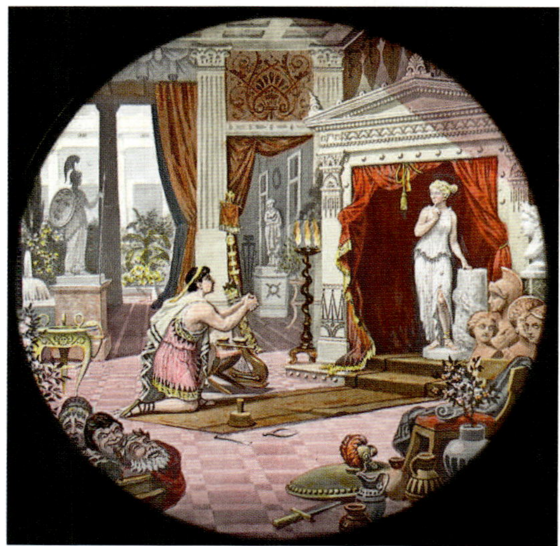

Fig. 4.33 Beale's slide 2 from *Pygmalion and Galatea*.

dramatic entrances and exits of the narrative.

The second slide (Fig. 4.33) is exactly like the first except for once crucial detail – the coloring of Galatea's skin. When the light shifts from the slide in one lantern to the other in order to make the dissolve, the whole scene shimmers because the two slides are always slightly off-register. Gradually, Galatea's color changes from white marble to warm living flesh, accented by her white drapes. Pygmalion is amazed, but so are our audiences. The effect is so magical that we have moved *Pygmalion* up to become the opening segment for our *Valentine Show*.

But Beale's art is not enough on its own. The showman plays a major role in determining the effect of the dissolve. In the case of the change from first to the second scene, I create a very slow dissolve, and then pause the dissolve at the very moment when the change in Galatea is barely perceptible. (I also use an early lanternist's technique, the ***finger flicker***,[35] to help create a sense of mystery, suspending three fingers in front of the lens and flicking them back and forth, so that mysterious shadows play over the scene, and the whole image seems to dance.)

In the third slide (Fig. 4.34), Galatea steps from her pedestal, and here the lanternist should make a quick dissolve, or the ***flash*** we discussed using with comic slides. That creates a sense of movement, much like that in the "anime" or stop action comics that were on the internet in its early days. Once the dissolve is finished, the attention of the audience is drawn first to the *dominant-contrast* movement, that of Galatea leaving the pedestal, and only later does it pick up the appearance of a new character, the wife, symbolically placed between the lovers in a *three shot* that sets up the next scene.

In the fourth slide (Fig. 4.35), love is consummated with a kiss. Here I use an even faster flash, one that throws the lovers into each other's arms. But this is also a *reaction shot*. The furious wife moves from her *subsidiary contrast* position to the very center of the image, the burning brazier no longer highlighting Galatea, but *symbolizing* the wife's fury.

The fifth slide (Fig. 4.36), in which Galatea turns toward her pedestal, again calls for a fairly rapid dissolve, as it imparts movement, but not as fast as the previous slide. The wife stands between the lovers. Galatea's hand extends into the dark of the proscenium. The drapes in this

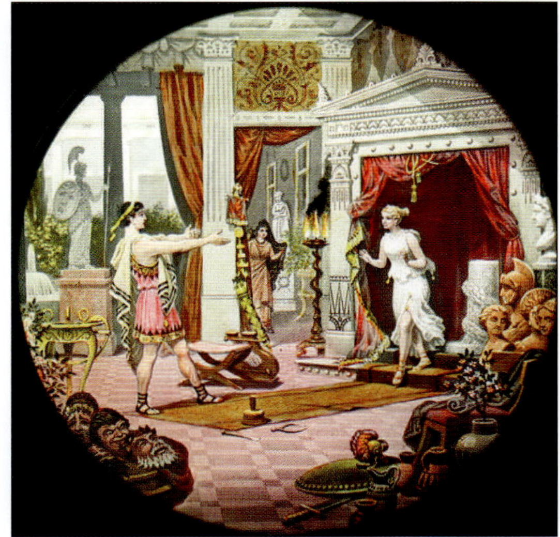

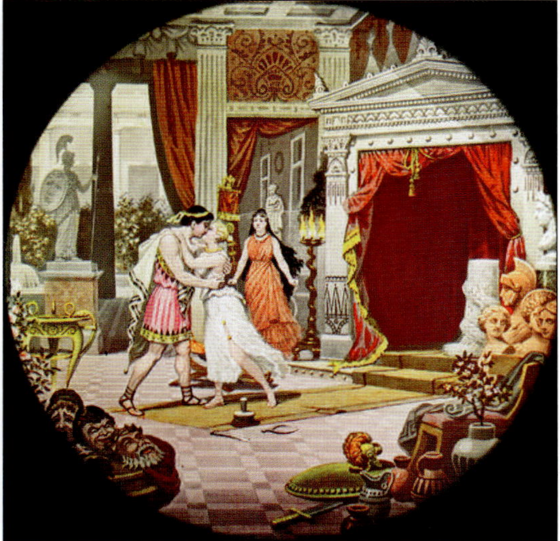

Fig. 4.34 (left) **Beale's slide 3 of *Pygmalion and Galatea*.**

Fig. 4.35 (right) **Beale's slide 4 of *Pygmalion and Galatea*.**

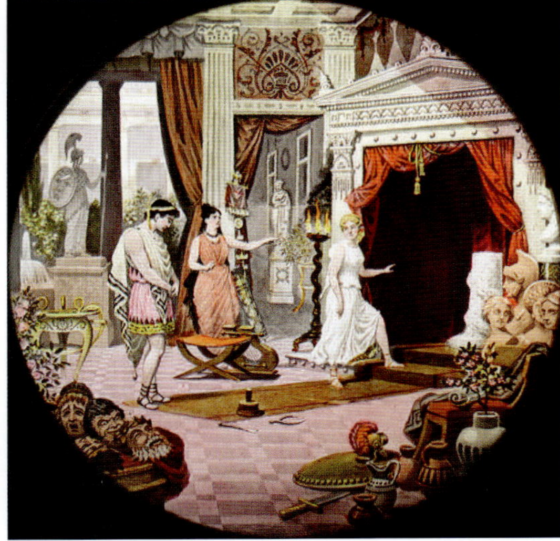

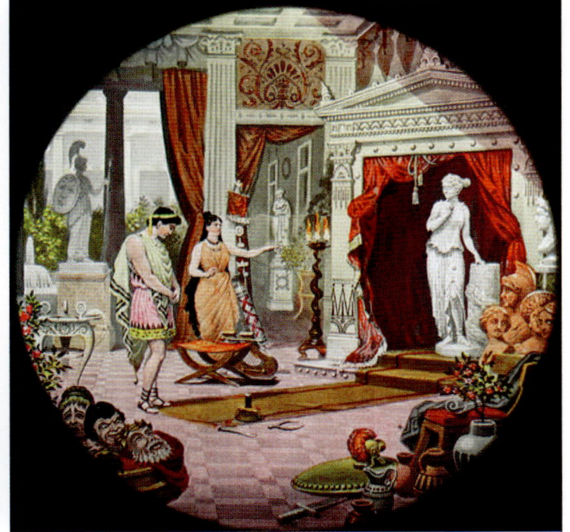

Fig. 4.36 (left) **Beale's slide 5 of *Pygmalion and Galatea*.**

Fig. 4.37 (right) **Beale's slide 6 of *Pygmalion and Galatea*.**

space have changed from red to almost black, implying the void to which she will return.

The sixth and final slide (Fig. 4.37) is not a simple ***mirror*** of the first. It is a *variation*, now containing the triumphant wife, combined with Galatea on the pedestal. During the dissolve to it, as Galatea disappears, suspense is created – will she, or won't she give up her earthly life and reappear as a statue? Careful control of the light creates at first a ghostly Galatea image in the arch way that gradually solidifies to her stone image.

When I began performing *Pygmalion*, I did not understand the sophistication of this sequence of dissolves, and did them all at a moderately slow speed. Only gradually did I recognize the subtleties. I learned how to dissolve quickly to avoid incongruous "double" images – like the one an early lanternist created when he made a "cow appear suspended on the point of a steeple".[36] But much more important than avoiding such problems was learning how to take advantage of the fact that I could control the speed and nature of the transition from one image to another – whether in "simple dissolves", or "effect dissolves" such as those in *Pygmalion*. I learned how to slowly dissolve to build suspense, or even stop a dissolve in mid-transition to freeze the action; how to "flicker" to suggest a magical transition; how to "flash" quickly from one slide to the next in order to create a shocking change. Beale had built material into his images that helped the lanternist make the dissolves an art, not simply a rote technique. But he was dependent on the skill of the lanternist to make the dissolves work artistically on the screen. As "The Practiced Hand", a lantern manual, emphasized, in a line that has become my mantra:

> It is on paying attention to [the] trifles [of slide manipulation] that much of the success of an entertainment depends.[37]

Indeed, the success of lantern entertainment often depends on the way in which the performers manipulate the changes from one image to another. This is a unique feature of lantern narrative art. It is not seen in any other visual media – not in film, not in comics, not in magna, not in graphic novels, not in ancient sequential images carved in stone. In all of those the time relationship between the sequential images is fixed by the media used. The viewer makes meaning out of the sequence at his or her own pace (except in film), but the media itself (the film, the paper, the stone) is unchanging, and cannot respond to the viewer. In contrast, the performers in a lantern show can vary the time duration and nature of the slide changes at will, *and can also* respond to the way the audience reacts to those changes. The performers can sense if the audience is "with them", or if they need to draw out the narration and slow the suspense, or race to leave the audience breathless, or "flash" to crack a joke. And the audience, in turn, can feel the performer responding to it, can sense how they are both dancing together, sharing the beats they create: The joint dance of performer and audience – the magic rhythms of a magic lantern show.

A Poor Beale Dissolve?

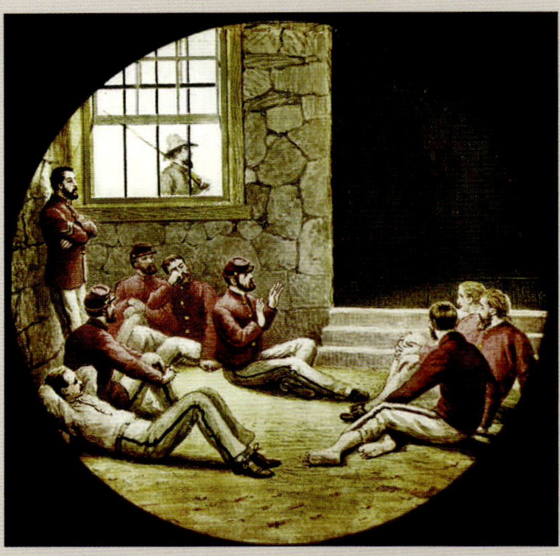

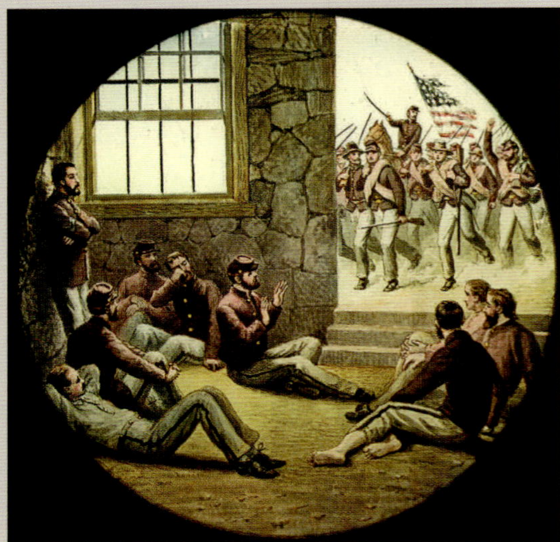

Fig. 4.38 Beale's two dissolving images, slide one and slide two, for the Civil War song, *Tramp, Tramp, Tramp.*

What's wrong with this Beale dissolving set of *Tramp, Tramp, Tramp* (Fig. 4.38)?

This set illustrates a song in which a Union soldier in prison dreams of being rescued, a dream he alone can see. The slide at right, scene two in the dissolve, illustrates this concept well. We see the soldier's amazement at the arriving Union troops, the other soldiers' boredom. But the scene at left, scene one of the dissolve, makes no sense. The scene inside the prison is exactly the same as it is in scene two. Why is the soldier in scene one amazed? He sees nothing in the doorway.

This set was created in an unusual fashion. Beale first painted a full-sized, complete image of scene *two*, which was sold alone for several years. Probably at Briggs' direction he created the scene *one* image by using a fold-over patch on the painting of scene two that covered the marching soldiers, and added the Rebel guard. That would have saved the cost of painting a whole new scene.

Sad to say, the result is a poor dissolve. At the very least the patch should have covered the dreaming soldier of scene one, creating a new image that gave him a bored or dreaming expression and posture. That way, when scene one dissolved into scene two, scene two would be a "reaction shot" of his deliverance.

But as is – it's garbage in, garbage out. When projected, the set has little impact.

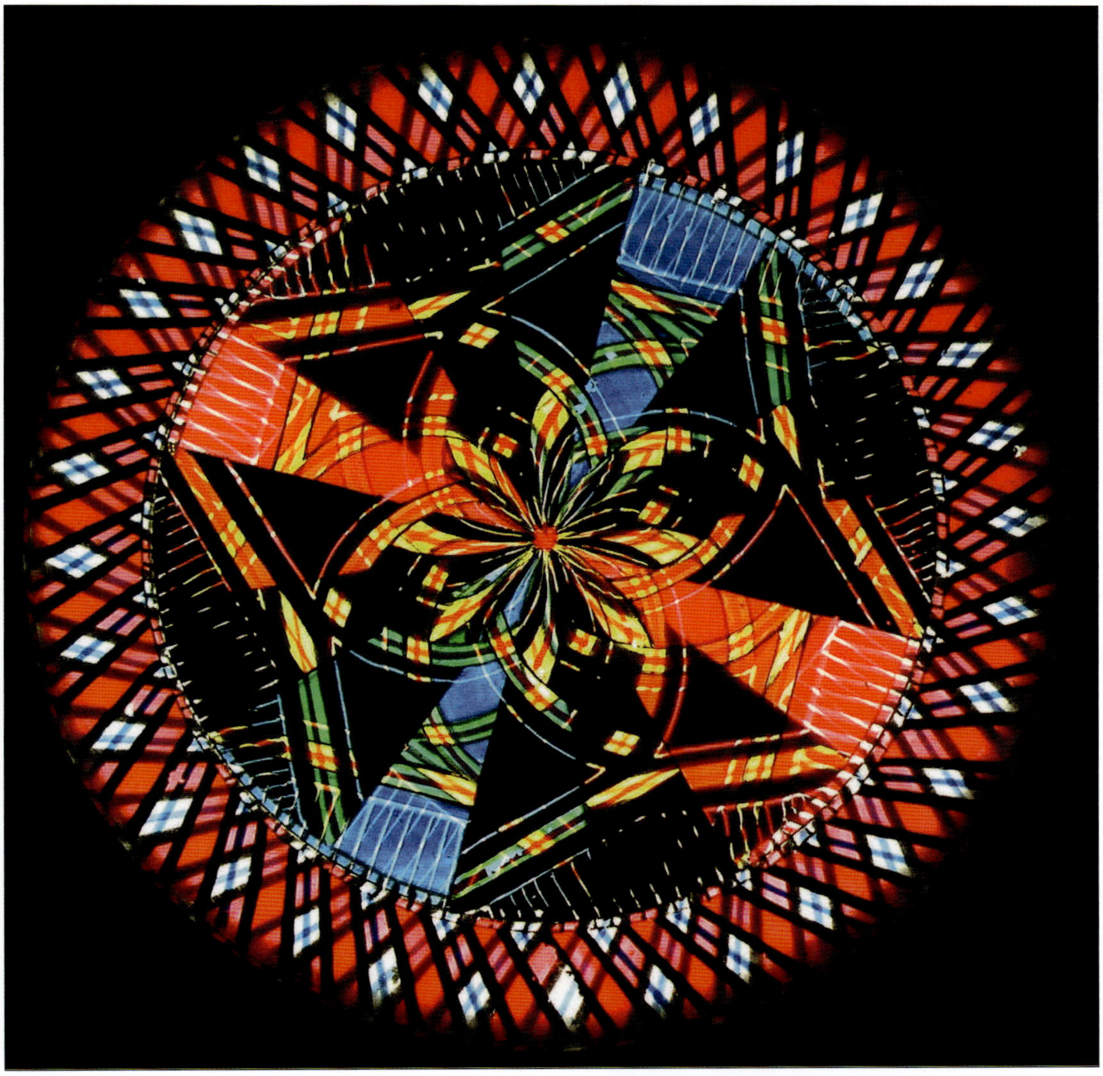

Fig. 4.39 Grandfather Carter's chromatrope, or rackwork slide. Two pieces of patterned glass revolve across each other to produce brilliant flashing patterns.

Other Special Effects

Henry Childe, who helped create the dissolving concept that Beale used so effectively, is often credited with creating another mechanical slide, the ***chromatrope***, or "color-throwing" slide. Chromatropes produced spectacular kaleidoscopic images by means of two geometrically painted glass plates that rotated over each other. By varying the patterns and the colors, a wonderful range of effects could be achieved,

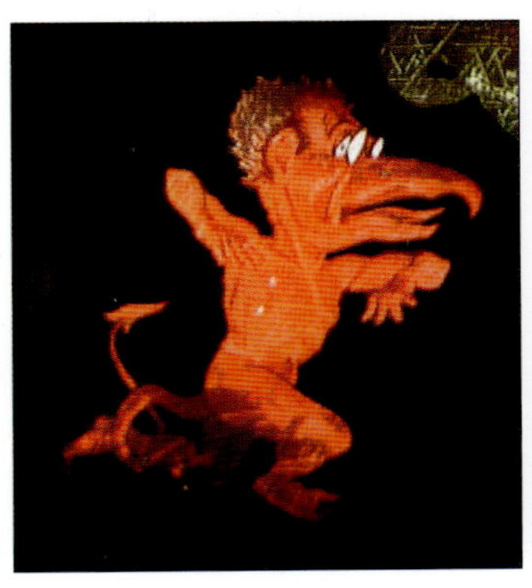

Fig. 4.40 (left) One of a series of monsters in Beale's revolving slide 2 for *Knights of Pythias, Third Rank, Pythagoras.* At right, the base slide of the set.

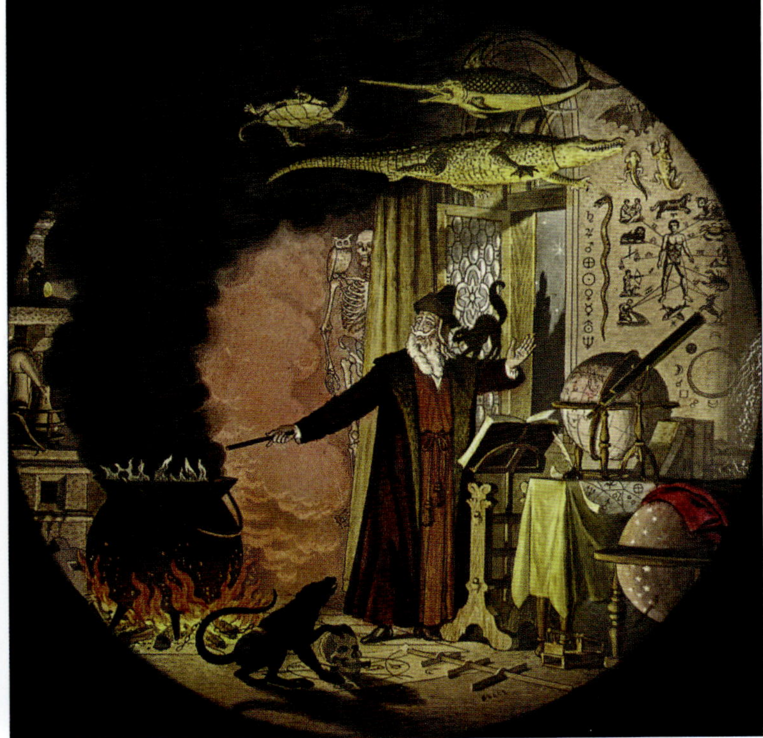

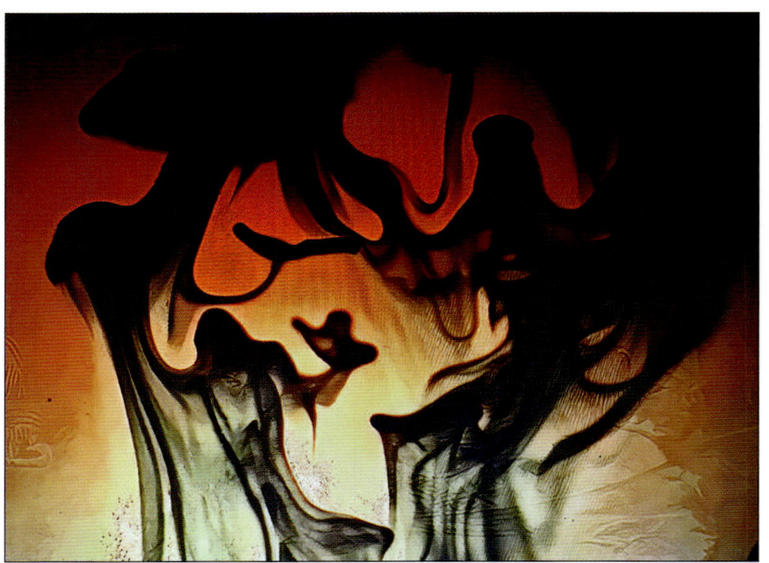

Fig. 4.41 "Ghosts" in a tank slide. The ghosts, created by black dye dropped in a small tank inserted in the lantern's slide chamber, swirl around Minnehaha in our production of *Hiawatha*.

especially if one chromatrope were dissolved into another (Fig. 4.39).[38]

(My first public show, some 40 years ago now, was for a local historical society. I used a chromatrope as the finale, a traditional practice. Just before the chromatrope faded, an old lady's voice was clearly audible: "If that's what you see when you smoke marijuana, I'm trying some"!)

Slides with a similar revolving "rackwork" mechanism can cause a windmill to spin its vanes, a waterwheel to turn, fire to pour from Mt. Vesuvius, or the planets to circle the sun. One of the secrets to performing with this type of slide is to control the onset and the speed of the motion.

We use a rackwork slide set of two images by Beale in our *Halloween Show*. One of the slides shows the magician at his cauldron. The second slide is a rackwork slide showing a series of devils, which are moved with a crank and *superimposed* over the magician's scene (Fig. 4.40). When the audience, egged on by me, tries to call the devils forth with Shakespeare's incantation, "Double, double, toil and trouble/ Fire burn and cauldron bubble", the devils at first refuse to appear. Then, when the audience chants with louder conviction, the devils emerge in *slow motion*. Even greater conviction will shift them into *fast motion*, and the devils pour forth in a shrieking blur. As with the movies, slow and fast motion can be used for dramatic and comic effect, but unlike the movies, the motion can respond to the tempo of the audience itself.

A variety of other lantern "effects" developed over the course of the century. ***Rain*** or ***snow*** *slides*, using cloth on a roller, could create a rain or snow effect. ***Negative images*** (glass negatives) were sometimes projected for their ghostly allure, and to give a 3-D effect. And hollow ***tank slides*** held liquids that could be used for science demonstrations, and in a variety of other fashions, as could ***cage slides*** that held live bugs.

Like the Ratcatcher, the tank slide is so dramatic that it makes its way into almost all our shows. For our *New Year's Show*, it is the "Magic lantern Crystal Ball", swirling with colors that create foreboding shapes to foretell the future, or create ghosts (Fig. 4.41). (The colors are created by food color dropped in the top of the tank.) For the *Patriotic Show* we use only red dye, the blood of the Civil War.

The Sad Tale of Two Lantern Stars

I can't resist telling you a story about two triops that performed in our tank slide, a hollow slide with water in it. They were "Wax" and "Wayne", the "performing bugs" of our Halloween Show.

These little half-inch shrimp-like fellows traveled with us in a thermos to prevent them from freezing, and created something of a security stir at airports. No security officer would believe our story of what was in the container, but none was willing to stick his finger down into the murky water to find out if our smallest cast members were indeed alive.

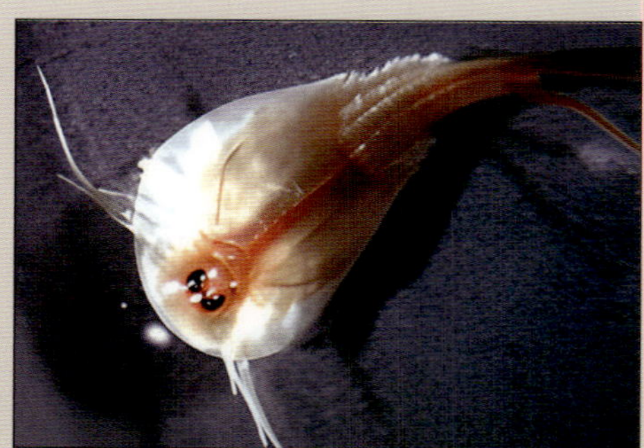

Fig. 4.42 Lantern Show Star Sau-cy.

Given the success of Wax and Wayne on screen, the next year I raised another set of triops, which I named See and Saw. They performed well, so after the Halloween tour season, I took them along to meet the family at Thanksgiving.

Unfortunately, Saw, the biggest, ate See for Thanksgiving dinner, right in front of my grandchildren.

We gave Saw a new name after that: "Sau-cy".

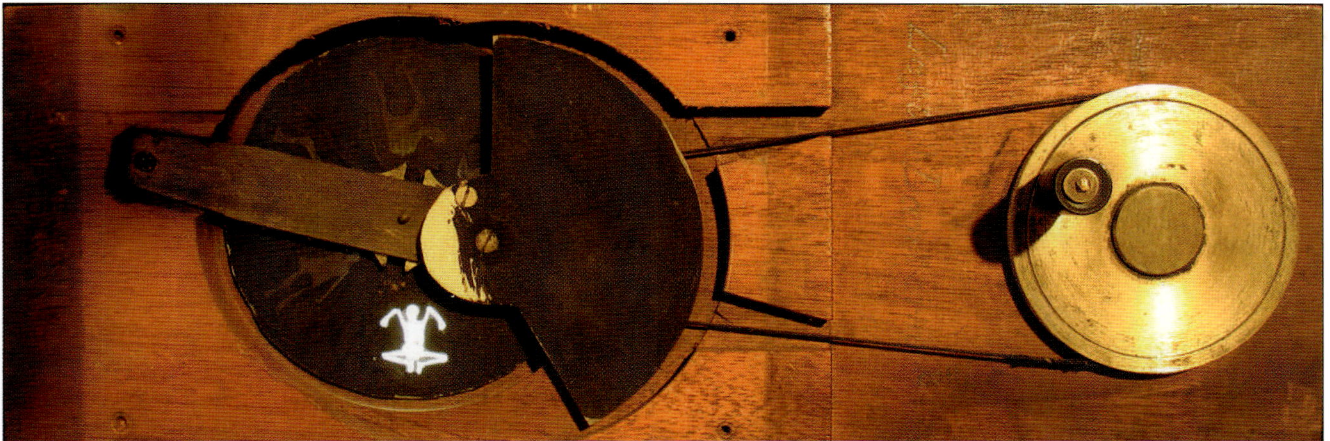

Fig. 4.43
A choreutoscope, with cover removed. A revolving wheel of different images made the skeleton dance, while an intermittent black shutter kept the images from becoming a blur.

And for *Halloween*, we sometimes use a early technique that I remember as a child reading about in Frank Baum's *The Marvelous Land of Oz*. We insert live bugs (three-eyed "Triops") into the tank (Fig. 4.42). The bugs appear on screen as giant moving creatures, just as they did in Oz when Mr. H. M. (for Highly Magnified) Woggle-Bug, climbed off the sheet to join the Oz adventures.[39] (We'll hear how one master showman, Henry Morton, "milked" this slide shortly.)

In the community of cinema scholars these days, a definite trend resists the old concept that today's movies "evolved" from earlier technology. In most respects I support this trend; certainly those early "pre-cinema pioneers" (including Beale) did not know they were headed to Hollywood. But some "film techniques" do seem to have come more or less directly from magic lantern experience. As cinema scholar Lipton says,

> There is every reason to believe that the motion picture directors of the celluloid cinemas earliest days were exposed to magic lantern-created effects like fades, dissolves and pans. The attribution of such effects to cinema pioneers probably constitutes giving credit for techniques that were invented many decades or centuries before the celluloid cinema.[40]

(Charles Musser, for instance, points out in *Before the Nickelodeon* how the early film maker Edwin Porter used dissolves and pans in *Pan American Exposition by Night*.[41] To Lipton's list of effects could be added several he cites elsewhere – *wipes*, *zooms*, and *animation* – and I would add *close ups*. Aside from these, many of the "cinematic techniques" that Beale used may have been picked up by early cinema practitioners from Beale's magic lantern art, or from that of others, but there is no direct evidence for this. They could just have easily been adopted from the fine arts, illustration and the stage.

Moving Images on Screen

From the 1820s on the lantern industry tried out many ways to create motion on screen. They weren't searching for the "movies", but for motion that was more dependable and adaptable than wiggling bugs; motion more subtle and continuous than slip and mechanical slides; motion more realistic than the moving patterns of the chromatrope. Some of these efforts were in the form of toys and scientific experiments not directly related to the lantern, like the phenakistiscope and the zoetrope. But many used the projecting lantern itself. Some employed unique magic lantern forms of creating screen motion, and some used techniques that would eventually appear in movie machines.

Filmed movies are just like lantern shows in that they are created with a series of still pictures. But in a movie shot, each picture is the same size, each evenly separated from the others, each slightly different from the others, each following another in rapid succession. What made possible the movie's greater subtlety and duration of motion was film, a flexible medium that could rotate through the projector and show the pictures at 24 frames a second, or higher. The phenomenon that makes us perceive movie motion has traditionally been called "persistence of vision", but no after-image persists in the retina. Rather, the brain is not able to distinguish between real motion and apparent motion if the images are similar and changing fast enough. But if the pictures are running in front of the projector lens, why don't we see half-frames on screen, making the pictures a confusing blur?

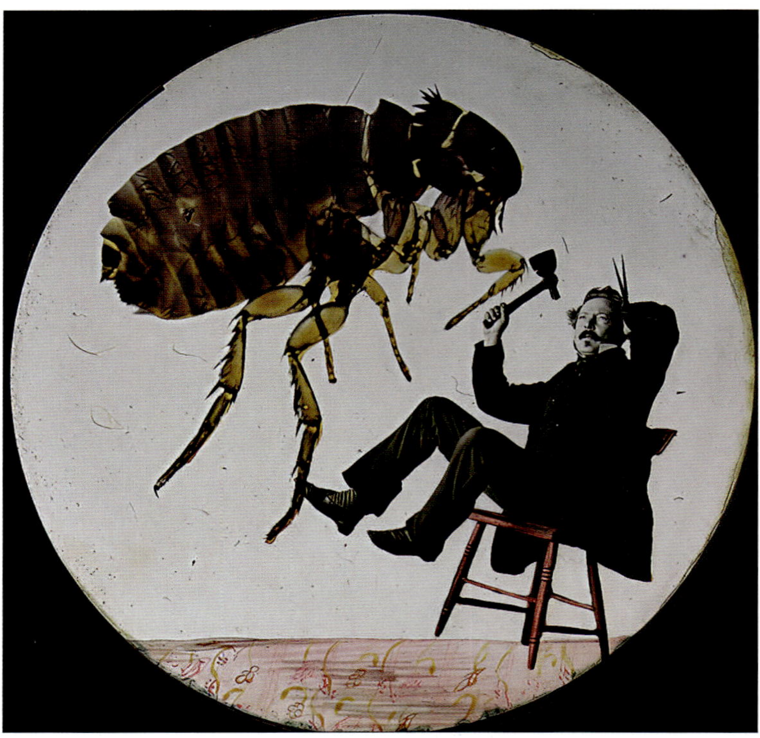

Fig. 4.44 A very early glass photographic slide created by the Langenheim brothers. The Langenheims enjoyed playing around with their new medium.

Fig. 4.45 Photographic lantern slide of a woman surrounded by spirit images.

The answer is that the film is moved by an intermittent drive that stops each image for a fraction of a second in front of the lens. We see it in that position and not when it is moving because an intermittent shutter cuts off the projected light when the film is moving – thus the flicker that led to movies being called "the flicks". What we see on screen is a rapid series of discrete still pictures that the brain interprets as continuous motion.[42]

(This whole subject of how we see the movie's illusion of motion as "real" is still a matter of debate, and the shutter is not necessary for all screen motion. For instance on YouTube you can see how in the 1870s the French pioneer, Émile Reynaud, created a kind of fairly rapid "stop action" screen motion by using a system of rotating mirrors to stabilize the images. And today, if you photograph your running dog with your phone's video camera you will see a moving image on your screen, even without a shutter. The pixels are being replaced so rapidly that your brain "sees" motion.)

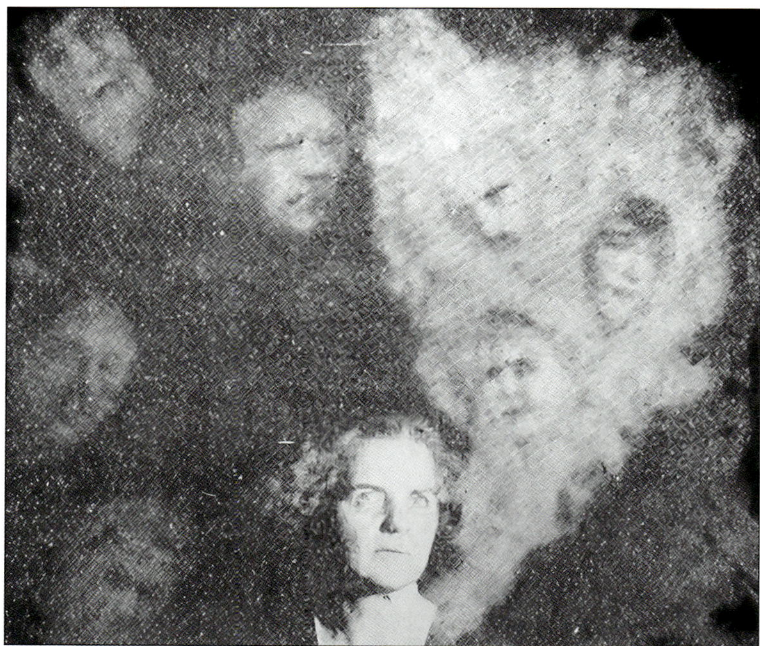

Before the invention of celluloid cinema, a variety of lantern devices experimented with motion, usually by modifying a lantern to insert wheels of images and shutters, or by creating a similar configuration within the slide itself. In 1869, Thomas Ross of England invented the "Wheel of Life" – a self-contained lantern slide that could make a group of skeletons dance, but the constantly revolving shutter made the image indistinct on screen.[43] About the same time L. S. Beale (no relation to J. B. Beale) produced a moving similar slide called a Choreutoscope that used intermittent motion of a panorama slide, producing a single skeleton image that moved more smoothly and was brighter. (The C. W. Briggs Co. developed a circular variant of the choreutoscope, called *The Dancing Skeleton* in 1874.) Choreutoscopes were widely available by the end of the century. They created true "mini-movies" on screen, but the "movie" was very mini indeed, and their complexity made them an expensive novelty (Fig. 4.43).[44]

The First Photographic Images on Screen

Another important step toward what would turn out to be the movies was photography, especially photography on a transparent medium that could be used for projection. The Langenheim brothers of Philadelphia were responsible for developing the first photographs on glass slides about 1848 (Fig. 4.44). They presented their new slides at the 1851 Crystal Palace Exhibition in London, and made extravagant claims for them:

> The new magic lantern pictures on glass ... must throw the old-style magic lantern slides into the shade and supersede them at once, on account of the greater accuracy of the smallest details which are drawn and fixed on the glass from nature ... with a fidelity that is truly astonishing.[45]

The claims of the Langenheims turned out to be true. Photographic views, especially of foreign countries, became extremely popular. In an age when few people could travel, photography showed foreign lands the way they "really were", and the public was fascinated. Professionally-made travel slides were common. Amateur slides were even more so, because of an important photographic development in the 1880s. The new "dry plate" photography did not require the use of wet chemicals while taking photographs, though chemicals were still used in the developing process. The dry plate process made it much easier for amateurs to take their own photos, and hence to make their own slides, and give their own shows – though such shows suffered from the *aleatory* or hit-and-miss nature of some of their photography. The heightened sense of reality depicted by photographic slides – both professional and amateur – led many lanternists to feel a "decided prejudice [against] the hand-painted slides". Photography, and hence "photographic realism" ruled; Beale's illustrated realism was a niche, albeit a significant one, in the overall market.[46]

In addition to its role in representing reality, photography could also be used to distort reality, and to create special effects. In our *Halloween Show*, we use a series of ***spirit photographic slides*** that were supposed to show the spirits of the dead hovering around the head of a living loved ones (Fig. 4.45). Many people believed they were seeing genuine photos of the dearly departed, projected on screen. The effect was created, of course, through a *process shot* or *double exposure*, the same technique that is used to create similar "ghost" effects in today's movies.

Photography was also a key element of the success of Beale's slides, since it meant that his single master design could be easily copied onto hundreds of identical slides. Photographic slide reproduction provided a standardized level of quality that was impossible before its invention, and in this sense, was similar to the movies – which depended on photography not only to create the image on the film, but also to reproduce standardized copies for mass distribution.

A Friendly Projector

In the late 1860's, two other things combined with the newly available photographic slides to create rapid growth in magic lantern use. First, kerosene from the Pennsylvania oil fields became plentifully available. It was an inexpensive and easily managed fuel that could give a light that was bright enough for a lantern show for 25 to 50 people.

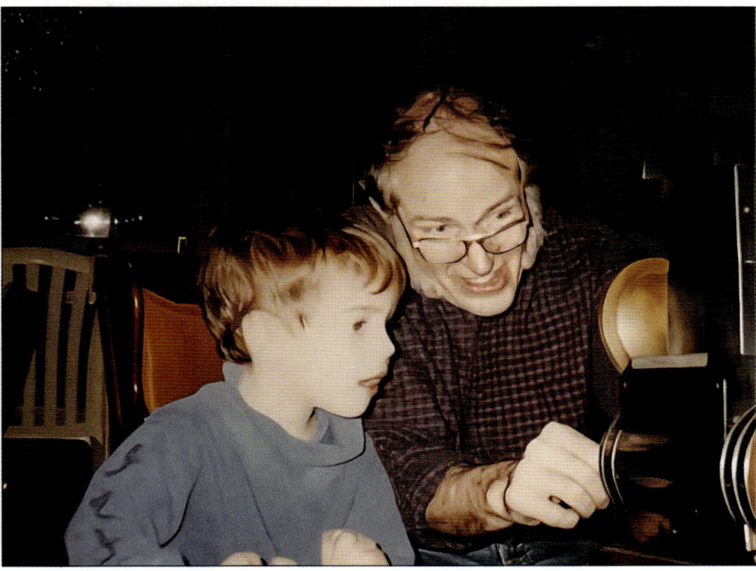

Fig. 4.46 My grandson Eric stares in wonder as I light the kerosene lamp of Great Grandfather's Marcy Sciopticon for a family show about 1992.

Second, in 1868–69, the American Lorenzo Marcy invented and perfected a new kind of

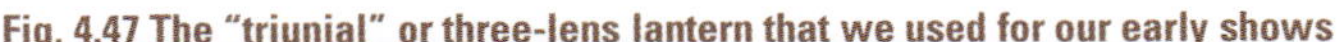

Fig. 4.47 The "triunial" or three-lens lantern that we used for our early shows

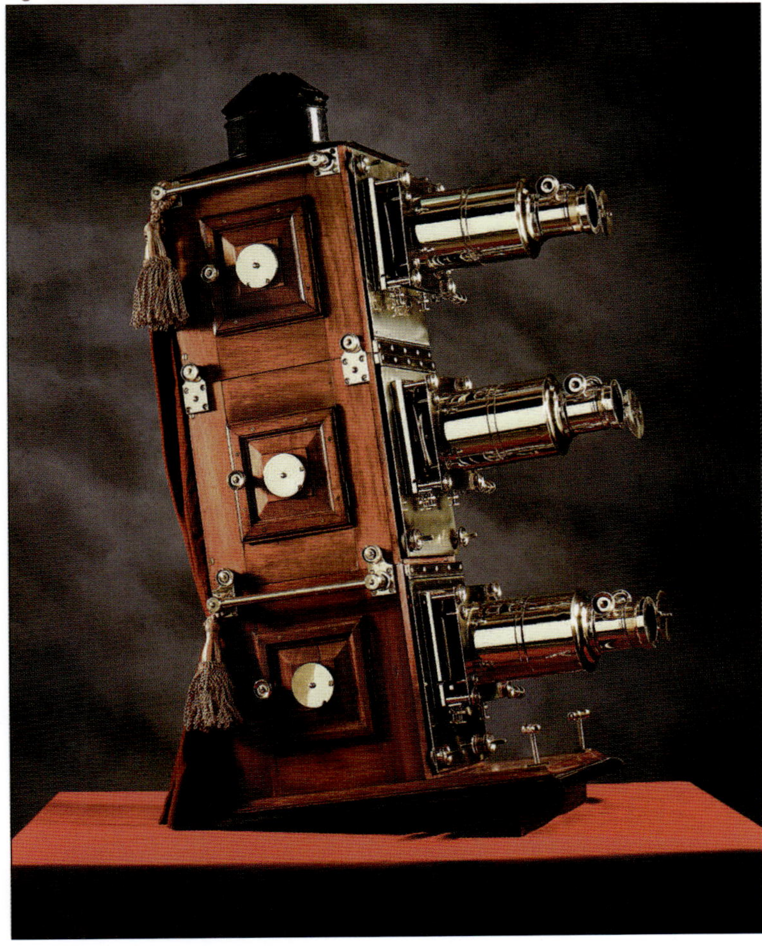

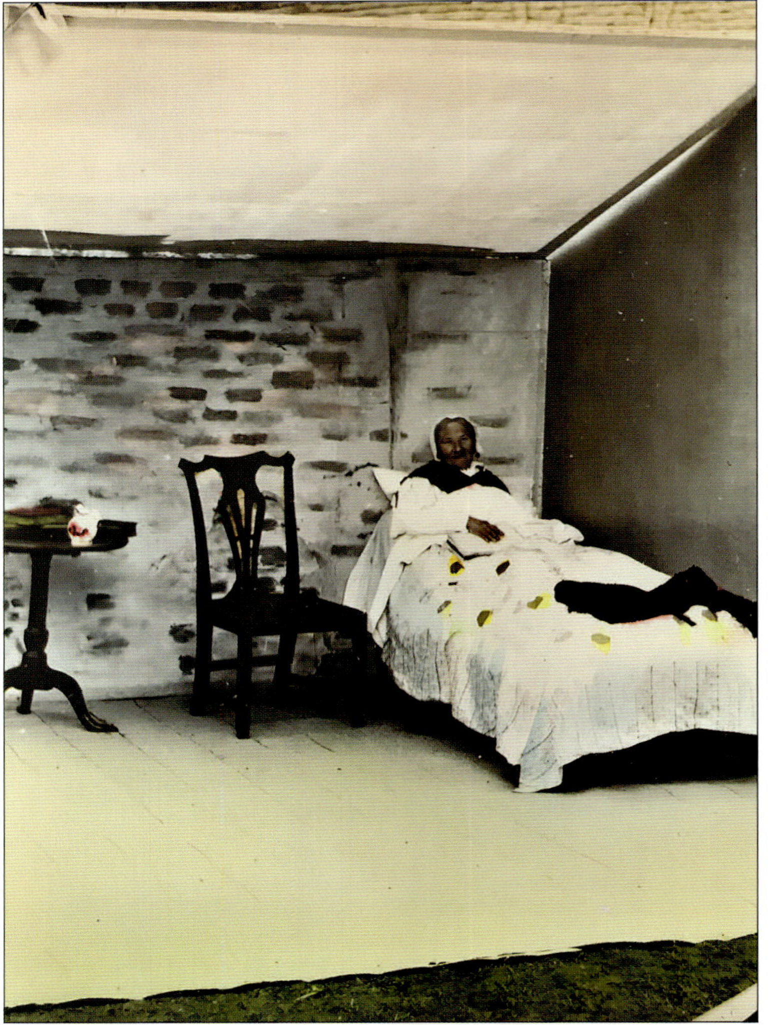

Fig. 4.48 "Life model" slide from the British *Old Rose* set. Life model slides like this were often photographed outdoors, in front of a painted set.

lantern called the "Marcy Sciopticon" that was especially made for the new fuel.[47] The ***Sciopticon*** lantern was a friendly little machine, with a compact and novel construction (Fig. 4.46). The combination of ease-of-use and a safer, brighter light made it an immediate success. The Marcy lantern became the model for many other manufacturers, and opened up a much larger market among schools, churches and families. This expanding market set the stage for the mass production of slides that made Beale's images so ubiquitous in the 1890s.

Great Grandfather Carter's lantern was a Marcy Sciopticon, and so it was this elegant little projector that gave me my first sense of the "magic" of the magic lantern. I still use this lantern in the summer to put on shows for family and friends at a camp without electricity in the Adirondacks. These shows serve to remind me of things I learned about kerosene lanterns from elderly people at our public shows back in the 1980s. They often recalled two things about their own family's magic lantern shows when they were children in the 1920s – the smell and the light. Kerosene lanterns like the Marcy Sciopticon work best when the wicks aren't turned up too high, and hence don't smoke too much. But the lure of getting a brighter image is irresistible, the wick gets pushed up a little, and then a little more. Pretty soon the lantern looks like the Little Engine That Could, puffing merrily away, with the smoke pouring from its tall chimney. The smoke adds to the sense of magic lantern mystery, and the smell of burning kerosene prints itself indelibly on the olfactory memory of the young – a fact mentioned by many who remembered such shows from their childhood.

The light given by these kerosene lanterns is striking too – very different from the clear steady white light of limelight, or of a modern projector. The kerosene burns quite yellow, giving a golden cast to all the pictures, a wonderful antique glow. And, since the flames flicker, so does the image on the screen, making every picture seem alive, mysterious.

While Marcy was making the lantern simpler for fathers and grandfathers to use in delighting the young, others were making it more complex and able to produce spectacular effects for larger audiences. By the 1870s the double lantern, or ***biunial*** had grown to the ***triunial*** or "triple" – a spectacular three-lantern combination of brass and mahogany that could handle dissolves and special effect slides simultaneously (Fig. 4.47). The massive gleaming presence of the triunial gave magic lantern shows a new splendor and dignity, especially when combined with the power of limelight. However, few show people performed with them, and their popularity did not last. I used to employ a triunial, but like my Victorian counterparts, I found that it is just too big and cumbersome to manage on the road. In our shows we now use a biunial, which can produce 95% of the cinematic effects of the triunial with a third less hassle.[48]

Photographing Live Actors for the Screen

In England the new lanterns were used to show the ***life model*** slides that were becoming popular in the 1880s. By photographing live models in front of painted backdrops, British lantern firms such as Bamforth & Co. gave a new illusion of reality to popular story sets and temperance moral tales.[49] These companies were the direct forerunner of the movie *studios*, and indeed several of the British life-model firms such a Bamforth, and Riley Brothers went into film production after the movie camera was invented. The painted backdrops of the life-model studios were often reused in different stories, a kind of production *back lot*. Often the execution was slap-dash, as in the slide depicted in Fig. 4.48, where grass and another flat can be seen in the foreground. Bamforth once claimed to have created an entire 12-slide set of *Excelsior* in a single day. His slide sets were the equivalent of *B-films*, mostly based on scripts of little or no literary merit, stilted action, and *shallow space* staging in a limited area. British users complained that these slides were "perfectly absurd", with the likelihood of obtaining good slides "greatly a matter of chance".[50] Nonetheless, a big market existed. By 1905, Bamforth and Co. claimed to have an inventory of more than two million slides on hand, and to be the "largest producer in the world". Though one might want to take these claims with a dash of salt, Bamforth and another competitor, York and Son, together produced about 850 different sets, totaling 12,750 images.[51]

Interestingly, though both Bamforth and Riley Brothers had American offices, and life model slides were regularly offered in McAllister's catalog and others, these English life-model story sets never really caught on in America until the song slides were developed after the birth of the movies. Perhaps this was because the photographed stories were so clearly "English" in their furnishings and clothing, and hence were rejected as "foreign" by the very working-class audiences they were designed to reach. Or perhaps it was because Briggs and Beale were already dominating the American market with their dramatic illustrated versions of stories and poems, leaving little desire for rather lifeless "life models".

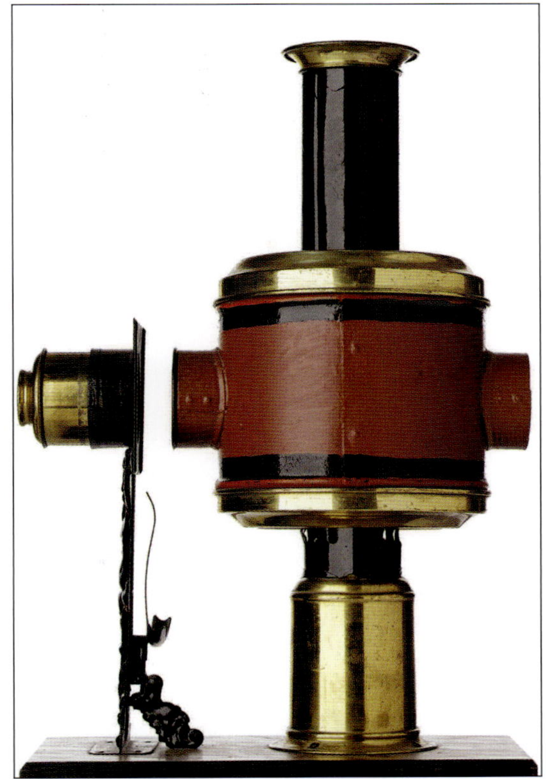

Fig. 4.49 A German toy magic lantern. The Germans dominated the toy-lantern trade in America.

Lanterns for Children

Children were one of the target audiences for life-model slides, as well as some of the sets developed by Briggs. The obvious popularity of magic lantern shows with children led to the development of toy magic lanterns, first, it would appear, about 1800 in the German toy center of Nuremberg (Fig. 4.49).[52] By the late nineteenth century, the industry had grown into

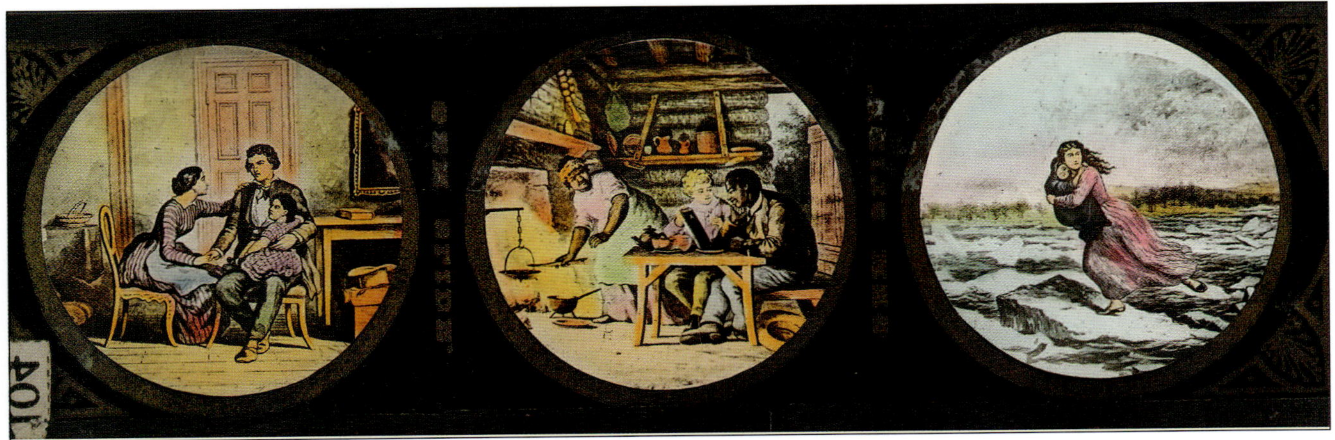

Fig. 4.50 A children's Gem Slide for Beale's *Uncle Tom's Cabin*, made by Briggs. Almost all Gems were black and white, unlike this example.

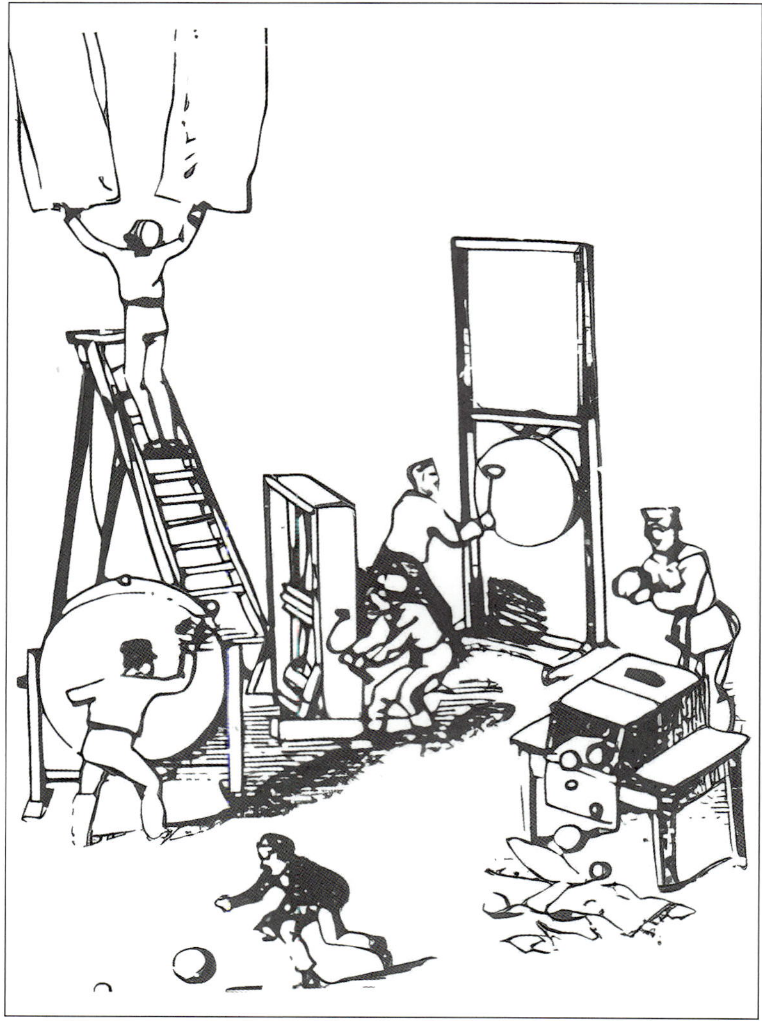

Fig. 4.51 Foley artists, or sound effects men, working at the "Poly." Effects shown are a thunder sheet, drum, giant clacker, gong, rolling cannon balls, tambourine, and clutter box. ©University of Westminster Archive.

a half-dozen competing firms of substantial size. In 1894, for instance, the Ernst Plank firm alone was manufacturing 150,000 lanterns a year. The German lanterns were often sold in boxed sets consisting of a lantern, half-a-dozen small slides, and a few tickets for the children to use for admitting their adoring relatives. They could project a picture a foot or so in diameter, enough for family viewing.

In France about 1848, a tinsmith named Auguste Lapierre made a toy lantern for his own children, and seeing their enthusiasm, set about manufacturing them. The Lapierre firm continued until 1908, shipping lanterns all over the world. Many French lanterns were much more elaborate than their German counterparts, with exotic patterns stamped in tin or brass, and then painted in brilliant colors. Several were in unique and elaborate shapes, such as a Chinese Buddha or the Eiffel tower – both now highly collectible. The French slides themselves, however, took a *minimalist* approach, often using delicate outline drawings with nominal color.

Americans made several attempts to develop a competitive product. The "Youth's Companion" lantern, and the "Gem" and "Home" lanterns were sold by McAllister, by Sears Roebuck, and by a number of other lantern distributors. Beginning in 1886, a total of 85 Beale slides were adapted to the Gem slide format, usually three pictures to each 2½ inch x 8" slide (Fig. 4.50). These were not, as might be expected, a continuation of the children's stories that had formed the early Gem repertoire, but primarily adult Literature, History, Religion, Temperance, and Spanish American War subjects, usually in black and white. Again, judging by eBay, the American children's lanterns and the Gem slides, never caught up with the German exports in popularity, though they are by no means rare, and *Uncle Tom's Cabin* is quite common.

I trust that it is clear now that the magic lantern show, whether a child's or a showman's, could have a profound effect on those who watched. A children's lantern had such an effect on the early imagination of one of the 20th century's most important film directors, Ingmar Bergman. Bergman, who called his print autobiography *The Magic Lantern*, celebrated its influence on him in a heavily autobiographical movie called *Fanny and Alexander*. In it, a young Bergman-like character discovers the mystery of his own creativity as he plays with his lantern alone at night. If you'd like to see a modern film director's homage to magic lantern art, find the video, and let your imagination soar with Bergman's as the magic lantern brings the fantasies of his youth to life.

The Royal Culmination

Just as children's lanterns extended their range and influence during the 19th century, so did the adult lantern. By the 1840's the magic lantern had reached an advanced enough stage of technological development to be used for a range of different shows. One of the most elaborate was that at the Royal Polytechnic Institution in London. The Polytechnic, the equivalent to our modern science museum and IMAX Theater, gave extraordinary productions that dazzled two generations, from about 1841 to about 1881. The shows often used as many as six giant lanterns. The glass slides were oversized, often 8½ x 6½", sometimes almost two feet long. They projected an image of incredible detail in an image about 33 feet by 27 feet. The slides

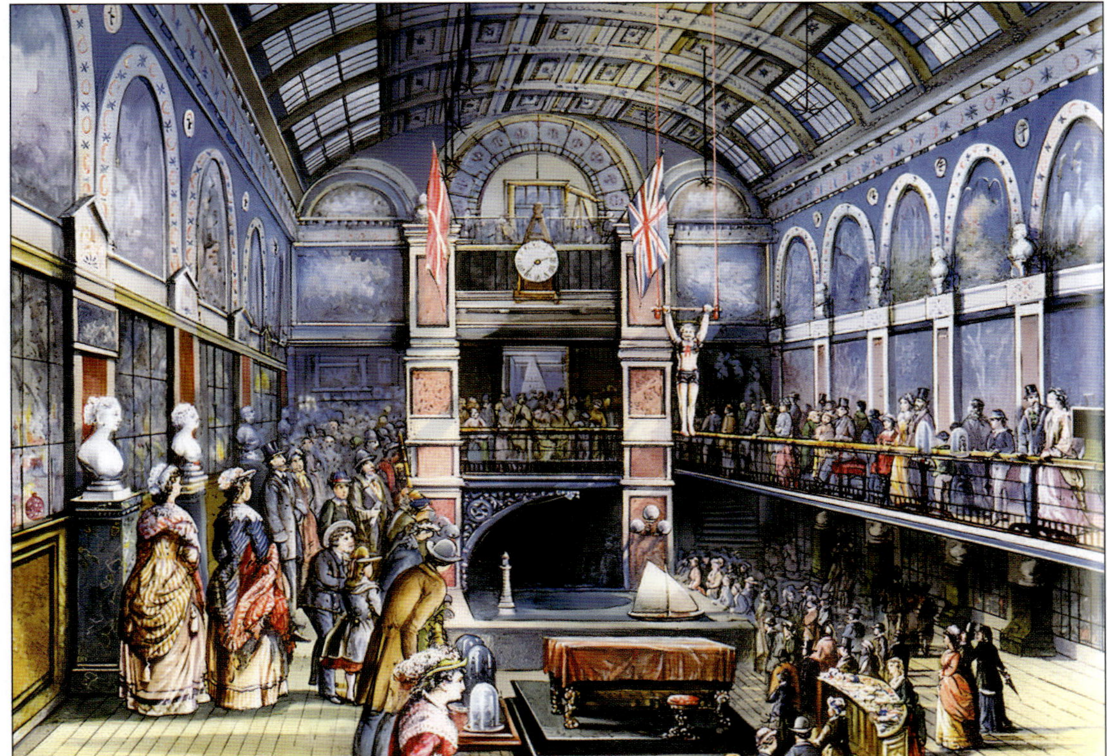

Fig. 4.52 Lantern slide of The Great Hall of The Royal Polytechnic in London. The "Poly" combined exhibits of all kinds, like our science museums, combined with a magic lantern theater.
Cropped image.

were painted for the "Poly" by Henry Childe and W. R. Hill. Childe's dissolving views and complex special effects were an important part of the shows' popularity. The program was changed regularly and included battles, fairy tales such as *Aladdin's Lamp*, and Christmas specials. An elaborate sound effects department of *foley artists* was behind the screen, producing *synchronous sound* to heighten the drama of the action (Fig. 4.51).[53]

In one sense the Polytechnic was the culmination of the magic lantern art of its time – the slides were dazzling and the theater remained the only venue where magic lantern shows were a main and the continuing attraction (Fig. 4.52). But Child's slides and shows were one-of-a-kind. And in this sense, the Polytechnic was atypical of the mass medium that the lantern was becoming, and of the mass media of film and TV that grew from it. What made the lantern a force to be reckoned with was not the singular spectacle in London. It was the thousands of shows, of every possible variety, put on by amateurs and professionals all over the world.

Americans shared this world-wide fascination with lantern shows. The shows proliferated in American theaters, churches, fraternal lodges, asylums, schools, and homes. As we will see shortly, a national lantern culture developed, featuring shows on every conceivable topic, presented by famous showmen and by amateurs, in venues big and small. In the midst of all this activity emerged Beale's employer, the visionary C. W. Briggs.

Chapter Five

The Magic Lantern Sweeps America

Fig. 5.17 An image of Yellowstone Falls, taken by Burton Holmes and used by him as the finale for his illustrated lecture on Yellowstone Park. The coloring of this slide is by his colorist, Katherine Gordon Breed. Discussed on p. 116.

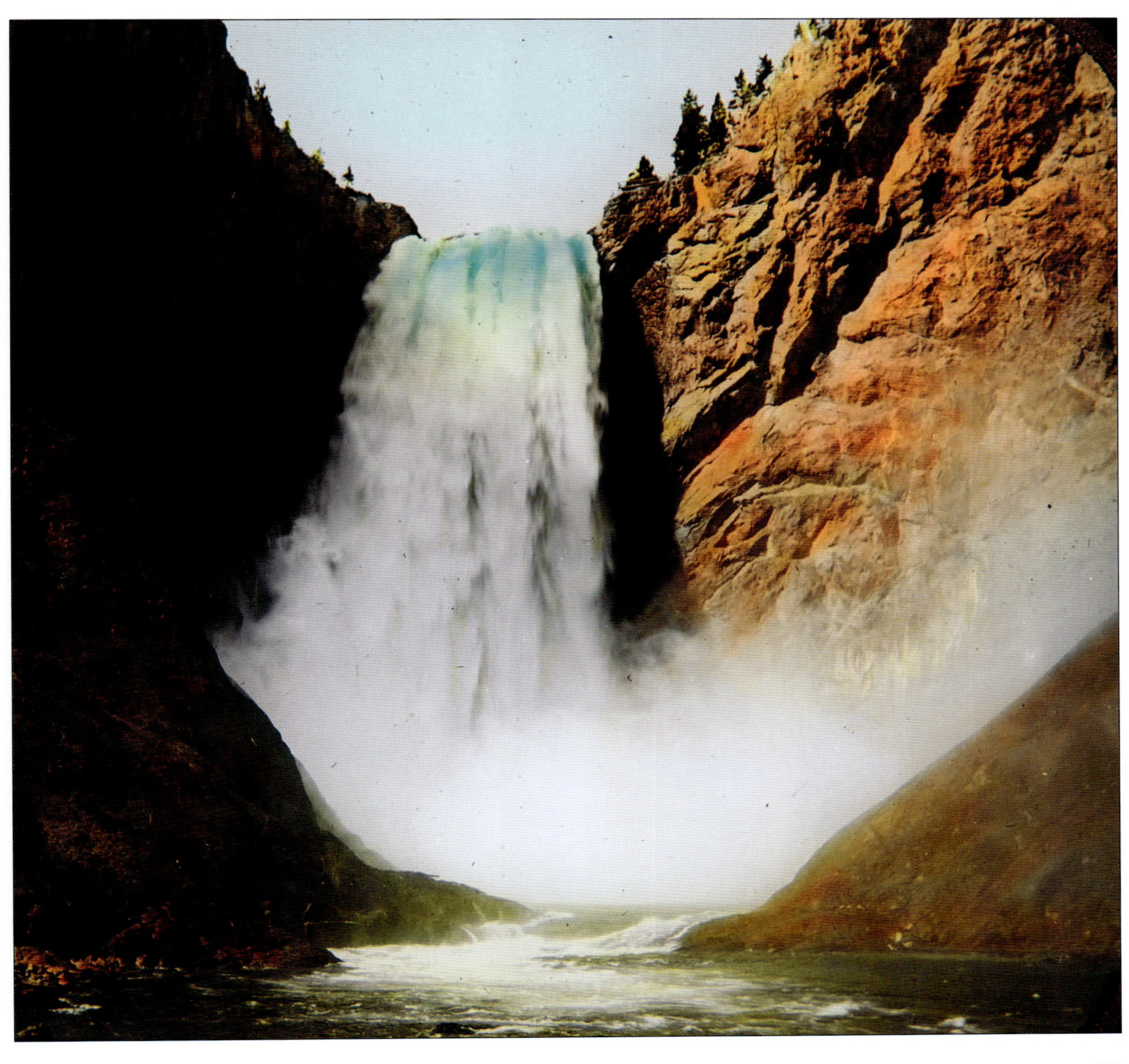

We have already seen how Beale himself, in just two years of his youth, 1863–64, went to *five* different magic lantern shows, including the new "stereopticon" show. His frequent attendance was on the leading edge of massive national interest. A short decade later, the magic lantern was sweeping the country. It is hard to overstate how pervasive the magic lantern became in America from the 1870s to the 1910s.

An Overview

Twenty years ago, I published a very rough estimate that in the 1890s, 30,000 to 60,000 lantern performers were giving 75,000 to 150,000 public performances a year. If we assume 100 people at a performance, then a total yearly audience of 7,500,000 to 15,000,000 people a year were watching lantern shows in America.[1] I was guestimating from a very small sample of public performances, excluding church, fraternal, college and school use. Today I think that original projection of public performances may have been overstated, but if church, fraternal, college, and school use are included, I think figures of that size are conservative. As one lantern scholar has said, endorsing that early estimate, "Any cursory survey of the literature and documentation surrounding the medium would support figures of this magnitude".[2]

What kind of documentation was this scholar thinking of? Consider a few facts: In the 1890s more than 300 lantern slide companies were operating in the United States, 112 of which offered Beale's slides. The top 15 of these companies, like T. H. McAllister and McIntosh Stereopticon, had catalogs of about 250 pages, each containing some 20,000 different slides for sale or rent (Fig. 5.1).[3] (At one point the McAllister company bragged that it had 150,000 different slides in stock, though he probably meant slide copies.)[4] The Taylor and Huntington Co. once sent out to Civil War veterans 100,000 copies of a flyer advertising slides and promotional materials for them to use in giving Civil War shows.[5]

Who was using all these slides?[6] A half-dozen superstar showmen come immediately to mind – you'll meet several shortly – but they used their own unique slides, not mass-produced ones. About 500 professionals might also be possibilities[7] – you'll meet a number of them too – but many of these also used their own slides. The vast market for the slides in the catalogs consisted of family showmen like Great Grandfather Carter, small-time amateur show people, pastors, secret society operators, college professors, and schoolteachers. While the professionals might reach 1,000 at a show, the amateurs might be lucky to draw 100 – or even 10. But thousands of them were in the field, tens of thousands. Together they became the major customers of the lantern industry. Every popular consumer magazine carried advertisements touting the money that could be made as a magic lanternist, or promoting the lantern's entertainment and educational value (Fig. 5.2). Enterprising Americans responded. Cumulatively, those small-time show people surely reached an audience of millions.

Fig. 5.1 Page from the "Economic Catalog" section of the T. H. McAllister Catalog. It lists each slide for various stories. Beale illustrated nine of the ten stories on this page.

McAllister, Manufacturing Optician, New York.

The Wreck of the Hesperus.

(With Poem by Longfellow.)

1. It was the schooner Hesperus.
2. Blue were her eyes as the fairy flax.
3. The skipper, he stood beside the helm.
4. Then up and spoke an old sailor.
5. Last night the moon had a golden ring.
6. The snow fell hissing in the brine.
7. He wrapt her in his seaman's coat.
8. And bound her to the mast.
9. Like a sheeted ghost the vessel swept.
10. A fisherman stood aghast.

Maud Muller.

(With Poem by Whittier.)

1. Maud Muller on a Summer's day,
   Raked the meadow sweet with hay.
2. And blushed as she gave it, looking down,
   On her feet so bare, and her tattered gown.
3. The Judge looked back as he climbed the hill,
   And saw Maud Muller standing still.
4. Oft when the wine in his glass was red,
   He longed for the wayside well instead.
5. She wedded a man unlearned and poor,
   And many children played around her door.
6. Alas for the maiden, alas for the Judge,
   The rich repiner and household drudge.

The Courtin'.

(With Poem by James Russell Lowell.)

1. Zekle crep' up quite unbeknown,
   An' peeked in thru' the winder.
2. An' there sot Huldy all alone,
   'ith no one nigh to hender.
3. She thought no v'ice had such a swing
   Ez his'n in the choir.
4. He stood a spell on one foot first,
   Then stood a spell on t'other.
5. That last word pricked him like a pin,
   An'——wal, he up and kist her.
6. Tell mother see how matters stood,
   An' gin 'em both her blessin'

Curfew Shall Not Ring To-night.

(With Poem by Rose Hartwick Thorpe.)

1. He with bowed head, sad and thoughtful, she with lips all cold and white.
2. "I've a lover in that prison"
3. "Bessie," calmly spoke the sexton.
4. She had listened while the Judges read.
5. She with quick steps bounded forward.
6. She has reached the topmost ladder.
7. Out she swung, far out, the city seemed a speck of light below.
8. Firmly on the dark old ladder.
9. At his feet she tells her story.
10. Kneeling on the turf beside him.

Old Kentucky Home.

1. "The sun shines bright in the old Kentucky home."
2. *Chorus*—"Weep no more my lady."
3. "They sing no more by the glimmer of the moon."
4. "The time have come when darkies have to part."
5. "A few more days and the trouble all will end."
6. "A few more days till we todder on the road."

A Leap for Life.

(With Poem.)

1. "Old ironsides at anchor lay."
2. "There stood the boy with dizzy brain."
3. "A rifle grasped
   And aimed it at his son."
4. "That only chance your life can save;
   Jump, jump, boy!"
5. "He sank—he rose—he lived—he moved—."
6. "His father drew in silent joy
   Those wet arms around his neck."

Faust.

1. Faust in his Study.
2. Vision of Marguerite.
3. Marguerite at the Church.
4. Faust and Mephistopheles Visit the Garden.
5. Faust and Marguerite in the Garden.
6. Marguerite Spinning.
7. Marguerite Sorrowing.
8. Death of Valentine.
9. Marguerite Going to Prison.
10. Marguerite in Prison.

Abide With Me.

1. Abide with me, fast falls the eventide.
2. When other helpers fail, and comforts flee.
3. Swift to its close ebbs out life's little day.
4. Change and decay in all around I see.
5. I need Thy presence every passing hour.
6. Who, like Thyself, my guide and stay can be?
7. I fear no foe, with Thee at hand to bless.
8. Where is death's sting? where, grave, thy victory?
9. Hold Thou Thy cross before my closing eyes.
10. Heaven's morning breaks, and earth's vain shadows flee.

From Greenland's Icy Mountains.

1. From Greenland's Icy Mountains,
2. From India's coral strand,
3. From many an ancient river,
4. From many a palmy plain.
5. What though the spicy breezes
   Blow soft o'er Ceylon's isle.
6. The Heathen in his blindness
   Bows down to wood and stone.
7. Shall we, whose souls are lighted
   With wisdom from on high.
8. Salvation, oh, salvation,
   The joyful sound proclaim,
9. Till each remotest nation
   Has learned Messiah's name.
10. Waft, waft, ye winds his story
    And you ye waters roll.
11. Till o'er our ransomed nature
    The lamb for sinners slain,
12. Redeemer, King, Creator,
    In bliss returns to reign.

Where is my Boy To-night?

(With Poem.)

1. "The boy of my tenderest care."
2. "As he knelt at his Mother's knee."
3. "O could I see you now, my boy."
4. "But bring him to me with all his blight."
5. "O where is my boy to-night?"
6. "My heart o'erflows for I love him, he knows."

What were their subjects? Magic lantern catalogs tell us what was being retailed, and from that we can infer what subjects were most popular. Figure 5.3 shows the subject contents of two of the largest catalogs, those of the McAllister and McIntosh companies, expressed as percentages of topic pages to the total.[8] We can use the same breakdown to look at what percent of the slides *in each category* Beale produced. Though some differences exist between the two catalog companies, in both "Travel" is by far the largest category of slides. As we shall see in what follows, that emphasis in the catalogs indeed correlates with a lot of travel "illustrated lectures" on the screen itself. The growth in travel lectures was a direct result of the new ability in the 1870s to print photographic images on glass with "dry plate" technology, which was much simpler to use than the old "wet plate". Suddenly it was possible for anyone to help audiences "travel" anywhere in the world, offering themselves as an experienced guide who had actually travelled … or at least as an experienced "Professor" who was an "expert" on his rented slides.

Other content areas are spread out fairly evenly, with the exception of "Religion" which is a big emphasis in the McIntosh catalogs. The one content area that the catalog percentages do not suggest the importance of is "Secret Society" slides. In fact, for reasons I'll describe in due course, the Societies generated one of the country's largest cumulative yearly audiences.

You may have noticed that there is no separate category for the kind of story, song and comics show that Great Grandfather Carter did, and that most re-enactors, including myself, do now. Such shows drew on categories like "Literature" and "Misc.", but, except for home use, they were a relatively small portion of the overall lantern activity. Most public lantern shows were so-called "illustrated lectures", that is, shows with a heavy educational emphasis. They covered an incredible variety of subjects.

In terms of Beale, the estimates given are for the percentage of slides in each category that were created by Beale, and are based on a count of catalog content. He had almost no impact on the largest category, Travel, and none on Science. But his impact on the Religion, History, Literature, and Secret Society offerings was very substantial indeed – one man producing between 25 and 50 percent of all the slides offered by the catalogs in these fields.

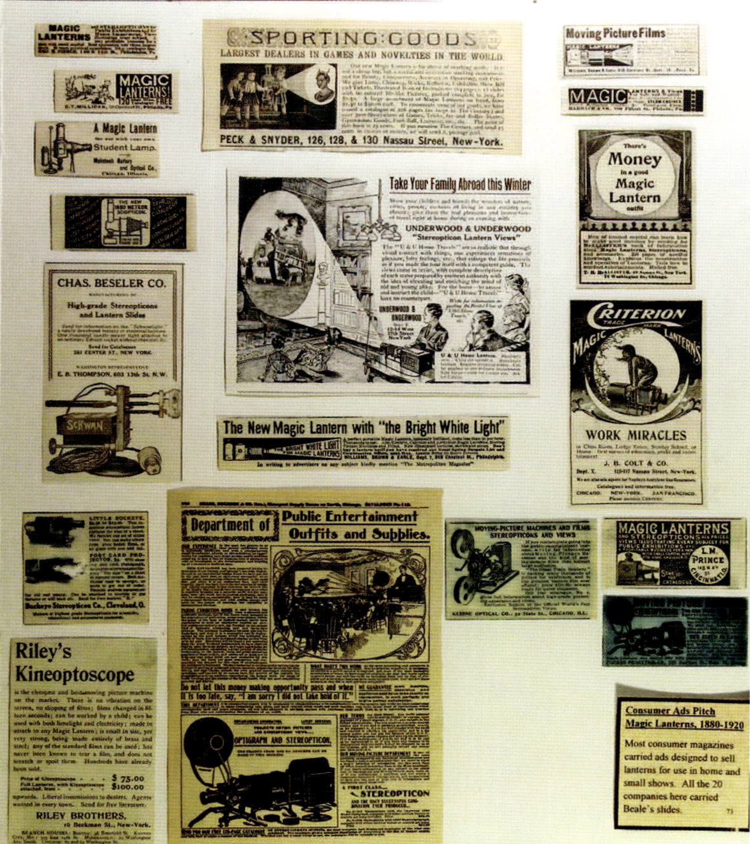

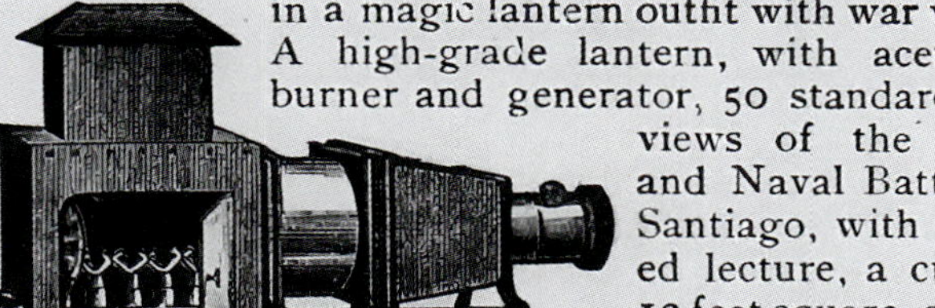

Fig. 5.2 Ads promoting magic lanterns. Such ads were in almost every popular magazine.

A Sampling of Lantern Shows

To give some concrete sense of all this lantern activity in America, I'll share with you vignettes of some 35 different performers, their advertising, and venues.[9] Most of the performers are professionals who made a significant portion of their income from illustrated lantern lectures, but we'll also see some very modest characters. Our survey of performers and venues begins with the overall context, then moves to the early (1850–1880) shows, and after that is organized by venue, type of performer, and content. Each performer or group of performers will be presented in a single page, which will include some examples of their broadside advertising and slides. Notes give more details and references about the artifacts shown.

Fig. 5.3 Percent Distribution of Catalog Slide Pages by Date, Subject, and by Beale.

Catalogs	*Date*	*Travel*	*Religion*	*History*	*Literature*	*Science*	*Secret Societies*	*Temperance*	*Misc.*
		%	%	%	%	%	%	%	%
McAllister	1892	68	3	4	4	2	1	1	16
McAllister	1900	67	3	12	2	3	1	1	11
McIntosh	1913	44	17	3	9	12	5	1	8
McIntosh	1916	61	20	1	11	2	—	2	4
Average		**60**	**11**	**5**	**7**	**5**	**2**	**1**	**10**
Est. % of Category Slides by Beale	--	0	25	25	25	0	50	10	10

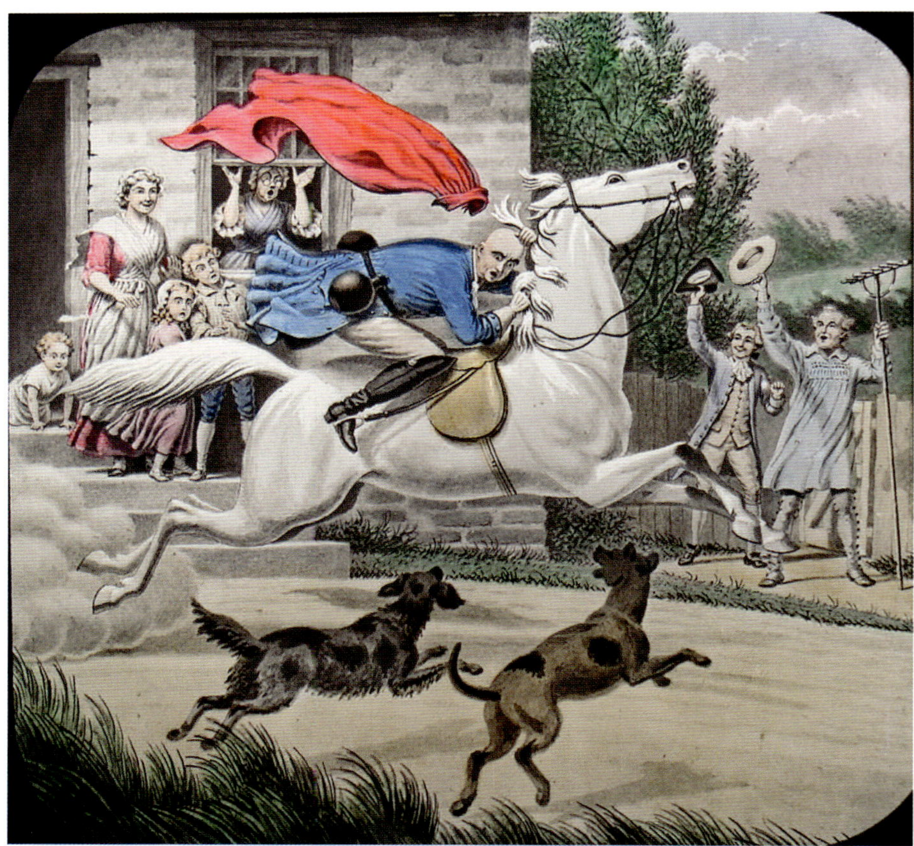

Beale's slide 8 from *John Gilpin's Ride*, a comic parlor poem by Cowper. Popular poems like these helped build Beale's presence in many catalogs.

Magic Lantern Advertising Plasters the Landscape

Fig. 5.4 When Beale began working with the magic lantern he faced a crowded field. The variety and ubiquity of shows was absolutely extraordinary. Advertising for them competed for space with many other attractions.[10]

Top right. A lantern slide of an English wall covered with broadside ads. Much of the advertising for lantern shows was with such broadsides – large posters pasted on building walls. Such advertising was as ubiquitous as TV advertising today, so magic lantern showmen faced stiff competition for space.

Center. N. Harkness flyer. The competition for advertising space led to the development of professional Bill Posters, who advertised in their own right.

Bottom left. Animated lantern lever slide. Broadside advertising was so common that it generated lantern-slide jokes on the subject, such as this animated cartoon. A man is posting an advertising bill, using a stick to hold up the bill while he spreads paste with a long-handled brush. Two kids are pasting up a "Stick No Bills" sign on the sign-sticker himself, their brush moved up and down with a lever.

Bottom right. Hammer for a Bill Poster. A special collapsible bill-poster's hammer was available, which could be assembled to become 3 ½ feet long. It mystifies people who see it in my collection. I love to explain and demonstrate it.

Two brackets near the hammer's head held the broadside and a thumbtack so that the advertiser could place the advertising up high, out of the reach of competitors and malicious small boys. The head was magnetized to hold other tacks so that they could be hammered in with a one-handed reach. When done, the bill poster could disassemble the hammer, put it in his suitcase, hop the train, and move on to the next town.

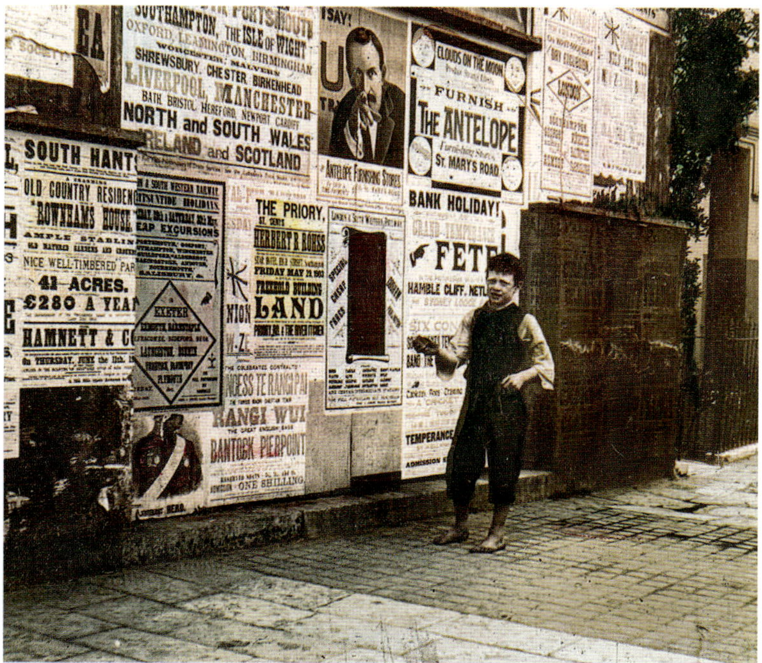

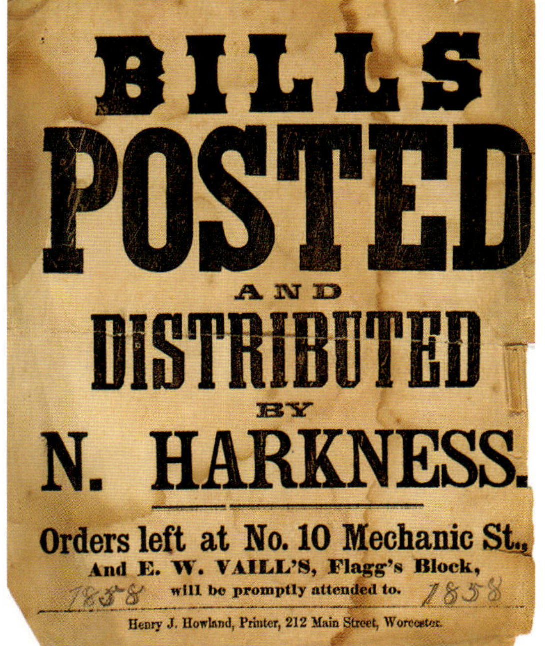

BILLS POSTED AND DISTRIBUTED BY N. HARKNESS.

Orders left at No. 10 Mechanic St.,
And E. W. VAILL'S, Flagg's Block,
1858 will be promptly attended to. 1858

Henry J. Howland, Printer, 212 Main Street, Worcester.

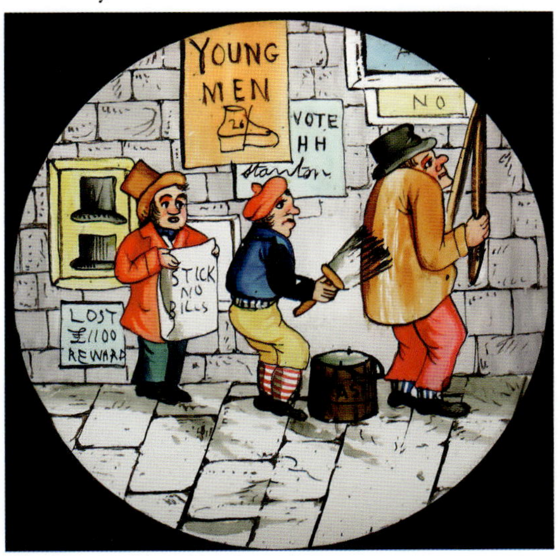

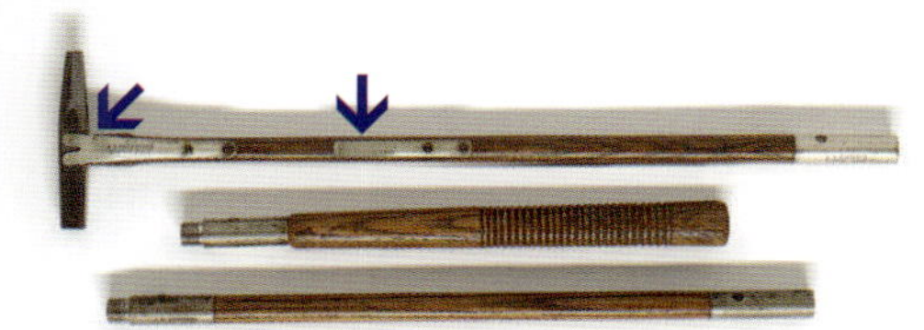

Early Shows: Barnum & Bunnell – Weird Shows

Fig. 5.5 Early lantern showmen included P. T. Barnum, the famous promoter, who regularly gave lantern presentations as part of the entertainment in his Philadelphia Museum in 1849, and later in his New York Museum. His presentations emphasized – you guessed it – a razzle dazzle of dissolving statuary, and "special effect" slides.[11]

Top right. "Fat Men's Show" broadside. George Bunnell, a protégé of Barnum's in the 1880s, was manager of a museum in Brooklyn, and also regularly promoted lantern shows. The Bunnell Museum's *Fat Men's Show* (portion of a flyer shown) was probably a combination of live comedy and the projected images of Dave Foy, "Pelicitous Photographer of Peculiar People".

Bottom right. Slip Slide. Making fun of fat people was a standard part of the lantern repertoire, as in this slip slide. The huge stomach is initially covered with a mask. Pull the mask slowly aside, and the stomach grows and grows and GROWS.

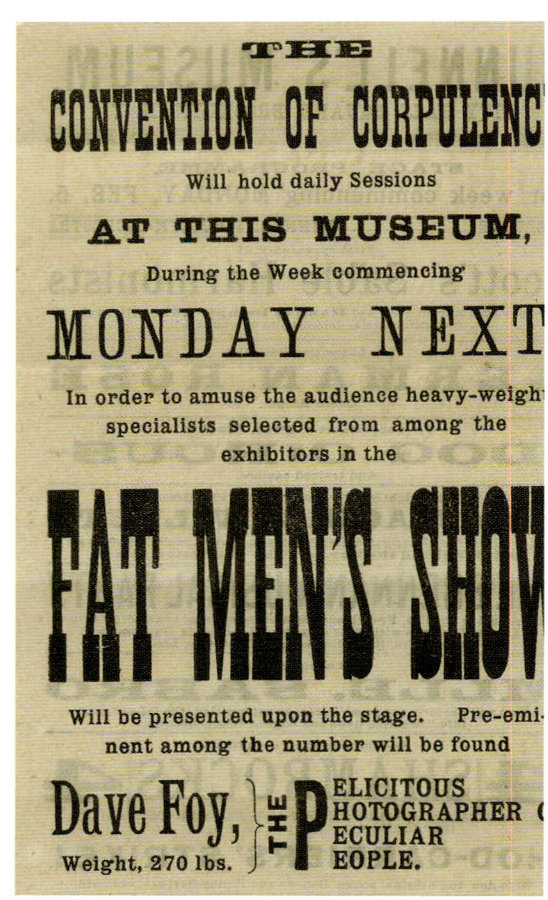

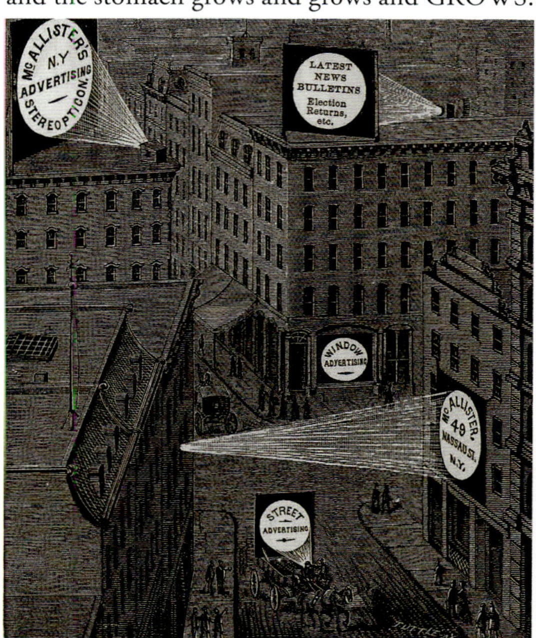

Left. Engraving. Stereopticon advertising was a regular part of the street scene in 19th century America, as is suggested by this engraving that promotes lantern advertising. Note the horse-drawn moving ad.

Bottom left. Order card. This order card for advertising using the stereopticon is for an unknown product to be displayed outside Barnum's "Greatest Show on Earth".

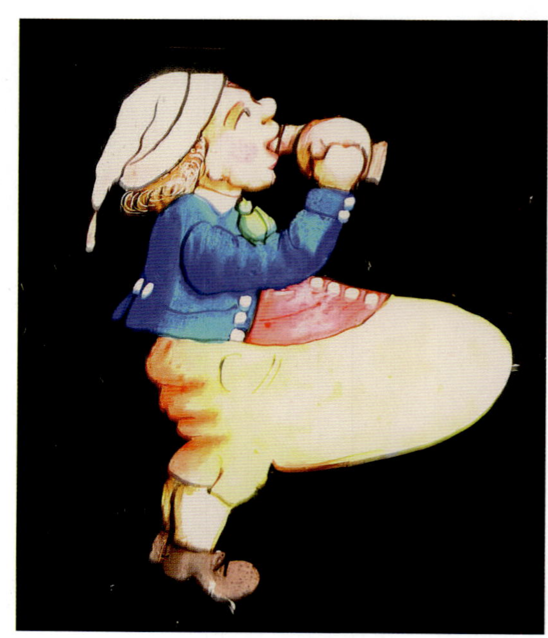

P. T. Barnum's New & Greatest Show on Earth.

Insert Advertisement as per copy to occupy One half upper of 8th page of Programme, for One day, and one written slide in Advance Stereopticon, (to be exhibited one night, wind, weather and location permitting,) for which we agree to pay to your order, ($ 10 00/100) Ten no/100 — Dollars, on presentation of copy containing Advertisement and return of this voucher.

H. SYLVESTER,
P. T. Barnum's Programme and Advance Stereopticon Ag't.

Name, [illegible] Brothers
Business, Grocers
Address, 175 Saginaw St

Bunn Dramatizes Shakespeare

Fig. 5.6 The stage was a natural place for the magic lantern to find subject material, and Shakespeare was the obvious candidate for high-quality entertainment.[12]

Top. Bunn broadside. This small broadside is for an early (1850s) illustrated lecture, given by an Englishman, Alfred Bunn, at the Masonic Temple in Boston. Bunn claimed he had already given the lecture 300 times in England.

Bunn was a well-known theatrical promoter in England. His book, *Old England and New England*, in which the Shakespeare flyer is pasted, is a lively tour of America.

Bottom. Beale's slide 1 of *Hamlet* (left), and slide 8 of *The Merry Wives of Windsor* (right), both created around 1910–1913. These images were not used by Bunn, whose shows were before they were created, but lectures on Shakespeare continued to be a popular subject throughout the lantern era.

The Beale Shakespeare sets were probably used in dramatic readings within the context of illustrated lectures, just as Bunn was doing fifty years earlier. Another market appears to have been schools.

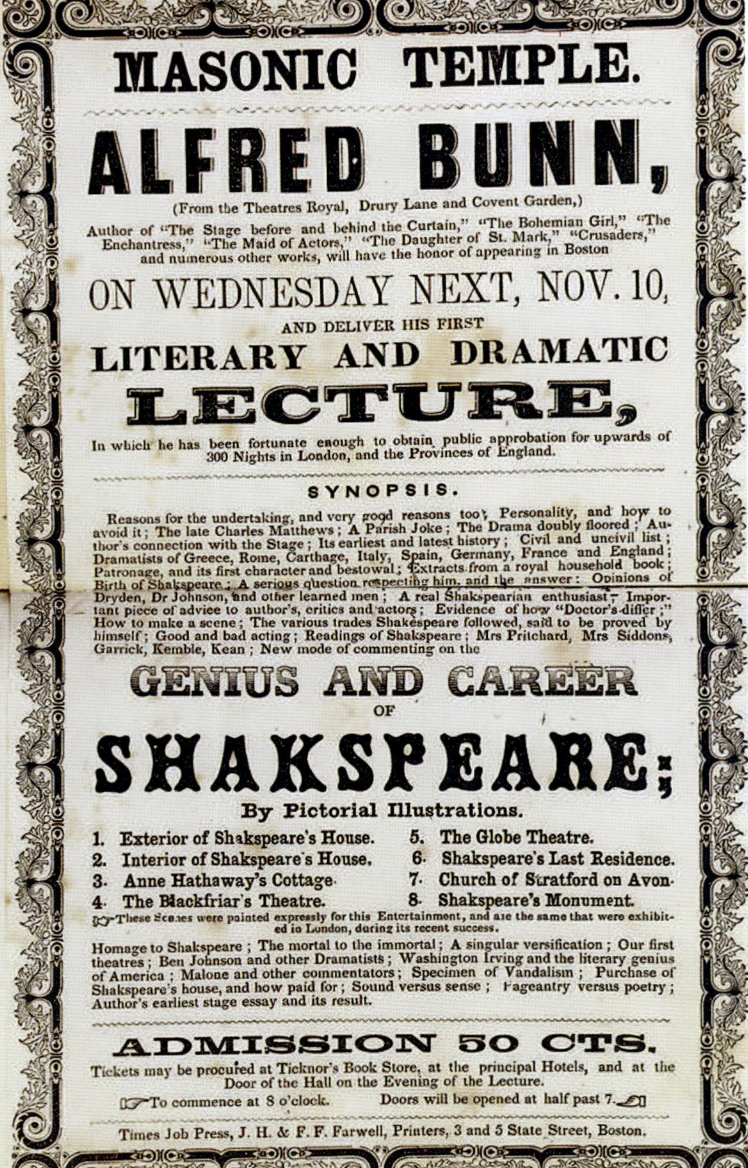

MASONIC TEMPLE.

ALFRED BUNN,

(From the Theatres Royal, Drury Lane and Covent Garden,)

Author of "The Stage before and behind the Curtain," "The Bohemian Girl," "The Enchantress," "The Maid of Actors," "The Daughter of St. Mark," "Crusaders," and numerous other works, will have the honor of appearing in Boston

ON WEDNESDAY NEXT, NOV. 10,

AND DELIVER HIS FIRST

LITERARY AND DRAMATIC

LECTURE,

In which he has been fortunate enough to obtain public approbation for upwards of 300 Nights in London, and the Provinces of England.

SYNOPSIS.

Reasons for the undertaking, and very good reasons too; Personality, and how to avoid it; The late Charles Matthews; A Parish Joke; The Drama doubly floored; Author's connection with the Stage; Its earliest and latest history; Civil and uncivil list; Dramatists of Greece, Rome, Carthage, Italy, Spain, Germany, France and England; Patronage, and its first character and bestowal; Extracts from a royal household book; Birth of Shakspeare; A serious question respecting him, and the answer: Opinions of Dryden, Dr Johnson, and other learned men; A real Shakspearian enthusiast; Important piece of advice to author's, critics and actors; Evidence of how "Doctor's differ;" How to make a scene; The various trades Shakespeare followed, said to be proved by himself; Good and bad acting; Readings of Shakspeare; Mrs Pritchard, Mrs Siddons, Garrick, Kemble, Kean; New mode of commenting on the

GENIUS AND CAREER

OF

SHAKSPEARE;

By Pictorial Illustrations.

1. Exterior of Shakspeare's House.
2. Interior of Shakspeare's House.
3. Anne Hathaway's Cottage.
4. The Blackfriar's Theatre.
5. The Globe Theatre.
6. Shakspeare's Last Residence.
7. Church of Stratford on Avon.
8. Shakspeare's Monument.

☞These Scenes were painted expressly for this Entertainment, and are the same that were exhibited in London, during its recent success.

Homage to Shakspeare; The mortal to the immortal; A singular versification; Our first theatres; Ben Johnson and other Dramatists; Washington Irving and the literary genius of America; Malone and other commentators; Specimen of Vandalism; Purchase of Shakspeare's house, and how paid for; Sound versus sense; Pageantry versus poetry; Author's earliest stage essay and its result.

ADMISSION 50 CTS.

Tickets may be procured at Ticknor's Book Store, at the principal Hotels, and at the Door of the Hall on the Evening of the Lecture.

☞To commence at 8 o'clock. Doors will be opened at half past 7.☜

Times Job Press, J. H. & F. F. Farwell, Printers, 3 and 5 State Street, Boston.

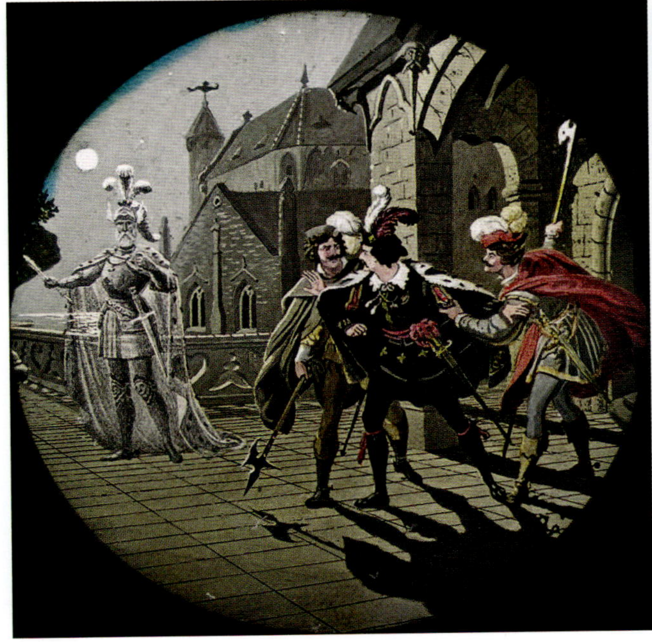

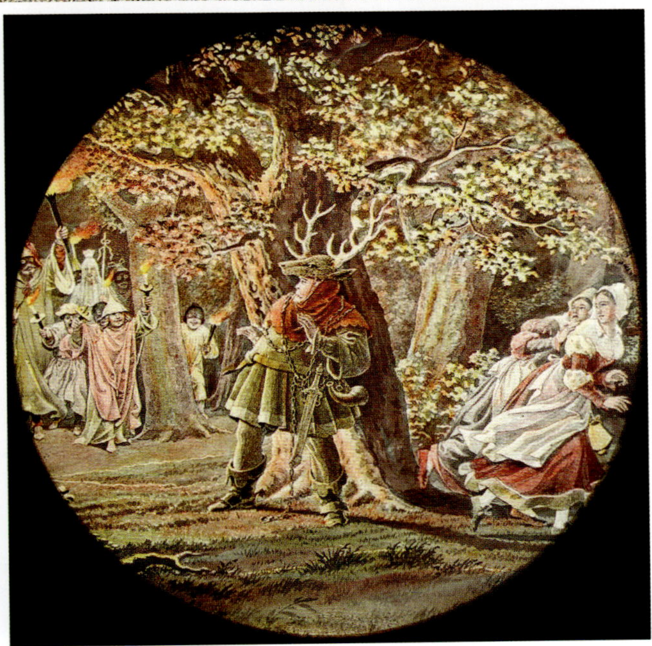

New Stereopticon Depicts Civil War Rebellion

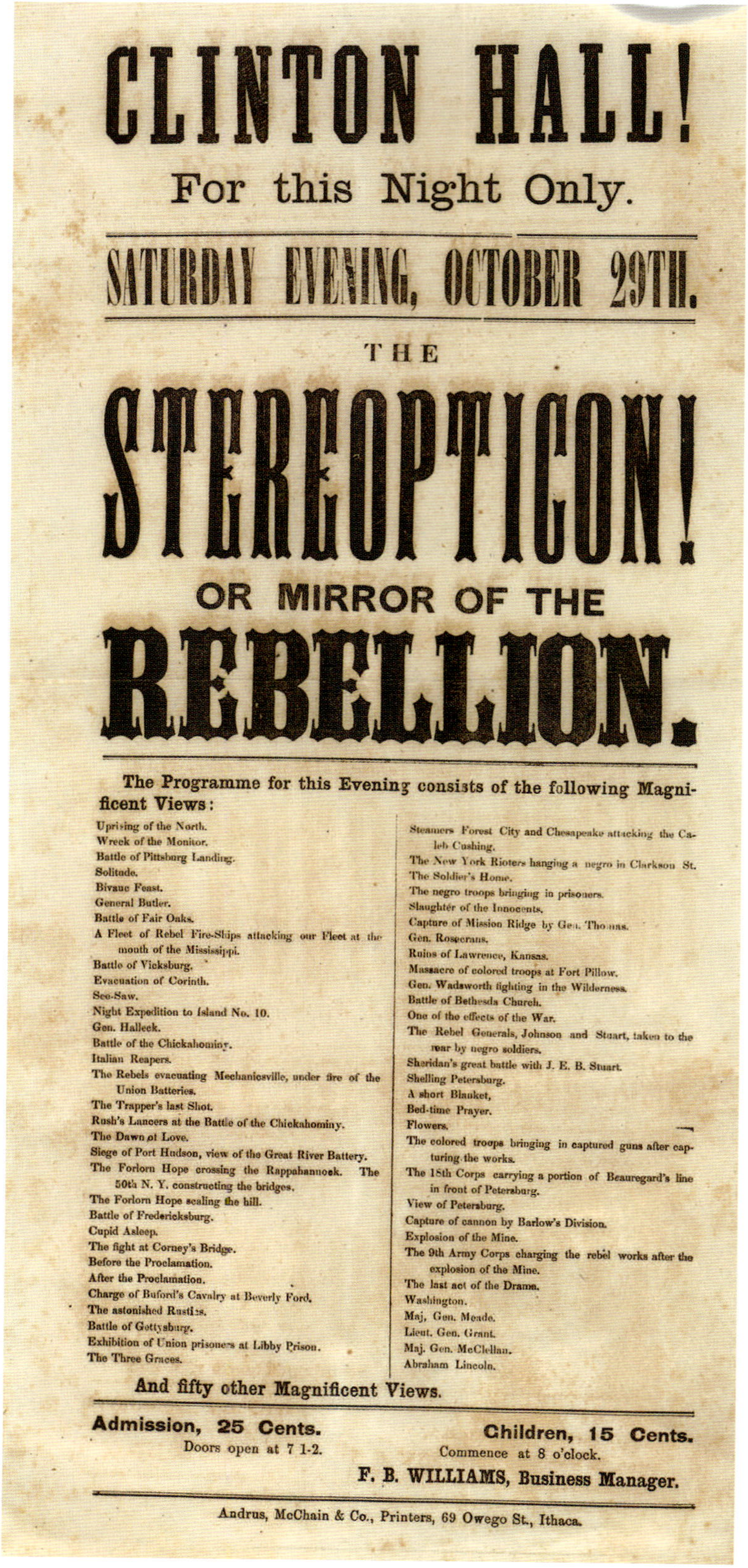

CLINTON HALL!

For this Night Only.

SATURDAY EVENING, OCTOBER 29TH.

THE

STEREOPTICON!

OR MIRROR OF THE

REBELLION.

The Programme for this Evening consists of the following Magnificent Views:

Uprising of the North.
Wreck of the Monitor.
Battle of Pittsburg Landing.
Solitude.
Bivauc Feast.
General Butler.
Battle of Fair Oaks.
A Fleet of Rebel Fire-Ships attacking our Fleet at the mouth of the Mississippi.
Battle of Vicksburg.
Evacuation of Corinth.
See-Saw.
Night Expedition to Island No. 10.
Gen. Halleck.
Battle of the Chickahominy.
Italian Reapers.
The Rebels evacuating Mechanicsville, under fire of the Union Batteries.
The Trapper's last Shot.
Rush's Lancers at the Battle of the Chickahominy.
The Dawn of Love.
Siege of Port Hudson, view of the Great River Battery.
The Forlorn Hope crossing the Rappahannock. The 50th N. Y. constructing the bridges.
The Forlorn Hope scaling the hill.
Battle of Fredericksburg.
Cupid Asleep.
The fight at Corney's Bridge.
Before the Proclamation.
After the Proclamation.
Charge of Buford's Cavalry at Beverly Ford.
The astonished Rustics.
Battle of Gettysburg.
Exhibition of Union prisoners at Libby Prison.
The Three Graces.
Steamers Forest City and Chesapeake attacking the Caleb Cushing.
The New York Rioters hanging a negro in Clarkson St.
The Soldier's Home.
The negro troops bringing in prisoners.
Slaughter of the Innocents.
Capture of Mission Ridge by Gen. Thomas.
Gen. Rosecrans.
Ruins of Lawrence, Kansas.
Massacre of colored troops at Fort Pillow.
Gen. Wadsworth fighting in the Wilderness.
Battle of Bethesda Church.
One of the effects of the War.
The Rebel Generals, Johnson and Stuart, taken to the rear by negro soldiers.
Sheridan's great battle with J. E. B. Stuart.
Shelling Petersburg.
A short Blanket,
Bed-time Prayer.
Flowers.
The colored troops bringing in captured guns after capturing the works.
The 18th Corps carrying a portion of Beauregard's line in front of Petersburg.
View of Petersburg.
Capture of cannon by Barlow's Division.
Explosion of the Mine.
The 9th Army Corps charging the rebel works after the explosion of the Mine.
The last act of the Drama.
Washington.
Maj, Gen. Meade.
Lieut. Gen. Grant.
Maj. Gen. McClellan.
Abraham Lincoln.

And fifty other Magnificent Views.

Admission, 25 Cents.
Doors open at 7 1-2.

Children, 15 Cents.
Commence at 8 o'clock.

F. B. WILLIAMS, Business Manager.

Andrus, McChain & Co., Printers, 69 Owego St., Ithaca.

Fig. 5.7 The American word "Stereopticon" was a new, more "scientific" name for a bigger and more powerful lantern, and helped distinguish it from children's "magic lanterns".[13]

Left. The Stereopticon Show broadside. The "stereopticon show" was introduced in Philadelphia in 1860 – the show Beale saw. The show's competitors, such as this one, rapidly picked up the name, and soon many "stereopticon shows" were competing for attention. The stereopticon was a dissolving two-lens, or "biunial" lantern. It showed photographic slides that were so sharp they seemed to have a 3-D appearance – though they were not actually 3-D.

This broadside promotes a Civil War Show featuring slides that were probably made from a combination of photographs and photographed etchings or wood engravings. (Similar slide shown at bottom.) The show includes a slide of the Battle of Petersburg, June 15, 1864, just four months before this lantern performance on October 29, so this show is an early form of current-events screen production. The Civil War remained a popular subject in lantern shows for the next 40 years.

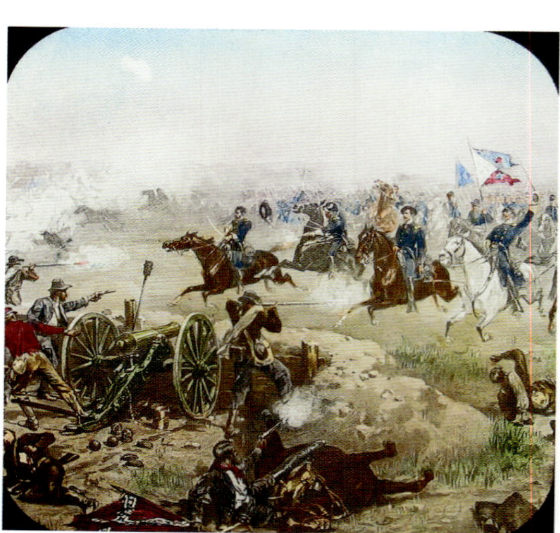

The Magic Lantern Variety Show

INSTRUCTIVE & AMUSING
EXHIBITION.

MESSRS. FUNK & PUTNAM

Respectfully announce to the Ladies and Gentlemen of this place and vicinity that they will exhibit

On Wednesday Evening, June 7

At Trenton N. J.

A GREAT VARIETY OF HIGHLY MAGNIFIED

DISSOLVING VIEWS!

Executed in the highest style of art, conveying to the mind of the Spectator an idea of the Scenes represented with a vividness and reality otherwise unattainable. Commencing with

Astronomical Diagrams

ALL MOVABLE:

1. The Solar System—showing the Revolution of Planets, with their Satellites, round the Sun.
2. The Earth's annual motion round the Sun, thus producing the Seasons.
3. A Diagram to illustrate the cause of Spring and Neap Tides.
4. The Earth's Rotundity, by a Ship sailing round the Globe. The Revolution of a Comet round the Sun. The Diurnal motion of the Earth, illustrating the cause of Day and Night. The Monthly Lunations of the Moon. Various Eclipses of the Sun and Moon.

BEAUTIFUL REPRESENTATIONS

OF THE

Prominent Events and Places

MENTIONED IN

HOLY WRIT

Expulsion from Eden; Abraham offering Isaac; Joseph sold by his Brethren; Joseph meeting his Father; Moses in the Bulrushes; the Ark of the Covenant; the High Priest; the Altar of Incense; David killing Goliath; the Handwriting on the Wall; the Fiery Furnace; Ruth and Boaz; the Ascent to Mount Sinai; Cedars of Lebanon; Valley of Brook Kedron; City and Lake of Tiberia; Bethlehem; Birth of Christ; Christ stilling the Tempest; Raising of Lazarus; Jerusalem; Garden of Gethsemane; Sardis; Laodicia; Alexandria; Palmyra; Patmos; Petræ; Treading of the Wine-Press, &c.

To be followed by a Series of Views, showing the Baneful Effects of

INTEMPERANCE

The Drunkard's Daughter. The Robbing Landlord. Facing the Enemy →

LONG-MOVING

PANORAMIC VIEWS!

Noah entering the Ark; Crossing of the Red Sea; Burning of the Missouri, at Gibraltar; Eruption of Mount Vesuvius; Hunting the Stag; Thames Tunnel.

A PLEASING VARIETY OF

HUMOROUS

MOVING FIGURES

Will be introduced for the Amusement of the JUVENILES:—The House that Jack built; the Old Man and his Ass, or the folly of trying to please everybody; Horse and Cow drinking; the Black Orator; the Banjo Player; the Dentist; the Cobbler; the Roast Pig; Feats of Horsemanship; Dog Trick; the Impudent Monkey; the Miser and his Gold; the Disappointed Miser; the Blooming Pink Rose; Flying Fish.

The whole to conclude with a Magnificent Display of CHROMATROPES, or

ARTIFICIAL FIREWORKS

GOOD NIGHT!

Admission, - - - Cents

Children under 12 years, Half-price.

Doors open at half-past 6 o'clock. Lecture commences at 7 o'clock.

Brown's Steam-Power Job Printing Office, Ledger Buildings, Phila.

Fig. 5.8 Variety shows were popular in the early days of the magic lantern because they cast a wide net, and because the exhibitor could easily keep the program fresh by changing a few segments.[14]

Left. Funk and Putnam broadside. Funk and Putnam presented an *Instructive and Amusing Exhibition,* in the early 1880s. This show combines different subjects – astronomy, Holy Writ, humor, etc. – a common format in early lantern history. It also promises a wide variety of slide types – Dissolving Views, Astronomical Diagrams, Moving Panoramic Views, Comics, and Artificial Fireworks (a chromatrope).

Bottom. Beale's slide 5 of *The Drunkard's Daughter.* In addition, Funk and Putnam offered this sad Beale temperance tale on the effects of drinking. Temperance (or "Intemperance") sets were relatively rare in America, especially compared with the hundreds of them in England.

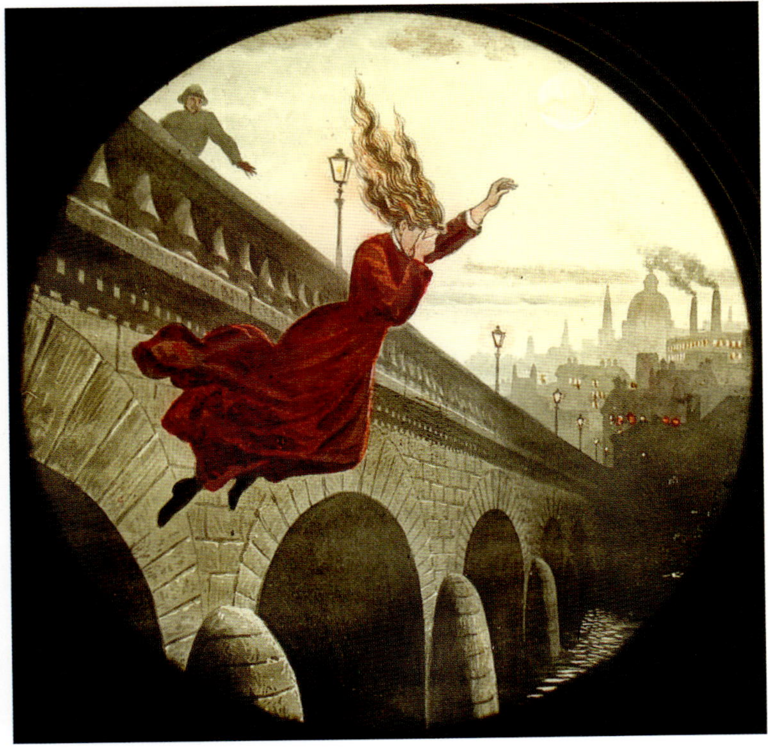

Lloyd Touts Photographs, Fun

Fig. 5.9 The invention of photographic sldies in the 1850s opend up a wide range of new subject matter, especially travel.[15]

Right. *Lloyd's Over Land and Sea* broadside. Lloyd offered a tour of America and England, probably using the black and white photographic slides popular at the time.

Bottom left. Photographic lantern slide. By the 1860s photographs were well on their way to becoming the dominant form of screen presentation.

Bottom center. Dissolving View. Lloyd also included Dissolving Views. Here, for instance, the view of the Statue of Liberty can slowly change from day to night, at which point the torch is lit with yet another dissolve.

Bottom Right. Animated cartoon, created with a slipping slide. At the bottom of the Lloyd's broadside comes one of the best lines in all of magic lantern promotion: "Nor is the Entertainment lacking in an occasional presentation of the FUNNY SIDE OF THINGS. But there is nothing tawdry, puerile, or coarse; nothing cheap excepting the price for Admission".

The "funny side of things" would have been animated slip-slide cartoons – the classic ending for many lantern shows, including my own.

Variety shows such as this one set the pattern for most modern recreations of lantern shows. The more serious "illustrated lectures" get short shrift today, although, as we will see, they attracted huge audiences in the late 19th and early 20th century.

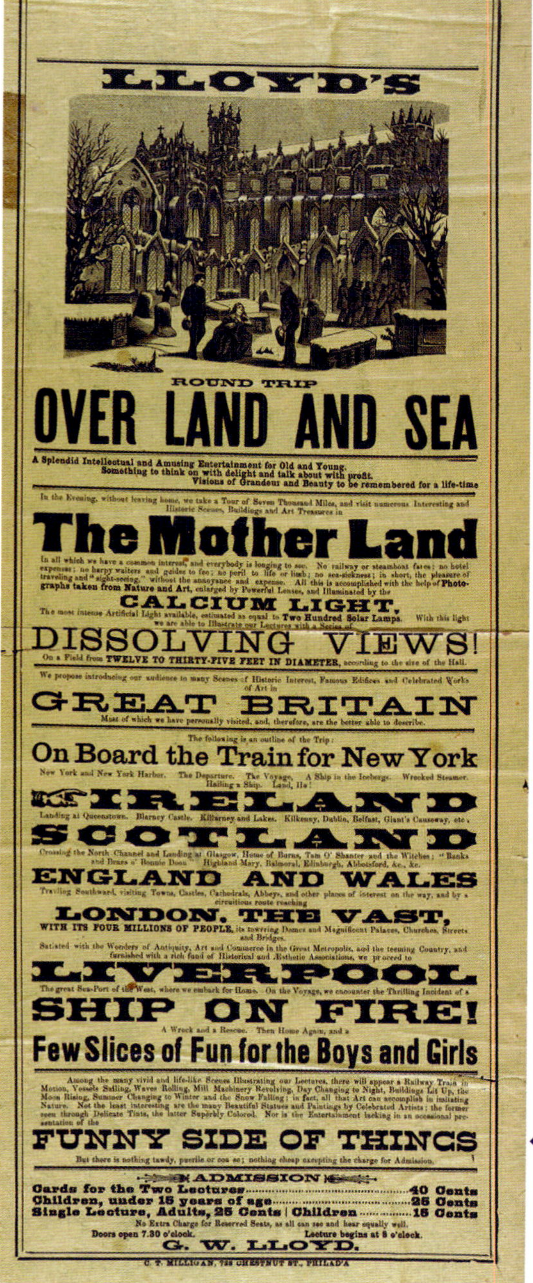

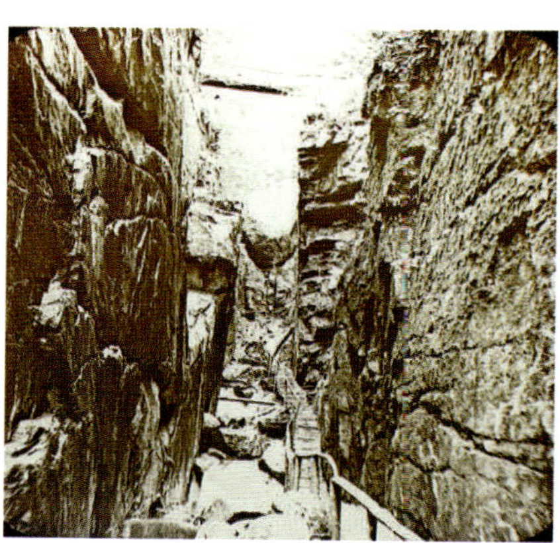

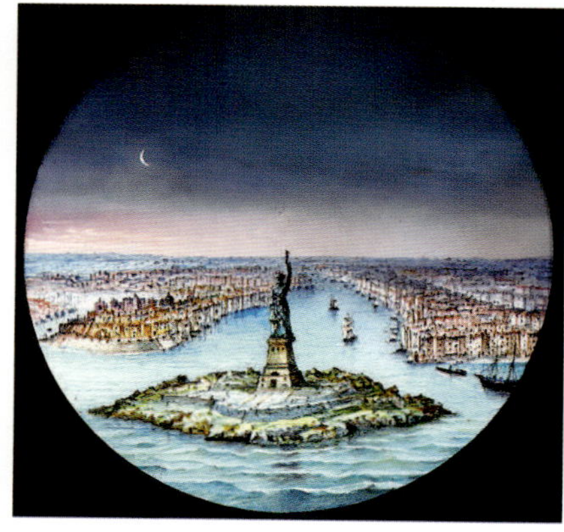

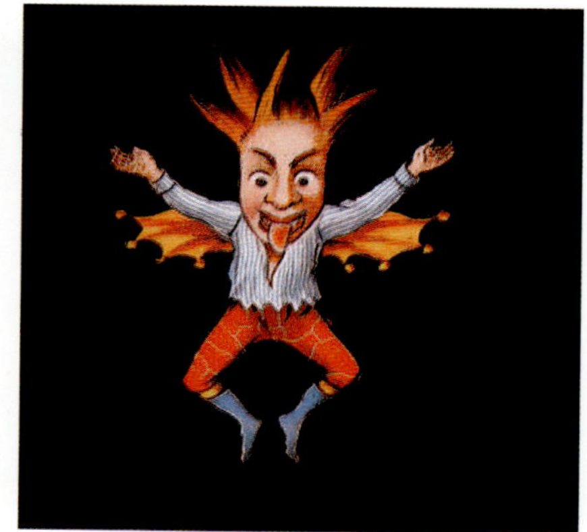

Venues – Slides in Every School

Fig. 5.10 The Keystone View Company, one of the largest lantern slide distributors in the U.S., specialized in sets of lantern slides for very targeted venues, the schools. Most notable was the "600 Set" – 600 images of America and the world.[16]

Bottom. Request to make photos. Keystone began in 1892 when photographer B. L. Singley used this "Free of Charge" flyer to build a stock of images to be displayed the next year at the 1893 World's Fair.

By 1905 Keystone claimed to be the largest company of its kind in the world, with offices across the United States, and 20,000 different views available for sale.

By 1922, Keystone boasted that every city with a population of over 50,000 had the Keystone System (600 slides and 600 stereo cards) for each one of its schools. That would mean that the Keystone slides were explaining the world to between three and six million children a year.

Top right/ Keystone color slide. Most Keystone slides were in the less-expensive black and white format, but the company also produced color versions such as the one shown here of Boston's Quincy Market.

Bottom right. Keystone information card. Each slide came with an explanatory card so that students could read about the image, either by themselves, or to the class. These little cards were produced in an easy-going, interactive format, designed to hold the attention of students. I'm sure they did, which is undoubtedly part of what made this set so popular.

States and cities also offered lantern slide collections. New York State, for instance, had 40,000 slides in circulation.

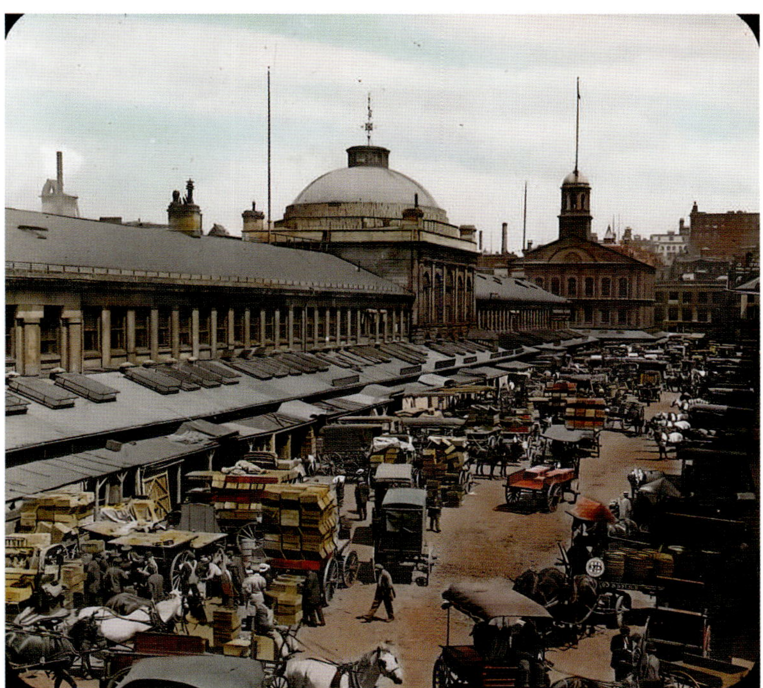

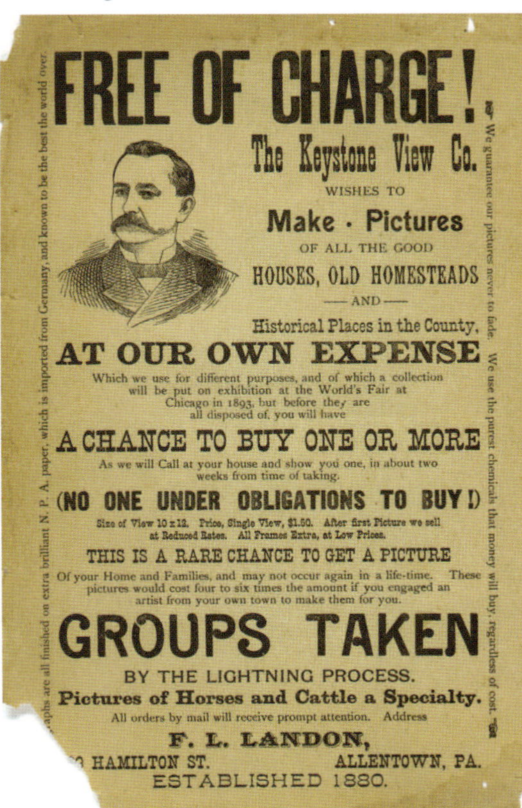

543—(20601)
WOOD CARRIERS OF SEOUL, CHOSEN

The northern part of Chosen (chō′ sĕn′) is crossed by a range of snow-capped mountains, heavily wooded. Following the foothills and the ravines there are hundreds of acres of forest untouched by the axe. Here are the wild animals sought out by Korean hunters. Wolves, wild dogs, and tigers, to say nothing of the smaller species of the furry tribes, are to be found. Wherever there are forests in Chosen, they contain fine trees of maple, oak, pine, ash, and birch.

But about the cities and along parts of the shore the woods have disappeared. The natives say the trees were destroyed by a great forest fire which raged for 7 years. Perhaps this is a myth, but it is likely that fires helped to make the country barren of trees. But some of the timber has been used for building purposes, and a great deal of it has been made into firewood and charcoal. Still the untouched forests of Chosen are one of

Lantern Lectures Delight the Insane

Fig. 5.11 One of the more unusual venues for lantern shows were "asylums for the insane", what we call mental hospitals today, where they were a common part of the programming.[17]

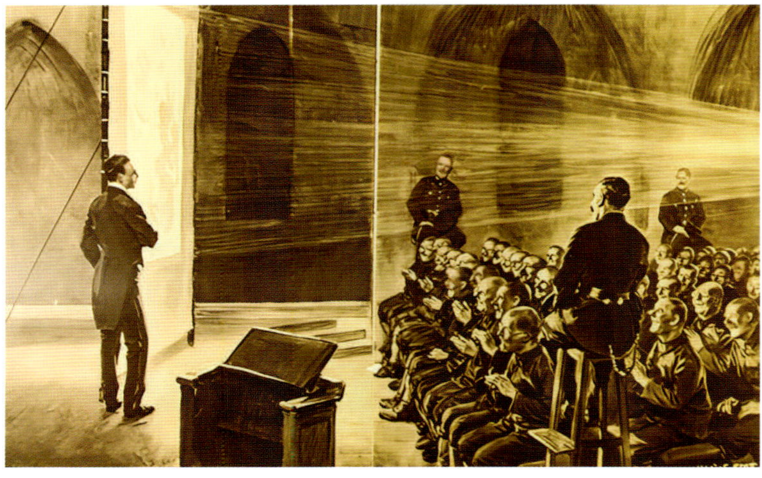

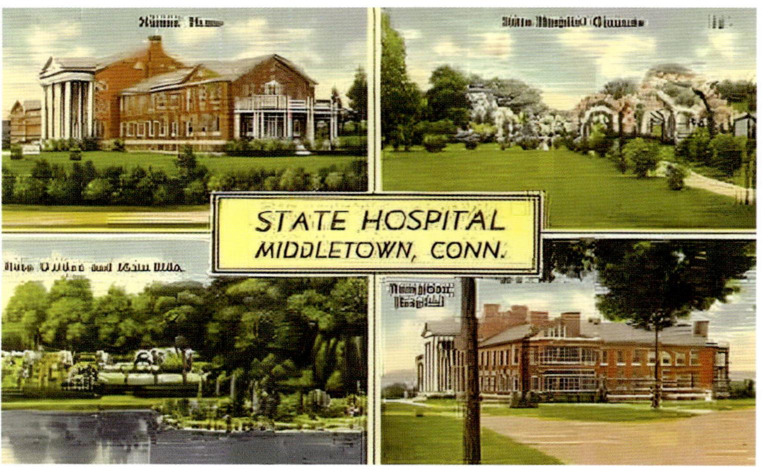

Top. Depiction of a lantern show in a British prison. Though not an image of an asylum show, this picture probably gives a good idea of both the close supervision at American asylum shows, and the delight that lantern shows brought inmates.

The idea behind lantern shows in asylums was that since the inmates could not be let out into the real world, the real world should be brought to them. Beginning in 1844, The Pennsylvania Hospital for the Insane in Philadelphia pioneered this concept, and by 1862 had built up a collection of a thousand slides. The idea spread to asylums all over the country.

Center. State Hospital, Middletown, CT. By the turn of the century, lantern programs were well established in most asylums. For instance, this asylum had a 600-seat theater built in part for this purpose, and offered lantern lectures monthly, most of which were travel lectures.

Bottom. Comic slip slides were common in asylum shows. Here are two images of the kind often used. A top-hatted prig becomes – **SLIP** – an ass. Inmates probably took special delight in images that poked fun at the gentry who managed the asylum.

At the time Dr. John Minson Galt explained that lantern "hilarity" in his asylum would help "supplant the place of delusive ideas and feelings … If you can get [the insane] to laugh natural, it is quite apt to explode the whole affair" – by which he meant, I think, that if a magic lantern show could get the insane to laugh naturally, it could break them out of their delusion, and put them on the path to sanity.

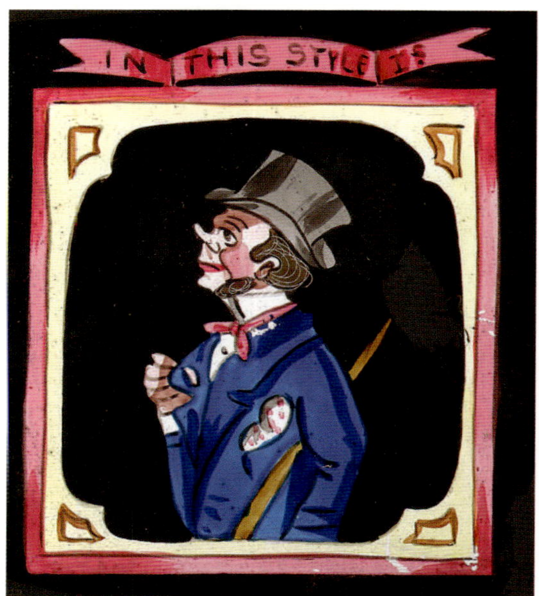

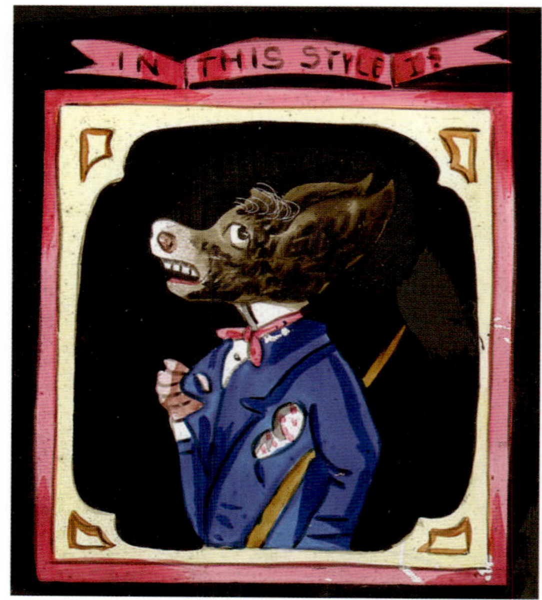

Traveling Chautauquas Educate Millions

Fig. 5.12 Magic lantern shows and illustrated lectures were produced in a bewildering range of venues. Among the most important were the *Traveling Chautauquas*, which were like circuses touring across the country by train, offering performances in tents.[18]

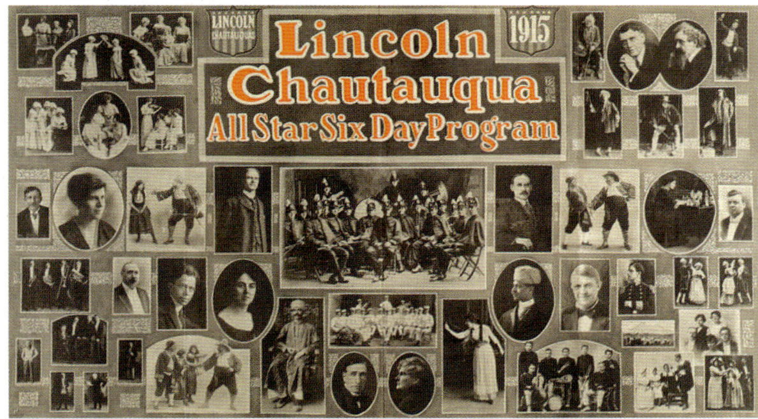

Right. Lincoln Chautauqua poster. The Circuit Chautauquas did not bring clowns and elephants to small town America; they brought cultural enlightenment. Six trains of equipment and performers would leapfrog each other along a rail line, providing six-days of changing performances in town after town.

In this large (2 x 3') poster, two of the performers pictured presented lantern "illustrated lectures" which were a staple of the Chautauqua circuit. Traveling Chautauquas reached over 9,000 towns – about a third of the people in the country every year. The height of lantern lectures in Chautauquas was about 1906; after 1920 their popularity dropped rapidly.

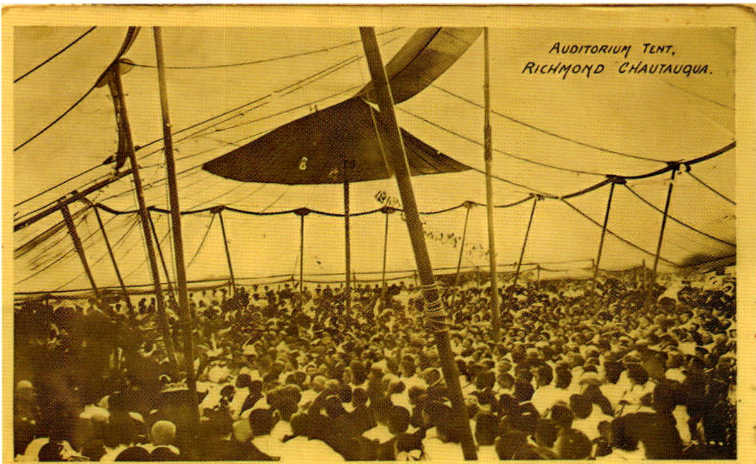

Center. Postcard of a Chautauqua tent. The tents usually held about 1,000 people. Try to imagine what it would be like to perform in this setting, in the heat, night after night all summer long, with no mike. Lantern showmen of the time had powerful lungs, and extraordinary endurance.

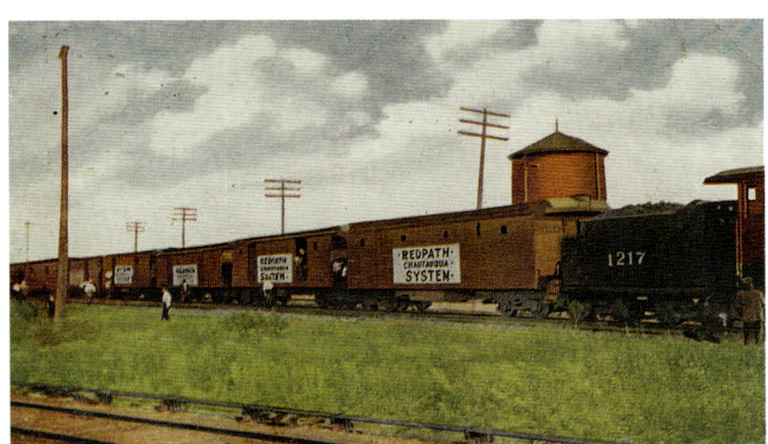

Bottom. Postcard of a Chautauqua train. The train carried the tent and chairs, and was met by a group of local young men who were hired to set them up.

Venues: Fred Gives "Grand Exhibition!"

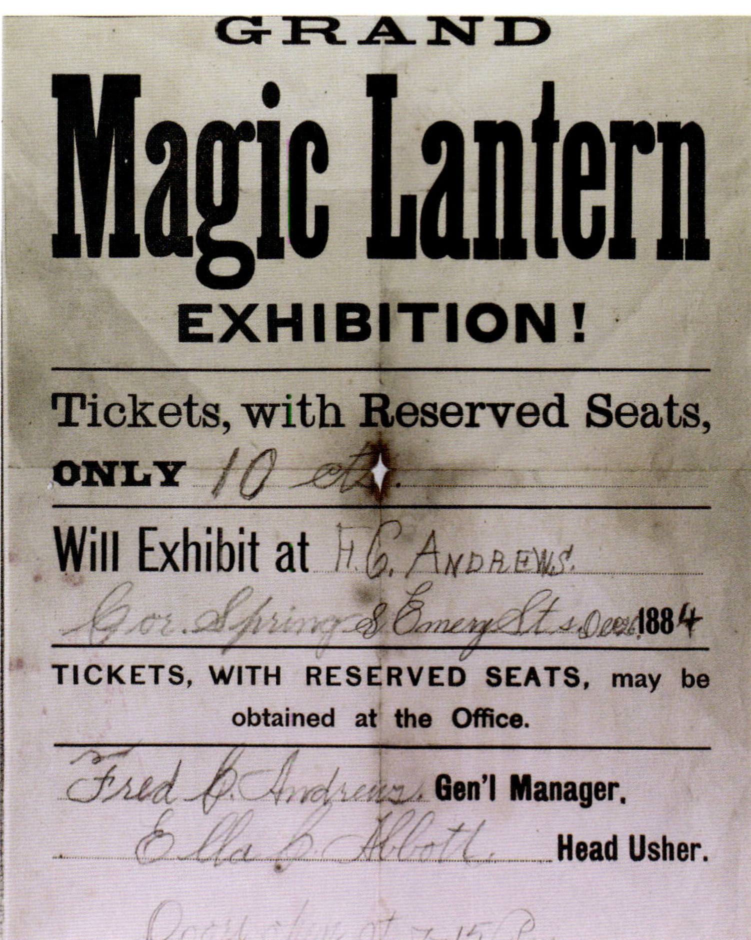

GRAND
Magic Lantern
EXHIBITION!

Tickets, with Reserved Seats,
ONLY 10 cts.

Will Exhibit at H. G. Andrews'
Cor. Spring & Emery Sts. Dec. 1884

TICKETS, WITH RESERVED SEATS, may be obtained at the Office.

Fred C. Andrews Gen'l Manager.
Ella C. Abbott. Head Usher.

Fig. 5.13 One of the most wide-spread venues for lantern shows were middle-class homes where shows were performed by children, using their own lanterns.[19]

Top left. Broadside for child's show. This show is performed at the home theater of "H. G. Andrews" and the showman is … who else but young Fred Andrews, probably age 8–10. He has just received a toy magic lantern for Christmas, 1884, and has organized his toy magic lantern show for Dec. 26.

Bottom right. The ornate box in which a child's lantern and slides might come. The "Laterna Magica" title allowed the box to be sold in many different countries.

Bottom left. Round slide for child's lantern. Round slides like this were unusual – most had several scenes in a rectangular format. This slide allows a child to tell the story of *Robinson Crusoe* in a guaranteed sequence. Animated comic slides were not generally included with toy lanterns, despite the fact that kids loved them – just too expensive.

Most toy lanterns were made in Germany. Because they were inexpensive they were enormously popular. Perhaps as many as 50,000 toy lanterns a year were sold in America – from the 1880s, when Fred got his present – to the 1920s. That would amount to two million lanterns, As a result, you'll find many for sale on eBay today, very inexpensively.

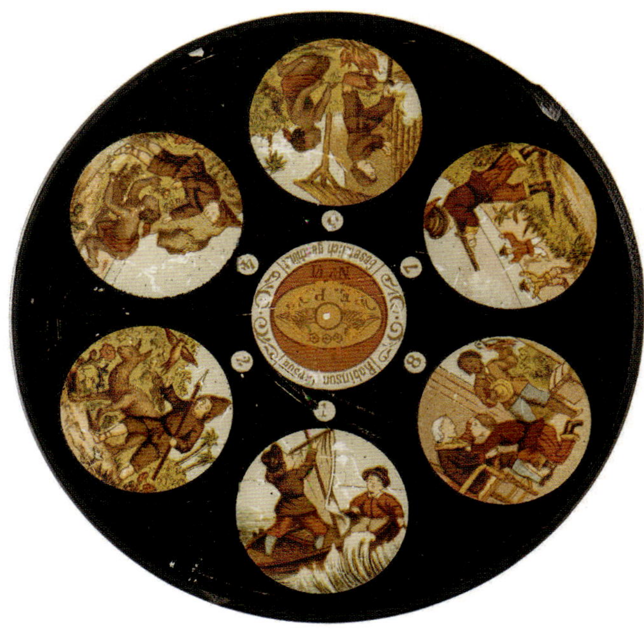

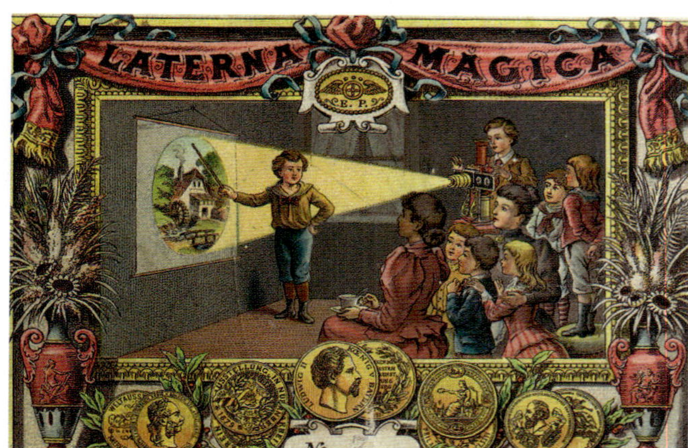

Superstar Performers: Stoddard – "Prince of Lecturers"

Fig. 5.14 Let's turn now to the performers. First the Superstars.[20]

Bottom. John L Stoddard. Stoddard was the most famous of the lantern industry's major performers. He was an extremely popular lecturer, capable of filling a 3,000-seat hall for two weeks straight with his photographs of foreign cultures. People would line up two days in advance to buy tickets.

Right. An ad for a Portfolio of Stoddard's lantern-slide pictures. The ad mocks those who think a guided tour abroad can replace *Stoddard's Portfolio* as an introduction to travel. This printed *Portfolio* was so successful that after Stoddard retired, he published his lectures in book form – 14 volumes of them. They made him a multi-millionaire.

Stoddard began lecturing in the late 1870's and ended in 1897, giving about 3,000 performances. He was an extremely professional and meticulous performer, traveling with an advance man, a stage manager, and his own lantern operator. He carefully wrote out and then memorized his lectures, signaling slide changes with pre-arranged phrases in his lectures, rather than a signaling device or saying, "Next Please". Specializing in European travel, he mixed biography, poetry, humorous anecdotes, and history into his lectures. His style exuded culture. He dressed formally and stood very straight, speaking with a rich, deep, well-modulated voice, but emphasizing his points with energy and passion. No matter what the size of the hall, he could be clearly understood.

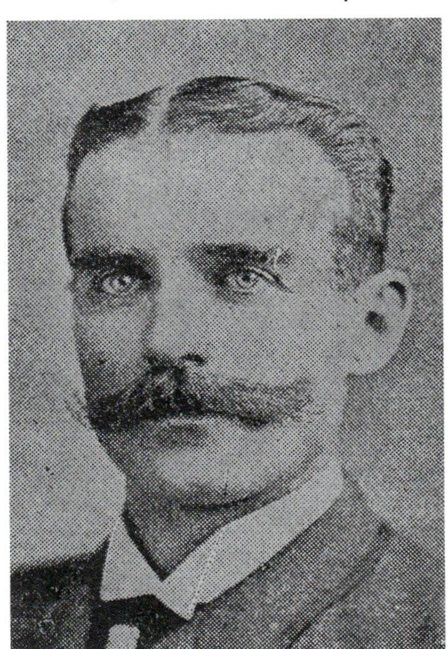

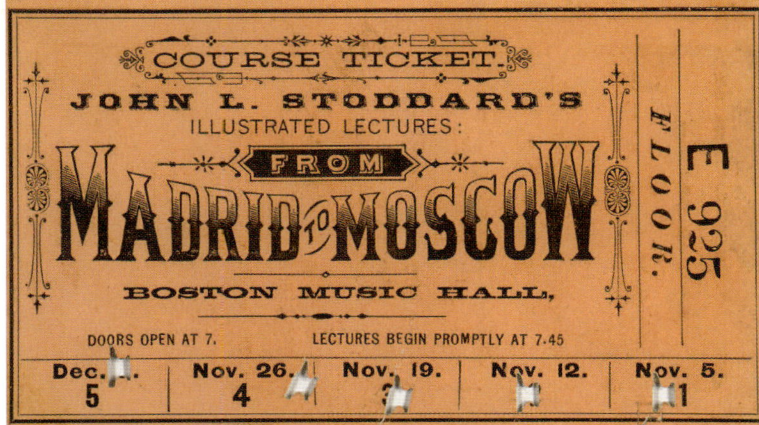

Above. Ticket to Stoddard performance. This 2½" x 4" ornate ticket for Stoddard's show in The Boston Music Hall gives a sense of the social event that his lectures became. The Hall seated 2,700.

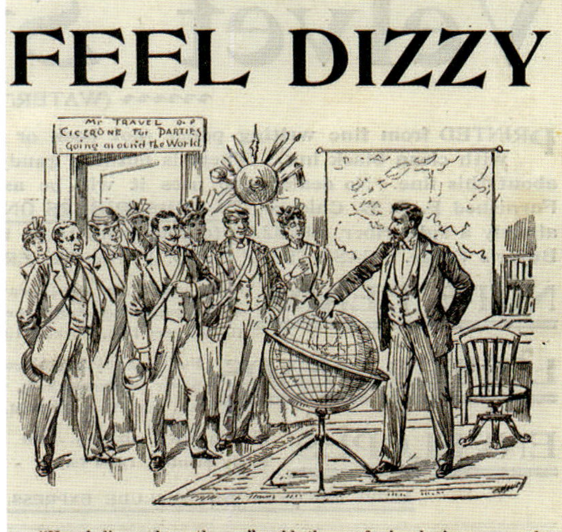

Superstar Performers: Superstar Burton Holmes Dons Gas Mask

Fig. 5.15 Superstars such as *Burton Holmes* rose far above amateur performers of magic lantern shows, or even the top 500 professionals.[21]

Right. Burton Holmes broadside. Holmes coined the term "travelogue" and created his shows first with slides, and later with slides and movies, eventually earning a Hollywood star.

Left. Holmes dressed for a show. Holmes generally cultivated an elegant persona on stage. But he also liked to appear in the costumes of the countries he visited, or, in the case of his *Victory Travelogue,* in one of the gas masks worn during WWI.

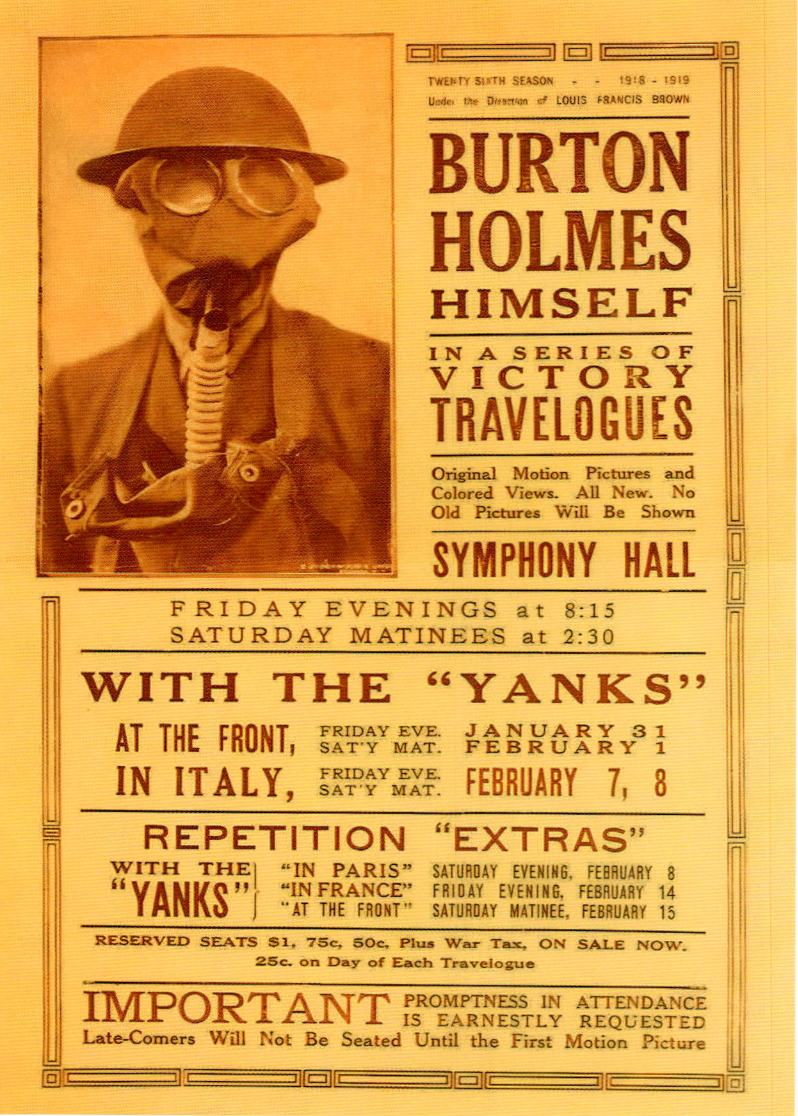

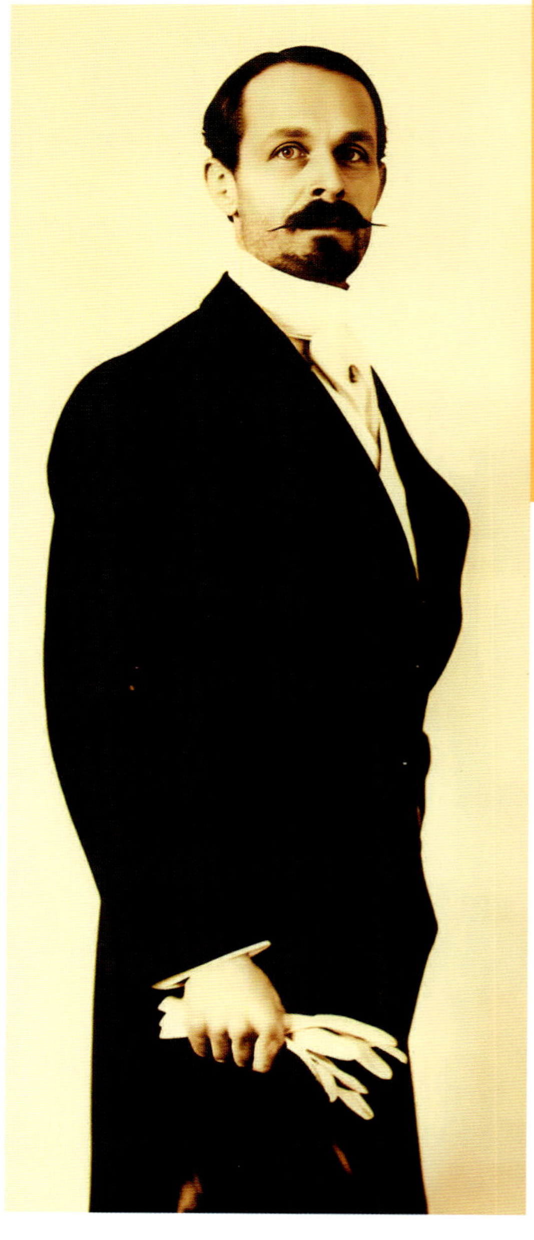

By his 50th anniversary year tour in 1946, Holmes had performed before 3,000 audiences, totaling ten million people. Superstars such as Holmes performed in large city halls, often before audiences of 2,000–3,000. They could be paid, in 2025 dollars, as much as $10,000 a lecture.

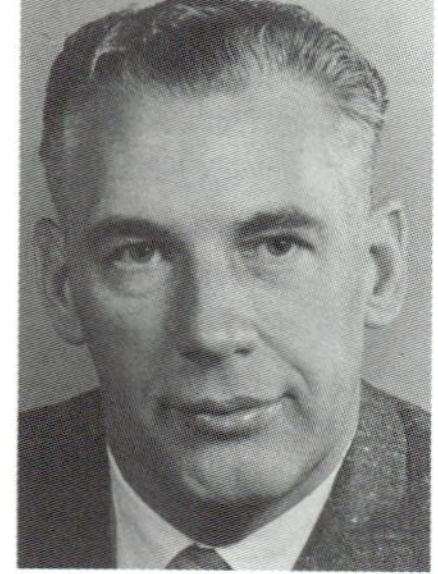

Bottom centre. In 1946, Holmes passed on the mantle he had inherited from Stoddard by pinning his lapel gardenia on Thayer Soule, who had sometimes given lantern lectures as a stand-in for Holmes. (In effect, Holmes had been franchising the "Holmes" brand.)

For 60 years Soule produced movie travelogues in all parts of the world, and presented them in person throughout the United States and Canada, including 28 performances in New York City's Carnegie Hall.

You can see movies by both Soule and Holmes on YouTube.

Pioneering Women Take on Men

Fig. 5.16 Five-to-ten percent of professional lantern lecturers were women.[22]

Annie Peck was a classics professor at Smith College, and also the first to climb several major mountains in South America.

Below. Annie Peck in climbing mask. At one point Peck climbed with a wooden face mask to protect herself from the elements. On it she drew an outlandish mustache to poke fun at the male competitors who were racing her to see who could climb the tallest mountain. She supported her climbing adventures by giving lantern lectures about her exploits.

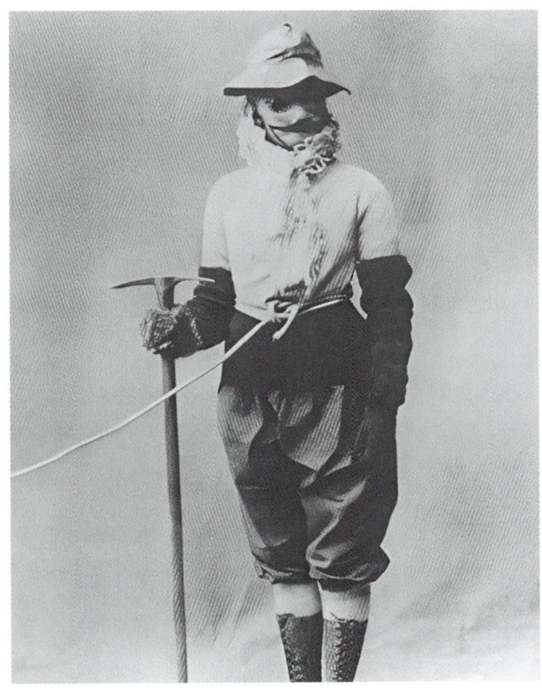

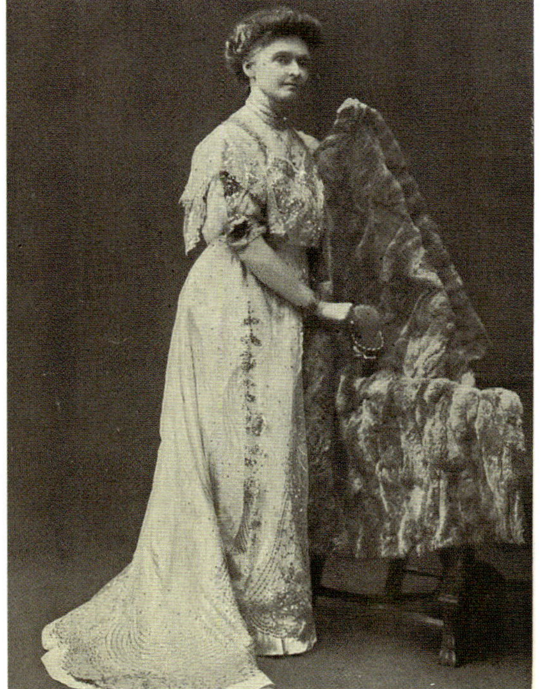

Left. Annie Peck advertisement. One of the most outstanding women lecturers was Annie Peck, seen in a 1908 advertisement for her lecture at the Academy of Music in Brooklyn.

Bottom left. Advertisement for Mrs. Leonidas Hubbard. A 1906 ad in *Talent* tells us that Hubbard presents, "her thrilling story in an exceedingly vivid and dramatic manner, illustrating it with many stereopticon views of the grand and beautiful scenery".

"Her youth, her slender and graceful figure, and the delicacy of her features are in striking contrast to the arduous and daring nature of [her] great undertaking".

Adventurous women such as Hubbard were not above using gender stereotypes to their advantage.

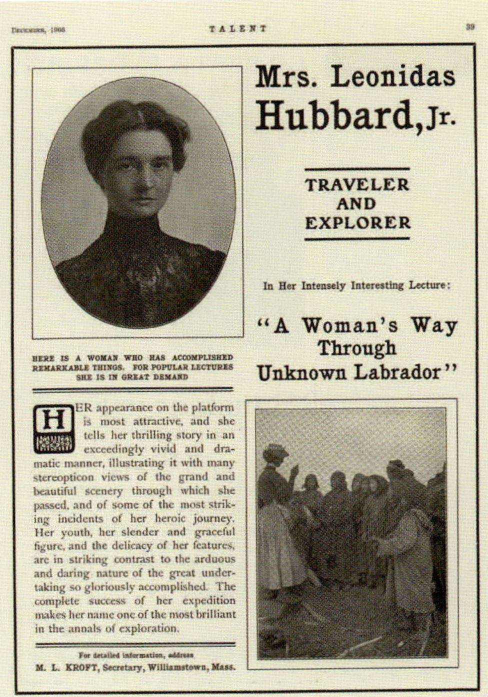

December, 1906 TALENT 39

Mrs. Leonidas Hubbard, Jr.

TRAVELER AND EXPLORER

In Her Intensely Interesting Lecture:

"A Woman's Way Through Unknown Labrador"

HERE IS A WOMAN WHO HAS ACCOMPLISHED REMARKABLE THINGS. FOR POPULAR LECTURES SHE IS IN GREAT DEMAND

HER appearance on the platform is most attractive, and she tells her thrilling story in an exceedingly vivid and dramatic manner, illustrating it with many stereopticon views of the grand and beautiful scenery through which she passed, and of some of the most striking incidents of her heroic journey. Her youth, her slender and graceful figure, and the delicacy of her features, are in striking contrast to the arduous and daring nature of the great undertaking so gloriously accomplished. The complete success of her expedition makes her name one of the most brilliant in the annals of exploration.

For detailed information, address
M. L. KROFT, Secretary, Williamstown, Mass.

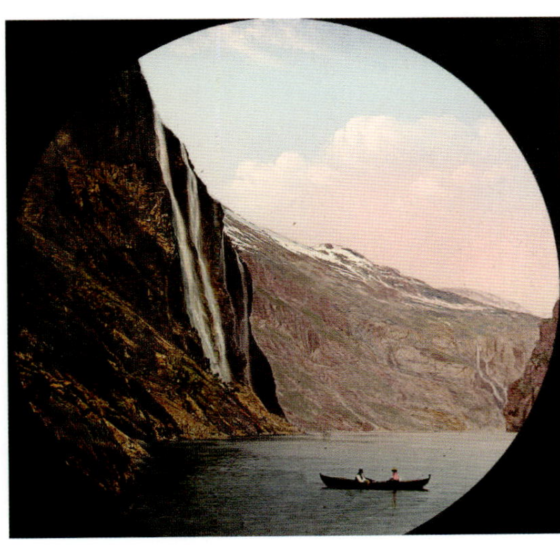

Bottom. Slide of Labrador scenery, such as Hubbard might have used.

Women Performers: Breed Wields a Single-Hair Brush

Fig. 5.17 Katherine Gordon Breed was, for a short time, a woman lecturer, but her more important role in lantern history was as the medium's most outstanding colorist.[23]

Right. Katherine Breed in a brochure for her illustrated lecture, the slides for which she presumably colored herself. The coloring for slides was applied in various mediums to the images on the glass. Though the work of the colorists contributed enormously to the success of lantern shows, the colorists themselves were usually anonymous. Breed was an exception.

She worked for two of the most famous illustrated lecturers, John L. Stoddard, and Burton Holmes. She travelled with both to get the colors of their images exactly right, and often painted with a single-haired brush, obtaining extraordinarily realistic results.

Below: A set colors of the sort that Breed might have used.

Bottom. Holmes helps Breed from the carriage at Yellowstone where they were preparing an illustrated lecture.

Chapter opening picture: Breed's slide of Yellowstone Falls. Coloring like this helped make this image the grand finale of the Holmes lecture on *Yellowstone National Park.* The slide is about 3 x 4". At that scale you'd have to look very carefully at the rock on the left to see the two tiny fishermen. The largest would be about an eighth of an inch high. He's colored in three different colors. That's Breed at work.

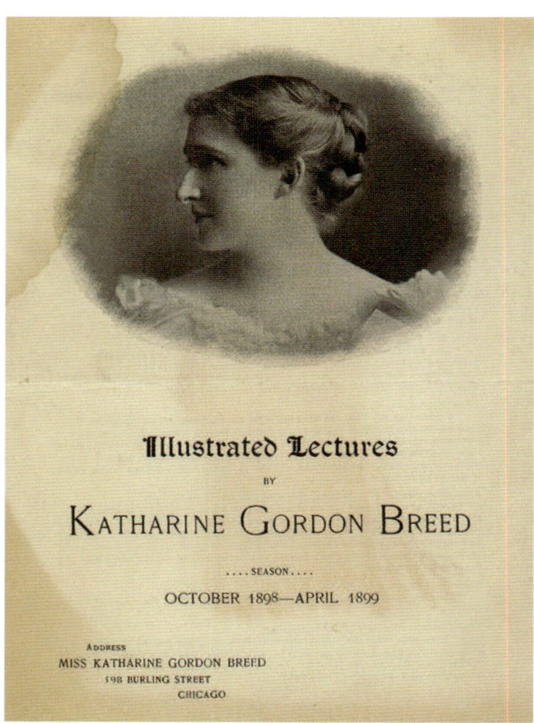

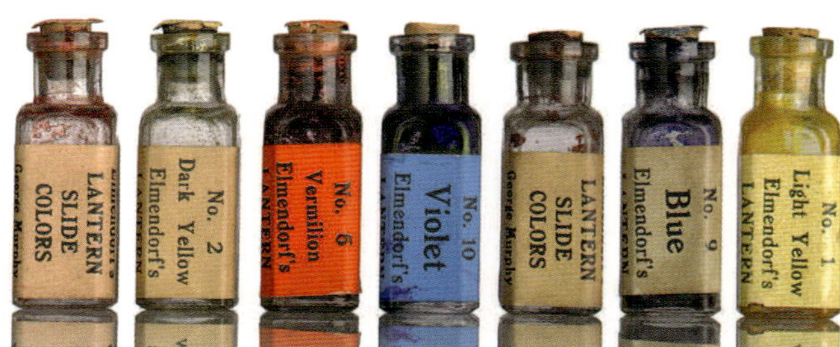

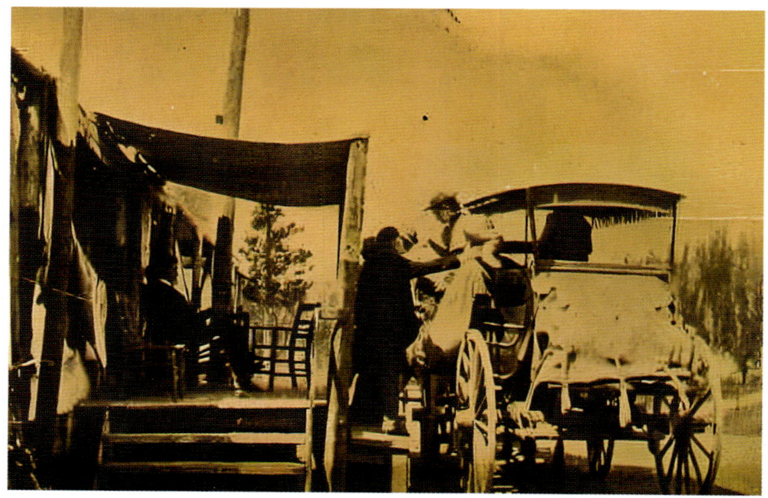

Black Performers: Shows Fighting Slavery, *Negro Looking Up*

Fig. 5.18 African Americans used the magic lantern in all kinds of ways – to protest slavery, for "negro improvement", for religious purposes, and to encourage emigration.[24]

Top. The frontispiece of Prof. W. G. Hynes booklet, *Negro Looking Up,* features his young son sitting on the American flag with a college in the background, exuberantly pointing the way upward. The subtitle of the book captures the message of Hynes' shows: "Out of Darkness (Slavery) Into Light, Future Hope, Onward to Victory". Hynes, who called himself "The Picture Historian", began his magic lantern career in 1871 at age six, when Santa gave him a $1 lantern for Christmas. From then on he was constantly upgrading his equipment and expanding his programs. At age 24 he finished his first six-month performing tour from which he cleared $96 (about $3,500 in 2025).

Below. Hynes and his wife setting up a combination lantern slide/movie show. Hynes took his first movie, of 400 feet, in 1905, and continued to take movies on a regular basis, especially at Baptist conventions. His shows had a heavy emphasis on "Negro improvement", showing pictures of successful Black doctors and merchants to inspire others to follow their footsteps – a radical position at the time.

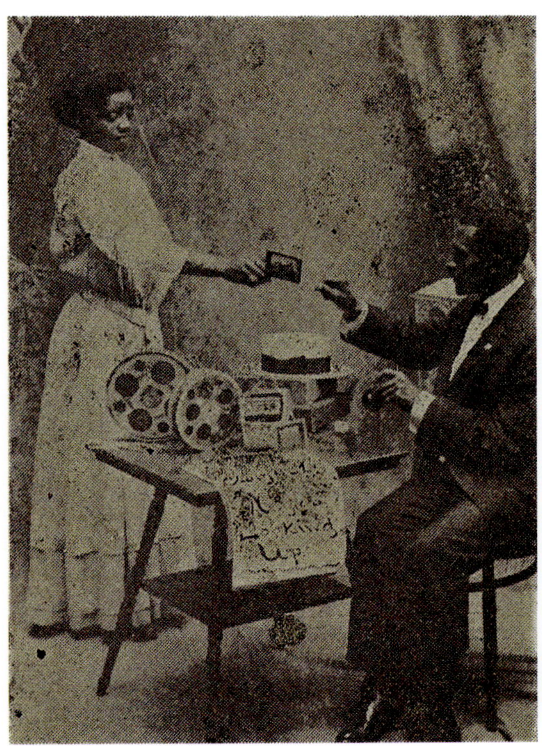

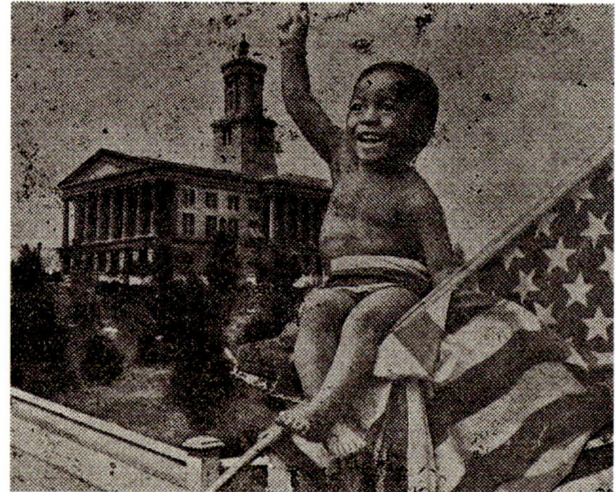

Hynes also used literature (Beale's *Uncle Tom's Cabin*), and Beale's images of the Spanish American War, which show Blacks and whites joining together in the war effort. Hynes lantern shows had a strong religious emphasis, and incorporated images of Bible History, likely by Beale, and hymns that were almost certainly by Beale: *Rock of Ages* and *The Holy City*.

Bottom right. Throughout his life Hynes was constantly on the road, making year-long trips, often with his family, travelling first by carriage, and after 1921 by car. While traveling on the Texas/Alabama border in an 1889-90 trip, his carriage was caught in the current at a ford. As he shows in his sketch, he and his horses were swept away, and he might well have drowned. He was saved by a man on shore who saw him, threw him a grapevine, and pulled him to safety.

To see a re-created Black History Show, search with Google for *Dr. Toer's Amazing Magic Lantern Show*.

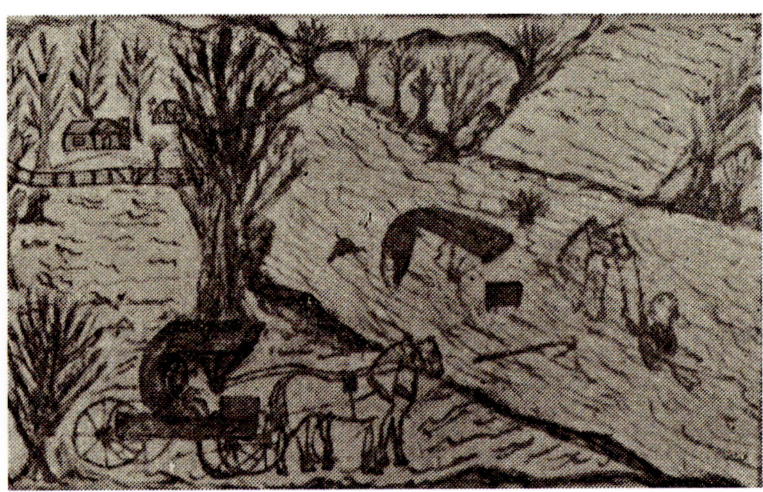

Show Recruits Black Colonists

Fig. 5.19 African Americans used the lantern for a wide variety of purposes, including promoting emigration.[25]

Right. Prof. J. C. Hazeley flyer. Hazeley, "a Native African", offers "Africa at Your Door", a "*Grand African Sciopticon Panorama*" in which Black American audiences can "see the Heathen African Women, the Hair Dressers, the Heathen African boys going to school, … the Heathen African Women with their babies on their backs".

Hazeley hits every note, pitching his message as well to concerns closer to home: "You all like coffee; then come and see the Tree that bears the Coffee you drink, and bring your children with you".

Hazeley sounds like a missionary, but his real purpose was to generate interest in colonizing Liberia.

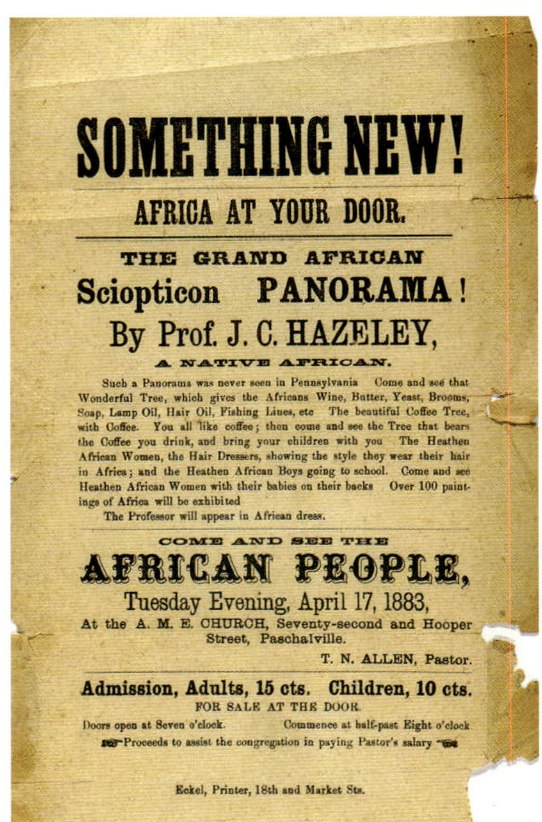

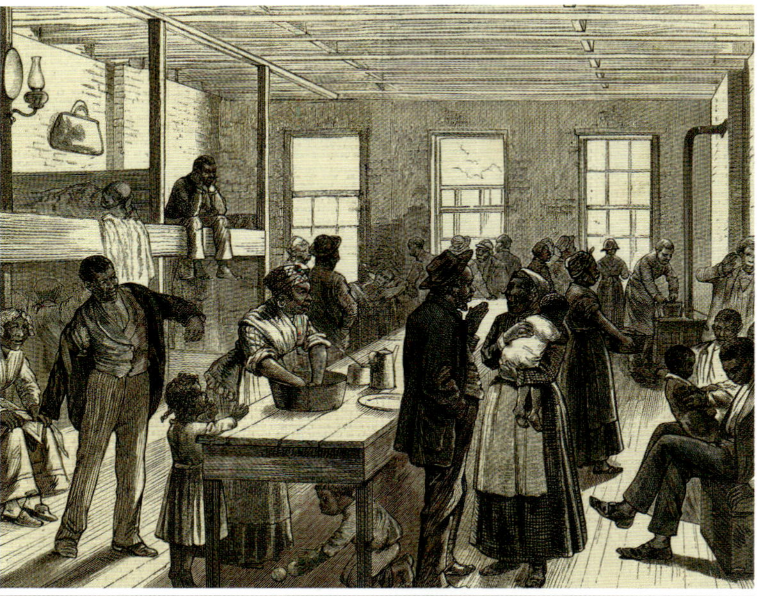

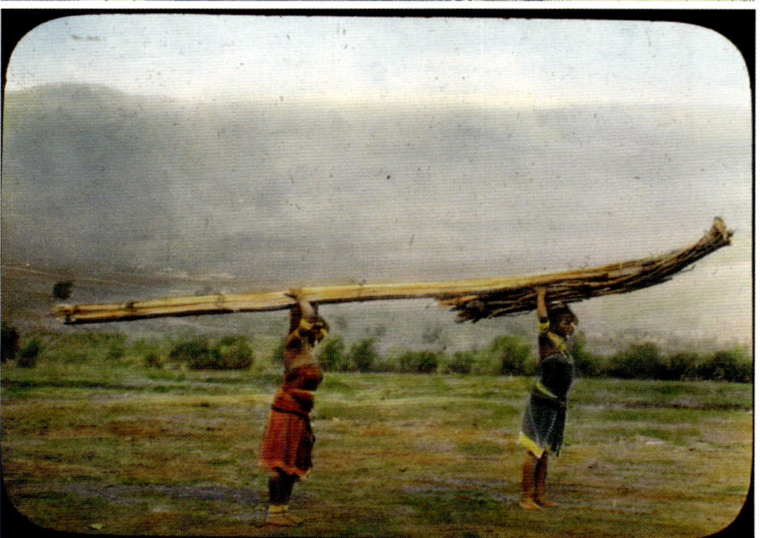

Upper left. Engraving of black emigrants. Hazeley was at least partly successful, and convinced a group in Conway, AR to emigrate. The etching shows a group of such Blacks waiting to board a ship for Liberia.

Lower left. Slide of Africa. The color slide is the sort that Hazeley might have used in his presentation. It shows "Heathen African women" carrying a boat made of reeds.

Black Performers: The Devil and the Church

Fig. 5.20 Black churches, just like white churches, were heavy users of the lantern.[26]

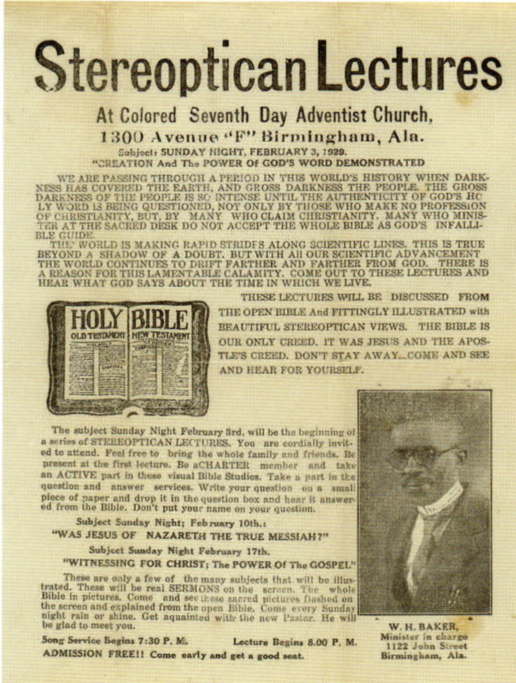

Stereoptican Lectures

At Colored Seventh Day Adventist Church,
1300 Avenue "F" Birmingham, Ala.
Subject: SUNDAY NIGHT, FEBRUARY 3, 1929.
"CREATION And The POWER Of GOD'S WORD DEMONSTRATED

WE ARE PASSING THROUGH A PERIOD IN THIS WORLD'S HISTORY WHEN DARKNESS HAS COVERED THE EARTH, AND GROSS DARKNESS THE PEOPLE. THE GROSS DARKNESS OF THE PEOPLE IS SO INTENSE UNTIL THE AUTHENTICITY OF GOD'S HOLY WORD IS BEING QUESTIONED, NOT ONLY BY THOSE WHO MAKE NO PROFESSION OF CHRISTIANITY, BUT, BY MANY WHO CLAIM CHRISTIANITY. MANY WHO MINISTER AT THE SACRED DESK DO NOT ACCEPT THE WHOLE BIBLE AS GOD'S INFALLIBLE GUIDE.

THE WORLD IS MAKING RAPID STRIDES ALONG SCIENTIFIC LINES. THIS IS TRUE BEYOND A SHADOW OF A DOUBT. BUT WITH All OUR SCIENTIFIC ADVANCEMENT THE WORLD CONTINUES TO DRIFT FARTHER AND FARTHER FROM GOD. THERE IS A REASON FOR THIS LAMENTABLE CALAMITY. COME OUT TO THESE LECTURES AND HEAR WHAT GOD SAYS ABOUT THE TIME IN WHICH WE LIVE.

HOLY BIBLE
OLD TESTAMENT NEW TESTAMENT

THESE LECTURES WILL BE DISCUSSED FROM THE OPEN BIBLE And FITTINGLY ILLUSTRATED with BEAUTIFUL STEREOPTICAN VIEWS. THE BIBLE IS OUR ONLY CREED. IT WAS JESUS AND THE APOSTLE'S CREED. DON'T STAY AWAY...COME AND SEE AND HEAR FOR YOURSELF.

The subject Sunday Night February 3rd, will be the beginning of a series of STEREOPTICAN LECTURES. You are cordially invited to attend. Feel free to bring the whole family and friends. Be present at the first lecture. Be aCHARTER member and take an ACTIVE part in these visual Bible Studies. Take a part in the question and answer services. Write your question on a small piece of paper and drop it in the question box and hear it answered from the Bible. Don't put your name on your question.

Subject Sunday Night; February 10th.:
"WAS JESUS OF NAZARETH THE TRUE MESSIAH?"

Subject Sunday Night February 17th.
"WITNESSING FOR CHRIST; The POWER Of The GOSPEL"

These are only a few of the many subjects that will be illustrated. These will be real SERMONS on the screen. The whole Bible in pictures. Come and see these sacred pictures flashed on the screen and explained from the open Bible. Come every Sunday night rain or shine. Get aquainted with the new Pastor. He will be glad to meet you.

Song Service Begins 7:30 P. M. Lecture Begins 8.00 P. M.
ADMISSION FREE!! Come early and get a good seat.

W. H. BAKER,
Minister in charge
1122 John Street
Birmingham, Ala.

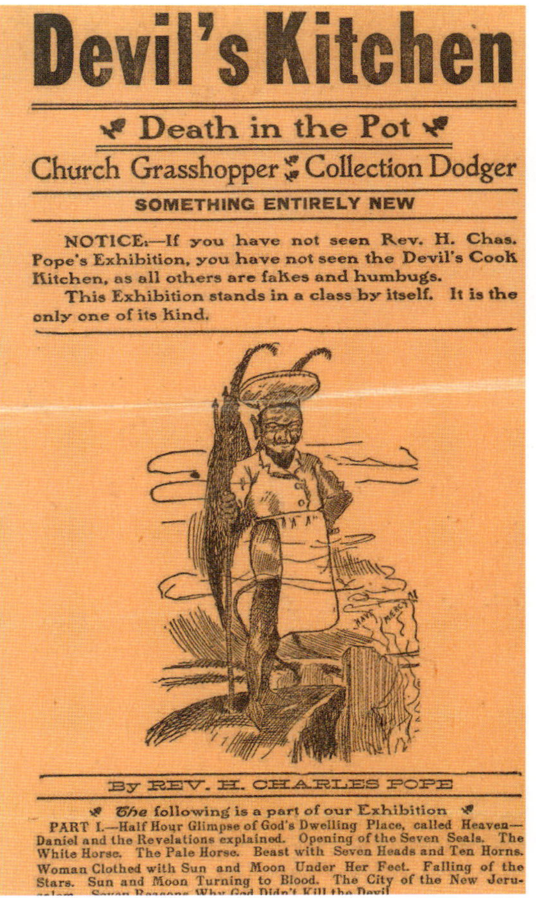

Devil's Kitchen

Death in the Pot

Church Grasshopper Collection Dodger

SOMETHING ENTIRELY NEW

NOTICE:—If you have not seen Rev. H. Chas. Pope's Exhibition, you have not seen the Devil's Cook Kitchen, as all others are fakes and humbugs.

This Exhibition stands in a class by itself. It is the only one of its kind.

By REV. H. CHARLES POPE

The following is a part of our Exhibition

PART I.—Half Hour Glimpse of God's Dwelling Place, called Heaven—Daniel and the Revelations explained. Opening of the Seven Seals. The White Horse. The Pale Horse. Beast with Seven Heads and Ten Horns. Woman Clothed with Sun and Moon Under Her Feet. Falling of the Stars. Sun and Moon Turning to Blood. The City of the New Jeru-

Left. Stereopticon Lectures by Rev. Baker. Baker, of The Colored Seventh Day Adventist Church, promises "real SERMONS on the screen". The sermons were to be held "every Sunday night, rain or shine". Baker was a new pastor in 1929, and chose illustrated sermons as a dramatic way to introduce himself to his parishioners.

Lower left. Detail of a broadside for *The Devil's Kitchen.* This program was a Black religious show produced in Birmingham, AL. The minister appears to have used commercially available slides, combined with one-of-a-kind slides of his own devising. The production combines theology and humor in a unique manner.

Middle right. Sunday School class using the magic lantern. The class is white, but similar scenes would have been common in Black churches. The screen is suspended with strings.

Bottom right. Slide by Albert Prieger. Prieger was a lantern slide manufacturer who specialized in images for Seventh Day Adventist churches. His image depicts a Biblical prophet imagining the things of the future that would foretell the End of Days.

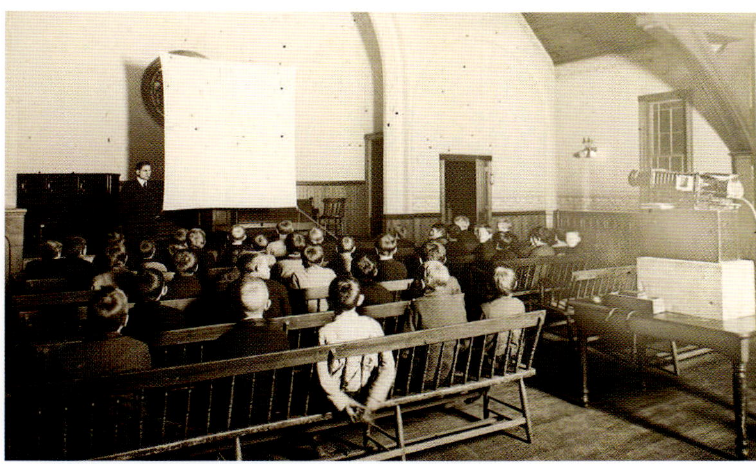

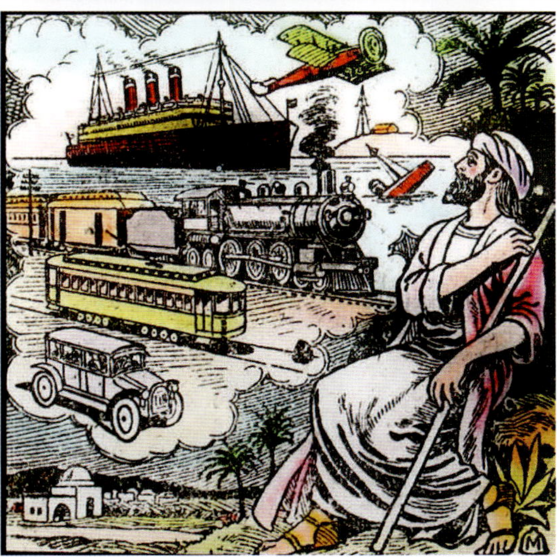

Small Time Performers – "The Terror of the West"

Fig. 5.21 At the other end of the spectrum from the superstars were the small-time performers.[27]

Bottom: "Terror of the West" cartoon. *Puck* magazine pokes fun at the tendency of small-time lantern showmen to exaggerate their subject matter. The lecturer's actual slide depicts a decrepit cowboy. The image the lecturer hopes his story creates is projected on screen – that of bloodthirsty desperado.

The aspirations of a real small-time showman are captured in a letter by one hopeful to a lantern distributor. A direct transcript:

> *Hicksville, Apr. th 22, 1857. Sirs thare is an article that I wish to purchas and I pen a fiew lines to you in order to ascertain if you have it in your possession namely a magic lantern and if not pease inform me whare I can get me and what the probable Cost of one would be enclosed is a pd stamp address Hicksville Defiance co ohio. Yours in haste L. B. Hoit (?) To Oakley & Son*

Yes, there really was (and is) a "Hicksville".

Left. The Williams Family, successful small-time performers, in the wagon that they used to transport their show from Chicago to the state of Washington in 1901–1904. They covered 4,000 miles, giving about 130 shows, mostly in small-town venues. Their first show netted $14.75, about $550 in 2025 dollars.

The tremendous number of showmen between the superstars and the small-time performers filled the nation's halls and supported the lantern industry.

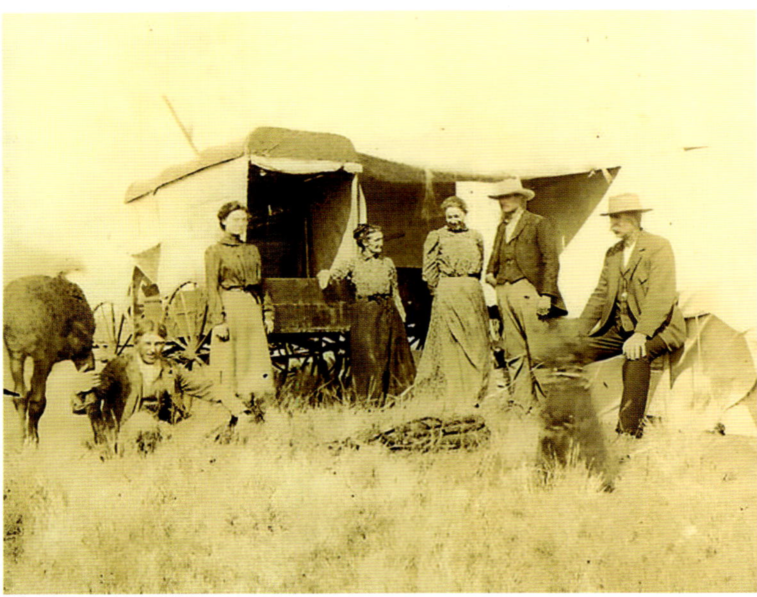

Courtesy Lynn Martin and Jackie Williams Fisher.

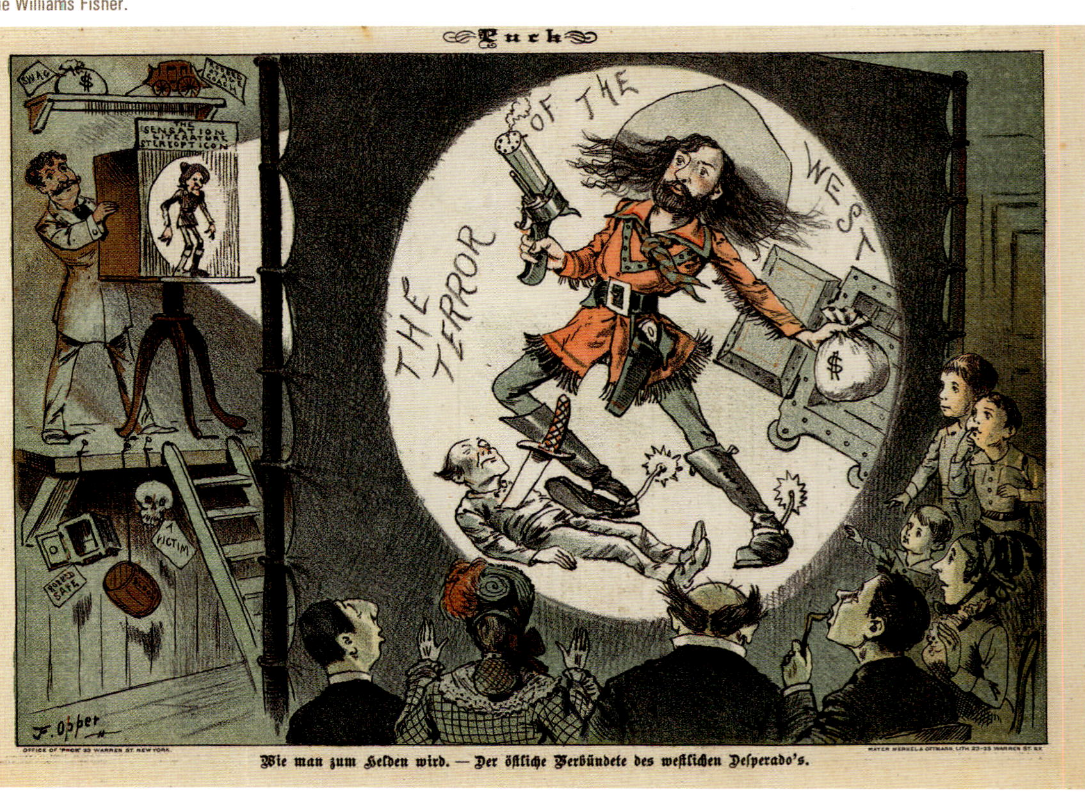

Illustrated Lectures – Gold Found in Alaska

Fig. 5.22 The "Illustrated lecture", became the staple of the lantern industry by 1890, largely supplanting the earlier variety format for professional magic lantern shows, and amateur shows as well.[28]

Right. Poster for an Alaska lecture. This large poster (17 x 23") for an illustrated lecture was produced by Sears, Roebuck & Co., which sold a package for the aspiring lecturer containing 100 copies of the poster, along with a lantern and slides. In 1908 Sears produced similar advertising material and slides for 13 other subjects (see Fig.5.37). The fact that a mass-marketer like Sears found it worthwhile to offer such a variety of sets is another indication of the wide-spread popularity of lantern lecturing by amateurs.

The poster highlights a "Talking Machine" to be combined with the illustrated lecture of "Magnificent Photographic Views". If you bought copies of this broadside, you had to buy the Talking Machine too, since it was pictured. Sears marketing!

Bottom. Slide of gold diggers. This slide image, by the Keystone View Co., is the kind that may have been used in the Alaska show. The miners panning for gold are trying to protect themselves from the ferocious Alaskan mosquitoes.

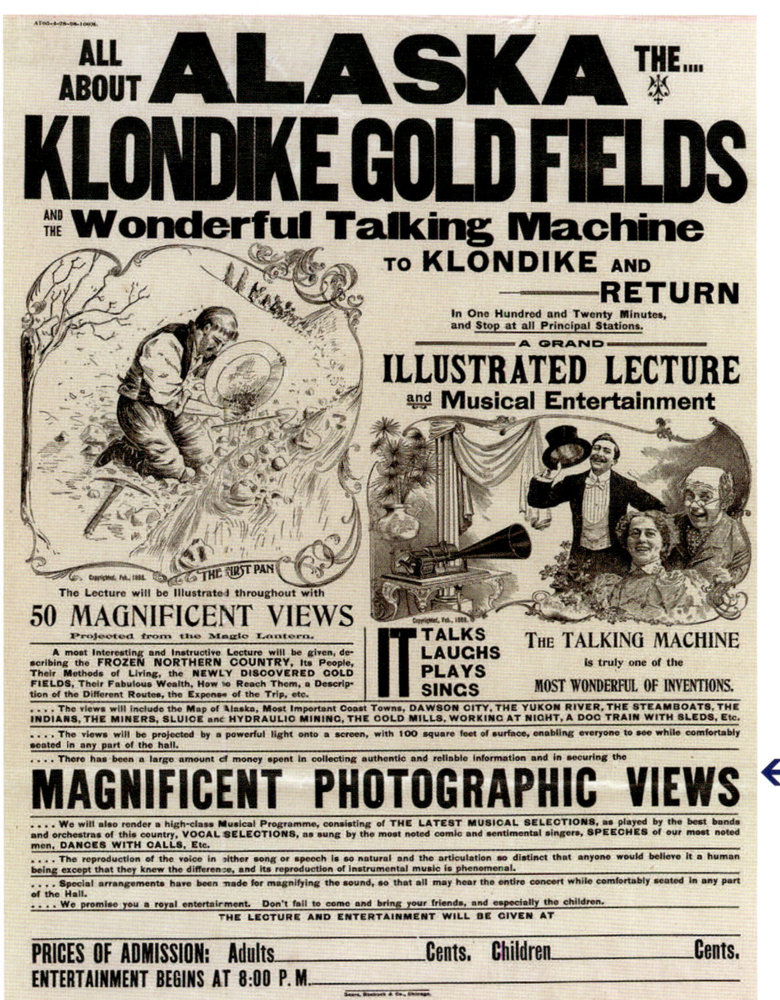

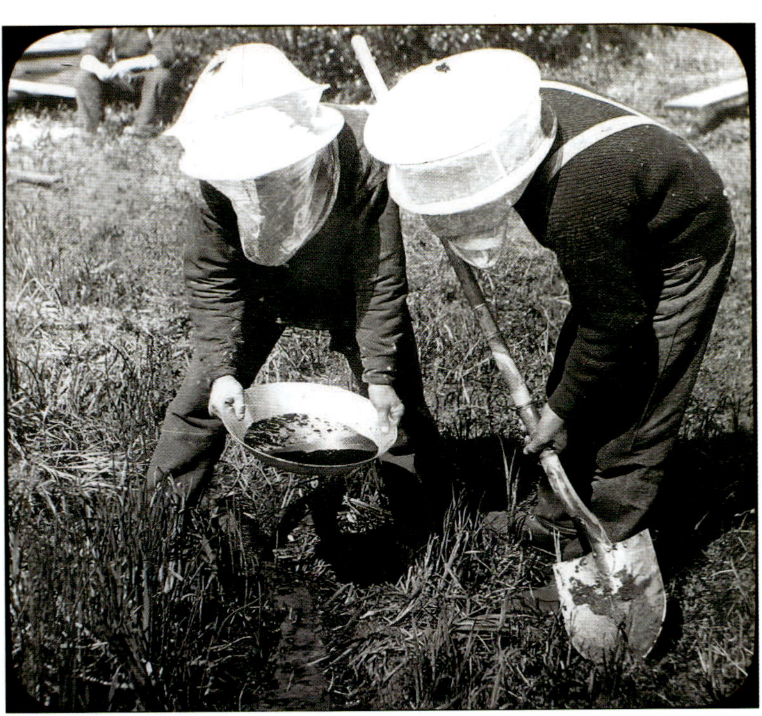

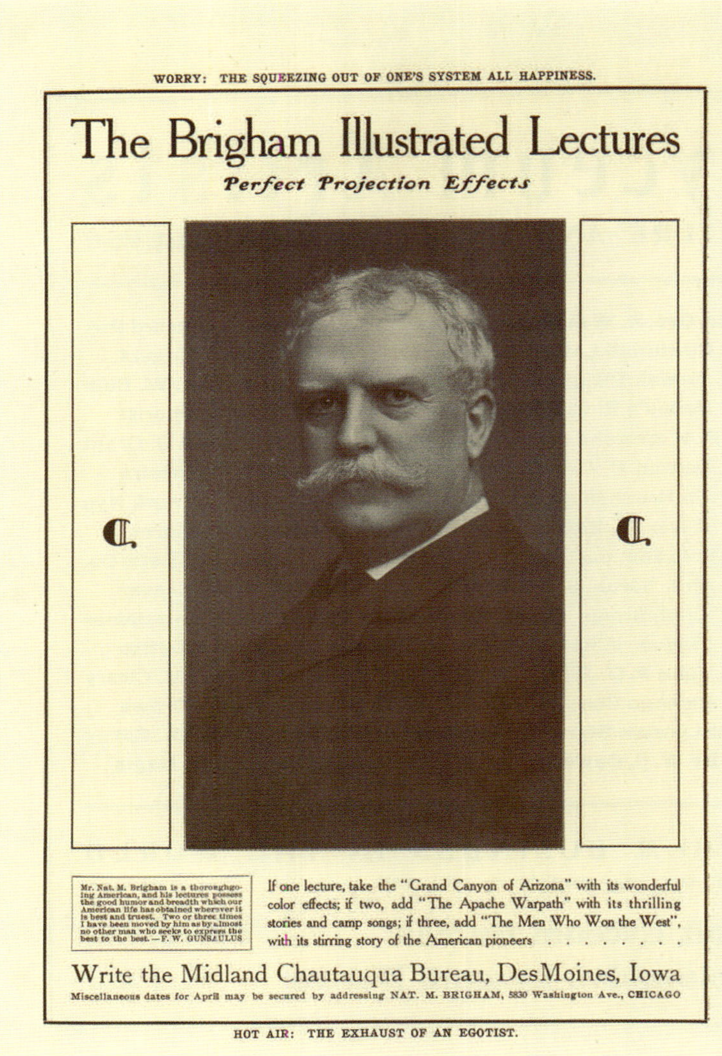

Nat Brigham Wows Unkapupa

Fig. 5.23 Nat Brigham was a talented lecturer who managed to win the praise of one of the industry's toughest critics.[29]

Left. Nat Brigham's in *The Lyceumite*, a trade magazine. In this full-page ad of March 1906 Brigham presents himself as he does in almost all his other ads – with a formal picture. He may appear a bit stern, but he was a very effective speaker who also sang during some of his shows about the American West.

Bottom left. Slide of The Grand Canyon. This slide suggests the kind of images Brigham might have used in his lecture on the subject.

Bottom right. Unkapupa. *The Lyceumite's* uncompromising and often caustic critic, Unkapupa, whose "cudgel and crown" logo is shown, summed up Brigham's appeal: "[He] is the best illustrated lecturer I have ever heard. That's strong, but true. He can make the average lecturer with illustrated accompaniment look like three dimes … I bow low to this gentleman of polished method".

From 1896 to 1906 Brigham gave 2,000 lectures – that's an average of 200 a year. If he had an audience of 500 at an average show (and he probably had a lot more), he was reaching 100,000 a year. If he was paid $100 a show (and he was probably paid a lot more), he would have grossed $20,000 a year, or about $750,000 a year in 2025 dollars.

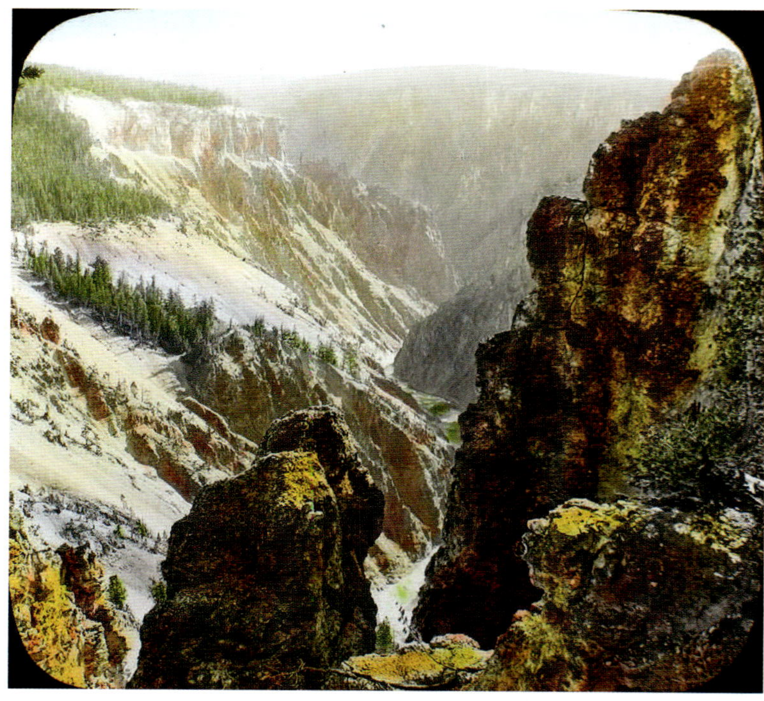

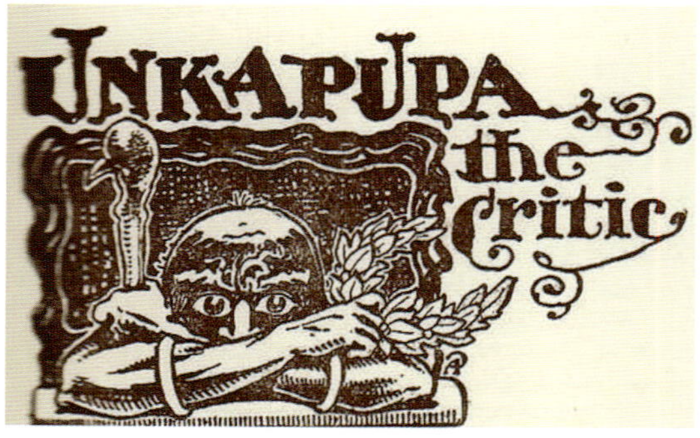

Religious Performances: Passion Play Attracts World

Fig. 5.24 The greatest use of lantern slides for religious purposes was undoubtedly the small presentations in Sunday Schools, evening programs, missionary activities and the like.[30]

Bottom. Flyer for Feicht's Oberammergau. Among professional religious shows, the most popular was re-creations of the *Passion Play* put on by the Austrian village of Oberammergau. This popularity was spurred by the success of John L. Stoddard's performance about the *Passion Play*, which was so powerful that Stoddard required a special team of ushers to remove the women who fainted when Christ was crucified.

The *Play* developed in 1634 when the people of Oberammergau were threatened with the plague. They promised God that if he would spare them its suffering, they would give a *Passion Play every* ten years thenceforth. By the 1890s Oberammergau had grown into a major religious pilgrimage site for Americans, spurred in no small part by lantern presentations.

H. E. Feicht's version employed an orchestra, chorus, and chimes, and was the only one endorsed by the villagers. Other versions of the *Passion Play* were available in the lantern catalogs for amateur showmen.

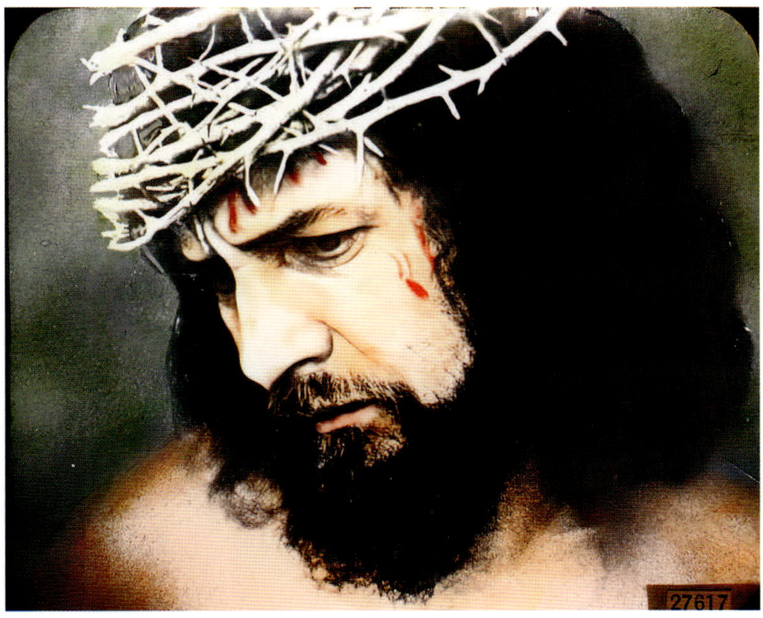

Top right, and bottom. Two color slides of the Oberammergau *Play*, though not from Feicht's show. They depict villager Anton Lang as Christ, and part of the Play's cast of 200, massed in front of the main set.

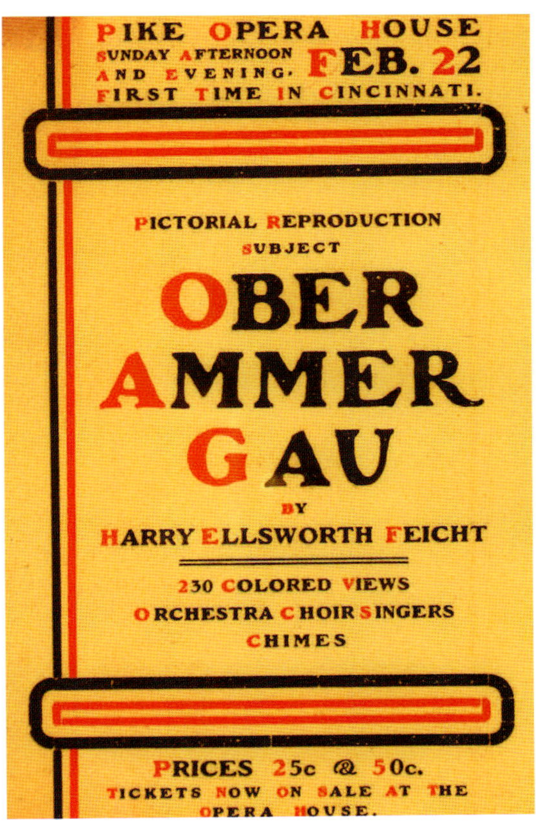

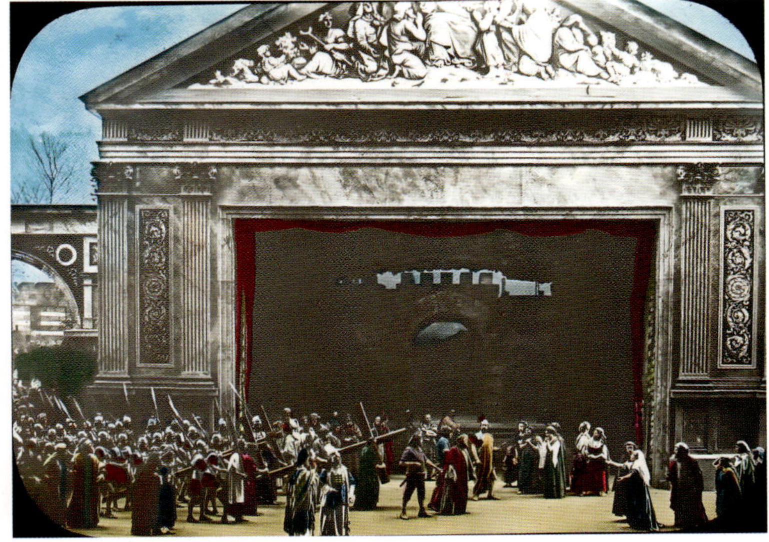

End of World & Missionaries

Fig. 5.25 The lantern's ability to excite and engage with the dramatic imagery of religion meant that it was widely used by those who saw the end of the world approaching, and those who wanted to reach out to the "heathen".[31]

Right. Broadside for Michael Paget Baxter's illustrated lecture on *Coming Prophetic Events*. Baxter toured the U. S., predicting that the world would end on April 23, 1908. He was author of *Future Wonders of Prophecy*, and editor of the *Christian Herald.*

COMING PROPHETIC EVENTS

Expected from Daniel & Revelation during next 12 Years before the End of this Age on the last day of Passover Week, April 23rd, 1908.

WARS AND REVOLUTIONS

in 1896-7, changing 23 into 10 Kingdoms (France, Britain, Spain, Italy, Austria, Greece, Egypt, Syria, Turkey, Balkan States) by 1898—Earthquakes, Famines, Pestilences—The Jews in Judea to Make a Seven Years' Covenant with Napoleon, on Passover Day, April 4, 1901, and to Restore their Sacrifices, Nov. 14, 1901, (Daniel vii. 24; viii 14 ix. 27)—Ascension of 144,000 Living Christians to Heaven without dying about March 12, 1903; Flight of Millions of Christians into a Wilderness; and Persecution of other Christians (while the Seals, Trumpets & Vials will be fulfilled) from 1904 until Passover Week in April, 1908, when Christ Descends and Reigns for 1,000 Years over the Nations (Rev. vi., viii., ix., xi., xii., xiii., xiv., xx.).

DISCOURSES BY REV. M. BAXTER

(Clergyman of the Church of England), and

REV. JOSHUA JAYE,

will (D.V.) be given

On these subjects, ILLUSTRATED BY COLOURED PICTURES, in

LESSER FREE TRADE HALL,

Peter Street, Manchester,

On Sunday, January 26th,

at 11 a.m., 3 p.m. and 6.45 to 9 p.m.

Second Address at Eight o'clock by Rev. Joshua Jaye.

And Monday, 27th, at 3 p.m. and 7.30 p.m.

SEATS FREE.

INDIA: HER HERITAGE AND HANDICAPS.

Slide 49 Neg. I-417

Hinduism teaches that it is sinful not to marry a daughter before puberty, and that there is real religious merit in marrying her very young.

Because of the high mortality among women, and the fact that widows cannot re-marry, wives are scarce. Hence, such a union as this one between a full grown man and a little girl - in this case nine years old - is not uncommon. Although but a child, this girl-wife has experienced much and her face has grown old and hard.

Bottom. Slide of lion. Baxter's lectures probably contained the same images as those in his book, like this lion symbolizing the evils of the Catholic Church. The horrific nature of such images, projected in a darkened room, certainly presented a vivid picture of the coming Apocalypse.

Left, and lower right. Script book. The hand-laced book contains the script and slide images for a missionary's illustrated lecture on India. The book and slides were meant to circulate to churches, in order to broaden the mission's reach. This page shown from the script bemoans the fate of a child bride.

Lectures like this were sponsored by many Christian missionaries. (Ten thousand missionaries worked in China alone.) Illustrated lectures were an excellent way of educating church audiences back home, and of raising money for further missionary work.

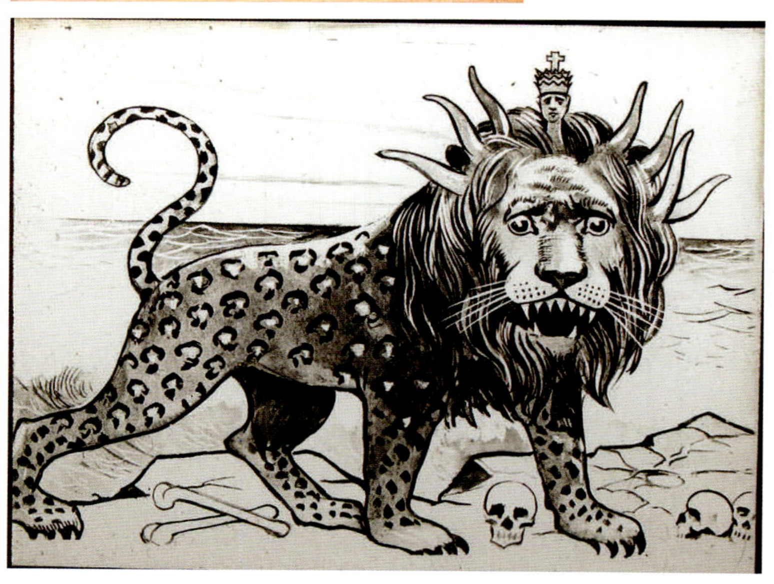

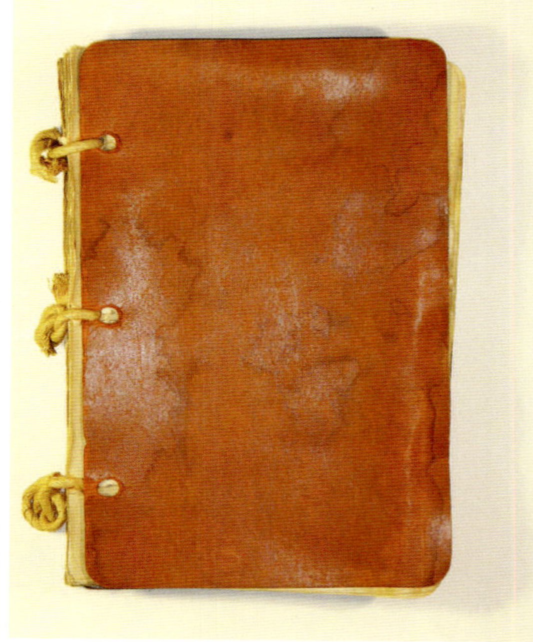

The Arts – *Indian Picture Opera*

Fig. 5.26 Shows related to the Arts accounted for about 15 percent of lantern productions.[32]

At right, Edward Curtis photograph. Curtis was one of America's foremost photographers. He spent 20 years collecting 2,400 images of Indians in the US and Canada, such as the dramatic photograph shown here.

During 1911–1912 he gave performances that mixed lantern slides of his images with movies, accompanied by a live orchestra. He sometimes called his production *The Indian Picture Opera*.

Below. The program, *The Intimate Story of Indian Tribal Life*, is for Curtis's November 18, 1911 performance at the Academy of Music in New York, which seats 4,000 people.

Bottom right. Red Fox flyer. A number of American Indians also gave shows about their own heritage. Red Fox offers a program "showing the various tribes in their quaint costumes, in the intimity [*sic*] of their home life in the great west".

In 1914, Red Fox rode 4006 miles to Washington to present a petition to the President asking him to name the second Saturday in May as "American Indian Day".

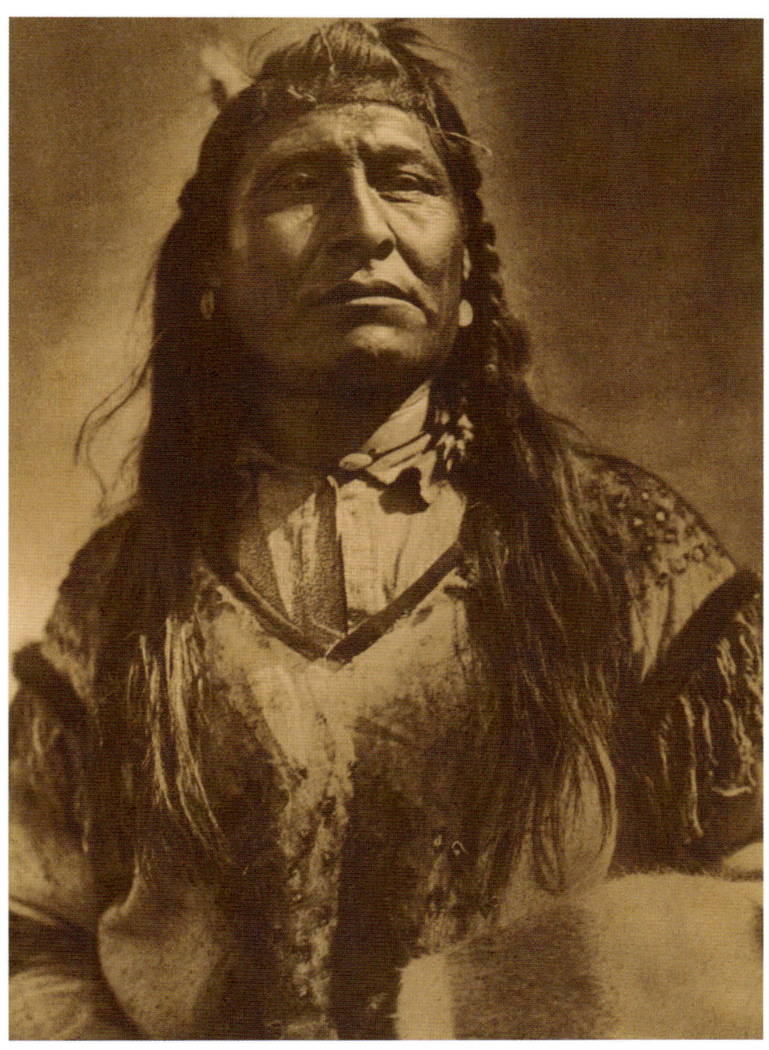

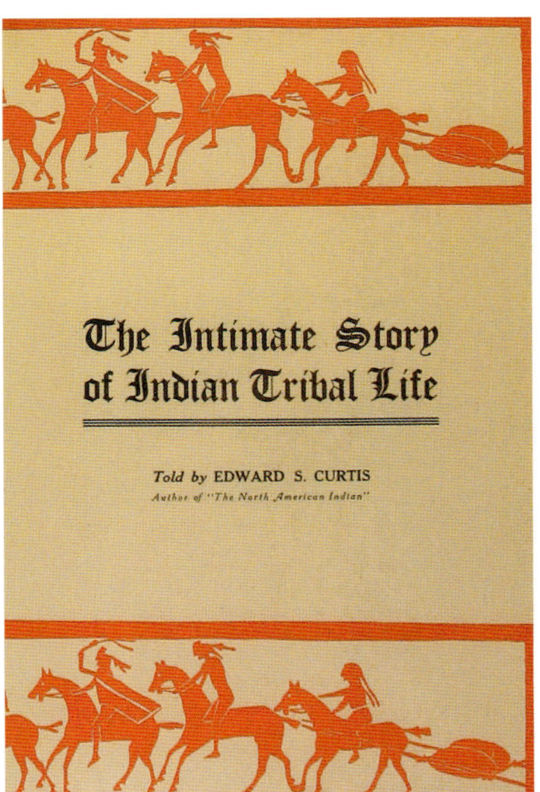

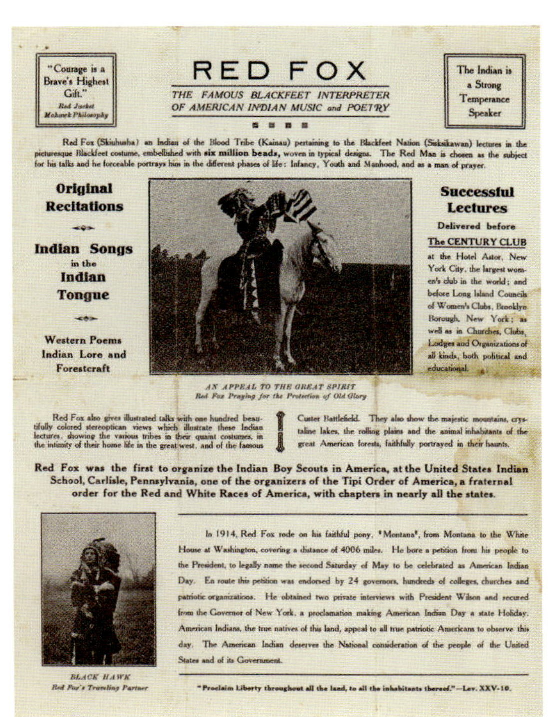

"Courage is a Brave's Highest Gift."
Red Jacket
Mohawk Philosophy

RED FOX

THE FAMOUS BLACKFEET INTERPRETER OF AMERICAN INDIAN MUSIC and POETRY

The Indian is a Strong Temperance Speaker

Red Fox (Skiuhusha) an Indian of the Blood Tribe (Kainau) pertaining to the Blackfeet Nation (Sisksikawan) lectures in the picturesque Blackfeet costume, embellished with **six million beads,** woven in typical designs. The Red Man is chosen as the subject for his talks and he forceable portrays him in the different phases of life: Infancy, Youth and Manhood, and as a man of prayer.

Original Recitations

Indian Songs in the **Indian Tongue**

Western Poems Indian Lore and Forestcraft

Successful Lectures

Delivered before

The CENTURY CLUB at the Hotel Astor, New York City, the largest women's club in the world; and before Long Island Councils of Women's Clubs, Brooklyn Borough, New York; as well as in Churches, Clubs, Lodges and Organizations of all kinds, both political and educational.

AN APPEAL TO THE GREAT SPIRIT
Red Fox Praying for the Protection of Old Glory

Red Fox also gives illustrated talks with one hundred beautifully colored stereoptican views which illustrate these Indian lectures, showing the various tribes in their quaint costumes, in the intimity of their home life in the great west, and of the famous Custer Battlefield. They also show the majestic mountains, crystaline lakes, the rolling plains and the animal inhabitants of the great American forests, faithfully portrayed in their haunts.

Red Fox was the first to organize the Indian Boy Scouts in America, at the United States Indian School, Carlisle, Pennsylvania, one of the organizers of the Tipi Order of America, a fraternal order for the Red and White Races of America, with chapters in nearly all the states.

In 1914, Red Fox rode on his faithful pony, "Montana", from Montana to the White House at Washington, covering a distance of 4006 miles. He bore a petition from his people to the President, to legally name the second Saturday of May to be celebrated as American Indian Day. En route this petition was endorsed by 24 governors, hundreds of colleges, churches and patriotic organizations. He obtained two private interviews with President Wilson and secured from the Governor of New York, a proclamation making American Indian Day a state Holiday. American Indians, the true natives of this land, appeal to all true patriotic Americans to observe this day. The American Indian deserves the National consideration of the people of the United States and of its Government.

BLACK HAWK
Red Fox's Traveling Partner

"Proclaim Liberty throughout all the land, to all the inhabitants thereof."—Lev. XXV-10.

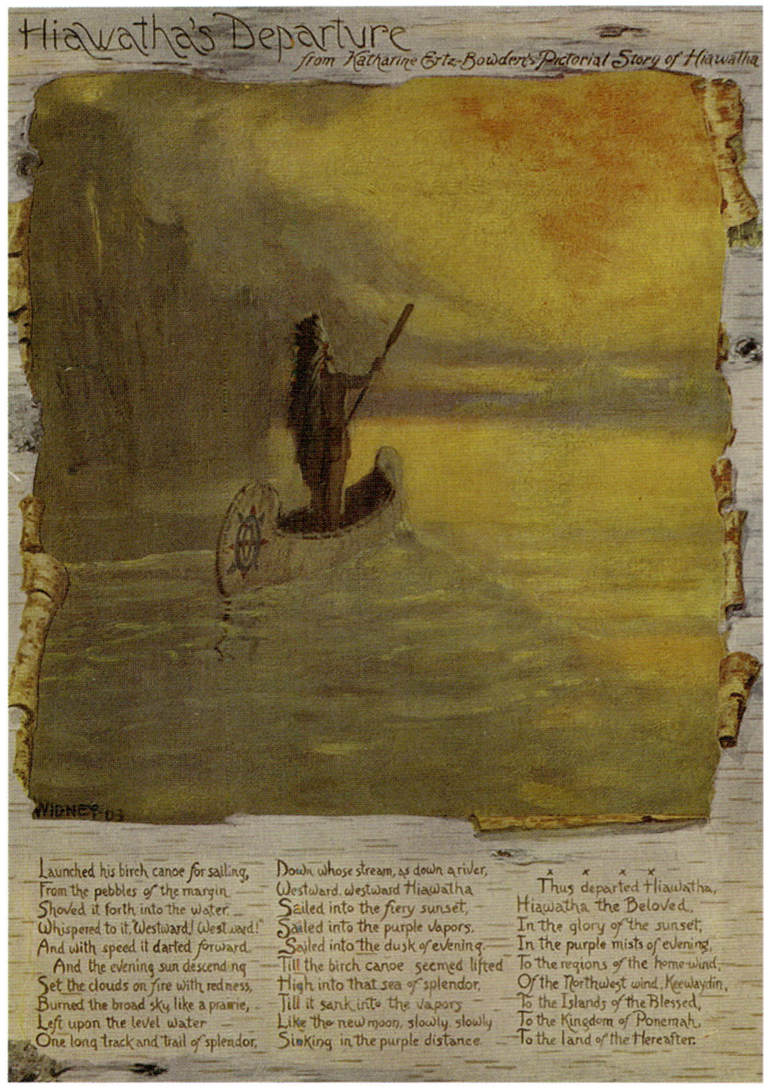

Courtesy of Valparaiso University Archives & Special Collections.

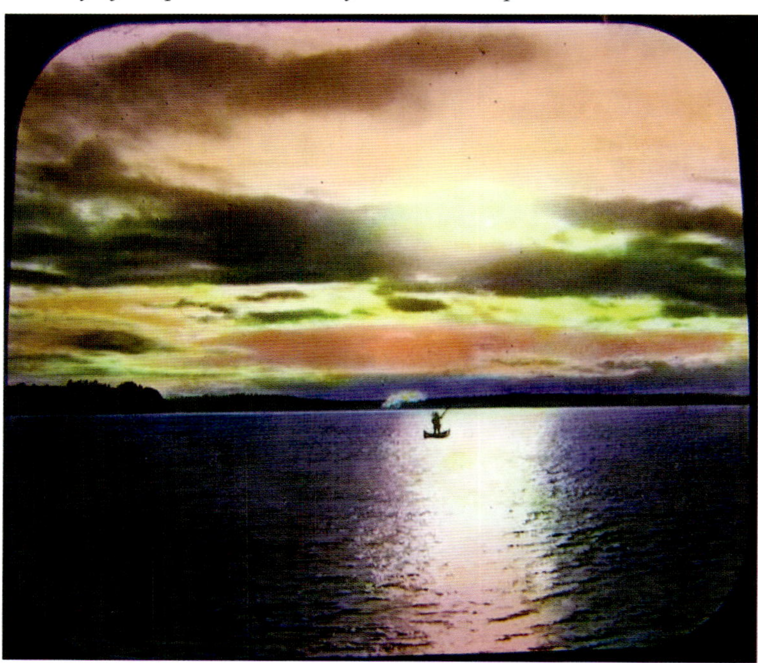

Katherine Bowden's *Hiawatha* Glows

Fig. 5.27 One of the most popular art performances was Katherine Bowden's *Hiawatha*.[33]

Left. Advertisement for Bowden's *Hiawatha*. This November 1909 color ad appeared in the trade magazine, *The Lyceumite*. It introduced what Bowden called a new "pictorial reproduction". Bowden's performance used slides and motion pictures of an Indian play that was based on Longfellow's famous story. It included "Indian" music, especially composed for the production.

Said *The Lyceumite*'s editor: "I have not seen all the things of an illustrated nature – no, not all – but I have yet to see anything that compares with [Bowden's] 'Hiawatha'".

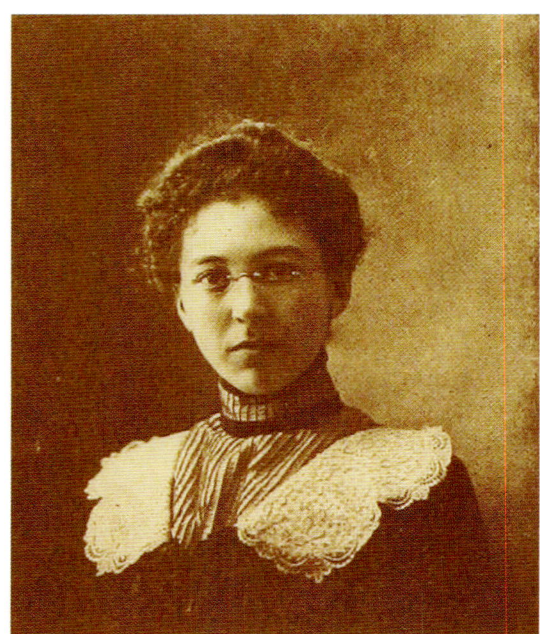

Professionals such as Bowden (pictured above) performed in major halls, and on the Lyceum circuit, a network that sponsored educational presentations and entertainment in about 6,000 communities around the country.

Left. Bowden slide from *Hiawatha*. The "Sunset" scene made a dramatic ending to Bowden's production. You can see some of Bowden's movies on YouTube.

Beale Brings Illustrated Drama to Screen

Fig. 5.28 Despite the craze for photographic lectures and shows such as *Hiawatha*, Beale's illustrated stories found their own niche.[34]

Bottom. Prof. D. B Nettz's broadside. Nettz's 1890s show used hand-drawn illustrations by Beale.

Nettz included four Beale sets – *Ten Nights in a Bar Room* (top left), *Life of Grant* (*top right*), *Uncle Tom's Cabin* (*bottom right*), and *Rock of Ages*.

Uncle Tom's Cabin, the famous anti-slavery polemic, and *Ten Nights*, at the time an equally famous anti-drinking novel, were two of Beale's earliest and most popular narrative sets.

The fourth segment of the Nettz show, *Peck's Bad Boy,* was a different way of telling a story, a set created by photographing live actors – "life model slides". The slides stories would later to be mixed with short movie stories to make a lantern/movie show.

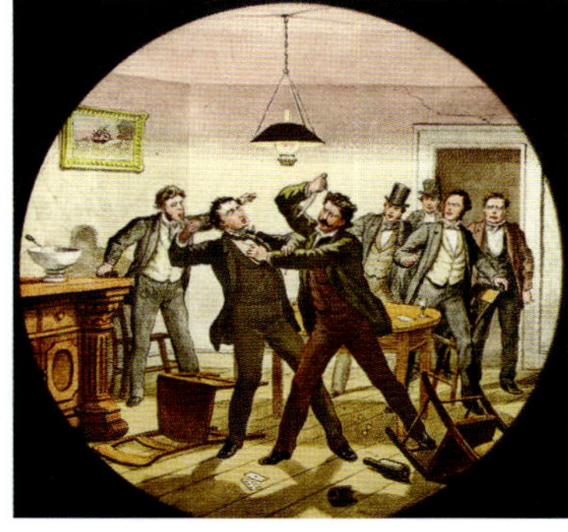

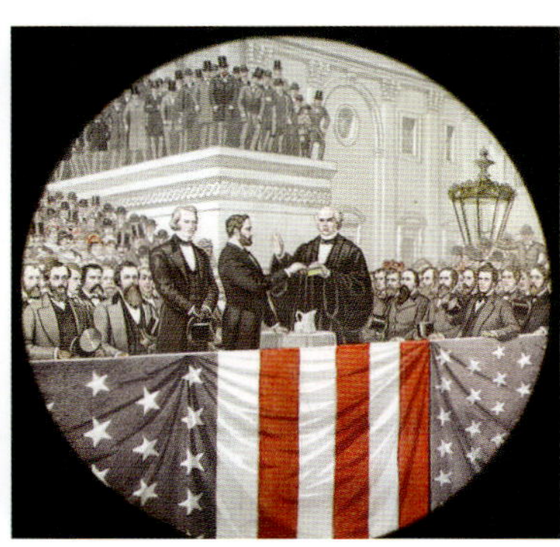

All the sets except *Rock of Ages* are described slide-by-slide, and the "150 Beautiful Pictures" gets prominent billing. Nettz wanted to distinguish his show from the showmen who might try to fill two hours with 60 slides.

Nettz promised **2 HOURS OF SIDE-SPLITTING SONGS AND FUN** – a rather remarkable claim for a show that features *Uncle Tom's Cabin* and *Ten Nights*. The price was 15 cents, about $5.00 in 2025 dollars.

On his tickets, Nettz spells his name as "Netts", but on the broadside, "Nettz". The Nettz family came from Germany/Bavaria. Perhaps they were still working out how to Americanize their name.

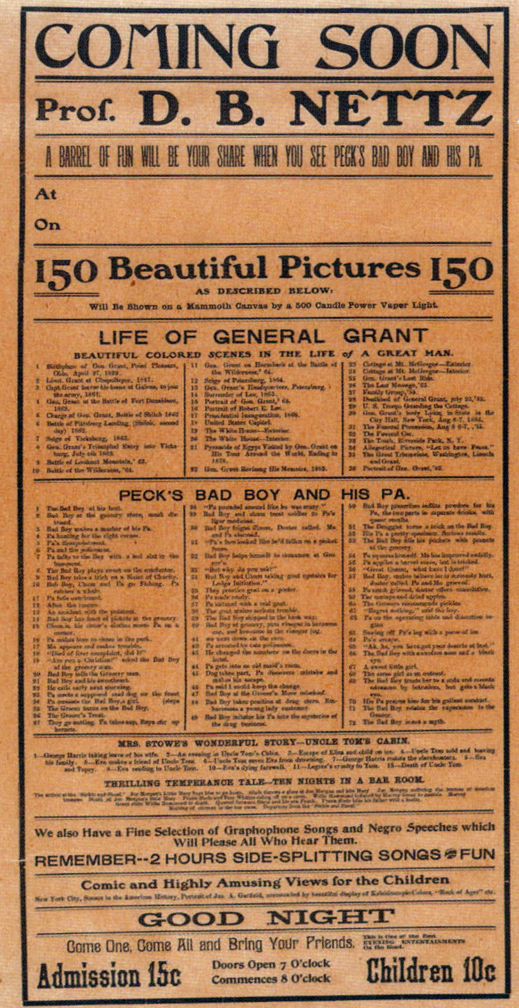

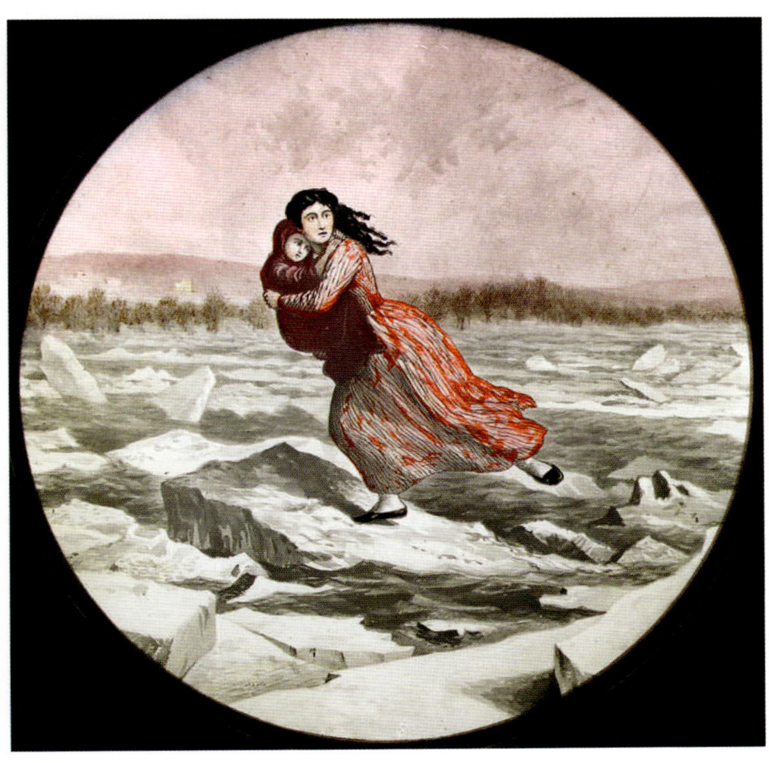

The Picture Play – A Stop-Motion Show

Fig. 5.29 The "Picture Play" was developed by Alexander Black, and was a series of lantern slides that changed about every 20 seconds to illustrate a feature-length story narrated by a single person.[35]

Below. Alexander Blacks's card, with his wry self-description, "Whomever he is, not so black as he is painted".

Black was a self-taught photographer, reporter, lecturer, and literati, who realized that the usual two-slide dissolve of the magic lantern show could be extended to create an evening's entertainment by photographing actors as they moved, and dissolving from one photograph to another. By doing so he created what one scholar calls "softened motion" – for a pre-cinema audience, a convincing avatar of real-life motion.

Black used up to 250–300 slides in a show, and took great care in making them. The background was staged to show off the actors to best advantage. The shots were carefully registered so that the background did not shift, and the actors appeared to be moving in the set. The slides followed the flow of the narrative, and concentrated less on capturing the highpoints, as Beale might have done, and more on ensuring continuity though the long sequences.

At *top right*, a slide from *Miss Jerry*. Black's first, and most successful Picture Play was *Miss Jerry*, which debuted in 1894. A fluffy little melodrama about an aspiring lady reporter, it was, as Black freely admitted, of no particular literary merit. But the novelty of the Picture Play made it a hit on the Lyceum lecture circuit, and Black quickly

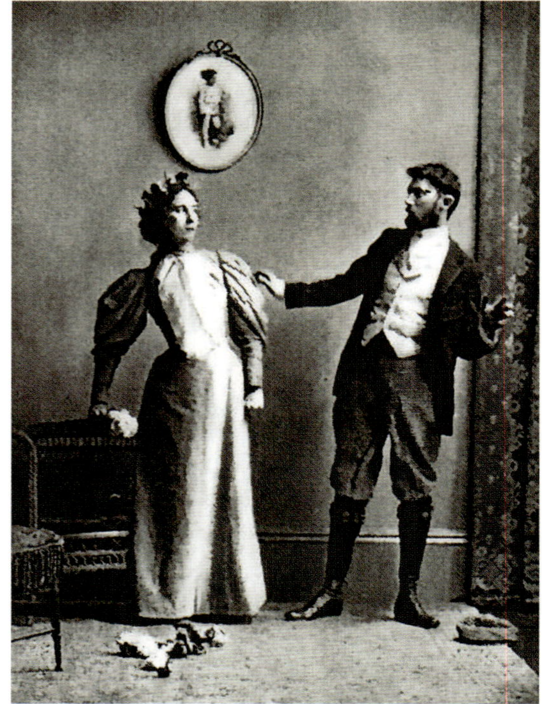

followed it with three more dramas, before the moving photographic images of the cinema made Black's work seem antique.

Black's Picture Plays were later celebrated as forerunners of the movies – as "slow movies". They were indeed examples of media experimentation in screen practice. But like Beale's illustrated stories, they did not fit well in a cinema history that concentrated on the development of the movie camera and projector, since they came just before or just after the first movie in America (1896) and used – unmodified – an ancient form of projection, the magic lantern.

There is an interesting YouTube on Black which includes some recreated Picture Play scenes, but be fore-warned: the images change every 5 seconds, not every 20 as they did in Black's shows.

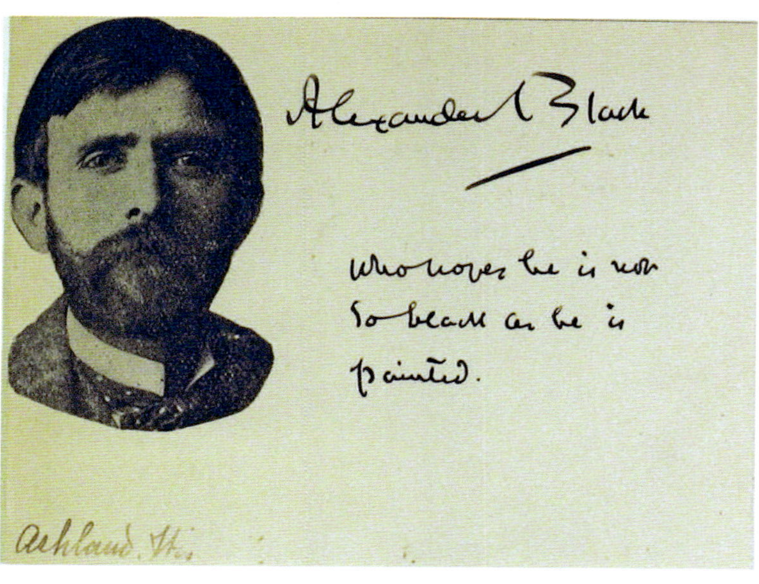

Science –
Are There Other Worlds?

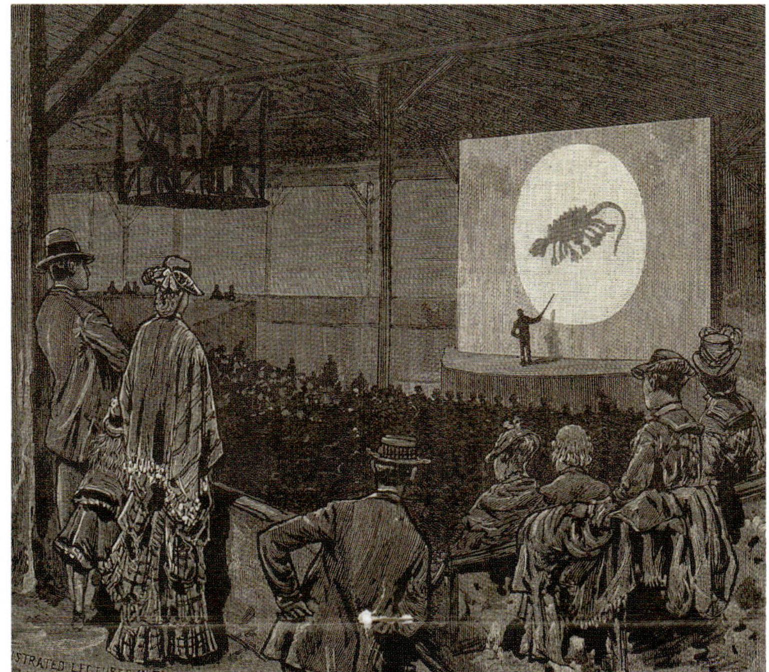

Fig. 5.30 Science, including Nature, was another major area of lantern performance.[36]

Right. Chautauqua science show. Science shows could draw big crowds. This one was held in the Amphitheater of the "Mother Chautauqua" in western New York – a 4,000 seat space. The lanternist and lantern are suspended from the ceiling, so that moving audience members, especially clowning children, did not cast shadows on screen.

We once performed at this Amphitheater, our biggest audience ever.

Bottom left. Charles Kellogg advertisement. In this March, 1905 ad in *The Lyceumite*, Kellogg promotes his popular Natural Science show combining bird whistling and lantern slides. "Bird Whistling" was a standard genre of stage performance. Bird whistlers were admired for their remarkable ability to imitate a wide range of bird songs.

Kellogg began his career in 1888, and by 1906 had performed 2,200 times. He claimed a ten-octave range, and said he "sang" rather than "whistled", using a second larynx like a bird's.

Bottom middle. Mary Proctor brochure. Proctor was the daughter of a famous astronomer, an accomplished astronomer herself, and a frequent lecturer on the subject. Photographs taken through the telescope literally opened new worlds to audiences when projected through the lantern. One of Proctor's most popular lectures was in fact called, *Are There Other Worlds Than Ours?*

Bottom right. Proctor 1897 letter. In her letter she proposes doing a lecture for $50, about $2,000 in 2025. She was represented by the Pond Agency, one of the best-known.

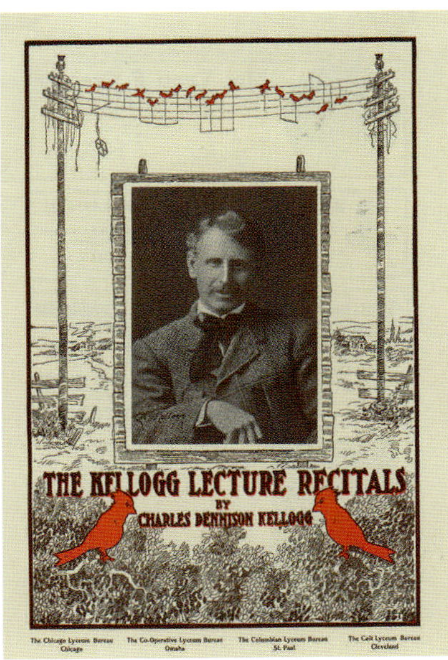

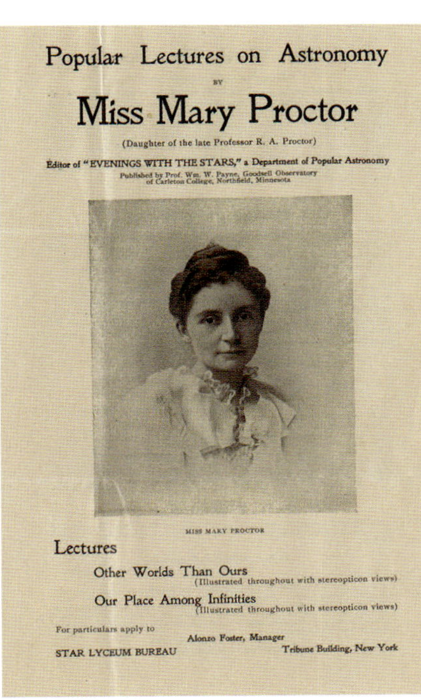

Popular Lectures on Astronomy

BY

Miss Mary Proctor

(Daughter of the late Professor R. A. Proctor)

Editor of "EVENINGS WITH THE STARS," a Department of Popular Astronomy
Published by Prof. Wm. W. Payne, Goodsell Observatory of Carleton College, Northfield, Minnesota

MISS MARY PROCTOR

Lectures

Other Worlds Than Ours
(Illustrated throughout with stereopticon views)

Our Place Among Infinities
(Illustrated throughout with stereopticon views)

For particulars apply to
Alonzo Foster, Manager
STAR LYCEUM BUREAU Tribune Building, New York

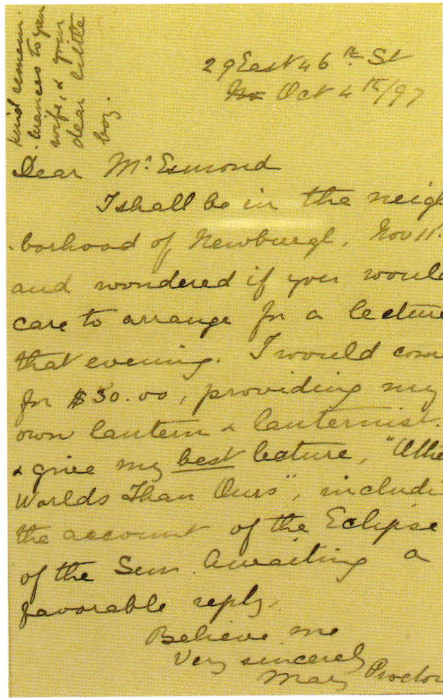

kind remembrances to your wife & your dear little boy.

29 East 46th St
~~Nov~~ Oct 4th/97

Dear Mr Esmond

I shall be in the neighborhood of Newburgh, Nov 11. and wondered if you would care to arrange for a lecture that evening. I would come for $30.00, providing my own lantern & lanternist. & give my best lecture, "Other Worlds Than Ours", including the account of the Eclipse of the Sun. Awaiting a favorable reply,

Believe me
Very sincerely
Mary Proctor

Social Issues – Bonnie and Clyde Star in Death

Fig. 5.31 Now for a magic lantern show that's a little weird.[37]

Right. Bonnie and Clyde poster. The death of the notorious gangsters, Bonnie and Clyde, created a sensation, and exploitation of it was almost immediate. The show promoted in this flyer combined a three-minute movie of the police ambush with 30+ lantern slides made from photos by Bonnie, morgue pictures of the bloody bodies, etc. You can see the movie on YouTube.

Left. Lantern slide of Clyde. This slide of a dead Clyde in the morgue was made by the Kansas City Slide Co., which specialized in producing slides to order. Usually, their customers were churches or advertisers, but in this case it was a showman exploiting the "Terror of the Southwest".

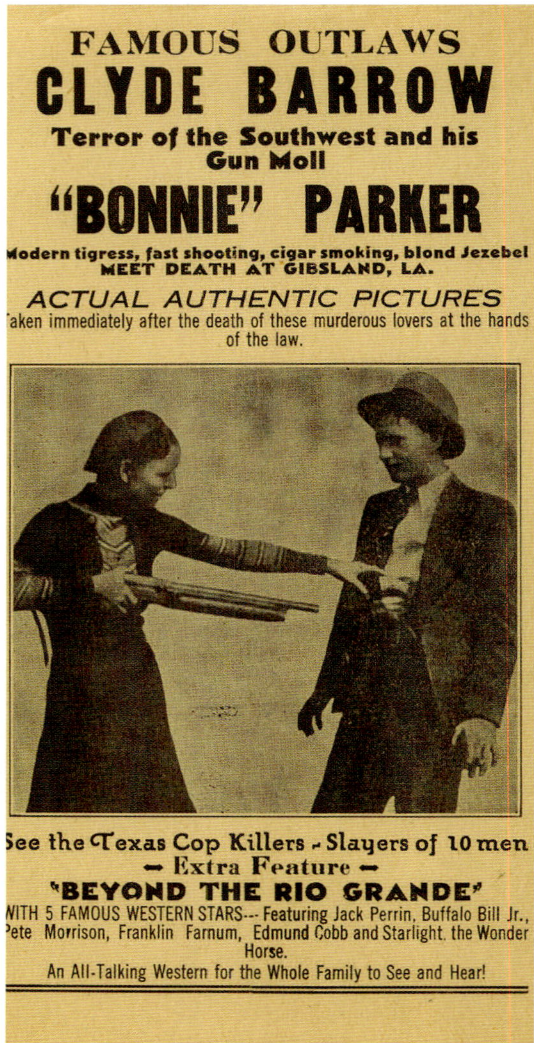

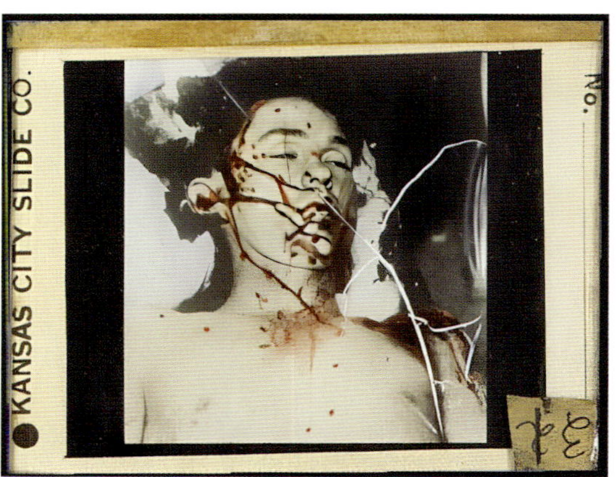

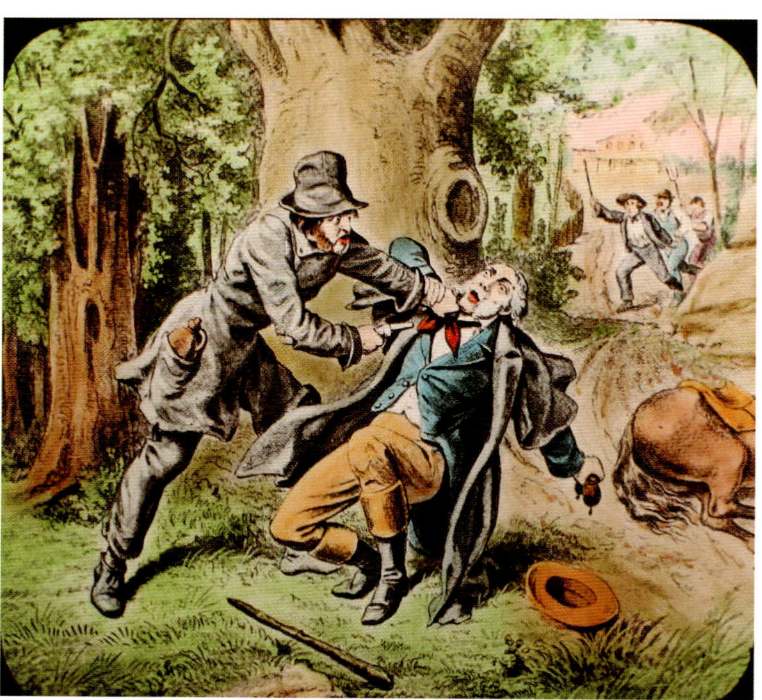

Bottom left. Temperance slide. Lantern slides featuring (non-Biblical) violence were rare. When they appeared, they were usually in the context of the effects of drinking, as in this temperance slide. An upright man has fallen into desperate straits because of drink and here is about to be apprehended while committing robbery and murder.

Lights & Shadows of a Great City

Fig. 5.32 Want to see on screen what you'd be afraid to see in person – the seedy side of New York? The lantern could take you into the Shadows, and was used in many efforts at social reform.[38]

Right. Broadside for *Lights and Shadows* lecture. This lantern production was based on a book by James McCabe, a colleague of Jacob Riis, the famous reformer who used lantern shows to try to reform the slums, and help the millions of immigrants who lived in them. This show employed images by both McCabe and Riis, as well as others.

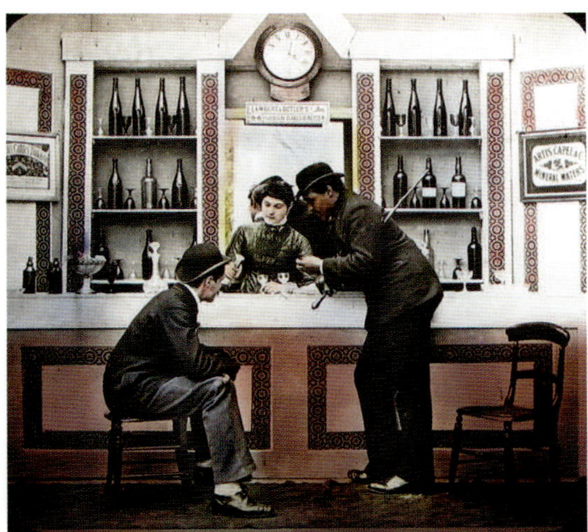

Above. Slide of bar. This picture of the bar shows racial and sexual mixing, a combination that was particularly troubling to viewers of the Victorian period.

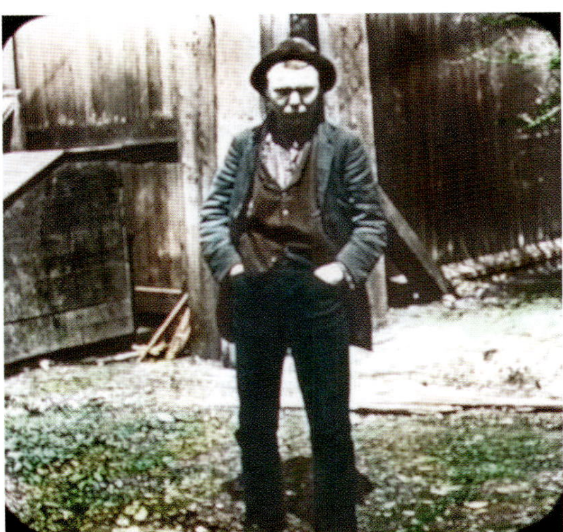

Left, bottom. Slide of a "tough", in an image like those Riis used. Riis is known today as a groundbreaking documentary photographer whose shocking images revealed the desperate lives of the poor, beset by "toughs" such as the one in this slide from *Lights and Shadows*.

Riis did not consider himself much of a photographer, and took very few photographs. He was primarily an illustrated lecturer, giving thousands of presentations to promote his cause. His performances mixed his slides with outraged passion, statistics, lively stories, and humor – a very effective, and popular combination.

On YouTube you can see a re-creation of Riis's lecture called "A Layman's Sermon" that I did for the Museum of the City of New York. I loved doing this. Working with Riis's own script and slides, it was easy to see why he was so successful.

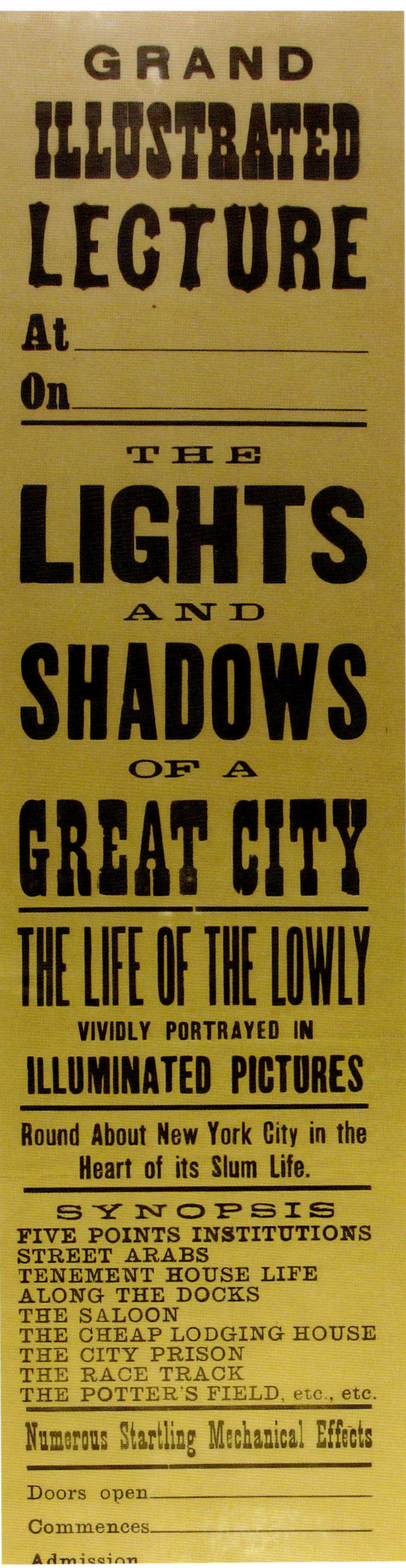

The Mississippi of Intemperance

Fig. 5.33 One authoritative source claims, "This 1882 poster is perhaps the most extraordinary and certainly one of the rarest temperance broadsides to emerge out of the 19th century". It may be right.[39]

Below. Designed by Dr. Nathan W. Tracy (1841–1919), *The Mississippi of Intemperance* employs the metaphor of the Mississippi River to describe the progression and dangers of alcoholism. The "river" itself flows from its tributaries of Wine Lake and Beer River to Delirium Tremens Falls and then to The Gulf of Despair, where reign a host of goblins from hell. The map of the river is surrounded with vignettes of the gradual decline of a happy family man – from homey bliss to bar life, wife beating, murder, and eventually the gallows.

Tracy was an extremely active temperance lecturer from about 1880 to 1913, drawing crowds of more than 2000 people. In his early performances, he used a large painting of the "Mississippi of Intemperance". Later he used both a magniscope (an early motion picture projector) and a stereopticon to present hundreds of images during a 2-hour temperance spectacle. His lecture almost certainly included some of Beale's Temperance stories, the names of which speak for themselves: *Ten Nights in a Barroom*, *The Drunkard's Daughter*, *The Drunkard's Reform*. Tracy's speaking circuit focused – logically enough – on the Mississippi Valley, often under the auspices of the Women's Christian Temperance Union.

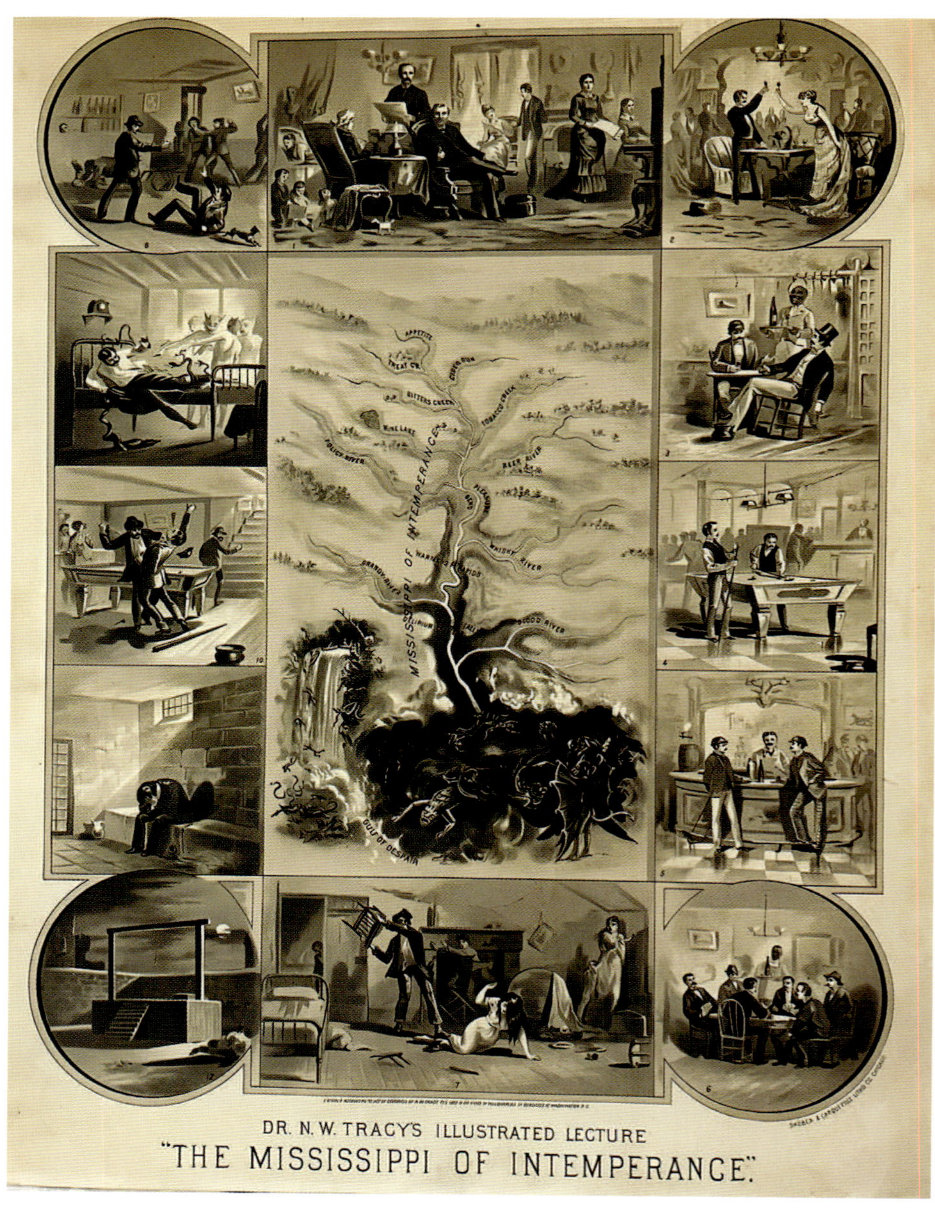

Stereopticon Dramatizes Elections

Fig. 5.34 The lantern was not only used for social reform; it was also used to report the results of the elections that often turned on those reforms. Slides were projected on a gigantic outdoor screen, or sometimes on as many as four screens at once.[40]

Below. Hand-tinted engraving of Election night, 1888, and (at right) an engraving of a similar scene, 1896. Stereopticon election shows were not simple one-shot reports like "So and So Wins". Just as in our modern election reporting,

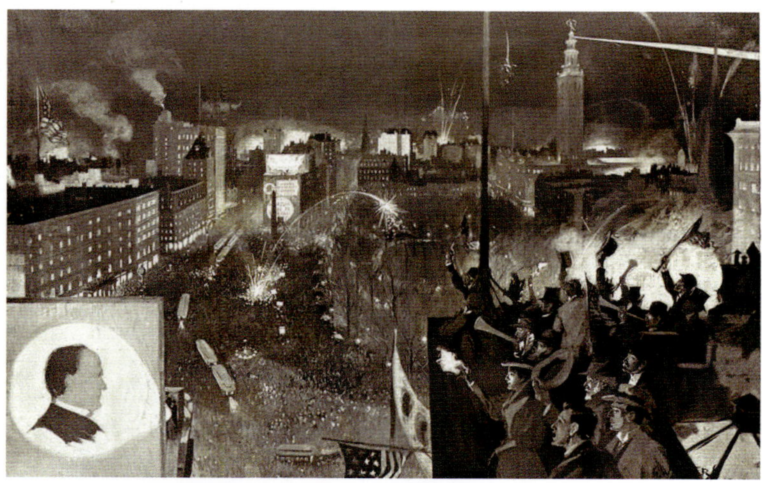

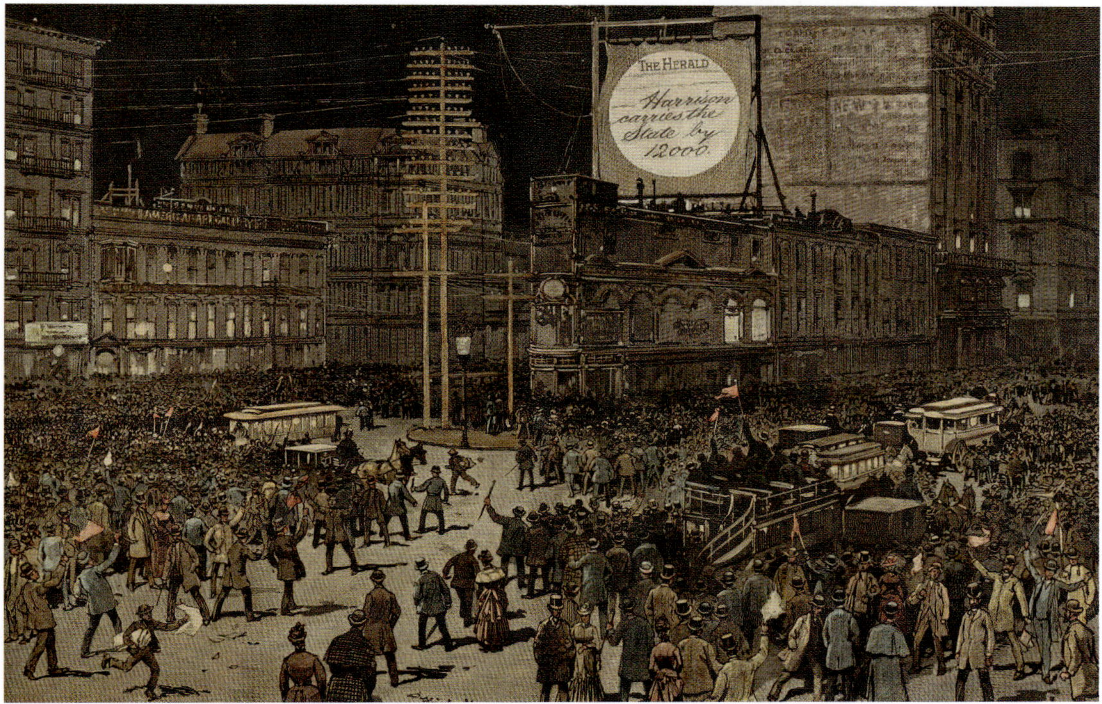

they were elaborate and dramatic "story-telling shows", spun out over time, with partial results reported as they came in. The "stereopticon man" could manipulate his multimedia storyline (and the crowd), with pre-packaged slides, or spontaneous ones, made on the spot.

> While the crowds were waiting for definite figures the graphic cartoons shown by the stereopticons at the new Eagle building attracted much interest. Those indicating a Democratic victory were received with cheers ... Then came the Eagle's handsome portrait of Flower, ... followed by cartoons showing that Flower had knocked Fassett out ... .

The response to such shows could be huge and riotous, as it was at the election of President McKinley.

> It is estimated that 125,000 people gathered in City Hall Park ... [and] on Broadway there were 150,000 more ... The roadway was one mass of howling humanity. Men as well as women were blowing horns and waving flags.

Wars – The Civil War
The Horrors of Andersonville

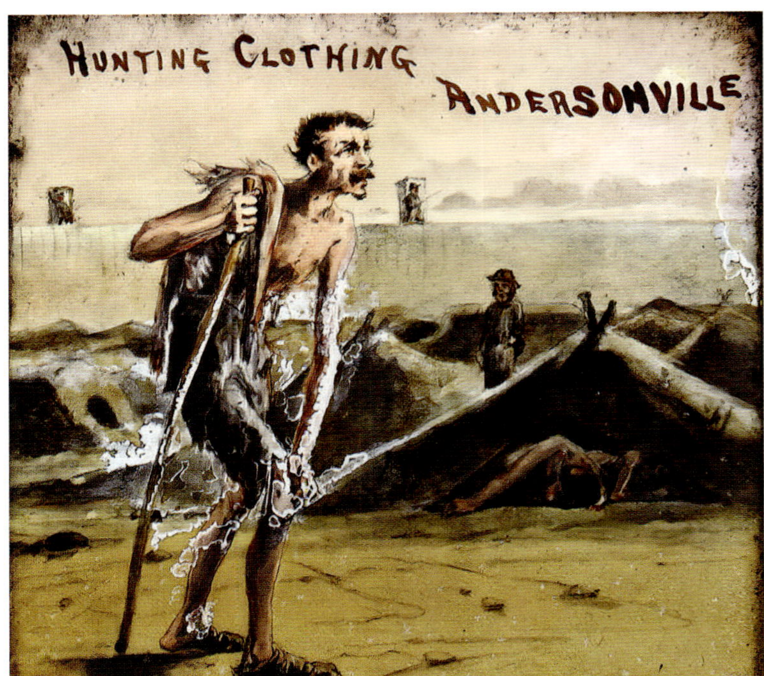

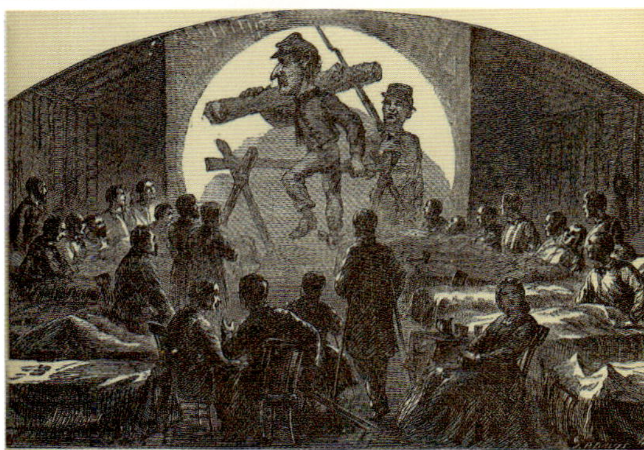

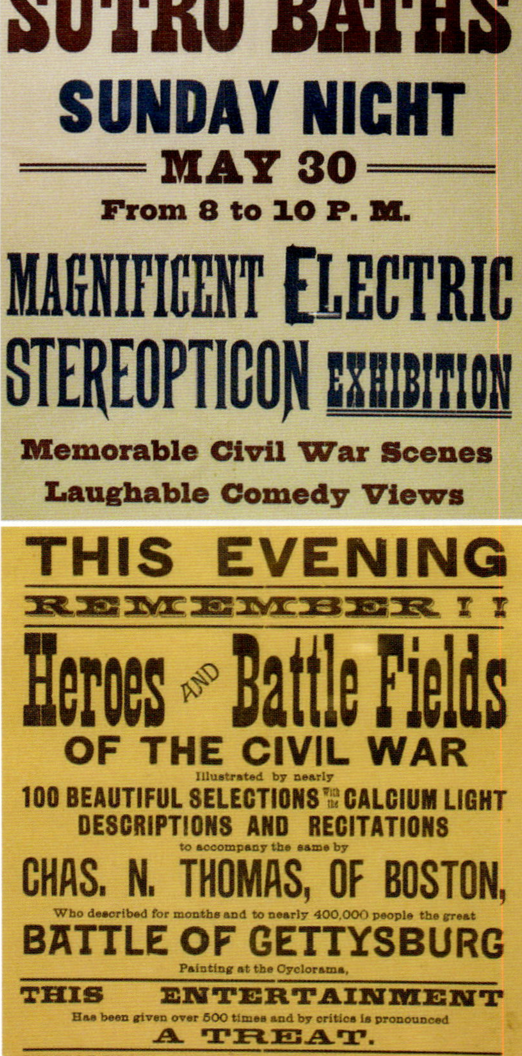

Fig. 5.35 War coverage was a continuing subject of lantern shows, from the Civil War to WWI.[41]

Top. Andersonville slide. James Taylor, an artist colleague of Beale's at *Frank Leslie's Weekly*, illustrated a lantern lecture about the horrors of the Southern Civil War prison at Andersonville, GA. This slide is similar to his work, which was in a rough, graphic style, appropriate for reporting on the grim conditions at Andersonville.

The lecture, by Ezra Hoyt Ripple, an Andersonville survivor, was called *Dancing Along the Deadline*. Ripple was the only performer using those images which were made especially for him by Taylor. His text survives in book form.

Above bottom. Soldiers in a Civil War infirmary watch a lantern show about the war in an image from Charles Coffin's *Four Years of Fighting*. Lantern shows were seen as a way to deal with "nostalgia", what we would call PTSD today.

Top right. Sutro Baths advertisement. A San Francisco cable-car placard advertises a *Civil War Show* at Sutro Baths, a large entertainment complex centered around swimming, but with seating for thousands. The ad ran in 1898, thirty years after the war. Interest in lantern shows about the War seemed to have no end.

Note that the Sutro Baths "Civil War Scenes" are mixed with "Laughable Comedy Views" – another indication of the enduring fascination with lantern animated comedy, and the willingness to mix the serious and comedic in lantern shows.

Above lower. *Heroes and Battle Fields* broadside. Charles Thomas's lecture was notable because of his previous experience narrating the *Gettysburg Cyclorama* – a giant circular painting of the Gettysburg battle, with the audience at center. The cyclorama is still at Gettysburg and is a major attraction there. Thomas gave his Gettysburg lantern performance over 500 times.

Lectures on War – "Bully Little War" on Screen

Fig. 5.36 The Spanish American War, with its drama and nationalistic fervor, was a natural for screen presentation, and many companies rushed to provide slides.[42]

Right. Broadside for Spanish American War show. The War began with the explosion of the battleship *Maine* in Havana Harbor on February 15, 1898. This large broadside (26 x 40"), produced by The Sears, Roebuck Co., is copyrighted the same month. Like the Sears broadside on Alaska (Fig. 5.22), it also offered recorded musical entertainment.

Bottom right. Spanish American War photographic slide. The 35 Spanish American War slides by Sears are a combination of 25 photographs, mostly of ships and generals – and 10 illustrations, almost all by Beale, who created 49 Spanish American War images. Though most of the show's photographs are rather static, the bleak image of the sunken *Maine* makes a telling statement.

Bottom left. Beale slide, "Landing of U. S. Marines" in the *Spanish American War* group. It is Beale's illustrations that portray the drama of war at a time when it was difficult or impossible to take action photographs.

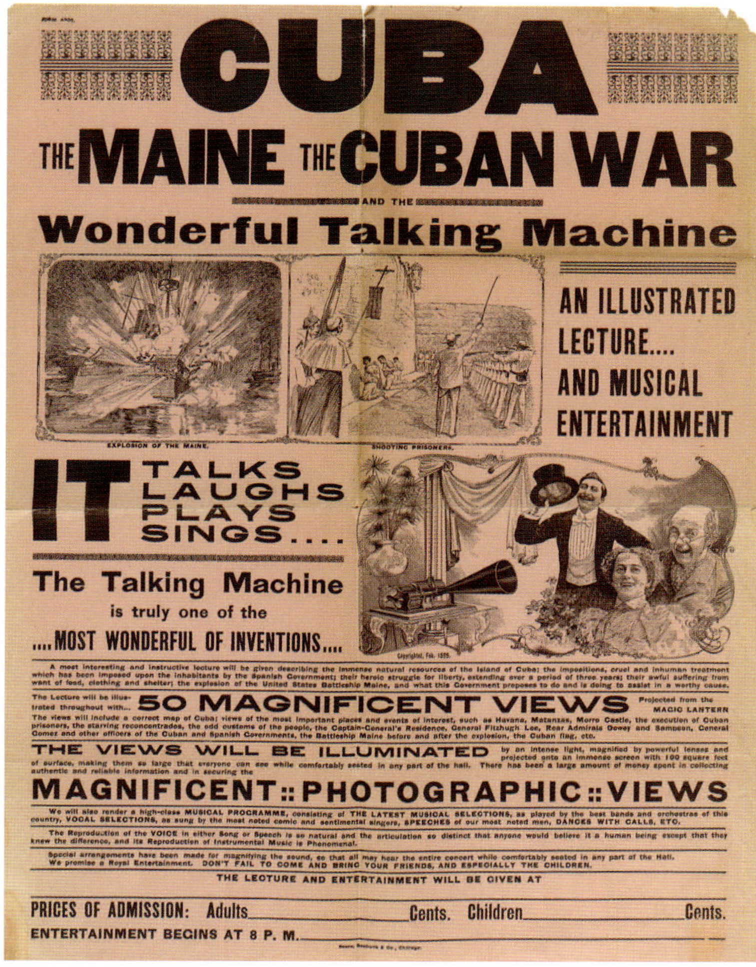

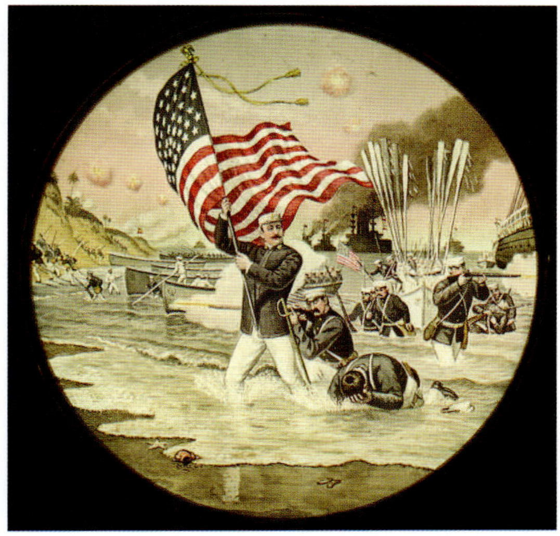

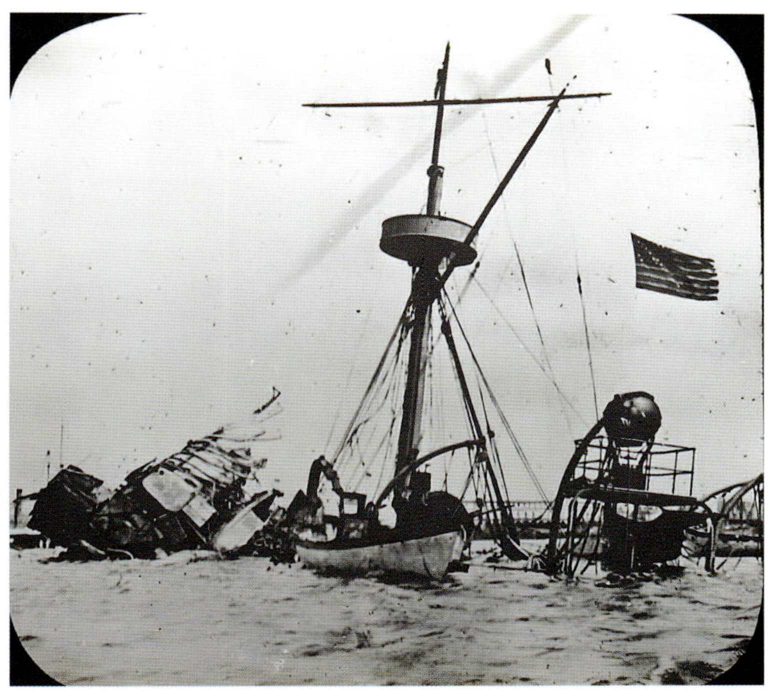

Movies Outshine the Lantern

Fig. 5.37 The Spanish American War coincided with the point at which the movies for the first time began to look as though they might be serious competition for the lantern.[43]

Left. Sears Spanish American War broadside. A Sears broadside presents a new Spanish American War show, probably produced in 1899, just a year after the Sears's show depicted on the previous page. That earlier show was presented entirely with lantern slides. But this new show *combines* movies and lantern slides.

The "Moving Pictures" get top billing, just three years after the first movies arrived in America. The lantern slides, the "Magnificent Photographic Views", are tucked in at the bottom.

Trouble was ahead for the magic lantern era.

Bottom left. A combination projector. In 1905, another sign of trouble for the lantern – a triple stereopticon and a movie projector, both built into one machine.

The heyday of the lantern was drawing to a close. And in fact, the height of popularity for American illustrated lectures was 1906. After that a slow decline set in until 1920, when the illustrated lecture's popularity dropped off sharply. But illustrated lectures persisted, using lantern slides for many years in a reduced fashion. In the mid 20th century they revived with 35mm slides and acetate sheets. Today they are ubiquitous. We call them "PowerPoint" lectures.

Bottom right. Pond Bureau catalog. In the 1933 catalog of the Pond Bureau, one of the most famous booking agencies, eight of the 14 lecturers were still using hand-colored lantern illustrations, or a combination of slides and movies.

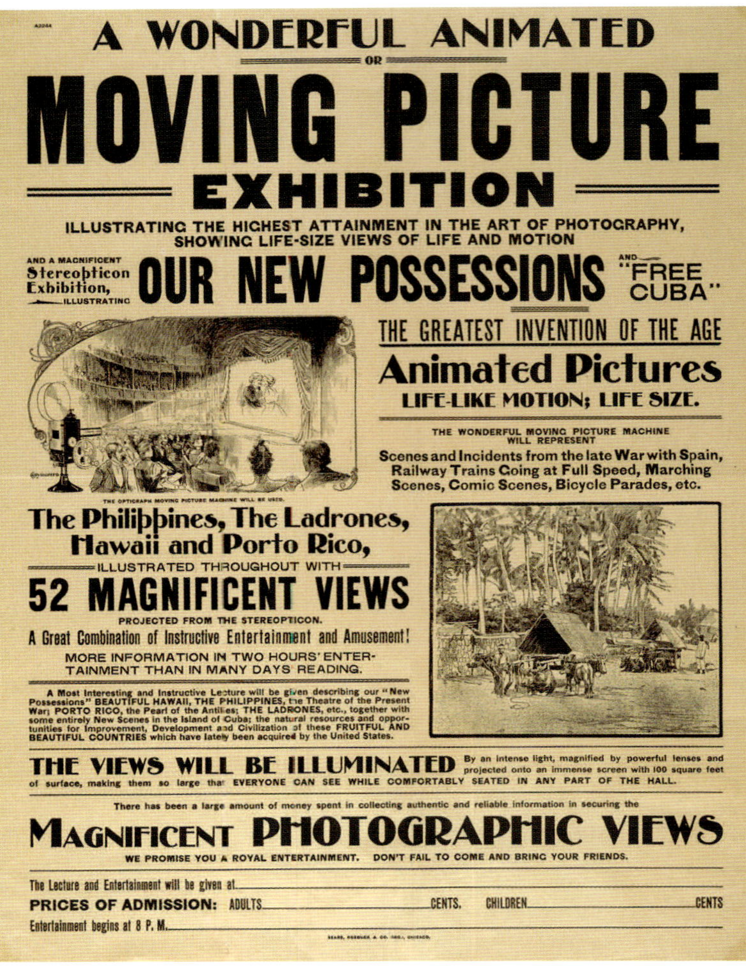

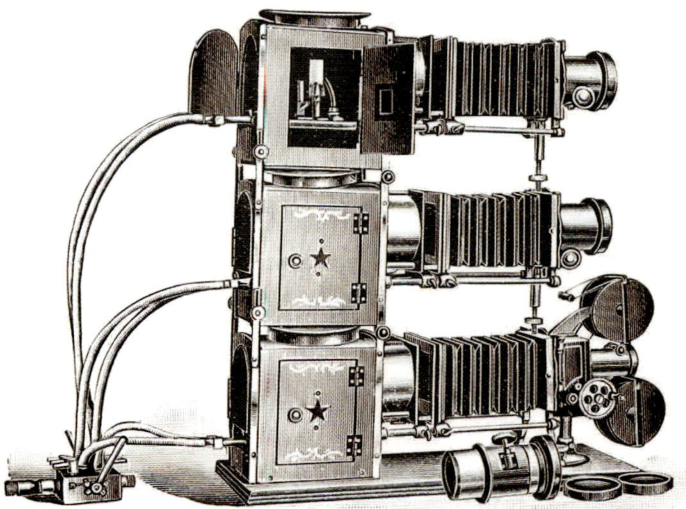

"Ideal" Triple Lantern.

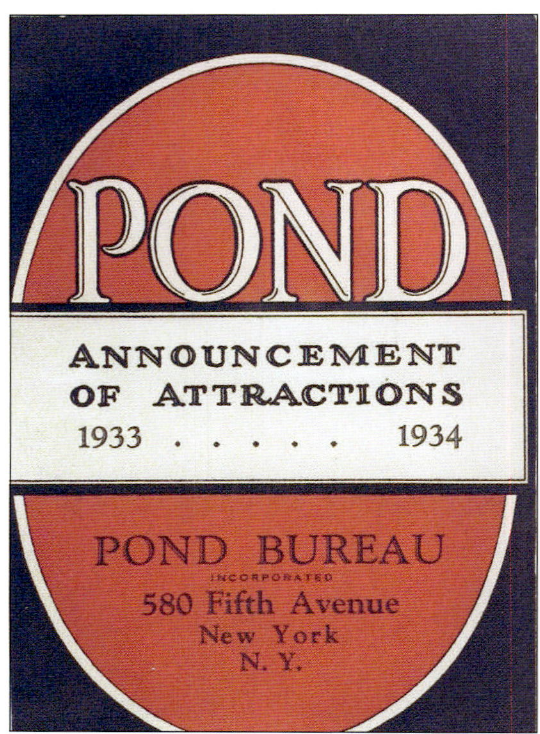

"Daring Photographs" of WWI

Fig. 5. 38 WWI was the last lantern war, the last war in which major reporting was done with lantern shows.[44]

Right. Poster for WWI show. This huge (26 x 40") poster on the *European War* was produced in 1914 by The Novelty Slide Co. of NY. As can be seen here, the company specialized in marketing disaster, presented in a big and bold manner. Its repertoire included lantern shows on the *Assassination of Duke Ferdinand, The Mississippi Flood,* and *The Titanic.*

The company claimed that the "remarkable" slide pictures were taken by their own "daring photographers", and a large part of the show's appeal was its timeliness and authenticity.

Unfortunately, the WWI shows themselves do not live up to their billing. Most of the slides are of castles and forts – standard travelogue material. The few images of troops mostly show the two sides standing around.

Bottom. Novelty Slide Co. WWI slides. The two slides shown are more interesting than most, but the slap-dash nature of The Novelty Slide Company's production is evident in the black exposure across the top of the dirigible slide. It was a sad comedown from Beale's dramatic and meticulously executed pictures of the Spanish American War.

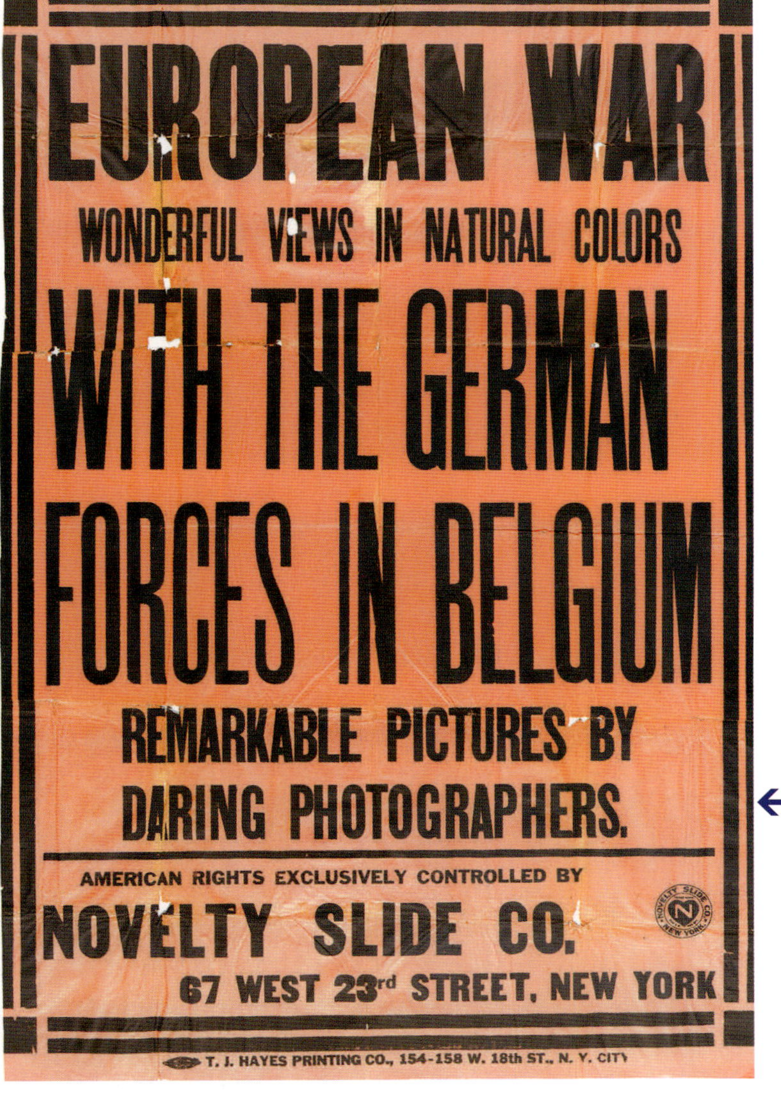

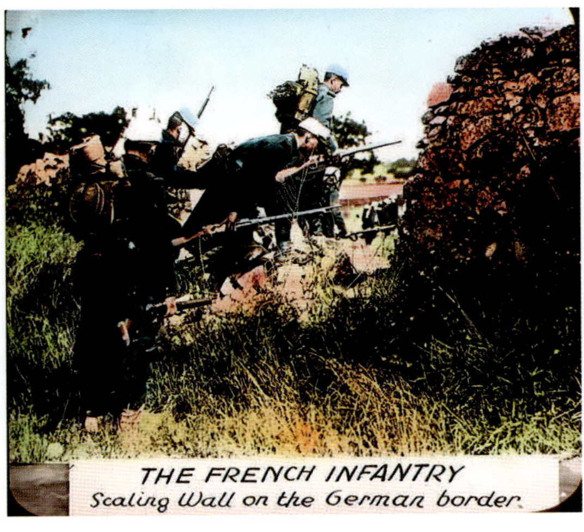

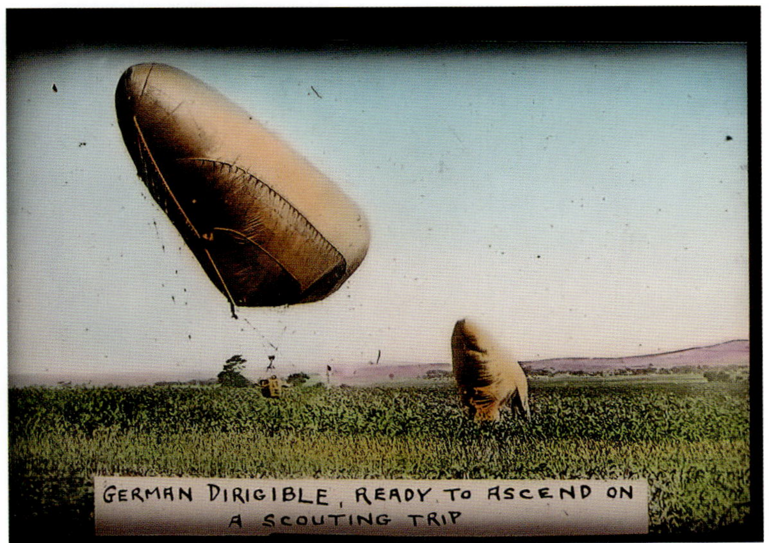

Summary and Conclusion

Fig. 5.39 From the 1870s to the 1920s, magic lantern shows proliferated across America, bringing delight and instruction to the nation's great cities and small towns.[45]

Right. In this 1860's tintype, an unidentified showman stands before the broadsides for his magic lantern show. (The image in a tintype is reversed, so his "Magic Lantern" headline reads backwards.)

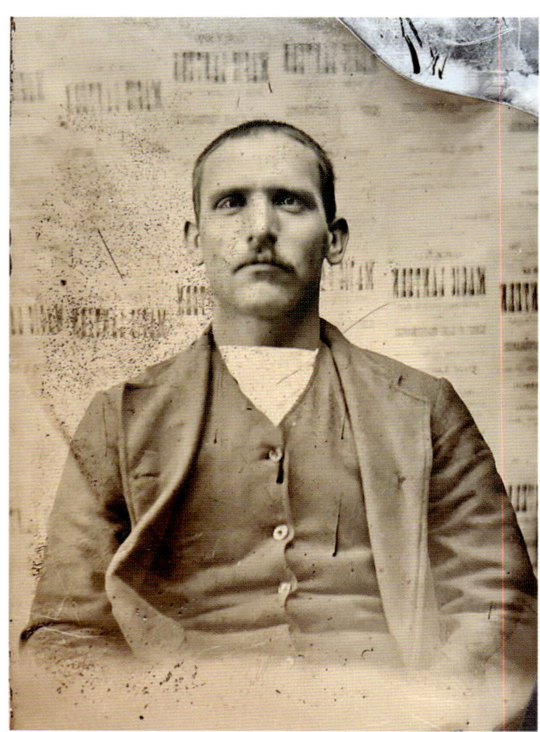

This showman is on the leading edge of a media explosion that would reach into every corner of American life. Lecturing had long been a common form of entertainment and instruction. After the 1870s, dry plate photography democratized photographic lantern shows and they spread rapidly. Suddenly it not only became easy to *tell* audiences about the world, but to *show* them its wonders.

From the 1880s showmen of all kinds leapt at the opportunity. Stoddard and Holmes transfixed audiences of thousands in the big cities, touring lecturers filled the Chautauqua tents of small towns, Keystone images reached into thousands of schools, and shows on the Passion Play filled church halls.

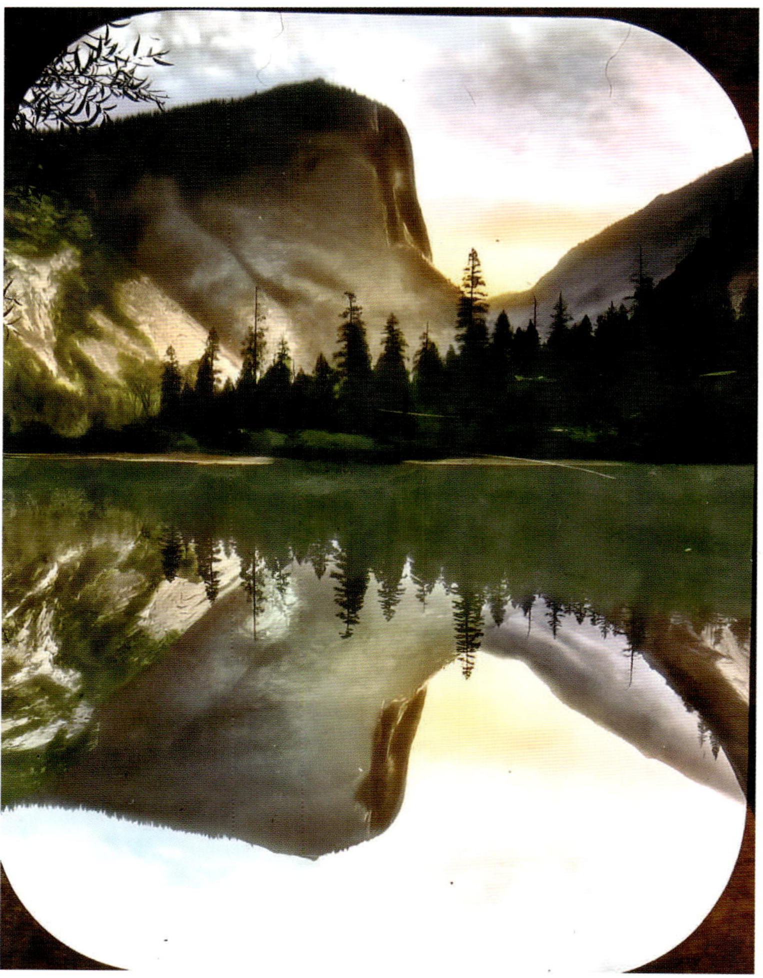

At left. What strikes me, reviewing the collection of primarily photographic lantern shows in this chapter, is the incredible variety of subject matter and presentation that the new photographic medium allowed – from spectacularly colored images such as this one of Yosemite, to the most mundane. (And I've left out the most mundane, like a set on "How to Build a Pig Pen".) If it was out there in Victorian life and could be photographed, the magic lantern was the way to share it with the world.

But what if it wasn't out there? Some subjects – important subjects, popular subjects, like literature, religion, history, rituals – were not easily covered with photography. That created an opportunity for the lantern firm of C. W. Briggs, which focused on hand-illustrated lantern images, and for his lead artist, Joseph Boggs Beale, who was soon to become a major force in magic lantern culture.

Chapter Six

The Business Vision of Briggs – The Screen Art of Beale

Fig. 6.18 Beale's slide 2 for the song, *Tenting on the Old Campground* by Walter Kittredge. Discussion on p. 152.

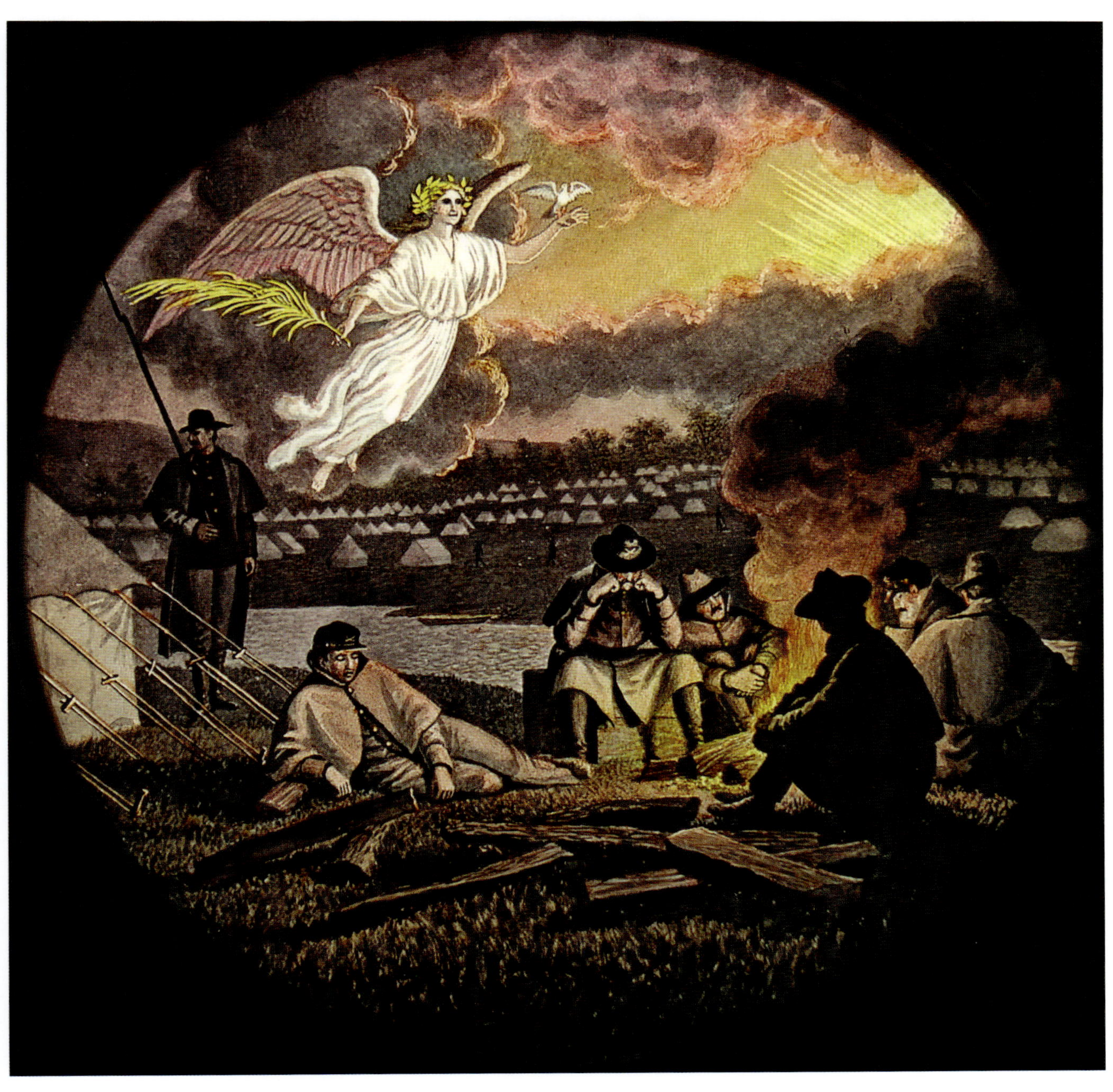

We've reviewed very briefly a wide range of lantern showmen and women, the kind of shows they performed, and the kinds of venues that hosted them. Now it's time to focus on the team of Casper W. Briggs and Joseph Boggs Beale, who had a unique and entirely different role in the magic lantern world. I used a letter from Briggs to Beale as a way of starting this book, and the two will have a major role to play in the following chapters, all the way to the end of the story.

C. W. Briggs Co. – A Unique Business

The C. W. Briggs firm, like the McAllister and McIntosh companies, was a slide manufacturer, though its product was different from all the rest.

Most of the companies feeding the enormous demand for slides provided images that featured photographs of travel sites, natural history, astronomy, etc. But important markets did not lend themselves well to such photographs because the action was not contemporary – Bible stories, secret society rituals, history, literature. A few companies attempted to cover these fields with photographic "life model" slides by posing costumed actors before painted sets and photographing them, but this format never caught on in America as it did in England. A new technique was developed for these subjects, a technique I'll call ***artist-illustrated slides***, made by photographing specially created lantern-slide illustrations. These artist-illustrated slides were carried by the catalogs of McAllister and McIntosh, in fact by *all* the leading catalog companies. But these companies did not make these slides themselves. The firm that for many years was essentially the only American manufacturer of such slides and which then wholesaled them to all the others, was the C. W. Briggs Co.

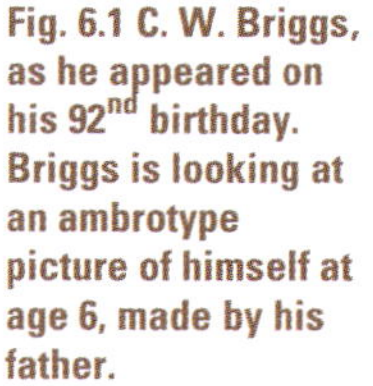

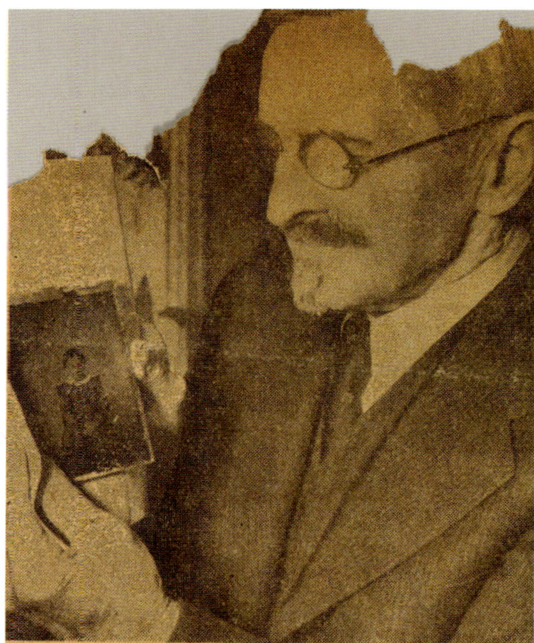

Fig. 6.1 C. W. Briggs, as he appeared on his 92nd birthday. Briggs is looking at an ambrotype picture of himself at age 6, made by his father.

The father of C. W. Briggs, Dr. Daniel Briggs, produced photographic slides during the 1850s in Massachusetts, using a process somewhat different from that of the Langenheim brothers in Philadelphia. The Briggs lantern-slide business flourished, specializing in scientific subjects. When Casper reached the age of 21 in 1868, he assumed active management of the firm. In 1872, he moved the company to Philadelphia, the center of the growing lantern industry. (Between 1864 and 1880, half of all lantern patents issued to Americans went to Philadelphians; most of the lantern catalog companies were also located there.)[1] In 1874, when William Langenheim died, Briggs bought the firm out and combined it with his own company, calling it "C. W. Briggs" (Fig. 6.1). He soon established the new firm as a leader in the industry, capitalizing on its established reputation in making photographic slides.

Briggs was a small, precise and energetic man, who lived at 59 High St. in the Germantown suburb of Philadelphia, the same area Beale lived in while he was making slide designs. Briggs cast his first vote for Grant, and continued to vote Republican in the next 16 presidential elections. He suffered repeated family tragedy, losing his first wife, and then a second, before he married for the third time. He had at least an amateur's artistic talent, and hung his home with oil and water-color sketches he had made during trips to Maine, Pennsylvania, and South Carolina. Active in several dramatic organizations, he wrote, acted, directed, and designed for them. He was an amateur authority on Dickens, a member of the Dickens Fellowship, and an avid reader of the novels of the day. He was also a member of the Philadelphia Camera Club.[2]

The Briggs purchase of the Langenheim's business added more than a thousand images to his existing catalog, including dissolving views, art, religious subjects, history (especially the Civil War), some literature, an assortment of comics and mechanical slides, and a few travel slides.

Some of the images were photographs. Many were simply photographic copies of engravings. Some images had been especially painted for the magic lantern. By one account at least, Briggs "dominated the slide producing business" in the country. That may have been an exaggeration, but certainly his company grew to become by far the largest manufacturer and wholesaler of artist-illustrated slides, and the leading ***slide coloring*** firm.[3]

Briggs seems to have continued to promote a mix of photography, illustration, and mechanical slides after the Langenheim purchase. In 1876, he was selling colored-patterned chromatropes and slip slides, and introduced his variant of the "Dancing Skeleton", a slide with rapidly changing multiple views of the skeleton's antics.[4] In 1883, he brought out four new "Walk Abouts" – sets of twelve photographs each of Boston, New York, Philadelphia, and Washington, with accompanying scripts. But such travel slides faced a tremendous amount of competition. Philadelphia alone had a half-dozen firms selling hundreds of such sets, comprising piles of images. Hundreds of photographers were eager to provide those firms with still more pictures. But even as late as 1892-94, Briggs was still offering a strange mixture of expanded travel series, the Langenheim repertoire, his own earlier anatomy and science slides, and Beale's new artist-illustrated sets, especially Temperance sets (Fig. 6.2).

However, soon after he combined with Langenheim, Briggs began making steps toward a new, much more focused direction.

The Vision of Briggs

Despite his firm's pioneering history in the field of photographic images, and despite the fact that the nation's lantern repertoire was primarily photographic travel slides, Briggs began to concentrate his business on artist-illustrated slides. That was a field where competition was much more limited, in fact, almost non-existent. No doubt he saw the potential of that vast market in secret societies, Sunday schools, and evening church programs. He also began developing slides in history and literature, a field where again almost no American-made competition existed. He was probably aiming at the school market with the stories and songs, and also at the markets for small public showman and home showmen.

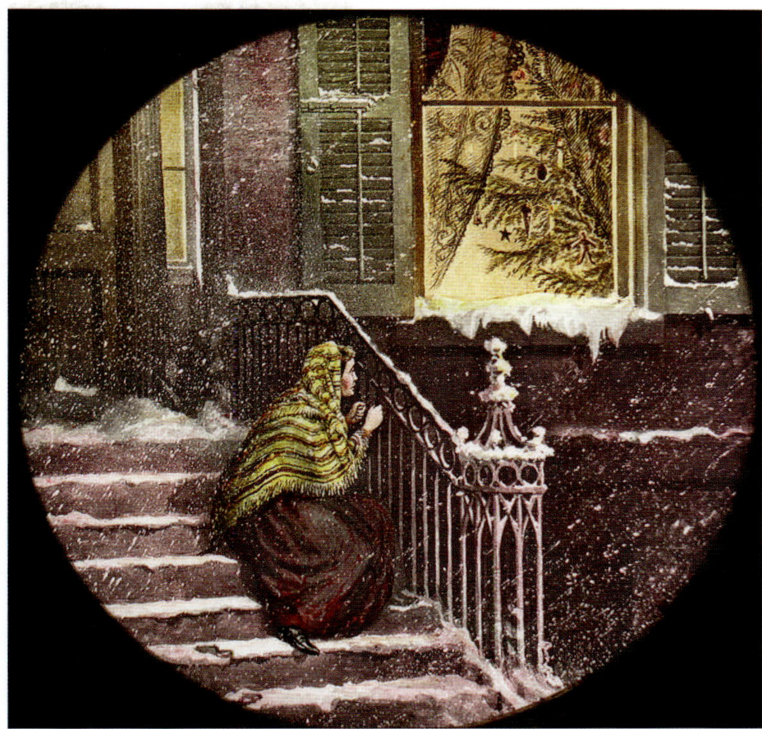

Fig. 6.2 Beale slide 4 *The Drunkard's Daughter* (1882). Already Beale's talent for the lantern medium is evident.

Gradually, Briggs developed a vision of creating "a great collection of educational and religious pictures, ... the most important stories of the Bible and ancient and modern history, and ... the best in literature".[5] By concentrating on imagery of the Bible, history, literature, and secret societies, Briggs was focusing on some of the most essential parts of the American experience – our religious faith, our history, our formative myths and stories, our fraternal communities. He imagined a time when people in opera houses, schools, church halls and homes throughout the country would not only watch travel lectures, but be entertained and uplifted by a broad range of exciting stories, poems, and songs – especially those with an American connection – all readily available on a local screen. He set out to be the leading manufacturer of the slides that would nourish this new visual culture.

It was an ambitious goal and was fraught with more difficulties than Briggs at first realized. His original plan had apparently been a simple one: Find the best available engravings or etchings that illustrated great literature, history, etc., photograph them for slides, and make them available to lantern audiences. But the meticulous Briggs was disappointed with the result of this approach.

Projected on screen, his photographic copies of engravings were not nearly as effective as the

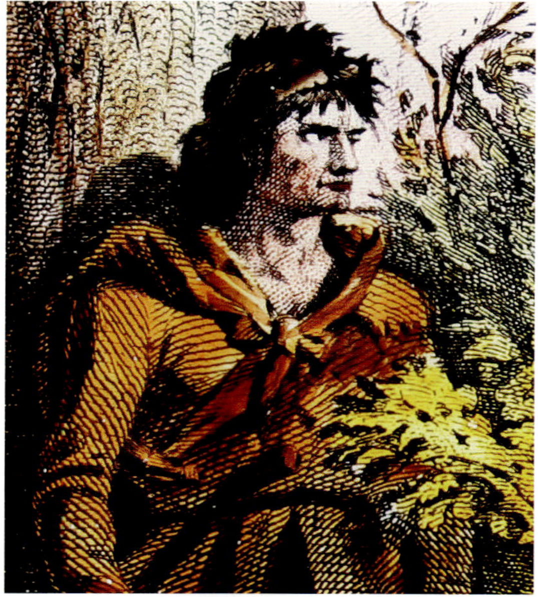

Fig. 6.3 Detail of a non-Beale slide made from an engraving.

engravings themselves had been when printed on paper. The fine hatch lines, which gave them their detail and sense of reality on the printed page, became giant scratches when enlarged and projected on screen, especially if the original had been a small engraving (Fig. 6.3). And the dark sections of the engraved image, formed with hatch lines and cross-hatching close together, made the lantern-slide color look muddy. Several known techniques for dealing with this problem existed.[6] The approach Briggs settled on was to make ***salt prints*** (very faint photographic images) of the engravings or etchings, and then have an artist ***overpaint*** the image in the design to make it more suitable for projection. It is probably for this purpose that he hired the artist Herman Farber in 1877. Farber's overpaintings were effective, though of course the technique was limited to improving an already existing image.[7]

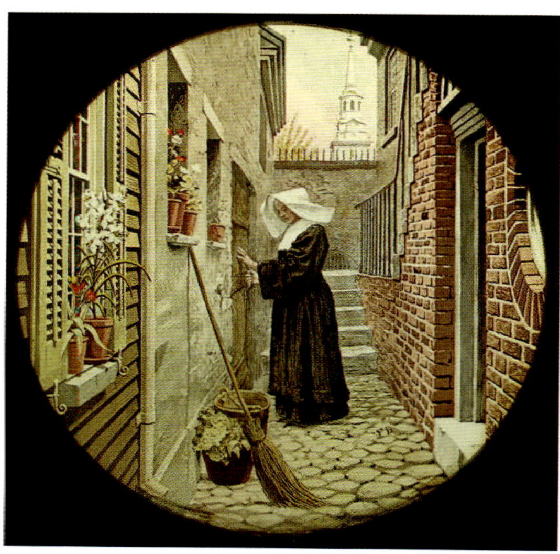

Fig. 6.4 Beale slide 23 of *Evangeline*.

A second problem that Briggs found in using existing images was that they were often of different sizes, shapes, and styles. I have run into this problem myself in our shows. Like the lanternists of old, I've sometimes patched together slides from different sources to dramatize a story or song. Laid out on a light box, illustrations drawn from hither and yon seem to work well enough, but projected on screen they are sometimes a significant problem. The different artistic styles can clash with each other, leading to inappropriate audience response. And the different sizes and shapes of the images (their different *aspect ratios*) make the pictures jump around on the screen, severely weakening any sense of visual *continuity*. Some lanternists were very much aware of this problem, calling it, "an eyesore not to be tolerated". In the later years of the industry, some said the sales of slides with a standard aspect ratio could be "almost 100 to 1" times greater than those without.[8]

To avoid such an eyesore (and loss of sales!), Briggs could either use a portion of the image and blow it up to fit the slide aspect ratio, or have the images ***pieced out*** or ***matched out*** – that is, extend the sky or bottom foreground vertically to create a standard aspect ratio. (The image was sometimes extended horizontally as well, but this took a more skillful artist like Beale, as it involved matching the style of the central portion of the picture.) The new matched-out section created with paint had to be indistinguishable from the original engraving when the slide was enlarged on screen by the magic lantern projector. In a scene from *Evangeline*, for instance (Fig. 6.4), Beale created a square image from a narrow vertical scene by the famous British artist Frank Dicksee. Beale hid the transition with the broom and the door jamb, creating a whole new scene. This matching-out technique worked well, and Briggs continued to use it during the next twenty-five years, applying it in many engravings, especially in the fields of history and religion.[9]

Briggs faced a third problem in creating his collection of great illustrated literature, and it was a much more difficult problem than either hatch lines or aspect ratio. He wanted a ***series of pictures*** to illustrate the narrative of each poem or Biblical story. Most artists and engravers had painted only a single scene from a poem or parable. At best, by combining artists, Briggs might be able to find two or three images for a story. For most stories not enough pictures were available to create any kind of *continuity*, or to hold the interest of an audience while the narrative was being dramatized during a lantern performance. Even if the images existed, they were episodic. They were book illustrations, designed to capture the action described in a particular page, to freeze a moment in time. They lacked the sequential continuity that would tell a story with a visually dramatic flow from beginning to middle to end, as one image dissolved into another in a narrative arc.

Briggs Chooses Illustration

To solve these problems Briggs showed no interest in developing an American version of the life-model photographic slides so popular in England, or in importing British illustrated slides. Instead, he embarked on his own project to create the world's greatest collection of *illustrated* literary, religious, fraternal, and historical slides. The choice was consistent with his interest in more complex *narrative forms* – the poems of Longfellow, the stories of Dickens and Whittier, the Bible, the plays of Shakespeare. This "high literary art" suggested a more elevated form of graphic presentation than the English slap-dash, life-model production, or the somewhat sketchy quality of England's leading slide illustrator, Nannie Preston. Beale's talents did in fact provide a more complex, more polished, more "literary" style for these works, as did the much higher-quality work of the British company, York & Son, and the French company, Maison de la Bonne Presse.[10]

Briggs's choice to pursue the artist- illustrated format, rather than a life model one, also led him and Beale toward a more "cinematic" presentation than would have been possible with photography at the time. This may sound paradoxical, since the cinema is so closely associated with photography, but a good artist could give a much greater sense of life and drama to a story than could still photographs of actors, no matter what the context. It was simply too hard to get photographs of natural action from multiple actors all at once. Look, for instance, at two temperance slides of the same subject, one done in the English life-model format, and one illustrated by Beale (Fig. 6.5).

Seen by itself, the English life-model slide makes its point. Mom and Dad sit in their "Happy Home", the title of the slide, their children around them. But the scene is stilted, static, as many life-model slides are. Indeed, one British lanternist joked that such slides should not be called "Taken from Life", but "Taken from Death".[11] Nonetheless, it must have taken many shots to get five people to look this natural – even portraying such a low-key emotion as contentment.

(Lantern scholars Joe Kember and Richard Crangle argue very convincingly that the minimalist nature of the life-model format, often using characters with their backs to the audience, was intentional. They see it as a way to draw the audiences into a scene by showing "folks like us", and hence sparking religious conversion or the taking of the temperance pledge. Perhaps for this reason these sets were very popular in England, and maintained their popularity over many years.)[12]

Briggs and Beale had a different objective than the British manufacturers, as can be seen by comparing the life-model slide with a Beale illustrated version of the same "Happy Home"

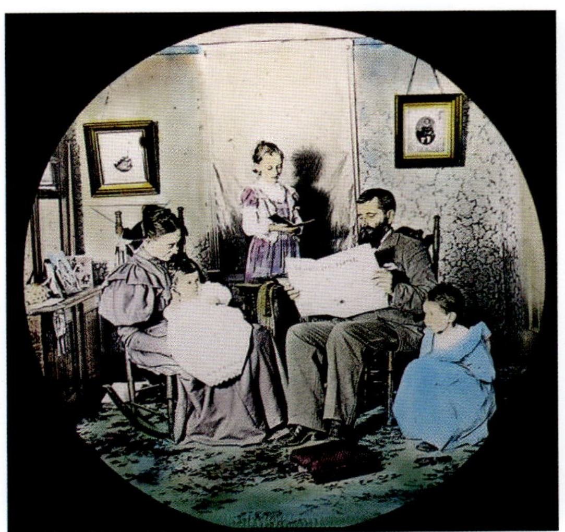

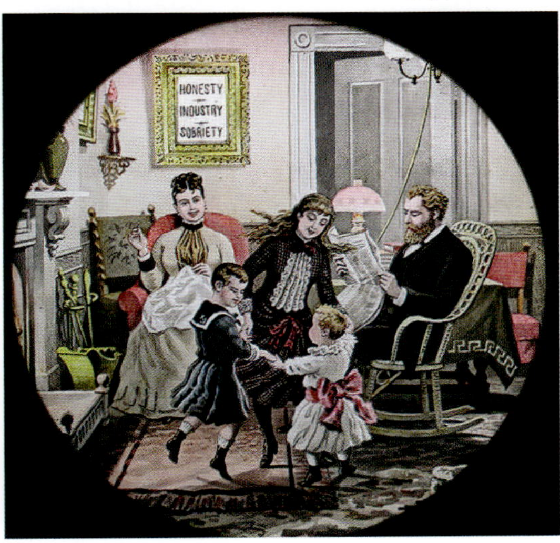

Fig. 6.5 ***Left,*** **a British "Life Model" slide of "Happy Home" and,** ***right,*** **Beale's slide of "Temperate Home" from the** ***American Mechanics*** **set.**

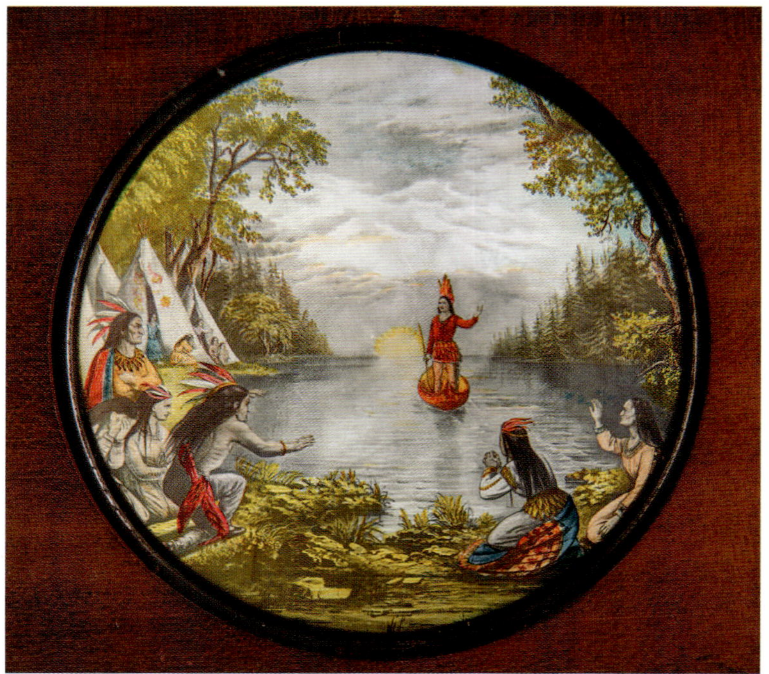

Fig. 6.6 Brigg's slide made from an 1868 Currier and Ives lithograph of "Hiawatha's Departure". The sense of anatomy, perspective, and design are minimal.

temperance scene. What a difference! Papa's actually reading, concentrating amid the happy confusion of his home – not posing with a prop. Mom beams at her children with pleasure, her sewing hand caught in mid-action. And the kids whirl in delighted animation, hair flying, feet off the floor, skirts a-twirl, joyously center stage in the life that "Honesty, Industry, Sobriety" has brought them.

My point here is not simply that Beale chose to portray a more vivacious and exuberant version of "Happy Home", with the more intense emotion of joy, rather than contentment. He did so in part because he *could*. He could create this drama with his paintbrush in a way that he himself would never have been able to do if he had photographed "from life" with the technology of the time. Thus, the Briggs decision to *illustrate* the great works of literature opened up the possibility for dramatic action, and for cinematic interpretation that would have been difficult or impossible using the still camera.

To create his illustrations, Briggs at first used existing engravings or lithographs, like the image of "Hiawatha's Departure" (Fig. 6.6), or artists who could supplement existing engravings, or create entirely new sets. He was following the steps of the Langenheim Brothers, who, in 1860, had hired an artist named Nisle to create a number of Civil War drawings; a set of 60 Old Testament slides; temperance stories; and a set of *The Lord's Prayer*. As such, Nisle might lay claim to being America's "first screen artist", but almost all of his illustrations were copied from previous work and he was hardly a "great artist". His output was meager compared to Beale's and his talent was meager as well. His designs are sketchy at best, and often feel like cartoons. Briggs probably wanted a new version of *The Lord's Prayer* (Fig. 6.7), not simply to update the clothing, but because of this cartoonish quality – Nisle's awkward figures, his crude anatomy like the man's arm, his faulty perspectives like the off-kilter railings. The whole scene seems unreal.[13]

Indeed, I tried to use Nisle's slides for *The Lord's Prayer* in our *Bible Show* but gave up because audiences – even religious audiences – laughed at his pictures of Victorians in prayer. Beale's remake of the set is certainly full of piety, but it has solidity, and a certain sense of grandeur.

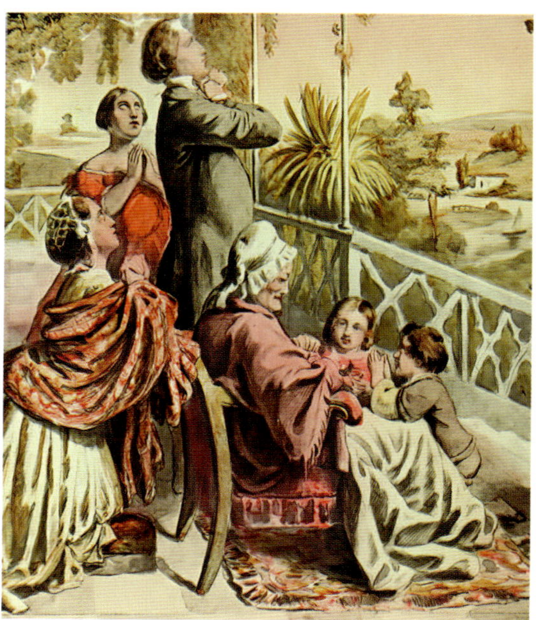

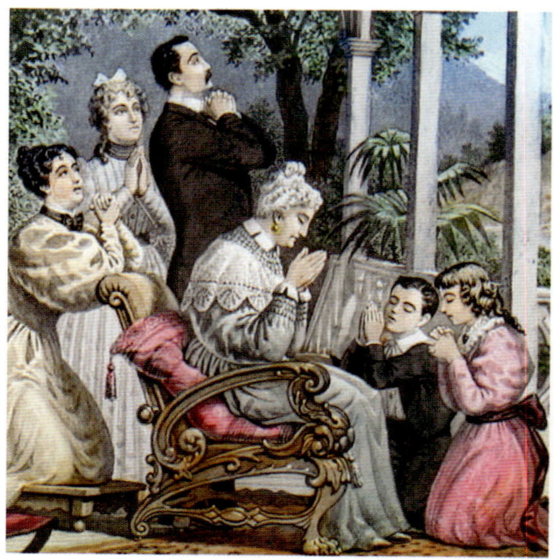

Fig. 6.7 *Left*, detail of Nisle slide 1 from *The Lord's Prayer*, and (*right*) a similar detail from Beale's version.

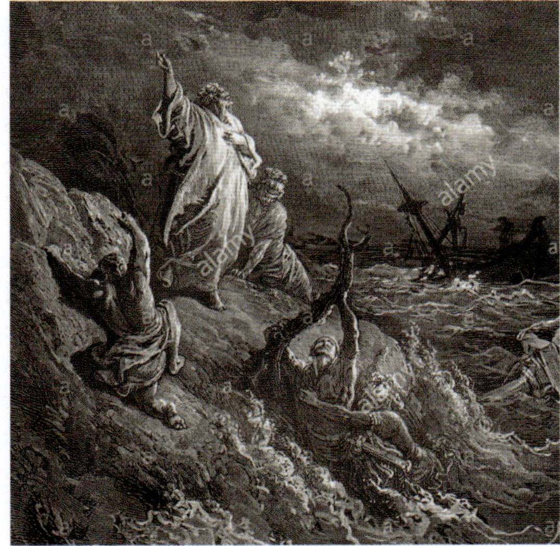

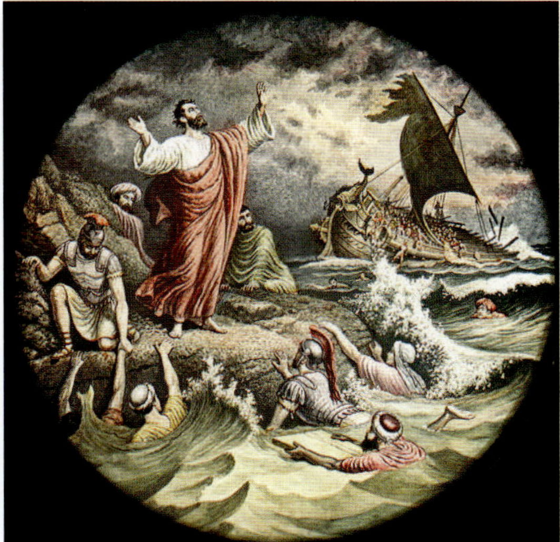

Fig. 6.8 ***Left,*** **engraving of "St. Paul Landing at Malta" by Gustave Doré, and,** ***right,*** **Beale's slide of the same name from The Life of St. Paul set.**

Audiences did not laugh; they joined in worship. A fair amount of Beale's output in his early years at the Briggs Company were similar re-conceptions of Nisle's slides. The 1908 McAllister catalog, for instance, listed as "by Nisle" only 10 of the 60 Bible subjects that had once been attributed to him.[14] Beale had redone all the others.

Briggs also tried several other artists: He hired Herman Faber (Fabre), a faculty member of the Philadelphia School of Design for Women, and Herman Tholey and his son, but none proved very satisfactory. It is unlikely that either Tholey or Faber were employed full time, as almost no signed designs by them exist. Briggs thought that Tholey was satisfactory for comic stories, and continued to offer his *The Farmer and the Calf* comedy and his re-do of Nisle's *Drunkard's Progress*, and to use him for fill-in work. But Briggs did not feel that either Tholey's style or his anatomy skills were up to par for literary illustration.

Briggs did not want the "cartoony", hard-edged style; nor, as we have seen, did he want to use the engraving technique commonly employed for literary illustration. The issue came to a head when Briggs tried to create a new religious series. He had purchased a collection of Gustave Doré's Bible illustrations, but the pictures were so dark and dense that they were almost unintelligible on screen, and his existing staff could not fix them by simple over-painting. Finally, he hired Beale to re-conceptualize the pictures (Fig. 6.8). Generally, a resemblance exists between the two images, but Beale's re-imagined scenes which use a greater tonal range, are much clearer when projected. And, as one Doré scholar has said, Beale's images are "more narratively complex".[15] In Beale's depiction of "St. Paul Landing at Malta", for instance, he packs the scene with details mentioned in the Bible – the 276 people aboard the ship, the stern broken off, the swimmers using planks, the centurion helping a prisoner. All of these details increased the drama of the scene, and helped to sustain audience attention as the passage was read. Altogether, Beale replaced 26 of Doré's slides, and to my mind, each of these replacements is an improvement – specifically, each is more successful when used as a screen projection.

Luckily Briggs found in Beale an artist who could not only "fix up" the designs of other artists, but who could make the visual story move on his own, who could, as it were, give still pictures a "cinematic" narrative feel. Beale's talents became central to achieving Briggs's great endeavor. But what made Beale's art so well suited to the screen? And how did Beale adapt his previous experience as an illustrator to the demands of this new medium?

The Challenge of Screen Art

After years working as an illustrator for newspapers and engraving companies, Beale was about to begin the role that would define his career, that of a magic lantern artist-illustrator. He would need all the talents we have already seen him developing in his earlier life, coming from many different experiences and media – from the panorama and street parades, from his training in the perspective and the symbology of academic art, from book illustration, from years working in the country's leading illustrated magazines. These experiences gave him the ability to create detailed "realistic" renderings

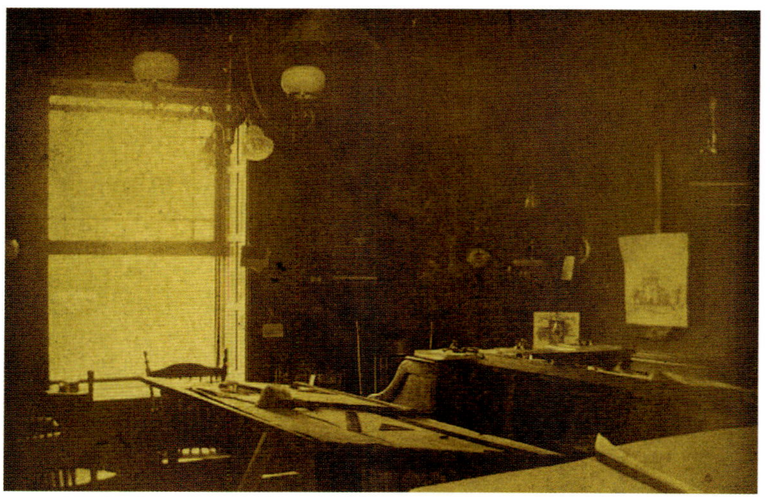

Fig. 6.9 Beale's studio in the attic.

quickly; an expert skill in perspective and stage setting; an ease with anatomy and hence the ability to create and cast characters; an understanding of how to put those characters into movement; control of lighting and the ability to use it dramatically; cartooning; and costume design.

But he would face new challenges with magic lantern art, many of them outside the world of print illustration, where he had worked all his life. New organizational issues faced him. Could he function well in the magic lantern business environment? Could he work out a new kind of artistic relationship between himself as "cinematographer" and his "producer", Briggs?

Artistically, he also faced a host of new questions. Painting for the screen was not like creating a design for a newspaper engraving, or for a painting hung on the wall. The space scale was vastly different. He was painting in a small scale for viewing on a large scale. And the purpose was entirely different. He was not creating a single view to be seen by itself, but a series designed to tell a story – sometimes a whole novel – with only a few slides. Could he find ways to extend the narrative power of each slide?

Those questions began to be answered when Beale started freelancing for C. W. Briggs in 1881, but he did relatively few lantern slide designs in the next nine years. Even though limited, the association was apparently a successful one. In 1890 Beale was moved to a "major account" in Briggs' ledger, bought a Milligan lantern through Briggs, and began buying copies of the Briggs slides he had already made. These slides were the start of that collection of "Beale Owned Slides" which he purchased one by one, as Briggs manufactured slides from his designs. He kept them in his attic, and may have used them for family performance. They form the foundation for my discussion of Beale's art in this book.[16] When Briggs was ready to plunge into the development of his vision of illustrating the world's great secular and Biblical literature, Beale was ready also. Sometime in 1892 he left Frank Harris and Company, where he had been employed as a full-time fashion illustrator, and began working full-time with Briggs. It was a critical career change, for he would soon become America's most popular magic lantern artist, and establish himself as a pioneer, though an unacknowledged one, in the coming American cinematic century.[17]

Artist in a New Business

As a magic lantern artist Beale functioned like the *art director* or the *cinematographer* of a movie – that is, the person who had direct responsibility for the artistic creation of the screen image. Briggs was like the *producer* or *producer director*, the businessman who selected the subject content, had overall responsibility for its execution, and ran the company. Beale worked at home creating the designs. Briggs worked at his factory, supervising the manufacture of the slides, and attending to the business side and distribution. The two communicated by sending designs and notes back and forth by post or messenger, and, occasionally in later years, by telephone.

Beale's studio was an attic room in the family home, with a tilted drawing table, probably near the north window to get the indirect "artist's light" (Fig. 6.9). Once electricity arrived, a number of electric bulbs were suspended overhead so that he could work late into the night if he was behind on deadlines. At the table was a straight-backed chair – on it a rule, triangle, compass, and pencils. Paints and paintbrushes were probably kept in a cabinet along the walls. A few framed pictures decorated the room; a few sketches were tacked up near the drawing table. In this room Beale worked alone, at a steady pace that had characterized his output since his boyhood panorama. He painted about 1½ to 2 original 13" x 13" pictures a week, on all kinds of subjects at once, and earned about $50 a week, or $2,500 for a 50-week year, about $85,000 in 2025 dollars.[18]

When Beale finished a design, he sent it down

to Briggs at his factory at 628 Callowhill Street in Center City, Philadelphia. Six photographers in the Briggs's factory photographed the painted designs, and photographically reduced them to about 3" square, adjusting the *exposure* of the negatives as they did so. The photographic process used was the ***wet collodion*** method that Briggs's father had used before him – a photographic emulsion on the glass made by dissolving gun-cotton (pyroxyline) in alcohol and sulphuric ether. It was a more difficult technique to manage than the "dry process" commonly employed by the 1880s, but Briggs liked its ability to capture detail and fine illustrations, and Beale soon learned to make the most of its ability to render grades of shading, as it was ideally suited for his images.[19]

Next the photographers printed black-and-white positives of the images to an emulsion on glass plates, four slides at a time, in a four-up ***light*** (Fig. 6.10). The slides were then cut apart and colored. Then each slide was covered with a thin piece of glass and bound around the edges with tape, or set in a wooden frame.

My wife and I spent several days in the bowels of the George Eastman Museum, studying their large collection of Briggs negatives for possible hidden Beale signatures and other hints to slide production. After we finished our search, and as we were packing up for the 5-hour drive home, the archivist asked us if we'd like to see the sleeves.

"Thank you. We saw the sleeves. We put all the negatives back in them. They're OK."

"No, no, not the new ones. The original ones. We kept them, and they have notes on them. Would you like to see them?"

God bless archivists.

We stayed an extra day, and what we found was fascinating. Briggs' notes make it clear that he was meticulous about the creation and use of his negatives. He wanted to avoid problems coming from collodion emulsions that were too ***thick*** or too ***thin***, or that were thicker on one side than another. A major Briggs' concern was to capture the details of a face, which – as any illustrator will tell you – is where the eye naturally goes in any illustration. Another of Briggs' special concerns was to capitalize on Beale's dramatic and varied use of light. In *Hiawatha*, for instance, Briggs specified that slide six was to

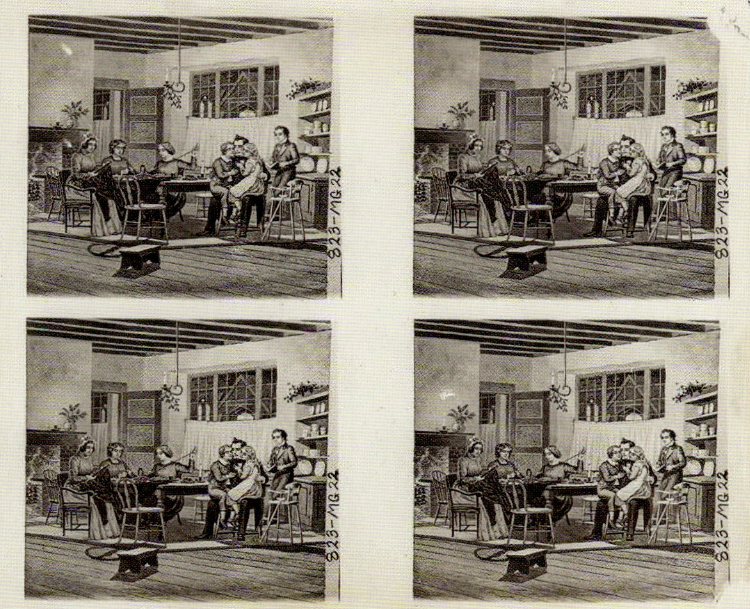

Fig. 6.10 A "light" of positives for a scene from Beale's *Marley's Ghost* (*A Christmas Carol*).

be, "Day, not dark storm", which did improve the slide. The upper third of the slide has been made very light, so that the dark thrown tree stands out dramatically (Fig. 6.11). Sometimes Briggs commented on ways to maximize the drama of images. In the cloud slides used to mask the dissolve between the angel images of *Flight of the Soul* (see p. 78), he directed that the outlines of the clouds should be sharp in the first image, but in later slides of the same image, the slide photographer should focus on the center of the image and let the edges be less distinct. This would create the effect of the real world slowly dissolving into Heaven.

(While generally strictly informational in his comments, Briggs sometimes got testy about poor printing, as he did with an image from *Drake's Ode to The American Flag*: "In God's names LESS! Thin, not quite fresh". Such comments may not have been entirely appreciated.

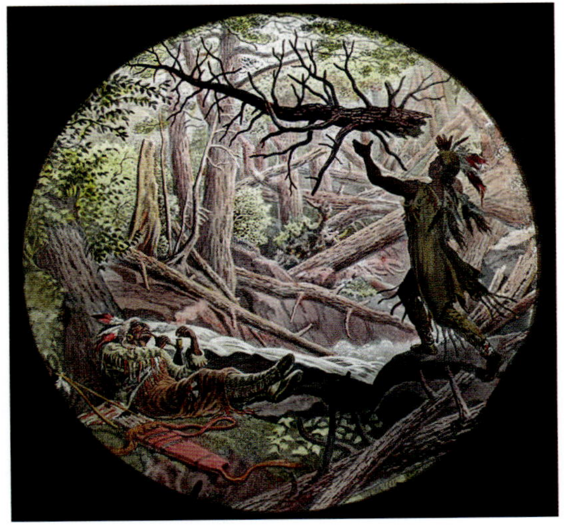

Fig. 6.11 Beale's slide 6 of *Hiawatha* by Henry Wadsworth Longfellow. Here Hiawatha's friend Kwasind clears the forest path for his resting father.

The Coloring Process

Once the slides were reproduced in black and white, they could be sold as is, or colored. (Coloring doubled or tripled the price of a slide.) Twenty colorists in the Briggs workshop hand-painted the color individually onto each slide, often working with large magnifying glasses (Fig. 6.12). It took between a half-hour to three hours to paint one slide; and a colorist could expect to make about four dollars a day, about $140 in 2025 dollars.[20]

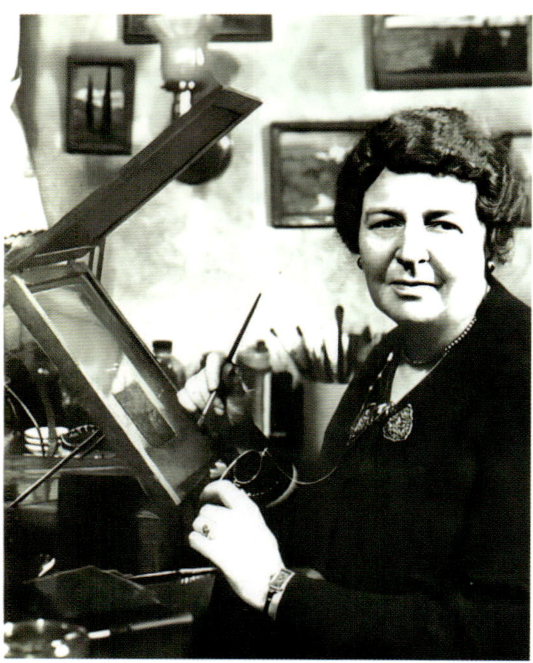

Fig. 6.12 Grace Nichols, a colorist for Burton Holmes the famous lantern lecturer, coloring slides about 1939. Courtesy, The Burton Holmes Archive.

Three main methods of coloring existed in the industry – watercolors, oil, and varnish. Briggs used the varnish method, in which pigments were mixed with diluted varnish, and applied in successive layers of color.[21] The work required great skill, because when the slides were projected the colors would not be seen in the same tints as they were when applied. On screen, they would be modified by both the shades of black in Beale's designs, and by the brilliant white of the lantern's light. And, as opposed to Beale's detailed painting done on a 13" x 13" sheet of paper, painting the color was entirely different because it was done on glass at such a tiny scale – a 3" circle or square. "It must be remembered", wrote *The Photo-Miniature,*

> … that in lantern-slide work we are, first and last, impressionists; that is, we do not separately touch each leaf, or blade of grass, or minute detail. A slight, even wash over the whole of the mass gives it the requisite variety and contrast of tint.[22]

The Briggs colorists were more meticulous than most, but still the point is well taken. Their skill was indeed that of the impressionists – to give the sense of multi-faceted color and light without in fact coloring every leaf or minute detail (Fig. 6.13). Coloring was a major part of the Briggs business – so much so that in the 1890s his letterhead did not mention his illustrated slides, but proclaimed that his was the "Only House in America supplying Colored Magic Lantern Slides to The Trade". The Briggs colorists were renowned throughout the industry for their expertise, as the editor of *The Magic Lantern* makes clear. The wise lanternist, he said, should beware of competitors who offered "spurious slides colored by foreign hands, on our own shores", slides which were of, "wretched quality" (Fig. 6.14):

> It has long been an open secret that there is only one party in America who can and does color lantern slides well … He colors for all the trade in this city [Philadelphia], New York, and

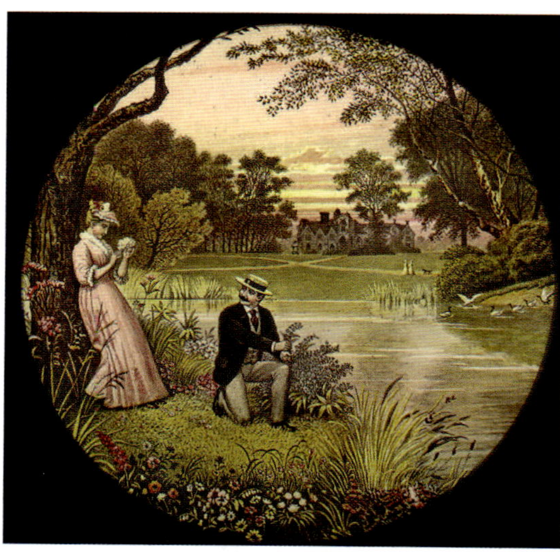

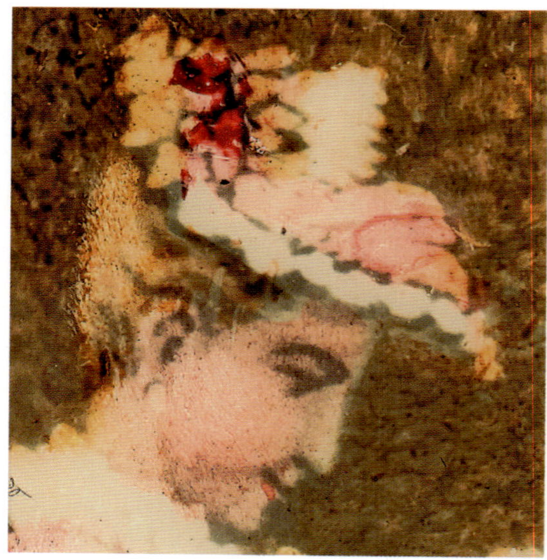

Fig. 6.13 Beale's slide 8 from *The Brook* by Alfred Lord Tennyson, at about the 3" size it was colored, and a detail from it, showing both finely-painted transitions, and an "impressionist" approach.

elsewhere, and no matter where you have made your purchase you have purchased his excellent work. The party we allude to is Mr. C. W. Briggs.[23]

Once the Briggs factory workers colored the slides, they sealed the paint with Canadian balsam varnish, which gave a hard, clear coating that protected the image and increased the brilliance of the coloring. The slides were then covered with a second piece of glass to further protect the painting, framed, packed, and sold wholesale to the nation's leading distributors:

> [The Briggs factory] was literally like a place straight out of Dickens. Each of the four floors had its own potbellied stove and was devoted to one feature of manufacture. The first floor had the shipping department and the fireproof vault for wet-collodion [glass] negatives ... The second floor was used for cutting the glass plates, each with four slides printed on it, into individual 3-1/4 x 4-inch slides, and for varnishing negatives and colored slides. The third and fourth floor of Briggs and Company held the photographers and colorists. Also on this floor were 16-inch pine shelves that held old readings [scripts] that went with the slide sets ... and title labels for slides in great quantity.[24]

The brilliance of the Briggs color, combined with the subtlety of his collodion printing and with the drama of Beale's art, continued to impress the industry right to the end of the magic lantern period. For instance, the authoritative 700-page tome, *Optic Projection*, published in 1914, lists Briggs among 12 American slide manufacturers. But it goes on to say that the Briggs company offers, "beautiful slides ... made by ... the collodion process". Briggs is the only company singled out for such a descriptor, let alone such praise.[25] The Briggs company's emphasis on high *production values* was also a happy fit with Beale's talents. Though it took Beale a while to find his style, he would soon realize that by combining his skills in depicting elaborately lighted scenes with the skills of the Briggs factory in color work, he could create truly breath-taking images.

I believe Briggs sold most Beale slides in color. I have no direct evidence on this; it is an impression born of reviewing thousands of Beale slides on eBay. Why might Beale's work tend to be in color, given that color slides were so much more expensive than black and white? It probably has to do with the nature of the Briggs market. Many, perhaps most, of his slides were purchased by institutions like schools, secret societies, and churches. These institutions could pool the resources of their members to afford quality, and could amortize the expense over many years of use. They each had a significant reason for using Beale's spectacular color: Schools to inspire the young, secret societies to impress their new initiates, churches to celebrate the glory of God.

Beale's Role in Coloring

What was Beale's role in this coloring process? His magic lantern paintings, after all, were in black and white. Though he did not do the coloring himself, he did have to prepare for the work that would be done in the Briggs factory. Luckily, his boyhood experience as a ***tinter*** for photographs had given him much more experience in moving from black-and-white images to color than was usual for an illustrator of his time, and no doubt he used that knowledge in his lantern work.

But making the transition was not easy. Preparing for the color at the Briggs factory required another kind of communication between "cinematographer" and "producer". Sometimes Beale would indicate in the margins of the designs he sent Briggs the colors for the final slides

Fig. 6.14 Detail of Beale's "The Capture of Stony Point" from the *American History* group, in three different grades of coloring quality.

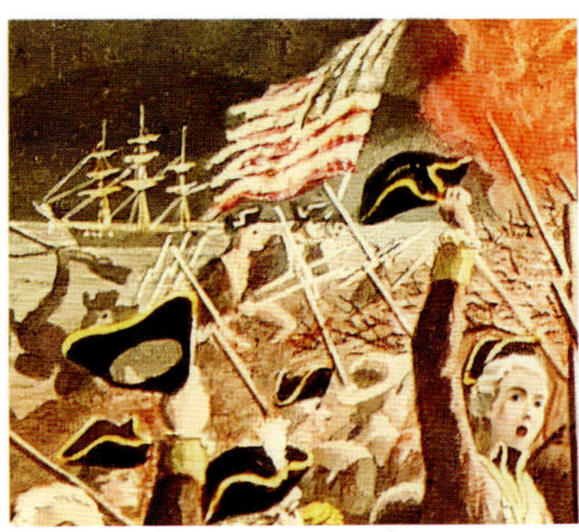

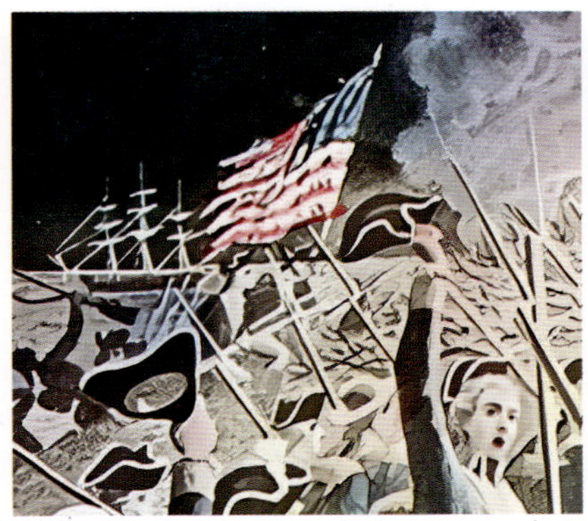

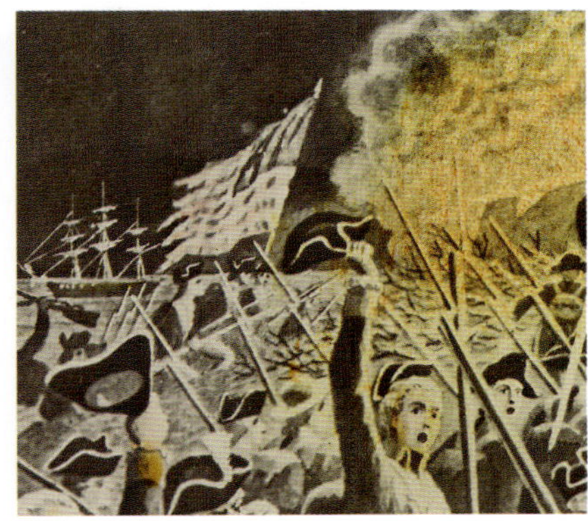

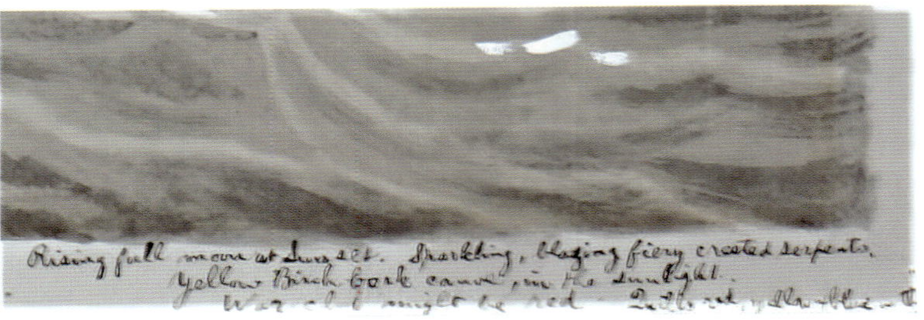

Fig. 6.15 Beale's coloring directions on the design for slide 18 of *Hiawatha*. Beale rarely provided such coloring instructions.

(Figs. 6.15 and 16). Sometimes, especially if the specifications were significant, as in military uniforms or flags, he would send detailed attached notes. In other cases, such as this slide from *Hiawatha*, it's not clear why he provided the instructions. Perhaps he wanted to balance the "blazing, fiery crested serpents" with the red of the war club in order to tie this complicated composition together.

On other occasions the coloration would be discussed in correspondence, as in this letter from Beale to Briggs (Fig. 6.17):

> In your letter of the 15th is mentioned "that everything looks too nice and new" in my drawing [of *Old Black Joe*]. To take away the new look, "Old Black Joe" in the graveyard should have his shoes and trousers painted mud color nearly to his knees … as they must have been; since I can only show light and shade, with black and white.[26]

But specific involvement in slide coloring was unusual for Beale. Not only did he not color his slides himself; in general, he did not direct the coloring either. As a result, he did not control one of the central features of his screen art. For that he was dependent on the skills of the colorists. Luckily for him the Briggs colorists were very skillful indeed, for their work had a profound impact on the screen image. The vivid colors and delicate shadings of Beale's slides produced by the Briggs company are one of the features of our shows that audiences react to most often. They assume that an art form that came before the silent movies must of course have been black and white, or worse ... probably a muddy blotch. They are always surprised and delighted by the dramatic coloring of Beale's lantern slides, an aspect of his images for which Beale himself had little responsibility.

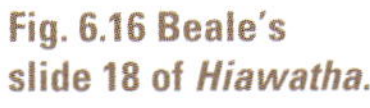

Fig. 6.16 Beale's slide 18 of *Hiawatha*.

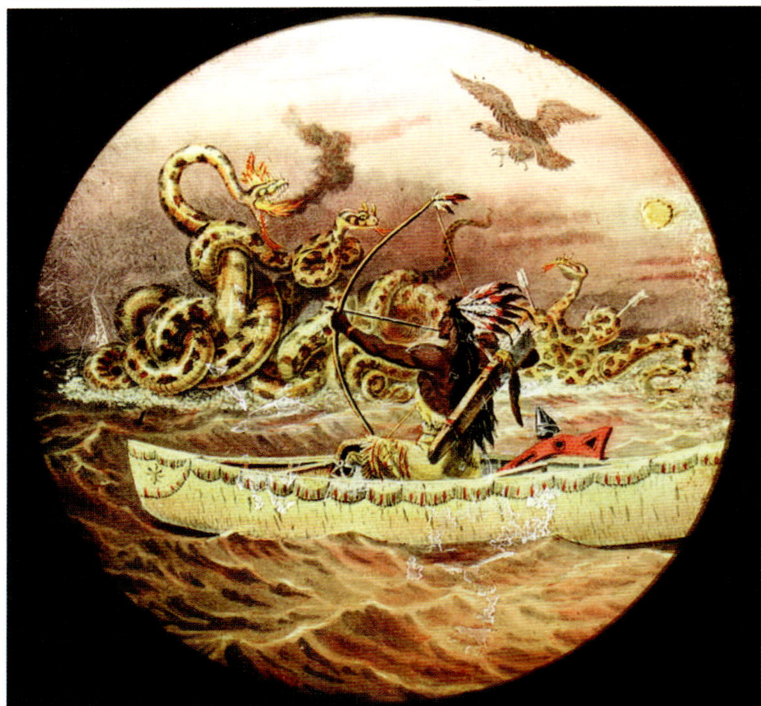

The very first movies of the Lumiere Brothers had no such color effects; they were in black and white. The contrast of these movies with the real world of natural color, or with the magic lantern world of artistic color, was striking. Maxim Gorki, the famous Russian writer, was dismayed by his first visit to a movie:

> Last evening, I was in the Kingdom of Shadows. If one could only convey the strangeness of this world. A world without color and sound. Everything here – the earth, water, and air, the trees, the people – everything is made of a monotone gray. Gray rays of sunlight in a gray sky, gray eyes in a gray face, leaves as gray as cinder. Not life, but the shadow of life. Not life's movement, but a sort of mute specter.[27]

Gorki's much quoted reaction was not typical, but he surely made a point, …and made it well. Certainly, one of the competitive disadvantages of the movies in the early years was its relative lack of color when compared with the lush palette and detailed coloring of magic lantern slides.

The movies tried to remedy this disadvantage by various methods. They frequently used the old lantern technique of tinting whole scenes – red to indicate sunrise, blue for night, etc.[28] Or they sent films to the magic lantern tinting studios and had each print tinted by hand. This did not require great artistic talent, but even with the early short films, this was a Herculean task. And even the finest tinting, such as that on Melies' films, is not up to even the crudest of lantern slides. It was just too difficult to paint so many tiny images. The longer the films became, the bigger the problem. Finally, black and white (or overall tints) prevailed.

The lantern continued to be the way to bring color to the screen, even at the movies. Announcement slides, advertising slides, and most especially song slides – all in color – were shown before and after the movie reels. As we shall see, it was the color, fantasy, and audience participation of song slides that helped sustain the movies during its early lean years.

The Briggs Business and Beale Slide Sales

The busy Briggs factory did not sell slides at retail; Briggs was a wholesaler, selling "to the trade". Thus, Beale images appear in many shapes and sizes of lantern slides, with many different distributors' labels. The Briggs/Beale illustrated slides of Literature, History, Secret Society, and Religion had, as we have seen, a significant role in the larger lantern slide industry, visually dramatizing important parts of human experience. But by 1908 they still occupied a relatively small niche – about 9-10 percent – amid the much larger sale of slides made directly from photographs, like travel and science slides. A niche perhaps, but Beale was certainly the largest single contributor of slides to the American lantern industry. Think about this for a second. Something like ten percent of all the slides sold in America were created by one man. To me, that seems quite extraordinary.

This level of Beale's sales in 1908 had been driven in large part by the steady increase year over year in the number of his slides that Briggs offered. That rose at the rate of about 110 new Beale slide images a year, so that by 1908 about 60% of the slides Briggs offered were by Beale. The second factor that drove sales was the rise in the number of companies carrying Beale slides, rising from 29 in 1890, to 121 companies by 1908. The third factor was the introduction in 1900 of the *Economic Catalog*. This was a catalog of 24 pages, rising to 34 by 1908, prepared by Briggs, but inserted into the catalogs of his distributors, or printed separately with the distributor's name on it. It offered Beale's slides at dramatic savings from the usual catalog prices. The *Economic* slides sold for $.25 for black and white, and $.50 for color – a 37% and 50% reduction respectively, bringing the price down to about $8.80 and $17.50 in 2025 dollars. The fourth factor that influenced Beale's sales were of course general business and cultural influences, such as the economic Panic of 1893, the Spanish American War, and, finally, the movies.

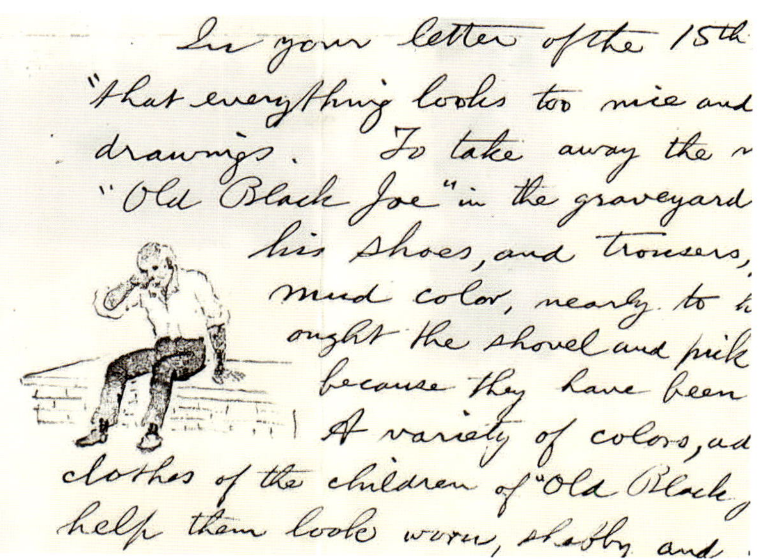
In your letter of the 15th
"that everything looks too nice and
drawings. To take away the
"Old Black Joe" in the graveyard
his shoes, and trousers,
mud color, nearly to
ought the shovel and pick
because they have been
A variety of colors, and
clothes of the children of "Old Black
help them look worn, shabby and

Fig. 6.17 Beale letter to Briggs, November 22, 1905, in which Beale sketched out his coloring idea for *Old Black Joe*. Photocopy of original made at The George Eastman Museum.

Pulling together all these factors, I estimate that cumulatively, from the period1890 through 1908, Briggs sold between 1,300,000 and 2,200,000 Beale slides.[29] That may sound like a lot, but given that Beale produced 2,621 total slide images in his career, and that these sales were over a period of 19 years, at the low end of the sale range that would mean an average yearly sale for individual slide images of only 26 copies per year. The cumulative sale of hundreds of thousands of slides, covering a wide range of subjects – shown again and again to audiences of twenty, or a hundred, or several hundred people over many years – surely reached a cumulative audience of many millions, and surely had a profound effect on American culture.

Just who were those people, and what kinds of showmen performed Beale's slides in what kinds of venues? That is not an easy question to answer. My studies of the major performers, the "professional" lantern showmen, does not suggest that many were using Beale's slides.[30] I think, rather, that smaller-scale showmen were the major users. A good indication of their nature can be inferred from the content of Beale's work. As we shall see, he produced many religious slides for use in churches, missions, and religious education. Secret Society slides, often with different content for the different societies, were to be used in fraternal halls. I think the major market for the story, song, history, and current events slides was small performers, and the schools. (When the Briggs business was sold, the new owner tried to adapt such slides to more modern formats like 35mm, and sell them to the schools.)

Briggs and Beale – A Collaborative Process

As Beale and Briggs began to work together, a pattern developed in their relationship, though it is sometimes difficult to always determine who was the *auteur* – the driving creative force for a given set. Certainly, Briggs made a major contribution and would be considered a *creative producer*. He always chose the subject, and usually gave Beale instructions for a slide set – varying from very explicit (perhaps choosing what scenes to illustrate), to quite vague. With few exceptions, we cannot tell the degree of his involvement by set. Sometimes, on religious slides where the potential existed for controversy, Briggs had a clergyman provide detailed art directions. Sometimes, as with *Doré's* images, Beale was given existing slides and simply asked to make new, better versions. This was also true of comic slides where a joke of proven appeal was to be given a new look, as in *First Cigar*.

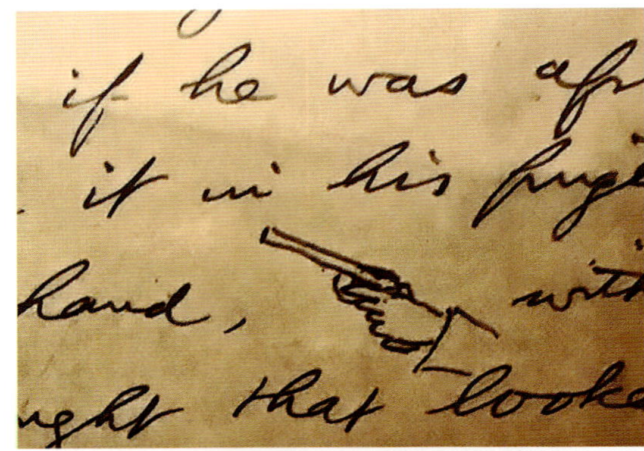
if he was afr
it in his finge
hand, with
ught that looke

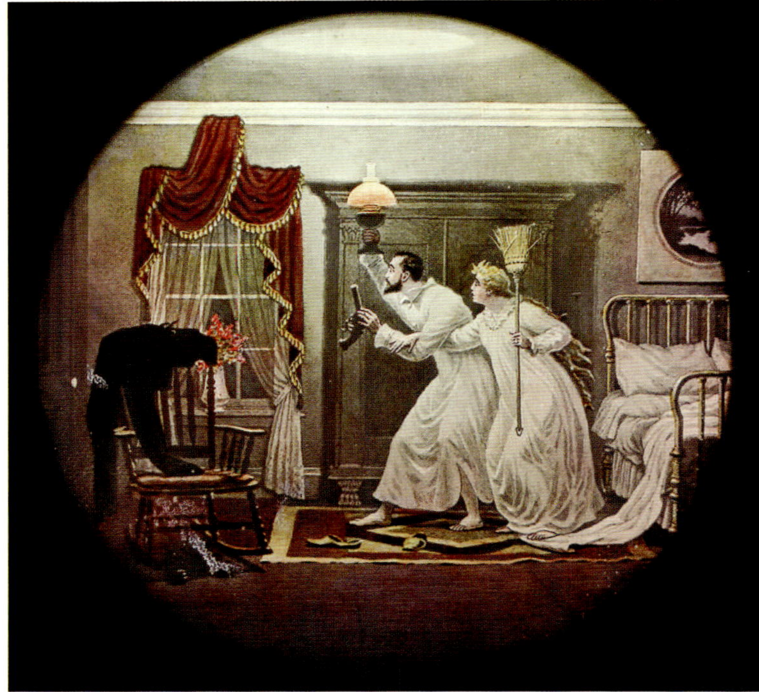

Fig. 6.19 Beale's slide 1 of *Mr. Timorous and His Bull-Dog*, and (top) portion of his letter to Briggs discussing this scene.

Sometimes Briggs provided a sketch for Beale to "work up". Sometimes there seem to have been conversations at which Beale took notes. And sometimes Beale seems to have been largely on his own, working out the artistic design of the piece, and then sending sketches to Briggs for approval.

One potential clue to the degree of Beale's creative involvement in a design might seem to be Beale's signature on the slide, as in Fig. 6.18, the image at the start of this chapter, where it is hidden just below the piece of wood at left. You might assume that he would sign those pictures on which he made the largest contribution. To some degree this is true. For instance, he does *not* sign designs that he simply adapted from another source. But beyond that, I have been unable to find additional consistent patterns in his use of signature. Sometimes it is there, sometimes not; sometimes on one slide in a series and not others; sometimes in a sketch but not in the final design. A signature is a sure sign that Beale did a design, and probably that he felt he made a major artistic contribution to it; the absence of a signature tells very little. Luckily, the lantern catalogs sometimes provide help in attribution. They name "Beale" as the creator of many slides, but only in the "Bible" and "Artistic Gems" sections, so they are not much use in sorting out the degree of his creative involvement in stories.[31]

Though Briggs was clearly the boss and made the final decisions, the artistic relationship between Beale and Briggs was fluid, and hence disagreements between "cinematographer" and "producer" were inevitable. For instance, in *Mr. Timorous*, a comic story for which Briggs had provided rough sketches, a discussion arose after the design was completed about how Mr. Timorous should hold a gun with which he is about to accost a burglar (Fig. 6.19). Beale wrote:

> I can make his fingers reach out covering more of the pistol, but I thought, from your sketch, he was holding it timidly, as if he were afraid of it, so I made him hold it with his fingertips ... [At first I had put] it properly in his hand, with his finger on the trigger, [as in the sketch] but thought that looked too bold. It's comic as it is, but I will make it as realistic as you decide.[32]

(Beale won the argument. It was Briggs's concept that ended up on the cutting room floor; not Beale's design. Mr. Timorous holds his gun in his fingertips to this day. And Beale's judgment was correct. We use *Mr. Timorous* in our *Spring Show*. After the introduction to the story, we begin in the dark. Suddenly, the pianist creates a noisy crash with the piano, a noise that awakens the sleeping Mr. Timorous. "A burglar"! screams his wife. He flashes up on the screen, dressed in his nightshirt, dangling his gun, terrorized by the prospect. Before I get a word out, the audience is laughing.)

Whatever disagreements existed between Briggs and Beale, their working relationship was certainly productive, and lasted 36 years. On Beale's part, his success was based on a subtle combination of technical manipulations to his base paint-on-paper medium, developing a art style specifically designed for the screen, and a mastery of narrative techniques. This combination was so different from his previous work that it is hard to believe the same person did both. Compare, for instance, any of Beale's slide images with his engravings on pages 38, 42, 45, 46, 53, 57 or 59. Beale's slides were also unlike anything he or any other American had developed before.

Creating a Technical Style for the Screen

Faced with the demands of a new medium – images for slide projection – Beale created a new technical style composed of small adjustments to ordinary artistic practice, each of which helped in making an effective transfer from a paper design to a luminous screen image:

After some initial experimentation, trying some designs at 11" square, and some at 20", Beale settled on a standard design size of about 13-1/2" square on 14-1/2"square paper – large enough to enable him to paint detail, small enough to be able to "see" a series of designs all at once, and to be able to handle them easily.[33] He was trying to find the right balance in a complicated size transition during a lantern slide's life: The image was painted at about a foot square, reduced about six-fold to a 3" glass plate, colored, and then projected up to 20 feet in diameter – about 6,000 times larger on screen than the slide itself (Fig. 6.20). In this enlargement process, "defects are magnified", as one lantern specialist dryly noted. Beale was not really painting a square foot of paper; he was painting 400 square feet of illuminated screen. Starting with the optimal size was essential for achieving the maximum effect when his picture

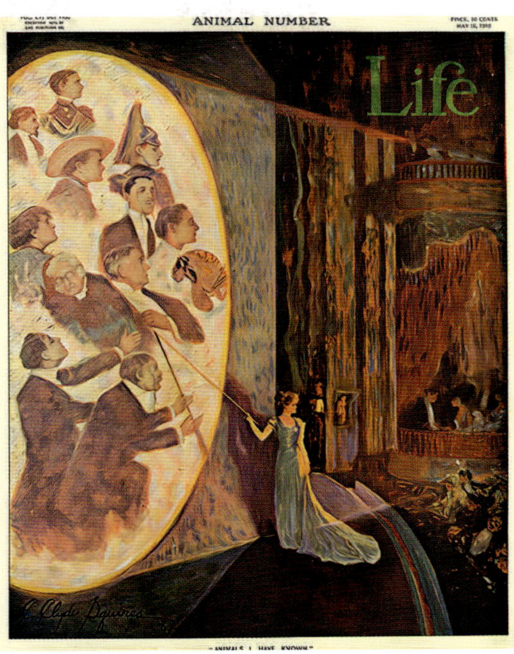

Fig. 6.20 Cover of *Life* magazine, May 19,1910. A woman lectures with lantern slides. The picture shows the size to which Beale's 3" images had to translate when projected.

finally hung in midair, spot-lit in a darkened hall.[34]

Beale drew for two different aspect ratios at once, the 3¼ x 4" "Economy" slides, and the "woodframe" slides, which had a circular 3" image in a 4 x 7" wooden frame. The Economy format, which was much cheaper than the woodframe, had largely replaced it by 1900. Beale was always careful to keep the important visual information ***within the circle*** of his designs so that they would work in the wood-frame format. The difficulties of coping with this double *aspect ratio* were similar to those experienced today in adapting movies to different sized theater screens, or to television – most obviously in adapting the wide-screen movies to TV with the "letter box" format (Fig. 6.21).

Building the Ideal Tonal Range

Tonal control was the single most important technical criteria for high-quality slides, a standard emphasized over and over again by photographic lantern-slide authorities. For instance, Alfred Stieglitz (noted photographer, editor of *The American Amateur Photographer*, and lantern-slide enthusiast) railed that slides lacking medium gradation were, despite their popularity, "an abomination to the refined eye". And of all the criteria for high-quality slides, a full tonal range was the most rarely achieved. Stieglitz and other authorities felt that it was unmet by 90% of both amateur and professional photographic slides.[35]

This sharp criticism was based on the fact that

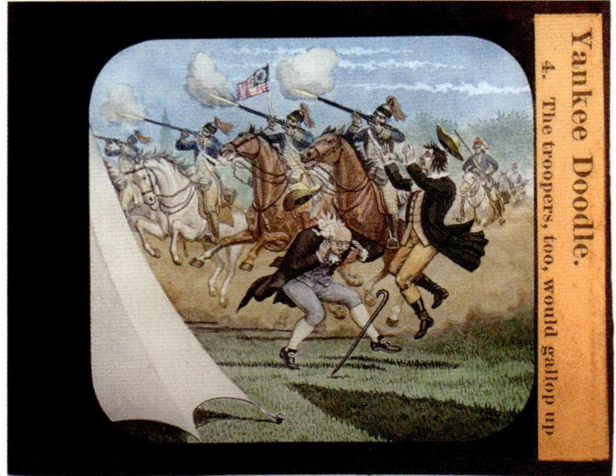

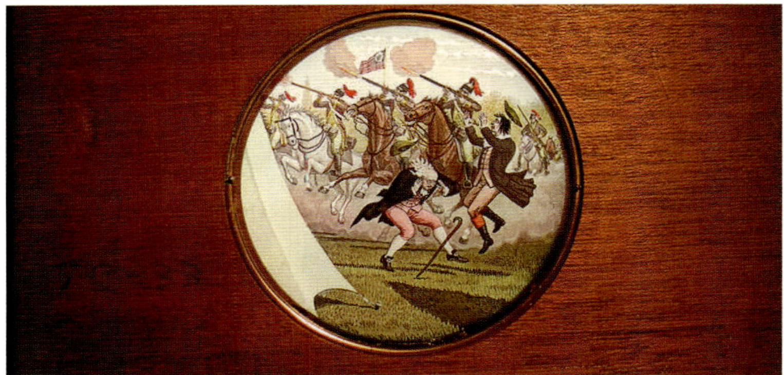

Fig. 6.21 The Beale image, Slide 5, from *Yankee Doodle*, in two different slide formats. Different artists or companies often colored slides of the same Beale image differently.

projected images could display more than twice the tonal range as the same image printed on paper (1/40 vs. 1/100).[36] The lantern's light created a white that seemed as brilliant as the sun; the blacks could have no light at all; and hence lantern slides could be close to the real tonal gradations of nature. The experts wanted to see this special capability of the lantern slide fulfilled. Again and again, they decried the juxtaposition of harsh black-and-white that was characteristic of most photographic slides, disparaging it as "tar and whitewash". Stieglitz advocated ***local reduction*** of values during the development process, and went so far as to add to some of his slides ***compensating cover glasses***. These overlaid the original image with tonal gradations in order to create the desired effect. Before his efforts, *The Photo-Miniature* editorialized, "The artistic possibilities of a [photographic] lantern-slide were never fully grasped".[37]

Beale's illustrated approach consistently achieved the full range of tonal values *The Photo-Miniature* was looking for (Fig. 6.22). Combined with the rich detail of his portrayals, it gave his images a naturalistic quality unmatched by all but a few of the photographic lantern slides of his day. Beale may have been painting with black and white, but what he saw in his mind's eye, and managed to convey, was the full range of natural light and color, shimmering on the screen.

For most images he abandoned the white or light brown paper used by his predecessors, and chose a light gray, usually the #1 weight paper produced by the firm of Carl Schleicher and Scheull. This provided the base tonality for his design, giving tonal *unity*. Perhaps one of his artist friends returning from Paris gave him this secret. John Singer Sargent's teacher, Carolus-Duran, had emphasized again and again, "Cherchez la demi-teinte". ("Find the middle tone".)[38] The gray paper allowed him to paint both lighter and darker on the tonal scale, and would not create ***hot spots*** or ***glare*** or ***false accents*** when photographed. Building from the gray paper tonal base, Beale created his pictures in shades of *monochrome*, primarily of ***gouache*** (an opaque watercolor). Almost all his designs used seven tones, six plus the paper itself, usually two tones that were lighter than the paper, and four darker, with gradations between them as they merged. Seven tones were considered the maximum that an artist could effectively manipulate; most artists used no more than five. Beale thus had superb control of tonal values throughout the image.

China-white oil paint was used to create the lightest shades, so that when the design was photographed, the projector's light shone through the glass slide with only the lightest of tones. The advantage of using oil paint for the highlights is that it could easily be painted over the gouache. When the slide was tinted, these points provided the brightest colors on the screen, giving Beale's slides their characteristic brilliance (Fig. 6.23). The very brightest spots, usually very small ones, were left untinted, or the negative itself might be re-touched with black to ensure overexposure, or the paint on the slide might be scratched though. These techniques ensured that the picture's tiny ***highlights*** were the blazing white of the lantern's light itself. This delicate use of highlights was another area in which Beale's work met the criteria of excellence promoted by the photographic experts, who lamented clear slide glass that "occupies any considerable area", because it contributed to ***dazzle*** – a blinding of the audience by a large area of brightly-lit screen. Conversely, they felt that highlights consisting of "very minute points of clear glass" gave ***sparkle*** to the very best lantern slides.[39]

At the other extreme of the tonal spectrum, Beale again followed the best practices of lantern art, "guarding against too much shadow", obtaining his tonal gradation by using the ***higher scale of light***. Unlike what might be true in creating a painting, *The Photo-Miniature* argued, "the deepest shadows must, if necessary, be sacrificed" in a lantern slide, because the loss of light from projecting the image meant that the "detail among the deep shadows" would be lost on screen.[40] (In fact, too much shadow was exactly what made so many of Doré's images so problematic as lantern slides.) Beale kept the darkest end of his tonal spectrum to a minimum, usually reserving it for very small areas. Even when he did use a large dark mass, he did so with gradations of dark.

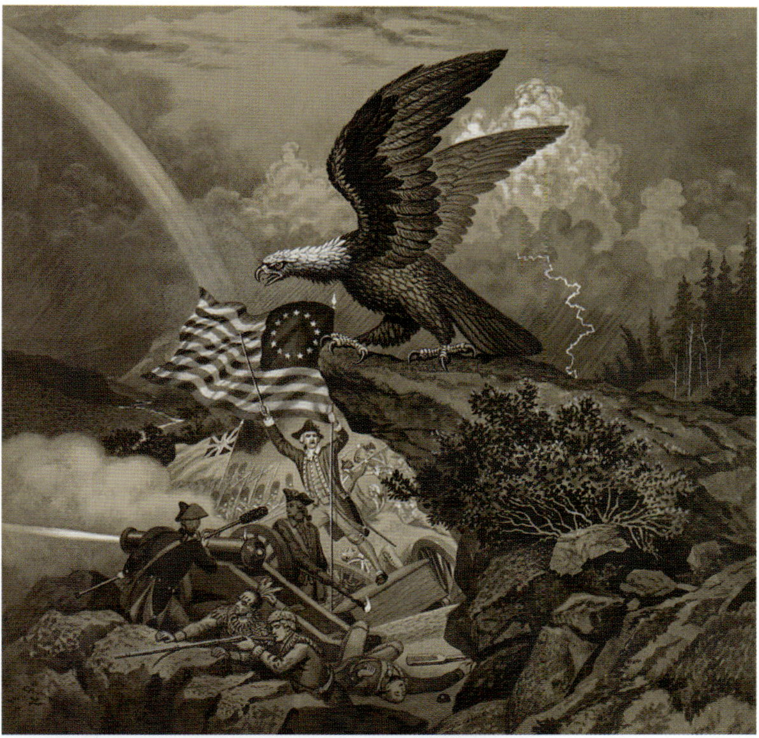

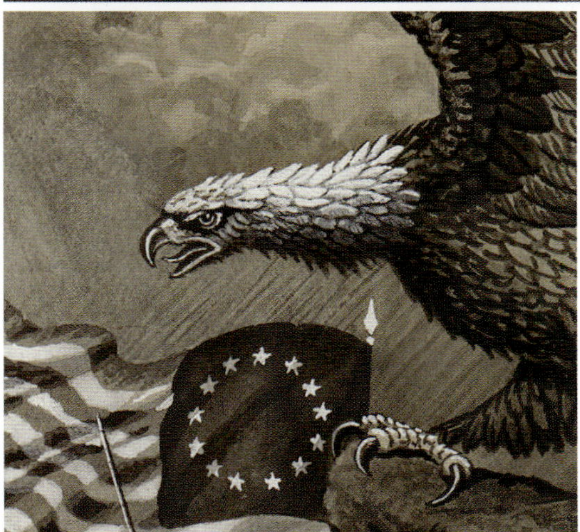

Fig. 6.22 Beale's design of "1777 American Flag" from the *U. S. Flags, Miscellaneous* group. The design and detail show Beale's skillful use of seven tonal gradations.

Centering on the Action

Beale centered his images so that significant detail was in sharp *focus* and nothing essential was lost by the fuzzy distortion at the lens' edge in those lanterns that lacked a flat field – a distortion so pronounced that it was sometimes called the ***vignette effect***. Keeping essential information "within the circle" was also important because slide images came in those two formats, round and square, both produced from the same design. Hence all important information needed to be kept within the more restricted round format. And the centralized image was also used for dramatic effect. For instance, In the scene from *The Old Oaken Bucket* (Fig. 6.24), the action is centered on the symbolic bucket, the "emblem of truth over-flowing". It is also highlighted by five design lines pointing to it – two sides of the well, the boy's figure, the pole and chain lift, and the grass edge.

Beale usually located the picture's action in the upper two-thirds of ***the circular image frame***, in part perhaps, so that important visual information would not be obscured on the screen by the large hats of the ladies in the audience (Fig. 6.25). This positioning also helped keep the central image in focus, for if the projector cannot be directly perpendicular to the screen, which is usually the case, some portion of the picture will always be out of focus and distorted, an effect called ***keystoning***. In our shows, to compensate for the keystoning effect, I've

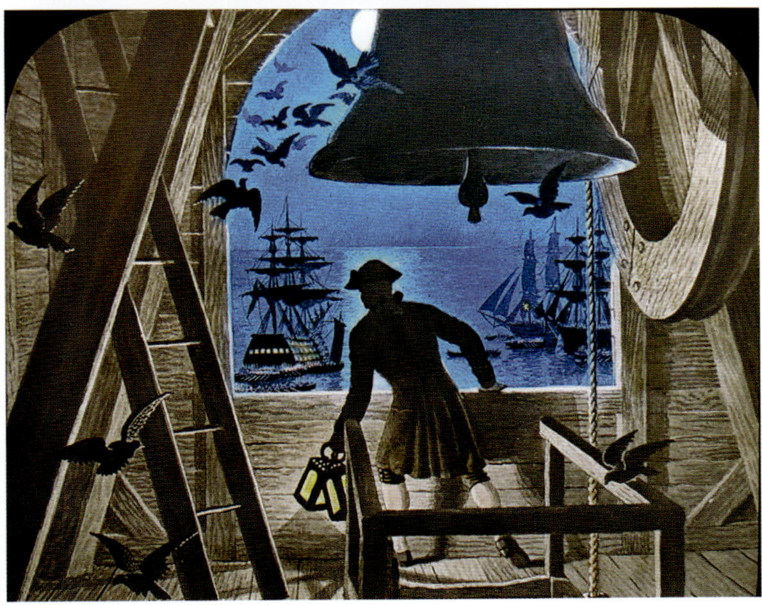

Fig. 6.23 Beale's slide 2 from *Paul Revere's Ride* by Henry Wadsworth Longfellow. The composition is dark, but tiny highlights on the ships give "sparkle" to the scene.

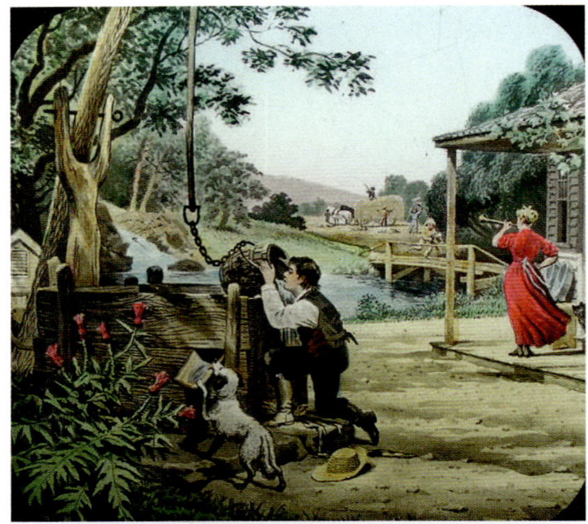

Fig. 6.24 Beale's slide 3 from *The Old Oaken Bucket*, a "Popular Song" set.

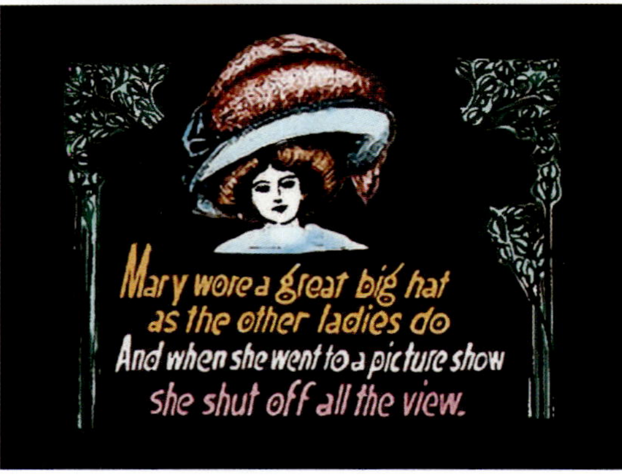

Fig. 6.25 An early movie announcement slide, used to try to keep women's hats from blocking the view of the audience. Courtesy Larry Cederblom Collection.

learned to focus at a point two-thirds of the way up the image, at the eyes of the painted actors on screen. This helps gives the *impression* of sharp focus, even when the bottom portion of the circle is a bit fuzzy.

Beale often presented scenes as though seen on stage (Fig. 6.26). This was by no means consistent, and occurs most frequently when the action is in a stage-like setting such as a room.[41] But wherever they are, the characters almost invariably behave as though they were "on stage", unaware of an audience on the other side

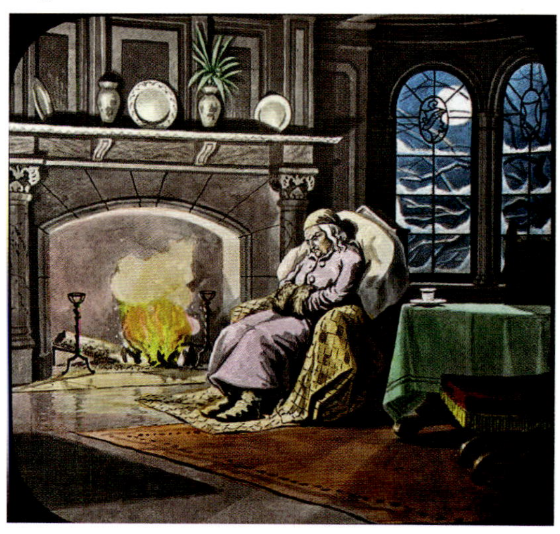

Fig. 6.26 Beale's slide 7 from *The Seven Ages of Man* by Shakespeare. "The Last Scene" has a definite stage-like quality.

of the *"fourth wall"*, the invisible wall separating the stage action from the audience. And almost always the ***vantage point*** of the perspective is at eye-level, consistent with a stage-like presentation.

Beale's Artistic Screen Style

Above and beyond these technical matters, Beale developed his own personal artistic style for screen projection, a combination of repeated motifs, controlled design, and a variety of narrative art techniques.

Beale treated certain *motifs* in a similar fashion throughout his career, and they help us distinguish his work (Fig. 6.27). Characteristic motifs are his human faces that are rounded with bold features, fully delineated; angels with the wings of doves; and complex architecture. Other motifs are part of Beale's repertoire for establishing perspective: patterned floors; rocks heaped in great mounds in the foreground; chickens, geese, dogs or objects in the foreground.

Beale's clouds and skyscapes form a motif used to provoke audience response, and capitalize on the well-known tendency for a "good sky" to "bring down the house" at lantern performances.[42] Spectacular sunsets lit the skies for years after the enormous 1883 explosion of the South Seas volcano at Krakatoa. The blast filled the stratosphere with dust particles that refracted the sun's light all over the world. Beale made the most of those sunsets, and the lantern's ability to infuse their color with light almost as brilliant as the sun itself (Fig. 6.28).

Beale developed two quite distinct artistic styles for creating slide images, a "literary" style, and a "comic" style.

Beale's ***literary style*** was used for literary and other serious works. It was rich with detail, often employing elaborate sets, and characters that were realistically portrayed. In his illustration for slide 8 of *Maud Muller* (Fig. 6.29), Beale depicts a rich old judge, pining for a poor woman (Maud) who once offered him her drinking cup filled from a lush roadside spring, and whose offered love he passed by. Beale creates a sumptuous set surrounding the lonely old man, full of the details of his wealth. Even the details of the details are detailed. But unlike some situations that we will see shortly, where Beale illustrates the details specifically mentioned in the poem, in this case the poem uses

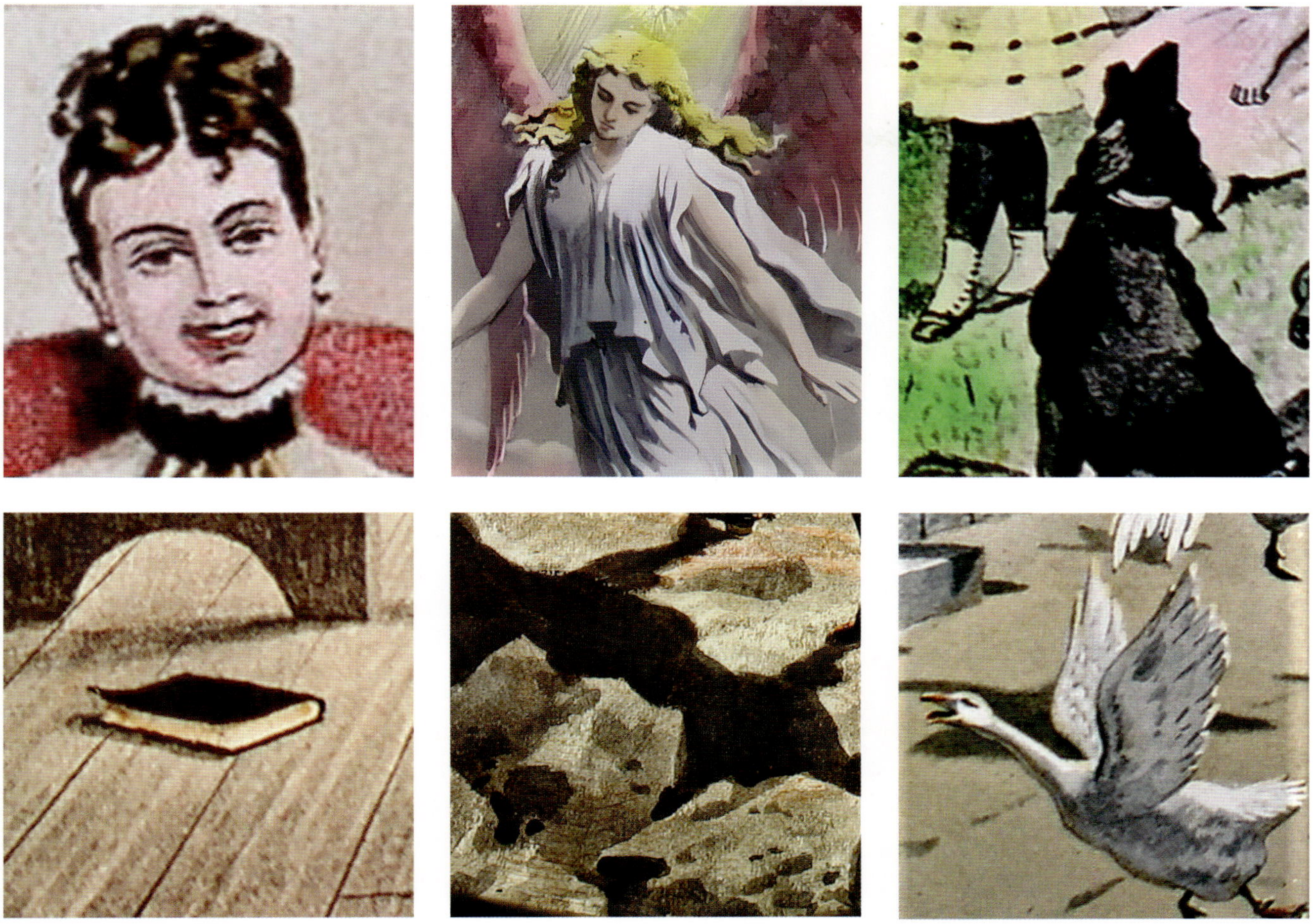

Fig. 6.27 Various details from Beale slides showing typical motifs.

only two words to describe entire scene: "rich repiner". Every detail in the image is Beale's literary-style invention, built around those two words.[43] Beale emphasizes not just the judge's wealth, but his loneliness, using carefully selected symbolic props – his discarded books; his only companions the two animals; his four empty chairs; his potted plants struggling for the sun; his collection of elaborate but empty cups and vases – a hollow echo of the cup of love Maud once offered him.

> Alas for maiden, alas for Judge,
> For rich repiner and household drudge!
> God pity them both! and pity us all,
> Who vainly the dreams of youth recall;
> For of all sad words of tongue or pen,
> The saddest are these: "It might have been!"

As I finish those famous lines from *Maud Muller*, I let Beale's image of the rich repiner sit on screen for a moment, like a stage tableau. It fades very slowly, as the music harkens back to the melody we heard when the judge first met Maud beside the spring. After the words are gone, his fading picture still fills the mind's eye, floating on the dying music, resonating with

Fig. 6.28 Beale's slide, "Erin", from the *Artistic Gems* group.

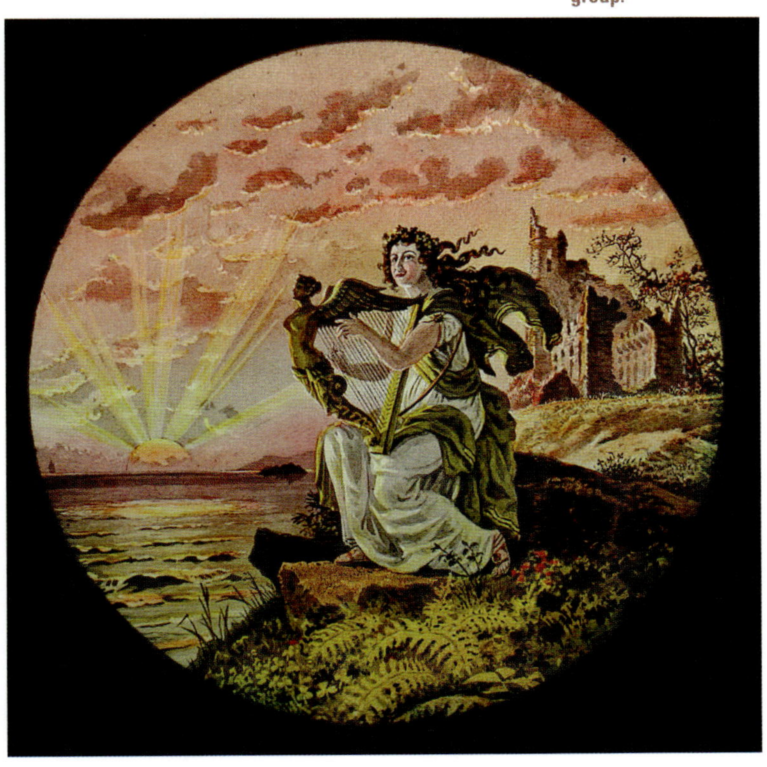

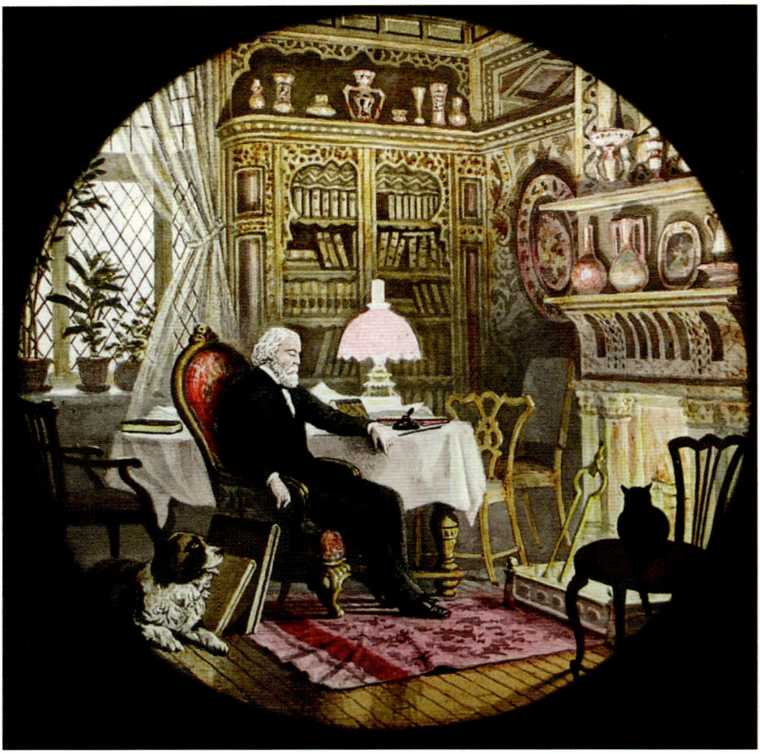

Fig. 6.29 Beale's slide 8 of *Maud Muller* by John Greenleaf Whittier, in Beale's "literary style".

the audience as the meaning of the words sink in.

Beale's ***comic style*** for the comic stories had much simpler sets, generally realistically portrayed, though often with comic touches. Characters had exaggerated faces and gestures, often (but not always) with stereotypic ethnic features. Animals with human expressions – especially pigs, goats, dogs and mules – were a staple. For instance, the comic slide of *"The Wicked Flea"* juxtaposes a wealthy gentleman in a work-a-day setting with the bizarre image of a giant flea (Fig. 6.30). Small details emphasize the contrast between the "normal" environment – the patterned stones, the grain of the fence wood, the latch on the shutter, the cellar door – with the huge size of the "abnormal" flea. Other details emphasize how out of place the man is in this working-class neighborhood – his potbelly, his top hat, his fancy watch fob. They stretch the comic contrast even further, as man and dog both react to the giant flea. Even the window at the top of the door reacts – its two "eyes" looking down in amusement, providing a second level to the joke.

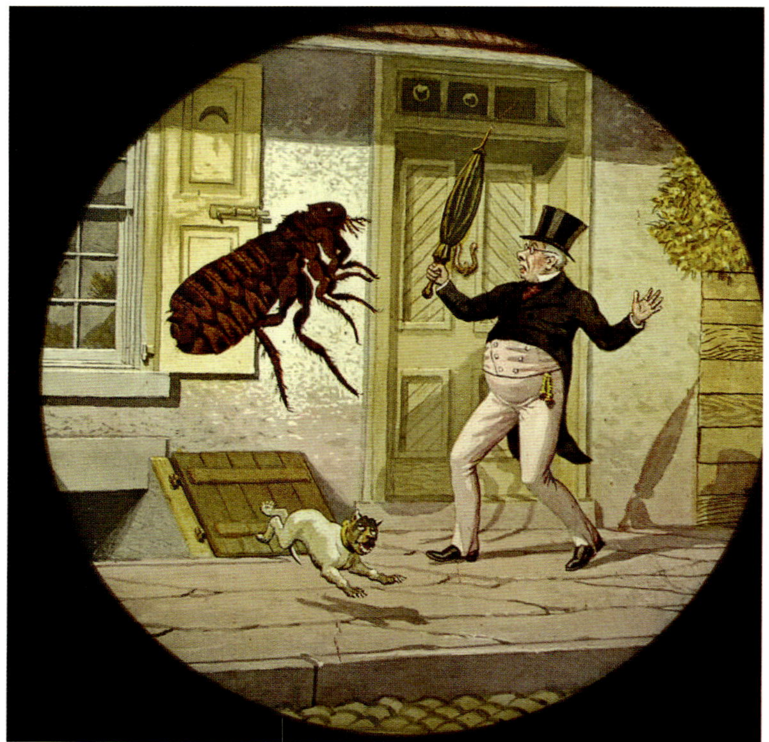

Fig. 6.30 Beale's slide of "The Wicked Flea" from *Comic Singles and Dissolves, Animals.*

Beale's compositional style was also strong and distinctive.[44] His scenes were of a *closed form*, carefully balancing and arranging elements (Fig. 6.31). *Tight framing* concentrated attention on central figures that otherwise might be lost in scenes jammed with detail. Artistic compositions were designed to make the eye move from the bottom of the image, across and around the space in order to follow the action to a focal point. The designs often employed strong diagonal, V-shaped, or circular patterns. The composition was not only intended to lead the eye in two dimensions, but in three. Diagonal, circular, and spiral forms and lines led the eye from the foreground, back into the distance, and out again, one shape mirroring another. Often objects or animals were placed in such a way as to direct the viewers from one area of a picture to another. The effects of Beale's extensive formal art training and his informal apprenticeship at *Leslie's* were evident in his compositional skill. His design sense fits well with the period's accepted criteria for both high art and art photography.[45]

Summary and Conclusion

Briggs and Beale worked together to create a remarkable body of work. Briggs brought to the partnership his vision of presenting great literature and history on the screen, and a prescient sense that illustrated slides were the best way to realize that vision. His high standards for printing and coloring made him the acknowledged master of the field. He was a shrewd businessman who ran his company successfully in a hotly competitive industry. Perhaps his most important business decision was to hire Beale, and

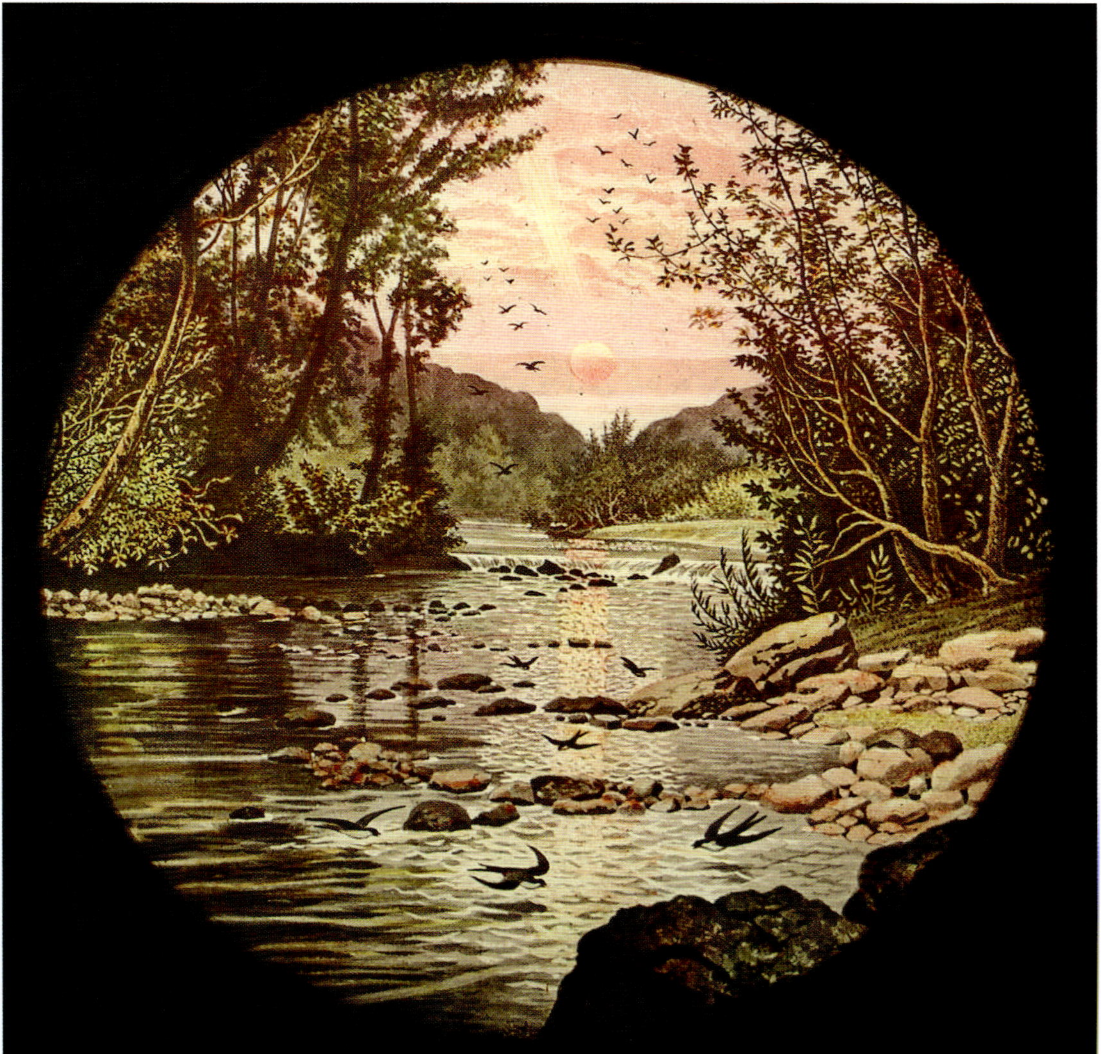

Fig. 6.31 Beale' slide 9 illustrating *The Brook* by Alfred Lord Tennyson. An "X" design through the trees and stones organizes the complex scenery, and leads the eye into the distance.

work with him collaboratively, ensuring a high quality of artistic output. Beale's production was very impressive indeed. Eventually he accounted for about 60% of the Briggs business, and, as we have seen, nine-to-ten percent of the entire industry's slide offerings.[46] Arguably, with the focus on illustrating essential human experience – religion, literature, history – those Beale slides represented the most important ten percent of the slides in the industry's catalogs. Beale brought to his partnership with Briggs a wide background in illustration. He was a steady, hard worker, who could produce on a schedule. Amenable to direction, he was also willing, inventive, and able to create the unexpected and the exciting. He could adapt to the lantern medium's unique quality of lighted images projected at a large scale. He developed a special screen style – a style that made the most of the medium's tonal range and color – a style that was distinctive and dramatic. When mixed with the narrative techniques we are about to explore, these qualities made him a visual story-teller without equal on the American screen.

Chapter Seven

Beale's Narrative Techniques

Fig. 7.1 Beale's slide 5 for *The Pied Piper* by Robert Browning. Discussed on p. 162.

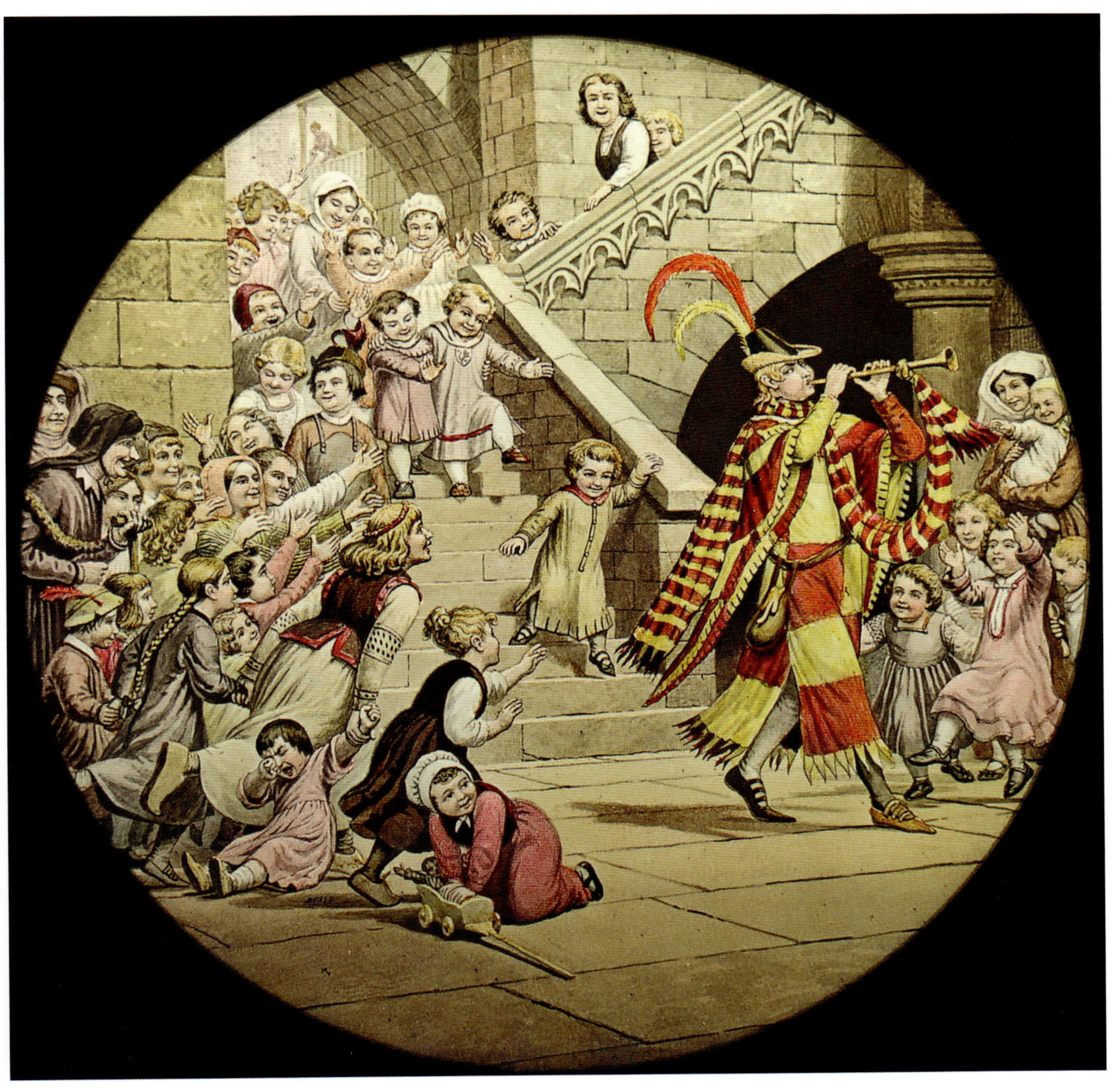

We've seen how the businessman Briggs developed a vision of bringing great literature to the screen, and how the artist Beale built a repertoire of techniques to present most effectively those screen pictures. But in themselves, Beale's technical choices such as finding the right tonal range and an appropriate literary style would not create great narrative art. To do that, Beale would need to develop a range of visual story-telling techniques – ways to capture audience attention, to sustain it while the image was on screen, to immerse the viewer in the action, to shape the arc of the story. Beale's success in these efforts – his ability to meld his story-telling images with an author's text – will take him from being a master craftsman to being a master narrative artist.

Capturing Attention

The very first thing that Beale had to do – the most important thing – was to capture the attention of his audience. And the best way to do that was to make sure that every picture had narrative punch, that it told a story. Beale had a genius for such visual storytelling; it's what accounted for his commanding position in the lantern field during his lifetime. Forty years after his death, it explained his commanding position in America's leading catalog of stock art. In 1966, the nation's foremost image-archivist, Otto Bettmann, founder of the Bettmann Archive, explained that he filled his catalog with artists who could "get to the heart of the matter". He explained that "An art director or editor buys a picture the way a housewife buys a steak. It's the meat that counts; the fat only adds to the poundage". Beale's pictures focused the viewer on that meat, which explains why Bettmann's catalog of 3,669 of his best images contained more pictures by Beale than by any other artist in the world.[1]

That drive to "get to the heart of the matter", had a long tradition. Beale's images were examples of what lantern expert W. D. Farrington called the "first rule" of lantern slide illustration. Though Beale filled his slides with detail, he composed his images so that – in Farrington's words – every slide "meant something":

> Every picture should tell a story ... The lights and shadows should be so arranged that the eye is irresistibly drawn to the primary object which it is desired to illustrate. ... [The] subject matter must be made prominent at the expense of the minor matters by which it is surrounded.[2]

Beale's slide 5 of *The Pied Piper* (Fig. 7.1), at the start of this chapter, is a good example of Farrington's point. Forty-two people jam the picture of the Piper leading the children to their doom, but we can't miss him. Flamboyantly dressed, he is the largest and brightest figure. The stone stair rail points directly at him. Hands reach toward him from every direction. The dark negative space below the arch of the stair frames and contrasts with his face and pipe. The feathers of his hat rise above him like swooping explanation points. The eye is indeed "irresistibly drawn" to the Piper. He leaps out at the audience.

A similar point to Farrington's was made by the famous American illustrator Howard Pyle, who taught at the Drexel Institute in Philadelphia and in Wilmington, Delaware during the period Beale was working nearby. Pyle taught his students to picture the "***supreme moment*** [of action], leaving to the imagination what precedes and follows". Though no evidence exists that Beale ever studied with Pyle, he would likely have known of Pyle's teachings. He certainly became an expert at finding these "supreme moments" in a story, and building a *series* of narrative images that paced the flow of the dramatic action to take maximum advantage of them.[3]

Concentrating on the "first rule" of storytelling illustration is also central to the movies, often described in movie criticism as "key emotional incidents" which are part of an "event" encompassing the cause and response to the incident.[4] This language points to another way in which lantern art differs from the movies. Modern

Fig. 7.2 Photographic lantern slide by Edward Wilson.

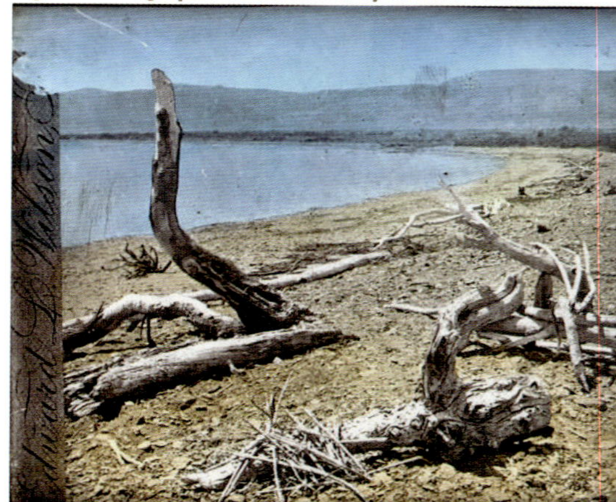

cinema does most of its storytelling about those "events" with rapid sequences of edited images. Because the lantern had so few slides to tell a story, it was essential that each slide tell as much of the narrative as possible. The effectiveness of a magic lantern slide set is not so much in the art of the editing between slides to show cause and response, as it is compressing that sequence within the individual slides themselves, such as in the "extended visual narratives" we'll discuss shortly.

Capturing Attention with Mise-en-Scène

A key part of creating story-telling images that captured audience attention was skillfully handling the mise-en-scène.

We've already explored in our discussion of *The Little Match Girl* a bit about Beale's use of *mise-en-scène* – the cinematic term to describe the combination of style, character, stage set, blocking, and lighting that gives a scene its unique quality.[5] It was a well-understood part of the lanternist's art, with an important legal basis. A photographic image (or illustrated design) could not be copyrighted unless "there is produced some *artistic effect* (my emphasis) in lights, shades, poses, etc".[6] That in itself was a major incentive to strive for unique mise-en-scène. Beyond the legal requirement, "artistic effect" was a marketing advantage. For instance, Edward Wilson, photographer, slide-maker, and editor of *The Magic Lantern* trade journal, introduced his catalog of photographic slides by describing with pride his unusual sense of mise-en-scène (Fig. 7.2). He claimed that even when he was taking pictures of "things often photographed before, I believe I have treated them differently". Wilson said that he tried to "introduce life into my pictures, thus making them seem not only more real, but more picturesque". This quality of Wilson's mise-en-scène accounted for much of his success and was recognized and admired by his peers:

> Mr. Wilson's slides show an artistic taste rarely met with; and his admirable choice of objects and position, ... have won him a place at the head of his profession.[7]

As Beale's handling of mise-en-scène demonstrates, he had great skill in this area, and, like Wilson, his mastery accounted for much of his success. It's worth examining his use of mise-en-scène again, this time in the popular parlor poem, *Annie and Willie's Prayer*, because in this case Beale's preliminary sketches exist. They are the only evidence that allows us to see *how* Beale went about achieving his effects. In *Annie and Willie* we can study his process of "introducing life into his pictures" in order to capture and hold audience attention.[8]

Often people underestimate the difficulties of creating something like the *Annie and Willie* designs, and assume that a drawing simply "arrives" whole in an artist's mind, by intuition rather than conscious thought. This is certainly not true in Beale's case. He is clearly working in what movie critics call the "classical" mise-en-scène mode in which changes in style are related to thematic developments. Nothing in a Beale design is there by happenstance. In the development of his *Annie and Willie* sketches, we can see how every aspect of his image is the result of a conscious decision, and often of considerable re-working to achieve drama by combining *unity* and *variation* within the confines of the slide format.

When creating a set of lantern slides Beale faced more than the usual issues involved in designing individual pictures. Those issues were compounded when creating a *series of scenes* that would tell a sequential story. Each individual design was interlocked with the whole *sequence* like a jig-saw puzzle. And since Beale was limited in the number of slides or "scenes" he could make – usually 4 to 12 images – he had to imply much of the action between them. In Beale's sketches we can see that he was making alternative *takes* of his scenes, testing them out until he found the one he wanted, just as movie directors would do when faced with the same problem.

The story Beale was illustrating is a sentimental little Victorian tale. Annie and Willie's father, embittered by the loss of his wife, sends the children to bed early on Christmas Eve, telling them that Santa isn't real. They pray for their father and mother as their mother had taught them to, but also that Santa will send them presents. Their father overhears them and has a change of heart. He goes out into a stormy night to buy a tree and presents, and sets them up in the children's room. Next morning, joy reigns, children and Dad celebrate together – a fitting *closure* for a Christmas story.

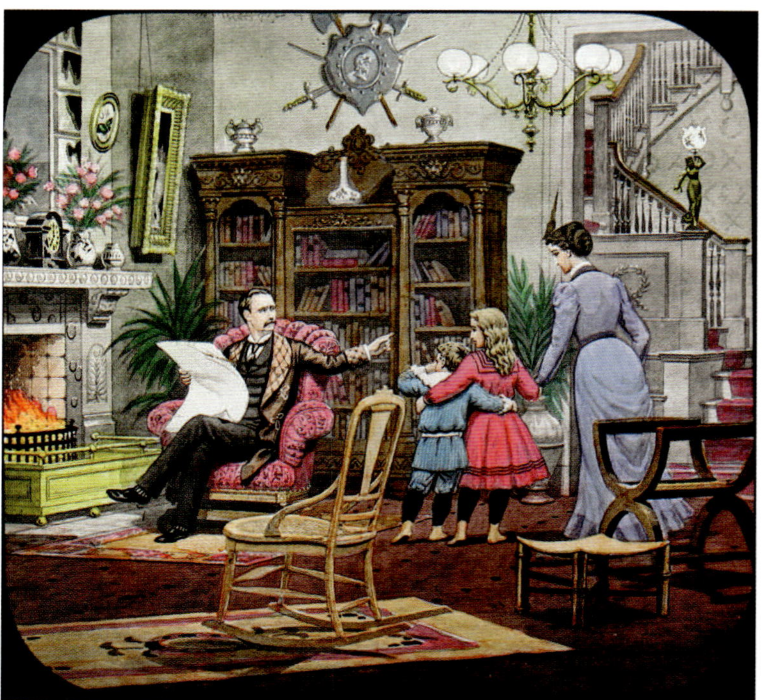

Fig. 7.3 Beale's slide 1 for *Annie and Willie's Prayer* by Sophia P. Snow.

Beale creates a dramatic beginning to the story with an ***establishing*** shot that immediately defines the mise-en-scène of the story world – the time and culture, the characters, and the narrative tension between them (Fig. 7.3).[9] At the center of what film critics call the "bull's eye", the dynamic of the story is set in motion as the bereaved father sends the motherless children upstairs early. The children huddle together for comfort, their backs to us, drawing us into the scene in sympathy. The aunt – mentioned later in the text – does her best to console them. Beale builds an elaborate set surrounding the characters, using his "literary style". Evidence of wealth is everywhere, but there is no evidence of Christmas. The mise-en-scène itself puts the story in motion.

Let's look next at a rough sketch that Beale created for two upcoming scenes, numbers 2 and 4. They are done in the same size as the final design – 13 x 13 inches (Fig. 7.4). Probably to save time, Beale outlined the two scenes in one single drawing of the children's room. It's a strategy that made sense for him, but creates some rather strange overlapping images for us to sort out, like the table leg of slide 4 sticking through the stool of slide 2.

In the sketch for slide 4 the father has returned with the tree and presents, and is arranging them in the bedroom, assisted by the aunt. As a first step in creating the design, Beale draws the ***line of horizon*** and establishes a pencil perspective grid of imaginary perspective lines – most clearly visible above the beds. The grid defines the overall scene set and allows him to control the elements more easily. Then, Beale begins sketching the scene, not only with a pencil, but sketching the tree directly with his paintbrush, just as he would create it in the final design. Gradually, he works out the elements of the mise-en-scène, including a chandelier very similar to the one in the living room, a *match cut* helping to tie the two rooms together in our minds, and in this scene highlighting the sleeping children.

He experiments with the *props*, at first creating a double bed, and then changing it to two singles, which allows him to add some feminine frou-frou to Annie's bed. He draws in a symbol of Mother, her empty rocking chair, the same symbol that he put front and center in scene 1. Here, the rocker will appear in scene 2, beside the praying children, but not thereafter. Beale probably removes the chair from the future scenes to facilitate the *blocking*, clearing the way for the overloaded father to maneuver around the room with all the presents. But he may also be suggesting that Father's love is now strong enough to compensate somewhat for Mother's loss. Mother's rocker is in fact replaced by a chair beside the bed, on which, in the final scene, Father sits, cuddling his children.

Beale places the new Christmas tree in the back left corner. In the following bedroom scene the grownups will have shifted the tree across the room to set it up in the right front, dominating a third of the screen. By keeping props like these shifting around the set, changing them from background to foreground, and changing their relative importance with size and positioning, Beale helps to capture our attention, adds to the sense of dynamic movement within the story, and creates a sense of three-dimensional space.

Once Beale had created the rough sketch, he would have drawn a light pencil outline for the final design directly on new paper – light enough so that it would not show through the gouache of the final painting. He might, at this point, make further changes. For instance, in the final version of slide 4 (Fig.7.4, right), Beale increases the sense of depth in the room by further angling the lines of the door to the rear. He adds a hall lamp with rings of light radiating from it – perhaps reminding us of the lost light of the mother. He adds a fire grate in the foreground that anchors the scene, and also allows him to

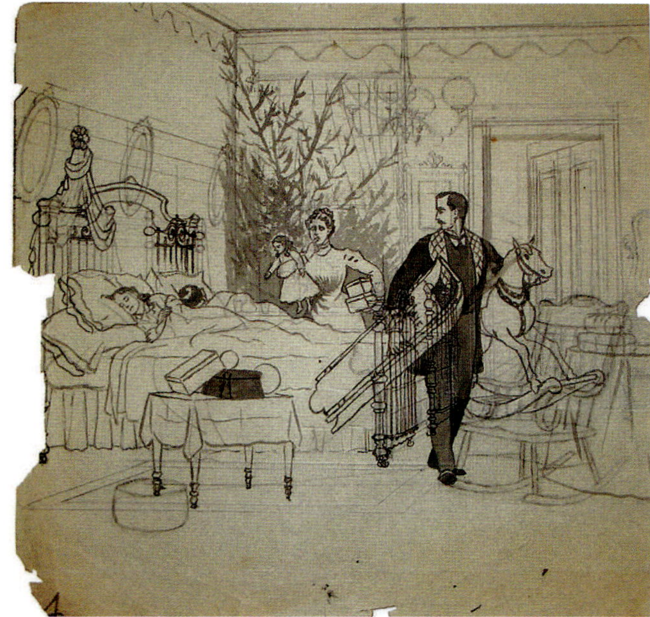

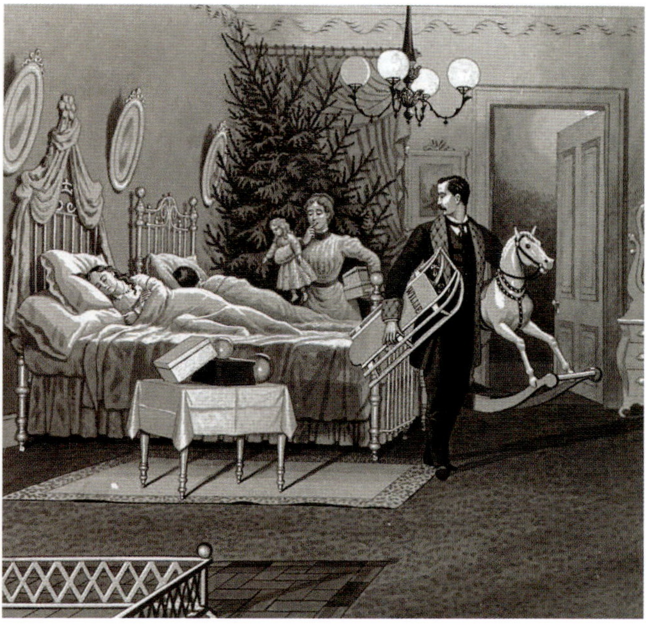

Fig. 7.4 Left, Beale's sketch for slide 4 of *Annie and Willie's Prayer*, and right, the finished image. The same sketch served as the basis for slide 2.

more dramatically control the lighting, shifting from *high-contrast lighting* in an earlier scene when the children knelt before the fire to pray for their presents, to *soft-key frontal lighting* in this scene. (The next scene shifts to dramatic high-contrast *back lighting* as the morning sun streams in the window.)

In these rough sketches and their associated final images we can see Beale actually working out the elements of mise-en-scène, making different *takes* until he arrives at a *final cut* as the movie makers would call it – the combination of elements that would capture audience attention with the most drama and vitality, and tell the story most clearly.[10]

Directing Attention

Two other aspects of Beale's narrative art are characteristic, and were especially important for success in the magic lantern medium – directing and sustaining the audience's attention to the image on screen.

An artist who paints a picture to hang on a wall knows that the viewers will not look at it long. (Today, the average museum visitor spends 15 to 30 seconds per picture.)[11] The artist who paints a picture for a book also gets little attention from the reader. After all, it's more critical for the reader to read the words than study the picture. In both cases the premium is on attracting attention, not holding it. But judging from printed lantern scripts, the average lantern audience watched an image for between one and three minutes, often more. Beale knew that he not only needed to attract the attention of his audiences, but that they would be looking at his images on screen for a considerable time, and could not easily turn their focus away. They were essentially locked in their chairs, and if not involved could become bored or unruly. Thus, it was especially important for him to create images that would not only *capture* attention, but that would hold attention. The movies did this with ever-changing movement, and in the early days of film it was movement itself that fascinated people. But Beale couldn't possibly create as much movement on the screen as did the movies. What could he do in a lantern-slide format that would serve the same purpose?

The first approach that Beale uses is to *direct attention*, to catch our eye and focus it immediately where he wants us to look. To do this he employs a whole range of artistic techniques. We saw how he directed the eye in *The Pied Piper*. Another good example is the slide of Annie and Willie waking up on Christmas morning (Fig. 7.5). Their figures, which in the first slide were small and turned away from us, are now large, facing us, and in the center of the image. Previously asleep, they are now very much awake, and very animated, hurtling through space toward their toys. Annie is backlit as the rising sun outlines her and turns her hair into an angel's halo. Willie is also backlit and semi-silhouetted against the window. He breaks across the frame of the curtain, which adds to his sense of movement. The curve of his body mirrors the shape of the horse's head. Leaping

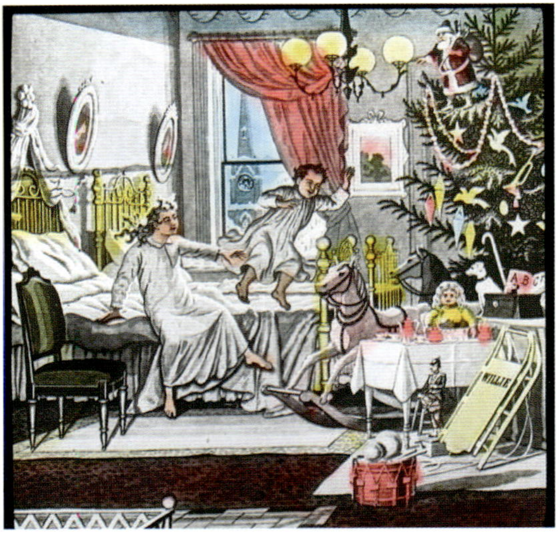

Fig. 7.5 Beale's slide 5 of *Annie and Willie's Prayer*, in a slide with – unfortunately – rather poor coloring.

off the bed in mid-air he is already molding himself to fit around the horse he wants so much. That leads our attention from boy to horse, and makes us imagine the next instant of action when the two unite. In our mind's eye, Willie moves.

With techniques like these – comparative positioning and size, centrality of image, dramatic action and contrast in action, control of lighting, mirroring of line and form – Beale directs our attention, and moves it within the scene. But how sustain that attention, how keep us involved as the slide sits on the screen for several minutes at a time?

Sustaining Attention with Detail

One of the chief ways Beale sustains our attention within a slide is with ***narrative detail***, using his art and the story itself to shift our awareness from one element of the image to another, so that we keep seeing something new, something that makes the story flow. The specificity of Beale's detail not only conveys the sense of "being there" as we saw in all those different-sized horseshoes in *The Village Blacksmith*. It also serves as a device for holding attention, because often the specifics in Beale's literary pictures are described in the poems themselves. As the narrator reads the poem, the audience "reads" the image, it gradually "sees" details that it may well have missed before.[12] Certainly, the audience would have missed the *intrinsic interest* and significance of these details without having heard the poem. Hence, though the same slide might be up on the screen for several minutes, the audience is continually discovering something more in the image. Beale's intent was not only to capture the emotive moment, as a modern filmmaker might with a brief close-up, but also to pack a single "scene" with several minutes' worth of on-screen attention.

Take, for example, the passage that describes the Christmas morning of *Annie and Willie's Prayer*.

(If you can, stop reading here and ask someone else to read to you the following poem section while you look closely at the picture in Fig. 7.5. If you can do this, you will be seeing the image just as Beale's audience would have seen it while hearing the narration.)

The poetry is not Shakespeare's, nor even Browning's, but it is sufficient for you to understand how Beale's narrative art used storytelling detail to involve his viewers in the story:

> Miss Dolly was seated beneath a pine-tree,
> By the side of a table spread out for her tea;
> A work-box, well-filled, in the centre was laid,
> And on it the ring for which Annie had prayed;
> A soldier in uniform stood by a sled,
> "With bright shining runners, and all painted red",
> There were balls, dogs, and horses; books pleasing to see;
> And birds of all colors were perched in the tree;
> While Santa Claus, laughing, stood up in the top,
> As if getting ready more presents to drop.

No doubt the first thing you saw when you looked at the picture was the dramatic overall image of the children's ecstatic joy. But then, Beale draws you into the specifics of the picture. As you hear the *narration*, these specifics emerge from the visual tapestry one by one. You "notice" things that previously you only "looked at". The slide image itself might be static, but Beale has developed another way to make your *eyes* move and create different *shots* within a single slide scene. He does this by avoiding *close-ups*, and instead using *long shots*, so that both the context and the particulars of the action can be seen and experienced all at once. He makes your eyes become like the movie camera, *zooming in* to create your own close-ups. You are prompted to do this by two things – the narration itself, and the visual details of intrinsic interest that Beale plants in the picture to satisfy your close-up attention.

So effective is this technique that after a modern show, audience members sometimes ask me to see "the close-up slide" in a Beale scene, a slide that was only a "close-up" in their imagination (Fig.7.6).

The single slide image on the screen becomes analogous to the *long take* in the movies, when the action is shot in a long sequence from one point of view, rather than being covered by *editing* different shots together. The famous movie director Stephen Spielberg frequently uses long takes because he sees them as a way for the audience to participate in the cinematic experience in just the way that audiences engage with the detail in Beale's images. He urges other directors to do the same:

> I'd love to see directors start trusting the audience to be the film editor with their eyes, the way you are sometimes with a stage play, where the audience selects who they would choose to look at while a scene is being played ... .[13]

Immersion

Beale went beyond capturing attention with story-telling images, directing it within the mise-en-scène, and holding it with detail. His pictures used a wide range of other techniques to further *immerse* his viewers in the story. so that it was not just watching the story from the outside, but was cooperating with him in creating the story's meaning. His immersive techniques are all devices to "stretch" the story visually. In the evocative language of narrative expert and brain scientist, Angus Fletcher:

> The *stretch* is taking ... a regular pattern ... of the story world ... and expanding the pattern further ... [It] is ... at the root of all literary wonders ... It's been linked in modern psychology labs to a shift in neural attention that flings our focus outward ... . We quite literally feel the borders of our self dissolving... . This neural feeling is why we can "lose ourselves" in a book or a film, forgetting our personal limits in the horizons beyond.[14]

All story illustrations "stretch" the text beyond itself because they provide it with a new visual meaning. To use a Victorian term, the text becomes ***realized*** – more real – as it moves "from the mind's eye to the body's eye".[15] Beale's realistic details in particular help an audience "see" the text in a new way, giving graphic specificity to the words. Often he stretches the text and our imaginations even further by add-

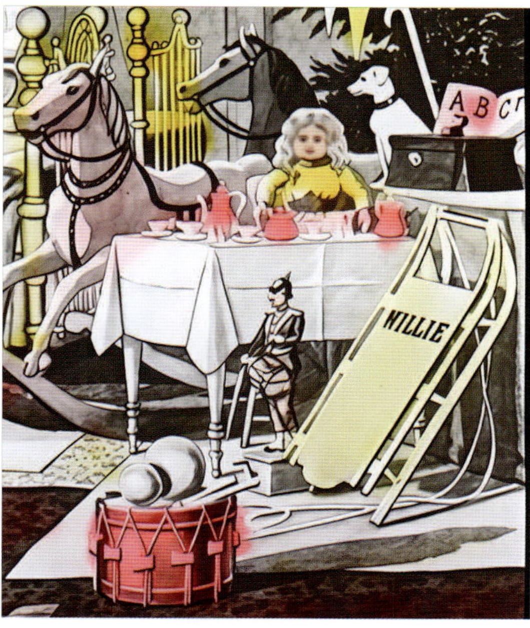

Fig. 7.6 Detail of Beale's slide 5 from *Annie and Willie's Prayer.* In the poem the sled is described as red. The slide colorist never got the message.

ing visual details that are not in the text itself. And because his illustrations are projected on screen, they are huge, often ten to fifteen feet square, sometimes twenty, larger than all but the largest museum paintings. They dominate the viewer's field of vision, and – literally – stretch the story to life-size, large enough for us to imaginatively walk into his images and lose ourselves in his screen world.

Beale sometimes stretches the text even more by creating an additional ***immersive*** layer to the story – a layer of visual ambiguity, of anticipation, of half-seen glimpses, flashbacks, symbols, dissolves, and motion. Unlike Beale's abundant details that make his pictured world concrete for us, these techniques are more oblique – they only hint at future action or deeper meaning. A teasing visual detail might suggest an upcoming scene, a symbol might suggest a character trait, a strange shadow might suggest a double message. These devices blur the line between the "fiction world" and our "real world" because they all invite our involvement to interpret their significance. They draw us in as we watch, making the story rich with meanings we help create. Even if we do not consciously notice Beale's immersive techniques, or fully understand them, we catch their "feel", we sense the "atmosphere", and interpret the story based on that subjective feeling. In fact, one of the most powerful aspects of Beale's immersive techniques is that they evoke our emotions. We not only "think" about the meanings these techniques suggest, but we also "feel" them. The more we feel the story world, the more "real" it becomes.

These days scholars are documenting the "reality" of visual stories – the way we comprehend them – by measuring body reactions of the audience like eye movement, heart rate and dopamine release. Though the field of research is still in its nascent stage, scientists can tell precisely what part of a pictured story creates what kind of mental, body and emotional response.[16] Their work helps to refine today's hyper-immersive media such as video games and artificial reality. But the same approaches can define the reactions to traditional narrative art, including magic lantern art. Less precisely but just as clearly, you yourself could hear and feel those reactions in any of our lantern performances. Even if the audience is composed of adults who certainly know the screen story isn't "real life", they laugh at the funny slides, tense up in the dramas, and choke up on the sad stories like *The Little Match Girl.* Their bodies and emotions react as they would in "real life". Beale's immersive images meld with the magic of the magic lantern medium itself – the voice in the dark, the music, the shared community of story creation. They lift us from the hard seats of an auditorium to the wonders of the screen world.

The immersive techniques Beale uses to create that world can be divided into three rough categories: Anticipating Coming Action, Creating Deeper Meaning, and Participating in the Action.

Anticipating Coming Action

A critical way that Beale immersed the audience in the drama was by planning slide content that would get them to Anticipate the Coming Action. He helped them to imagine the story's development, to create their own narrative, and thus to become more involved. Anticipation is a central principle of cinematic storytelling, described in David Bordwell's *Narration in Fiction Film.*[17] The same principal operates in the field of graphic novels. Will Eisner, in his classic book, *Graphic Storytelling and Visual Narrative*, describes the power of anticipation in the old-time Sunday comics, a power strong enough to bring the audience back to the story after a week's absence, week after week after week.[18] I myself remember those days back in the 1940s and '50s when the Sunday paper held continuing adventure stories that I did not want to miss.

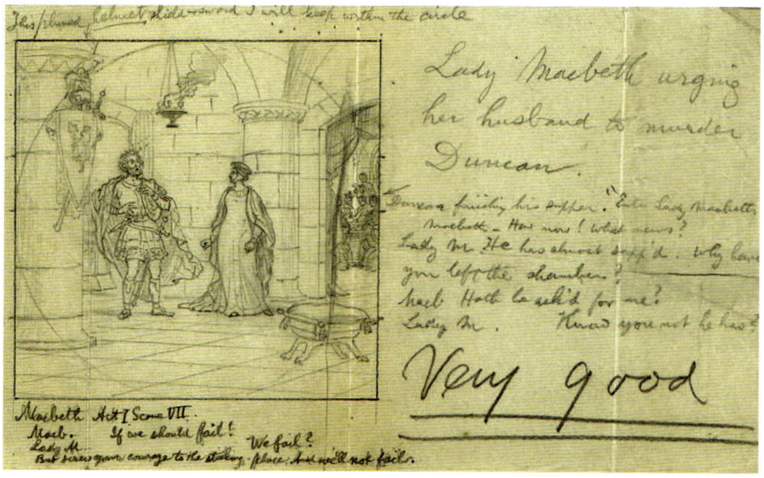

Fig. 7.7 Beale's sketch for slide 4 of *Macbeth* by Shakespeare. Beale's note at top assures Briggs that the final design will keep the shield "within the circle" of circular slides. The large "Very Good" is by Briggs.

In discussing the techniques that artists used to build such anticipation, Eisner concentrates on Harold Foster, who created one of my favorite comics, "Prince Valiant" – an adventure story set in the age of King Arthur. Eisner points out that at first Foster had trouble controlling his complex narration, having to number his panels so readers could find their way through the jumble of images. But gradually Foster learned to simplify, to "illustrate the whole of the action", to concentrate on the visual flow. Then, to end the week's installment, he would interrupt that flow at a key moment, delaying resolution, leaving his readers hanging, anticipating the next episode. So involved were my friends and I in "Prince Valiant" that we would spend the week debating what would happen next, creating our own versions of the story. Foster's techniques to build anticipation worked. Our immersion in the Sunday comics and in comic books drove our parents to distraction. (Today, what drives parents – and spouses – to distraction is the video game, an immersive medium full of anticipation, and direct participation.)

Extended Visual Narrative

In the lantern format, Beale could not use the week-to-week cliff hanger to create immersion through anticipation, but he used his own magic lantern devices for that same purpose. One device might be called the ***extended visual narrative.*** This involved merging two scenes in one slide to suggest a secondary story, or future action, or cause and effect. Beale learned this technique of compressing a narrative sequence into a single image at *Leslie's Weekly*, where it was standard practice.[19] The approach was designed to encourage active viewer involvement by creating a context around the defining moment of action. It shaped the moment's meaning, suggesting a contrasting action, or action before or after the defining moment. It extended the scene's viewing time, but also made the audience wonder where the story might go, actively involving them in the plot. A Beale sketch for a scene from *Macbeth* (Fig. 7.7), shows how he could compress two scenes into one, while in addition foreshadowing action at a more distant point in the future, and set us to wondering what will happen next.

Beale first draws attention to Lord and Lady Macbeth, who, at the center of the scene, are planning their king's murder, their plotting *top lit* by a smoldering torch overhead. Then Beale places their future victim, King Duncan, in *deep space* through an archway, dining with his men, unaware of the danger to come. As the scene unfolds, we gradually learn that Lady Macbeth plans to prolong Duncan's party so she can get his guards drunk, murder Duncan while they are unconscious, and blame the murder on them.

This particular way of extending the visual narrative has the wonderful Dutch name of "*doorkijkje*", or ***see-through doorway***. It permits the spectator to view something outside the main pictured space, and often allows Beale to immerse the viewer in the scene by telling one story while making the viewer anticipate another. In this case he quite literally *highlights* the immediate murder plot with the torch above Macbeth's head, and, at the same time *foreshadows* a future scene by – again, quite literally – placing the victim and his companions in the background shadows. The *intrinsic interest* of those companions, their future role as pawns in a murder plot, is only revealed toward the end of the scene. Briggs is right on target to mark the sketch, "Very Good".

Beale could also extend the visual narrative by creating a "doorway" where none is actually in the scene by placing a subordinate image within the primary image – for instance the image of Jesus approaching Jerusalem in the background of the scene when Ben Hur finds his mother (Fig. 7.19). Or he could insert a ***balloon*** or ***cloud*** in one corner of the image – a magic lantern convention that provided great narrative flexibility, as well as extending the visual potential of a single slide, and building anticipation. It was employed to indicate that a character was having a dream or vision, or to flash backward in time to memories of the past, or to flash forward with visions of the future. It was effective in stories, but especially in songs and in religious slides. The technique could be used either within a single slide, or with two slides, so that the vision could be superimposed over the base scene with a biunial (double-lens) lantern, and made to appear and disappear as part of the unfolding story (Fig. 7.8).

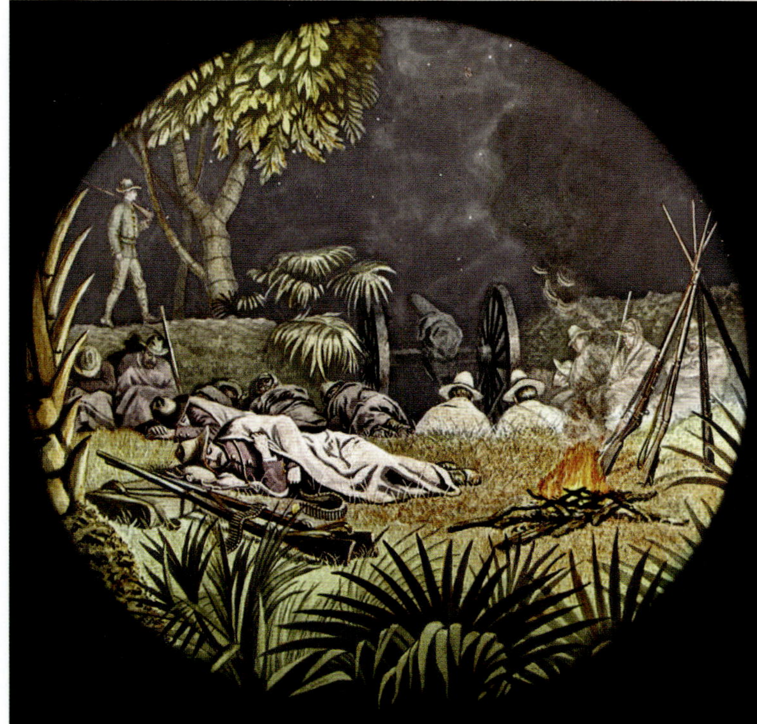

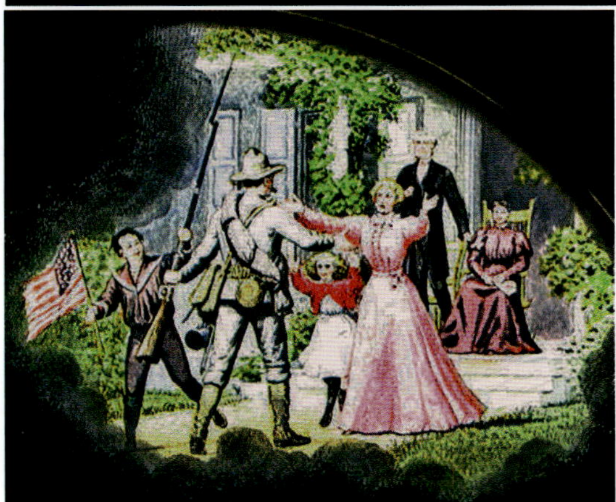

Fig. 7.8 Beale's slides 1 and 2 of Thomas Campbell's song, *United States Soldier's Dream of Home.*

Point of View and Teasing Details

A second way Beale built anticipation was through point of view scenes. This could be a *point of view shot* in the movie sense, in which the camera is often "over the shoulder", seeing what the character sees, as in Fig. 7.26. In Beale's case we are ofen beside the character in one scene as he literally peers into the next. We cannot see what he sees, we must imagine it, which builds anticipation. We find ourselves

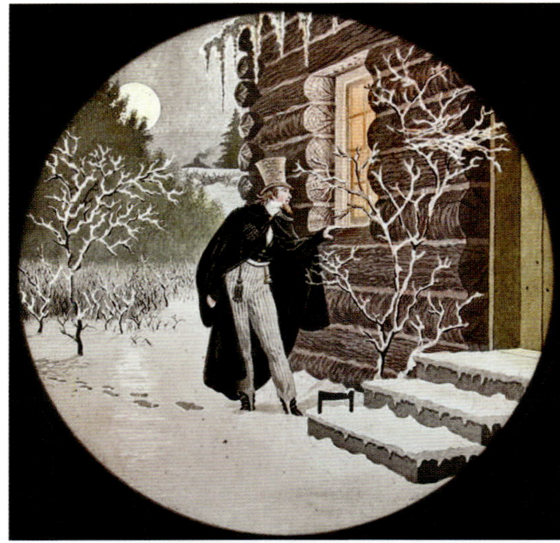

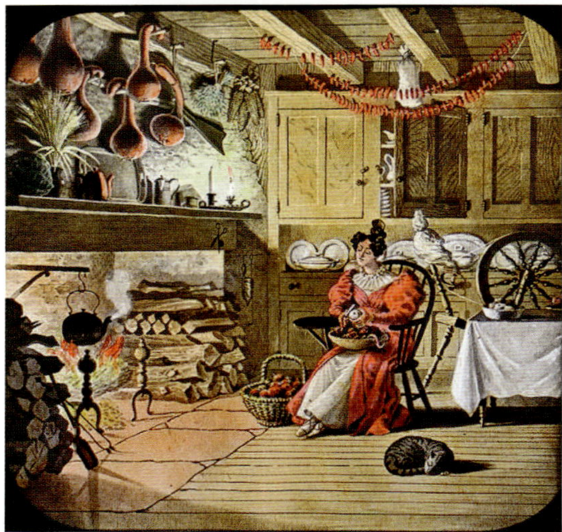

Fig. 7.9 Beale's slides 1 and 2 of *The Courtin'*.

creating the second scene, and become more involved in the story as we do so.

For instance, when at the opening of the dialect poem, *The Courtin'* (Fig. 7.9, top) we are outside in the cold with Zekle.

> Zekle crep'up quite uhbeknown,
> An peeked in thru' the winder".

We wonder what he sees. Beale lets us imagine the scene for him and in doing so pulls us into the action. Then, in the next slide (7.9 center), the point of view shot, we do see what Zekle sees.

> An' there sot Huldy all alone,
> 'ith no one night to hender.

Where might the story go from here? We anticipate a happy ending, but we can't be sure. As the poem progresses, we see further Beale images of the lovers admiring each other, but afraid to act.

Zekle builds up his courage, but then falters again. Will he ever make his move, we ask ourselves? Finally, toward the end of the poem Beale, resolves our questions with a flamboyant kiss scene (Fig. 7.10).

> Says he, 'I'd better call agin;'
> Says she, 'Think likely, Mister;'
> Thet last word pricked him like a pin,
> An'... Wal, he up an' kist her.

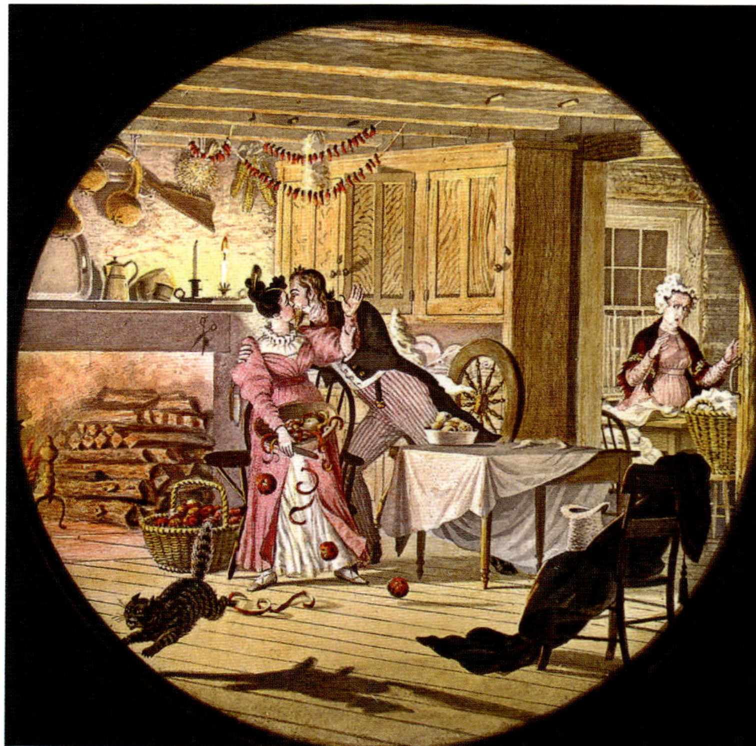

Fig. 7.10 Beale's slide 5 of *The Courtin'*.

I don't think it's too much to say that we ourselves enjoy that kiss, because, like the characters, we have been immersed in the story, anticipating, torn between fear of failure and hope for a happy ending.

A similar procedure to increase anticipation occurs when Beale plants teasing details in the slide that imply action either before or after the present, and sets our minds to imagining what those scenes might be. In *Darius Green and his Flying Machine* (Fig.7.11) Darius is "an aspiring genius", intent on flying. A gangplank, tied down to the workbench, sticks out the window. Bat skins are nailed to the wall above it. That's all we need to anticipate what will happen next, to immerse ourselves in the story by creating a meaningful story in our own "mind's eye" – the scene of Darius's takeoff and landing.

Flash Forward

Another major Beale technique for immersing the audience in the story – long used to build anticipation in literature and much used later in the movies – is the *flash back*, or *flash forward*. Reaching back in time allows us to gain perspective on the current action, see it in a new light, anticipate what may come next. And reaching forward in time gives a hint of the end of the drama, and makes us anticipate "the rest of the story". The classic example of this, in both literature and the magic lantern genre, is *A Christmas Carol*, called in magic lantern language, probably for copyright reasons, *Marley's Ghost*. Beale's slides for the set are beautifully executed. It was often used in evening shows for church audiences, and was much appreciated. "Awe-inspiring and amusing", said one reviewer.[20]

Following Dickens, Beale moves back in time to Fezziwig's Ball (Fig. 7.12, left), when Scrooge was a young man; and then to the present, when Scrooge meets the aptly named Christmas Present (center). Finally, Scrooge sees the future (right). Bob Cratchit's family grieves for the dead Tiny Tim, whose chair sits empty, casting its shadow on the Cratchit Christmas. It is this movement backward and forward in time that creates the anticipatory tension, and keeps the audience wondering what will happen next, especially, of course, wondering about the fate of Tiny Tim.

Creating Deeper Meaning – Shadows

A second class of techniques that Beale used to immerse his audience in his stories was Creating Deeper Meanings to the surface plot. These techniques engaged the audience, and got them thinking in a more complex fashion about the screen images. Beale's main ways of creating deeper meaning were by using multi-layered visual textures of shadows, symbols and parallel editing.

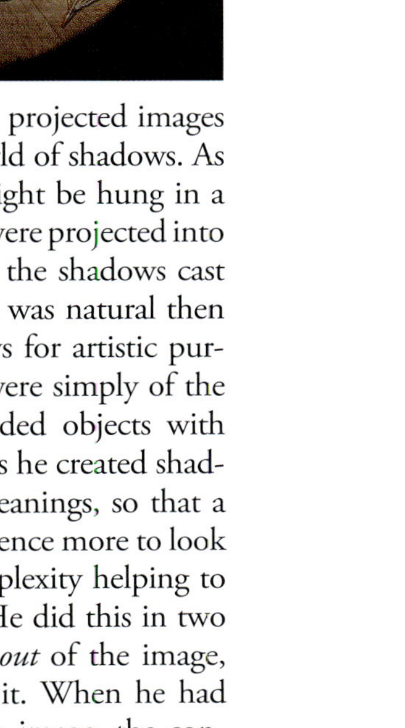

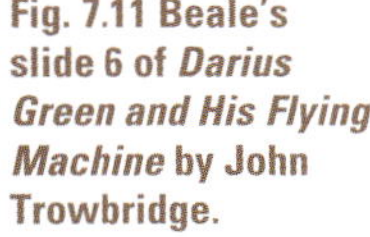

Fig. 7.11 Beale's slide 6 of *Darius Green and His Flying Machine* by John Trowbridge.

First, Beale's shadows: Beale's projected images were actually seen amid a world of shadows. As opposed to "wall art" that might be hung in a well-lit museum, his pictures were projected into a darkened room, filled with the shadows cast by the light of the lantern. It was natural then that Beale would use shadows for artistic purposes. Usually, his shadows were simply of the ordinary kind – they grounded objects with light and dark. But sometimes he created shadows that suggested deeper meanings, so that a "shadow world" gave the audience more to look at and think about – its complexity helping to immerse them in the story. He did this in two ways: having shadows reach *out* of the image, and having them reach *into* it. When he had the shadows reach out of the image, the connotations were often foreboding.

For instance, In *Annie and Willie* (Fig. 7.13 left), we see Father out shopping for a tree on a snow-swept street, having relented from his stern stance against Santa. In the background, another man carries off his tree, and even further back, another is loaded with presents. But Father is without tree or presents. The dominant thing in the image is not his Christmas tree, but his

Fig. 7.12 Slides 11, 14, 22 from Beale's *Marley's Ghost*, the lantern name for *A Christmas Carol*.

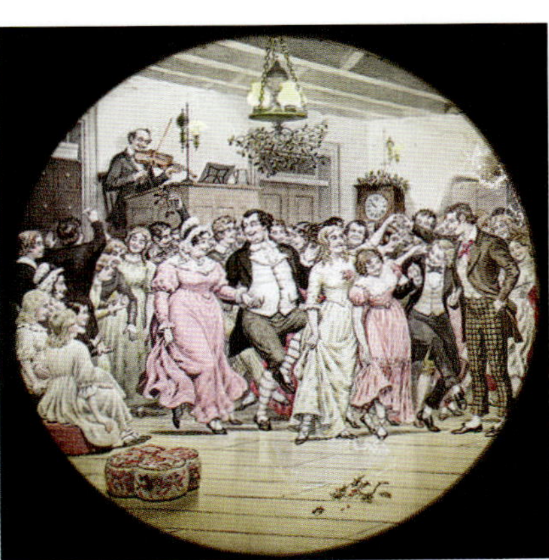

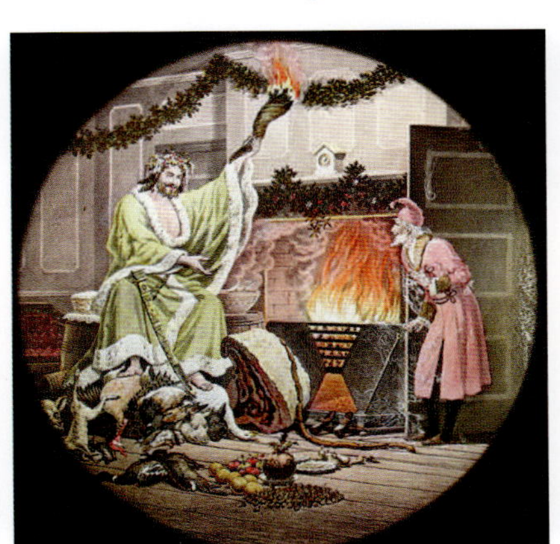

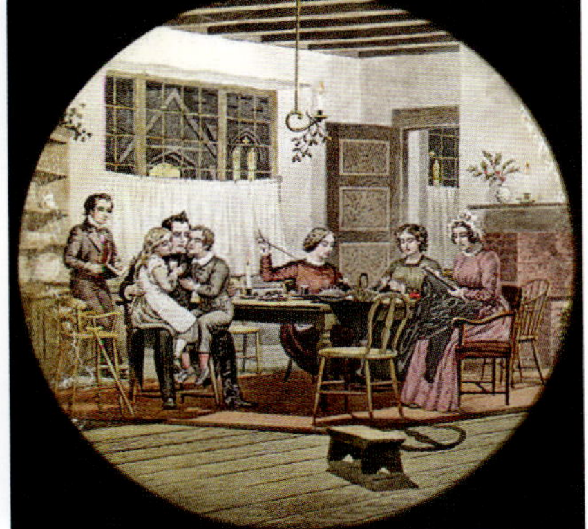

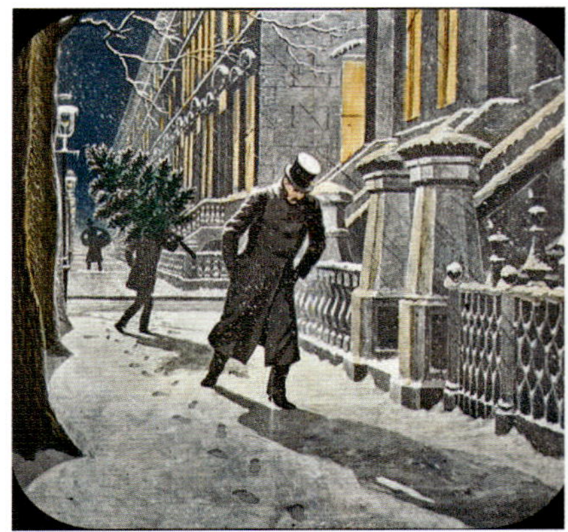

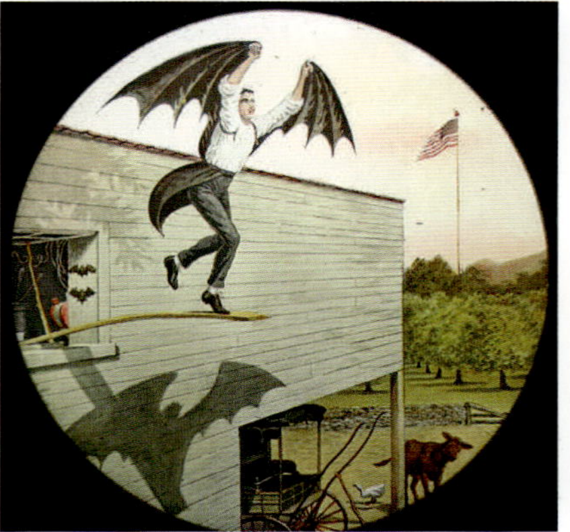

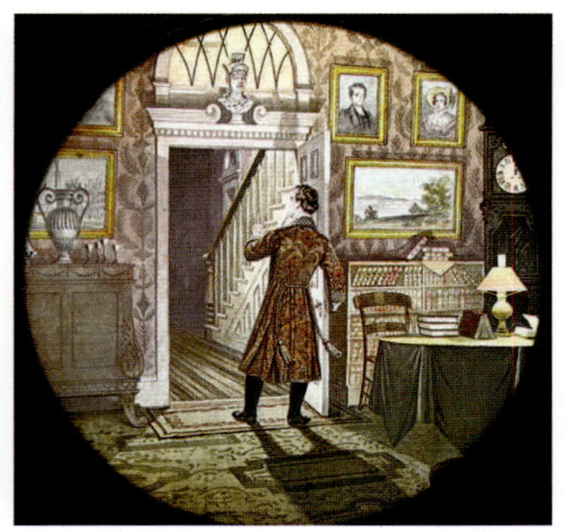

Fig. 7.13 Left, Beale's slide 3 of *Annie and Willie's Prayer.* Center, Beale's slide 7 of *Darius Green and His Flying Machine.* Right, Beale's slide 2 from *The Raven..*

shadow, a huge dark nothing that fills the foreground, emphasizing his loneliness, reaching out toward us, calling for a deeper understanding of this tormented man.

In *Darius Green and His Flying Machine* (Fig. 7.13 center), Darius is gazing up at the sky, at last ready for his test flight. His daring figure breaks across the line of the barn roof, half in the air already, dominating the top part of the picture, mirrored by the proudly waving American flag. But below his feet, the bottom half of the picture paints quite a different story, a deeper meaning beneath his daring. There the aspiring figure of Darius becomes a lumpish shadow, perched on a shadow plank that is not angled up, but down toward the ground. A calf looks askance at this strange shadow figure, seeming to wonder at the absurdity. We, the audience, are suspended between the two images, top and bottom, real and shadow, wondering which will become reality in the next slide, wondering how the story will end.

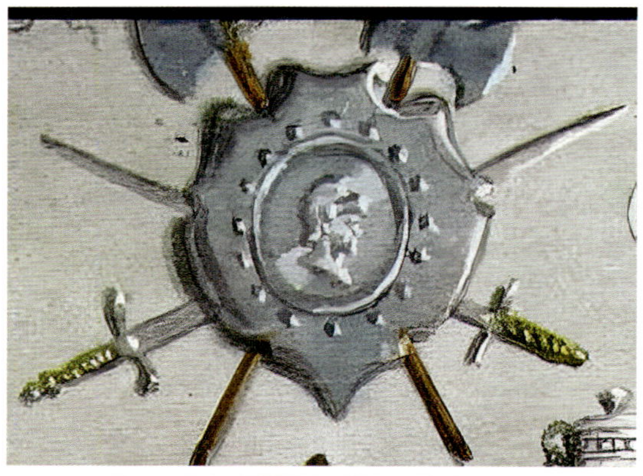

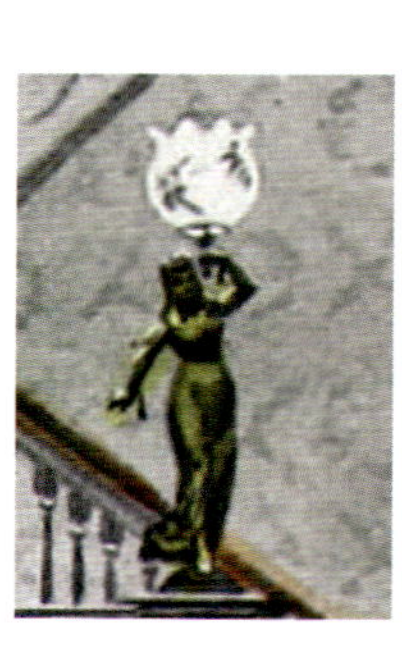

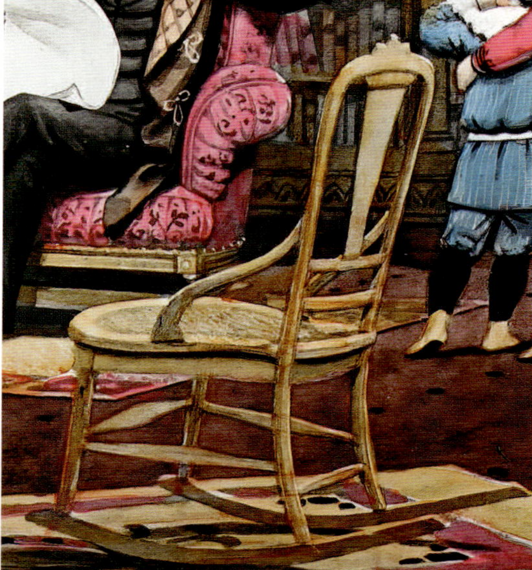

Fig. 7.14 Details from Beale's slide 1 of *Annie and Willie's Prayer.*

And in *The Raven* (Fig. 7.13 right), when the protagonist – his back to us – first opens the door to investigate the strange tapping, a realistically rendered shadow extends out toward us, to the slide frame. It creates a phantom path for us to enter the screen world. We join the protagonist at the door to investigate the deeper meaning of this strange noise. As the poem continues and the protagonist's grip on reality diminishes, the shadows in the room become more and more unrealistic, until at the end it is the Raven's shadow that envelops all.

> And my soul from out that shadow,
> That lies floating on the floor,
> Shall be lifted – nevermore.

In all three cases the shadow is a major and ominous element in the slide, sometimes seeming to cross into our world, sometimes raising questions about the "real world" depicted on screen. These shadows, in Beale's hands, were a powerful way to create greater involvement with the image, to suggest multiple layers of meaning, to help us lose ourselves in the story.

Symbols

The deeper meanings of shadows are by their nature implicit. But Beale could and did use symbolism and metaphors to create much clearer ways of suggesting deeper meanings and immersing us in his stories. He did not resort to a standard set of symbols except in illustrating religious texts and secret society rituals, each of which had their own symbolic systems.[21] Instead he created symbols from ordinary objects. Because of the context in which Beale placed these objects and the way he handled them, they implied meanings that they would not have had elsewhere. They became transcendent and suggestive, as we will see with the symbolic details in *Maud Muller*.

Annie and Willie's Prayer offers three other examples – all in the opening scene (Fig. 7.3). None of the symbolic details in the scene are mentioned in the poem itself. The empty rocking chair and the ethereal figurine – positioned on the newel post and lighting the way up the stairs to the children's room – would have no particular interest or meaning in another context. But in *Annie and Willie* they certainly evoke the absent mother, and suggest that her spirit is still watching over her children as they are dismissed from the family fireside and sent off to bed. Similarly, the shield and swords positioned directly over Father's head become emblematic of the hard edge to his character as he banishes his children from Christmas (Fig. 7.14). This symbolic level of the picture influences us whether or not we understand the symbols. Even if we do not "read" their meaning explicitly, they create an ambiance in the scene. They generate an undertone, a deeper mood and meaning, a "feel" that helps draw us into the characters and immerse us in their story.

In poems like *Annie and Willie*, where a great deal of written detail already describes the scene, Beale primarily concentrates on "illustrating" that detail to help sustain our attention. He adds his own symbolism only lightly. Similarly, *The Raven* is already full of Poe's verbal detail and symbolism such as the symbol of the raven itself. In this case Beale again adds his own symbolic touches lightly – for instance, a curtain in the background that becomes a great claw (Fig. 8.19).

But in those works where the text itself gives little detail or explicit symbols to prompt Beale's illustration, he is free to add his own symbolic layer to the images, and to make it carry a major portion of the narrative. This is particularly true of songs, which often have a minimal text. We will look at the symbolism throughout the song of *Where is My Wandering Boy Tonight* in detail later, but here is one brief example (Fig. 7.15). The wandering boy stands drinking in a bar, toasted by his new "friends". A statuette on the bar symbolizes exactly the opposite from the one in *Annie and Willie*. It is a beautiful Nubian, a dark angel that is about to lasso the wandering boy. Though not mentioned in the song itself, it is a dominant element in the scene, paired against a good angel, a clergyman who has just appeared in the barroom door to take the boy home. In this case, it is Beale's symbols that carry the import of the visual story.

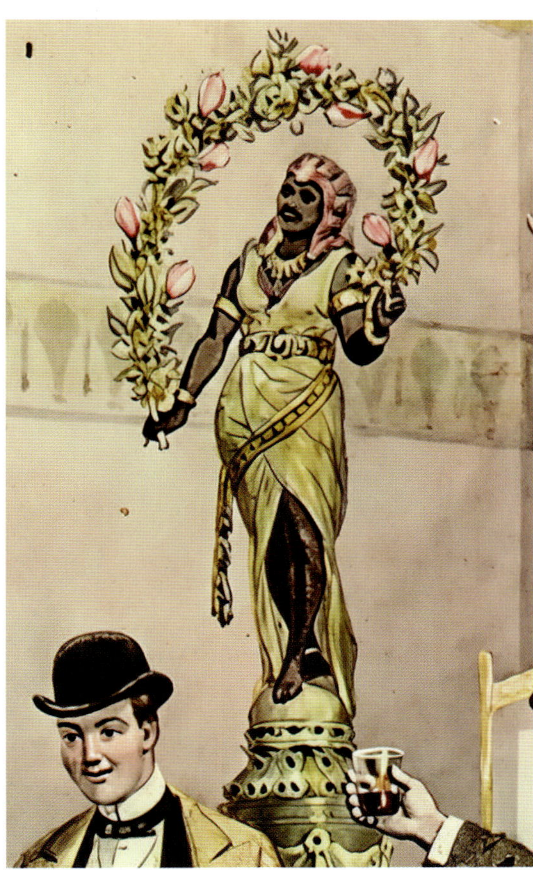

Fig. 7.15 Detail from Beale's slide 4 of *Where is My Wandering Boy Tonight.* (Fig. 9.23).

Not surprisingly, Beale's religious slides are full of traditional symbolism – angels, the good shepherd, the sheep, etc., and he illustrates them in many different contexts. But several of the religious hymns employ extended secular metaphors or allegories, often involving the sea, like *Let the Lower Lights Be Burning*. In this instance, each image in this life-saving drama has implied meanings. In the opening slides Beale realistically portrays the most obvious metaphor, a lighthouse. In later slides like Fig. 7.16, he also shows the fishermen hurrying to set out the "lower lights" along the shore that would mark a safe entrance to the harbor. The fact that ordinary fishermen are preparing such lights suggests the possibility that everyday people like us – not just the lighthouse keepers, the lofty ministers – can assist in the salvation of souls.

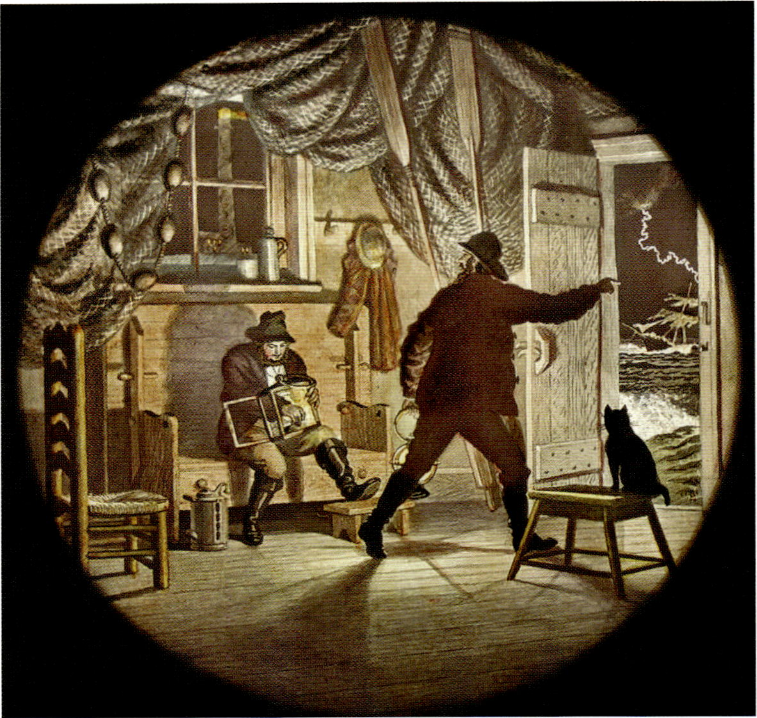

Fig. 7.16 Beale's slide 4 of the hymn, *Let The Lower Light Be Burning* by Philip Bliss.

Let the lower lights be burning!
Send a gleam across the wave!
Some poor fainting, struggling seaman
You may rescue, you may save.

Since terrible shipwrecks were a common part of 19th century life, Beale's detailed depictions of such lifesaving metaphors helped make spiritual matters gripping and concrete – drawing his audience into the deeper significance of the hymn.

Fig. 7.17 Beale's slide of "The Bride and One Year After" from the *Comic-Love* group.

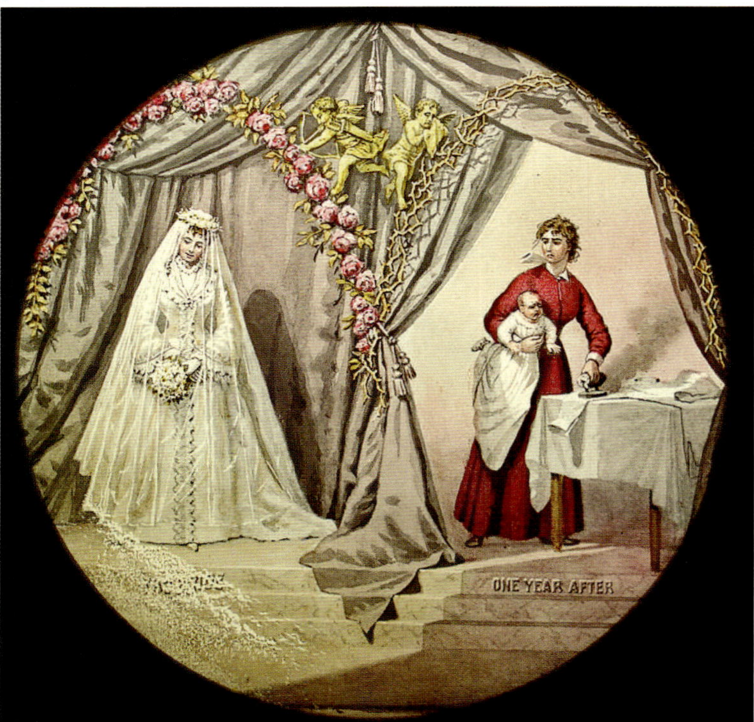

Parallel Editing

An entirely different way of creating deeper meaning and immersing the audience in the story was through *parallel editing*, also called *cross-cutting* or *intercutting* in the movies. The contrasting stories increased the dramatic tension, with one story illuminating the implications of the other.

At the simplest level, Beale presents a single split-screen image, juxtaposing two stories, as in *The Bride and One Year After* (Fig. 7.17). The "before and after" contrast of the blushing bride and the harried mother – juxtaposed side-by-side in a single slide – has a greater impact than the two images would have if projected separately. Everyone in the audience understands the contrast. This image never fails to get a rueful laugh when projected as part of our *Valentine Show*. Symbolic cupids above the bride's flowers and the wife's thorns react to the two different worlds – providing a second level to the joke.

Beale uses a more complex form of parallel editing to convey meaning in longer works like *Evangeline* and *Uncle Tom's Cabin*. Perhaps one of his most interesting uses is in *Ben Hur*, the story of a Jewish boy seeking spiritual salvation in a Roman world of war, "the most thrilling and interesting points" of which, as one reviewer described it, "being illustrated by means of handsome stereopticon views".[22] Ben Hur's mother and sister are thrown in jail after the accidental injury of a Roman near their house, and Ben Hur himself is sent to the galleys (Fig. 7.18). We follow his life as he rescues the galley captain, becomes his adopted son, enters a chariot race against his Roman tormentor, and decides to raise an army to protect the new King of the Jews, Jesus. At the end he realizes that Jesus does not want protection, but stands for love, and Ben Hur becomes a Christian. Meanwhile, he searches for his mother and sister. In a parallel story we follow them as they languish in prison, and are discovered by a kindly Roman warden. They are released, but are sent to the Valley of the Dead because they have contracted leprosy. The picture of them in prison is grim. Their clothes and flesh are both rotting away, a parallel to Ben Hur's life in the galley.

The two parallel stories are brought together in one of the most dramatic sequences of the set. An ecstatic Ben Hur recognizes his Mother and

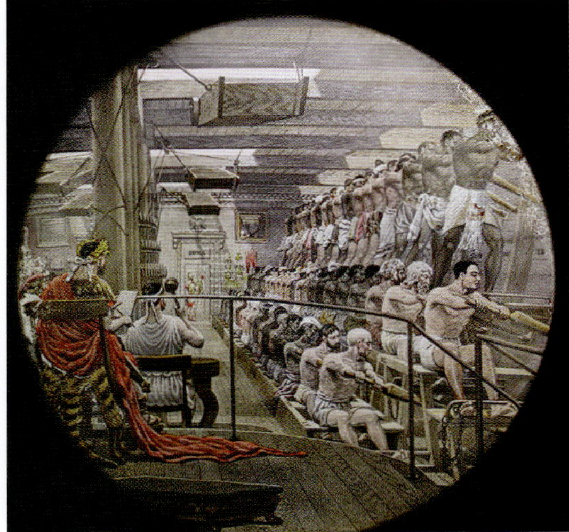

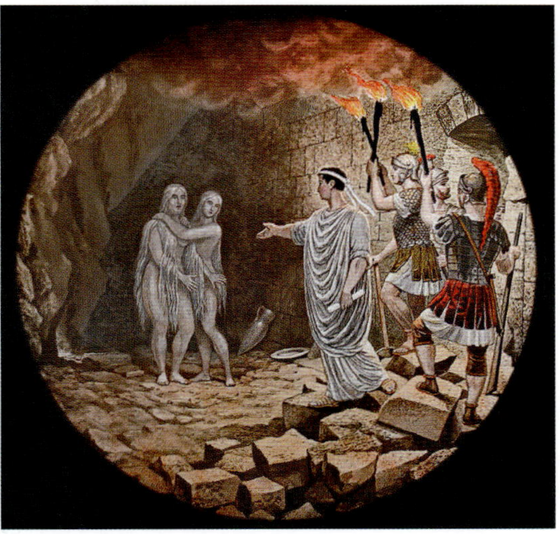

Fig. 7.18 Beale's slide of "Ben Hur at the Oars" and slide 19 of *Ben Hur* by Lew Wallace. The two images capture the two parallel stories of the set.

Sister, now made whole again, just as Jesus enters Jerusalem in the background (Fig. 7.19). The image epitomizes the transformation of the lepers' bodies, and Ben Hur's spiritual transformation. The merging of the two juxtaposed stories gives a greater richness to them both, making the physical spiritual and the spiritual physical.[23]

Why did Beale, (or Porter and Griffith in their early movies) use parallel editing in stories? In both cases the answer is the same: they were simply following the story that had been laid out for them by the book's author. It had long been a common literary technique because authors had recognized its power. (Think, for instance, of Shakespeare's double identity comedies.) Indeed, Griffith himself saw nothing extraordinary in his use of it. His wife reported this conversation, presumably with someone in the "front office":

> "How can you tell a story jumping about like that? The people won't know what it is about".
>
> "Well", said Mr. Griffith, "doesn't Dickens write that way?"
>
> "Yes, but that's Dickens; that's novel writing; that's different".
>
> "Oh, not so much, these are picture stories; not so different."[24]

Griffith adapted the established literary and magic lantern technique of parallel editing to the needs of silent film. He did so using a speed and flexibility of movement that created new possibilities for telling a story. But he was extending – consciously or not, coincidentally or not – a well-developed magic lantern screen "grammar" for creating deeper meaning for "picture stories", not inventing a new one.

Participating in the Action – Body Position

A third class of techniques that Beale used to immerse the audience in his stories was to help viewers actually Participate in the Action. Like the shadows that reached from our world into the screen scene, these devices blurred the distinction between the two worlds, encouraging us to vicariously enter the scene and join the action. Beale used body position, breaking the frame, and screen motion for this purpose.

I mentioned earlier that the British Life Model slides drew viewers into the story by using characters positioned with their ***back to the audience.***[25] Beale sometimes uses the same device. At first, he did this in such a way that he blocked the rest of the view (Fig. 10.5). Briggs must have commented because that approach quickly disappears. Later Beale used characters with their backs to us to give a three-dimensional sense, and to involve us in the scene, as when Annie and Willie were sent to bed, or in Figs.

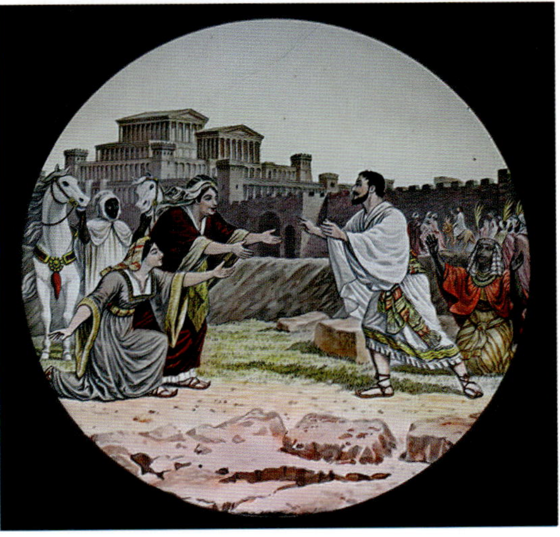

Fig. 7.19 Beale's slide 23 of *Ben Hur*.

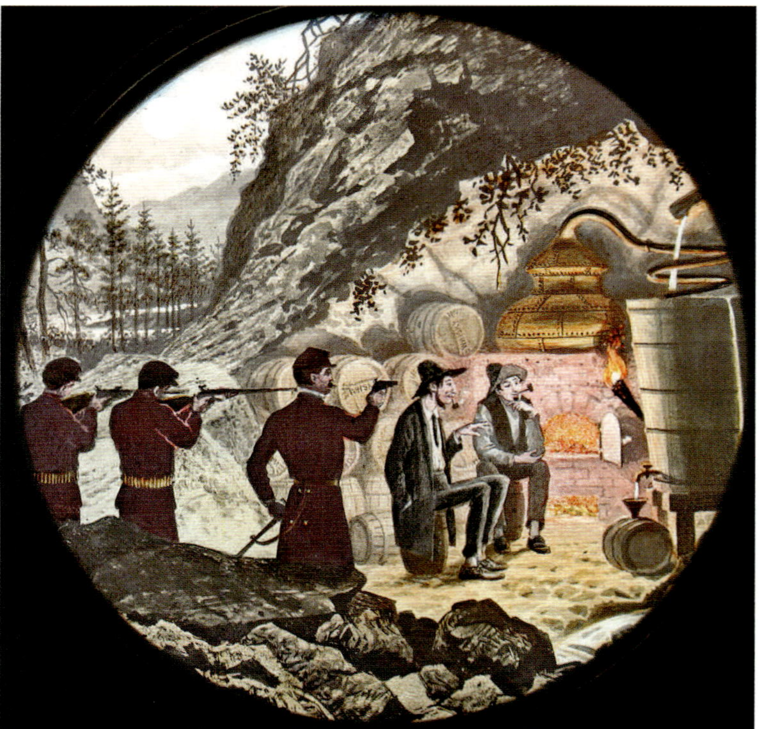

Fig. 7.20 Beale's slide 2 of *Raid of the Moonshiners*.

7.13 and 7.16.[26] In cases where Beale uses this technique he often places us, the audience, in a physical position to become the character, or join the action. In *Raid of the Moonshiners*, for instance, the moonshiners sit watching their still, while the raiding police, all with their backs to us, line up to capture them. The artist's vantage point, and hence our point of view, positions us just behind the rocks, as backup to the police and next in the line of figures. It is easy for us to imagine ourselves – guns drawn – participating in the dramatic arrest (Fig. 7.20).

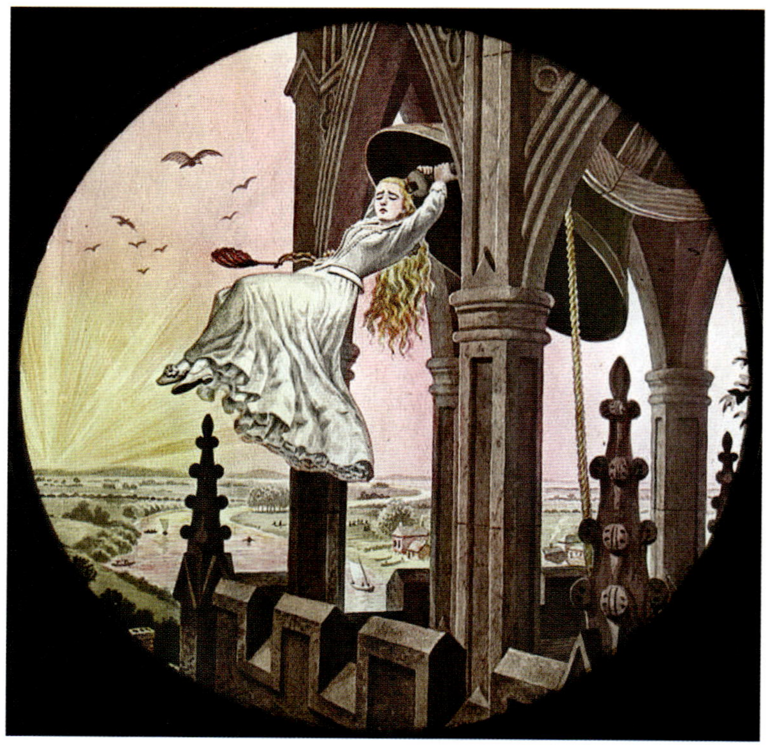

Fig. 7.21 Beale's slide 7 of *Curfew Shall Not Ring Tonight* by Rose Hartwick Thorpe.

Breaking the Frame

Another way Beale gets us to participate in the action and immerse us in the story is to weaken the boundaries of the screen world by breaking the frame of the image. This is a common technique in other forms of narrative art. In graphic novels and comics, for instance, characters sometimes break outside of the panel frame – as when a monster bursts from the panel and seems to rage toward us.[27] Obviously Beale cannot break through the frame of the slide format itself. But he can create more subtle forms of "breaking the frame" by defining a frame within the boundaries of the slide, and then having a character break through that.

We saw a bit of this in *Annie and Willie*, when Willie's leap broke across the line of the curtain. A much more spectacular example is the image from *Curfew Shall Not Ring Tonight* that my wife and I chose for the cover of our earlier book about Beale, *Before the Movies*.[28] In the story, Bessie tries to save her lover by silencing his funeral knell. She swings out over the city, hanging onto the bell's clapper, her flying form breaking across the frame of the bell tower (Fig. 7.21). The scene is very dramatic when performed. It would be much less so if Bessie were before a solid background, rather than breaking the frame of the church spires. And it is not simply more dramatic. Because Bessie is breaking free from her surroundings, it is easier for the audience to participate in her daring, joining her in crying the chorus of the poem, "Curfew shall not ring tonight!"

Shadows

We have already discussed how Beale capitalized on the dark and shadowy world of lantern projection, and used shadows reaching ***out of the image*** toward the audience in order to suggest "Deeper Meanings". But he also employed shadows to break past the slide frame ***into the screen image***, and allow us to "Participate in the Action". These shadows are from imagined "real people" in the off-stage world who enter the screen image in shadow form. Their shadows become avatars for the audience, helping us to immerse ourselves in the action by allowing us to participate in it. Through our shadow avatars, we become *extras* on the *set*, and assume a part in the story world.

We've seen Beale use shadows in this way in *The Village Blacksmith*. There he showed the shadows of children running from the off-screen world, our world, into the screen world of the blacksmith's shop, carrying us along with them into the excitement of the scene.[29] A similar use occurs in the Comic Sketch of *Mr. Spurt and His Auto* (Fig. 7.22). Mr. Spurt buys a fancy car, lords it over the country people as he tootles along, has a breakdown in the rain, and is rescued by a kindly farmer. In the final scene, the shadows of the forgiving off-screen country people wave a cheerful goodbye while a farmer's horse hauls off the auto. The shadows also represent us, waving goodbye to Mr. Spurt, and to his comic story, as a rainbow celebrates the happy ending of his little drama.

Beale used a similar shadow technique for a more serious purpose in a popular patriotic song that called for an end to war, *Tenting on the Old Camp Ground* (Fig. 7.23). As soldiers resolutely march off – waving the flag – to join the Spanish-American War, two strange ghost-like shadows appear before them from the reality of our off-screen world. A dog, probably belonging to the cheering family, reacts to the ghosts, howling in fear. These shadows entering the screen are not of "living people" like the country people in *Mr. Spurt*; they are shadows of the dead – our dead. Their ghosts illustrate the song lyrics for this slide:

> We are tired of war on the old campground,
> Many are dead and gone.
> Of the brave and true who've left their homes,
> Others been wounded long.

Using shadows, Beale managed to combine in a single image the war's flag-waving patriotism, and its grim reality, helping his audience participate in that uneasy tension, immersing us visually in the nation's conflict.

Finally, there is another, quite different way for shadows to increase audience immersion and participation in magic lantern stories, but it involves the showman, rather than the slide artist. The showman can use his *own* shadow to dramatize the action. I am not positive that 19th century showmen did this, but they certainly could have. It is an obvious and very effective technique, one that I use often. For instance, in the story of *Evangeline*, the British invade a

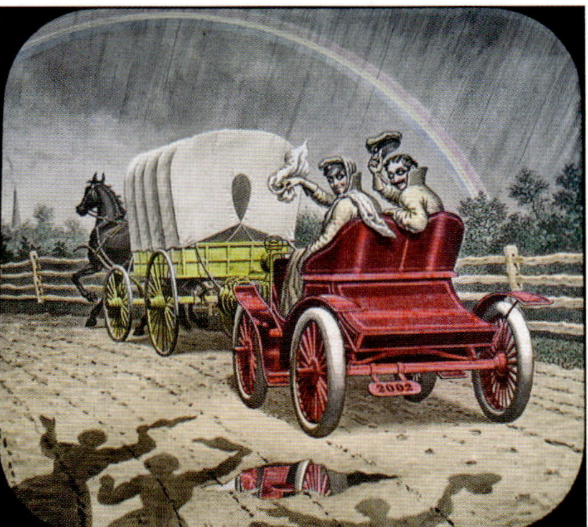

Fig. 7.22 Beale's slide 6 of the Comic Sketch, *Mr. Spurt and His Auto*.

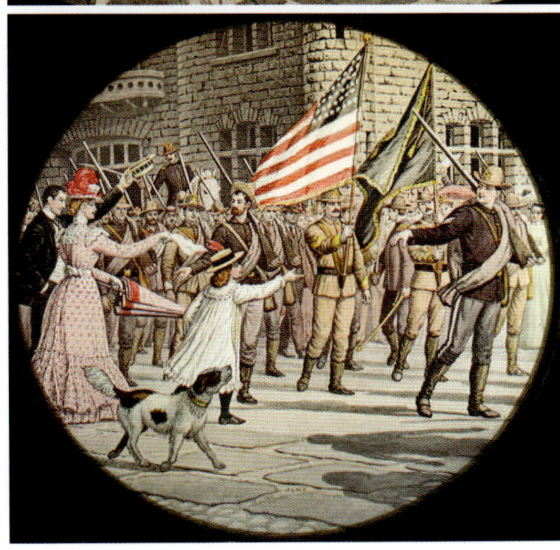

Fig. 7.23 Beale's slide 4 of *Tenting on the Old Camp Ground*, by Walter Kittredge.

French Acadian community in Canada. The British commander demands that the Acadian men come to the church. Once there, he surrounds them with soldiers, and makes an announcement that turns their world upside down (Fig. 7.24).

> All your lands, and dwellings, and cattle of all
> kinds
> Forfeited be to the crown; and that you
> yourselves from this province
> Be transported to other lands... Prisoners now
> I declare you!

When performing the previous sections of the poem, I have had my back to the crowd as I operated the lantern, and I have been using a French accent. But to make this announcement I walk in front of the projected image. Suddenly I'm facing the audience, speaking directly to them, now with a British accent, my face lit by the light of the projector. My shadow is huge on the screen behind me, melding with the image of the Acadians, gesturing as I speak. I have crossed into the screen world, pulling my audience with me, immersing them in the story.

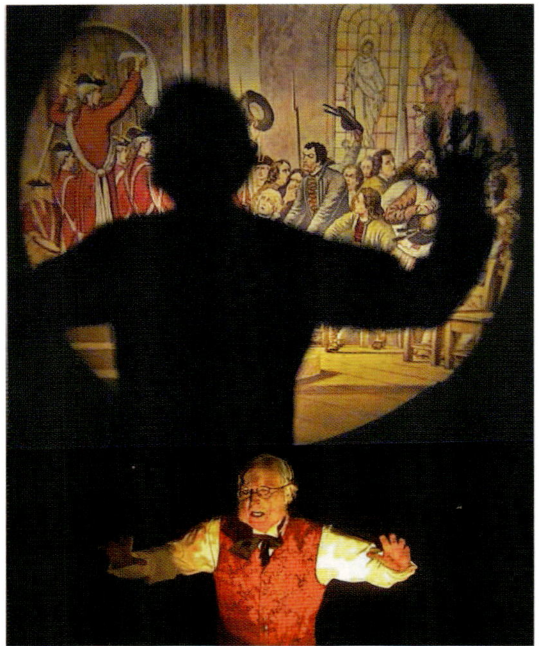

Fig 7.24 Video screen shot, Beale's slide 11 of *Evangeline* by Henry Wadsworth Longfellow, with my shadow projected into the slide image. Bob Suter photo.

They *become* the Acadian prisoners in the church.

There's another way for the showman – not the artist – to get the audience to participate in the action. In fact, the technique is often called "audience participation". I use it in every performance. The showman can spontaneously pick up on a remark from the audience, or lead it in rhythmic clapping for a jumping clown. He can prompt the marching feet of the soldiers in *Barbara Fritchie*, or the rumbling rats in *The Pied Piper*. He can encourage the audience to join in singing *Auld Lang Syne*. Audience participation techniques such as these allow the audience to physically join the action and become part of the show. More broadly, they create a participatory climate that draws people into the story world. Audiences love it. The magical dance between the showman and the image and the audience is one of the great attractions of a Magic Lantern Show.

Dissolves

Returning again to the artist's role in encouraging participation: The magic lantern dissolve provides Beale with another way to encourage the audience to immerse itself in the story. I've mentioned how he uses the "standard dissolve" to move smoothly from one scene to another, or uses "effect dissolves" to produce special effects. In the cigar smoking scene, for instance, the effect dissolve creates comic action; in *The Little Match Girl*, it helps drive the narrative as the Christmas Tree dissolves into its lights. But there is an aspect of the effect dissolve that we haven't yet explored, and that is the way it invites us to participate in the action.

For early 19th century audiences, the effect dissolve had enormous appeal. The slowly changing images, one scene morphing into another, seemed truly magical. "Dissolving Views" were heavily promoted in lantern broadsides, in some cases becoming the central feature of the show. And the power of the dissolve was not confined to the early lantern period. In the 1960s there was a resurgence of interest in the form, with elaborate shows produced by dissolving images using multiple 35mm projectors.[30]

What is it that gives the effect dissolve such power across the centuries? I don't think it is simply that one image changes to another. I think the explanation is that at some point in the transition *both* images are half-visible, two images in one, a demi-world of ambiguity and mystery. As art historian Isobel Armstrong puts it, at her most lyrical:

> [It is] a transformation scene which is also a dissolution. It is a de-formation and re-formation simultaneously, after-image and prior image, past superimposed on the present, the present on the future. Layers of transparency halfway between appearance and non-appearance, matter and non-matter, the borderline between substance and light; mist, shade, shadows of shade, gleams of light and half-differentiated radiance, this is perceptible as the imperceptible.[31]

The shifting images of the effect dissolve create a tension that draws the audience into the scene. The dissolve demands participation as the viewers try to discern what the new image is, what it might be, what it might suggest.

The second explanation for the power of the effect dissolve, in Beale's case, is that he uses the effect dissolve not only to create motion from one place to another as in the joke slide, or from one time to another, as in winter-to-summer changes. He builds on the ambiguity of the dissolving images to create a ***transformational narrative dissolve***, shifting from one state to another. To do this Beale often uses dissolves as the dramatic high points of longer narratives that are otherwise illustrated only by single slides. The dissolve transformation stands out from the rest of the story and suggests its deepest meanings.

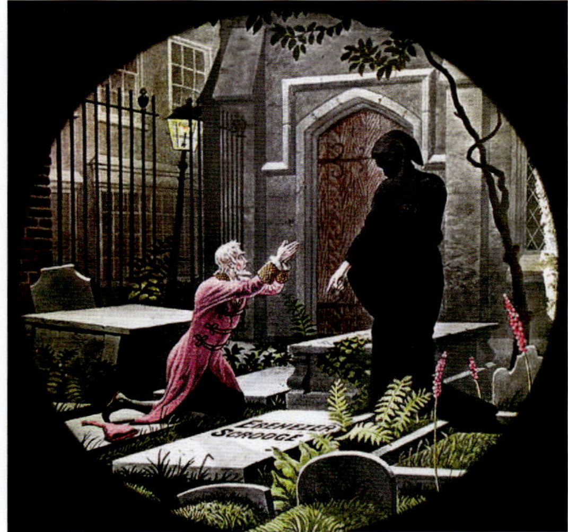

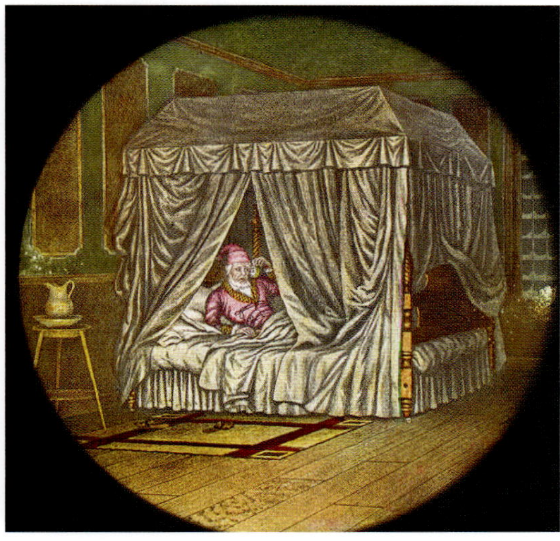

Fig. 7.25 Beale's slides 23 and 6 of *Marley's Ghost* (*A Christmas Carol*) by Charles Dickens.

Beale's version of *Marley's Ghost* (*A Christmas Carol*) is a good example. Indeed, cinema scholar Fred Guida, in his book on screen versions of *A Christmas Carol*, describes how Beale "infused his slides with a decidedly cinematic sense of composition and exposition".[32] For instance, toward the end of the story, we see Scrooge in the graveyard with the Ghost of the Future. As Scrooge pleads for a new chance at life, the music comes up full of drama, and at the same time the scene begins to flicker into a very slow dissolve (Fig. 7.25).

> No, No, Spirit, No! Hear me! I'm not the man I was! Why show me this if I am past all hope? Assure me that I yet may change these shadows by living an altered life!

If we do not know the plot, we do not know the answer to this plea of Scrooge, which voices the central issue of the story. The answer is revealed by the dissolve, as we see the Ghost begin to flicker. Its grim presence slowly disintegrates and turns into a bed post. The grave stone transforms into the bed of a newly-compassionate Scrooge as he awakens on Christmas morning to begin a new life. In that moment when the Ghost is disintegrating and Scrooge is reborn, the two images flicker between each other. The dissolve draws us into participating with the story, imagining different answers to Scrooge's question. That ambiguity, in turn, drives home the transformational meaning of Dickens' story.

Even if we do know the plot of *A Christmas Carol*, and we surely do, the transformative dissolve retains much of that power. We may know *what* happens in the Dickens story, but we do not know *how* it happens in Beale's art, so we try to imagine what forms will emerge as the dissolve occurs. The dissolve drives our involvement. Just suppose, for instance, that Beale had simply created two different images, without a dissolve. The moment would have been much less immersive because it lacked that transitional double image when we could see a change occurring but could not yet tell what it would be. Resolving that ambiguity pulls us into the story, whether we know the plot or not.

Motion

An unusual form of immersing the audience in the story through participation involves screen motion.

Lenny Lipton, in his book, *The Cinema in Flux*, defines two types of screen motion, real motion, and apparent. He describes "real motion" as the kind that we have seen in slip slides where the image actually moves on screen, and "apparent motion" as that created by movies where the image only appears to move, but is actually an illusion created by rapidly changing still images. Beale produced very few slides with mechanical "real motion", but they are striking.[33] One slide, part of a dissolving set called *The Enchanted Grotto* (Fig. 7.26), uses two pieces of glass, one with the overall scene on it, and the other, a lever slide, containing the arm with wand, and the birds and butterflies. When the lever is moved, the goddess waves her wand, and is encircled by the moving birds and butterflies. The slide then dissolves into a closer view of a rival goddess, seen approaching in the boat. The dissolve encourages our participation with the story, in the manner explored earlier. The moving arm of the pictured goddess increases this participatory effect, as it creates a more mysterious demi-world of transitional images.

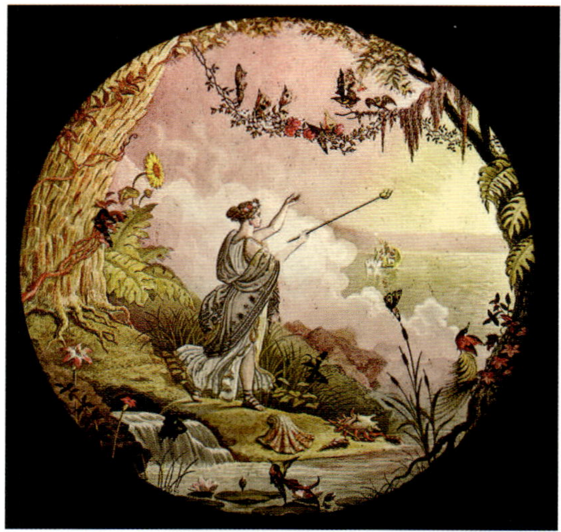

Fig. 7.26 Beale's slide 1 of *The Enchanted Grotto*.

If the movement from one slide to another, such as in Beale's comic slides, continued for more than two images, then the lantern showman could not make the slide changes fast enough to make "real motion" without a special slide like the Dancing Skeleton, and even there the movement was very limited. Without film, it was impossible to create "apparent motion", the illusion of continuous motion created by very rapidly changing still images. Was another alternative possible?

Beale created many motion slides in a category between "real" and the "apparent" that I would call ***simulated motion***. He did this in several different ways. One way used several slides with a registered background, and the figures in different positions in each slide. We have seen this in *Pygmalion and Galatea*. Six slides with the same background change about every 20 seconds – a kind of stop-motion drama – "simulated motion".[34] Simulated motion creates its own sense of immersion. Because there is a time interval between the images as they are being changed, it allows room for the audience to participate. Indeed, the audience *has* to participate in order to imaginatively move the figures from one position to another. That in turn helps immerse us in the story.

A more complex way that Beale created simulated motion was with sequential images of a figure moving through a *changing* background. In the movies, this would come to be called a "*dolly shot*", or a "*travel shot*" because the camera filmed the scene by travelling on a dolly along with the action. Beale used this approach in a limited way in several sets, but his most extensive use was in the comic sketch of *Mrs. Casey and the Goat* (Fig. 7.27).

In terms of "narrative art" the Comic Sketches like *Mrs. Casey* presented unusual challenges for Beale. In the Sketches he was not "illustrating" an existing narrative. There was no text prepared for him by an author. He was creating narrative art that had to tell the story with the pictures alone. In *Mrs. Casey and the Goat*, which I've reproduced in full on page 182, you can see four ways he does this. He creates a story that is simple, with a clear narrative line. His pictures depict the story almost in real time, as opposed to the illustrations of a story like *Evangeline*, in which he selected 24 highlights for a poem that covered 50 years. That means each Comic Sketch slide moves the action forward in time and through space. And the action of the story itself is fast-moving and dramatic, so almost every slide is a new comic scene.

The slides for Comic Sketches do not illustrate known poems, so they do not have lines from the poems printed on the labels as do the Parlor Poems. Rather, they have a short description of the scene such as, "He takes the goat by the horns". The exhibitor can simply project the slides rapidly, one after the other with no dialogue at all. Or, in my case, I've created a brief poem to accompany the slides. When I perform *Mrs. Casey*, the slides are only on screen for about 10 seconds each. With 12 slides to the set, that means two minutes of fast-paced zany action, about the same length as some of the early movies. The slides for *Mrs. Casey and the Goat* are clearly designed for such a fast-paced presentation. The slides are overlapping edits that follow a rapid chase. In this *screwball comedy*, not only do multiple slides depict the action in close to real time, but the depiction *tracks* the action down the street, keeping Mrs. Casey

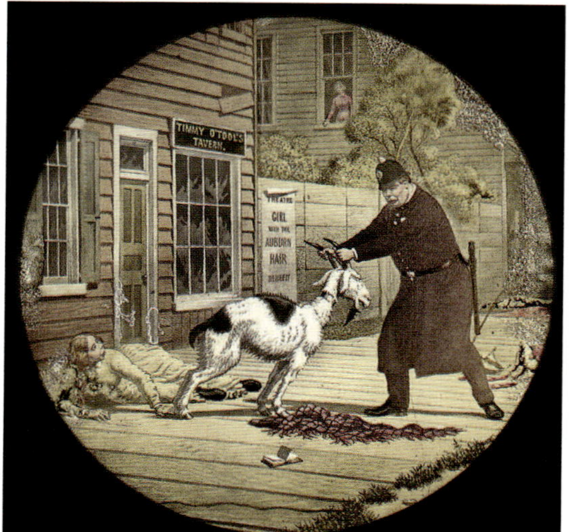

Fig. 7.27 Beale's slide 7 of the Comic Sketch, *Mrs. Casey and the Goat*.

and the goat in the frame as the goat charges and the background shifts. Almost every slide has a slightly different view of the action and its background. At the conclusion, the "camera" of Beale's drawing pad swivels aside and pulls back to bring the church once again into view – the happy ending to this little drama.

Both kinds of simulated motion, that in *Pygmalion* and that in *Mrs. Casey*, create stop-action intervals between the slides. This might seem like a weakness of the magic lantern medium, but it actually helps immerse us in the story. For comparison, think about a movie of the same scenes. The time between the slide images would be filled with filmed motion, leaving no room for us. Here we participate in creating the visual story, and that makes it more our own.

I've presented the images here along with my "Irish" doggerel. To get a sense of how the story plays, have someone read it to you (dramatically!) while you look at the pictures, one at a time, through a circle made with your thumb and forefinger. (Note that I've changed the original title character from "Mrs. O'Casey" to "Sally O'Casey", just to add a little love interest to my story (Fig. 7.28). And yes, the images stereotype the Irish. Interestingly, I've never had an objection.

1. "Sure, and it's a rosy Spring now!"
Said Sally Casey, going to church.

2. "Oh dear, there's that Billy goat now",
Said Sally Casey with a lurch.

3. The goat, he lowered his curving horns,
And Sally Casey, her parasol.

4. "My God", she cried, "he'll not be turned",
And in her mind, she saw her fall.

5. The horns of the goat, like an Irish lyre
Twang sharp, as butt to butt they butt.

6. Just then, O'Grady arrives.
"Sure, what do we have here? What?

7. O'Grady, the man of the hour is he,
And grabs the goat's offending horn,

8. But the goat, to get his goat is free,
And drives him to a trough well worn.

9. Ah, Timmy O'Toole's 'nere seen more flow
Than Officer O'Grady made that day.

10. He rose, and his Irish ire rose too –
T'wod be the red coat devil to pay.

11. "Oh my, that uniform, it shines!"
Said Sally, her eyelids all aflutter.

12. Well now, the goat may have claimed the mountain top
But Casey and O'Grady claimed ...
each other!

Fig. 7.28 Beale's slides 1–12 of *Mrs. Casey and the Billy Goat*
See following page.

Controlling the Narrative Arc

We have explored Beale's use of a wide range of techniques to help immerse his audiences in the story – devices anticipating the action, creating deeper meanings, participating in the action. But besides immersing them in the plot, Beale needed to control the narrative arc in order to build maximum impact. He did this by maintaining continuity through storyboarding, by creating narrative momentum through slide pacing, and by carefully controlling visually the beginning and the ending of his stories.

It was essential for Beale to maintain *continuity* among the images, particularly with long or parallel stories. As we have seen in *Annie and Willie* and in the sketch from *Macbeth*, when Beale was creating one slide, he was also thinking forward and backward in the slide sequence, editing each scene so that it fit into the narrative whole. Given the limited number of slides devoted to a story, this effort was by its nature *elliptical editing* – omitting parts of the story, yet keeping the essence of the whole. With so much left out, it was essential that Beale clearly establish the flow of the action. Unintentional *dis-continuity editing* was common in the lantern trade, a truth that drove famous lantern expert T. C. Hepworth to exasperation. "Look again at the life model sets, there are dozens of them which have important pictures omitted, probably because they would entail some trouble or expense". Or, at the other extreme, there was the problem of too much material. Hepworth recommended *cutting to continuity*: "If a part of the subject is of such a nature that it may be likely to prove tedious to an audience ... that part should either be compressed, or lightened by a good anecdote ...".[35] (The movies faced similar issues with continuity, hence the concept of having a "continuity editor".)

Mrs. Casey and the Billy Goat

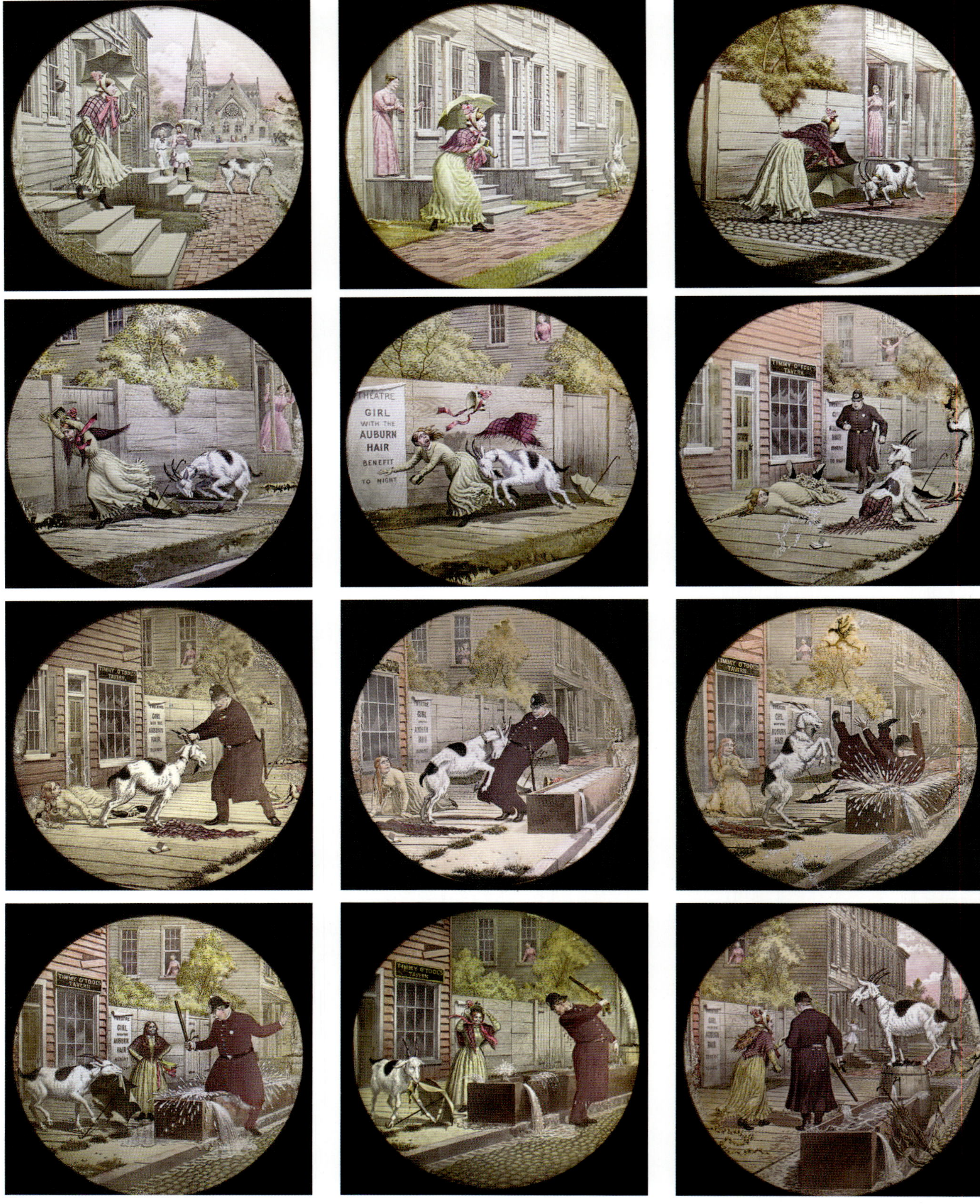

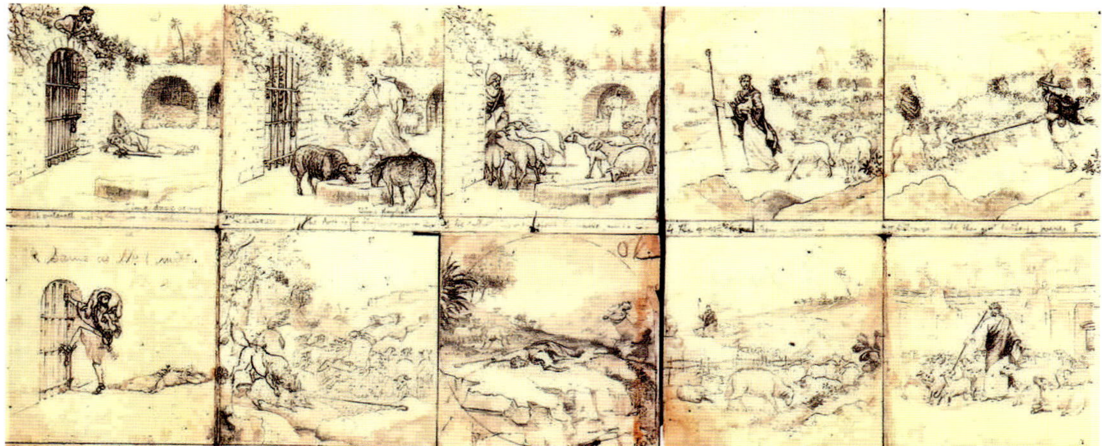

Fig. 7.29 Beale's storyboard for the Bible parable, *The Good Shepherd*.

Once Beale had worked out on his full-sized "roughs" exactly how each scene would look and how they would all fit together, he would sometimes prepare for Briggs a series of clean "thumbnail" sketches about two inches square – what in movie production would later be called the *storyboard*, or *beat board*.[36] The storyboard was an easily managed summary that Briggs could use to check continuity – to make sure that all the important action of the story was covered, and that the details of scene, costume and actors were consistent. If satisfied, Briggs would send the storyboard back to Beale with his "OK", and Beale would complete the final designs. (The process may have worked in reverse too, with the storyboard coming before sketches, or the storyboard used to explore options. In the Beale storyboard for *The Good Shepherd* (Fig 7.29), for instance, he shows two different positions for the wolf in panel 7, presumably so Briggs could pick the one he liked best. Unlike Beale's rough sketches, however, which are full of alternative *takes,* the rest of the storyboard is almost identical to the finished slides).[37]

The parable of *The Good Shepherd* is a complex set of allegories, contrasting the good shepherd (Jesus) with robbers and hired hands – religious charlatans or mercenaries. Beale keeps the action straight by using a number of different continuity techniques: *casting* for easily differentiated characters; *costuming* to differentiate the characters even further through their dress; *spatial continuity* to anchor us firmly in several different sets;[38] *temporal continuity*, with a defined time frame of dawn to dusk; and finally, *narrative continuity*, with the words of the parable themselves clarifying the sequence of actions (Fig. 7.30).

Fig. 7.30 Beale slides 2, 7, and 10 of *The Good Shepherd.* Shifting locales, from earth to Heaven, make this a demanding parable in which to maintain continuity.

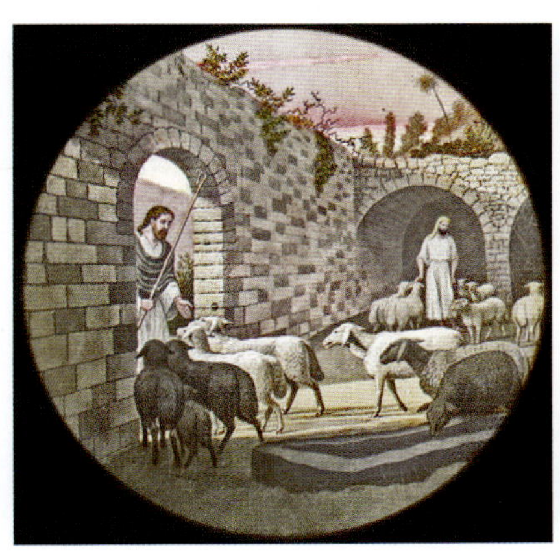

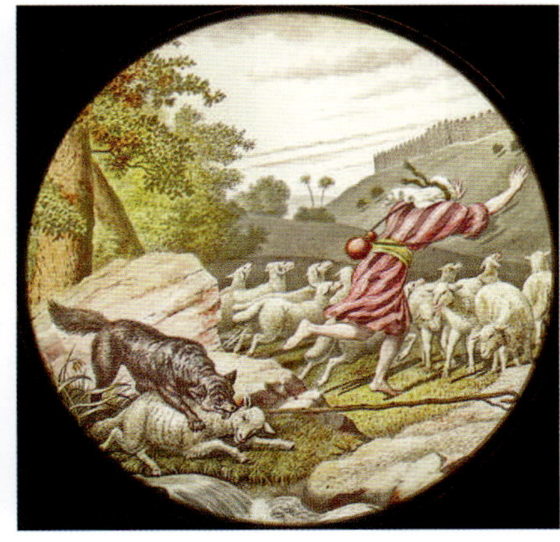

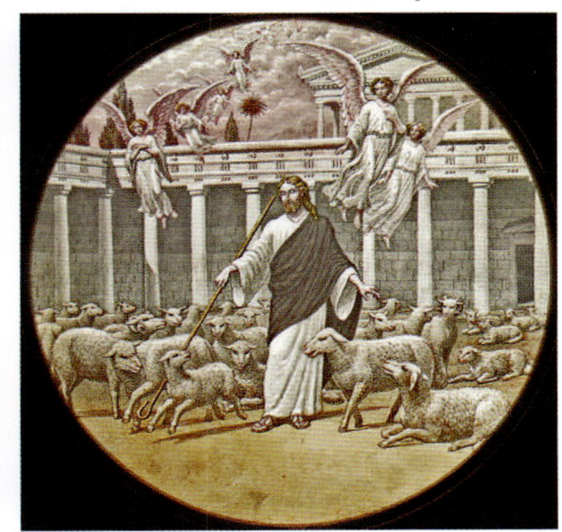

A Beale Mistake in Continuity?

The importance of continuity issues to the magic lantern cinematic art is evident in an incident involving *The Night Before Christmas,* also called *Visit of St. Nicholas.* The set had originally consisted of 4 slides, then was expanded to 6, then dropped back to 4, then expanded to 6 again. Among Beale's effects after he died were two versions of slide 2. What in the world was going on?

Slide 1 is the establishing scene of the children nestled asleep in their bed (Fig. 7.31, left). Briggs was apparently displeased with the first version of slide 2, (Fig. 7.31 center). It is easy to see why. Though at first blush, it looks like an appealing view, continuity problems abound: A baby, not mentioned in the poem, has been introduced for no reason. The parents' bedroom is different from the children's room in the previous slide. In particular, the parent's room has no fireplace. As a result, Papa cannot say, "As I drew in my head, and was turning around /Down the chimney St. Nicholas came with a bound". He'd have to sprint to the next room.

The second version of slide 2 (Fig. 7.31 right), fixes these problems. We can see the same rug as in the opening scene at left – the same wallpaper, the same fireplace, which is right beside the children's bed. Continuity is maintained. And now, as a plus, we can also see the "moon on the breast of the new-fallen snow", the set-up for the next slide, Santa's arrival.

But why did this continuity problem occur? How could Beale, who takes such care with continuity in *The Good Shepherd* (and in everything else), miss so badly here?

I don't think he did. Look closely again at the center image. Note the way the man's nightshirt falls without form or response to his actions. Compare it to the nightshirt at right. Note, at center, the disconnect between Papa's head and his shoulders. Note, at center, the way the baby seems suspended above the crib, Ma above the bed, and the glasses above the book. In that center image, nothing is anchored in its own space.

I don't think Beale painted that picture. I think Briggs first asked another artist (probably Tholey) to fill out the set. That artist made a mess of it, so Briggs sent the slide to Beale and asked him to fix it.

But there's no proof of that theory. The extra slide is a mystery.

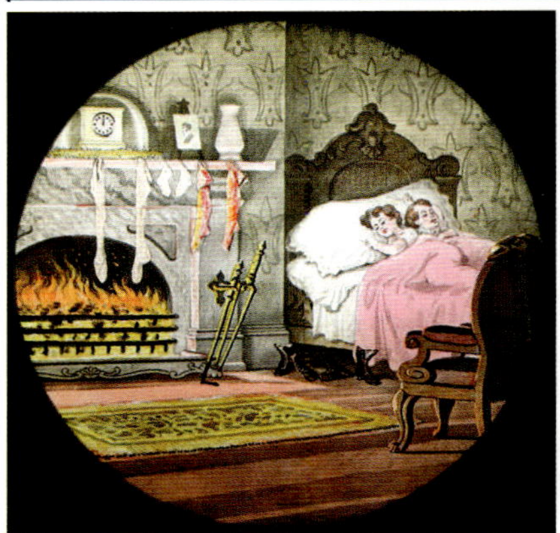

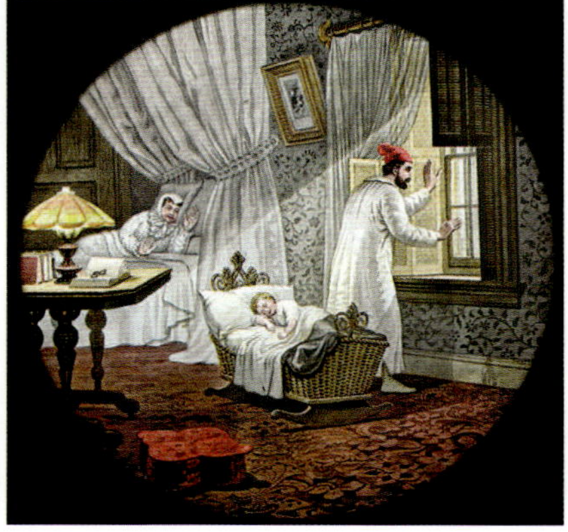

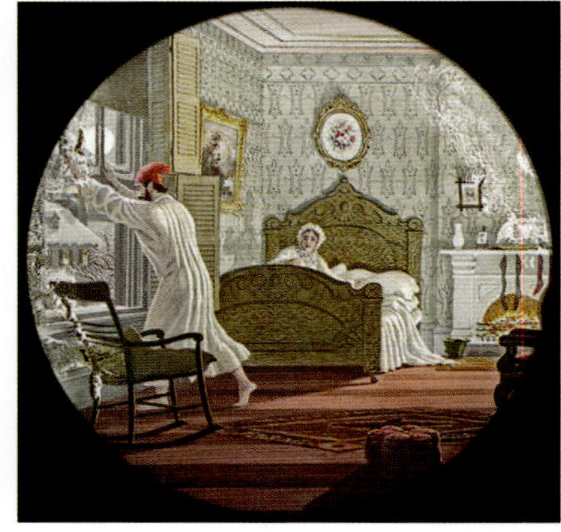

Fig. 7.31 Beale's slides 1, and 2 and 2a? from *Visit of Saint Nicholas*, by Clement Moore.

Building Momentum

Beale frequently controlled the narrative arc by building momentum in the way he paced the slide images with the story. He could have taken a story, divided it into roughly equal sections, and then illustrated the most "telling moment" in each of those sections. But he did not do this. Rather, he changed the ***pacing of the slides*** so that the visual action on screen was changing faster at the most dramatic point, creating a sense of visual momentum and excitement that matched the pace of the narrative.[39]

I've already mentioned how a quick change from one slide to another could alter the momentum of the story, and create impact. A similar logic holds true for the larger arc of the story, as in *The Spectre Pig,* by a 16-year-old Oliver Wendell Holmes (Fig. 7.32). This is a whacky comedy in which a butcher slaughters a pig, despite the hysterical pleas of his son and daughter. "Ah! Woe is me! Alas! Alas!/The Pig. The Pig. The Pig"! All of the early action is depicted with three or four stanzas for each slide, so each slide is projected for at least a minute.

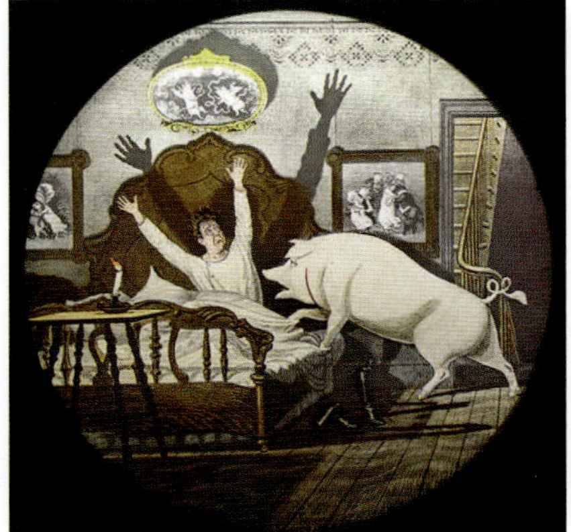
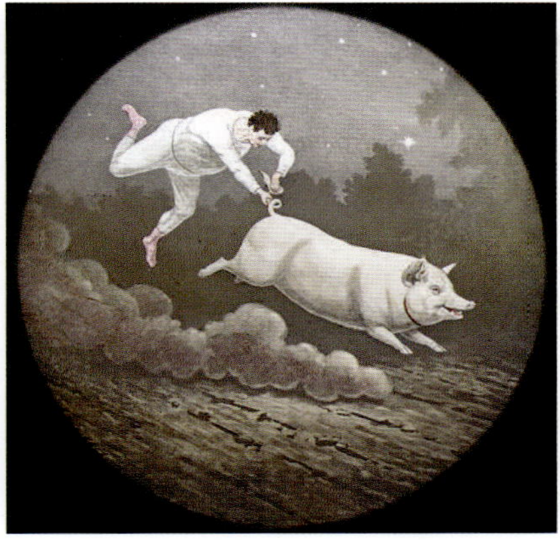
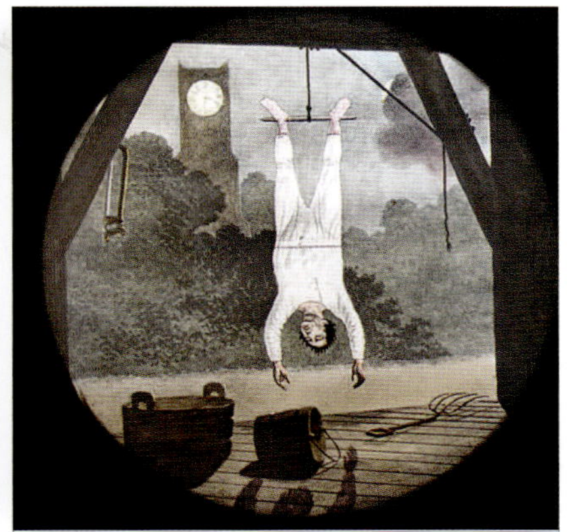

Fig. 7.32 Beale's last three slides for *The Spectre Pig* by Oliver Wendel Holmes. Slide 6, "Now wake, now wake, thou butcher man!" Slide 7, "The shadowy spectre swept before". Slide 8, "A ghastly shape was hanging there".

Then, when the butcher's work is done, he goes off to bed. The clock strikes twelve. The pig shakes free from the beam on which he was slaughtered and makes his way to the butcher's house. At this point the action picks up dramatically, as depicted above. The butcher is accosted in bed by the pig, dragged to the barn, and hung from the very beam the pig was slaughtered on. There is only one stanza per slide, 20 or 30 seconds, and indeed, when I perform the poem, I pick up the verbal pace, speaking faster and faster, voice taut with impending doom. When I get to the last lines of the last stanza, I suddenly slow down. "A ghastly shape was swinging there". I pause, not showing that final slide until the very last words of the last line:

"Yes, it was ... *the butcher man*"!

Ah, yes, ... I do love delivering that last line! Slowing down before it and waiting to project that grizzly last slide until the final three words, gives the ending a very dramatic punch. Throughout the poem, the changing pace of the slides and of the narration controls the momentum of the story, and helps give it life.

Beginning and Ending

Whether an author (or Beale) developed a story with a single through-line, or a parallel structure as in *Ben Hur*, it was critical that Beale shape the drama of the visual arc, with a beginning, a middle, and an end. Sometimes the story's text defined this for him, but sometimes, as in Comic Sketches with no text, he was on his own. At the beginning of a story I've pointed out how Beale often uses establishing shots to open it by defining its culture, time, characters, and tensions. Sometimes he even went back and added an establishing shot to increase the drama of the story. The tale of *Paddy and His Pig* originally jumped right into the chaos which the run-away pig caused.[40] Then Beale added an establishing scene of Paddy strutting off from the Pig Fair, showing off his well-behaved prize pig on its leash. This image contrasts dramatically with the pandemonium of the central section of the story, a series of slides in which the loose pig creates a new kind of havoc in each scene. It also contrasts with the final image of both Paddy and the pig being led off to the pen, making the ending all the more poignant (Fig. 7.33).[41]

Fig. 7.33 Beale's *Paddy and His Pig*, slides 1, 6, 12.

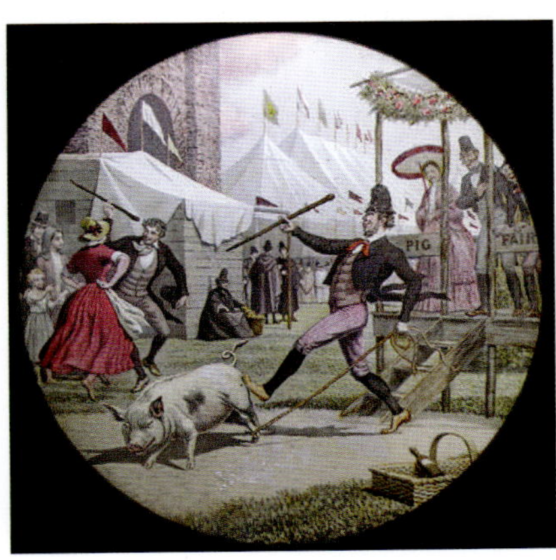

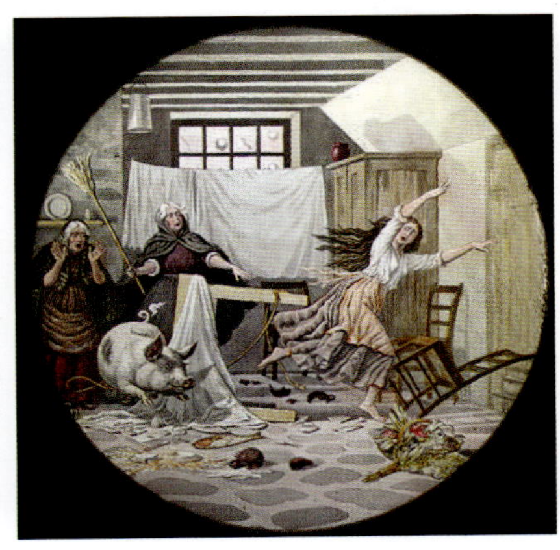
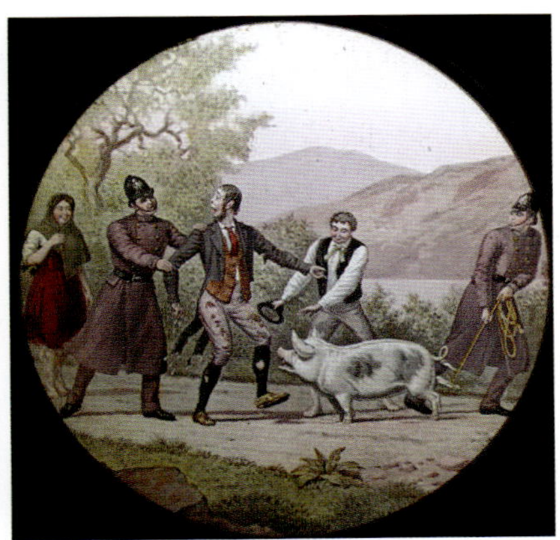

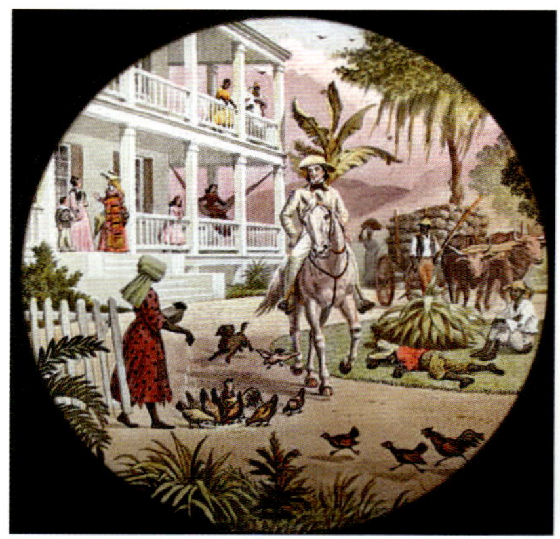
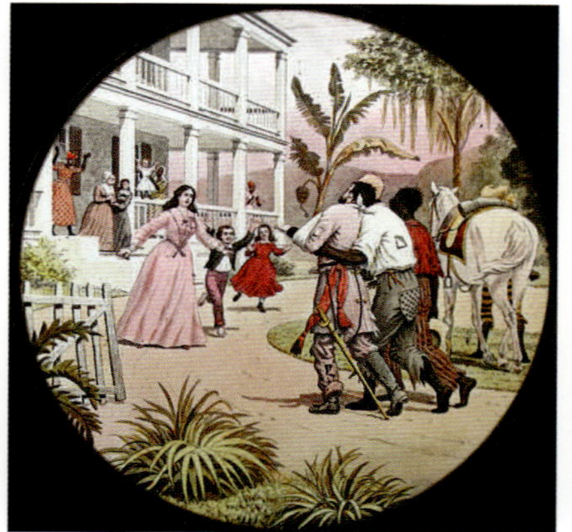
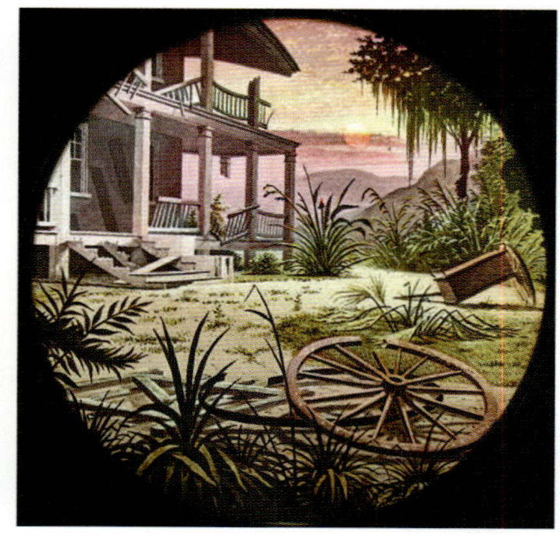

Fig. 7.34 Slides 2, 7, 8 from Beale's *Dixie's Land*. Each slide is from the same vantage point, but the scene changes dramatically over time to emphasize the arc of the story.

(By the way, I've used *Paddy* in many shows, not to tell the story as originally outlined, but to illustrate the song, "Oh Dear, What Can the Matter Be"? The song's rollicking rhythms and repeated question are the perfect counterpoint to the pig's antics. And though the slides clearly present a stereotyped view of Irish life, I've never had a complaint, perhaps because the whole story is so whacky.)

A powerful way that Beale often shapes a story's narrative arc is to end it with a ***parallel visual device***, mirroring its beginning images. *Dixie's Land* is a striking example (Fig. 7.34). This set does not illustrate the pro-South "Dixie" song you know, but, presumably, one of the many Yankee parodies meant to show how the fixation on slavery destroyed the fabled Southern land.[42] The song begins with an establishing view (not shown) of the "land of cotton" – sixteen slaves, sympathetically portrayed, bent at their work in a cotton field with an idealized plantation mansion filling the background. The next slide (shown) depicts the owner on horseback before his mansion, lording it over his slaves. In the background, a huge, wheeled wood cart heads to market, suggesting the booming economy of the plantation. The middle images of the set (not shown) depict the slaves at work, dancing, and praying in the forest; then the owner leaving for the war; and then (shown here at center) returning from the war, badly injured, supported by a slave. The house still stands unchanged as the owner returns, except that the hammock, a symbol of leisure seen in the first slide, is now gone. In the final image, a huge broken cartwheel dominates the foreground. The cart itself is gone. The wheels have literally come off the Southern economy. The mansion is all but destroyed, a dramatic contrast to the way the song began and a stunning closure to this story of *Dixie*.

(Planting a large-wheeled cart in the early part of *Dixie's Land*, and then using its broken wheel as a major symbolic image in the last slide, is an example of Beale's use of the "Chekhov's gun" principle to shape narrative structure. The Russian playwright Anton Chekhov explained this idea by saying, "If in the first act you have hung a pistol on the wall, then in the following one it should be fired". What seem like incidental details in Beale's images often take on greater import as the story develops, and influence our understanding of the story's meaning.)

Summary and Conclusion

Beale became a master of screen narrative art. He commanded attention with the mise-en-scène. He directed it with careful composition, blocking, and rhyming forms. He sustained attention in each slide with detail, both that described in the poem, and with detail he added on his own. He created immersive experiences through techniques that anticipated coming action, created deeper meanings, and helped the audience participate in the action. He shaped the narrative arc by controlling continuity and narrative momentum.

In time Griffith and others would use many of these same techniques to turn the movies from a flagging industry based on novelty, to a vibrant one that enthralled audiences with its stories, using many of the techniques discussed here. Did they get the techniques from Beale? Though possible, there is no evidence for that; more likely they found them in other sources or invented them on their own. But in the meantime, Beale was employing these narrative techniques to create his own sweeping world of screen entertainment and education – a world that we will tour in the next two chapters.

First though, I want to end this description of

Beale's artistic techniques by going back to our discussion of how Beale immerses us in his imagined worlds, and looking at another very unusual example of how he helps us participate in the action. It forms a fitting conclusion to this discussion of his narrative art.

While Beale frequently uses shadows in order to break through the slide frame and immerse us in the story realm, he also reaches across the slide frame to his audience in yet another way – not with shadows, but by using the eyes of his characters. He does this rarely. Ninety-nine percent of the time the characters in Beale's images look only at each other, ignoring the invisible "fourth wall" between stage and audience, and never even looking toward it. But in a few cases Beale's characters are like what film critics call *self-conscious narrators*; that is, they are engrossed in their story, but they also sometimes address the audience.[43] In these Beale stories the characters address the audience visually – they look through the fourth wall, as though reaching out to us to involve us in the action (Fig. 7.35). All the characters are young children. Perhaps Beale used children in this role because their innocence might allow them to "see" us beyond the boundaries of the slide frame. All play their roles in their story worlds, but simultaneously reach out to ours, pulling us into their lives.

We've already met two of these children, though in discussing their images I did not point out the way they directly address the audience. Let's refocus our attention on those slides, concentrating on how the children use their eyes. The little girl in *The Wreck of the Hesperus* sets off for a sail with her father, and, looking right at us, cheerfully waves goodbye, making us part of her well-wishers. All of us, those in the story world and we in the real world are unaware of the deadly hurricane that will leave her washed up on the Reef of Norman's Woe. Similarly, the Little Match Girl, homeless on the street at Christmas, holds up her matches as she looks out at us, pleading with us to buy matches so that she can eat.

Two other children that we have not met before also reach out to the audience with their eyes, inviting us to participate with their stories. The little girl in *America*, surrounded by American flags, looks out at us in the audience as she encourages everyone to join her in singing patriotic songs. And a little child on Noah's Ark is situated in the center of a circular slide, in the center of the ark's window, in the center of the only life left on earth. The child looks out at us solemnly when the dove arrives, as though asking us if we will create a better future than the past that has been destroyed.[44]

Beale has these children view us with eyes that speak their hearts, inviting us to participate in their different lives. It is another telling example of how he keeps his visual drama clear and direct, but also employs subtle narrative techniques to help immerse us in his story worlds.

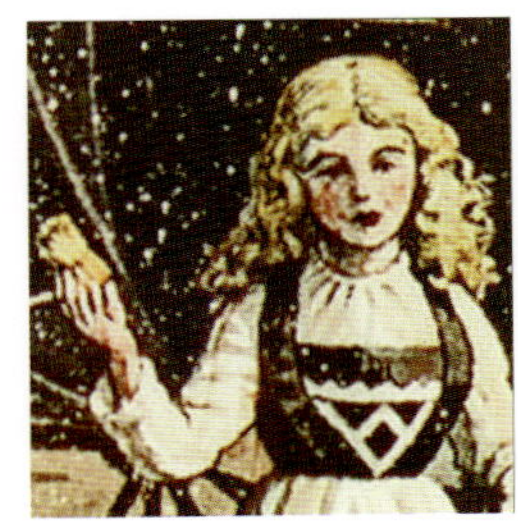

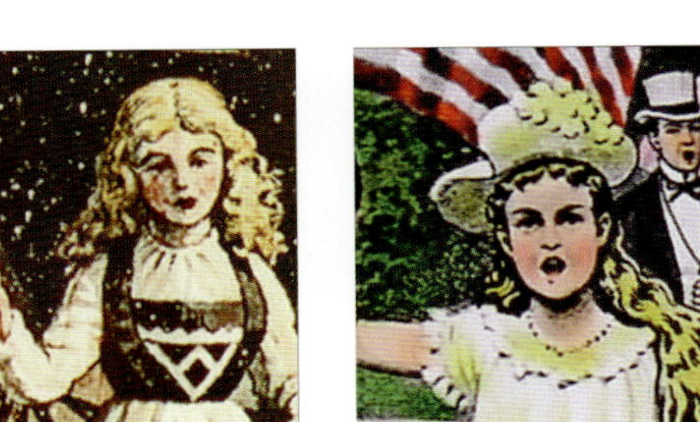

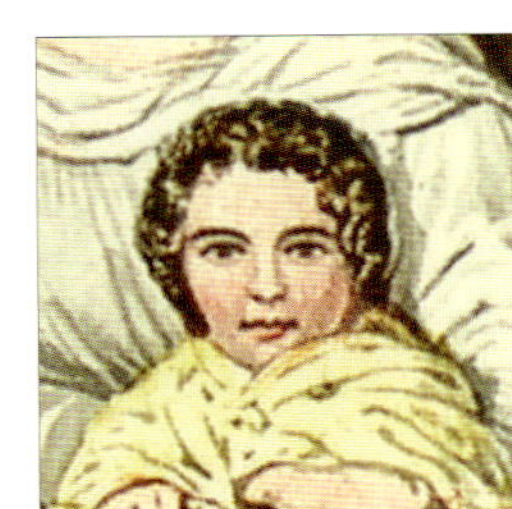

Fig. 7.35 Far left, Beale's slides for slide 1 of *The Wreck of the Hesperus* (Fig. 4.21); middle left, slide 1 of *The Little Match Girl* (Fig. 3.13); middle right, "America" from *Popular* Songs; *right,* "Return of the Dove" from the *Noah* group.

Chapter Eight

Beale's On-Screen World: Part One – Literature

Fig. 8.26 Beale's slide 5 of the twelve-slide set of *Home, Sweet Home*. Discussion on p. 200.

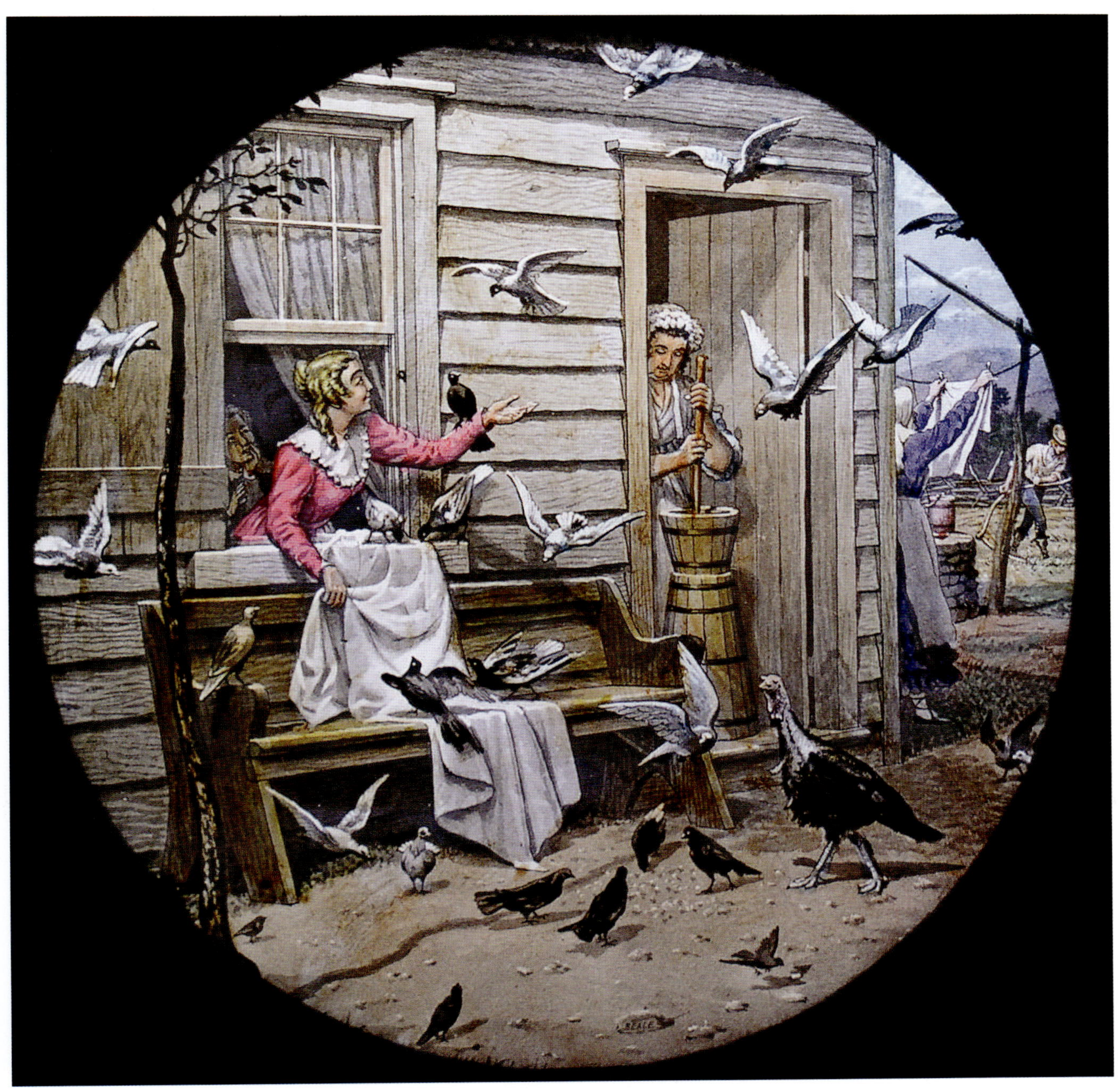

Introduction

The big-screen world that Beale created was fascinating – a world of literary chestnuts and Bible stories, of stirring history, of bizarre comedy and of even stranger Secret Society iconography – all re-imagined in a new kind of narrative art. Beale produced 2,085 lantern slide images.[1] Figuring one minute of screen time per slide (which is conservative, as lanternists often had a slide on screen for two or three minutes or more), that would equal 35 hours of programming. A movie today is a little more than an hour and a half long, so Beale's work would be equivalent to 20 full-length movies.

This prodigious output followed the broad tastes and interests of middle-class 19th and early 20th century culture, and the opportunities provided by "niche markets" for lantern-slide sales. Beale's *oeuvre* of 258 sets or groups[2] can be divided into six broad subject categories – Literature, Religion, History, Temperance, Secret Society, and Miscellaneous. I'll examine each of these categories in turn, looking at examples in each, following the order established in *Before the Movies*, which includes much more information about each set and slide than can be detailed in the lists here.[3]

Literary Works

This chapter will explore the first category, Beale's Literary works; the other categories will be handled in the next chapter.

The Literary works comprise 89 sets, totaling 789 slides. They make up some 30 percent of Beale's output, and account for about 25 percent of all literary slides offered in the lantern catalogs.[4] They include 5 Long Poems, 3 Novels and Long Stories, 8 Plays and Operas, 28 Parlor Poems, 19 Popular Songs, 7 Works of Religious Literature, 6 Short Stories, and 7 Comic Sketches. A list is at the chapter end. Except for the comic stories, the style Beale used for these Literary slides was his most detailed and sophisticated. Every aspect of setting, costume, and character was painted with extreme care. That gave these old "literary chestnuts" new excitement in a new medium, much as we today may "see anew" an ancient Shakespearean play portrayed in a movie with modern cinematic style.

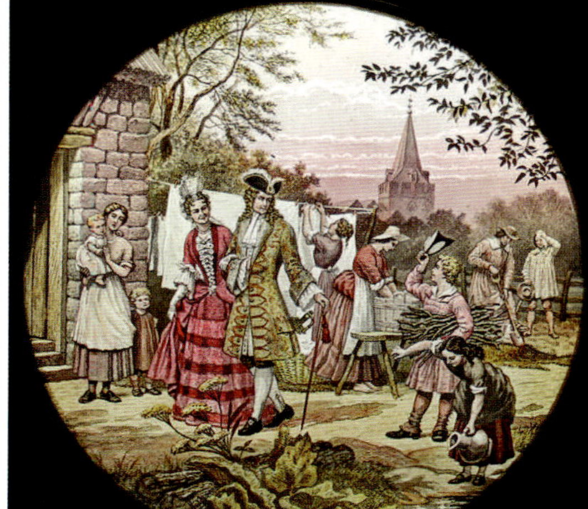

Fig. 8.1 Beale's slide 8 from *Elegy Written in a Country Churchyard* by Thomas Gray.

Literary – Long Poems

Among the most impressive of Beale's sets are some of his Long Poems. (Fig. 8.1).

We've already seen images from *Hiawatha* and *The Lady of the Lake,* subjects that gave Beale plenty of material for dramatic scenes in exotic settings. In addition to *Hiawatha,* two of Beale's other longer poetic works (*Evangeline* and *The Courtship of Miles Standish*) (Fig. 8.2) are by Henry Wadsworth Longfellow, as are four of the parlor poems.[5] In the Beale cannon, this puts Longfellow on a par with Shakespeare, who also has a total of seven works represented. That is about where the Victorians would have placed Longfellow in their literary pantheon. Though he is currently out of fashion, in the 1890s he was a revered and popular figure. His technical mastery, gripping stories, and melodious language earned him the privilege of having his bust placed in the Poet's Corner of Westminster Abbey, the first American to be so honored. Longfellow won his fame partly by creating mythic historical epics for his raw new country.

Of these *epic* poems, only *Hiawatha* has survived in the modern imagination, though those of us over 60 may also remember *Evangeline.* It is a sad, sad story, based on an actual event, the English "ethnic cleansing" of French Acadia in Nova Scotia from 1755 to 1764. Villagers were forcibly removed from their homes as their village burned, were put on ships and dropped at various ports in America. Many eventually made their way to Louisiana, where they became the people we know today as the Cajuns, an Americanized form of the French word "Acadians". In the poem, a young woman (Evangeline) and her lover (Gabriel) are separated in the upheaval.

She spends the rest of her lifetime searching for him throughout the American landscape. After finally becoming a nun, she eventually finds him dying in an almshouse.

The poem, *Evangeline*, though written by an American in English, has become a kind of national epic of the French-speaking Acadian Canadians, and of the Cajuns in America. We performed it, in English, at the cathedral in Quebec City to a packed audience. Although they had probably heard of the poem before, many had never actually *heard* it, and of course none had seen Beale's magic lantern version. I could feel them sinking into Evangeline's world, right from Longfellow's famous opening lines, which immediately convey a sense of sadness, "This is the forest primeval. The murmuring pines and hemlocks". Long poems and stories like *Evangeline* have become the central "core" of our shows. Without them, the full-length theater versions of our magic lantern shows seem like collages of bits and pieces. With them, the shows take on a feeling of substance, in part because these longer works deal with more complex themes, and in part because the audience has time to find their way into a unique literary and cinematic world.

In the *Evangeline* slide set, Beale's original pictures are mixed with close copies of those by another artist, Frank Dicksee, a British Pre-Raphaelite painter who rose to become President of the Royal Academy (RA), and who illustrated a deluxe 1882 printing of the poem.[6] "Borrowing" from another artist's work had several advantages as far as Briggs was concerned: It saved time and effort, and it built on an *iconography* that the audience already associated with the poem. In the case of Dicksee, it also borrowed the cachet of the "RA" stamp of approval. Whether or not Dicksee or his publisher were paid for these images is unclear; probably not. Intellectual ownership was treated rather cavalierly in the magic lantern trade, just as it was in the early days of the movies.

Of the 24 slides in the *Evangeline* set, eight are related to Dicksee. Four directly copy Dicksee's central image, "matching out" the picture to fit the lantern-slide aspect ratio. But even when Briggs and Beale are using so much of another artist's work, we can see their cinematic sensibility at work. In the disembarking scene (not shown) for instance, Briggs instructs Beale to "match out" the edges, and to make the next

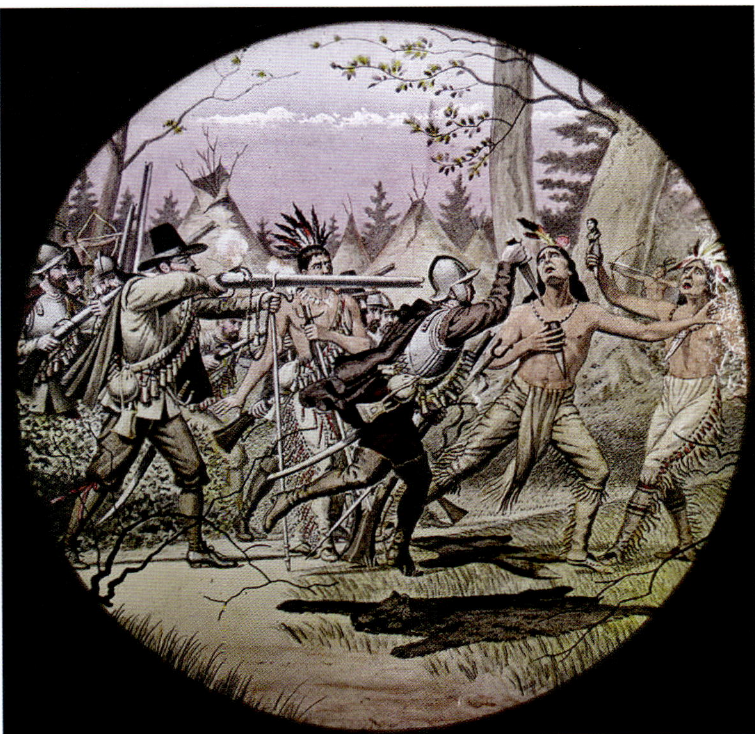

Fig. 8.2 Beale's slide 19 of the Long Poem, *Courtship of Miles Standish* by Henry Wadsworth Longfellow.

scene, which is a Beale original of Evangeline mourning her father (Fig. 8.3), "in ***harmony*** with it", thus ensuring continuity.[7]

In two images, Beale uses substantial portions of Dicksee's pictures, but also makes significant changes, and it is here that we can most clearly see Beale at work at changing book illustrations into sequential magic lantern art. The first image is a "matched out" copy of a Dicksee picture, a daytime *shot* of Evangeline at the prow of a boat on the Mississippi, searching for her lover (Fig. 8.4).

Beale largely ignores Dicksee's second picture of Evangeline in the swamps. Instead, he uses the same basic boat scene of Fig. 8.4 again, but

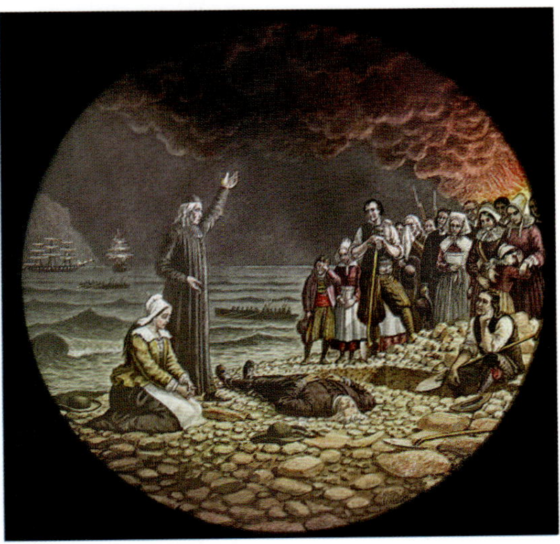

Fig. 8.3 Beale's slide 15 of *Evangeline* by Henry Wadsworth Longfellow, a Beale original.

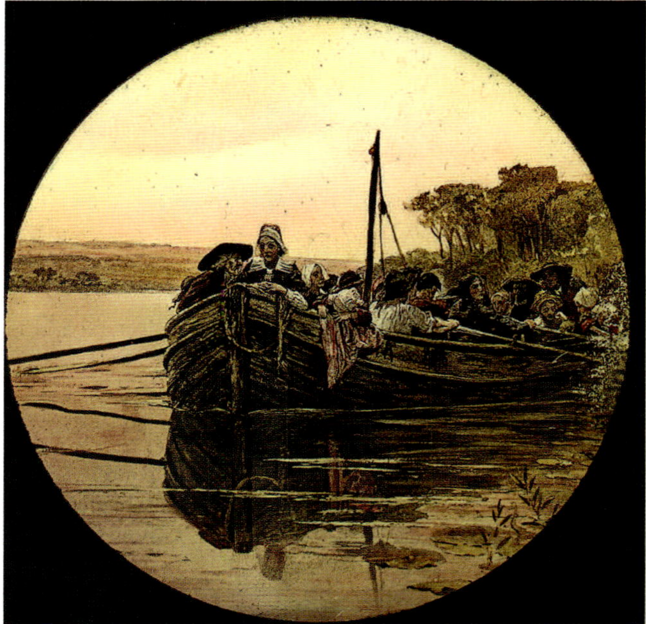

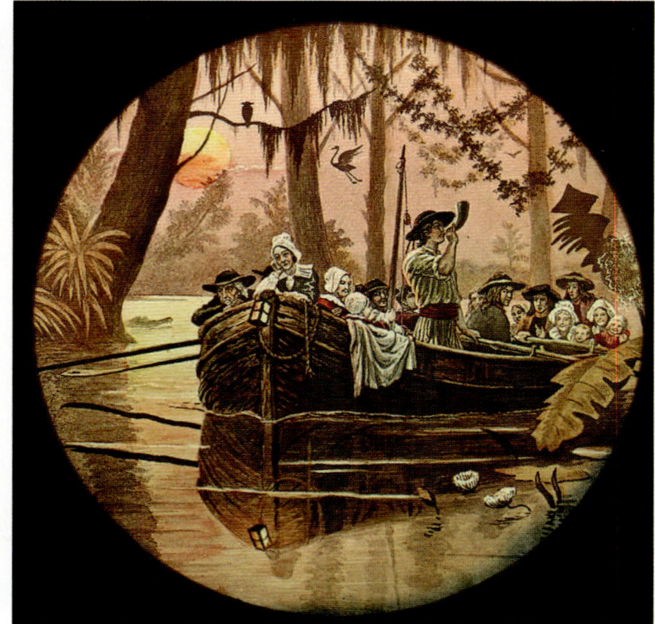

Fig. 8.4 ***(left)*** **Beale's slide 16 of** ***Evangeline,*** **a close copy of an image by Frank Dicksee.**

Fig. 8.5 ***(right)*** **Beale's slide 17 of** ***Evangeline,*** **a Beale original dissolve.**

completely transmutes its environment to create a moonlit night for greater visual drama. He frames the boat in almost exactly the same position that it was in before. This gives him the deep space to pack in the pictorial reinforcement for Longfellow's verbal detail, but also makes the two views into an effect dissolve, suggesting that day and night, Evangeline's search goes on (Fig. 8.5).

I always love to come to this point when presenting *Evangeline* in our *Valentine Show*, for the moment is a heart-stopper for the audience, and for me as well. The dissolve is spectacular. In the second slide, a blood red sun sinks behind the boat, casting a red glow over everything. "Tenebrous boughs of the cypress", and "trailing mosses" – details described by Longfellow – emphasize the maze in which Evangeline is now lost. An owl greets the moon "with demonic laughter", and a "grim alligator" suggests the "sad forebodings of evil" that Evangeline faces. As before, the boat is jammed with refugees – men, women, children – their bed linen hanging over the side. Evangeline's face remains, as ever, at the prow of the boat, always seeking Gabriel. But now Beale has *underlit* her face with a lamp. The lamp itself is reflected in the water before her, like the will-o'-the-wisp of hope she pursues:

> But Evangeline's heart was sustained by a vision, that faintly/
> Floated before her eyes, and beckoned her on through the moonlight.

What began as Dicksee's murky illustration becomes in Beale's hands a dramatic, attention-sustaining, image of perseverance, as once again Evangeline ends another day in her lifelong search. The image is made all the more telling because we learn as the scene *fades to dark* that Gabriel is in fact nearby in the swamps, but does not hear the horn being blown in Evangeline's boat, and so does not answer its call:

> But not a voice replied; no answer came from the darkness;
> And, when the echoes had ceased, like a sense of pain was the silence.

It is the closest the two lovers come for 30 years, and Beale has found the way to give the moment its full narrative impact.

Literary – Novels and Long Stories

In addition to long poems, Beale also illustrated three long stories and books – *Marley's Ghost, Robinson Crusoe*, and *Uncle Tom's Cabin*.

We perform *Marley's Ghost* (*A Christmas Carol*)[8] every year at Christmas, and you've already seen several of Beale's wonderful slides from it. As you might imagine, it's an audience favorite. Everybody loves to hear, once again, the old Christmas stories.

Uncle Tom's Cabin was one of the most popular books of the 19th century. Briggs did not produce his lantern set until 1882; attribution of it to Beale is "somewhat uncertain".[9] The 1882 slide images were very closely based on the book's illustrations by Hammatt Billings. In 1894 Beale created a new version of a key scene, "Eva's Dying Farewell", which replaced the original Billings-like illustration (Fig. 8.6).

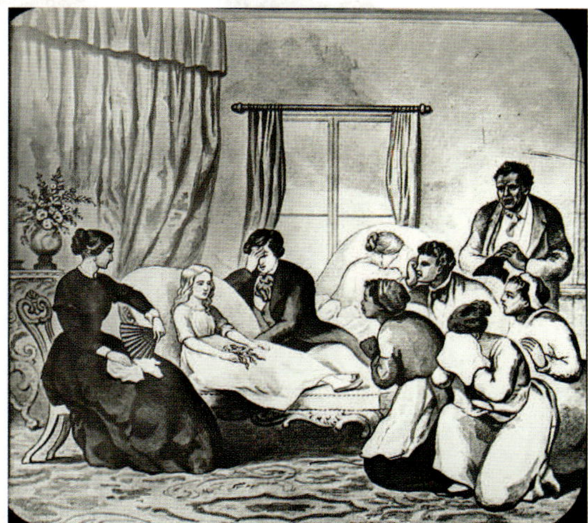

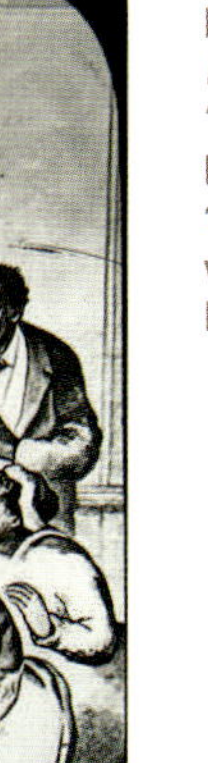

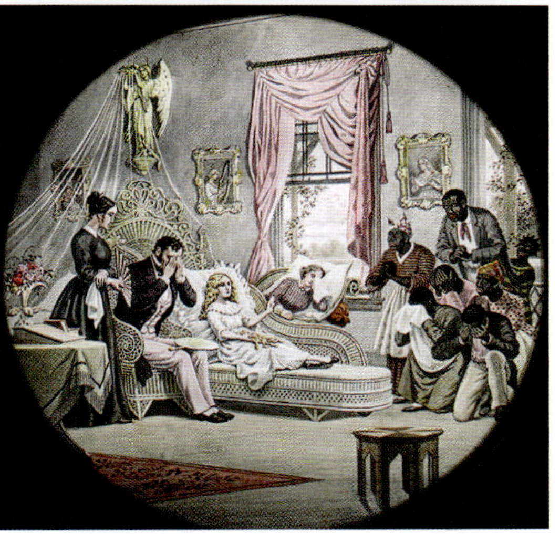

Fig. 8.6 Slide 10 of *Uncle Tom's Cabin*, "Eva's Dying Farewell", in the 1882 Billings-copy version, and the 1894 Beale version.

Several things stand out when comparing the two images. Beale's *mise-en-scène* is much more elaborate, as befits Eva's wealthy home. Eva is surmounted by a large angel, holding over her a gauze train, symbolic of her ascension to Heaven which is soon to come. The slave girl Topsy now appears among the slave mourners, harkening to the past when she and Eva appeared in slide 8 as friends. These kinds of changes are just the sort that we have seen Beale make in many other instances – part of his skill as a lantern-slide illustrator, where he often hints at action before and after the moment depicted in the slide. Finally, I'm sorry to say, the Beale depiction of Tom and the other slaves is much more stereotyped than it was in the Billings illustration.

Uncle Tom's Cabin is an example of how reactions to a lantern story can change over time. The book, and the lantern show, were extremely popular among Victorians. In the modern period, we performed *Uncle Tom's Cabin* for a half-dozen years at the home of the book's author, Harriet Beecher Stowe, in Hartford, Conn. But today, live performances of this piece are problematic because many Black people see "Uncle Tom" as an offensive term meaning excessively obedient. To forestall objections, we introduced the performance by explaining that the book was an anti-slavery polemic. In fact, Lincoln is reputed to have greeted Stowe by saying, "So this is the woman who started the war". But after Stowe's death, stage performances turned the story into an entirely different comedic production, featuring a chattering Topsy, and a groveling "Yassa Boss" Uncle Tom, which led to the term's current meaning, and the current difficulties in presenting it.

In the two parallel stories of the book, Tom is not the firebrand that another slave named George Harris is, but he never accepts the idea that his soul can be owned by another, and defies the slaver Legree in the ending scene. Still, even within the context of the author's home, *Uncle Tom* was hard for a white man such as myself to present to modern multi-racial audiences. We kept the lantern show alive by producing a version for the University of Virginia's massive academic website on *Uncle Tom's Cabin* where it ran for 20 years. Unfortunately, it was created with a digital program that is now obsolete, so for the time being, the video has been taken down, and the "*UTC*" lantern show is rarely seen today.

Such long works as *Uncle Tom's Cabin* presented Beale with a problem not found in the poems and short stories, where the original short piece of literature itself was the script for the lantern-slide presentation, though perhaps edited down a bit. With a parlor poem, relatively few slides could keep the action moving. But how could Beale create a 12-slide narrative version that was a *faithful adaptation*, to say nothing of a *literal adaptation*, of a novel such as *Uncle Tom's Cabin*, or *Robinson Crusoe*, a 330-page book?

Several different options were commonly employed in the lantern industry. A book of British *scripts* for *Robinson Crusoe* is interesting because it contains several different approaches in one publication.[10]

The first approach is what might be called the ***explicit summary***.

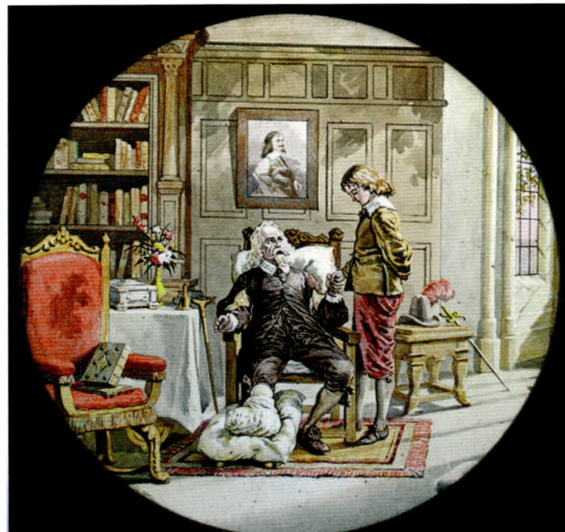

Fig. 8.7 Beale's slide 1 of ***Robinson Crusoe*** by Daniel Defoe.

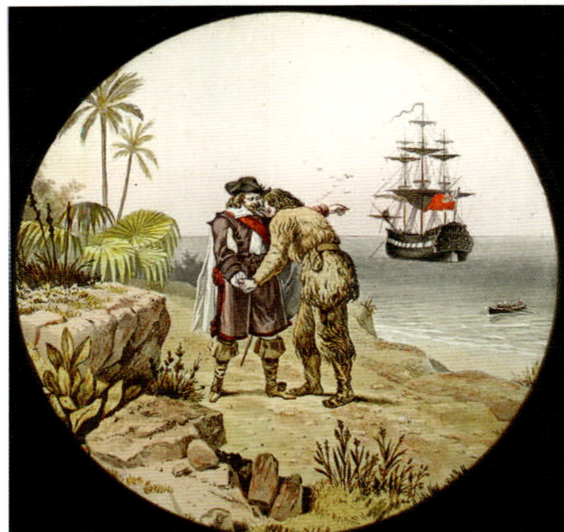

Fig. 8.8 Beale's slide 12 of ***Robinson Crusoe***.

> In the ... picture we see Robinson Crusoe filled with the stories he had read, and the tales he had heard, announcing to his father who is laid up with gout that he has fully made up his mind, and wants to go to sea (Fig. 8.7).

Here there is an explicit link to the slide ("in the ... picture") and a summary of the action, without using the words of the author. Clearly the lantern scriptwriters felt a freedom to cut by using *elliptical editing* and changing the *plot* elements when moving from the literary work to the magic lantern medium.

The problem with the summary approach is that it loses all flavor of the original literature, and, since it is a synopsis, also loses vivid detail. Hence, from a magic lantern art point of view, it also loses any possibility of linking word and image, as Beale was so skillful at doing. (The summary could be quite dramatic in its own right. Writes our author, or "compiler" as he calls himself, "A ship in sight! Yes! It really seemed true at last! But surely his eyes must deceive him! Crusoe calls Friday and together they both look ...". (Beale choses not to show us the ship sighting, but Crusoe's meeting with his rescuer, Fig. 8.8).

In the compiler's second approach, contained in this same publication, he writes an entirely new, ***versified*** version. This one seems to be designed to make the story more appealing to very young viewers:

> But though from the waters he thus had been spared,
> Most wretched was now his condition:
> Night saw him wet, hungry, and bleeding, prepared
> In a tree to take up his position.

Whether this dreadful poetry would actually hold the attention of the young better than would the original or the summary I doubt, but the attempt at least shows an effort to adapt the same material for different age groups.

The third method the script writers used is what we might call the ***summary/quote*** or ***abridged*** approach – providing summaries and transitions when necessary, dropping out unnecessary material in ellipses, but using as much of the original language as possible, including the dialogue. A Briggs script for *Uncle Tom's Cabin* – the only one extant for a novel – uses this technique, which suggests that it was the usual Briggs approach. No Briggs script for *Crusoe* exists, but here is another company's abridged version. Almost every word is from Defoe. Many pages of the novel have been condensed to a few lines (Fig. 8.9).

> He set up his tent – made of part of an old sail ... . He made a fence so strong that neither man nor beast could get over it. Into the fence or fortress with infinite labour I [sic] carried all my riches, all my provisions, ammunition and stores; and I also made a large tent to preserve me from the rains that in one part of the year are very violent there. I made it double, vis. – one small tent within, and one larger tent above it, and covered the uppermost part of it with a large tarpaulin.

I prefer this summary/quote approach, despite this compiler's awkward shift from third to first person. It gives the greatest feel for the author's language; it is often livelier than a summary, especially in the dialogue; and it makes maximum use of Beale's visual links to details in the *sound track*.

Like the *Crusoe* "compiler", I have not hesitated

to move the story and the slides around to make the most coherent and exciting narrative possible. One of my techniques for telling long stories when few slides are available is to add slides drawn from other sources, so that the story will flow more smoothly, just as the movies used *cover shots* for this purpose. I have found old lantern-slide scripts where lanternists used this same approach, penciling in extra slides.[11] In the case of *Crusoe*, I add a fabulous (non-Beale) slide of a double waterspout to explain Crusoe's shipwreck more fully (Fig. 8.10). I also add the swirling ghost shapes of a tank slide to provide frightening effects when Crusoe discovers a human footprint, and a pastoral English scene to show him home again after his ordeal on the island. Taking the opposite tack, I sometimes delete slides in order to simplify the story and remove sub plots that would detract from coherence in relatively short presentations to audiences who may not be familiar with the book.

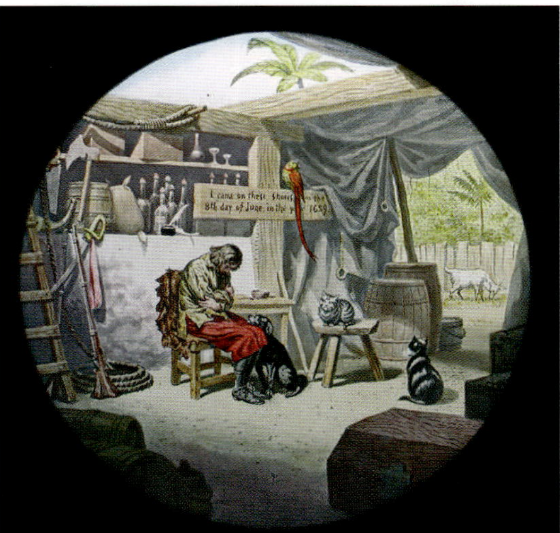

Fig. 8.9 Beale slide 4 of *Robinson Crusoe*.

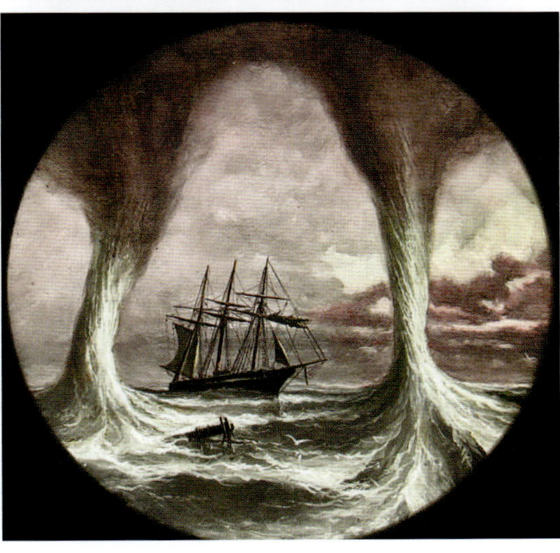

Fig. 8.10 Slide, not by Beale, of two waterspouts.

Literary Slides – Plays and Opera

Drama was another literary subject in Beale's repertoire. He illustrated seven plays, and one opera. We use his opera, *Carmen*, in our *Valentine Show*, switching around the slides so that they illustrate the opera's most famous aria, the "Habanera", and that works very well. One play, *Pygmalion and Galatea* by William Gilbert, we have already discussed at length in Chapter 2.

The other six plays are by Shakespeare. The choice of Shakespeare is obvious enough, but I must admit that the depiction of Shakespeare's plays is generally disappointing. That is probably because Briggs chose to make most of the sets by overpainting existing engravings – the outline drawings of Moritz Retzsch we have already mentioned – and then filling out the set with a few new Beale pictures.[12] Many of the slides look like photos of a stage production, with the characters all prerforming in a row. The famous "three witches" scene of *Macbeth* is an exception. It is certainly dramatic, and backed with details from Shakespeare's text, like the line of kings in the background. (Fig. 8.11).

Just how these play and opera slide sets were meant to be used is unclear. No "dramatic readings" or scripts are extant, though a condensed story for *Pygmalion* exists. I've never tried to perform the Shakespeare plays, and as a result, I have had no first-hand experience with audience reaction. Nor have I ever read any 19th century descriptions of a magic lantern play being performed. My best guess is that these slides were designed for school or lecture "educational summaries", or "play readings" in chautauquas and homes – a common pastime of the period in which people would gather together to read a play out loud (Fig. 8.12). This hypothesis is supported by the fact that though the sets generally cover the entire play, they put great emphasis on the high-points. Most sets concentrate many slides on one scene – a pattern found elsewhere in Beale's work, where the same practice is used to speed up the momentum of dramatic story moments.[13]

Literary Slides – Parlor Poetry

If we're looking for popular literature with a clear audience, we need only turn to Parlor Poetry – poems so well-known that they were often performed by family members in their parlors. These poems are the mainstays of our

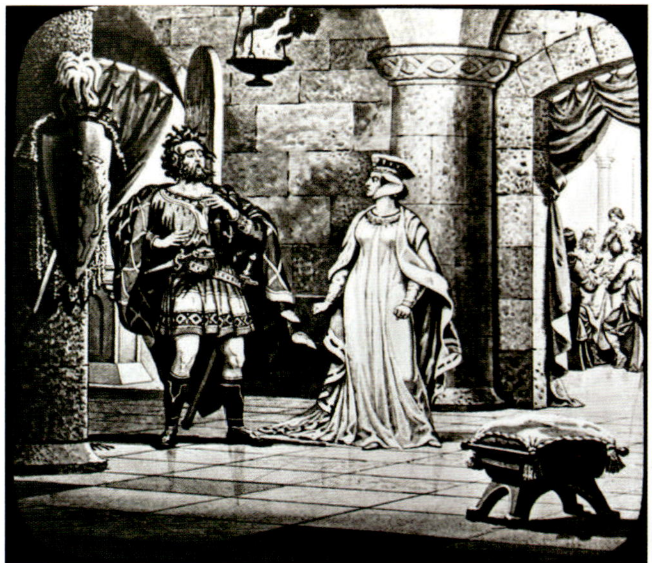

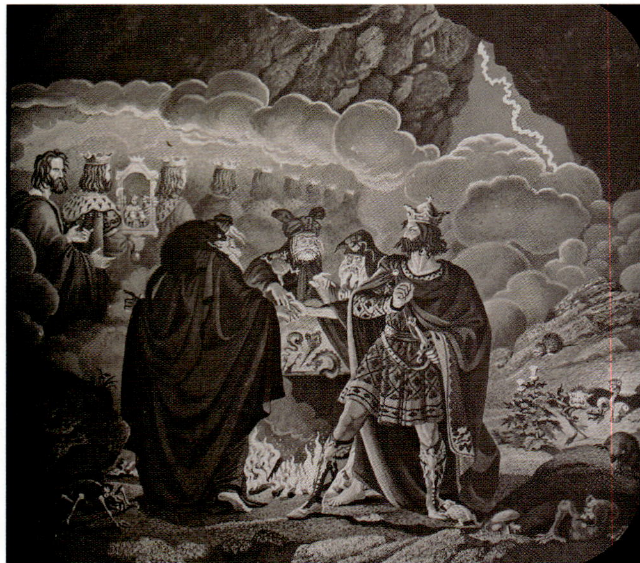

Fig. 8.11 Beale's slides 4 and 9 from *MacBeth* by Shakespeare. At left, the slide that we saw him sketching earlier. At right, the slide of the witches' scene, copied directly from Moritz Retzsch.

shows – short stories, in rhyme, that really grab and hold an audience's attention. Altogether, Beale dramatized 28 of these short poems, totaling over 200 slides, or about 10% of his entire output. These poems have clear moral teachings, and exciting drama – the product of a middle class bent on solidifying its *centrist* values. In them, heroes always arrive in the nick of time, laborers prefer their life of honest toil, lovers navigate their *rites of passage*, and children are killed off with distressing frequency ... but of course their deaths impart a moral lesson.

Parlor poems were tremendously popular in the lantern period, many of them known, in that telling phrase, "by heart". Today, almost everyone can recite portions of only two, *The Night Before Christmas* (Fig. 8.13), and *The Raven*. At our *Christmas Show*, I can hear the audience following my narration under its collective breath, and it *never* fails to supply the missing words when I pause for them at the end of the line, "Not a creature was stirring, not even a ... ". Many adults also know the key line, "Quoth the Raven … ". But beyond those two, modern knowledge of Victorian parlor poetry falls off sharply.

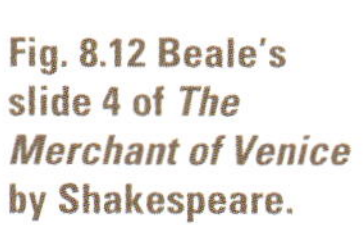

Fig. 8.12 Beale's slide 4 of *The Merchant of Venice* by Shakespeare.

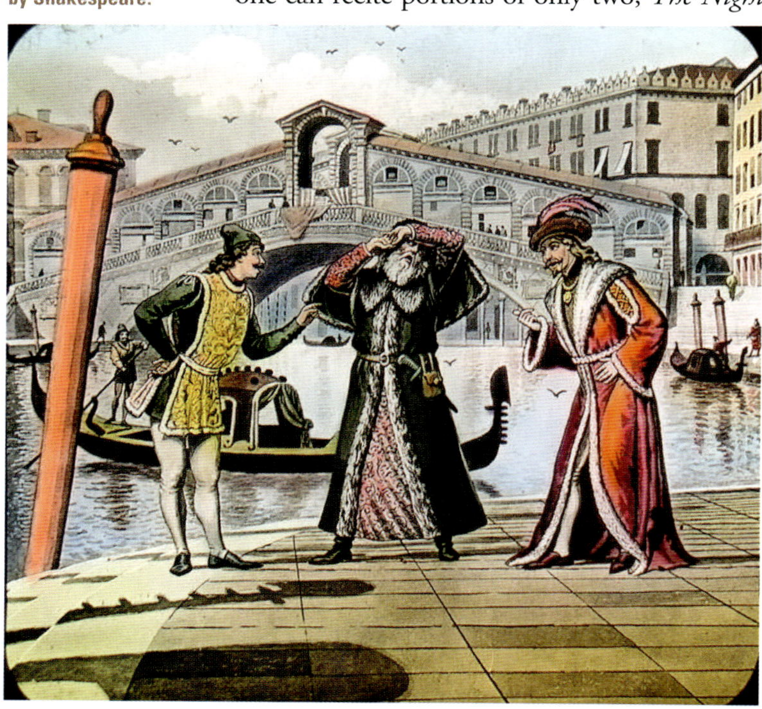

One hundred years ago that was not the case. My father, born in 1901, used to impress me by being able to recite a dozen of these poems. I've since discovered that he wasn't unusual. Many, many of his contemporaries could do the same. They learned the poems in school, recited them in class, and performed them as part of family entertainments. Adults performed them for their friends too, as did professionals in music halls and vaudeville shows. It's easy to see then why parlor poetry would be a major portion of the magic lantern literary repertoire. Fathers might buy slides to impress the relatives with their own *voice-over* performances or to encourage the oratorical genius of their children. Schools might buy them for literary and elocution lessons. Church groups might present "moral entertainment", and professional performers might use them to enhance their theatrical presentations.

Of all the parlor poems, *The Raven*, is one of Beale's most spectacular production of magic lantern art, the images unique in portrayals of Poe's poem.[14] When we perform it in our *Halloween Show*, accompanied by Beethoven's Sonata, Opus 10, No. 3 on the piano, I've often seen its combination of reality and fantasy rivet children as young as three or four, despite the poem's archaic language, lack of plot *linearity*, complex *symbolism*, literary *allusions*, histrionic acting, and adult subject matter.

A one-room set defines the constricted physical and *psychological space* of the poem, a *mise-en-scène* that Beale uses brilliantly to stretch the meaning of the text. At first the room is presented realistically, in great detail, but then gradually changes as the protagonist's madness increases (Fig. 8.14). Charles Musser, in his classic book, *The Emergence of Cinema,* describes Beale's "camera work" this way:

> The perspective shifts, "moving in" and "panning" from right to left for the first three slides and then "pulling back" for the fourth. This spatial disunity creates a mood of unease and disorientation, well-suited to the poem. It also sets up the next slides, in which specters appear. Specifically, the progression from slides four to five, and then from seven through ten retain single perspectives, and display excellent continuity. By dissolving from one view to the next, the exhibitor could thus create a particularly haunting series of images.[15]

The effectiveness of Beale's treatment of the poem is not only in the "camera work". In the first scenes of *The Raven*, Beale presents an abundance of sharply-defined reality – individual paintings on the wall, complex rug patterns, ornate book bindings. The lighting of the first slide is high key and even, with three-point lighting (fire, lamp, door) providing the sense of a warm and comfortable home, though a sad one. Everything throughout the depth of field is in sharp focus. But even these first "realistic" details of the room prefigure the protagonist's fraught imaginative mind. Portraits on the wall may remind him (and us) of those loved ones he has already lost. The grandfather clock not only tracks time during the poem, but the decorations over its face foreshadow the demon's eyes that will be mentioned later in the poem. A billowing curtain at the open window is portrayed realistically, but is a set-up for the final scene.

As the poem progresses, the first-person protagonist, the "I" who narrates the poem and who looks very much like Poe, never leaves the room. He moves from fireplace, to door, to window, to chair – so that the audience is continually seeing something different in the three-sided set. And, while Beale's "camera" *tracks* him, we feel his agitation as he stalks restlessly about his caged mind, trying to comprehend the meaning of the raven croaking above him. The sense of manic action is heightened by the theatrical stance of the protagonist, using a series of Victorian oratorical gestures that Beale was an expert on, since he had illustrated a textbook on the subject (Fig. 8.15).[16] (This melodramatic style was also common in the early movies, which often used the same kind of frontal and mannered acting.)

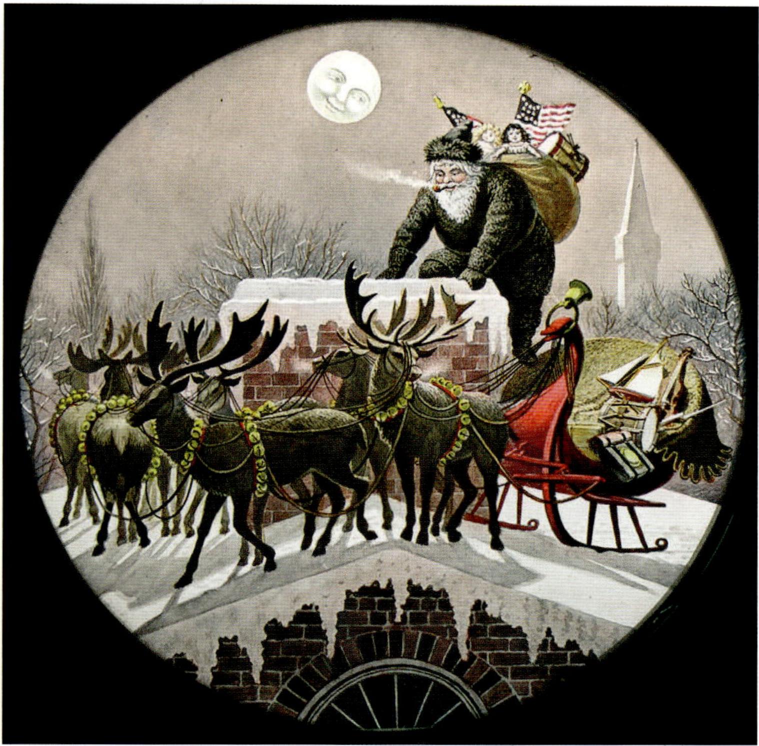

Fig. 8.13 Beale's slide 4 for *Visit of Saint Nicholas*, as *The Night Before Christmas* was called in the lantern catalogs.

A flashback (not shown) depicts Poe's protagonist as he once was, curled in the chair with his lover. A truly chilling effect dissolve – the one Musser describes – begins with this *lyrical* scene

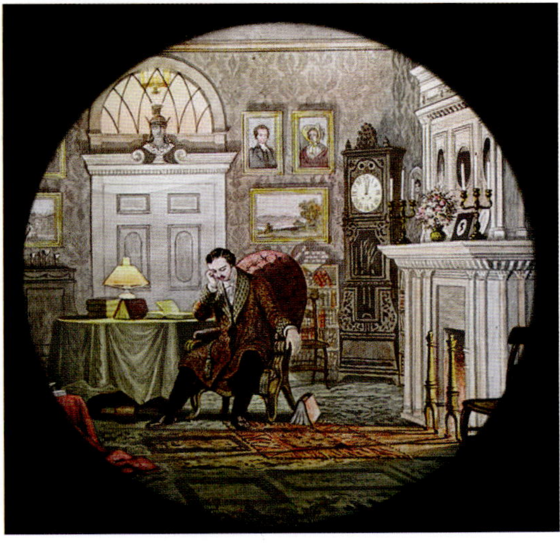

Fig. 8.14 Beale's slide 1 of *The Raven* by Edgar Allen Poe.

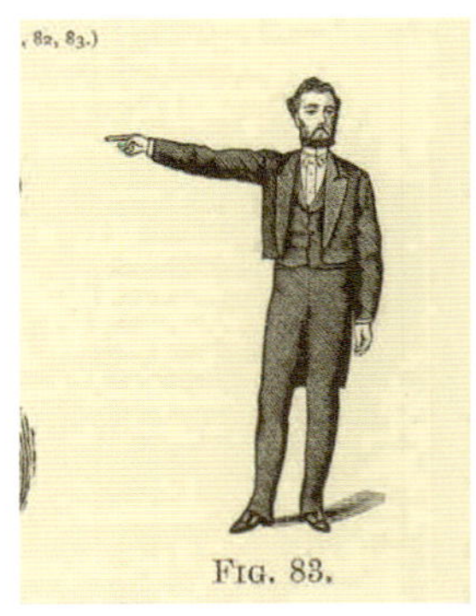

Fig. 8.15 Beale's drawing of the gesture for "Emphatic Designation" in *A Manual of Gesture*, which he illustrated.

of former bliss, and then transforms it. Spectacular angels take his lover to Heaven (Fig. 8.16), an image directly suggested by the text. But then, in an image entirely from Beale's imagination, the protagonist associates the raven with a ghastly vision of winged Death wielding his scythe (Fig. 8.17). "'Prophet!' said I, 'thing of evil! – prophet still, if bird or devil'!"

While these transformations are occurring, Beale changes the mise-en-scène, slide by slide, to create a new reality, again using images not mentioned in the poem text itself. As the action turns from the initial slide, we lose track of the fire, and can no longer see its warm glow. The scenes gradually become darker, and the lighting harder and more stark. The details of the room recede, as *sharp focus* gives way to *soft focus*. The lamp, once a bright yellow, burns steadily lower. In the next-to-last scene it sputters out in smoke. The pictures on the wall turn, slide by slide, along with all the rest of the room, into a ghostly blur of soft focus, as the real world disintegrates (Fig. 8.18).

These changes do not just happen in the mind of the protagonist. The "screen world" Beale shows us is no longer the "real world" that we

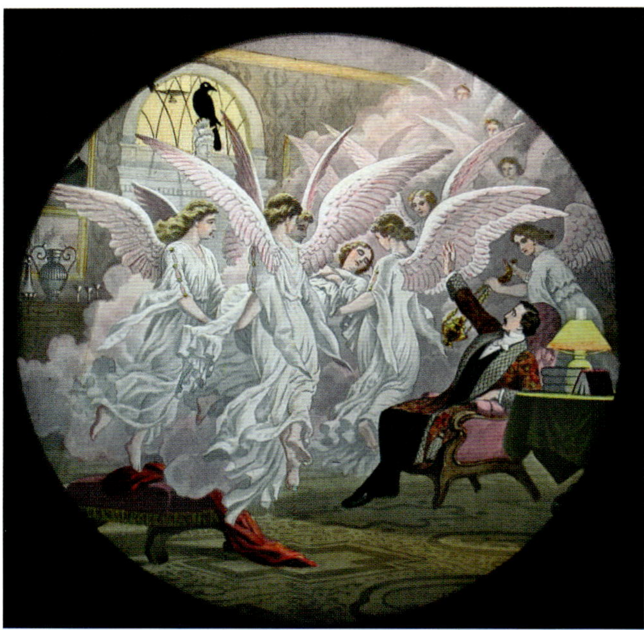

Fig. 8.16 Beale's slide 7 of *The Raven*.

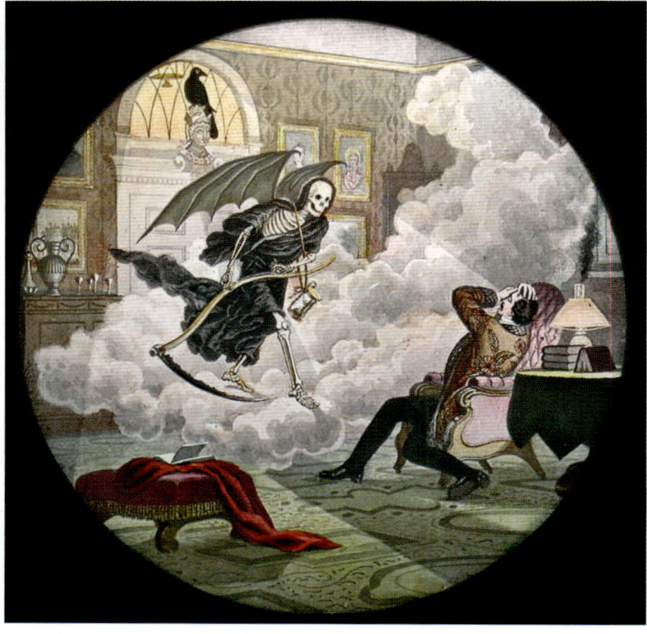

Fig. 8.17 Beale's slide 8 of *The Raven*.

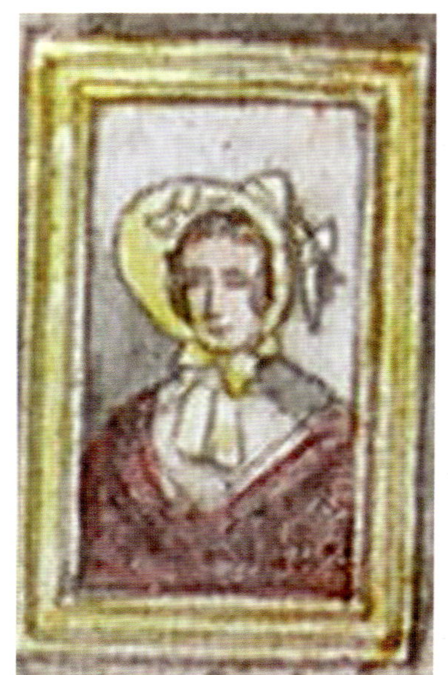

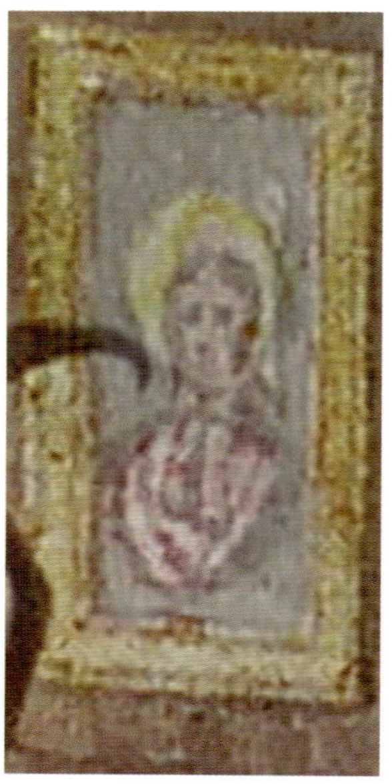

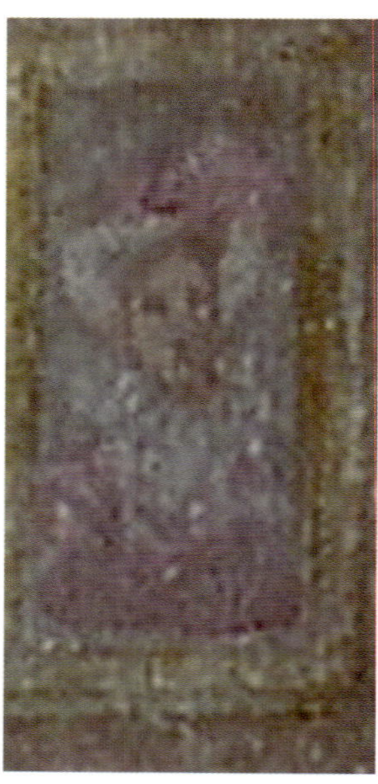

Fig. 8.18 Detail of pictures on the wall in slides 1, 8, and 12 of Beale's *The Raven*. "Reality" slowly disintegrates.

saw in the first image. We now see the room the way *the protagonist* sees the room. As it changes in his deteriorating mind, we experience the same changes ourselves, seeing it all from his point of view. In effect, we enter his consciousness, and lose contact with the real world along with him. We lose our own reality in his reality. His eye becomes our eye. His "I" becomes our "I".

In the final scene, the protagonist has collapsed and lies prostrate on the floor (Fig. 8.19). The snows of winter blow over him through the open window. The curtain now looks like a hooded phantom, reaching toward him with a giant claw. The details of reality such as the pictures on the walls are almost completely lost. No light comes from the fire. The lamp is dead. The only lighting is outside the room, coming through the transom. It leaves the room a maze of low-key shadows. The raven is entirely a silhouette, emphasizing its sinister blackness. It sits above the statue of Pallas, goddess of wisdom and freedom, and completely dominates it. Their combined shadow overwhelms the man, his body, his life. It even reaches out to the edge of the slide frame, toward us. As the poem hurtles toward its final line, the protagonist's soul merges with our own.

> And my soul from out that shadow,
>
> That lies floating on the floor,
>
> Shall be lifted, ... Nevermore.

Literary – Popular Songs

Closely related to the stories and poems were Beale's Popular Songs. In the lantern age, when almost every middle-class family had a piano and almost everyone played it, songs were a natural genre to develop into lantern-slide sets, and they are among the most frequently found sets today. Lantern slides for songs could be used in home settings, as well as in schools, and in theatrical venues, where professional voices would lift the production to a whole new height. In addition, since many stories had opportunities for songs within them, songs could be woven into other lantern-slide presentations. The Lucas Museum's collection contains one lantern story "reading" where the music for the songs is included in the printed *script*, and another where song titles have been added with hand-written notes.

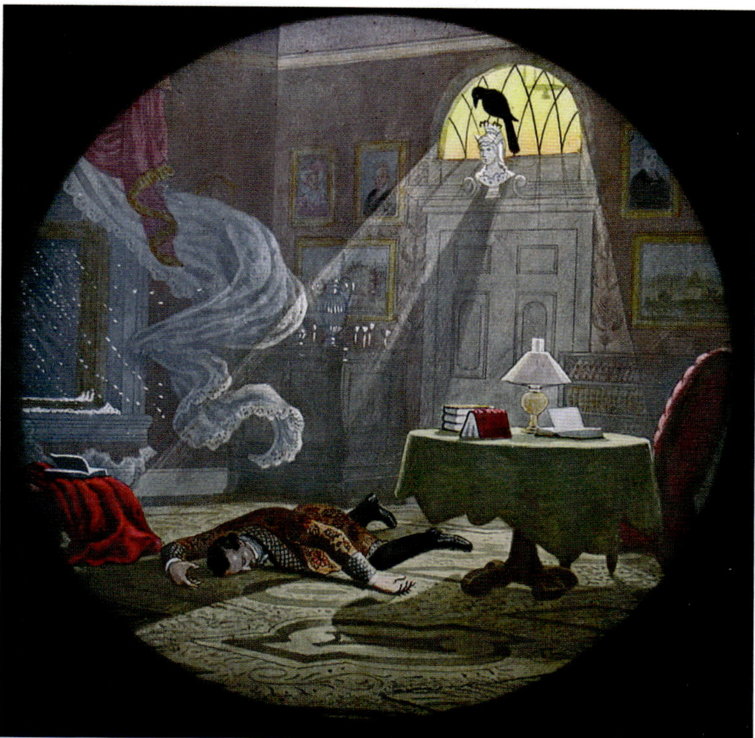

Fig. 8.19 Beale's slide 12 from *The Raven*.

Four of Beale's song sets are patriotic (e.g. *America),* eight are about war (*Tenting Tonight*), seven are sentimental songs of home – *Auld Lang Syne* (Fig. 8.20) and *Swanee Ribber* – plus one group of comic songs.

Many of the patriotic songs Beale illustrated are still well known. When we perform our *Patriotic History Show* for schools, we send the music to the music teacher in advance, and encourage her to make each grade responsible for a differ-

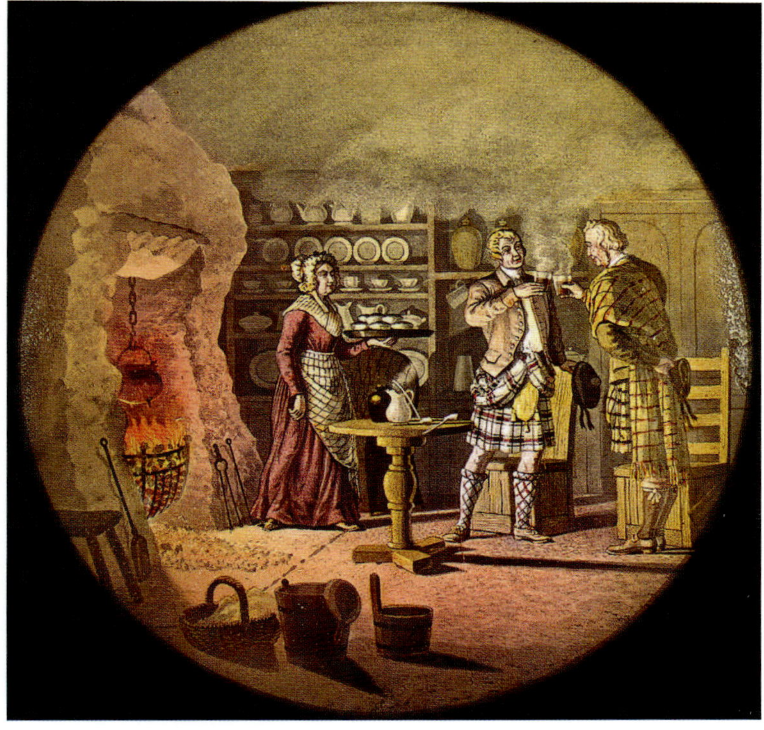

Fig. 8.20 Beale's slide 2 from *Auld Lang Syne*.

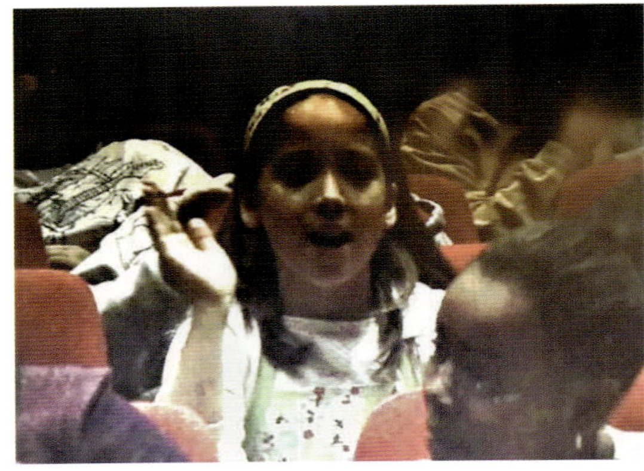

Fig. 8.21 A fifth grader at one of our shows claps the beat as she sings "Yankee Doodle".

ent song. Hearing modern kids belt out *Yankee Doodle* gives some sense of the energy that was generated by the shared culture of public singing a century and a half ago (Fig. 8.21). But even in our adult shows, where no opportunity exists for advance coaching, everyone swings right into the patriotic songs, especially in times of war. They also join readily in the chorus of *Home Sweet Home* – the most popular secular song of the nineteenth century. All modern audiences know at least one line, which I'm sure you know too, as it was imbedded in modern consciousness by the movie of *The Wizard of Oz* – "There's no place like home".

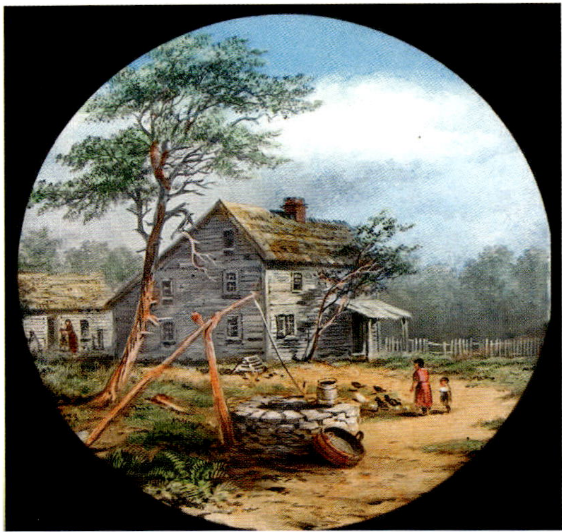

Fig. 8.22 Slide 1 of the four-slide set of *Home, Sweet Home* by John Howard Payne.

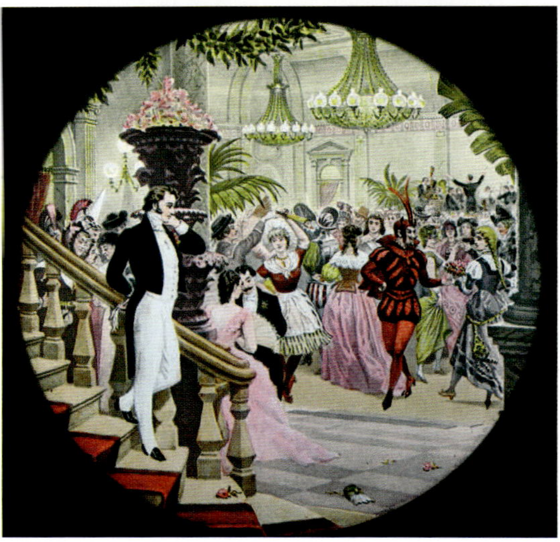

Fig. 8.23 Beale's slide 2 of the four-slide set of *Home, Sweet Home.*

Home, Sweet Home is one of Beale's most touching sets. It was so popular that it was expanded from one slide to four in 1887, and then again to 12 by 1906, but the set of four gives a sense of its impact.[17]

In the first slide of the four (Fig. 8.22), we see the old homestead in an image that is not by Beale. The house is a small and run-down, but it is still the beloved home of the young American who leaves it to travel abroad.

The second image is a dramatic contrast to the simple homestead – a scene "mid palaces and pleasures" (Fig. 8.23). The young American has been invited to a fancy dress ball. He is elaborately dressed himself, but he stands off to the side, an outcast. At the center of the whirling dancers struts a red devil, symbolizing the dangers of this fancy life. The devil dances with a lovely girl holding a bundle of roses. Perhaps it was she who rejected the young foreigner, discarding one of her roses at his feet.

In the third slide (Fig. 8.24) we see a flashback scene of the old homestead which contrasts with the lonely merry-making of the dress ball. This time we see the young man basking in the warmth of a roaring fire, luxuriating in his family's love, making music together with the lovely girl.

In the final slide (Fig. 8.25), the prodigal son finally returns from his travels. His parents are old and gray. The mantle is no longer decorated with flowers, but the fire still burns bright, and, at the center of the image, loving hands reach out toward an embrace. There *is* "no place like home", and the contrasting images that Beale creates make us feel the meaning of those famous words all the more deeply.

When Beale came to expand the *Home, Sweet Home* set in 1906, he added a number of wonderful images, both of the young man wandering in the cities and ballrooms of the world, and of farm life back home – feeding the chickens, basking in the sun, skating on the pond. My personal favorite is of a beautiful young girl, perhaps a sister or "the-girl-left-behind", Fig. 8.26, which is used at the start of this chapter. She is feeding the doves that swirl around her, while her top-lit hair burns like gold. The doves suggest purity, and perhaps hovering angels.

Their *overlapping* wings create an extraordinary sense of depth that leads the eye directly in toward the door and window, and then into Home itself, where Grandmother is just visible. Various other family members go about their chores in the distance, all working happily together to support their simple life. A turkey, symbol of American Thanksgiving, struts proudly toward a slender young tree, sure to grow with time. As indeed it does. In slides depicting the farm some 20 years later the tree takes on stately form.

Even with just the four initial slides, we can see Beale building up a layer of narrative art with roses and devils that is not described by the song lines. And, since the words of a song do not provide as much descriptive detail as does a piece of literature, when he gets to the 12-slide set Beale is free to generate even more specifics on his own, creating his broader immersive symbolism of flying doves, strutting turkeys and growing trees – all to stretch the lyrics, and help us lose ourselves in this tribute to the American Home.

Three of Beale's sentimental songs are set in a Black context, *Swanee Ribber (Old Folks at Home)*, published in 1851, *Old Kentucky Home* in 1853, and *Old Black Joe*, in 1860 – all before the abolition of slavery. They were composed by Stephen Foster, probably the most popular 19th century song writer, whose popularity continued well into the 20th century. The three songs, and Beale's images for them, form a fascinating commentary on slavery.

Because Foster was white and his subject matter was Black, there has been a wide variety of opinion about the appropriateness of the songs for use in a modern context, though two of them are sung regularly (in somewhat altered versions), as the official songs of Florida (*Swanee River*) and Kentucky (*Old Kentucky Home*). I grew up in the 1940's singing these songs in school, and hearing a record of them performed at home by the great Black singer and political activist Paul Robeson. Robeson made his own accommodations to the sensibilities of his time, using Foster's word "darkies" in his rendition of *Old Kentucky Home*, but changing *Old Black Joe* to *Poor Old Joe*.

Foster's *Old Folks at Home* (*Swanee Ribber)* was written in dialect as a minstrel song. It sugar-

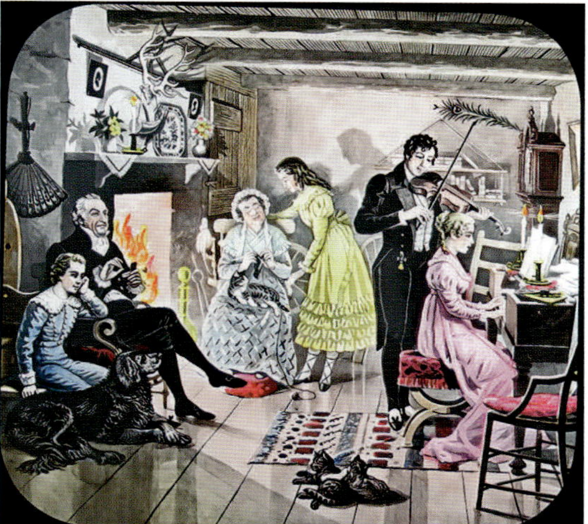

Fig. 8.24 Beale's slide 3 of the four-slide set of *Home, Sweet Home*.

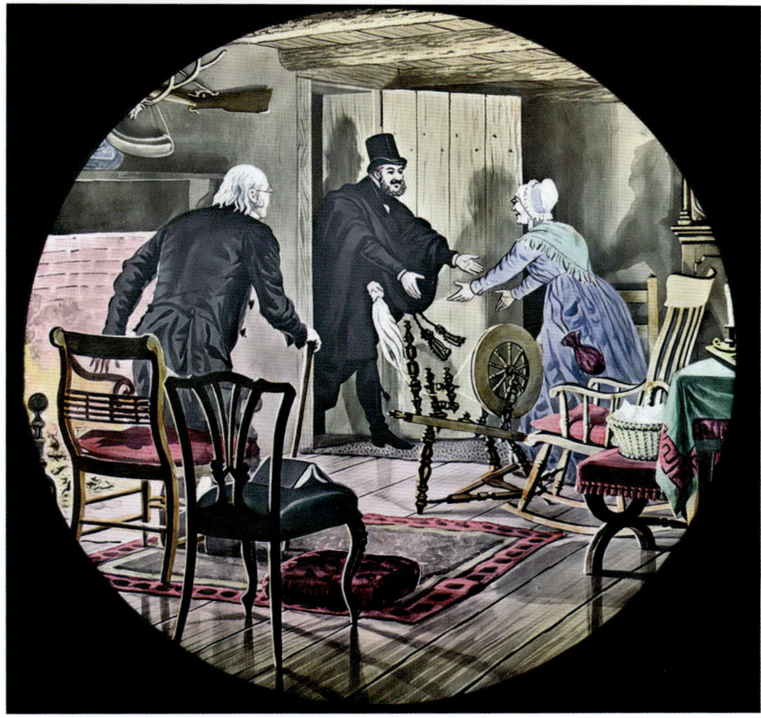

Fig. 8.25 Beale's slide 4 of the four-slide set of *Home, Sweet Home*.

coated slave life, depicting a slave "still longing for de old plantation", and fondly remembering how, "When I was playing wid my brudder/Happy was I;/Oh! take me to my kind old mudder,/Dere let me live and die". Beale's pictures follow suit (Fig. 8.27). Two of the six images show a desolate Black man wandering a desolate landscape, longing for home; the rest show happy scenes of slave home life. No slave labor is shown, no overseer, no master.

Old Kentucky Home, written without dialect, was an anti-slavery song inspired by *Uncle Tom's Cabin*. Indeed, it originally had the title of *Poor Uncle Tom, Good Night.* The song follows the pain of a slave separated from his family. Frederick Douglass, said it, "awakens sympathies for the slave, in which antislavery principles take root, grow, and flourish". Despite its clear

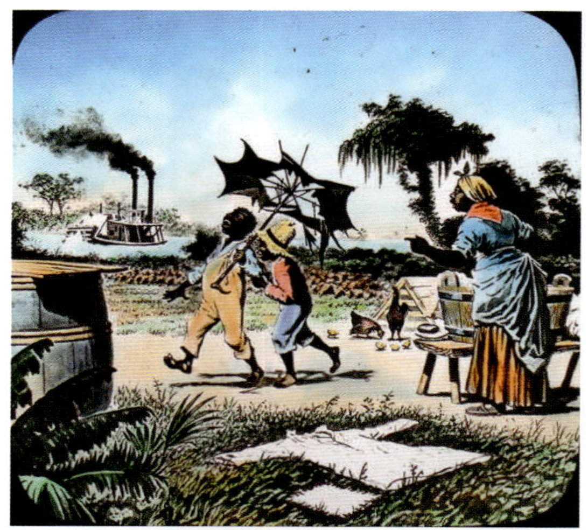

Fig. 8.27 Beale's slide 6 of *Swanee Ribber.*

anti-slavery view, over time the song's message, with some word changes, was reversed, much as happened with *Uncle Tom's Cabin*, and it became a glorification of planation life. Beale's images follow the original intent, and show a happy slave family devastated as the man is auctioned away (Fig. 8.28). The early images show the family dancing and on a coon hunt, but then the wife is shown weeping for her loss. The slave is sold at auction, works cutting cane under an overseer's whip, and finally wanders the world alone. It is a very sobering depiction of slave life.

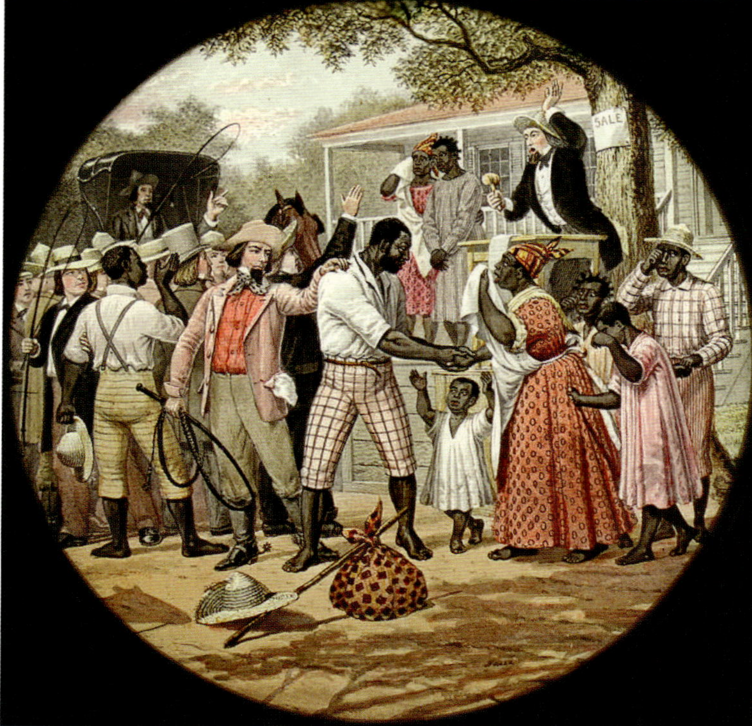

Fig. 8.28 Beale's slide 4 of *Old Kentucky Home.*

Old Black Joe, also written without dialect, tells the story of an elderly slave longing for the old plantation. The opening image is of slaves picking cotton, and having a good old time doing it. Everyone is laughing. As Joe remembers his earlier life, angels appear over him, and in the final scene, the angels beckon him to join them. In it, Beale depicts the angels as white, visually demonstrating – probably unintentionally – an incongruity in the Christian religion that the slave owners had encouraged among the slaves (Fig. 8.29). It is doubtful if they, or any of the white buyers of lantern slides, would have liked being reminded that they were promising Blacks would be welcomed into a "white" Heaven. The set does not seem to have sold well.

What did sell well, I'm sorry to say, was *Old Folks at Home*, with its heavy dialect, dancing slaves and watermelon-toting picaninnies. Other than *Home, Sweet Home*, it is probably the most common Beale song set seen on eBay.

Literary – Religious Stories

Longer religious literature like novels, allegories, and biographies were widely popular in the 19th century. *Ben Hur* remains well known to this day, though most people remember the chariot race better than the religious message. Such religious novels, which combined edification and entertainment, were widely adapted to plays, lantern-slide sets, and, later, to the movies. (In fact, a lantern adaptation prompted a landmark copyright suit that helped establish the rights of an author to his work in all media.)[18]

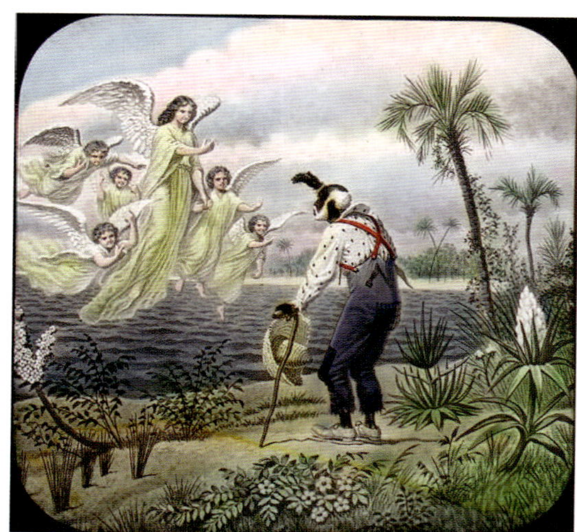

Fig. 8.29 Beale's slide 8 of *Old Black Joe.*

Beale's *Ben Hur* makes up most of the second half of our *Bible Show*. Of course, the chariot race is the most exciting part (Fig. 8.30). The audience participates, one side cheering for Messala, one for Ben Hur, just as they did in the

Victorian theater versions, when real horses galloped on a giant stage treadmill. But for a religious audience, the kind that attends our *Bible Show*, two other moments are just as affecting. The first is when Ben Hur is at last re-united with his mother through the miracle of Jesus, joining the two parallel stories that I mentioned earlier. The second is when Jesus is on the cross, and the soldier Ben Hur gives him drink, just as Jesus had given Ben Hur water when he had been a slave years before. It is then that the message of the book sinks home. The water is "a gift of love and of charity, the only service a soldier could render his King of Kings".

Pilgrim's Progress (Fig.8.31), the panorama version of which I mentioned in Chapter 2, is an allegorical story of Christian's search for salvation. Written in 1678 by John Bunyan, it was one of the most popular books of the 18th and 19th centuries, and continues so today – by some accounts the most widely-read religious book ever, next to the Bible. It was often the featured attraction in lantern shows. The Briggs set is comprised of 12 earlier Langenheim images, and 12 Beale images that were added sometime between 1893 and 1897 – interlarded between the originals. *Pilgrim's Progress* has lots of adventure, as the book is an episodic allegory. We have not tried to perform it, but I'd like to, just to see if it could hold a modern audience.

The Other Wiseman is a disappointing set. The story itself, as the title suggests, is about a fourth Wiseman who was never able to see Jesus. It is, interesting enough, still available in paperback. But the slide set, created late in Beale's career, has little to recommend it. The same set of characters seems to stand around in slide after slide, not doing much. It is as though Beale had finally lost his mojo.

With the exception of *Ben Hur* and *Pilgrim's Progress*, the Religious story slides are, to my mind at least, among Beale's least appealing. The problem with *Quo Vadis*, and *Tabernacle* (where Beale did 2 of 10 slides) comes from choices made by Briggs – the decision to put together sets by compilation rather than original creation. That destroyed the opportunity for Beale to use his skill at giving a story life on screen through continuity, dramatic pacing, and special effects.

The *Quo Vadis* set combines 8 original Beale images with 22 others drawn from pre-existing inventory. Even Beale's fabulous image of Nero fiddling can't save this mash up (Fig. 8.32).

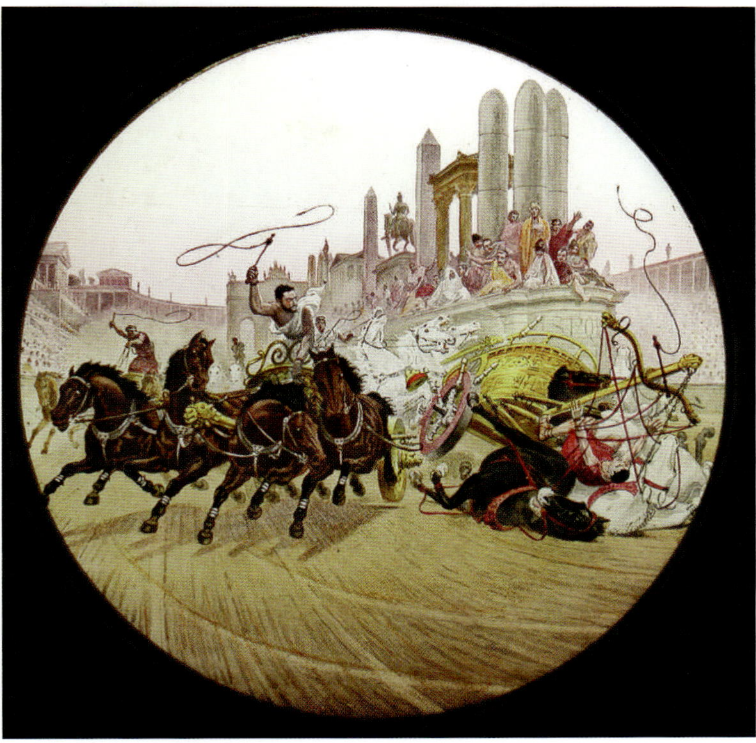

Fig. 8.30 Beale's slide of "The Winning Chariot" from *Ben Hur*, by Lew Wallace.

Literary Works: Short Stories

Short stories have always been a popular literary genre. Why then do only six Beale Short Stories exist, while there are 28 of a similar art form, the Parlor Poems? I think the answer is in the rhyme. The Parlor Poems were easy to memorize; not so the stories. And that "known by heart" script would have been a tremendous asset is selling slides.

Not only do fewer Beale short stories exist, but Beale only created one slide apiece in two of them. Two more stories, *Legend of Sleepy Hollow*

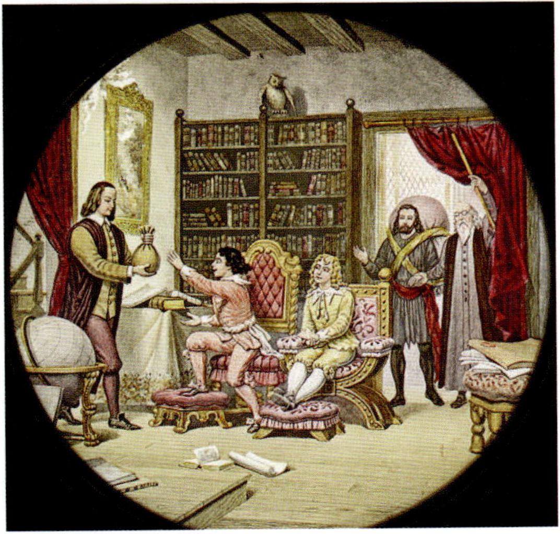

Fig. 8.31 Beale's slide 8 of *Pilgrim's Progress* by John Bunyan. Pilgrim is at right, with his pack of sin on his back.

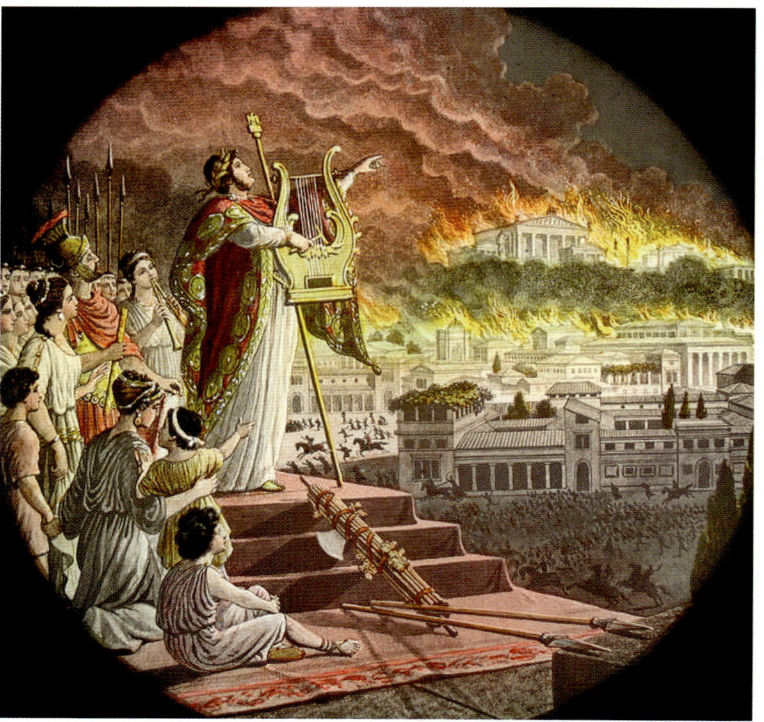

Fig. 8.32 Beale's slide of "Nero Playing Lute while Rome Burns" from *Quo Vadis* by Henryk Sienkiewicz.

and *Rip Van Winkle* are such close copies of drawings by F. O. C. Darley that they hardly count as Beale at all.

That leaves *The Little Match Girl*, which, as we've already seen, is a real classic of magic lantern art, and *The Man Without a Country.*by Edward Everett Hale (Fig. 8.33), Beale's last set, created in 1917 when he was 76. This story is not well known today, but it should be. It's the heart-wrenching tale of an American soldier who is punished for an act of treason, and condemned to spend his entire life isolated aboard ship, never seeing America again. (The story is the centerpiece of our *Patriotic Show*. In this hyper-partisan time of American history, it serves to remind our audiences that they all share love of country.)

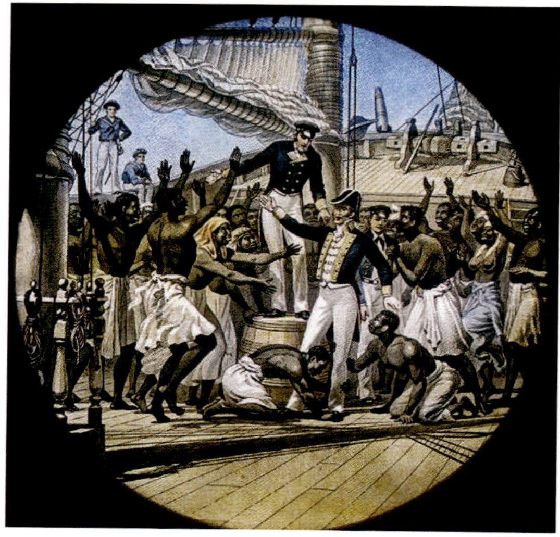

Fig. 8.33 Beale's slide 14 of *The Man Without a Country* by Edward Everett Hale. Nolan tells freed slaves that they can return to their own country, something that he could never do.

Literary – Comic Sketches

The Comic Sketches are a unique literary form in the Beale canon, quite different from all the others. He produced seven of these comic sets, although that number is a little arbitrary, since several of the parlor poetry sets could also be considered comic. I've placed sets in this category largely based on their exaggerated comic style, and the nature of their titles – often in the form; "Somebody and Something Else". Also, they do not illustrate well-known poems, though they clearly fit into well-known genres; and most seem to assume a rapid pace of slide changes.

One of the story sets is Black humor – *Uncle Rastus;* three are Irish humor – *Paddy, Mrs. Casey, Bridget's Dream*; two are what might be called "Suburban humor" – *Mr. Spurt, Mr. Timorous*; and one makes fun of fraternal organizations – *How Jones Became a Mason.*

As in the movies, physical slapstick is a staple. However, rather than being *interpersonal* slapstick, as in the movies, the Comic Sketches tend to involve *interspecies* slapstick. Berserk mules, pigs, dogs, and goats create chaos among hapless people. (I suspect that this species difference between lantern shows and movies is because it is very difficult to get a pig or a mule to perform slapstick on cue for a movie, but was easy for Beale to draw such scenes for the magic lantern. And, since the Victorians lived much more closely with large animals like pigs, goats and mules than we do, they had plenty of first-hand slapstick experience to relate to.)

All of the Comic Sketch images are drawn in Beale's comic style. Action and faces are exaggerated, with plenty of stereotyping or *typage*, much of it racial or ethnic. (Beale was quite capable of creating non-stereotypic Blacks, and indeed did so in a number of cases like *My Old Kentucky Home*. Unfortunately, *Uncle Rastus*

Fig. 8.34 Details of Beale's slide 9 from *Uncle Rastus and His Mule*, and slide 2 from *My Old Kentucky Home* by Stephen Foster. They represent two very different depictions of Black men.

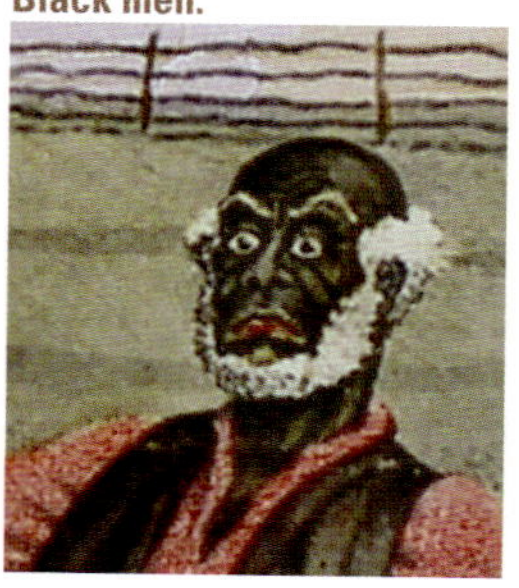

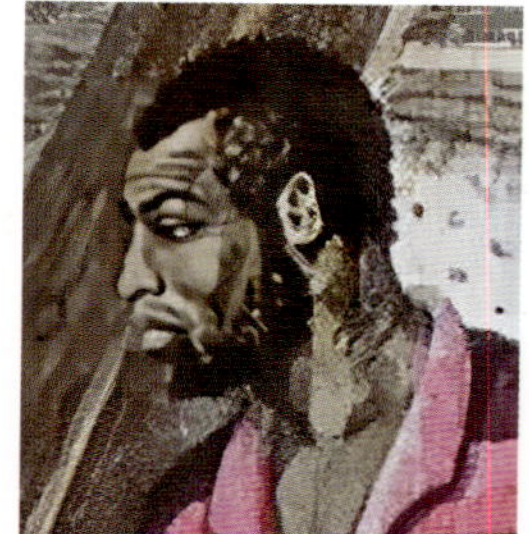

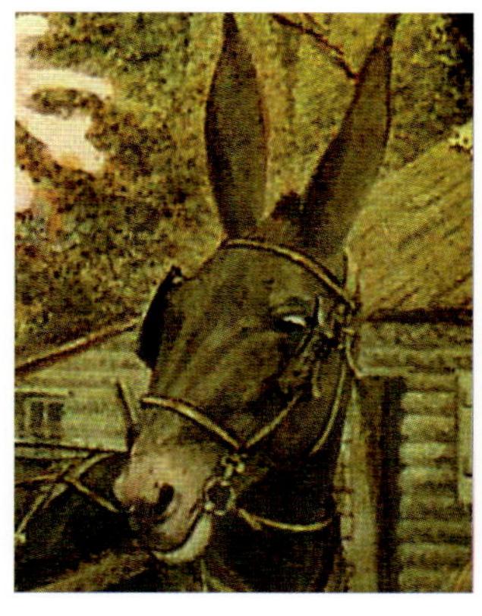
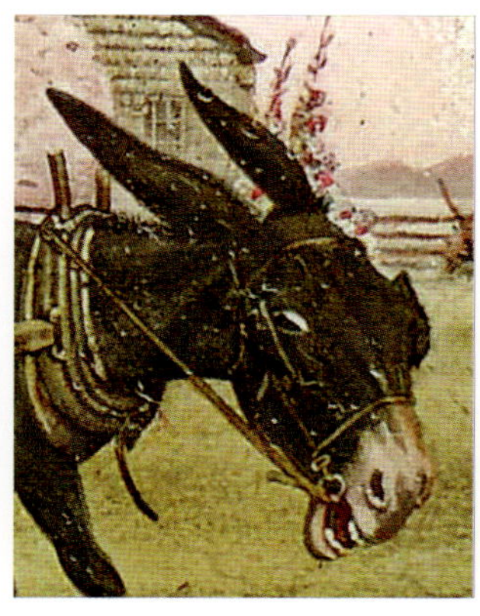
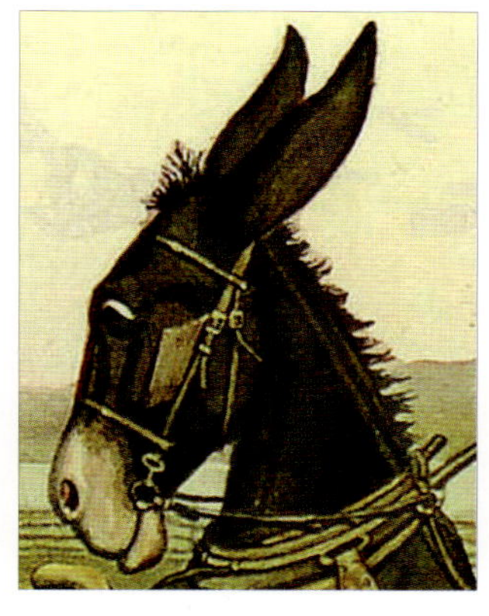
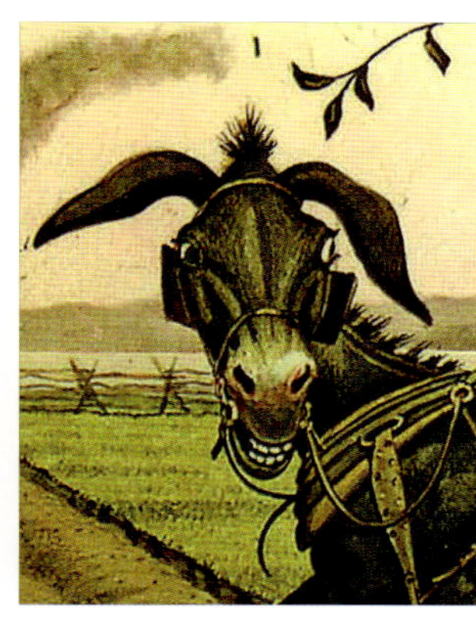
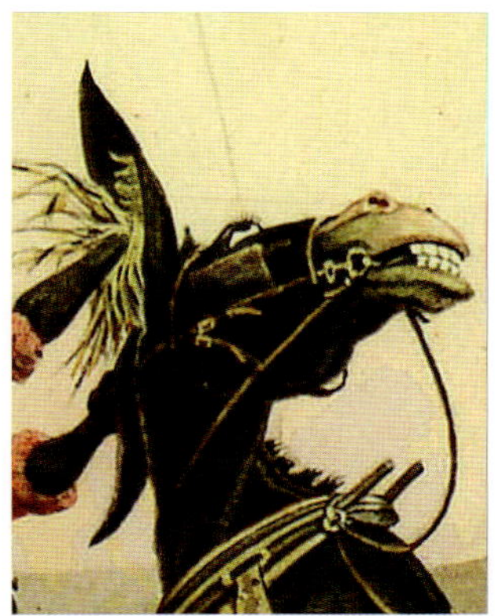
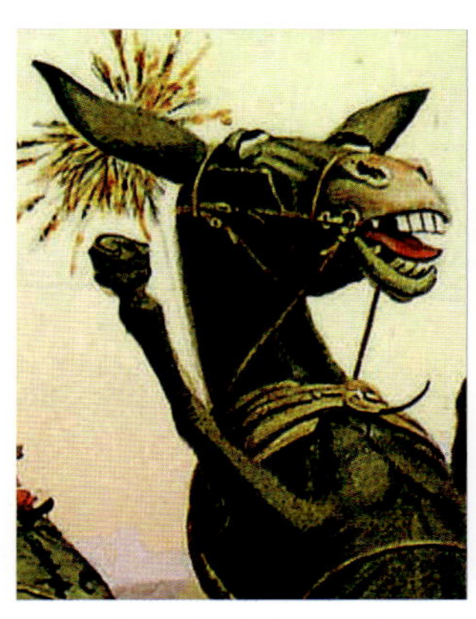
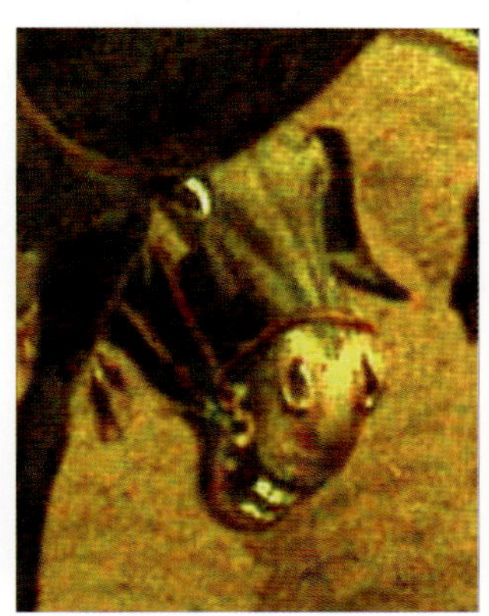
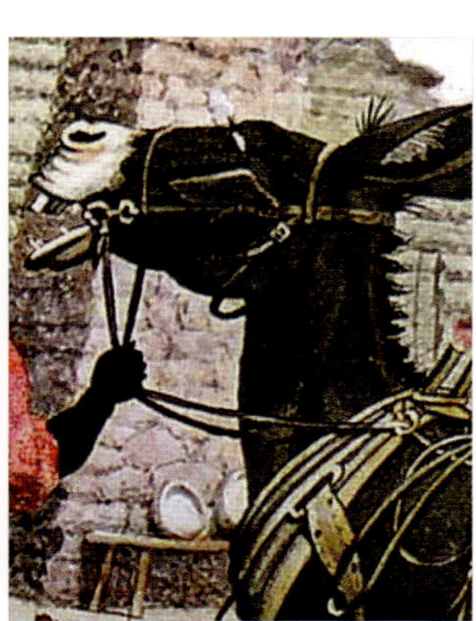

Fig. 8.35 Details of Beale's slides 2, 3, 5, 6, 7, 8, 11, and 12 of *Uncle Rastus and His Mule.*

and His Mule is not one of them (Fig. 8. 34). Beale also had a special gift for drawing comic animals, especially pigs, which take on delightfully demonic expressions as they fly through the air, charge through crowds, and climb into the beds of their terrified victims.

He was pretty good with mules too. The farmer, Uncle Rastus, in *Uncle Rastus and His Mule* is Black and depicted stereotypically. I've never tried to perform this set because of its racist content. A modern audience would reject it out of hand. That's quite different from how Victorian audiences would have responded, when racist humor was accepted, even in the most "polite" society. But the racist depiction of Rastus aside, it is the mule's expression that drives Beale's narrative art and tells the story. If you concentrate on the mule, who does dominate the action, this is a delightful story of animal antics. We can see the set in just this way by looking at the slides through a series of details that focus only on the mule's face (Fig. 8.35).[19] The images move from the mule accepting the days' task, to his vehement objection, to bemusement at Rastus's efforts to tame him, to rebellion, to an explosion of anger when Rastus tries to move him by poking his ear with straw, to hope that he has won the battle, and finally, when Rastus gives up, to delight at being taken home for dinner.

Conclusion

Beale's Literary works are a wonderful compilation of American and world literature, ranging from the great Victorian classics like *Evangeline* and *Ben Hur*, to whacky comics like *Uncle Rastus and His Mule*. The strongest subcategory, the one with the most sets and the most slides, is Parlor Poetry. That fact gives a clearer sense of what Briggs was thinking of in his vision of bringing great literature to the screen. He meant, in essence, popular literature – not quite as popular perhaps as the dime novels with their lurid illustrations, or the cartoons that were beginning to fill the newspapers, but not as great and hoary as Homer and *The Iliad* either. He wanted literary works that would sell, which meant, especially in the case of Parlor Poetry, works that were well known, and well loved. Beale gave to these works a new visual appeal that captured their varied themes with a style appropriate to each, and helped bring them to life, in many cases giving them a whole new visual layer of interpretation and meaning.

We'll turn now to examining the rest of Beale's slide creation. It is a broad-ranging collection, and includes two areas that were major markets for Briggs – Religious and Secret Society slides.

But first, it's time for an intermission (Fig. 8:36):

Chapter 8 Appendix
Beale's Literary Sets by Category

This table summarizes all Beale Literary sets by categories such as Long Poems, Songs, etc., and gives the title of each. The number after the *category title* – e. g. "Long Poems" – indicates the total number of *Beale* slides in that category, and does not include any non-Beale slides that might also be in it. The number after a *set title* indicates the same type of information for that set. Some slides appear in multiple categories and sets. For detailed information on each set and each slide within the set, see Borton, Borton, *Before the Movies*, 93–116.

Novels, Long Stories (Non-Religious) (48)

Marley's Ghost (24)
Robinson Crusoe (12)
Uncle Tom's Cabin (12)

Long Poems (127)

Courtship of Miles Standish (23)
Evangeline (24)
Gray's Elegy (32)
Hiawatha (24)
The Lady of the Lake (24)

Plays/Opera (94)

Carmen (12)
Hamlet (14)
Macbeth (12)
Merchant of Venice (11)
Merry Wives of Windsor (12)
Othello (12)
Pygmalion and Galatea (6)
Romeo and Juliet (15

Parlor Poetry (213)

Annie and Willie's Prayer (6)
Barbara Freitchie (1)
Blue and The Gray (1)
The Bridge (4)
The Brook (10)
Casabianca (6)
The Courtin' (6)
Curfew Must Not Ring Tonight (10)
Darius Green and His Flying Machine (8)
Drake's Ode to the American Flag (6)
How Persimmon's Took Ca ob der Baby (4)
Independence Bell (6)
John Gilpin's Ride (20)
John Maynard (10)
Leap for Life (6)
Little Breeches (8)
Maud Muller (6)
Nellie's Prayer (12)
Paul Revere's Ride (8)
The Pied Piper (8)
The Raven (12)
Shakespeare's Seven Ages of Man (7)
Sheridan's Ride (6)
The Spectre Pig (8)
Thanatopsis (12)
The Village Blacksmith (6)
Visit of St. Nicholas (7)
Wreck of the Hesperus (9)

Popular Songs (89)

America (2)
Auld Lang Syne (4)
Comic Songs (3)
Dixie's Land (8)
Home Sweet Home (12)
Killarney (2)
Marching Thro' Georgia (7)
Maryland, My Maryland (1)
Old Black Joe (6)
Old Kentucky Home (6)
Old Oaken Bucket (3)
Rally Round the Flag (2)
Red, White and Blue (4)
Star Spangled Banner (6)
Swanee Ribber (8)
Tenting on the Old Camp Ground (5)
Tramp, Tramp, Tramp (2)
United States Soldier's Dream of Home (2)
Yankee Doodle (6)

Literary – Religious (101)

Ben Hur (34)
The Game of Life (3)
Healing of the Daughter of Jairus (6)
Pilgrim's Progress (12)
Quo Vadis (8)
Story of the Other Wiseman (36)
Tabernacle in the Wilderness (2)

Short Stories (37)

Beauty and the Beast (1)
Bluebeard (1)
Legend of Sleepy Hollow (6)
The Little Match Girl (8)
Man Without a Country (15)
Rip Van Winkle (6)

Comic Sketches (80)

Bridget's Dream (12)
How Jones Became a Mason (12)
Mr. Spurt and His Auto (8)
Mr. Timorous and His Dog (12)
Mrs. Casey and the Goat (12)
Paddy and the Pig (12)
Uncle Rastus and His Mule (12)

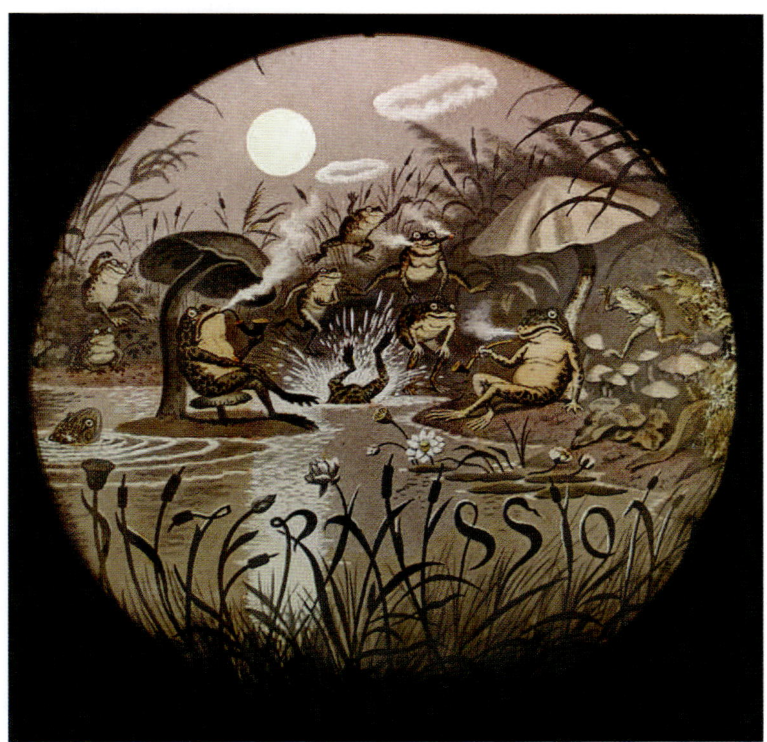

Fig. 8.36 Beale's "Intermission – Frogs in Pond" from the *Mottos* group.

Chapter Nine

Beale's On-Screen World: Part Two – Religion, History, Secret Society

Fig. 9.27 Beale Secret Society slide from *Knights of Pythias, Third Rank, Pythagoras*, "Where Hideous Creatures Climb". Discussion on pp. 226–227.

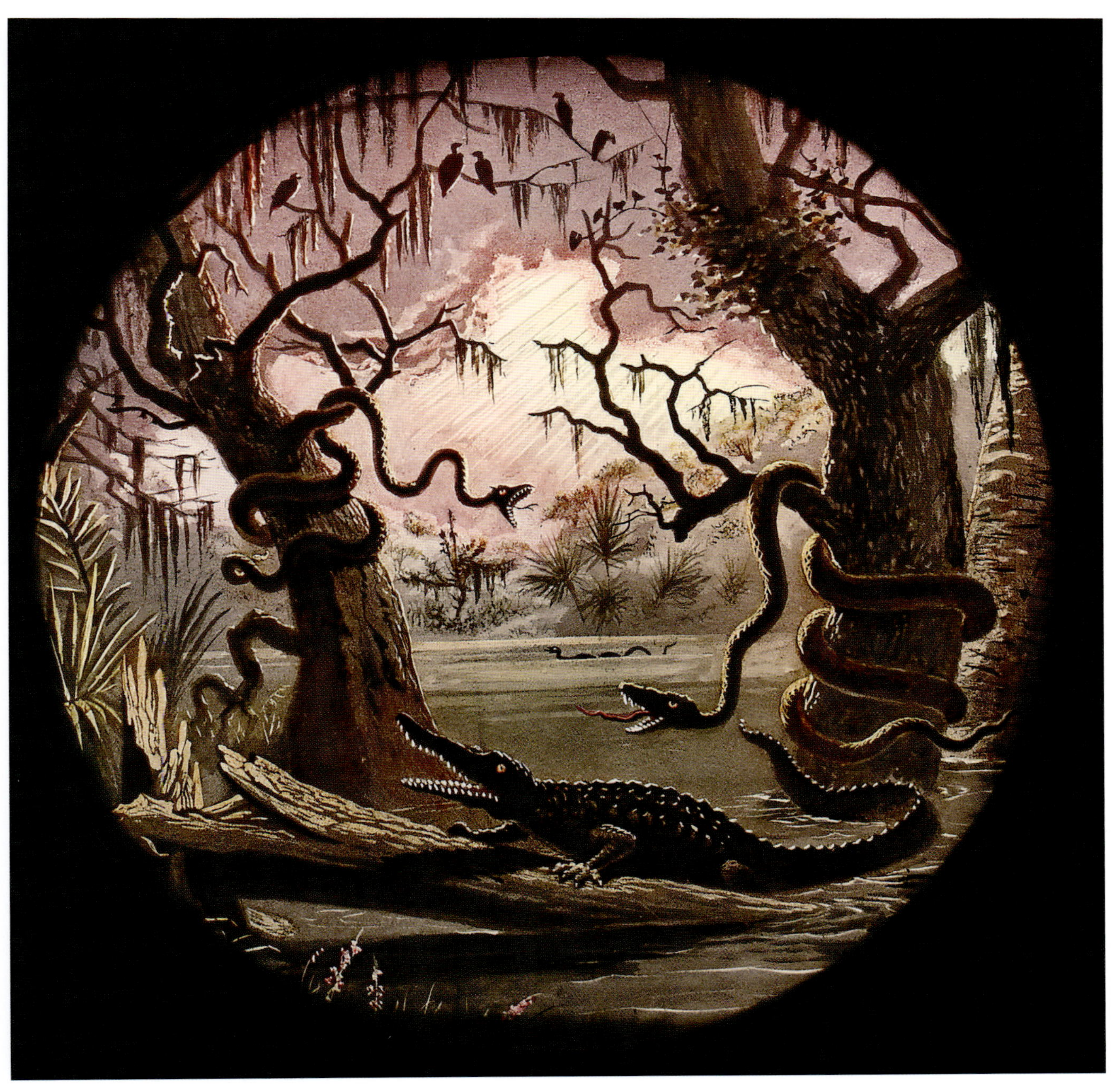

The 89 Beale Literary sets I explored in the last chapter are those most closely associated with his full narrative style, so I concentrated on them first. But they account for only about a third of Beale's total creative work. The other two thirds consisted of 78 Religious sets or groups, 32 History, 10 Temperance, 36 Secret Society, and 15 Miscellaneous. Beale also used his narrative skills in all these sets, sometimes surprisingly. A set list is at the chapter end.

Religion

Like Literature, Religion was a major category of Beale's work, accounting for about 700 slide images, roughly 34 percent of his slide output, and about 25 percent of all religious images offered in the magic lantern catalogs. Religion slides can be broken into four sub-categories of sets – 21 Hymns, 11 Works of Biography and Bible Texts, 19 Old Testament, and 27 New Testament and Miscellaneous.

Religious lantern presentations were deemed appropriate for those who might appreciate a "pictorially illustrated evening devotion", for "pictures draw ...their interest, … they clinch the story". In order to protect the solemnity of religious occasions, lanternists were warned that, "slides that are not of the highest order should in no case be used".[1] Of course, Beale's artistry, care, and precision helped make his slides "of the highest order". But in the catalogs, they had to compete with images by well-known painters of the day whose works were listed by name – Heinrich von Hofmann, Gustave Doré, and even the classical greats like Raphael. Certainly, in order to compete Briggs was very aware of the importance of filling religious slides with appropriate "accessories and surrounding[s]", and all of Beale's religious slides follow this guideline.

Religion, specifically "main line" Protestant Christianity, was a dominant and public part of 19th century middle-class life in a way that is not quite so true today, bracketed as it is by secularism, Catholicism and Judaism, burgeoning native-born sects like the Mormons and the Jehovah's Witnesses, and new imports like Buddhism and Islam. But in the 19th century, the dominance of Protestant churches meant that Sunday Schools, fellowship meetings, Bible study groups, and church-sponsored entertainment constituted a major market for the lantern. However, the use of slides could be controversial (Fig. 9.1).

> We protest against the practice ... of making the pulpit the organ for catchpenny advertisements. If a man comes along with a show of some sort, an exhibition of paintings, magic lantern, or what not, and only lugs in something about Palestine, or Jerusalem, or India, or the heathen, he will consider himself entitled to the free use of a meeting house, for his exhibition ... The pulpit is no place for such things.[2]

The lantern was not commonly used in the service itself, but in the many other forms of religious practice – Sunday School, youth groups, study sessions, evening events, missionary work. Judging from the plethora of religious slides produced, the clergy indeed got over its prejudice. In fact, churches were one of the main venues for pre-Civil War magic lantern shows.[3]

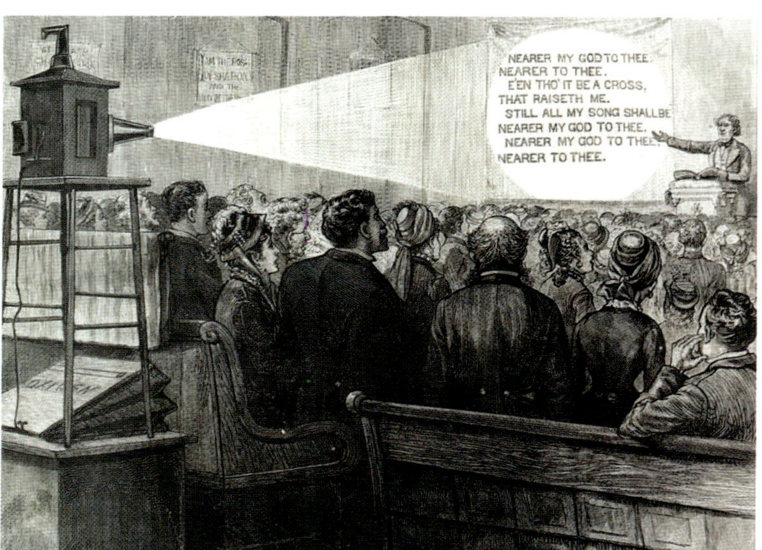

Fig. 9.1 Engraving, from *Leslie's Illustrated Weekly*, March 8, 1879.

Fig. 9.2 Beale's slide for *Hold the Fort*, an Illuminated Hymn.

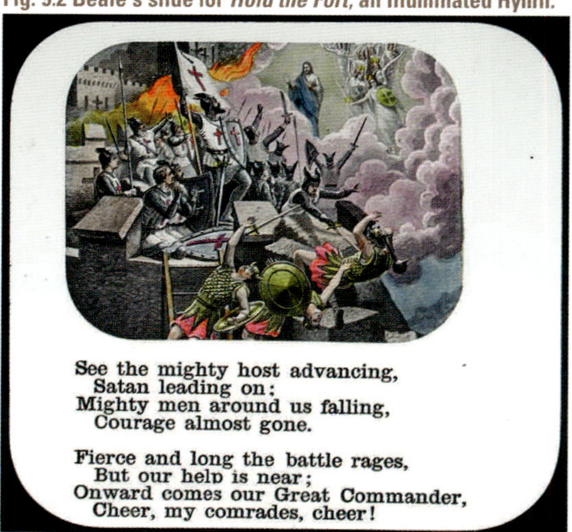

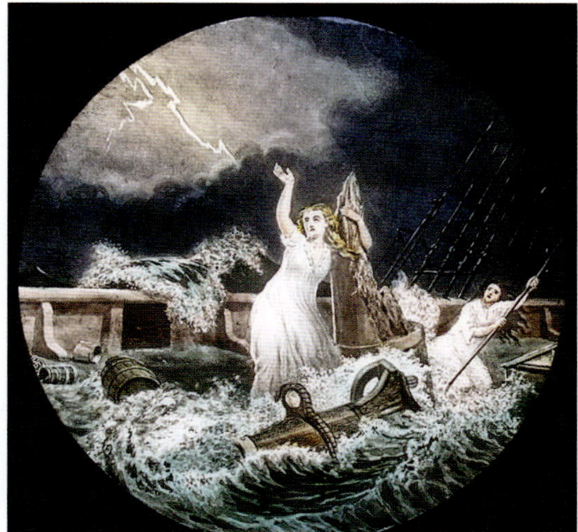

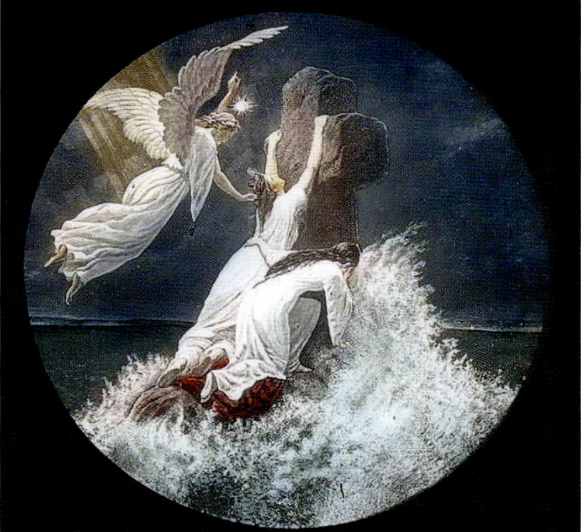

Fig. 9.3 Beale's slides, labeled A, H, K and O, for *Rock of Ages*.

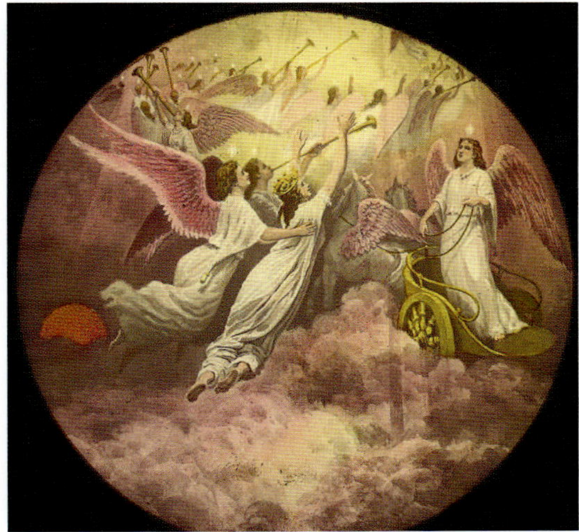

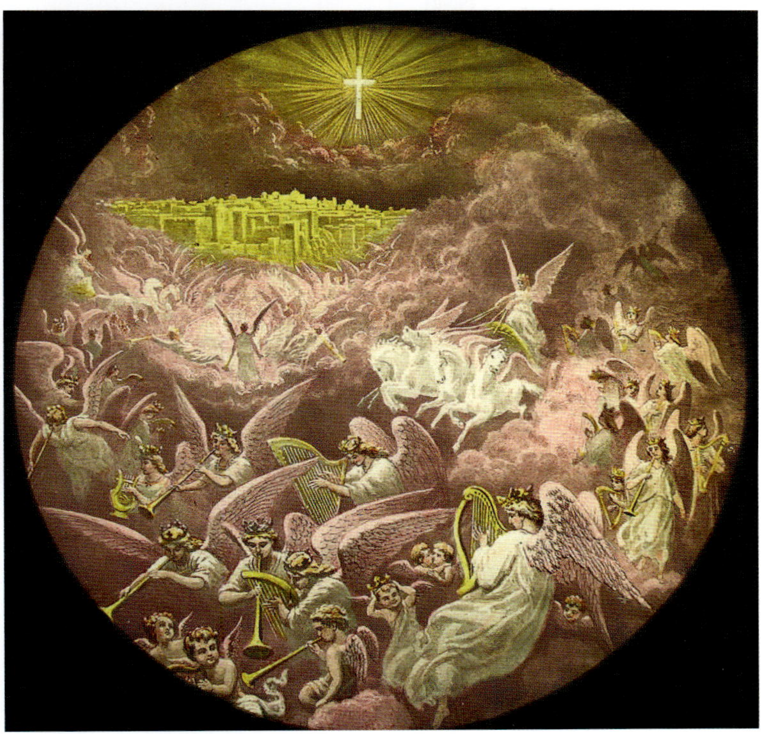

Hymns

The hymns Beale illustrated lent themselves to the cinematic technology and artistry of the magic lantern because of the flowing way their words were presented with music. Hymns called out for *cuts* and *fades*, multiple *dissolves*, *effect dissolves*, and *superimpositions*, with one image slowly changing into another in a visual legato. Often the lyrics involved extended *metaphors* that made it easy for Beale to put religious concepts in visual terms such as shepherds herding their flocks, lifesavers rescuing foundering ships, medieval battles (Fig. 9.2), or the rock of the church.

A good example is Beale's *Rock of Ages*, a hymn set used in both churches and Secret Societies. The first version of the set was a single slide of a woman clinging to a cross, based on a painting by Johannes Oertel. A four-slide set adapted from this image appears in the catalogs well before Beale, but in 1894 he increases the set to twelve slides, adding material before, after and in the middle of the original four. The slides pictured here (plus some others I will describe) show how Beale worked from Oertel's single image to create a 12-slide cinematic extravaganza to be projected as the choir sang one of the most rousing hymns of the Victorian age (Fig. 9.3).

Two women (Faith and her companion) are in the midst of a terrible shipwreck. A lightning streak is superimposed over the scene, the lanternist flashing both slides off and on to enhance the effect. Then (not shown) a rock appears in the sea, with the foundering ship in the distance. A rainbow is superimposed over the rock, suggesting that it is the Rock of Ages. A series of dissolves carries the symbolism further: a huge stone cross emerges from the sea; Faith climbs from the water and clings to the cross; her companion's hand reaches from the water; Faith pulls her up; then both women cling to the cross. Over them, a vision of angels is superimposed. Then one of the angels descends (in an effect dissolve) to crown Faith. A standard dissolve gives us a *low-angle* view of the ascension to Heaven over the clouds of the storm; another dissolve brings them to Heaven and another to the throne of Jesus. It is a beautifully realized series of images, transitioning smoothly from the realistic shipwreck through the *Rock of Ages* symbolism to Salvation.

I've used eight of Beale's hymns in various shows. All worked well. The music, and a beautiful soprano voice flow as the pictures flow. It's magical, even if you're not religious.

Religion – Biography and Bible Texts

These two groups of Religious sets, particularly the "Texts", lack what the hymns have, that lyrical flow. The Texts are by their nature short collections of words without a story connection. Thus, though Beale comes through on an image-by-image basis, these texts do not provide much opportunity for sequential art. Still, something is always fascinating in his rendering. Compare, for instance, the Biblical setting of *The Beatitudes* to the contemporary setting for *The Ten Commandments* (Fig. 9.4). I'd love to know what Beale's audience thought about that image. It might have hit a little close to home.

Religion – Old Testament

The Old Testament Religious area is a gold mine for any artist, full of fascinating characters, dramatic action – everything larger than life. We use several of these stories in our *Bible Show*, and they certainly grip an audience.

I particularly like *The Creation of Earth*, which I begin by using the tank slide of liquid pigments to create the effect of swirling chaos, and then gradually dissolving from one scene of the emerging Earth to another, as we see it slowly form and give birth to life.

The story of *Noah* has long been a favorite, not only because of its dramatic narrative, but because of the complex character of Noah himself, and, of course, the fascinating questions of how he handled all those animals. A model "Noah's Ark" was a common toy of the time for children, but the story is anything but child's play.

What strikes me about *Noah* is the way Beale visually weaves together the contrast between good and evil, the character of Noah, his management of the animals, and Biblical symbolism. It's all the more impressive because this group was not created at one time. The earliest slides focused on the flood and Noah's escape. Later slides in the set filled in both before and after the flood to give it greater context and to give great power to the portrayal of Noah. Clearly Beale worked hard to give this grouping continuity.

In the final version of the set we first see "The

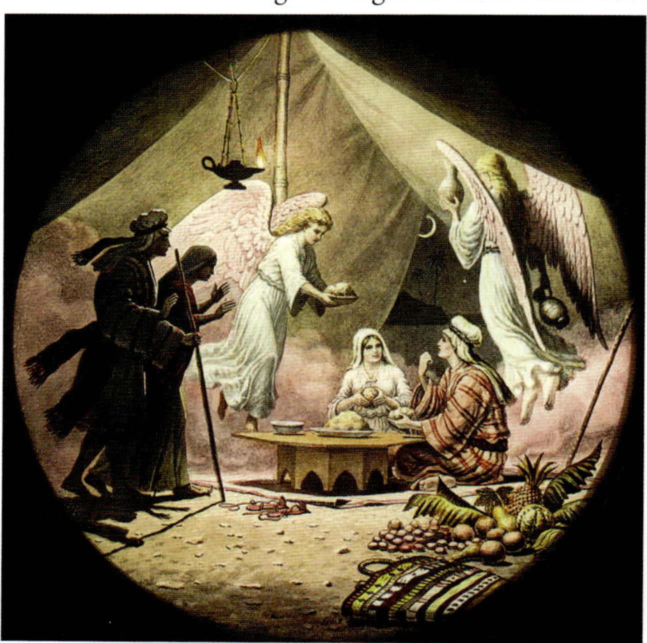

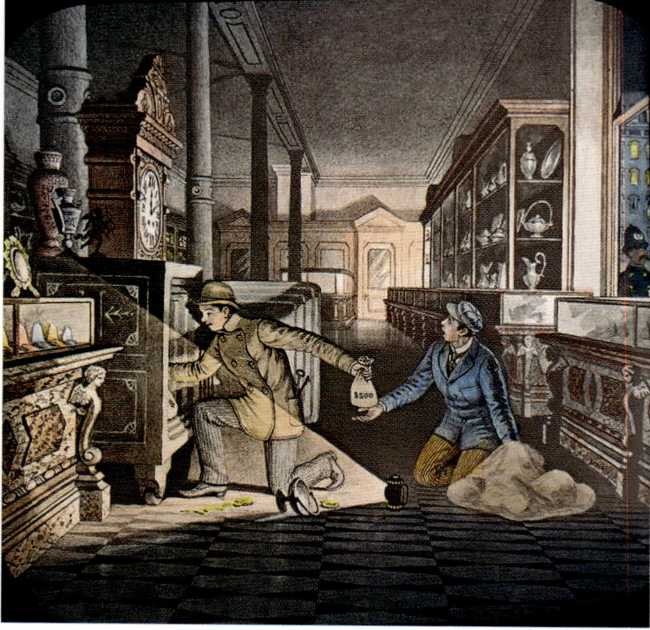

Fig. 9.4 Beale's slide 4, at left, for *The Beatitudes* – "Blessed are they that hunger and thirst for righteousness", and, on the right, slide 8 from *The Ten Commandments* – "Thou shall not steal".

Wickedness of Man Before the Flood" – in the foreground, vanity, corruption, lechery, slavery, brutality (Fig. 9.5). Through the "doorway" we can see even more – idol worship, human sacrifice, infanticide. A long diagonal runs down from the contemptuous king to the pleading slave below him. Beale has certainly crammed a lot of real-world wickedness into one image.

In dramatic contrast, the next scene shows Noah setting out on his great project (Fig. 9.6). He is holding his head in his hand, knowing the wickedness of the world, wondering how he will ever complete his celestial task using only real saws and real logs. This time the diagonal in the design runs upward, through the log and Noah, to the soaring stem of the ark, reaching above the real world.

The flood hits, the flood that Noah had been predicting. Men and women fight to survive on their tiny bit of rock (Fig.9.7). All their forms are twisted and tortured. Dangerous animals – a hippo, a lion, a bear – are about to drive the humans into the water. It is a scene of chaos, the only organizing design element a diagonal that follows a lightning bolt through the old man, the frantic people, and into the water.

Aboard the ark, it's an entirely different world (Fig. 9.8). Yes, all are crammed together, Noah's family despairing, the animals one on top of the other. But the animals are all (except the leopards) at peace. In the foreground one zebra sleeps on another; in the background, two elephants nuzzle; two giraffes touch nose to nose. Noah's family is framed and symbolically protected by sleeping animals, doves, and the great peacock's feathers, symbol of resurrection.

Finally, the rain stops. Noah tries to find out if dry land exists by sending out a dove who finally returns with an olive leaf. The waters recede, and the ark lands. All leave in a great swirling "S" design, the air aflutter with birds (Fig.9.9). The peacock's feathers flow across the foreground as Noah explains how God will not let a flood happen again, and how a new world awaits mankind.

The meticulous realism that we have seen to be characteristic of Beale's work is very much in evidence in *Noah*. It might be hard for us to imagine, realistically, how all those animals lived in the ark, but...there they are, presented in Beale's imagination as concretely as if they were in the farmyard or jungle. They look perfectly natural, and yet the way they are arranged suggests something more. In the ark even the camels look composed. It's a jungle in there, but a peaceful jungle, foreshadowing a new beginning for the world. Beale's detailed style gives this mythic story a sense of the everyday that makes it seem very real, while the subtle symbolism of

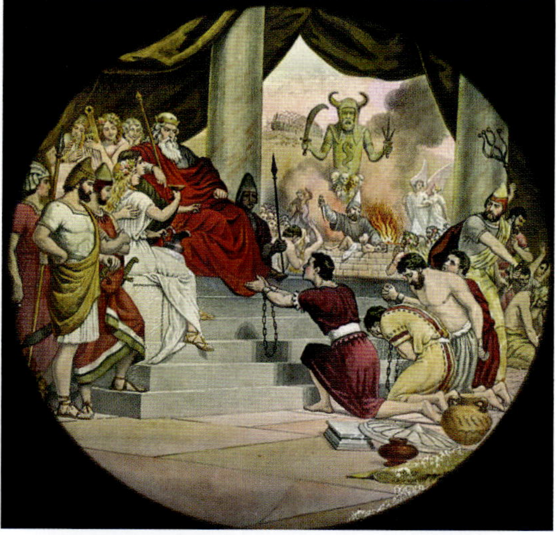

Fig. 9.5 Beale's slide 1 of *Noah* – "Wickedness of Man Before the Flood".

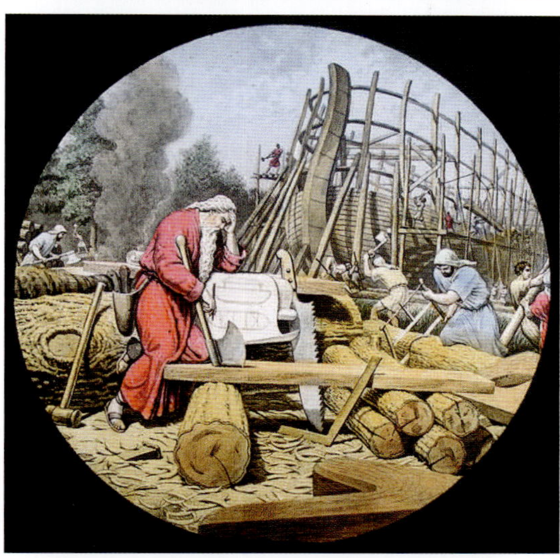

Fig. 9.6 Beale's "Noah Building the Ark" from the *Noah* group.

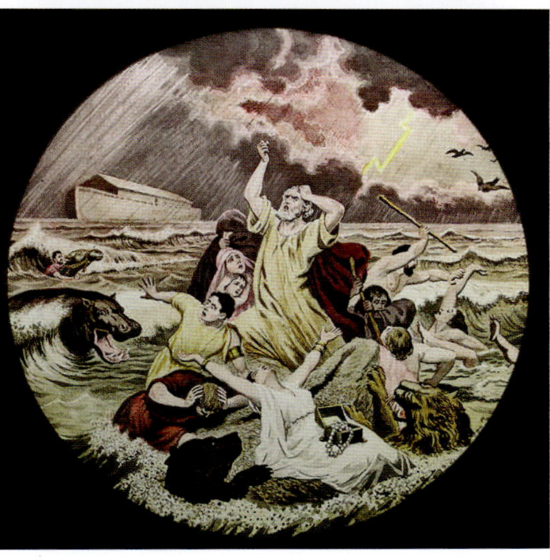

Fig. 9.7 Beale's slide, "Flood Destroying Man and Beast", from the *Noah* group.

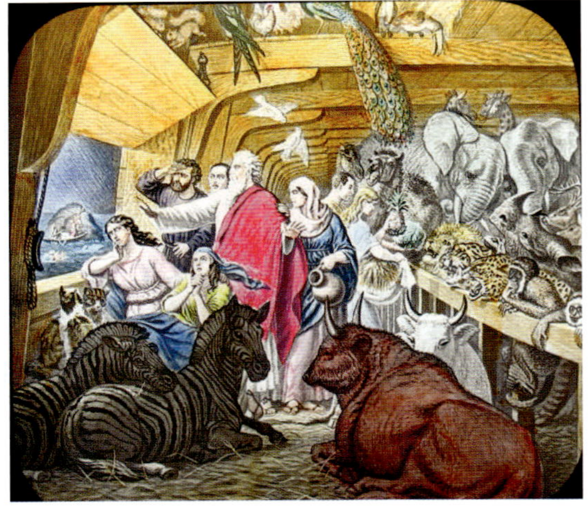
Fig. 9.8 Beale's slide of "Interior of the Ark" from the *Noah* group.

the ark's stem, the peacock's feathers, and the animals nuzzling adds an extra layer of rich meaning that draws us into the story.

The same could be said of all Beale's Bible stories, which is why they were so popular. They were probably used primarily in Sunday School or Sunday evening groups, and during more informal religious gatherings, especially for children around religious holidays. (You may remember that as a young man Beale himself brought the family children to two Christmas magic lantern shows at churches, which no doubt included Bible stories.)

Religion – New Testament and Miscellaneous

The New Testament Religious area, and the Miscellaneous[4] slides continue Beale's depiction of the Biblical universe, though the images devoted to Christ's life are much less dramatic than those in the Old Testament, with its floods, parting seas, and merciless plagues.

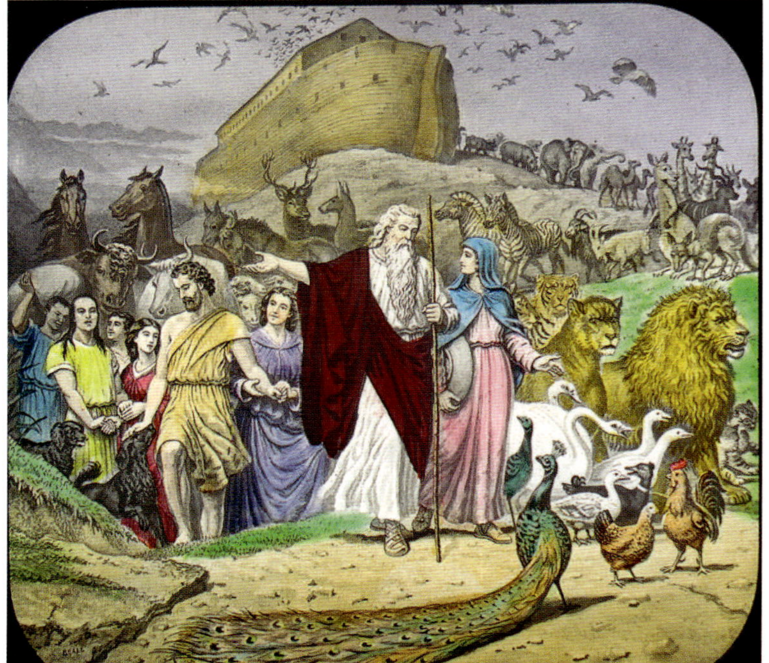
Fig. 9.9 Beale's slide of "Noah Coming Out of Ark" from *Noah.*

In the New Testament, if you're looking for drama, the place to turn is the Parables. They came in two forms. A single slide represented each of 40 Parables. Beale expanded 12 of these into a full story like *The Good Shepherd* or *The Good Samaritan* (Fig.9.10).

We've already seen how *The Good Shepherd* was developed, and captured the complex parable of Jesus in an understandable visual narrative. Most of the other parables were much easier to portray, as they had a much clearer storyline. For sheer size of audience, the most popular would certainly be *The Good Samaritan.* That's because it was not only used in church, but also by several fraternal groups, most notably the Masons.

These two parables were set amid the common people in common settings. But often the parables were set in exotic locales, or with exotic groups of people. Beale could use these situations to create stunning narrative images that would certainly have helped to drive home their point. A quick selection (Fig. 9.11): In *The Faithful Servant* the faithful servant is waiting to serve his master when he returns from the wedding feast. In *The House Built on Rock and Sand* those who hear the words of Jesus and do not follow them are like the foolish man who built his house on sand. In *The Talents* a returning master rewards his servants with money according to their performance. And in *The*

Fig. 9.10 Beale's slide 4 from *The Good Samaritan.* Behind the Good Samaritan (in red), we see figures from earlier slides in the narrative.

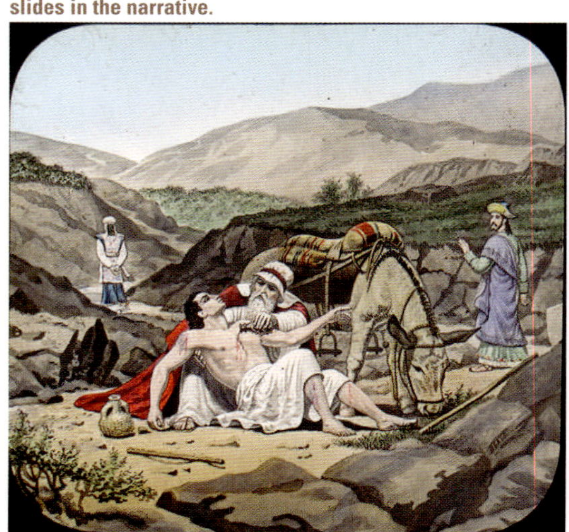

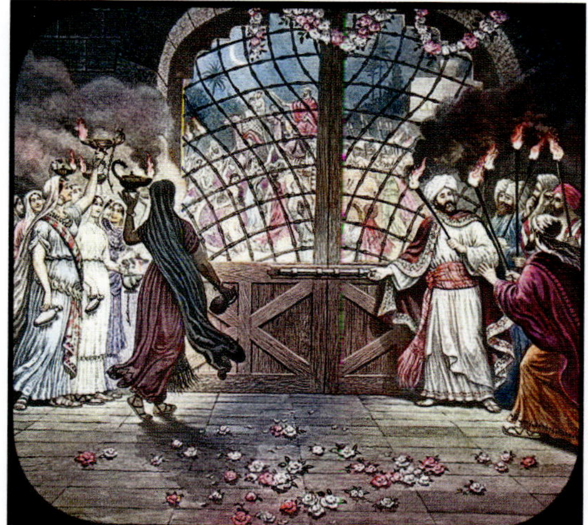
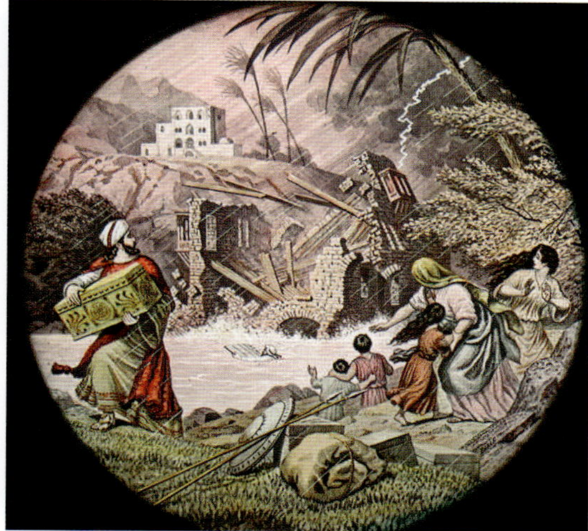

Fig. 9.11 Beale's slides illustrating four Parables: *The Faithful Servant* (top left); *The House Built on Rock and Sand* (top right); *The Talents* (bottom left); *The Wise and Foolish Virgins* (bottom right).

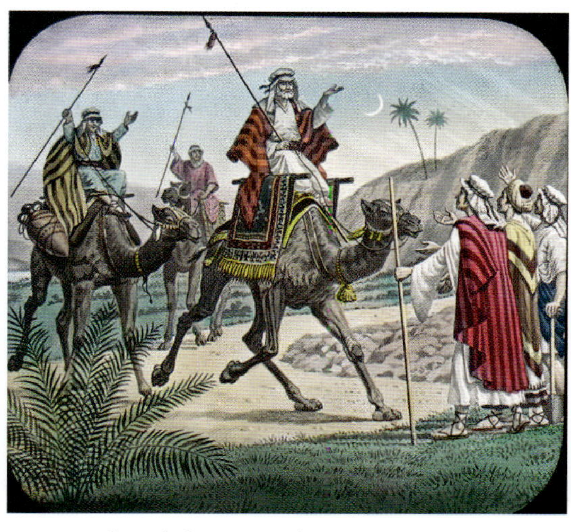
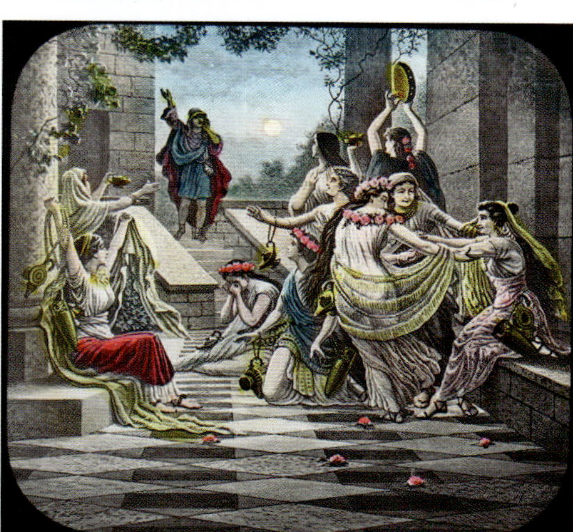

Wise and Foolish Virgins the wise virgins conserve the oil in their lamps to be ready for the bridegroom's late return; the foolish do not and are shut out of the wedding. Each picture draws you into its world – the scatted wedding flowers, the spears laid across the bedroll, the winding road, the patterned floor and flowing garments. Each captures a dramatic moment where something important is happening or is about to happen. We may not know exactly what happens next, but these pictures certainly make us want to know "the rest of the story".

Beale Dominates the Religious Market

Religious slides existed in the magic lantern catalogs before Beale began working – largely the work of Nisle, Doré and "famous artists". But gradually Beale's images begin replacing such slides in the catalogs, though at first he is not given specific credit. Beginning in the McAllister catalog of 1893, however, Beale's contributions are listed by name. The slides for all the *Parables* are also specifically described as by "By Beale unless otherwise noted". In 1905, McIntosh uses the same "By Beale" rubric for the *Old Testament, Life of Christ*, and the *Parables*. Beale had taken over the Religious market.

Why did Briggs have Beale replace existing views, often by much more famous artists? And why did the catalogs begin listing Beale by name in the Religious area? Clearly the catalog companies thought Beale's work was superior screen art. And since they kept promoting him for many years, we can assume that their patrons thought so too. But what exactly made Beale's slides so superior for Religious work?

First, they were very tightly targeted to their market. Religious slides not only had to be appropriate for use in church, but they also had to avoid religious controversy, a particularly difficult matter since the slides were being sold to a number of different denominations. As with *The Good Shepherd*, sketches seem to have been reviewed by a clergyman, but everyone, including the distributors, could, and did, express an opinion. One of the designs for a hymn set,

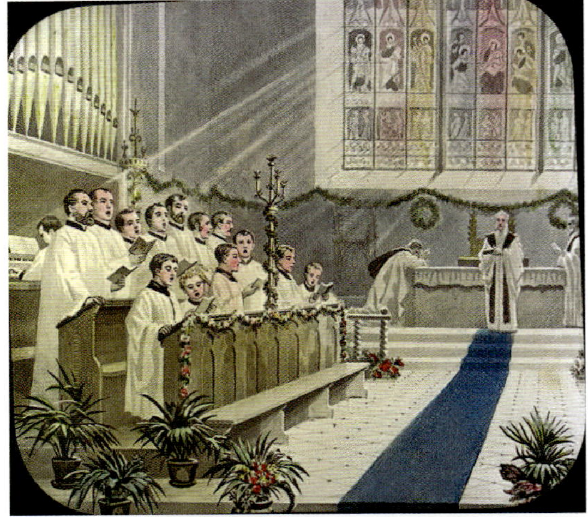

Fig. 9.12 Beale's slide 8 of *From Greenland's Icy Mountains*, a missionary hymn.

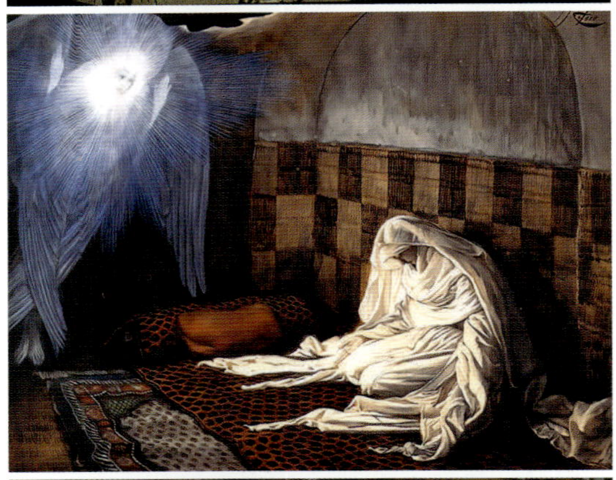

Fig. 9.13 James Tissot's slide of "The Annunciation". *Wikimedia Commons.*

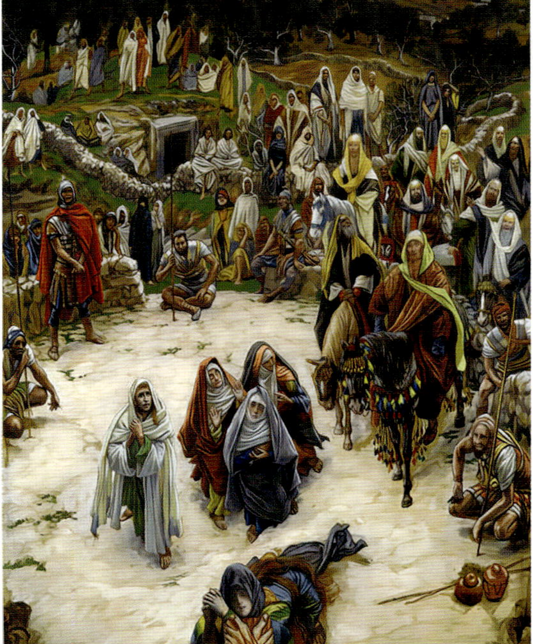

Fig. 9.14 Slide of Tissot's image, "What Our Savior Saw from the Cross". *Wikimedia Commons.*

Greenland's Icy Mountains, is an example (Fig. 9.12). The image shows a chorus singing in what certainly looks to me like an Episcopal church. On the reverse is a note from Briggs:

> McAllister suggests that this might not suit all creeds but he says he does not think of any way to improve it so you had better make it as it is. [Signed] "CWB" [C. W. Briggs]

Attention to customer concerns was important, but it was Beale's cinematic treatment that most accounted for his popularity. He did not just create single images, but often images in a narrative series that told a story with continuity. And, because the text of Bible parables and stories was often short, the slides tended to change faster than in a normal lantern reading. *The Good Shepherd* is a good example of this, changing on average every 10-20 seconds, which gives it a "movie-like" feel. This rapid projection would have increased the sense of a rich, nuanced visual presentation.

The second cinematic aspect of Beale's religious slides was his ability to dramatize supernatural subject matter. The slides were often full of *archetypal* images – angels, devils, burning bushes, giants felled by small boys, seas parting, disasters by flood and fire – images of truly "Biblical" proportions. The "greatest story ever told" was an ideal subject matter for Beale's typical deep focus treatment, allowing both a dramatic central image, and that rich supporting detail.

Religious Competition: The Slides of Tissot

By 1906, Beale's talent completely dominated the Religious area of the two major catalogs. Then in 1907 McIntosh introduced a new contender, James Tissot (1836–1902) touting his slides as, "the finest illustrations of the Life of Christ ever produced" (Fig. 9.13).[5]

Tissot, a Frenchman who spent a great deal of time in England, and who was a friend of famous artists on both side of the Channel, is a particularly interesting comparison to Beale. During the first half of Tissot's career, he concentrated on painting scenes of the fashionable – albeit often with an ironic twist. These pictures made him famous, but then, in the mid-1880s, Tissot turned to religion, whether because of personal conviction or because he saw a new market is not quite clear. He created 365 illustrations for the New Testament and, another 95 for the Old Testament. Tissot wanted his images to be "authentic", and to that end made three trips to the Middle East to sketch the sites and the customs and attire of the people – assuming that nothing had changed in the intervening 2,000–4,000 years.[6]

The paintings were used to illustrate various editions of the Bible, went on touring exhibitions, and were sold to major museums. During their American tour, they were accompanied by a magic lantern show of other Tissot art.[7] Some of Tissot's *Life of Christ* slides are indeed stunning, with dramatic new conceptions that make Beale's look staid and traditional. Particularly striking are Tissot's "The Annunciation", with a bird-like blue angelic seraph radiating fine halo lines all around her, and "What Our Savior Saw from the Cross", pictured from Christ's *point of view* with a most un-Beale-like use of negative space surrounding the foreground figures (Fig. 9.14).

But overall, Tissot's slides do not work as well on screen as do Beale's. Part of the problem is that they are all in different shapes and aspect ratios, so that when projected, the images jump around on the screen; Beale's were consistent. Part of the problem is that the rich color, dark palette, and complex design of Tissot's originals could not be reproduced well when photographed and then colored on the much-smaller slides. Beale's style was specifically designed for slide creation, tinting, and projection. Part of the problem may have been the "Catholicism" of some of Tissot's designs – an emphasis on the Virgin Mary, etc. Beale's images were Protestant, depicting Protestant church services and hymns, and the traditional Religious slide market was largely Protestant. But the most fundamental problem was that – despite the unusual "camera angles" – the Tissot slides lacked a strong narrative flow. Beale's slides had it – the quick sequences that told a Bible story with visual continuity, detail supporting the text, extended visual narrative, clarity of composition, dissolves, superimpositions, parallel editing. Perhaps as a result, McAllister did not join McIntosh in carrying Tissot, and, Beale's slides, even those created after 1907, are much more easily found today than are Tissot's.

Beale continued to be the pre-eminent illustrator of Bible stories and hymns on screen. It is likely that most American Christians of his time got their conception of the Holy Land from Beale's imagery. He must have profoundly influenced and inspired the millions who grew up from early childhood with his view of the spiritual world. Even in our Christmas shows today, Beale's angels – with their great out-swept wings and their ethereal beauty, hovering above us all on the screen – take the breath away from audiences, especially the children (Fig. 9.15).

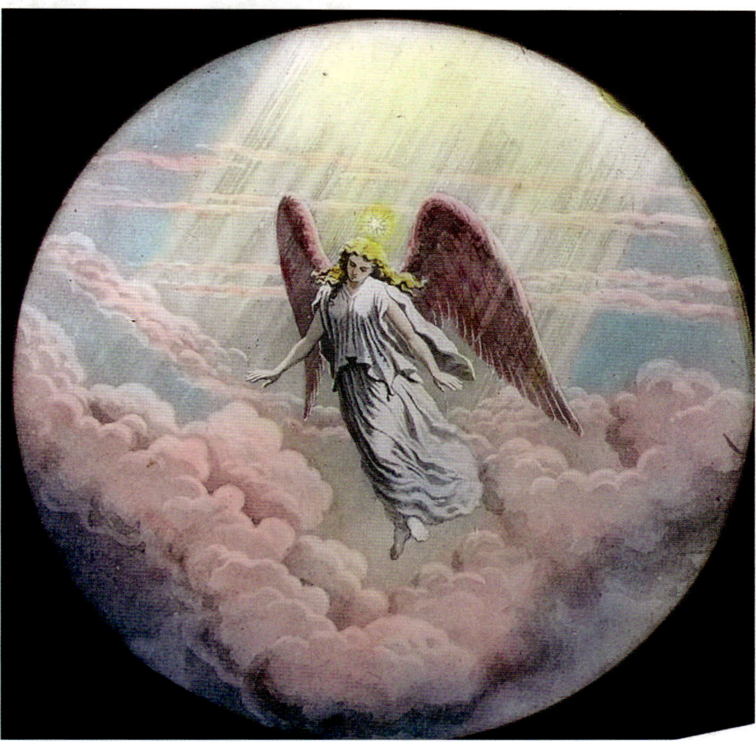

Fig. 9.15 Beale's slide of "Rays of Light from a Heaven of Peace", in *Knights of Pythias, Third Rank, Monitor*.

There was a downside, however, to Beale's visualization of Bible stories, a downside true with all audiences, but especially when his slides were used in missionary work, as many were. Curriculum-studies scholar Younsun Choi has pointed out that although the background of Beale's illustrations was the Middle East, the characters were all Caucasian. Moreover, the servants portrayed in such stories were almost universally Black and often portrayed in a stereotypical manner.[8] So when a missionary taught the parable of "The Wedding Feast" to an African or African American or Asian audience using Beale's slides, he was sending a double message. The explicit message of the text suggested that Heaven was open to all who heeded the call; the imbedded visual message of Beale's images was that People of Color would be the servants in Heaven.

I must also tell you also that not all was solemnity in 19th century churches. At my very first public show in the 1970s, at a neighborhood historical society, an old man came up to say that he remembered lantern slides from church when he was a child. At that point I knew almost nothing about the magic lantern except that my great-grandfather had one. I had never imagined that the lantern might be used in church, so I asked him to tell me more. He explained how

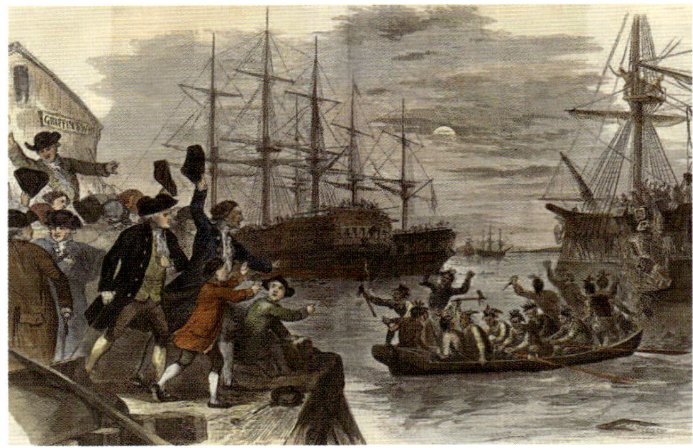

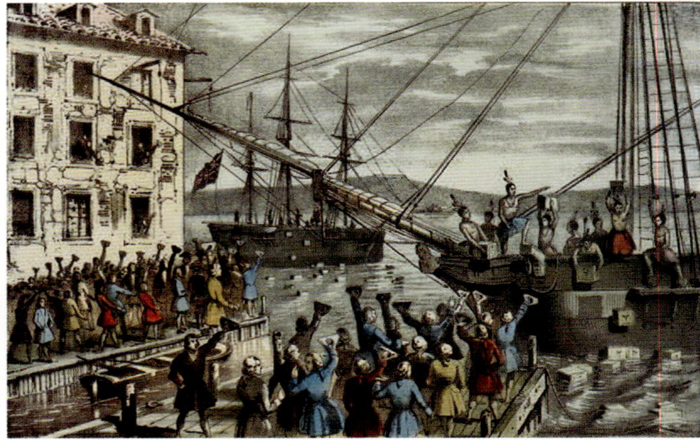

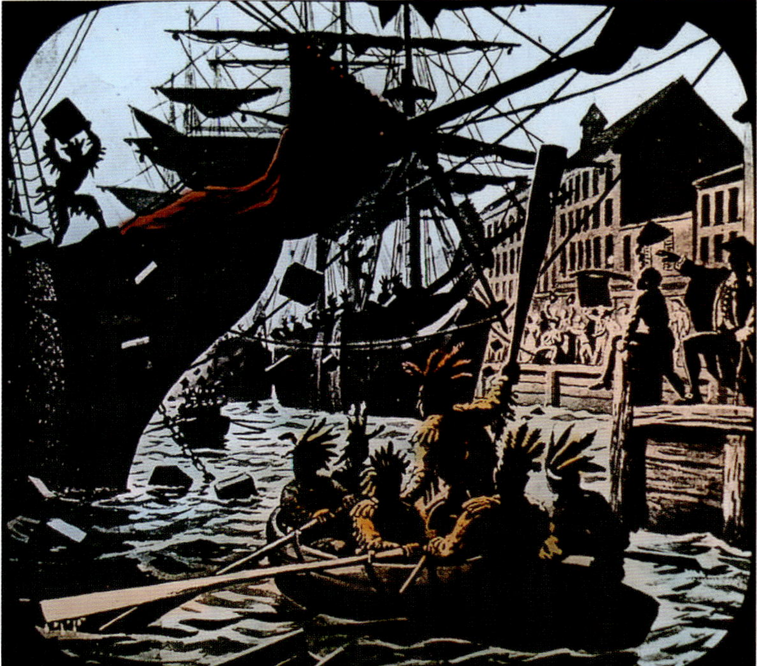

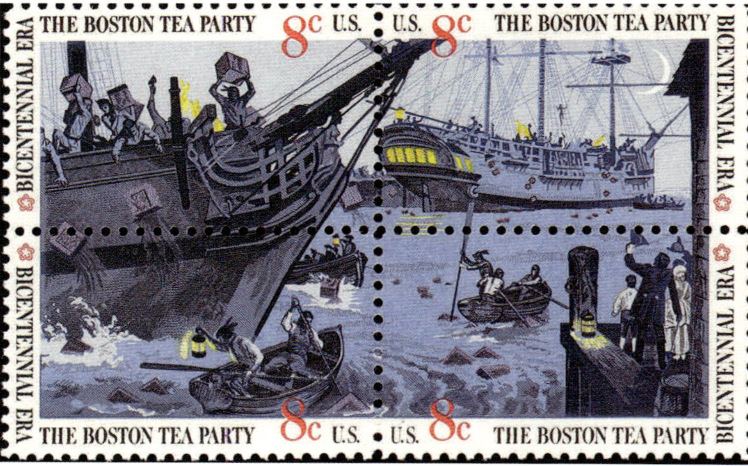

Fig. 9.16 Four views of "The Boston Tea Party". Beale's image is at the center.

he had seen illustrated Bible stories and hymns in Sunday School, and then, he said, "The teacher used to tell us that if we were really good, we could see the cartoons".

"The cartoons?" I asked. I didn't understand. I couldn't even imagine.

"Yes. You know. Like you showed tonight. The man with the growing nose". He grinned. "And the man who eats rats".

I don't think the Ratcatcher has made it into modern religious practice, but in other ways magic lantern religious imagery was clearly a pacesetter. Not too long ago we gave our *Bible Show* at a huge church in Tidewater, Virginia, hometown of the Christian Broadcasting Network. As I was setting up, I noticed that microphones blocked the white wall on which I intended to project our show. I asked the custodian if he could move them. "No need to do that", he said. "Nobody'll notice them. Every week the minister does a PowerPoint presentation of pictures on that wall to illustrate the sermon and hymns. You can't hardly see the microphones".

Magic Lantern PowerPoint – very modern, very high tech – alive and well in the churches of today.

History/Biography/Current Events

For many years art that depicted history was considered the "highest" genre of art, in part because of its narrative power. Beale's History slides were another major area of concentration in his work, providing a sweeping panorama of American and world events – 349 slides, or about 13 percent of his work, in 32 sets. They accounted for about 25 percent of all such slides offered in the magic lantern catalogs, and consisted of three distinct categories: Histories; Biographies, and Current Events.

Beale's *style* in the History slides suited the heroes and heroines who made up the nineteenth century's *centrist ideology* of history as a progressive story of civilization – the Story of Man. Heroic historical figures represented the force of character – the courage, intelligence, and discipline – that were part of every American's heritage, and to which all could aspire.

The market for these slides was primarily schools, and, as we shall see, secret societies. Most of the magic lantern catalogs carried History well before Beale began work, though the number of images was limited. Beale's role was to both re-draw existing pictures in order to make them more effective on screen, and to create new slides that would make historical events real for his viewers.

Some of the History slides are in sets telling a story that Beale narrates in a series of pictures, much as he illustrated Literature. But others tell a well-known story in a single picture, and this presents new challenges for his narrative art. We can see how he handles them by comparing his depiction of a well-known incident, the Boston Tea Party (center), with roughly contemporaneous illustrations – an engraving by John Andrews (top left), and Currier and Ives engraving (top right) (Fig. 9.16).

The most striking difference between Beale's image and his contemporaries is that Beale places the action not in daylight or dusk, but at night, when it did in fact occur. By doing so he has already added realistic information to the image, and, with his silhouetted composition, added drama as well. Both of the other illustrations are also crowded with people who clutter the foreground, detracting from the story. The main action, the rebels dressed as "Indians" throwing tea overboard, is completely lost in the picture at top left, and largely lost in the one at top right. Large crowds fill Beale's illustration also, but they are minimized in the background, their energy represented by the single hat-waving boy at right, who is visually separated from the tea-tossing action by an Indian's upraised oar.

As a result, in Beale's version the *rim-lighted* Indians in the foreground dominate the image as they approach the ship, their rebellious intentions represented by an Indian above them hurling a tea box. He is literally *highlighted* against the sky so that our eye goes from the Indians in the rowboat to this silhouetted focal point.[9] Beale has chosen to present the story in the middle of the time sequence. The Indians are not yet all on board, but tea is already raining down into the water. When the additional boatloads of Indians swarm the looming British vessels, even more tea will fill the air. Like the depiction in *Macbeth* of two scenes within one slide, this is a version of the "extended visual narrative" technique – presenting one scene while implying another that will complete the story.

Another difference between Beale's depiction and the others is that Beale moves his audience much nearer to the story's events. Our ***vantage point*** is not among the distant spectators, as in the other two versions, but as close-up eyewitnesses. Beale's framing places us just a few feet behind the Indian's rowboat. It is as though we were Indians ourselves, in another boat rowing toward the action. Beale has, in effect, immersed us in the revolt, and made us participants. It's no surprise then that when the US Postal Service decided to create a four-block US stamp of The Boston Tea Party (bottom left), Beale's image provided the model.

Beale uses these eye-witness techniques in many other History situations, and in other areas as well, especially when the action is dramatic and he wants to involve us. In "Battle of Bull Run" he places the audience right in the path of the panicked Union retreat. In "Volunteer's Return" he pulls in close to the joyful family and has the soldier turned away – becoming a generic solider – so we're tempted to follow the girl in and hug him too. And in "Admiral Dewey Directing Movements of the Fleet" he puts a gatling gun so close to the frame that it seems to be firing right over our heads. All such views immerse us in the action, adding to its drama – most especially if we are sitting up front in the audience (Fig. 9.17).

It is Beale's original slides like these that make his History come alive. His revisions of History slides are infused with the same sensibility, not only making the pictures clearer for projection, but adding intriguing details, striking design, action-packed adventure, and provoking symbolism. His combination of story-telling action and his attention to audience sensibilities made his History images a standard of American historical *iconography*, which, as we will see, persisted after his death into the mid twentieth century. Indeed, if you search Google images today for a picture of most important American events before 1910, you are likely to find a Beale image (though not identified by his name), and it is likely to be the best available from his period.

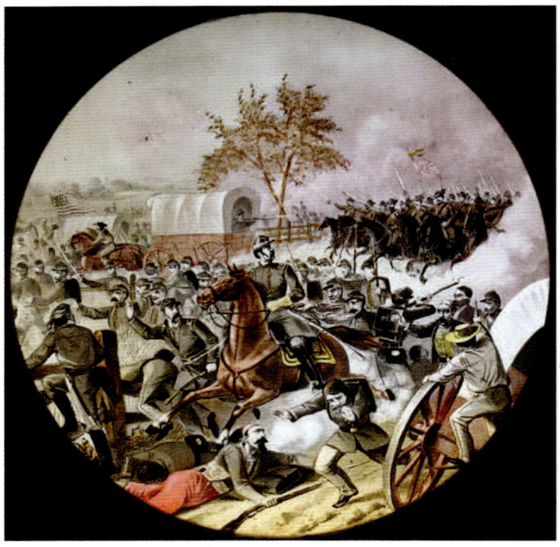

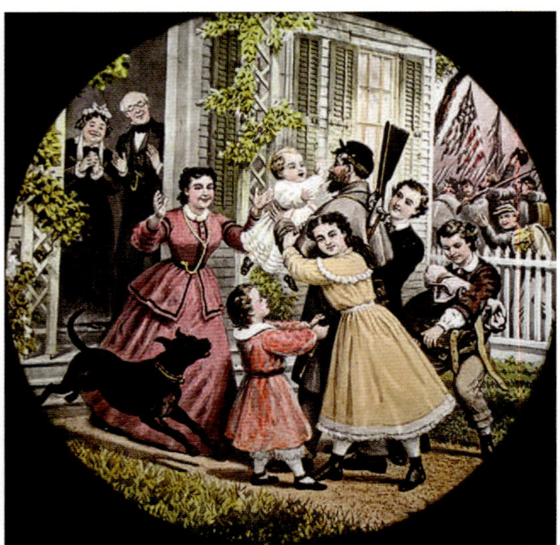

Fig. 9.17 Three Beale war slides draw us into the action: "Battle of Bull Run" (left); "Volunteer's Return" (right); and "Admiral Dewey Directing Movements of the Fleet" (bottom right).

Beale's History slides are the driving force in our *Patriotic Show*, which blends history, story and song to depict the American saga from the time of the Indians to 1900 (Fig. 9.18). This show is our most popular school program, and we have performed it many, many times before this most demanding of audiences. Beale does an excellent job of holding them. Usually, the teachers sit with the kids to help keep order, but at one show the teachers said they had a meeting. First one left. Then a half-dozen. Then all of them. Then the principal walked out too.

There we were, in the dark...two performers, 400 kids, and Beale. No problem.

Well, not much.

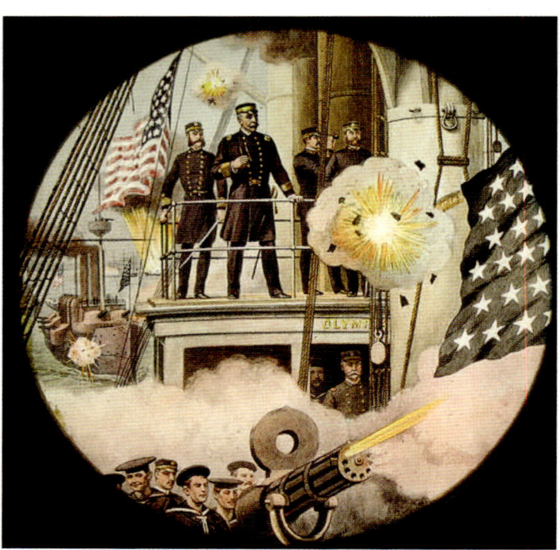

Fig. 9.18 Beale's slide of" Goddess of Liberty" from the *Patriotic Sons of America* set.

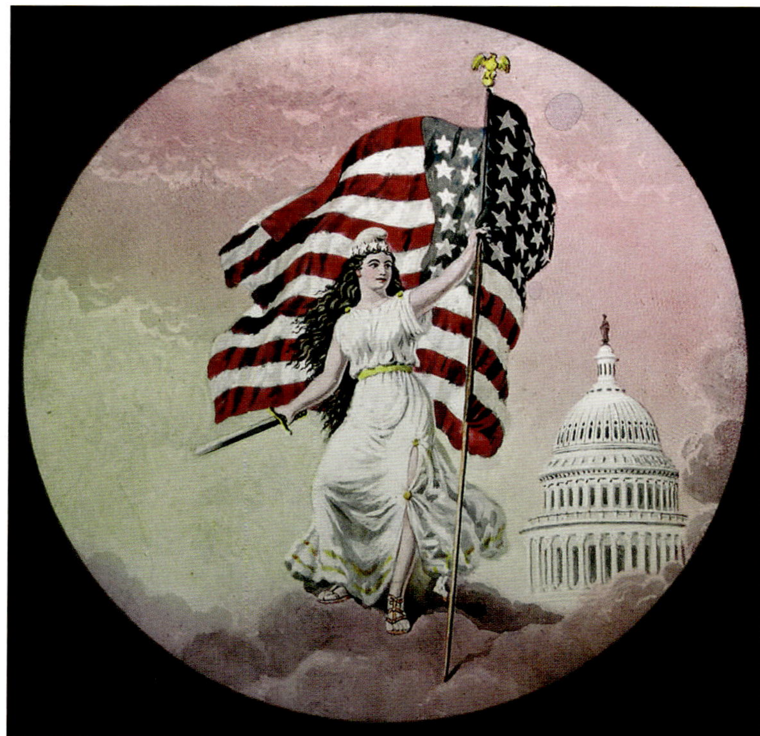

(When I first began performing school shows, I had a lot of trouble maintaining control, Beale or no. I was miserable; the teachers were not pleased; neither were the students. But bit by bit I discovered that my stage character gave me a license that I would not otherwise have had. I could stamp on the floor with my cane, speak in a theatrical voice, demand respect. The kids accepted control from me in my showman's character and costume that they would not have if I had been in jeans and a tee shirt.)

Historical Biographies

The "Life of" sets form a distinct Beale category of biographical work. Like the General History sets, some of the "Life of" sets were in the catalogs before Beale began working, so his slides are mixed in with others, notably in *The Life of Washington.*

The most striking set is *The Life of Lincoln.* The colorful early manhood of Lincoln and his long,

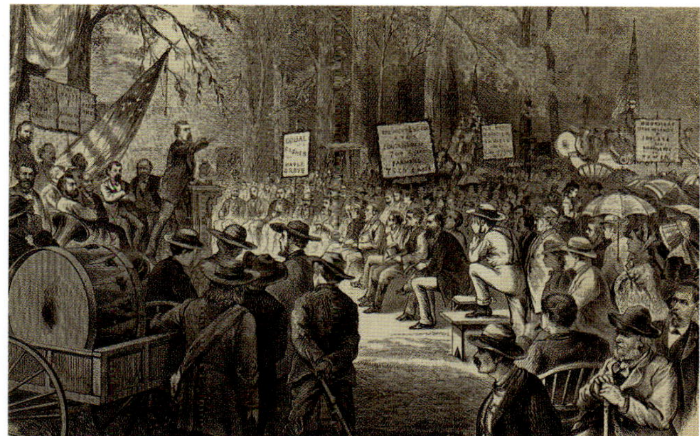

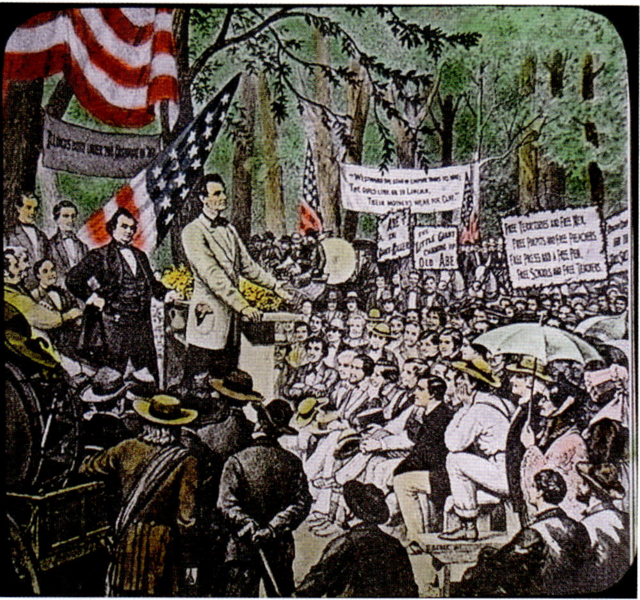

lanky frame provided both stirring story content and a visually dramatic actor to inspire Beale's patriotic brush. The development of one image, "Lincoln's Debate with Douglas", gives a fascinating glimpse into how Beale worked, and how his slide images were later used. While Beale was free-lancing for *Leslie's* in Chicago he was assigned to cover a Grange meeting, and produced a striking August 20, 1873 image of a large outdoor session. When he was later asked to produce a *Life of Lincoln* set, he simply took his earlier image, substituted Lincoln for the Grange speaker, and made a few other minor changes. He ended up not only with an excellent lantern slide, but a 1958 U. S. stamp as well (Fig. 9.19).

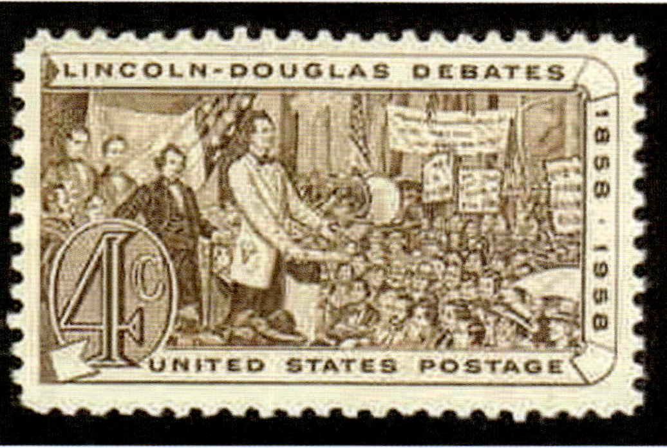

Fig. 9.19 At top left, Beale's 1873 etching in *Leslie's Illustrated Newspaper*. At top right, his 1898 adaptation of his own earlier image to make slide 3, "Lincoln's Debate with Douglas". At bottom, a 1958 U. S. Stamp made from Beale's slide image.

In general, we use individual slides from the *Life* sets in our shows, rather than the entire *Life,* since modern audiences do not share the earlier-period hunger for biography. The exception is *Lincoln* which we present as part of our *Civil War Show,* not as a straight *Life of Lincoln*, but as illustrations for "The Gettysburg Address". I'm not sure this is something that the lanternists ever did, but they certainly "could have" (one of the guidelines for our shows), and seeing Lincoln's life as a visualization for a government "of the people, by the people, and for the people" adds a new depth of meaning to Lincoln's famous words.

Our *Civil War Show* has a problem presenting a balanced treatment of North and South. Since "the victors write the history", and since the

"Cinema Verité" – The Children's War

Another way to assess the dramatic "cinema verité" quality of Beale's images is to contrast them with photographic images of war, and some children's slides of the Spanish American War allow us to do just that.

In 1902, a number of Beale's Spanish American War views were mixed with photographs, four images to a slide, and sold by Sears Roebuck for their children's lanterns. Sears refers to them all as "actual photographic views" – technically correct since Beale's slides were also reproduced photographically.

But why did Sears mix illustrations and photographs in the War series? The answer is clear enough from looking at the slides: The photos show the "actuality" – the steam rising from the cooking kettle, the slump of the soldiers carrying their dead. But it is Beale who shows both the actuality and the drama of the fight – the blaze of guns and the blaze of adrenalin. Photographers had not captured the action and emotion of war as powerfully as did Beale's designs. See note 20.

magic lantern business was located in the North, very few slides of the Southern army's victories exist. Though I've tried very hard to present a balanced picture, I'm conscious that I'm straining, especially when presenting to Southern audiences, or Southern re-enactors. The same comment applies throughout Beale's "history of the present", his Current Events coverage. You don't see much of the "other side" in his reporting.

Current Events

Covering current events was a part of the magic lantern tradition from its beginnings. I have already mentioned how early 18th century slides depicted battles of the time, and how reports from the front were a part of the Royal Polytechnic shows in mid-19th century London. In the United States, only one year after the start of the Civil War, the firm of N. B. Chamberlain & Sons in Boston was continuing the tradition, rushing out colored magic lantern pictures of the American Civil War, from the beginning of the bombardment of Fort Sumter to the date of publication.

Current events coverage by Beale was also concentrated on war, with occasional commemorative *Lives* such as that prompted by the assassination of President McKinley, and the two-slide dissolving set, *Martinique Disaster*, showing the volcanic eruption on St. Pierre Island in 1902. *The Spanish-American War* sets were by far the most popular of these Current Events productions, totaling 65 sides in all, a hot *property* for Briggs because the Spanish American War was a defining moment in American history.[10] It was against one of the great colonial powers of Europe; it came at the symbolic end of one century and the beginning of a new; it brought American Yankees and Southern Rebels together to fight under one flag again; it had the exuberant participation of Teddy Roosevelt; it was easily won by America; and it made America a world power for the first time. Plus, it was the first war to be covered by and celebrated by the movies, a feature that we will discuss in the next chapter.

Developing slides for Current Events like the Spanish American War presented Beale with a number of challenges. His assignment was not like being a "regimental artist" during the Civil War. He was not on the scene, and thus he had to make up images that gave a sense of "*cinema verité*" without having actually seen the action itself. To do this he seems to have relied primarily on the pictorial news reporting from his old print employers like *Leslie's*. Once he had a sense of what had happened, Beale still had to balance accurate reporting against the demands of a public hungry for heroic images. His treatment of Lt. Richmond Hobson's exploits is an illuminating example.

Hobson was a fiery, extremely handsome, but awkward young man who was a military construction specialist. He was assigned to bottle up the Spanish fleet under Admiral Cervera in Santiago harbor by sinking an old ship, "The Merrimac", across the entrance. (This was a coal ship, not the famous Civil War iron-clad.) Unfortunately, Hobson's ship was spotted, shelled, and lost its steering. By the time the ship sank from the bombardment and Hobson's own explosive charges, it was no longer blocking the harbor channel. Hobson and his men escaped to a raft, where they were rescued by none other than the Spanish Admiral himself, imprisoned, and subsequently released in a prisoner exchange.

The drama of this action, even though unsuccessful, caught the American public's imagination, as it was considered a suicide mission. When Hobson eventually returned home he was treated as a hero, and mobbed by adoring female fans, hundreds of whom demanded a "Hobson kiss" – still known to us today by the chocolate confection it inspired, the "Hershey Kiss".[11]

Beale's first treatment of this incident is fittingly dramatic, and quite realistic (Fig. 9.20). The *distance of framing* is close, so that the great bulk of Hobson's ship dominates the scene as it explodes and sinks in the background. In the foreground, Hobson and his crew, dressed in life-vests, and indistinguishable from each other in the water, struggle to help one another toward a shattered life raft that itself looks on the verge of sinking.

Realistic, yes, but apparently it was neither dramatic enough nor heroic enough to suit the public demand.

In Beale's second version, he creates a new image (Fig. 9.21). In this approach he pulls back the distance of framing so that the ship is further in the background, and we can see more of the foreground scene. He adds the Spanish shore battery blazing away in the distance, and the American flag, still fluttering defiantly over the sinking ship. In the middle distance, sailors don't swim for their lives; they ride safely in a spiffy-looking catamaran. No one wears a wimpy life-vest. Hobson is no longer indistinguishable from the others. Now he stands heroically upright on the raft amid the bombardment, dressed in full military regalia. He gestures toward his sinking ship with one hand and with the other points the way past some treacherous rocks that have conveniently appeared in the foreground to increase the dangers to be overcome by our dauntless hero. The depiction may not be accurate, but Beale has certainly found ways to extend the visual narrative.

The revision was a great popular success. Five different magic lantern catalogs used *"Hobson's Sinking of the Merrimac"* or other Beale images to promote their war coverage. Harbach's 1903 catalog assured its customers:

> The sight of this view will be thoroughly appreciated and applauded by all lovers of patriotism and bravery .... With such views, the exhibitor will often be requested to repeat the performance the next night.[12]

Harbach's catalog gave the war an eight-page spread – an unprecedented amount of space to devote to a single subject. Two other catalogs each devoted two illustrated pages to the war, a commitment of precious space was in itself unusual. Their spreads included up to four Beale images; another image was featured on the preprinted poster offered to advertise the war slide program. The fact that Beale's treatment of the war received such extensive promotion five years after it was over is a testament to the grip it had on the public imagination, and to the impact of Beale's visual reporting.

But not every Current Events slide set had such sales. Beale's 1905 slides on the Russo-Japanese War were a vain effort to duplicate the earlier success. They dropped from the catalogs almost immediately.

Temperance Slides

The Temperance slides form a distinct though relatively small category of Beale's output – ten sets, a total of 53 slides, or about 2% of his work.

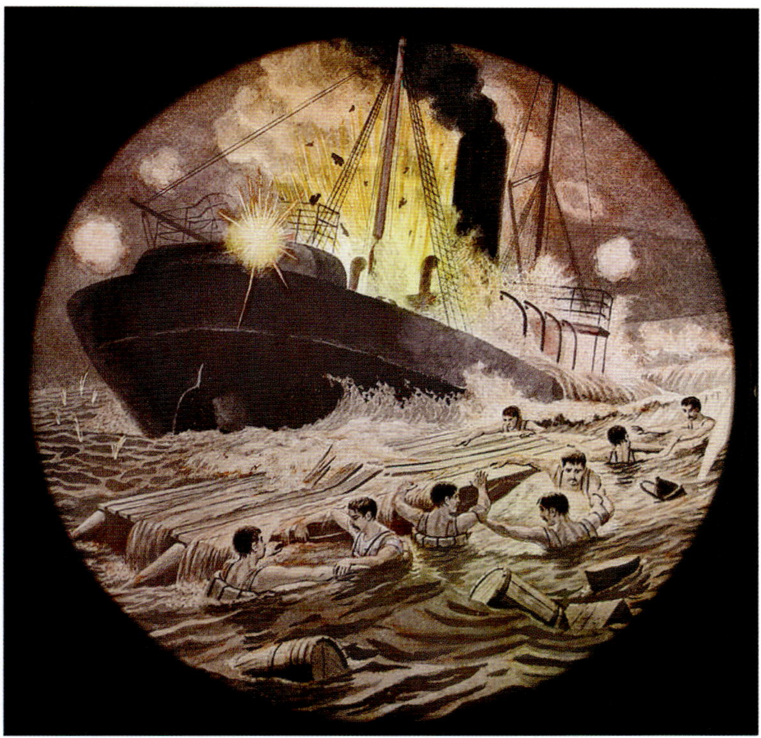

Fig. 9.20 Beale's first slide of "Sinking of the Merrimac" from the *Spanish-American War* set.

The Temperance Movement was in full-swing by the latter 19th Century, spurred by the creation of a third "single-issue" political party in 1869 (the Prohibition Party), and the organization of the National Woman's Christian Temperance Union (WCTU) in 1873. At its height, the WCTU had forty staffed state offices, and ten thousand local unions. As its name implies, the movement was closely associated with churches. Its mission was to combat

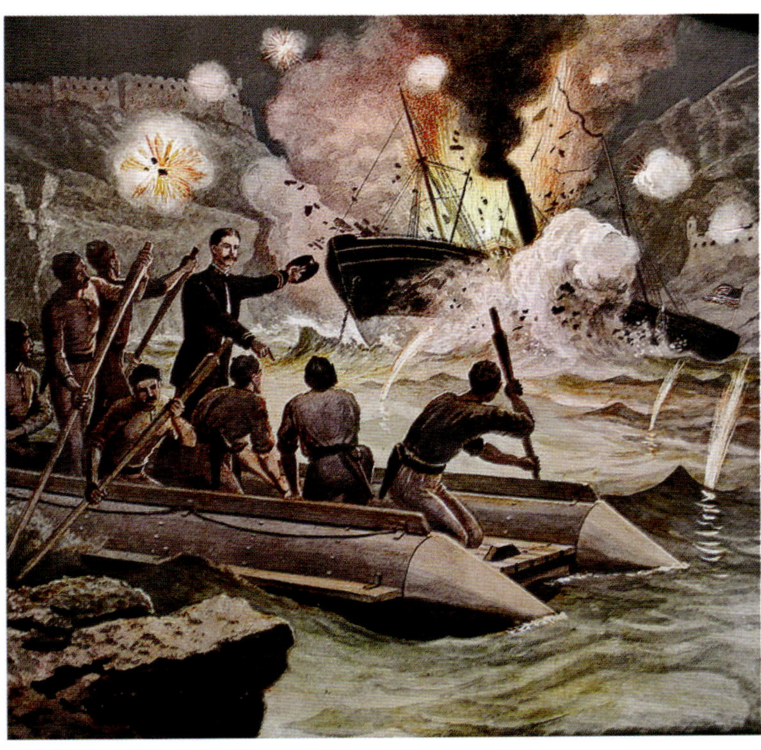

Fig. 9.21 Beale's revision of "Sinking of the Merrimac" from the Spanish-American War set.

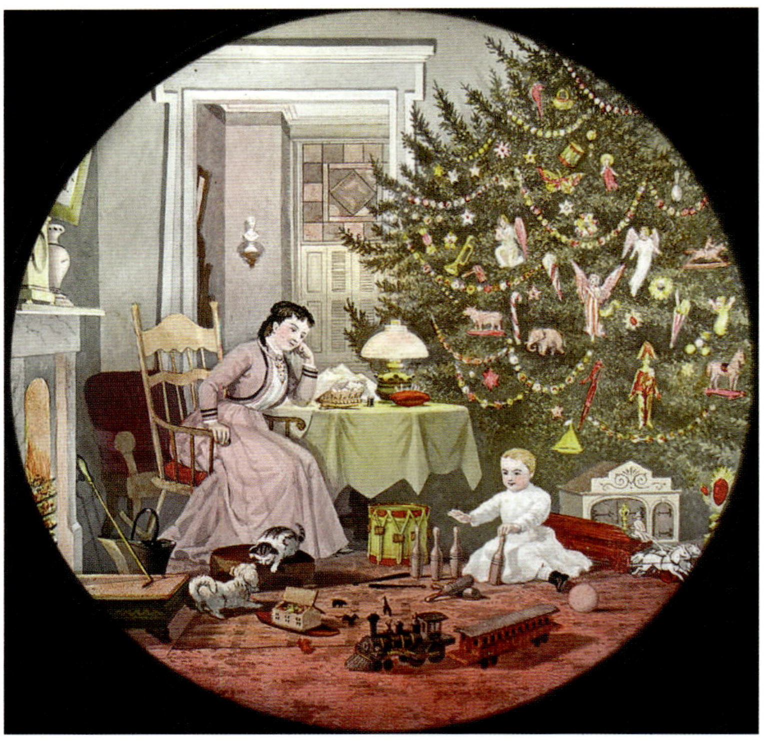

Fig. 9.22 Beale's slide 1 from *Where is My Wandering Boy To-Night?* by Henry Burr and Robert Lowery.

Fig. 9.23 Beale's slide 3 from *Where is My Wandering Boy To-Night?*

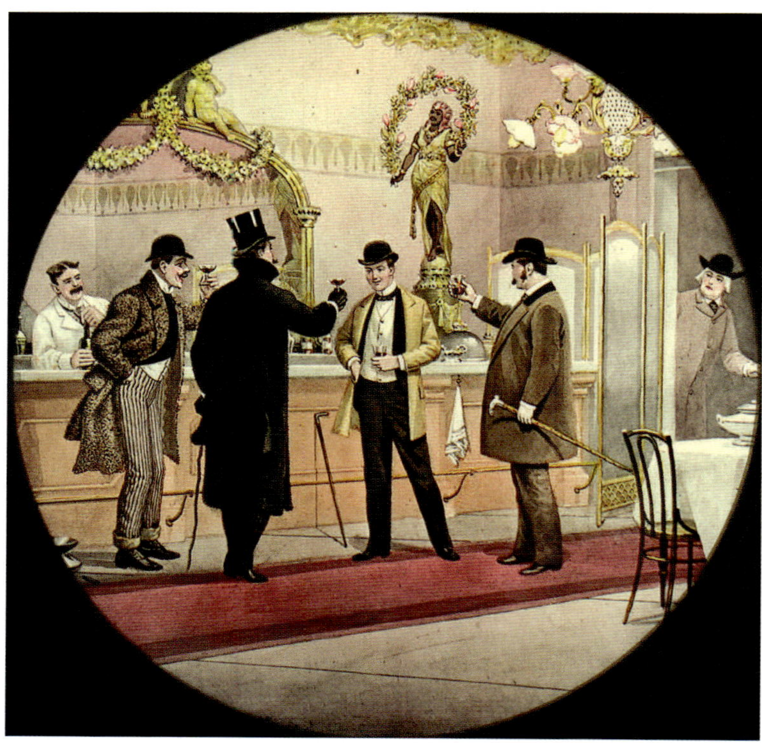

alcoholism – a curse that one modern historian has called "the major pathology of American society almost from its inception".[13]

In England, as I have already mentioned, firms like Bamforth and Co. produced and marketed "life model" temperance slides, dramatizing specially written moral tales about working men who took the temperance pledge, or who wished they had. One of Bamforth's major customers, the Band of Hope organization, gave 12,300 lantern lectures over a 50-year period. But despite the need for temperance in America, no similar wide-spread campaign with the lantern seems to have occurred. The British "From Life" temperance slides were never popular in America, perhaps because the stories were too mawkish for the American sensibility or too "English" in their depiction. Even the English lanternists complained of the lantern fare they were fed:

> Mr. Moss states that goody goody or preaching is not wanted for entertainments and that he fails to see what good it will do us to have our sympathies awakened – children do not always care to go to an entertainment which finishes up with a good cry.[14]

Some American lantern lectures of the *rhetorical form* tried to persuade people of the error of their ways, and a few temperance stories were shown, but not many, and those tended to have a harder edge to them. Briggs himself carried several sets inherited from Langenheim, but did not have Beale re-do them – a clear sign that they were not a high priority.

Where Is My Wandering Boy Tonight? is a temperance song which Beale did illustrate in its entirety. Since the song gives only the bare bones of the story, he created his own rich visual narrative, layered with suggestive symbols.

Slide 1 (Fig. 9.22) shows a young mother sitting by the fire, watching her baby play with toys beside a beautiful Christmas tree and under its protective angel decorations – establishing at once a religious connotation, and a sense of innocent happiness. In the next slide (not shown) we see the child a few years later, as a youngster, saying his bedtime prayers.

When next we see the boy, he is grown, and no longer at home (Fig. 9.23). We find him in a bar, being toasted by a gentleman in black cloak and top hat whose face and hands (significantly) are hidden. A "dark angel", a statue of a lascivious Nubian maiden, hovers above the boy, and seems about to capture him with a flowered garland. At the door, in the secondary story of this picture, is a "good angel", recognizable from his dress as a teetotaling Quaker or parson, sent by Mother to bring the boy home.

The slide used to depict the chorus (Fig. 9.24), shows Mother waiting for her "wandering boy" in the same room as before. Older and much worn with worry, she sits in her rocker with a Bible in her lap. She is framed by two looming shadows, one of herself in the chair, the other of an empty chair, suggesting the unknown forces contending for her son. His picture is framed above her. The empty doorway and his empty chair beside her are testaments to her anguish, and the lead-ins for the visual narrative of the next scene.

In the final scene (Fig. 9.25), the wandering boy appears in the doorway, and mother and son are re-united, thanks to the boy's "good angel" who stands behind them. The boy recognizes the error of his ways. He places his "man about town" hat and cane in his chair beside the home fire, ready to settle down and embrace his mother's love.

Despite this set's clear story, beauty, and effective use of symbolism, we have had a great deal of trouble getting modern audiences to accept it on its own terms, and to appreciate it. When we first began performing it, and I announced the title, *Where Is My Wandering Boy Tonight?*, the audience laughed, no matter how I changed my inflection. They probably shared the 19th century concerns about drug use, but they took Beale's entire song as a campy joke.

Finally, I stopped announcing the title of the song in my introduction. Our singer simply began as the first slide faded in. That worked much better. The audience became caught up in the story, until, that is, they saw the boy in the bar. Then they began laughing again. My problem was the jump cut between the two slides. Gradually I learned to make the transition from boy to barfly not a jump cut but a very, *very* slow dissolve, suggesting the span of many years from childhood to manhood. The laugh usually disappeared, especially if the singer also eased into the verse. Modern audiences were touched by the tale of a mother's anguish, and were generally able to accept this morality play as a meaningful expression of the pain of alcoholism – pain that is as real in modern times as it was in Beale's day.

Though there were period parodies of *Wandering Boy*, I don't think Victorian showmen had the problems I have had presenting it, especially when they were presenting to church and temperance audiences. It was very popular. Slides from it pop up all the time today on eBay.

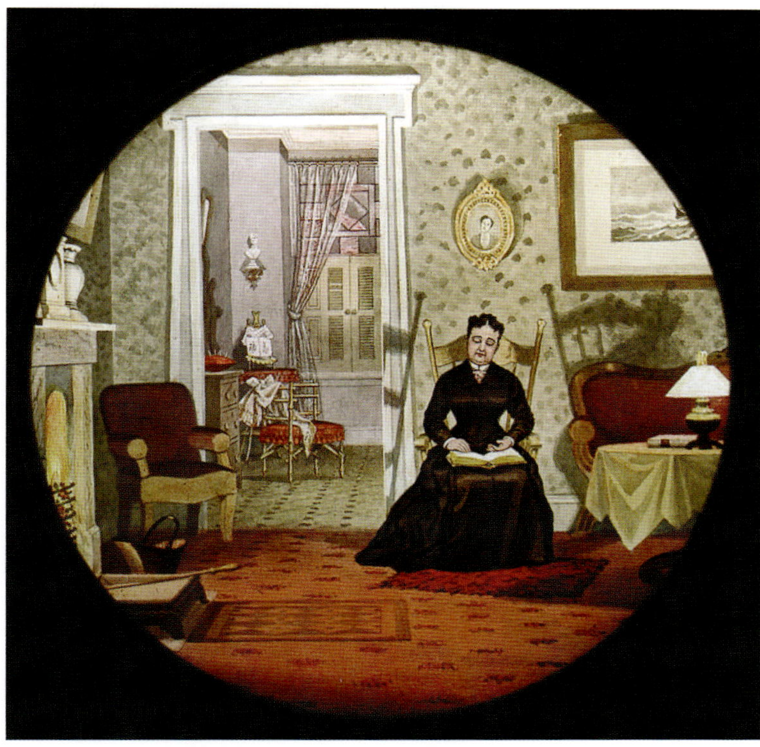

Fig. 9.24 Beale's slide 5 from *Where is My Wandering Boy To-Night?*

George Olney, a turn-of-the-century lanternist who made it a centerpiece of his shows, claimed to have "lectured in 4,000 churches".[15]

Secret Society Slides

Slides for Secret Societies may seem like an odd category, but it was a major one for Beale, totaling 406 slides in 36 different sets, or about 15 percent of his output. Those Beale slides

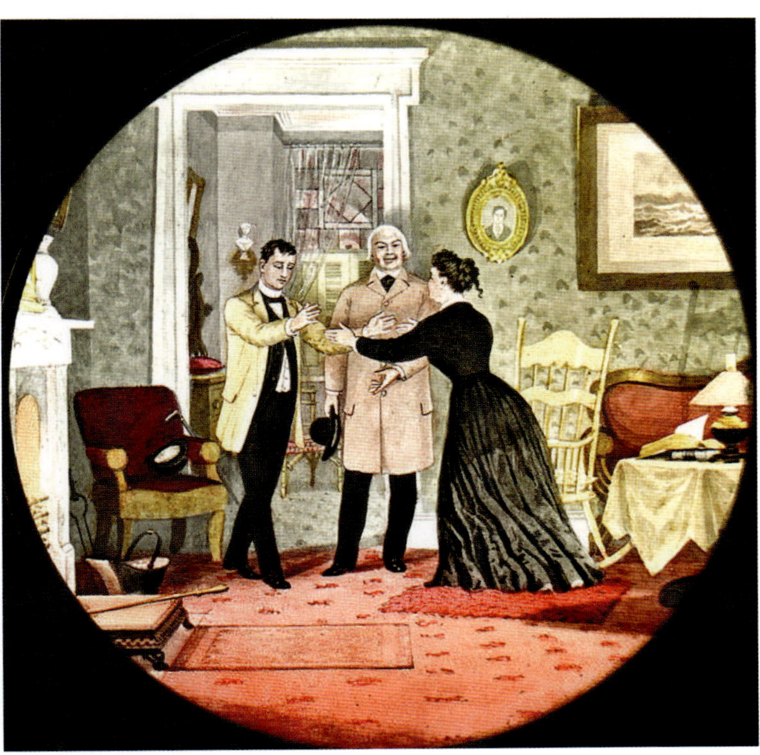

Fig. 9.25 Beale's slide 6 of *Where is My Wandering Boy To-Night?*

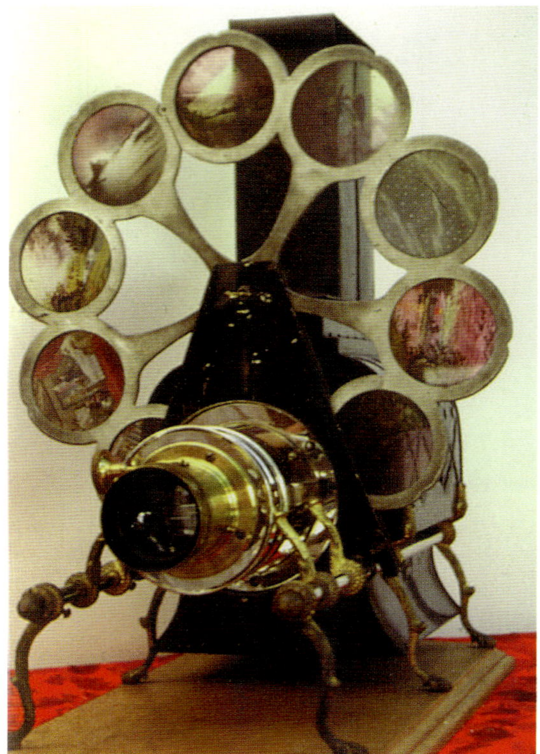

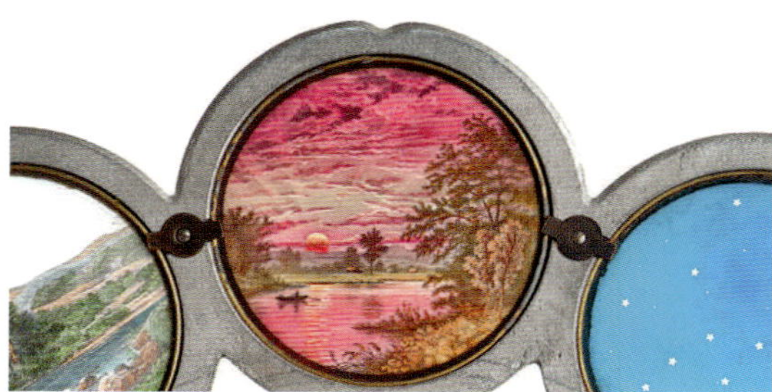

Fig. 9.26 Top, a Pettibone "Peacock" lantern of The Knights of Pythias. Bottom, Beale's "Sunset Glows with Rubies", one of a set in the Peacock format.

accounted for about 50 percent of all Secret Society slides offered in the magic lantern catalogs.

Many of Beale's Secret Society images are used elsewhere in the catalogs, especially in Religious sets. About 165, or 41 percent, are used in both areas – most of those first appearing in the Religious sections, and then adapted for Secret Society use. In addition, patriotic societies like The Patriotic Order of America had a heavy crossover with History sets. Such dual use of Beale's images made Secret Societies a very attractive marketing opportunity for Briggs.[16]

Visit any of the small Eastern or Mid-Western towns that have preserved their 19th Century Main Street heritage, and you will easily see why Briggs emphasized Secret Societies. The lodges (or "Temples") of the societies tower over the street: the Masons, the Knights of Pythias, the Oddfellows – each one trying to outdo the others in grandeur. These fraternal lodges were a mainstay of 19th century social life. The Masons, the largest of the societies, had 860,000 members at the turn of the century and was a road to power. By the 1890s, eight of America's 23 presidents had been Masons. But the world of secret societies was much broader than the Masons. Probably one in three adult males at this time belonged to a fraternal organization, including many members of the poorer classes. The non-Masonic secret societies may not have been as prestigious, but they provided ready fellowship, and their elaborate rituals, costumes, and titles gave a sense of importance to people whose lives might otherwise be consumed only with work (Fig. 9.26).[17]

The magic lantern was a widespread, almost ubiquitous, method of presenting the rituals and secret ceremonies of these Societies. There were magic lantern manufacturers and catalogs that catered almost exclusively to this market, and it was a major part of Briggs's business. Indeed, the use of ritual slides continues in the modern era. At our shows I have met several current-day lodge members who told me that their old magic lantern is still projecting its 100+ year-old Beale images, and, in fact, Beale Masonic images are still being sold in their more modern 35mm format.[18]

The scenes depicted in fraternal images ranged from the simple outlines of mystical objects ("The All-Seeing Eye", or the "Skull"), to stories, religious icons, patriotic subjects, and evocative landscapes. Here are four slides from the *Knights of Pythias, Third Rank, Pythagoras*, and the script (very significantly shortened) that would have been read to initiates as the slides were projected. I have boldfaced the key words related to the slides (Fig. 9.27), the final image of which is also the display image at the start of this chapter).

> Centuries before your eyes had opened on the light of day, I had attained the **knowledge of all the ages** ... . The journey before you is to you unknown. It lies, perhaps, through **flower-bespangled plains** and verdant meads, where summer sunshine sifts through interlacing boughs, and perfumed zephyrs sigh ... . It peradventure winds its devious and uncertain way along **the mountain side**, where unscaled peaks lift their towering summits amid the thunder's sullen roar ... . Mayhap it leads through bog and fen and foul morass, **where hideous creatures climb** and crawl, and slimy serpents cling and coil, and nameless, countless horrors lurk unseen.[19]

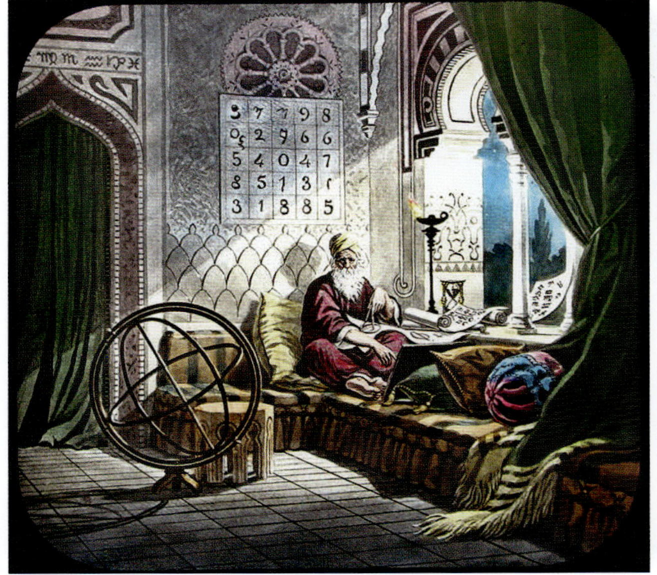
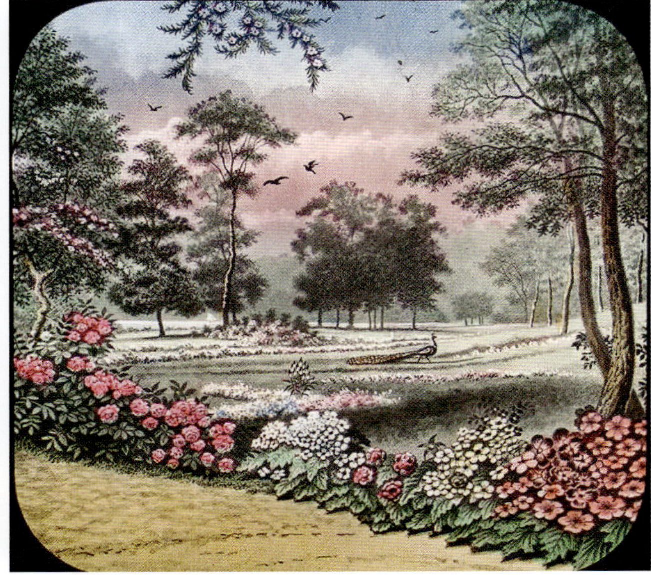
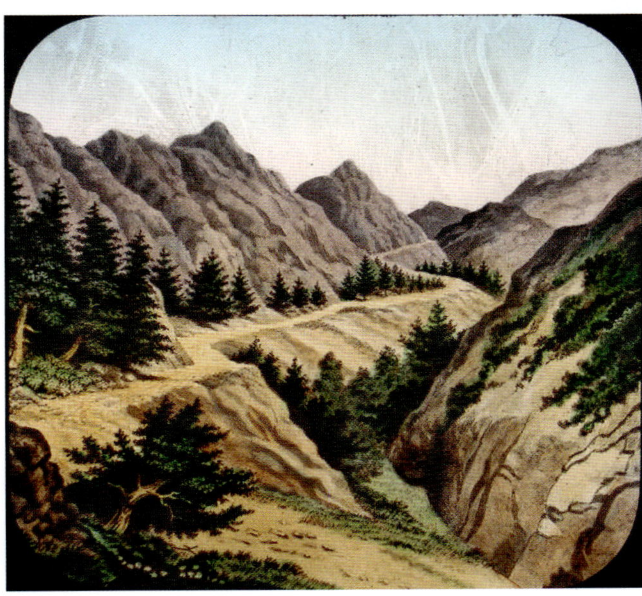
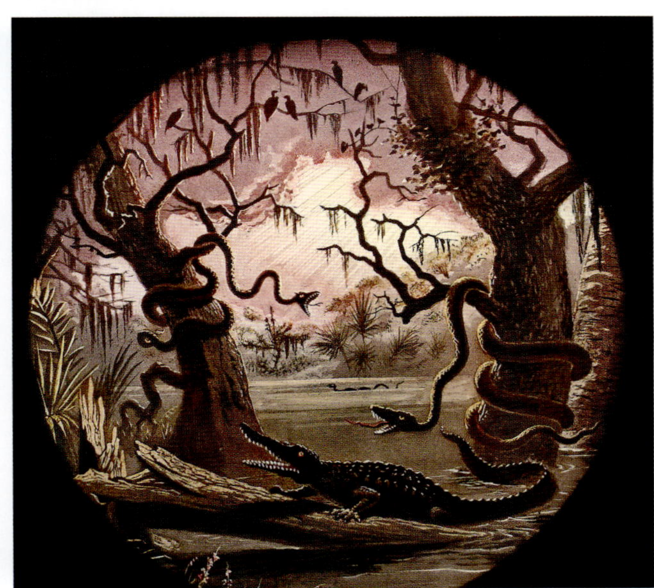

Fig. 9.27 Four Beale Secret Society slides from *Knights of Pythias, Third Rank, Pythagoras.* Top left, "The Philosopher". Top right, "The Flowery Plain. Bottom left, "The Mountain Side, Winding Road". Bottom right, "Where Hideous Creatures Climb".

Beale's mythical landscapes and scenes for Secret Societies are among his most *painterly* and *lyrical* – soft-edged, colorful images brimming with evocative appeal. The dissolve sequences and superimpositions must have added considerably to the mystical feeling that was essential to the Secret Societies' hold on their members' imagination.

Many of these images do not seem to be intended, as were the Parables, to invite a viewer into the story. They were used to overwhelm the initiate. Try to imagine yourself coming to an ornate lodge "temple", filled with strange trappings and men dressed in the elaborate costumes of "ancient orders". You are kept apart, then asked to come into a large, darkened room and stand alone before a screen. A voice in the dark leads you on a guided meditation as the images change. You are so close to the screen and so alone that when Beale's slides are projected, you feel totally immersed in their imagery, surrounded by evocative scenes and landscapes. It must have been quite an extraordinary experience.

It is easy now to poke fun at these fraternal societies, but for the nineteenth century they provided essential functions – fellowship, life and burial insurance, a sense of fun and drama, a connection to a larger world. And of course, Beale's lantern slide rituals were spectacular. "Lodge night" was not to be missed. By 1920, I estimate that about six million men were watching Beale's slides every month in fraternal settings.[20]

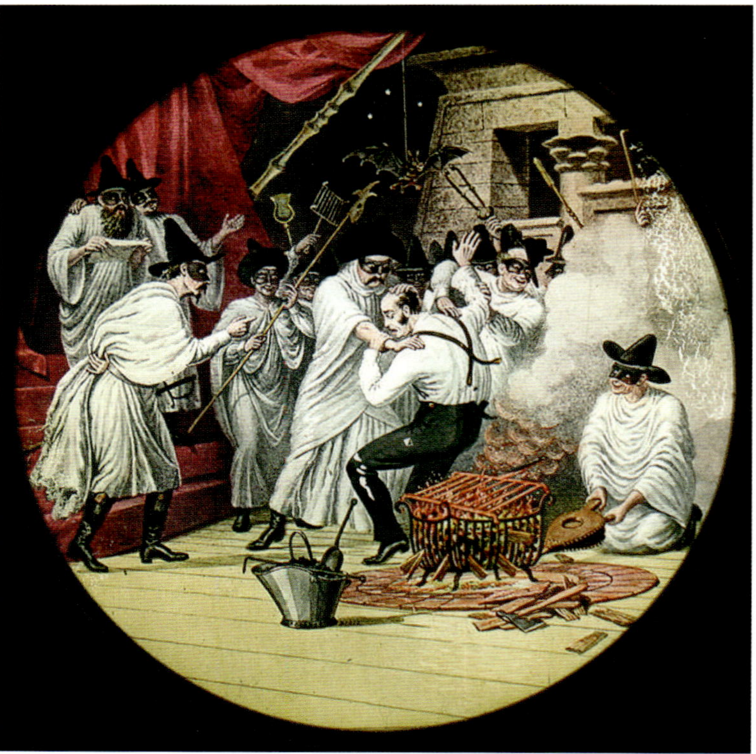

Fig. 9.28 Beale's slide 10 of *How Jones Became a Mason*. The set satirizes Masonic rituals.

How Jones Became a Mason

There is one other set that deserves to be discussed under the "Secret Society" rubric, though I've listed it above in the "Comic Sketches" section, since it has no script, and is certainly not a ritual set, but a parody of fraternal practices. In *How Jones Became a Mason*, Jones strides off with confidence to be inducted into his lodge where he is subjected to an incredible hazing (Fig. 9.28). As Beale follows the action we see Jones react to a decapitation, ride on a rambunctious goat, climb a greased pole, fly in the air, and be roasted on a red-hot griddle. On his return home to his wife, he is a shambles.

When I first began performing this story (to the audience chant of "Jones is Bones!"), I thought that all these tortures were the fruit of Beale's imagination. But then we gave a show at a Masonic museum, and there, on display was the "goat" – a stuffed goat fastened to poles that was made to buck under the initiate by four husky Masons.[21] Many of the other trials like the "decapitation" and "flying" and the hot "griddle" were illusions of the same sort. In others, such as the "Lowered into his Grave" scene, the experience was real enough, but Jones had no way of knowing how long it would last. Such hazing – the bucking goat in particular – was a common part of the initiations at many secret societies at the end of the 19th Century. Public criticism and parodies such as Beale's have largely put an end to the practice.

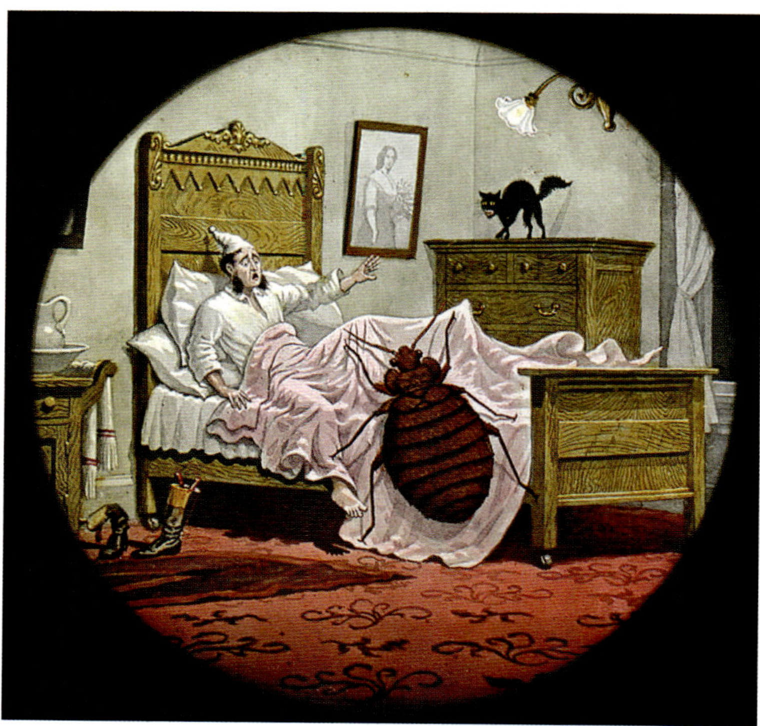

Fig. 9.29 Beale's slide of "Attack of the Monster, The Boarding House Bedbug" from Comic Animals.

Miscellaneous Groups

The Miscellaneous Group contains 138 slides, or about 5% of Beale's work, divided into Comic Singles, Artistic Gems,[22] Dissolves, and Other[23] (Fig. 9.29).

Beale's comic singles, most of them anyway, make a delightful ending for our review of his screen world, as giant bugs invade sanctuaries and farm animals go berserk.

What keeps the Comic collection from being an unalloyed delight is the Ethnic group, which includes a number of slides that are racially offensive. Beale was not unusual in his attitude, but it is hard to stomach today. Needless to say, I do not present the Ethnic Comedy slides in our shows (Fig. 9.30).

The "Dissolving Sets" in the Miscellaneous category was a place for the catalogs to showcase the lantern's ability to create the *dissolve effects*. Beale's additions to the category were relatively minor, though sometimes spectacular. We have already looked at one Dissolving Set slide, *The Enchanted Grotto*, the goddess with the moveable arm. In the accompanying slides, her Rival comes gliding over the water toward her in a series of effect dissolves. The dissolve format could also be quite telling, even if it were not an "effect dissolve". The Christmas Dissolves

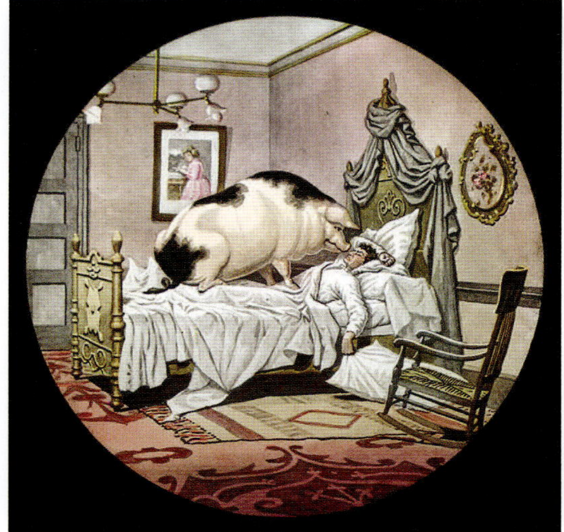

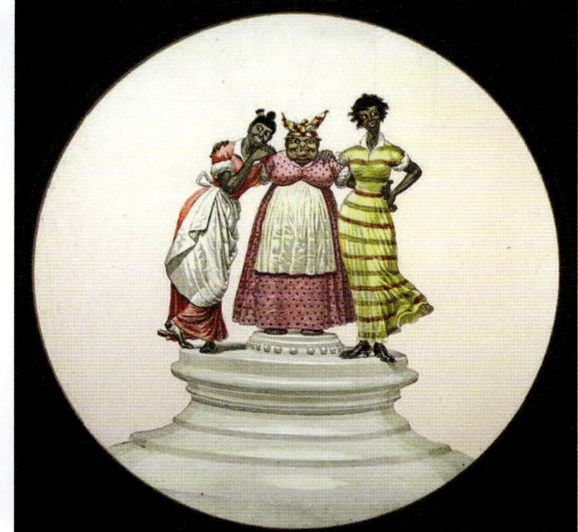

Fig. 9.30 Two of Beale's single comic views: "Why Did You Sup on Pork", and "The Three Graces". The first gets a laugh as soon as I project it. I don't project the second.

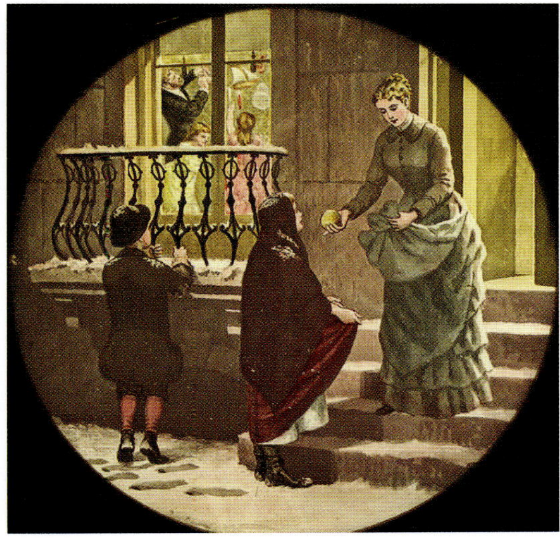

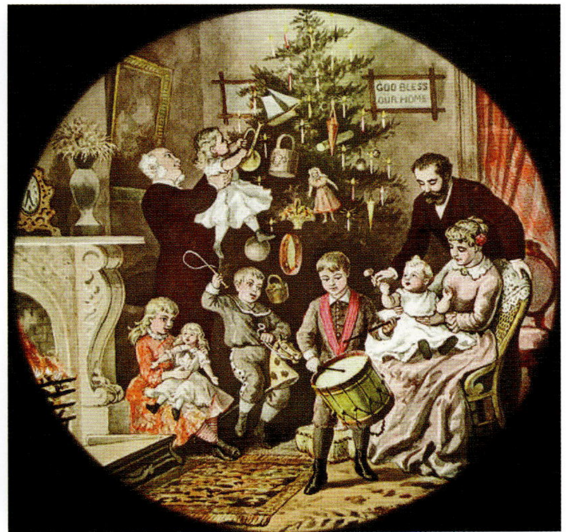

Fig. 9.31 Beale's Christmas Dissolve set, "Christmas Evening, Homeless", and "Christmas Evening, The Happy Home".

(Fig. 9.31), for instance, contains this two-slide comparison of poverty and plenty, telling in part because of the "through the window" view in the poverty scene that connects them.

Conclusion

Think back on the repertoire we have just reviewed in this chapter and the preceding one. In subject after subject – in genres ranging from novels, to poems, to songs, to religion, to the latest war hero, to fraternal rituals – we have seen Beale's skill in using the narrative arts. Time after time we have seen him adapt to meet the needs of his audience, whether they were magic lantern showmen, or schoolteachers, or ministers, or Masons. Here was a superb craftsman who could take an existing single painting and rework it so that it was infused with screen drama. Even more important, he could create whole original sequences of images that used all of the lantern's potential for visual storytelling. Despite a few weak spots, Beale has shown the power of his narrative art in almost every genre.

But how did that power develop over time? How would Briggs and Beale adapt to historical events around them? What would happen when a new, more flexible method of creating screen art was invented, the movies?

Chapter 8 Appendix
Beale's Religious, History, Temperance, Secret Society and Misc. Slide Sets by Category

This Appendix lists all Beale non-Literary sets by categories such as Religion, History, etc., and gives the title of each. The number after the *category title* – e.g. "Religion-Hymns" – indicates the total number of *Beale* slides in that category, and does not include any non-Beale slides that might also be in it. The number after a *set title* indicates the same type of information for that set. Some slides appear in multiple categories and sets. For detailed information on each set and each slide within the set, see Borton, Borton, *Before the Movies*, 117–168.

Religion – Biography & Bible Texts (102)

Life of Luther (2)
Life of St. Paul (25)
Life of John Wesley (8)
The Beatitudes (10)
Ecclesiastes (10)
The First Psalm (6)
Golden Bible Texts (13)
The Lord's Prayer (7)
The Palms (5)
Psalm XXIII (6)
Ten Commandments (10)

Religion—Hymns (152)

Abide With Me (12)
Calvary (3)
A Christmas Hymn (4)
From Greenland's Icy Mountains (12)
God Be With You Till We Meet Again (5)
Hold the Fort (2)
Holy City (14)
Jerusalem The Golden (4)
Jesus Lover of My Soul (8)
Lead Kindly Light (4)
Let the Lower Lights Be Burning (4)
My Mother's Bible (4)
Near The Cross (4)
Nearer My God to Thee (6)
New Born King (5)
Ninety and Nine (10)
Onward Christian Soldiers (4)
Rock of Ages (14)
Tell Me the Old, Old Story (5)
Throw Out the Lifeline (5)
Illuminated Hymns (23)

Religion – Old Testament (197)

Creation of Earth (8)
Creation of Life (11)
Cain (4)
Noah (8)
Abraham and Sarah (9)
Jacob (5)
Joseph (12)
Moses (32)
International Sunday School Lessons for 1895 (12)
Story of Esther (12)
Story of Daniel (12)
Story of Job (8)
Story of Ruth (8)
Samson (7)
Samuel & Saul (5)
David (16)
Captives in Babylon (10)
Elijah (6)
Jonah (2)

Religion – New Testament & Misc. (436)

Christmas (12)
Christ's Youth (5)
Christ's Ministry (44)
Calling the Disciples (5)
Easter (25)
Acts of the Apostles (8)
Peter and Philip (8)
International Sunday School Lessons for 1895 (12)
Parables of Christ (41)
Story of the Blind Man (8)
The Good Samaritan (8)
The Good Shepherd (10)
The Great Supper (10)
Laborers in the Vineyard (6)
Marriage of the King's Son (11)
The Prodigal Son (10)
The Sower (6)
The Talents (8)
The Unmerciful Servant (6)
The Wicked Husbandmen (8)
The Wise & Foolish Virgins (8)

Miscellaneous

Bible Story in Pictures (89)
Catholic Catechism (4)
Jewish Life (26)
Photodrama of Creation (36)
Story of the Very First Christmas (13)
Miscellaneous (9)

History/Biography (349)

American History (130)
Americana (20)
Early Period (5)

Colonial Period (18)
French & Indian War (4)
Revolution (27)
War of 1812 (10)
Mexican War (6)
Civil War (16)
Transportation (4)
Origin of U. S. Flag (12)
U. S. Flag, Misc. (7)
Passing of the Indian (1)

Biography (39)

Life of Columbus (2)
Life of Benj. Franklin (9)
Life of Lincoln (12)
Life of Washington (4)
Life of Mary, Queen of Scots (12)

History, General (77)

Seven Ancient Wonders of the World (7)
Greek/Roman/European (11)
English/Irish (42)
French (16)
Misc. Flags (1)

Current Events (103)

Life of Garfield (1)
Life of U. S. Grant (11)
Life of McKinley (12)
Destruction of St. Pierre (2)
Maine Disaster (4)
Spanish-American War (49)
War in Cuba (12)
War with Filipinos (4)
Boer War (4)
Russo-Japan War (4)

Temperance (53)

The Drunkard's Daughter (6)
The Drunkard's Reform (6)
Father, Dear Father, Come Home with Me Now (6)
Intemperance Subjects (5)
Raid of the Moonshiners (3)
Ten Nights in a Bar Room (12)
Two Paths of Virtue and Vice (4)
Where is My Wandering Boy Tonight (6)
William Jackson's Treat (4)
Miscellaneous (1)

Secret Society (409)

Masonic (164)
Royal Arch (46)
Scottish Rite (3)
Commandery (21)
Ascension (6)
Moveable Ascension (1)
Blue Lodge (21)
Blue Lodge Addl. (37)
White Shrine of Jerusalem (11)
Order of the Eastern Star (17)
Knights Templar (1)

Oddfellows (47)
Oddfellows (40)
Daughters of Rebecca (7)

Knights of Pythias (44)
First Rank (19)
Third Rank, Monitor (8)
Third Rank, Pythagoras (9)
Sixth Senator (8)

Other Secret Society (154)
Woodsmen of the World (15)
Knights of the Mystic Chain (6)
Patriotic Order Sons of America (16)
Patriotic Order of America (17)
Brotherhood of the Union (3)
Grand Army of the Republic (5)
Knights of Malta (17)
Sublime Order of the Great Cross (4)
Knights of the Golden Eagle (11)
American Mechanics (2)
Jr. Order of Am. Mechanics (8)
Brotherhood of Locomotive Fireman (6)
Knights and Ladies of Honor (2)
Foresters of America (1)
Orangeman (4)
Order of Maccabees (1)
Moose Lodge (22)
Tribe of Ben Hur (7)
American Insurance Union (2)
Miscellaneous (5)

Miscellaneous (138)

Comic Singles (57)
Animals (8)
Children (16)
Ethnic (19)
Love (5)
Misc. (9)

Artistic Gems (27)

Dissolves (26)

Christmas Dissolves (4)
Enchanted Grotto (4)
Fire in New York (2)
Steamboat Race in Mississippi (3)
Miscellaneous (13)

Other (28)

Mottoes (3)
Announcements (14)
Skirt Dancing Effects (6)
Hymns with Limited Distribution (5)

Chapter Ten

Change Over Time – 1881 to 1909

Fig. 10.37 Beale's "Destruction of Schenectady" from the Colonial Period group. Discussed on page 260.

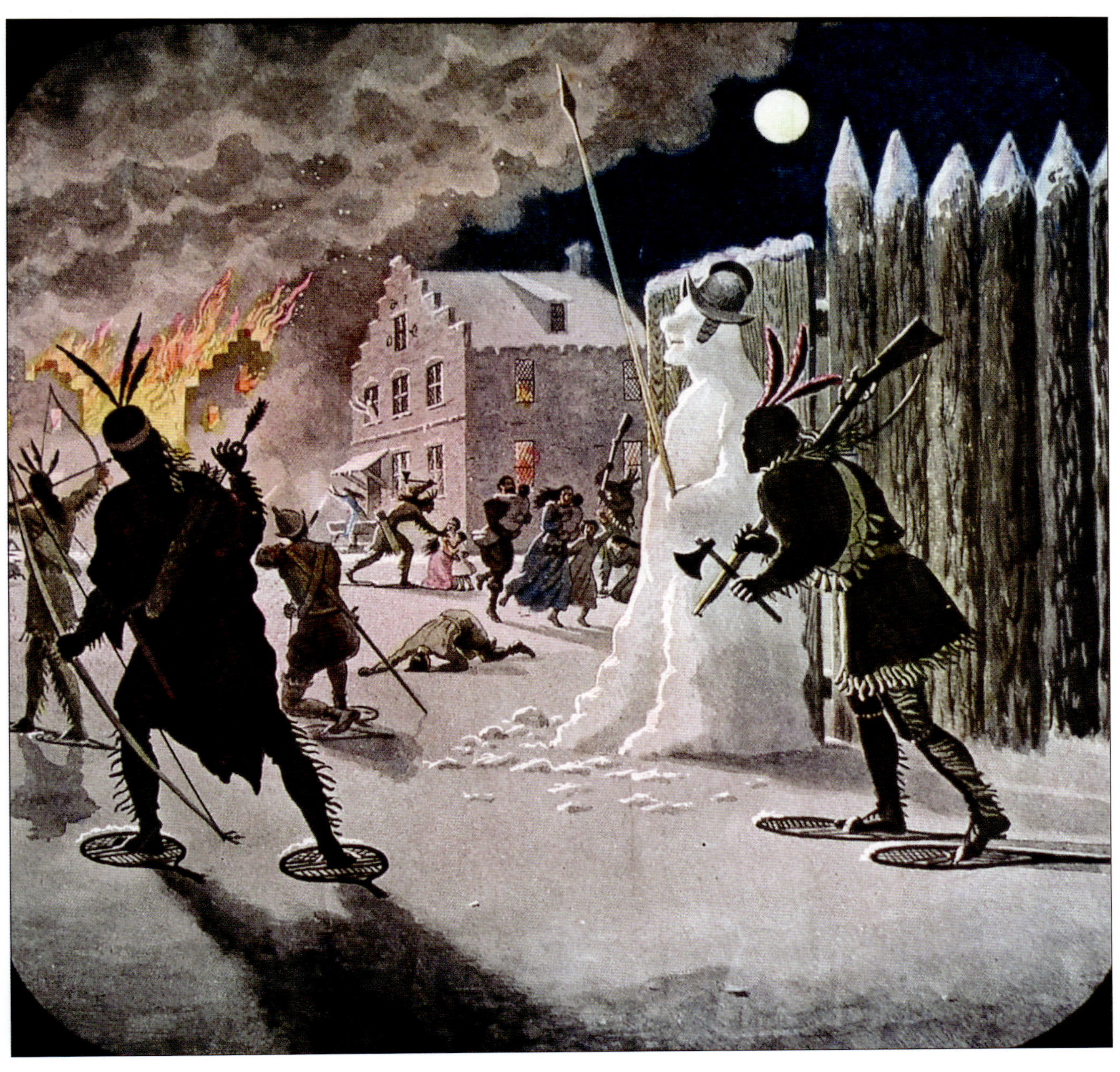

In the previous chapters regarding "Beale's On-Screen World" we've seen the range and cinematic sophistication of his narrative art in many different fields. But this body of over 2,000 images did not arrive whole, all of a piece. Some of it was produced in fits and bits in two freelance periods; others in great spurts of creativity; others at a steady pace over years. Some was produced in response to the vision of Briggs; some because of outside factors like wars and the emerging competition of the movies; some to take advantage of market opportunities. In this chapter we'll examine Beale's output over time, and place it in the context of events in the larger world, and related lantern and cinema developments. By doing so we can see something of *why* his body of work contains the slides that it does, and *how* his style and format changed as circumstances changed and as Beale himself learned more about creating sequential narrative art for the screen (Fig. 10.1).[1]

1881–1891 Beale's Early Freelance Period

From 1881 to 1891, Beale worked for Briggs in a freelance capacity, creating, over these 10 years, only about 135 images, or about a dozen a year. Much of the work was "fix up this, fill in that". But Beale also took the first steps toward fulfilling Briggs' vision of a great catalog of literature on screen – slide sets for two books (*Uncle Tom's Cabin* and *Ten Nights in a Bar Room*),[2] and four parlor poems like *Leap for Life* and *The Night Before Christmas*.[3] But aside from these beginning literary efforts, two things stand out in this early work: the heavy emphasis on Temperance, and Beale's increasing sophistication in narrative art.

Six of Beale's total of ten Temperance sets were created during this time, and it's easy to understand why. The Women's Christian Temperance Union had been organized only seven years before Beale began working for Briggs; by the 1880s the WCTU was at the peak of its educational crusade. The temperance novel, *Ten Nights in a Bar Room*, published in 1854, had become one of the most popular books in the country, selling over a million copies. A stage version played continuously during the last half of the nineteenth century, and featured the song, *Father Dear Father Come Home with Me Now*. So, it made good sense to develop slide versions of *Ten Nights* and *Father Dear Father*, as well as other temperance subjects.

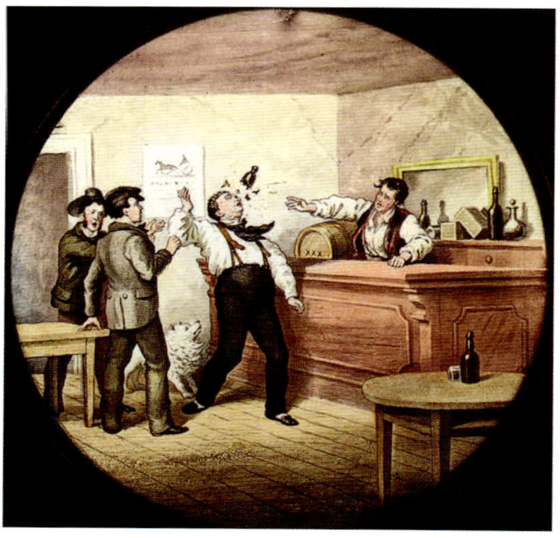

Fig. 10.1 Beale's slide 8 of *Ten Nights in a Bar Room* by T. S. Arthur (1881?). This set by Beale is one of his first, probably closely copied from an earlier illustration.

But this would be the last period in which Temperance was a major emphasis for Beale and Briggs. Why? The answer probably lies in the changing nature of the Temperance crusade itself. As it matured, the American Temperance movement became much more political than educational, running its own candidate for president in 1888. After that effort failed, it began using third-party tactics to put pressure on the political system, a drive that culminated in the passage of the Prohibition amendment in 1917. The Temperance magic lantern stories and songs that had been such an important part of the early educational programs were simply not as useful in this political effort.[4]

Beale's Style in the Freelance Period

Beale's *style* in this early period is, as might be expected, one of testing. The Temperance tale *Two Paths of Virtue and Vice,* an early example of parallel editing, is particularly interesting as it is the first Beale "story" that appears to be drawn "from scratch". We can be positive Beale himself created it because he signed three of the designs.[5]

Beale's style in slide number one, of the good and bad boys, shows the figures outlined in ink in much the same way that Nisle did, with much the same results. The boys look like cartoons, especially when projected, when the hard black edges seem highlighted (Fig. 10.2). This cartoony trait rapidly diminishes, as Beale gets the hang of outlining the figures with his brush, rather than his pen. The composition uses a dividing line between the two boys to emphasize their "two paths" – a visual device that is maintained throughout the set. In the first slide the divider is a faint fence line in the background, but its effectiveness is greatly diminished by the dark fence at right, which actually cuts the good boy off from school. It's an example of something that could be a small problem in a small engraving becoming a much bigger one when the same image is enlarged to a 10 or 20-foot diameter.

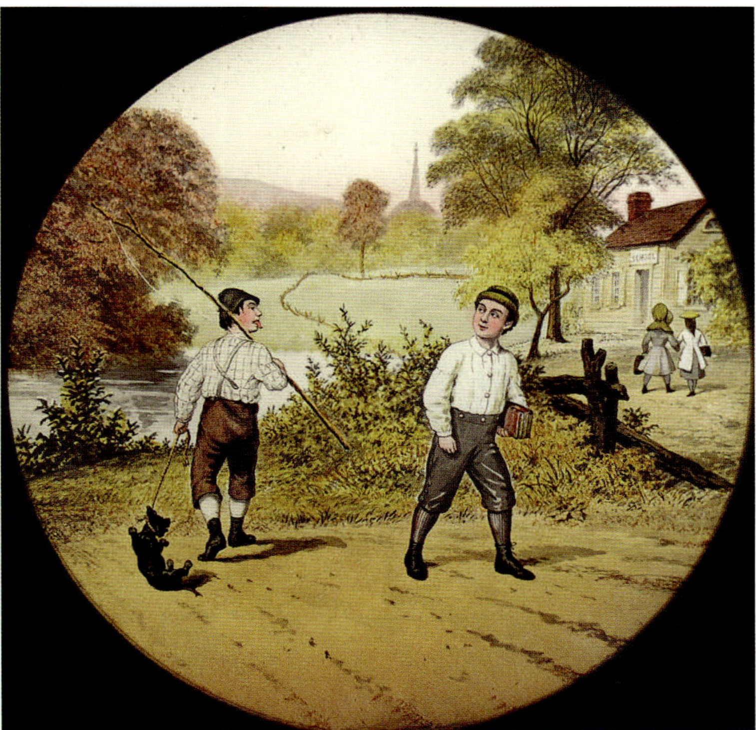

Fig. 10.2 Slide 1 of Beale's *Two Paths of Virtue and Vice* (1881), Author unknown.

The set as a whole has other problems. Beale naturally began by using the compositional forms that had been successful when he was illustrating for magazines, newspapers and other print media. He seems at first to have had some trouble adapting to the screen at a time when the screen was thought of as a stage set. In the first two slides (Figs. 10.2 and 3) he uses that stage-set convention, showing normally sized characters in a context that provides space above and below them.

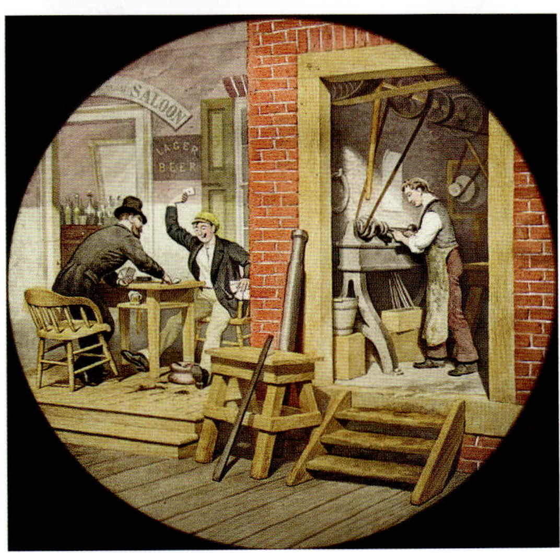

Fig. 10.3 Beale's slide 2 of *Two Paths of Virtue and Vice.*

In the next two slides he moves his "camera" – his vantage point – up closer to the action, closing the distance of framing. In the third slide he has moved so close that he cut off the leg of the table, forgetting how the slide would look in a circular format (Fig. 10.4). In the last slide, when he moves in still further, the figures are cut off at the chest and neck by the close framing, which also increases their size dramatically (Fig. 10.5). It is a form of composition that was common enough in Beale's earlier magazine and book illustrations, and common enough in the cinema today, but was disparaged by Victorian commentators on lantern slides because, "the figures are very much too large, the heads on a ten foot screen being monsters".[6] Beale soon drops this *medium close-up* composition, and almost never uses it thereafter, instead backing away from the scene so that the sense of a stage set is clearly maintained.

The problem of the composition in slide four of *Two Paths* is compounded by the fact that Beale has one of the figures in the near forefront turned away from the audience. In a magic lantern show this form of *blocking*, of having a major figure in the forefront, and turning his back to the audience, meant that the bottom of the picture was filled with a giant black blob. It looks as if a member of the audience were in fact *blocking* the screen. Briggs must have objected, for Beale almost never repeated this kind of obstructive composition. In scenes developed later he sometimes had characters facing away from the audience, but, as we have seen, positioned in such a way as to invite the audience to follow them into the scene, rather than blocking the audience view or involvement. Beale was generally at great pains to have all the actors on stage facing their audience, or each other.

In the early period Beale also took the screen as

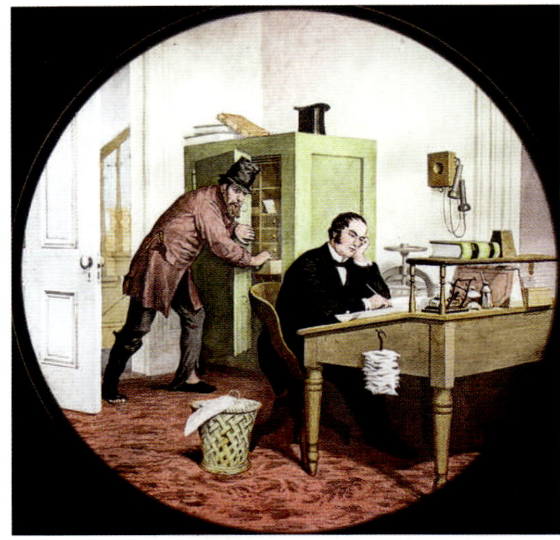

Fig. 10.4 Beale's slide 3 of *Two Paths of Virtue and Vice.*

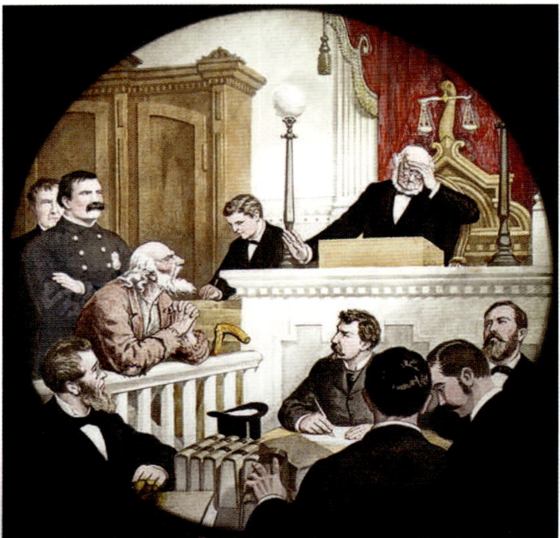

Fig. 10.5 Beale's slide 4 of *Two Paths of Virtue and Vice.*

"stage set" idea very literally. The sets often have minimal production values, looking as if they might be painted stage drops, with relatively little detail, presented in a flat, high-key light, as in the temperance song, *Father, Dear Father* (Fig. 10.6 and 7). In such stories a single stage set, a single mise-en-scene, might be used in slide after slide. In *Ten Nights in a Bar Room* for instance, five of the 12 slides repeat exactly the same shallow focus view of exactly the same flat set.[7] The actors simply alter their poses in front of the bar, though each picture is painted separately. A little later in this experimental period, *Pygmalion and Galatea* (1890), also uses a fixed backdrop. But as we have seen, in *Pygmalion* Beale developed a much more elaborate deep space set for the characters to use as they move about the set. The repetitive approaches to set design were less expensive to produce, of course, but they lacked variety and interest, and Beale rarely used it after this experimental period.[8]

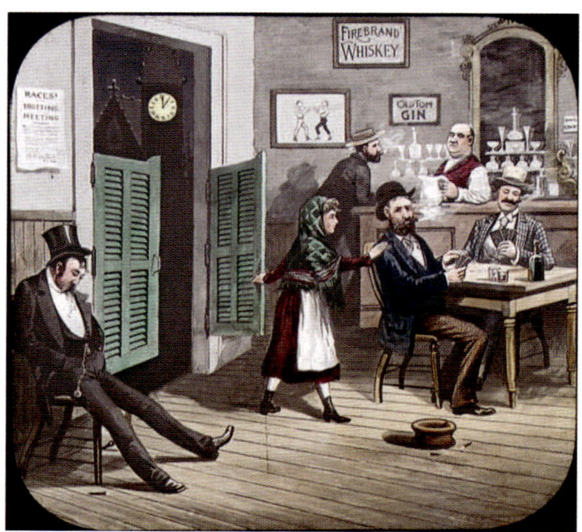

Fig. 10.6 Beale's slide 1 of *Father, Dear Father* (1887), by Henry Clay Work.

Freed by a combination of his imagination and a technical mastery of perspective Beale was learning how to give his productions a narrative fluidity that transcended the static form of the usual lantern slide. He also was using the cinematic story-telling potential of the magic lantern itself – the dissolves from one life-stage to another in *Two Paths of Virtue and Vice*, the dissolve effects that transform a statue into a living woman in *Pygmalion and Galatea*, a ***phantasmagoric superimposition*** of the Devil into a window frame in *Faust*. He was beginning to master his art.

The Larger Magic Lantern World

Elsewhere in the American lantern world, as reported by the trade publication, *The Magic Lantern*, this period was one of increasing confidence that the magic lantern was becoming a more and more important factor in entertainment and education. Since its inception in 1874, *The Magic Lantern* had been the first, and "the only magazine in the world devoted to the magic lantern". By the mid-point of Beale's freelance period, its editor, Edward Wilson, had become downright optimistic about the publication's future. He seemed to relish his role as tutor to the field, and was full of editorial good humor.

Most of *The Magic Lantern*'s coverage of show content focused on the most popular aspects of the then-current repertoire – statuary, special effects like the *Flight of Mercury* sequence, photographic travel lectures, temperance stories, and secret society views. Wilson mentioned that color slides had come back into fashion, after having been discarded in favor of black and white because lanternists thought "plain photographic slides" were more esthetic. This was a development that would augur well for the color capabilities of the Briggs factory that Wilson often promoted. But *The Magic Lantern* paid almost no attention to the ***illustrated slides*** of literature that was at the center of Briggs's vision, nor did a similar publication in England.[9]

In America, the later part of Beale's free-lance years was in fact the beginning of a ***photographic lantern-slide*** craze that can be tracked in the comments of various authors in *The American Amateur Photographer*. Its editor tied the "greater amount of interest" in photographic lantern slides to the better quality of plates available, and to the spreading use of the dry-plate development process. The American lantern industry was about to enter a period of unprecedented expansion, and though Briggs's niche as a wholesaler of illustrated images was not the main focus of that expansion, nonetheless, the British publication, *The Optical Magic Lantern Journal* (*OMLJ*), acknowledged that, "lantern readings on illustrated book subjects [were] very popular". Few such subjects had been made into commercially available slides; those who wanted them were forced to make their own. Briggs was ideally positioned to ride the rising tide.[10]

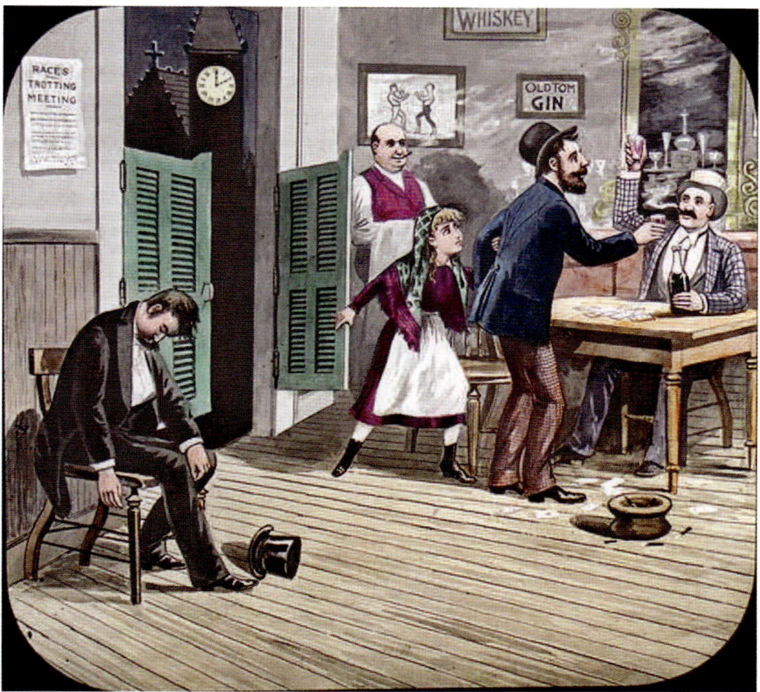

Fig. 10.7 Beale's slide 5 of *Father, Dear Father.*

Other Cinema Developments, 1880–1891

Outside the magic lantern field, other important developments in the cinematic arts occurred, not so much in the art of telling stories on screen, but in adapting the magic lantern machine itself toward becoming a more flexible means of projection, culminating in the movies. The process was enormously complex, multi-faceted, and international. I will not detail nor document that history here; that has been comprehensively discussed by such writers as Musser, Robinson, Rossell, and others. Rather I'll very briefly summarize their work, especially that related to Philadelphia, providing notes only for unusual items or direct quotes.[11]

After the Langenheim brothers of Philadelphia became the first to project photographic images on screen in the 1850s, the city became a hotbed of interest in projection. As early as 1861 Coleman Sellers of Philadelphia patented a device for depicting movement with a series of photographic images. It used a series of stereo photographs on a vertically mounted drum that turned fast enough to simulate movement. The device was a toy, however, and found few further

Kan yoo gett their bi rale?

The Magic Lantern *tried to increase the sophistication of many of the "professors" who ran lantern shows by satirizing their ignorance, as in this mock letter from May, 1877.*

DEAR SIR: I se yu hev hin too Uroap agen, end down too ejipt. I wornt yore noo vews, orr at lest som ov them. If yoo doant sel em chepe enuff, I think ov starting ther miself. How farr is it?

Kan yoo gett their bi rale, end kan yoo goa bi pensilvaineah sentral? I worn't too take with mee sum nise mann too pointe owt 2 mee thee piramyds and thee Neil and thee mediterranian and floreda and ingland wen tha heve inn site. Kant yore fatt frend Maips go to? I mit pa harf hiz meles att thee ralewa stashuns. If hee wunt go, ime going too heir stoderd if I kan gett him too go with mee on this tripp. I shaint go how ever if you kan sel mee sum slids. I warnt Maips too pik them owt. Hee iz a good phelow, butt hee doant rite long leters enuff too intelijente litterari men li me. Goodbi now.

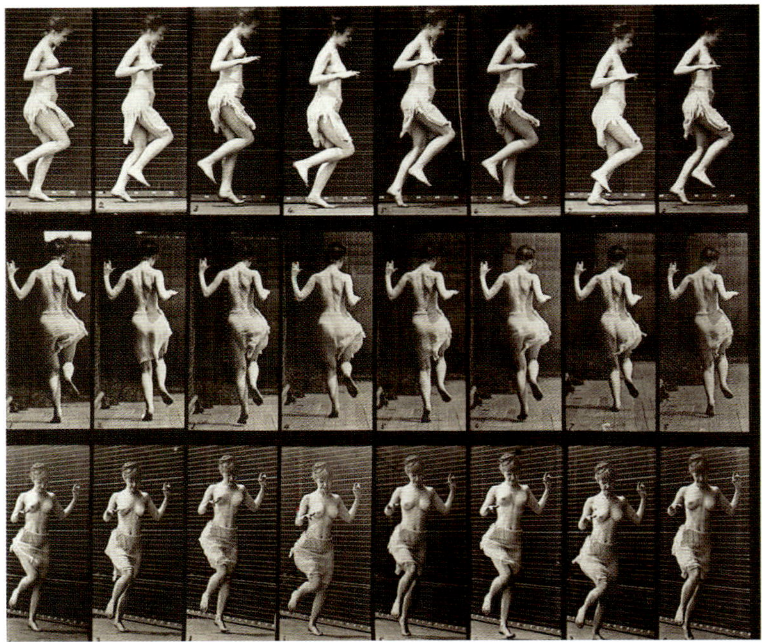

Fig. 10.8 Eadweard Muybridge's "Woman Hopping" from *Animal Locomotion*.

applications. A second Philadelphia innovator, Henry Hyle, is often cited for presenting before 1500 people a 1870 production consisting of moving images projected with a magic lantern and synched with sound. However, this story appears to be apocryphal; there is no contemporary evidence for it.[12]

Much betterr substantiated is the work of Eadweard Muybridge who in 1878 first showed his series of rapidly changing photographs, using what was later called the "Zoopraxiscope". One journalist called it "A Magic lantern Run Mad".[13] The images of moving people and animals changed about every 25th of a second, providing a sense of continuing and subtle movement which was much greater than the lantern could provide (Fig. 10.8). It created a sensation, partly because of the nudes that were included in the program. Muybridge worked in Philadelphia during much of 1884–85, creating over 200,000 pictures. Briggs and Beale likely knew of his work. In fact, Muybridge may have had some of his photographs altered by the Briggs artists to make the projected photographs appear more realistic.[14]

Muybridge's famous *Animal Locomotion*, published in 1887, may well have influenced Beale's horse drawings. In Beale's earlier slides, like "Damon's Homeward Flight" (1891), Beale's horses "galumph" in the artistic style of the day – fore legs forward and hind legs rearward – all extended to the maximum. But *Sheridan's Ride* (1902) shows five different views of a racing horse, all of which fit the Muybridge depiction of horse locomotion (Fig. 10.9).

The device Muybridge used for his shows was an adaptation of the magic lantern and had many of the lantern's limitations. It employed slides, though the slides were in a circular frame, or were circular glass, which allowed the images to change more quickly as they rotated. The slides were also often photographic (or appeared to be so), and hence more "realistic", but they did not provide a significantly greater duration or flexibility of motion than was already available in common lantern slides like the "Wheel of Life" or "The Dancing Skeleton". Limited though it was, Muybridge's lectures all over the world drew great interest; "motion" was in the air.

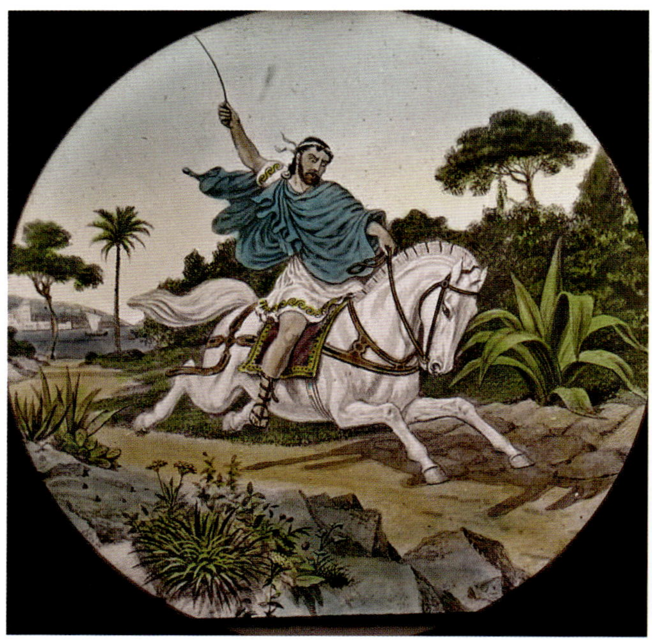

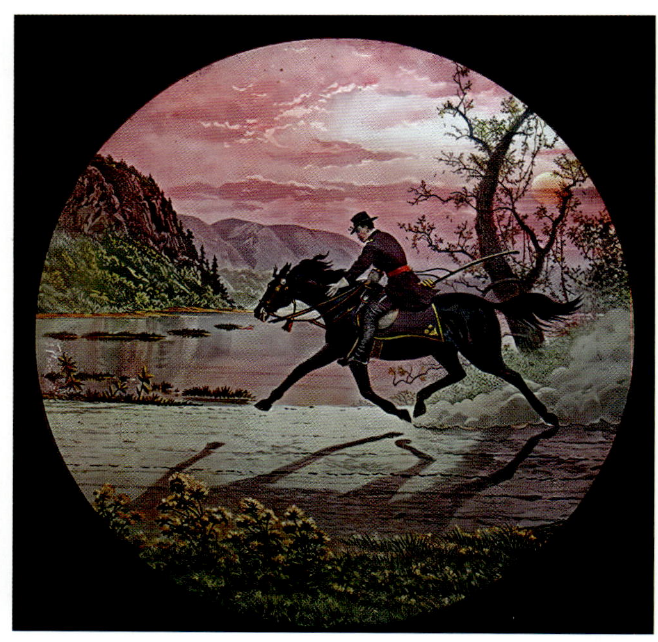

Fig. 10.9 Beale's slide of "Damon's Homeward Flight" (1891), from *Knights of Pythias, First Rank*, left, and slide 2 of *Sheridan's Ride* (1902–03), right.

From Slides to Film

The real break with the magic lantern tradition and the major advance in the cinematic arts, was the change from slides to film, or transparent cellulose, developed by George Eastman in 1889. Here was a flexible, transparent medium that could carry a photographic emulsion, and hence, when projected, give flexibility to motion on screen.

Thomas Edison was not initially interested in film; he was trying to create moving images based on a revolving cylinder. He picked up the idea of using film from a French scientist, and, with an employee named William K. L. Dickson, began working on filmed images to be seen with a peephole viewer. Their "kinetoscope", was unveiled to reporters in May of 1891 (Fig. 10.10). The images were round, like most lantern slides. The content was simply demonstrative "actualities" – an athlete doing his routines, a close-up of a workman smoking. It may not have been very entertaining, but, as one reporter noted, "Every motion was perfect, without a hitch or a jerk". In August, Edison applied for patents. The age of filmed cinema had begun.

But for the time being the experience of viewing cinema on film was very different from being at a magic lantern show, or at the movies as we know them today. The kinetoscope Edison had devised was a viewing environment in which one person at a time peered into a machine to see pictures flickering by on the rolling film. It was a solitary, slightly voyeuristic experience – no threat to the large-group participative immersion of magic lantern art. Edison explicitly rejected that model because he thought he could make more money with his individual peephole machines.

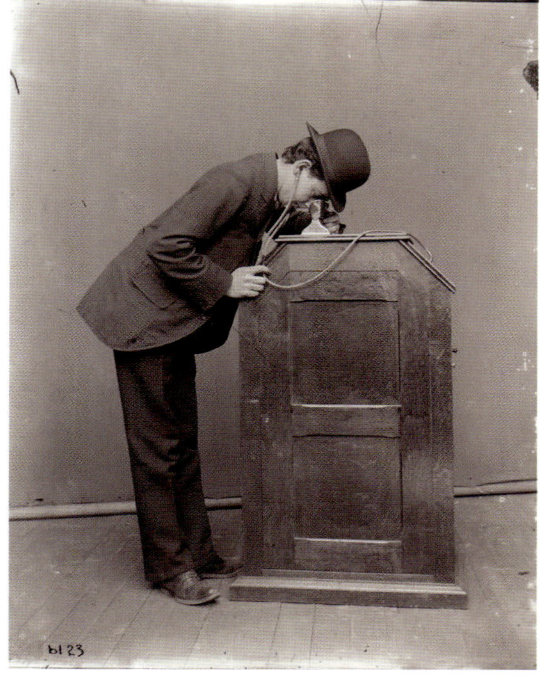

Fig. 10.10 Edison's Kinetoscope. *Wikimedia Commons.*

But the clock was ticking. Film rolled relentlessly on.

1892–1894 Beale Begins Full-time Work

Sometime in 1892, Beale began working full-time for Briggs, which makes a convenient marker for the start of a new period of our discussion, one that will end just before the birth of the movies in 1896. At the start of this more expanded collaboration Briggs and Beale faced two external factors, one likely to be encouraging; the other potentially disastrous.

On the positive side, in the period 1892–1894, views about illustrated lantern material (as opposed to photographic) were changing, a change that can be seen most clearly in the pages of the English lantern journal, *OMLJ*. Its earlier issues had been replete with a sense of the superiority of the photographic lantern lecture. Now it waxed nostalgic for the "good old days" of the grand illustrated lantern shows at the Royal Polytechnic which had closed in 1878. This nostalgia was matched with concern about the "decadence" of the modern photographic lantern lecture, and fears that the field was in decline. The decline was blamed on a combination of the easily-managed dry plate photography, the "hire" system in which anyone could rent a set of slides, the consequent rapid increase of incompetent amateurs entering the field, and the poor quality of many slides themselves:

> It is natural [that lantern exhibitions are not looked up to as they used to be], when the rubbish in the form of slides is taken into consideration. [Dry plate photography] has brought a lot of cheap (and nasty) productions ... into the market. Then comes the colouring (?) of these same slides; it might be poured on from a jug for all the artistic skill which is used

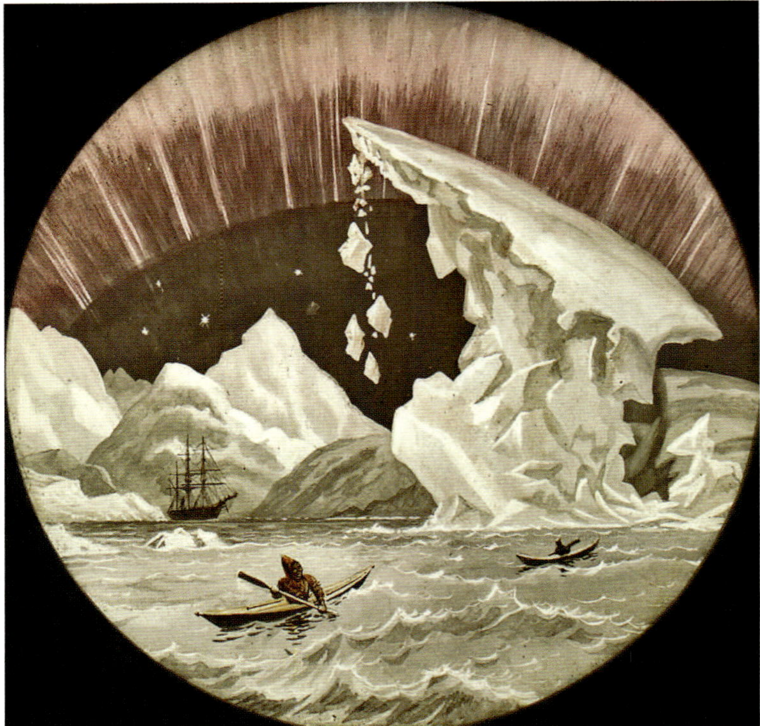

Fig. 10.11 Beale's slide 1 of the hymn, *From Greenland's Icy Mountains*, 1893, by Reginald Heber.

Fig. 10.12 The 1892–94 Briggs "Blueprint Catalog". George Eastman Museum

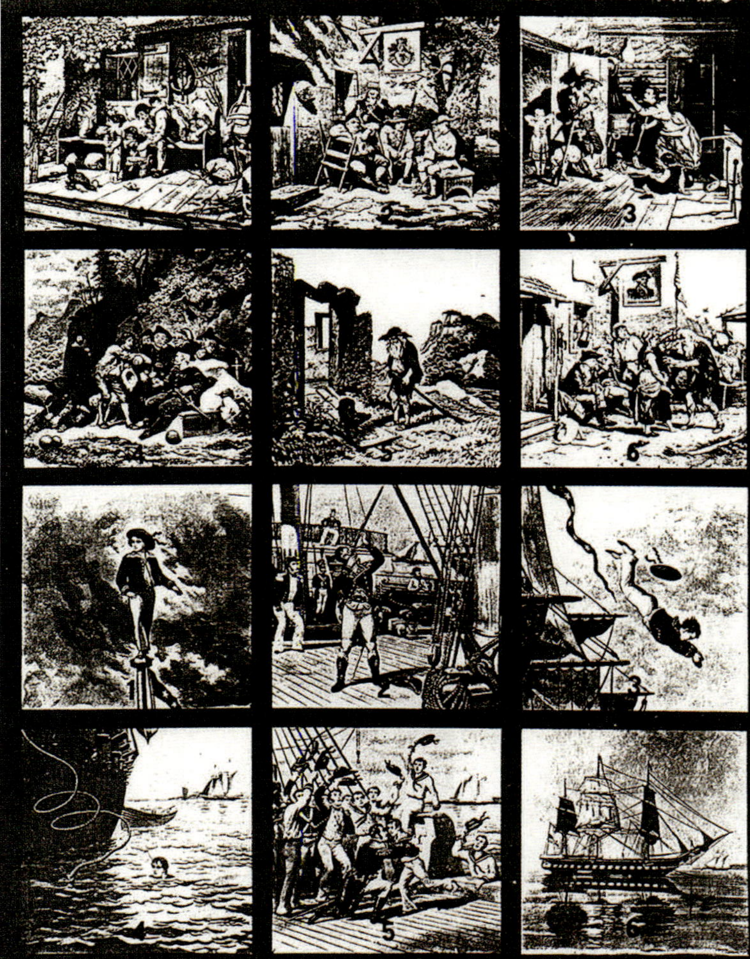

> – cheap, cheap, cheap being the order of the day, and nothing really good or artistic wanted.[15]

If a similar decline in the quality of lantern slides led to a decline in lantern *exhibition* in America, that would obviously not be good for Briggs's business, but this was not the case at all, at least for photographic slides. In fact, in 1892 *The American Amateur Photographer* reported that, "to some extent, lantern-slide exhibitions in America have crowded print-making to the wall". Photographic amateurs were consumed by "slide fever" and they were looking for quality.[16]

This then was the situation in 1892 when Briggs hired Beale to work full time. Production values and quality color were both areas in which the position of Briggs was unparalleled. It was an ideal time for him to broaden his niche of illustration and to pursue his vision of bringing great literature to the screen. And Beale, in turn, had hit his stride, as *Greenland's Icy Mountains* suggests (Fig. 10.11). Dramatic conception, composition, perspective, and lighting make this image a spectacular opening for what was also called *The Missionary Hymn*.

Over the period in which Beale worked full time under Briggs's direction, 1892-1909, Beale produced about two slides a week – a little more than 100 slides a year – about a dozen *sets* a year. In total Beale created about 1700 designs in this period, building the repertoire that defined American magic lantern illustration.

The strength on the artistic side was matched by the marketing department. For instance, Briggs produced a large catalog of his slides, contained full-sized pictures of each slide from each set – a feature not found in any other company's catalog. Such an approach was financially feasible because this "blueprint" catalog was sent only to lantern-slide distributors, not the general public. Fig. 10.12 shows two Beale sets, *Rip Van Winkle*, and *Leap for Life* displayed in such a blueprint catalog. Briggs wholesale marketing effectively froze those "cheap and nasty" British life-model slides out of the American market, and kept off the home-brewed competitors as well.

The Panic of 1893

At just the time that Briggs decided to hire Beale full-time, and just at the time that Beale himself decided to put his entire financial future into the magic lantern business – just at that time, calamity struck in the form of the Panic of 1893. Sparked by bubbles and by an overabundance of silver, the Panic rapidly spread throughout the economy. Fifteen thousand companies and 500 banks closed. Unemployment in Pennsylvania hit 25%, and then 35% in New York. By some accounts it was the worst economic crisis ever to hit the country, and it lasted four years.

No records show exactly how the Panic affected the Briggs Company, but as my own magic lantern theater company learned in the financial crisis of 2007–08, magic lantern shows are not an essential industry. My bookings collapsed; surely that happened 100 years earlier to many of the thousands of performers who bought the Briggs slides through his network of distributors. And yet, despite the turmoil, Briggs kept Beale on, and Beale kept producing, week after week. For both of them that must have built a sense of shared commitment.

The key to the Briggs Company survival during the Panic of 1893 lay not just in the dynamism of Beale's developing artistry, but in some shrewd production and marketing decisions by Briggs, especially in the Religious area.

Religion in a Time of Panic

Briggs continued to build his Literary category with classics, particularly American classic stories like *The Raven*; songs like *Swanee Ribber*, and *Tramp Tramp, Tramp*; and religious literary classics like *Ben Hur*. But the big changes in subject matter at the time of the Panic were in the fields of Religion and Comics.

In the Religious area a distinct difference occurs from the earlier freelance period, when Beale had been largely simply replacing individual Nisle designs. In 1892-94 Briggs suddenly begins introducing complete Biblical stories and parables like *The Prodigal Son* and *The Good Samaritan*, and illustrated hymns like *Rock of Ages*, and *Greenland's Icy Mountains*.

What probably drove this new emphasis on Religion was a rapidly-growing, cross-denominational movement to provide religious education, activities, and entertainment for the young. The Christian Endeavor Society, a co-educational, ecumenical movement founded in 1881, had 7,000 societies by 1887, and a half-million members. A similar and even larger society, The Sunday-School Movement, dated back in America to the 1790s.[17] By the 1890s it had become a national effort to draw all Protestant churches into one Bible education program. The headquarters of The Sunday School Movement was at 1122 Chestnut Street in Philadelphia, right in the middle of the "magic lantern quarter" where several of the national lantern catalog companies were based. It was natural, then, that the religious educators would look to the lantern to keep children involved with religion.

It was equally natural that Briggs and his colleagues would be interested in the Sunday School Movement. At its height, it involved 215,000 schools. Think of it: Almost a quarter-million Sunday Schools with about twenty-five million students in them, plus 7,000 Christian Endeavor Societies, plus thousands of similar denominational organizations like the Methodist Epworth League – all looking for a way to engage young people in wholesome, inexpensive educational and recreational religious activities. And these schools were not like the single lantern showmen, battling to scrape in enough bookings to survive the Panic. These were organizations, not individuals, with members who saw it as a religious duty to support the organization's programs. Now *that* was a ready-made slide market![18] And so Briggs expanded his Religious sets as rapidly as he could, filling out the basic New and Old Testament offerings.

Then in 1895, McAllister's offered an additional opportunity in the Religious area. He and Briggs agreed with The International Sunday School Movement to begin what must have seemed like a remarkable opportunity: The chance to produce an entire yearly curriculum based on Beale's slides, a curriculum to be followed by all those two hundred thousand schools. One slide a week was designated to cover a verse of the Bible. The first two quarters covered the New Testament; the last two the Old Testament, a total of 44 slides, some of which would surely have caught the attention of Sunday School students (Fig. 10.13).[19] During 1894, Beale must have been working furiously to meet the demand. As late as October, two-months before the program was to begin, McAllister's *Bulletin* mixed the claim that the "Lessons for 1895 can be made doubly impressive by our Pictorial Illustrations" with the caution that the slides, "are now in course of preparation, and will be ready for sale by the New Year".

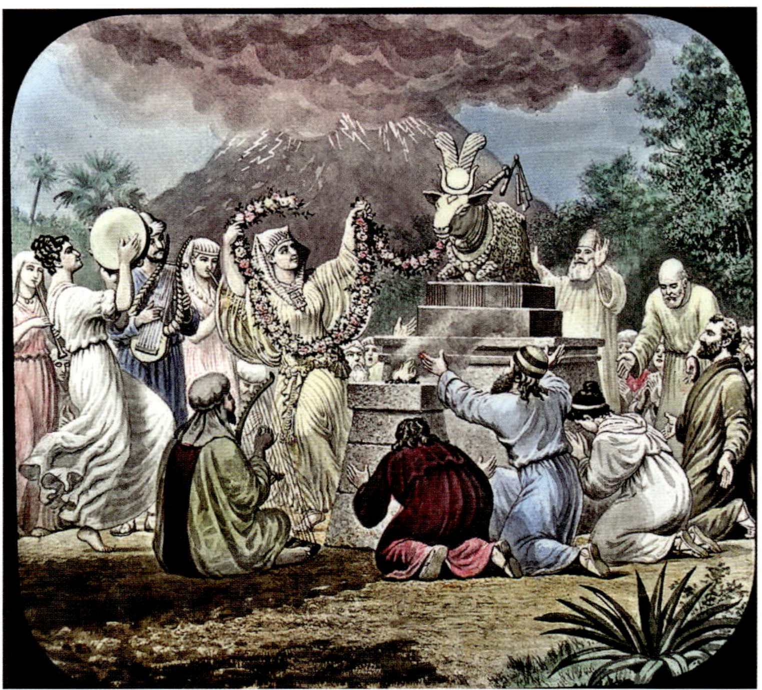

Fig. 10.13 Beale's "The Golden Calf", produced for The International Sunday School Lessons of 1895.

Obviously, production was lagging behind promotion.

But despite the rush, it made a great deal of sense for Briggs to go after this religious market through the McAllister catalog. Religious people were suffering from the Panic just like everyone else, but their organizations had thousands of local chapters in which individuals could pool their money to buy slides for the common good. In the midst of financial chaos, the religious slide market would have been – quite literally – a godsend. And, as we would say today, the religious market "had legs". As late as 1929, Beale's religious work was still being promoted in lantern-slide format by the Victor Animatograph Company.

However, the idea of a "slide a week" was not god-sent, and had no "legs" whatsoever. It was not repeated, probably because it made no sense. Even I, if I were a Victorian Sunday-School teacher, couldn't imagine going to the trouble of firing up a lantern just to show a single slide each week. But given how I've seen modern religious audiences respond to Beale's Bible stories and illustrated hymns, I'd jump at the chance to show my Sunday-School class, at a single sitting, complete illustrated parables like *The Wicked Husbandman*, Old Testament stories like *David*, or hymns like *Ninety and Nine*. Besides, I could promise my students that if they were good, I would show the Ratcatcher at the end of the lesson.

It's no surprise then that after 1895 Briggs and McAllister dropped the "slide-a-week" idea, and emphasized instead the religious format of complete stories and complete hymns. The work Beale did for the Sunday School project was not lost; the slides were simply folded into the regular catalog listings. And in that context, they definitely had staying power. One scholar estimates that "Missionaries and Sunday schools continued to use the lantern well into the mid-twentieth century".[20]

Comics in a Time of Panic

The development of a series of comic slides, begun in 1894, may have had a similar eco-

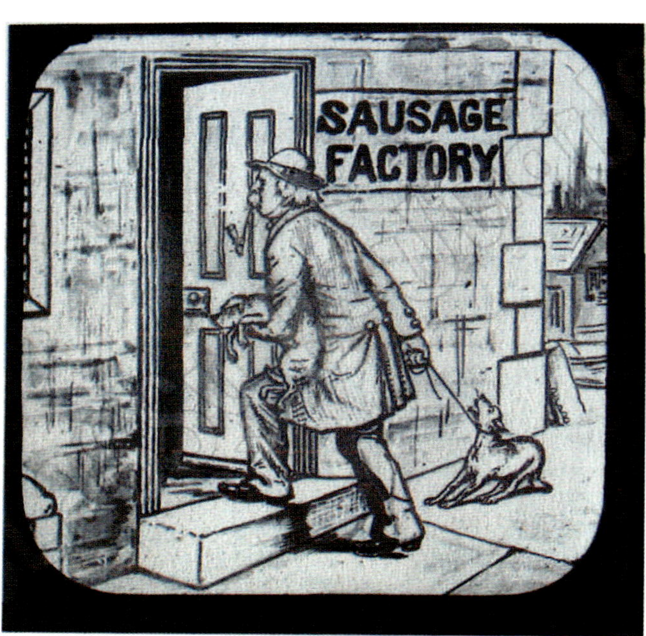

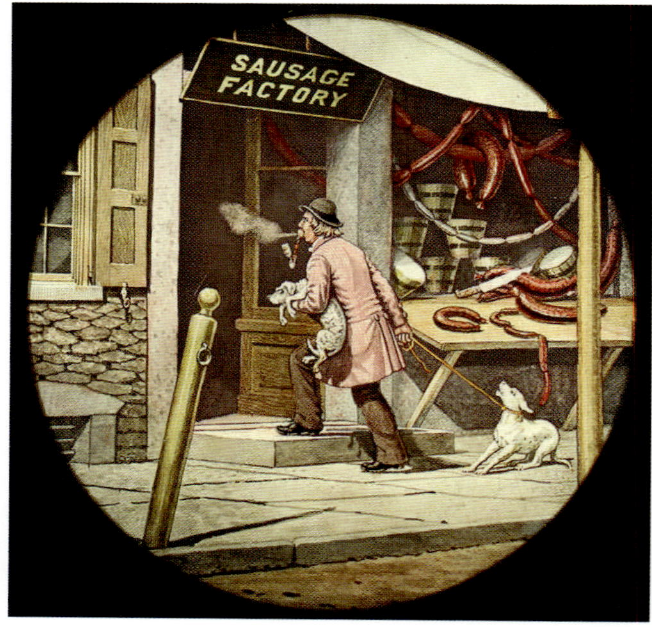

Fig. 10.14 Original slide of "Every Dog Has His Day", and Beale's version, from Comic Animals. Beale strengthens the original joke by adding the sausage display.

nomic incentive as the concentration on religious slides (Fig. 10.14). Beale was paid less than normal to create them because they were revisions of pre-existing, mostly black-and-white "crayon transparencies".[21] Paying Beale less, of course, would have cut Briggs' cost, though, unfortunately, at the same time it cut Beale's income. The creation of these comic slides was not an attempt to open up a new market, like the International Sunday School project. Rather, it upgraded the black and white sketches that had been a decidedly weak area in the Briggs catalog, and hence in that of McAllister.

In 1894 McAllister touted this upgrade. His *October Bulletin* announced a "special line of colored slides ... for the first time brought before the public". They were colored in a "cheaper style of finish" – part of the expanding format of all-glass slides that were sold at $.65 apiece rather than $1.50 for wood-frame slides. Some were Currier and Ives comic scenes, but many were the old crayon transparencies, revised and updated by Beale. Probably it was Briggs or McAllister who selected the most popular of the transparencies, and asked Beale to re-do them. Unfortunately, from my point of view, the upgrade was not the start of a trend. During the rest of his career, Beale neither revised many more comic slides nor created new ones like them. It's a shame. In our shows today they always get a laugh. That's just what was needed in the Panic of 1893, and during the hard times that lay ahead.

Taken together, these two groups of Religious and Comic slides accounted for most of the designs Beale produced from 1892 to 1894. But the largest *single* group was still the Literature category – 89 slides in all. While not ignoring quality control (upgrading the comic slides) or missing targets of economic opportunity (the Sunday Schools), Briggs was nonetheless pursuing his vision of building up an inventory of great literature for the screen with classics like *The Raven, Paul Revere's Ride, and Ben Hur.*

In terms of Beale's style, by the time he begins full-time work in 1892 all the elements that characterize his magic lantern technique are in place. The sketchy rendering of *Two Paths* is replaced by extravagant detail, used to give a sense of realism and to sustain attention. Sophisticated perspective techniques create a sense of depth. The shallow focus stage sets of *Ten Nights* give way to deep focus shots crammed with action. Diverse "camera angles" keep the action fluid; we no longer see the same set from the same point of view five times in succession. And, increasingly, complex lighting is used to heighten the drama, and to portray subtle changes in feeling. *Curfew Shall Not Ring Tonight* demonstrates how Beale used these techniques to create dramatic images, and make one slide of the story flow smoothly to the next, so that we're pulled into the narrative. The heroine, Bessie, tries to save her lover by keeping the sunset curfew bell from ringing. In Fig. 10.15 we see Bessie, we see the bell, we see the setting sun. But how will she stop the bell from ringing? Beale builds tension for the dramatic climax in the next slide when Bessie grabs the clapper of the bell, and swings out over the city as the sexton pulls the bell rope. (See Fig. 7.21.)

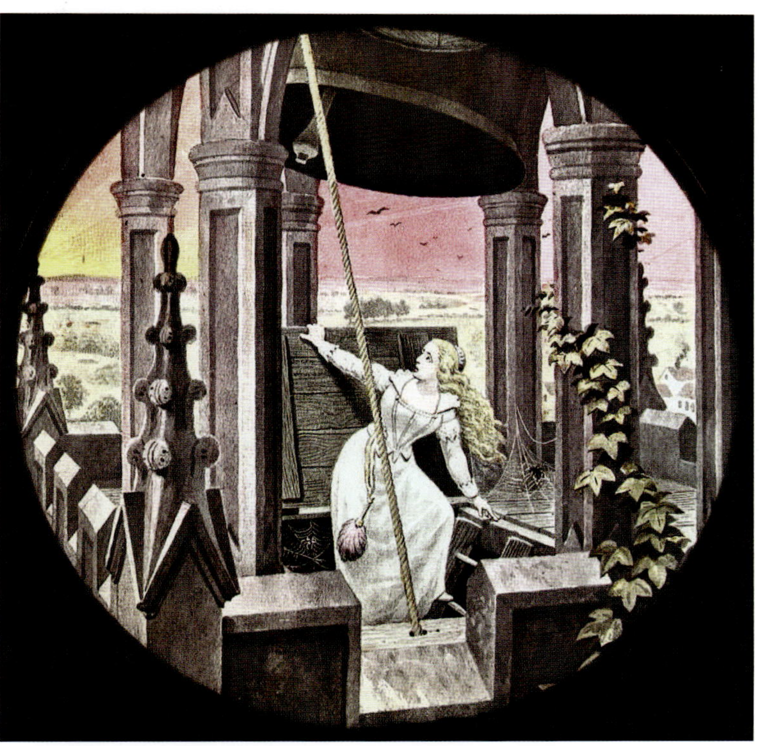

Fig. 10.15 Beale's slide 6 of *Curfew Shall Not Ring Tonight* (1894).

Beyond the increasing sophistication of Beale's style, new developments began to change the concept of both the lantern's ability to create "motion" on screen, and the nature of screen motion itself. Thomas Edison was at the center of them.

1895–97
The Birth of the Movies

The period of 1895–97 is the time when the three key ingredients that were to make the movies possible all came together: magic lantern projection, photographic images on film, and the intermittent mechanism for momentarily stopping the film in front of the projector aperture.

OMLJ had proudly claimed credit for being the first to publicize the "cinematograph" effect in 1889, in a version of the movies developed by an Englishman, William Friese-Greene. It went on to prophesy that, "we shall, by the aid of photography, the phonograph, and the optical lantern, be able to hear and see the facial expression accompanying recitations and songs uttered by our artists... .We may then expect to find [such things soon] in the dealers' catalogues".[22]

But in America, photographic lantern lectures – not movies – remained at the center of lanternists' attention. The *American Amateur Photographer* was heavily focused on lantern-slide creation, and reported that "many, if not most" amateur photographers were involved. Alfred Stieglitz, a leading photographer, became *AAP's* editor in 1893, and used his position to vigorously promote lantern slides as an art form.[23] This is the period in which three lantern performances a week occurred in my Connecticut hometown, and the newspapers were filled with their notices and reviews – in one case, three notices on a single page. The excitement of slide fever was evident across the country.[24]

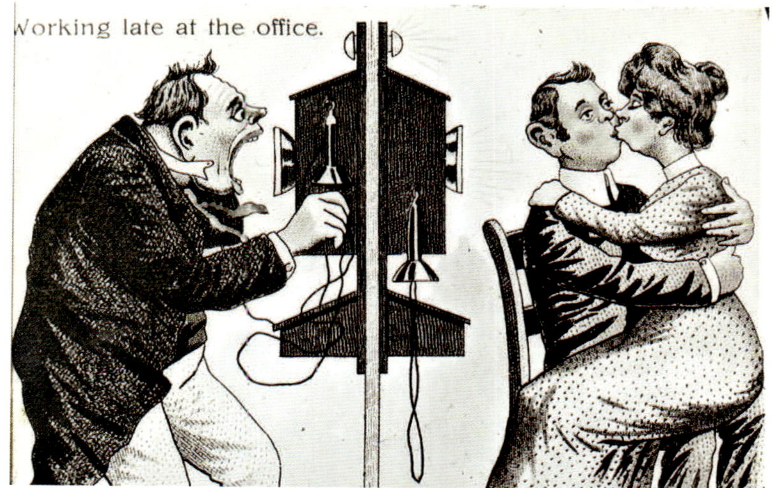

Fig. 10.16 A lantern slide by Siegmund Lubin, "Working late at the office". It is doubtful if Briggs would have published such an image.

Edison Finds a Movie Projector

But the idea of moving images on screen was advancing. Edison introduced the first ten peephole machines to show cinema on film, the kinetoscopes, on April 14, 1894 in New York. The films lasted 20 seconds each, and featured a combination of variety acts. They were successful but their success was short-lived.

Edison had ignored the idea of marrying magic lantern projection and images on film, but others did not. In the United States, C. Francis Jenkins and Thomas Armat had developed a "stereopticon phantoscope" that could project larger images. They patented it, but poor promotion kept them from capitalizing on what would turn out to be the missing ingredient of the movies.

If one person knew how to capitalize on an idea it was Edison. Realizing that screen projection with the "stereopticon phantoscope" might have success at a time when peepshow viewing with his kinetoscope was clearly falling off, Edison arranged to buy the rights to the phantoscope. After some minor improvements, many of them made by Armat, the phantoscope was re-christened with the "Wizard's" brand name as the "Edison Vitascope". The "new" machine, projecting "life-sized" images, opened with great fanfare in New York on April 23, 1896. Edison, everyone thought, had invented the movies. And at first Edison's movies were a smash success, though after that initial flash, the movies struggled for several years.

Another person saw the Jenkins machine in action, and also saw its potential. That was a Philadelphia colleague of Briggs in lantern-slide manufacture, Siegmund Lubin (Fig. 10.16). Lubin was a German Jewish immigrant who had a thriving downtown optical shop, and had begun making slides in the 1890s. He specialized in "song slides" – illustrations of popular songs that he sold primarily to local theaters and vaudeville houses. Lubin met Jenkins, purchased his movie machine, improved it, and gave his own cinema premier at Philadelphia's Brandenburg's Dime Museum in 1896. By 1897 he was in the movie business, offering his "Cineograph" and films for sale. To supply his customers, he became an agent for Edison's films, and then augmented his supply by simply copying his competitor's products, and selling the "dupes" as his own, or by remaking them – practices that engendered repeated lawsuits. When Lubin did make original films, he concentrated at first on using exotic acts from the local theaters. Dancing midgets, trained dogs, and a contortionist who did the "splits" – they all made their film debut in the Lubin back yard. (An early stag film of copulating horses was filmed on location in the country. Lubin's city neighbors missed that action.)[25] Lubin might be starting local, but he would soon become a major national figure, and an example of a slide maker who successfully made the transition into film.

Beale and Briggs Ignore the Movies

Briggs basically ignored all this frenetic movie activity in his own back yard, and in Edison's laboratory over in New Jersey. For Beale and Briggs, this same period was a time of steady lantern-slide production along the lines we have already seen. Literature continued to be the single largest category, particularly Parlor Poetry like *Paul Revere* and *The Village Blacksmith*. The set of *The Village Blacksmith* demonstrates the sophistication Beale had achieved by this point, and his ability to embody Briggs vision. The slide shown in Fig. 10.17 uses the same "stage set" as the image at the start of Chapter 3. but here we see it from a different point of view. The horse, previously central, is now almost off screen, and only pokes his nose into the scene. The children – in the previous slide seen only as approaching shadows – now crowd center stage, framing the blacksmith, watching in excited fascination. One little girl literally dances on air. The shadow of yet another child races in from off-stage, her arms flung wide in excitement. One slide is thus anticipating the next, so that the changing mise-en-scene itself helps drive the narrative, again providing an "extended moment" of action. The approaching shadows, seeming to come from our world off screen, help involve us in the on-screen excitement. Subject matter aside, this is a much more dynamic form of narrative art than the earlier *Father, Dear Father*.

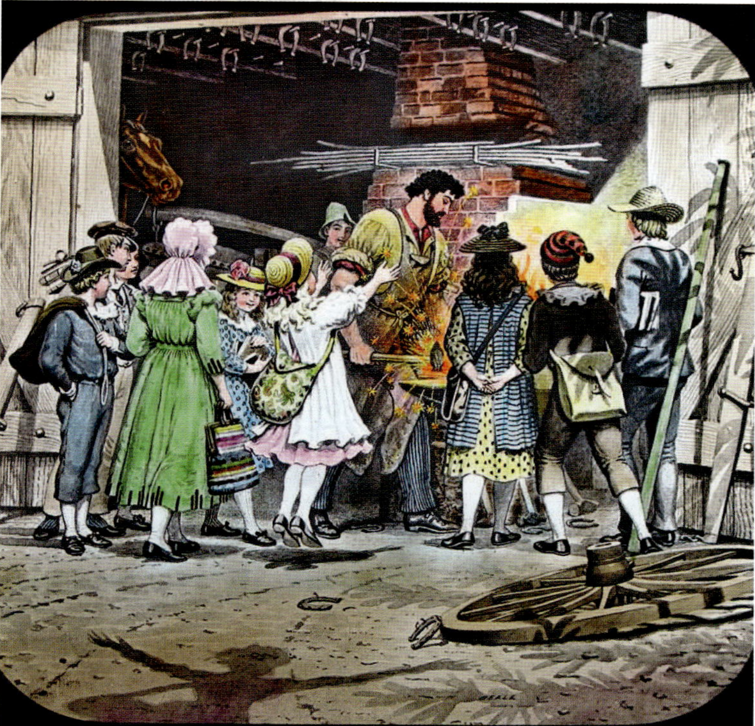

Fig. 10.17 Beale's slide 3 of *The Village Blacksmith* (1896).

A major new category emerges as a significant market in this period of Beale's work, the Secret Societies (Fig. 10.18). Though little documentation exists, Briggs would presumably have had to make arrangements with such organizations to obtain their ritual images, and to get a seal of approval for pictures that Beale created.[26] Like the Sunday-School Movement, the Secret Societies represented pre-formed organizations in which thousands of local chapters could be expected to follow the recommendations of national leaders to purchase slides for local use. With the Panic of 1893 still gripping the country, sales aimed at pre-existing groups continued to make excellent business sense. And since the Societies used a great deal of religious imagery, the many Secret Society slides could also be sold to the Religious markets and visa versa. The detail and drama of Beale's depictions made the mythic images seem real, and helped both groups become immersed in their traditions.

1898–1900
War Fever

Then came an unexpected development. Tensions had been building between the United States and Spain because of troubles in Spain's Caribbean possessions. The U.S. sent the battleship *Maine* to show the flag. When it was blown up under suspicious circumstances in 1898, the U.S. was soon ready to go to war. This "Spanish-American War" would be a major factor in both the lantern and movie industries, and in the interaction between them.

A look at Briggs' production shows the effect of the War on Beale's work. The Literary vision is pursued with a steady pace, adding such classics as *Quo Vadis* and *The Pied Piper*. But suddenly the previous emphasis on building Secret-Society views and Comic Slides is dropped. Instead, a war focus takes hold. It begins with *The Maine Disaster* set, a two-slide dissolve (Fig. 10.19). That, in turn, was followed by detailed coverage of the war, 64 slides in all.

By its very nature, Beale's coverage of the war must have been a demanding project – combining unusual production deadlines with the vagaries of reporting a complex conflict that he had not actually seen. But it was well worth it. The slides were a tremendous success, were heavily promoted in the catalogs, and continued to sell for years after the war. In particular, his dissolving set of *The Maine Disaster* became one of his most widely used. In our shows, its effect is very dramatic. Quiet music plays as the *Maine* lies sleeping at anchor. Suddenly a piano CRASH breaks the slumber, and, with a quick dissolve, a "flash", the *Maine*'s explosion erupts. Ship parts and sailors go flying everywhere. Even modern audiences gasp in shock.

Fig. 10.18 Beale's slide 36 for *The Blue Lodge Masons*.

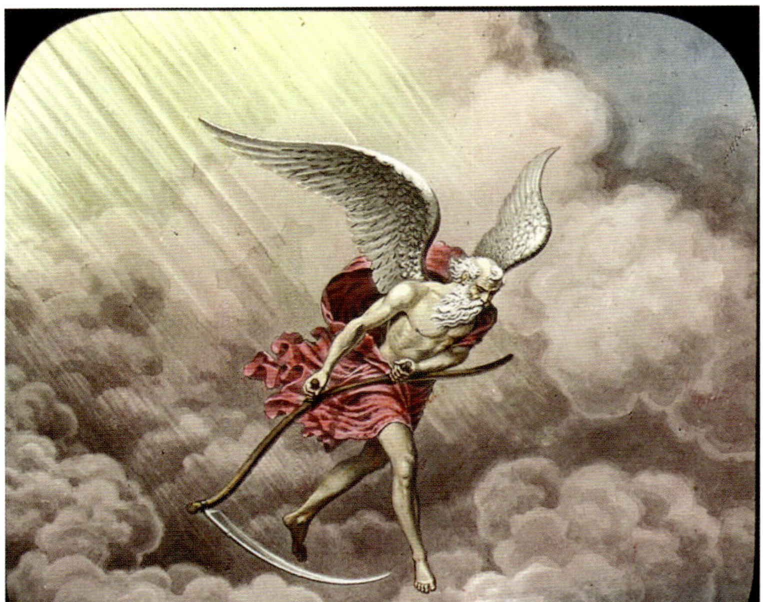

The Movies and the Lantern Go to War

By early 1898, the novelty of the movies had worn thin, Philadelphians had so little interest that periods of several weeks passed when no movies at all were shown. Edison's film production was falling, and in 1898 less than five percent of that was made up of story films. Lubin was still struggling, though he had built a studio atop the Bradenburgh's Dime Museum in Philadelphia, and was beginning to exhibit

Fig. 10.19 Beale's slides 1 and 2, "The Destruction of the Maine" (1898–99) from *The Maine Disaster*.

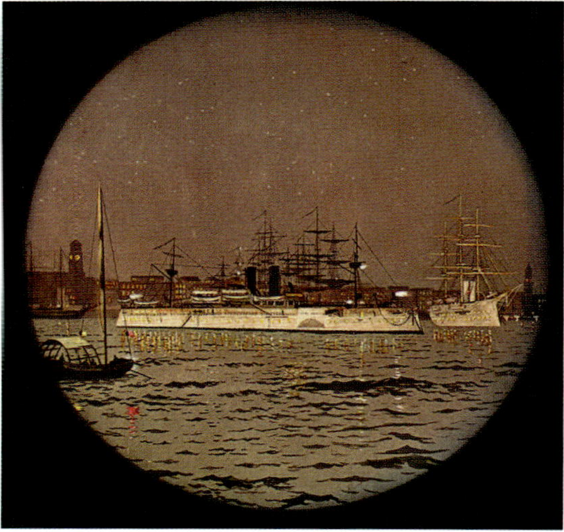

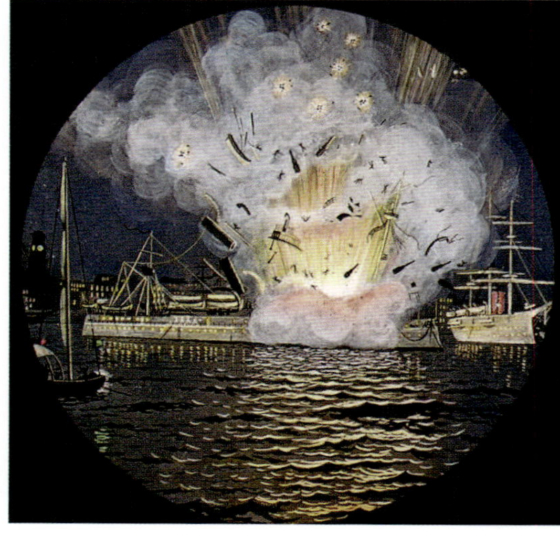

regionally. Only The Biograph Company was expanding, in part because about half of its films were acted stories, often with erotic overtones like the movie, *Peeping Tom*. But patent suits among the various "inventors" of the movies tied the entire industry in knots. Few wanted to invest when the legal outcomes were so uncertain.

Then, the *Maine* blew up, beginning the Spanish-American War. Biograph jumped on the opportunity, took an existing film about the "Iowa", retitled it *Battleship "Maine"*, and showed it to wildly patriotic crowds. The company followed this success with an effort to get real pictures like *Divers at Work on the Wreck of the "Maine"*. When the war action began, Biograph provided action in films like a staged charge of *Roosevelt Rough Riders*. Edison likewise had a camera at the war, and brought back films of the troops preparing for the invasion. A new company, American Vitagraph, re-created the *Battle of Manila Bay* with miniatures. Almost no scenes of actual conflict appeared in the movies of the period, but showmen and exhibitors put together shows of whatever film was available, usually combined with lantern slides, and christened them "wargraphs". They were enormously popular.

John P. Dibble's 1899 wargraph is a good example of how the movies and lantern slides complemented each other. Dibble had begun his career as a young man in 1875 giving lantern shows in opera houses and church halls throughout New England, and had been an active showman ever since. When the movies arrived, he immediately started mixing movies into his shows, and in fact won a 1923 *Moving Picture World* contest that gave him the right to create a promotional lantern slide and call himself the "PREMIER EXHIBITOR IN U. S. AND CANADA, DATE 1875" (Fig. 10.20). While this claim cannot be verified, he was clearly a very early exhibitor.

In his autobiography, Dibble says that "to a certain very limited extent" the Spanish-American War "increased the interest in Moving Pictures":

> Yet there were very few genuine scenes of that war taken... . The naval battle scenes were made with small toy models of battle-ships, and fire-crackers, taken in some tank of water, or bath-tub, most any old place. I had some of them and was mighty ashamed to show them.

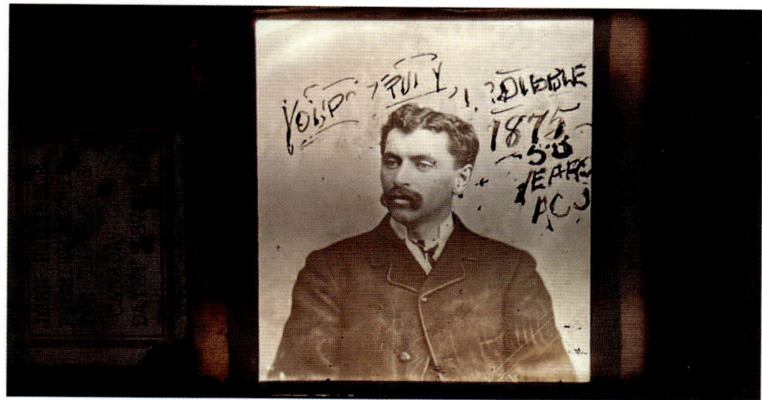

Fig. 10.20 John P. Dibble in a promotional lantern slide he made up to celebrate 50 years of performing.

> To me they looked so foolish, yet they seemed to go over with the public all right – or at least nobody did anything to us for showing them, as I feared they might. Yet I had some very fine short films ... [that were] all genuine, though short shorts, and probably they were good enough to balance out the rottenness of the fake scenes.

Mixed in with these films were "the best stereopticon slides I could find":

> War views, portraits of prominent commanders, ... the battle-ship *Maine*, and even one stereopticon view – faked up of course, showing the explosion, and destruction of the *Maine* in Havana Harbor, which I still have, and it looks quite realistic too.[27]

That, of course, was the Beale dissolving set. In addition to *The Maine Disaster*, Dibble's show used other sets that were almost certainly by Beale – "patriotic song" slides and "patriotic Stereopticon views". Beale's "American Flag", (Fig. 10.21) may well have been one of these slides. It gives the flag a kind of celestial transcendence, designed to elicit just the kind of audience reaction that Dibble describes.

Dibble gave a combination magic lantern and

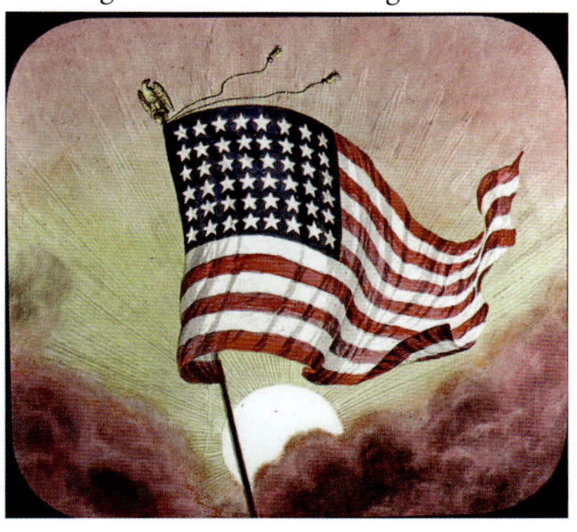

Fig. 10.21 Beale's slide 6 of *Drake's Ode to The American Flag* (1881–1893).

movie show on the Green in New Haven, Connecticut on May 1, 1899. The show, celebrating Admiral Dewey's victory at Manila Bay, was a huge success. The lights had been turned off in all the buildings around the green. People packed the windows, and an immense crowd, all standing, viewed the show. According to a front-page report in the *New Haven Union*, 20,000 people were in attendance, with "every inch of the lower part of the Green covered".

> "War scenes [the movies] were frequently shown, and met the hearty appreciation of the crowd".

But, as the *Union* makes clear, Beale's slides were appreciated just as much:

> 'Oh's and ah's' were heard as the colored pictures were thrown on the screen. The American flag got a thunderous greeting".[28]

Standalone magic lantern shows about the war could be just as popular. In Philadelphia, a lantern show at Keith's theater ran for weeks, with large advertisements listing the details. In fact, the popularity of lantern lectures had increased to the point that Gould W. Hart, of Brooklyn, formed "what might be termed a lecturer's agency", providing stereopticon equipment, operators, and an impressive roster of speakers including Alexander Black. And in England at least, the first blush of the movies seemed to be over. Though *OMLJ* had originally been an enthusiastic promoter of the cinema, and had urged lanternists to incorporate it into their programs, by the end of 1899, their enthusiasm had cooled. Commented "The Showman":

> We have now arrived at a time when many users of the cinematograph have become painfully aware that the best days of that at one time promising instrument are over, and no doubt some will be looking about for a new means of attracting the public taste, without departing from the realms of optical projection.[29]

To the lantern community, the movies seemed to be, at best, an adjunct to the traditional magic lantern show. Several firms, including Lubin and the Stereopticon and Film Exchange of Chicago, were now offering combination movie and slide projectors. Such machines allowed the exhibitor to switch easily from one format to the other, supplementing the limited supply of films with lantern slides, or visa versa, and using each medium for what it did best. The movies, it seemed, would provide the sense of real movement, actualities, and comic sketches. The lantern slides would provide longer, more complex dramatic stories, spectacular color, stirring visual symbolism, and illustrated songs.

Beale's Patriotic Hymns

Besides covering the war, the other major Beale emphasis of the 1898-1900 period was Religion, with 69 slides in all. What is striking about these Religious slides is the number of new Hymns in this three-year period – five in total – about equal to the production over the preceding 17 years. Obviously, the idea of illustrated hymns was catching on, the religious counterpart of what was to become a secular craze for illustrated songs.

Fig. 10.22 Beale's slide 1 and 3 from the song, *The Red, White, and Blue* (1899), celebrating the American victory in the Spanish-American War. Beale was especially proud of Slide 1.

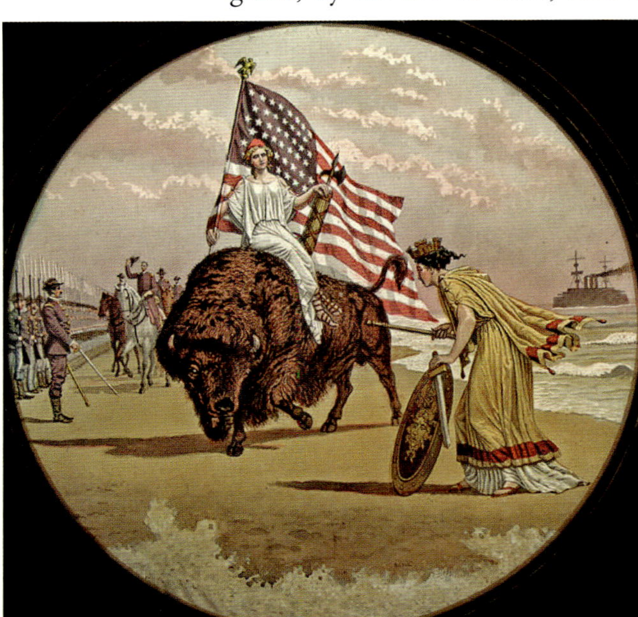

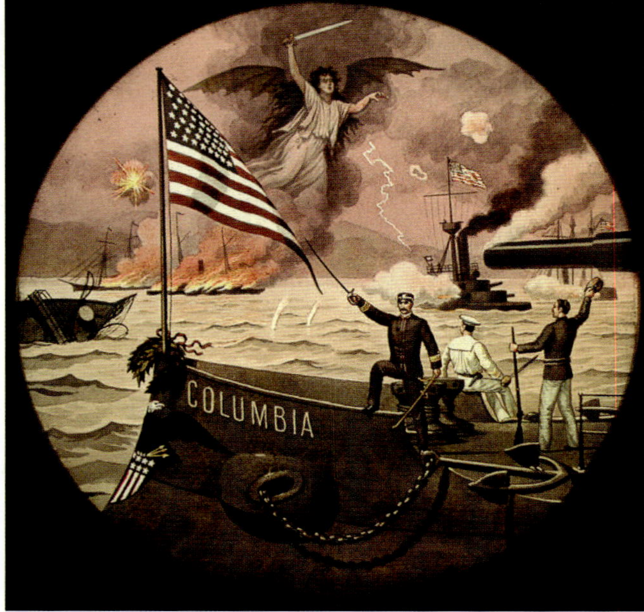

Strange as it may seem, war fever may have contributed to the new popularity of hymns. A Beale patriotic song, *Red White and Blue* (Fig. 10.22), was not a quite a hymn, but contained religious imagery explicitly tied to the war – for instance, an avenging angel pointing the way for American battleships. Two of Beale's hymns of this period, *Throw Out the Lifeline* and *Let the Lower Lights Be Burning* have a nautical theme. That would surely have resonated with a nation sending its boys on a dangerous naval crusade, as would *God Be With You Till We Meet Again.* The hymn *Onward Christian Soldiers* is so martial that it has been dropped from the hymnals in many modern peace-loving churches. If it was a singing war, and it was, then Briggs was ready to feed the market.

The "Economic" Catalog Vastly Extends Beale's Impact

It was not only the war that drove Beale's sales in this period; it was a new marketing strategy developed by Briggs and McAllister.

This major development at the C. W. Briggs company in 1900 is not immediately evident from the slide list, but it was one of the most important in the history of the firm – the introduction of the "Economic Catalog". The all-glass (rather than wood-framed) Economic slides had been available for years, and gradually, more and more lanternists began using them, until by the turn of the century they were becoming the dominant form of lantern slide. But the transition from the old format of wood-framed slides to the new created a problem. Once the Economic slides became common, what showmen would pay three times as much for the wood-framed slides?

I've already mentioned that McAllister tried to solve this pricing/income problem in 1894 by establishing a series of Economic slides (including Beale's comics) that were in a "cheaper style of finish than our *Fine Colored,* [with] the subjects ... in no instance duplicates of those". But this approach had an obvious downside. Poor quality McAllister slides would undermine the traditional "top of the line" McAllister image.

At the start of the new century, McAllister offered a new solution. This was a distinct 24-page "Economic Catalog" – sometimes issued separately, but usually bound into the larger McAllister listings. The first of these catalogs was accompanied by a letter from McAllister, dated Jan. 1, 1900, addressing the quality issue and emphasizing the point that, "These slides are of the 'McAllister' quality, and in every instance the best obtainable on the subject". The letter also said that this new line of inexpensive slides was possible, "owing to our increased facilities for making this line of Slides in large quantities".[30] The discount was substantial. The regular price for 3-1/4 x 4" slides in the same "standard" catalog was $.40 for a single black and white (in lots of 100, $.35) and $1.00 for colored (in lots of 100, $90.) In the Economic Catalog the price was $.25 and $.50, respectively, with no discounts for larger orders.

The "increased facilities" that allowed these dramatically cheaper slides in fact belonged to C. W. Briggs, who not only manufactured the slides, but also prepared the catalog. It must have been a risky move for Briggs and McAllister – cutting their price drastically in the hopes of making up the difference in greater volume of sales. Apparently, it worked, for Briggs continued to market his slides in the new "Economic" format. And from 1900 to 1907 he also gradually increased the size of the catalog by a third, from 24 pages to 32. His business was growing steadily, despite the movies.

The changeover to the "Economic Catalog" and its production within the Briggs company were indeed brilliant marketing strategies. For Briggs not only provided the catalog to McAllister. He also supplied the same catalog to at least seven of the other leading slide distributors of the day, each of which put its own name on it. It appears that any company could get the Economic catalog, stamp its name on it, and distribute the Briggs slides.

This meant that these distributors could not "cherry pick" among the Briggs wholesale offerings, but had to distribute the entire Briggs repertoire directly to their customers. Since a large part of the Briggs repertoire was Beale's art, the "Economic Catalog" vastly increased the dissemination of Beale's work – both because high-quality slides were now much less expensive, and because the advertisements for them were offered by almost all major companies in the market. It was the "Economic Catalog" – along with Beale's talent – that made his work the most widely used illustrated slides in America.

1901–1903
The Movies Falter

The 1901–02 catalog of the Stereopticon and Film Exchange, begins with this doubt:

> Will It Pay?
>
> This is the question that naturally rises when one anticipates embarking in a new enterprise. Ten years ago, it was prophesied that the stereopticon, as an entertainer, would be less used in the future than it was at that time. This, however, was a mistake, for the demand has been increasing ever since and today it is used more for entertainments than ever before. When you add a moving picture machine to the stereopticon, you double its value.

The catalog continues for seven paragraphs to explain the many opportunities for making money with the magic lantern by lecturing and by showing advertising slides. It devotes only one paragraph to the movies:

> Moving pictures are still in their infancy, and as improvements are made will grow in favor with the public. The fact of being able to bring to our very door all the important events of the world *in actual life and motion* is sufficient proof that this class of entertainment will never grow old.

In the aftermath of the Spanish-American War, the movies are seen as recorders of current events, a "visual newspaper" (a term used in *OMLJ*) that may show promise, but cannot yet hold the public. *OMLJ* worries about a "dearth in lanterndom" – a "scarcity of interest, a "barren excitement", and in consequence, a "scarcity of business", all, it is thought, due to the movies – but the setback for the lantern is seen as temporary.[31] Plenty of evidence supported this view. Legal wrangles – both patent and copyright – continued in the movie industry, so that investment seemed hazardous. Competing forms of technology meant a limited supply of films for each type of projector (Fig. 10.23). Prices dropped. "Actualities" – movies of actual events like feeding the baby or the surf on the beach – were wearing thin, and the lack of story-telling skill was obvious. Audiences across America, despite the catalog's assurances, became easily bored with film. Dibble summed up the films he bought in this period in his usual pungent prose:

> I'll tell the world [what they were like], for I was right there, and purchased them as they appeared – good, bad, and indifferent – *mostly indifferent.*[32]

Theaters refused to show such fare; in Philadelphia, for instance, only Keith's and Bradenburgh's (Lubin's base) were showing movies. Across the country the movies were becoming the "chasers" in the continuous programming of the vaudeville houses – the inexpensive act used to close the show and "chase" the customers out so that the theater could be emptied for the next round. The major magic lantern catalogs were experimenting with film, but only tentatively. A supplement featuring Lubin's films had been made "Expressly for T. H. McAllister" in 1898, but no evidence shows that he carried it after that. The cover of the 1902 McIntosh catalog suggested the customers write away for a list of films, but did not include them. Both companies saw the lantern and slides as the mainstream of their entertainment business at this period.

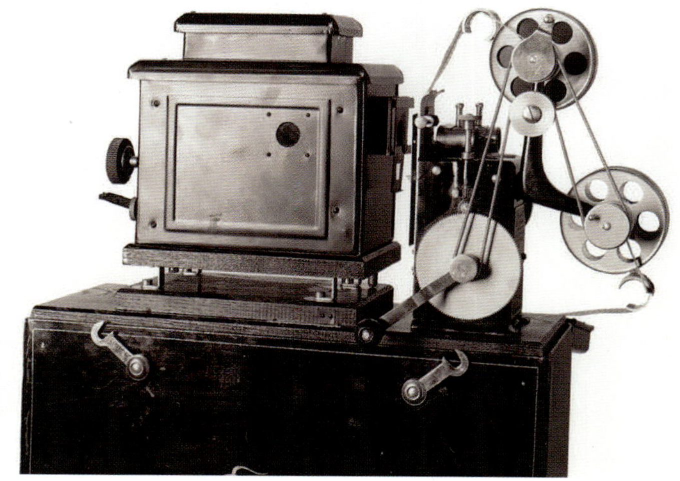

Fig. 10.23 Edison's 1901 "Projecting Kinetoscope". The Kinetoscope looked like a lantern, but it carried a movie reel. *Wikimedia Commons.*

This new, stronger confidence in the lantern's role is obvious in the subject selection of Briggs in the first years of the new century. The Secret Societies (his backup) get little attention; the Literature group gains steadily. The time seemed right for Briggs to realize his vision. Several of his title selections can be seen as building upon the stronger sense of nationhood created by winning the war: The sets of *Hiawatha* and *Evangeline* (both a year earlier, in 1900) are visual dramatizations of Longfellow's mythic history of America. *Sheridan's Ride* harks back to the Civil War to commemorate the action of an American hero in another war, while *Dixie's Land* presents the Southern fighting song in visual images with a Northern point of view. *Yankee Doodle* is, of course, the great American patriotic sing-along. Clearly Briggs thought it was time for "American" literature and song.

Longer Lantern Sets to Compete

Another trend was becoming evident in Beale's presentation of literary works. In the first period we discussed, 1880–91, both novels, *Ten Nights in a Bar Room* and *Uncle Tom's Cabin*, were presented in sets of twelve slides. The number of slides in a set began to change in 1892-97, perhaps in response to the popularity of Black's "Picture Plays" with their rapid change of images, or perhaps in response to the movies. *Ben Hur*, a novel no longer than *Uncle Tom's Cabin*, is presented in 32 slides, and *Pilgrim's Progress* is increased from 12 to 24. Even the comparatively short poem *Evangeline* gets 24 slides.

Having more slides to a set had obvious advantages. It was much easier to tell a long story with more images. For instance, with enough slides Beale could concentrate several of them around highpoints of the action, like Evangeline missing her lover in the fog. More slides meant more revenue from a given set. But that fact translated into higher cost for the customer, which presumably decreased sales. (For comparison, while a 12-slide color set of Economy slides sold at retail for about $200 in 2025 dollars, a 24 slide set would be $400 and a 32 slide set would be $535.)

This tension between rising "revenue-per-set" and declining "number-of-sales" can be seen in the treatment of *Quo Vadis*, a literary sensation

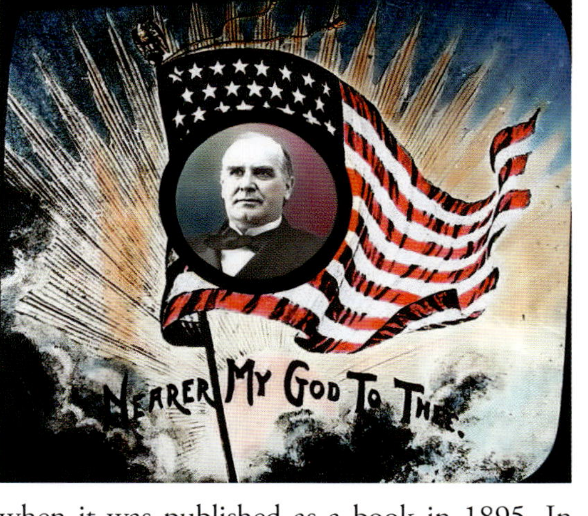

Fig. 10.24 Beale's slide 6 of Drake's *Ode to The American Flag*, modified to make a tribute to President McKinley, and introduce the hymn, *Nearer My God To Thee*.

when it was published as a book in 1895. In 1898 McAllister offers a 38-slide set cobbled together from pre-existing images (including nine by Beale), saying, "Should success warrant our efforts in this direction we will add from time-to-time special designs illustrating the most important situations recorded in the work". Success did not warrant much. McAllister dropped the set the following year.[33]

Despite the tradeoffs of providing more slides per set, the numbers do increase in this period. *Hiawatha* increases from four to 24. Gray's *Elegy in a Country Churchyard* goes from 20 to 32. *Lady of the Lake* is 24.

Illustrated Songs – Religious and Secular

Hymns are the other major concentration in the 1901–03 period – building on the chorus of religious song begun the previous period. This increase in the number of hymn lantern slides may have been because of the assassination of McKinley in 1901. Of course, the assassination prompted an immediate *Life of McKinley* set, but *Nearer My God to Thee* had been McKinley's favorite hymn (Fig. 10.24). Accord-

Fig. 10.25 Beale's slides 2, 4 and 6 of *Nearer My God to Thee* (1895). The set contains a spectacular series of effect dissolves.

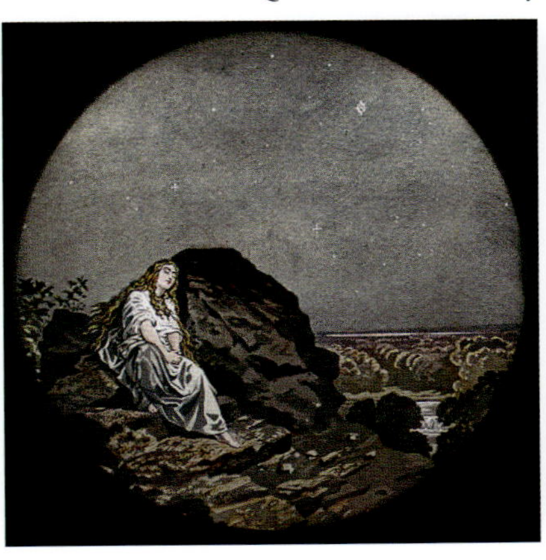

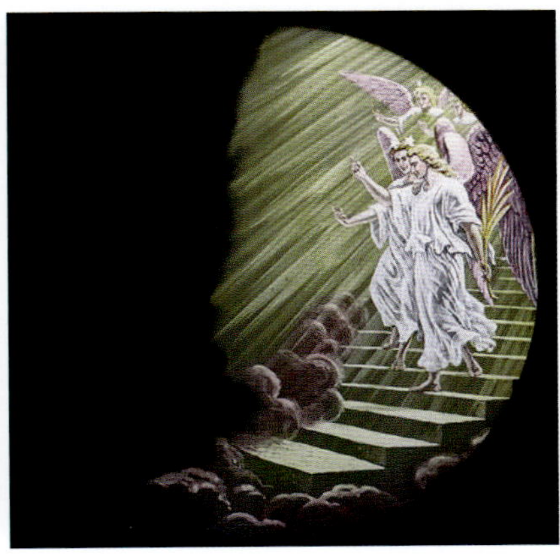

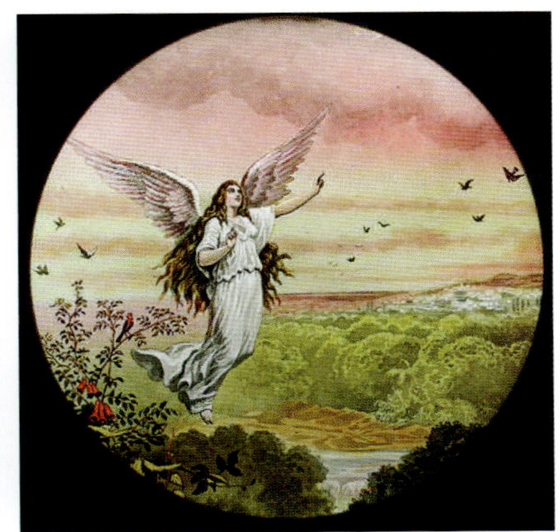

ing to newspaper accounts he mumbled the words as he was dying.[34]

Because Beale's 1895 version of the song (Fig. 10.25) was readily available, it was used in major commemorative services, and, no doubt, in many of the smaller services held in individual churches throughout the land. Briggs, alert as ever, followed the next year with four more hymns, all illustrated in Beale's rich, detailed nineteenth-century style.

Dibble describes the result of shows mixing such lantern-slide hymns with movies about McKinley's last days in Buffalo and his subsequent funeral:

> For months after the Buffalo tragedy it was not an unusual thing at our exhibitions to note ladies sobbing in genuine grief as these pictures were shown, and men too were often evidently deeply affected while viewing the wonderfully realistic scenes [of the movies] and listening to the sacred music of *Nearer My God to Thee* ....[35]

Contemporary "Illustrated Songs"

It is not surprising that Briggs would quickly rush to fill the market's desire for religious hymns. What is surprising is what he did *not* do. He did not offer any popular, current secular songs to complement the "chestnuts" like *Home Sweet Home* and *Swanee Ribber* that Beale had already produced. Contemporary "illustrated songs" were becoming increasingly fashionable, both as "standalone" entertainment, and to keep audiences happy while the reels were being changed between movies. ("Illustrated songs" is a confusing term. Most of these slides were made with life-model photographs, not artist-created illustrations. The "illustrator" was the *singer* who presented the song as the slides were projected. The audience often joined in singing the chorus, prompted by a ***chorus slide*** that contained the words.)

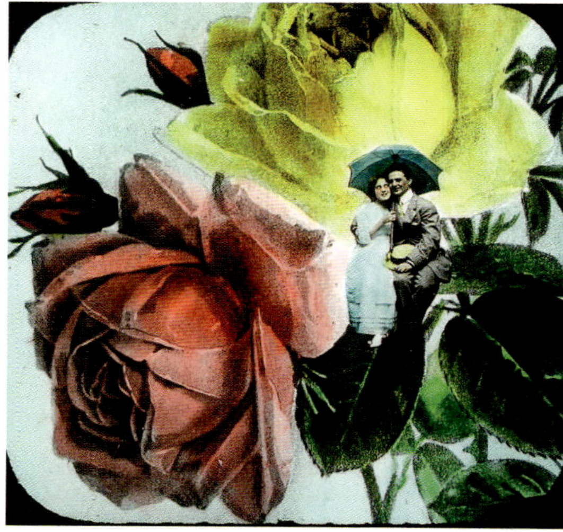

Fig 10.26 An Illustrated Song Slide. Such slides were a major part of the movie-going experience from 1900–1920.

By 1901–02, Dibble was making contemporary songs, "one of the leading attractions of his show",[36] and the Stereopticon and Film Exchange catalog was offering 62 different sets. The catalog mixed war songs like *Break the News to Mother,* lilting love ballads like *I Love My Dolly Best*, and melodramatic tearjerkers like *The Face Upon the Barroom Floor.* These sets were almost always ballads that told a story in song, contained from 12 to 20 slides, and were illustrated with a very different kind of "life model" photograph than those used by the British life-model slides so often disparaged – much more colorful and elaborate.

Credit for creation of the first of these contemporary song slides is generally given to George H. Thomas, a stage electrician and amateur photographer, who in 1894 got the idea while watching a vaudeville performance of *The Old Homestead.* During the performance a quartet sang *Where Is My Wandering Boy Tonight?* which was illustrated with a single slide. (Probably this slide was from the set by Beale that had just been released.) Thomas apparently realized that if he made life-model song slides, he might have a popular new form of entertainment that would fit well into a live-action vaudeville program. Teaming up with a pair of song writers he produced *The Little Lost Child*, which was an immediate success. Manufacturers of magic lantern slides such as Van Altena jumped into the business, and came to dominate it, operating after 1904 as Scott and Van Altena.

A song slide craze evolved that lasted through the early years of film and produced some narrative art that was as remarkable in its own way as Beale's was in his. These slides were bursting with the energy and bravado of America in the new century – expressed both in the subject matter of the songs, which often featured the latest inventions and fads, and also in vibrant colors and complex photo montages or composite shots (Figs. 10.26 and 27).

A very significant part of George Thomas's innovation was to get the producers of piano sheet music to pay for the manufacture of the song slides, which were then shipped gratis or for a small rental to the theaters. In effect, Thomas opened up a new market for slides, and, like the religious and secret society markets that Briggs had concentrated on, it was a group market where one sale to a theater syndicate could involve hundreds of sets.

As it turned out, the song slides market was also one with explosive growth potential, driven by a combination of audience appeal and shrewd marketing. The theaters hired local vocalists (the illustrators) who sang the songs and then urged everyone to join in on the chorus. After a few repetitions ("One more time!") the tune would be firmly planted in the memory of those in the audience. Once the performance was over, the audience would hurry off to buy the sheet music so that they could sing the song on their own. Many all-time favorites were embedded in the nation's consciousness by this immersive experience – *Down by the Old Mill Stream*, and *Take Me Out to the Ball Game*. The manufacturers of sheet music who provided the slides sold a great many copies of their product – often in the lobbies of the theaters themselves.[37]

In effect, these magic lantern slides turned what might have been a gray, wordless and inactive night at the movies into entertainment suffused with the color, song, and audience participation. Particularly before 1903, at a time when the movies were struggling to hold an audience, illustrated songs were critical to the success of screen entertainment. And their popularity only grew with the increased popularity of movies. By 1910, at the height of the illustrated song craze, they were a staple of every movie-house, large or small. Many of the historic movie theaters we have performed in had a special little "song illustrator" balcony from which the illustrator performed – right up there beside the box seats. The magic lantern had become the music video of the era. The demand was huge.

Where was Briggs during this explosive growth of lantern-slide images, telling stories in song? Nowhere to be found. We can only guess at the reasons. In large part it was probably that these song slides were photographic, life-model slides, and Briggs defined his niche as hand-drawn images. Part of his neglect of this market might have been the subject matter, which, though not as offensive as Lubin's movies, was still not quite Briggs's cup of tea. And Beale's style might have been a problem, even if Briggs wanted to give contemporary illustrated song slides a try. While Beale's images were still being heavily used to promote Spanish-American War coverage, his approach did not fit the light-hearted, insouciant attitude that many of the illustrated songs conveyed.

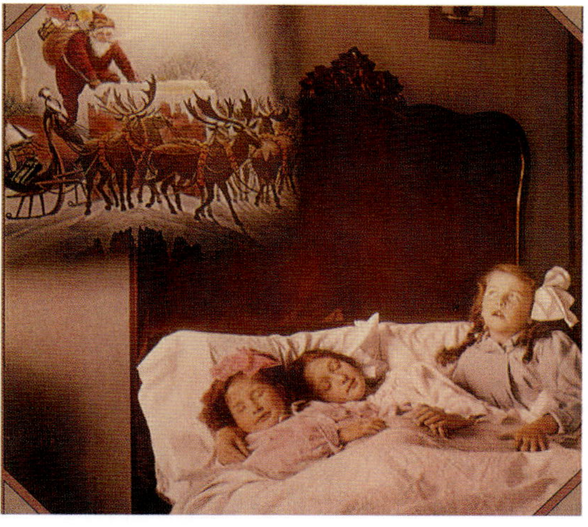

Fig. 10.27 Slide from *The Dawn of Christmas Day* (1909) by Scott & Van Altena. The song incorporates three Beale images from The *Visit of St. Nicholas*. Courtesy, The Marnan Collection.

By 1902 the catalog of The Chicago Projecting Company had begun to separate Beale from the "Illustrated Songs" under the rubric "Songs That Never Grow Old". By 1907, Sears was using the same heading. The company tried to update the "Never Grow Old" songs and a number of Beale "Sacred Songs" with "Talking Machine" cylinders or disks, to give them a new multi-media life, but this approach does not appear to have been successful.[38]

Moore, Bond & Co. directly attacked the Beale "Never Grow Old" songs, including such illustrated chestnuts such as *Swanee Ribber* (Fig. 10.28).

> If a song call[s] for scenes of the Swanee River, we send a photographer to the Swanee River to get them. Our songs slides are therefore true to life and correctly represent the sentiment of the song.[39]

This argument sounds persuasive. But despite it, Beale's *Swanee Ribber* is one of the most commonly found of all American illustrated song sets today. I have never seen the Moore-Bond photographed slides. What I *have* seen are pirated Moore-Bond "dup" negatives of such Beale song "chestnuts" as *Home Sweet Home* and *The Star Spangled Banner*, plus a dozen Beale stories. I saw them when I was asked to review a 40,000-slide Moore-Bond collection left after the company closed. There they were, nestled down amid original Moore-Bond material. Moore-Bond probably created those negatives in the 1920s. Certainly they copied

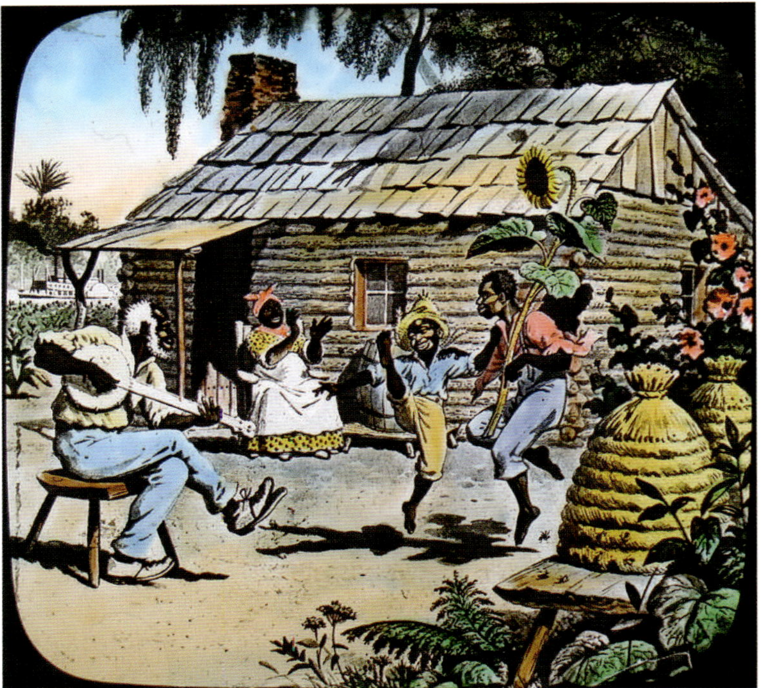

Fig. 10.28 Beale's slide 8 for *Swanee Ribber* (1893), by Stephen Foster. We find such images offensive today, but they captured the spirit of Foster's song, and were very popular.

them directly from the Briggs slides – the Briggs labels are still visible on the negatives. If imitation is the sincerest form of flattery, then Moore-Bond must have come to realize that Beale's style *was* well-suited to "The Songs That Never Grow Old" and life models were not.[40]

Some hopeful signs for the movies were hidden beneath the general sense of malaise that dominated the new industry, and that led people to

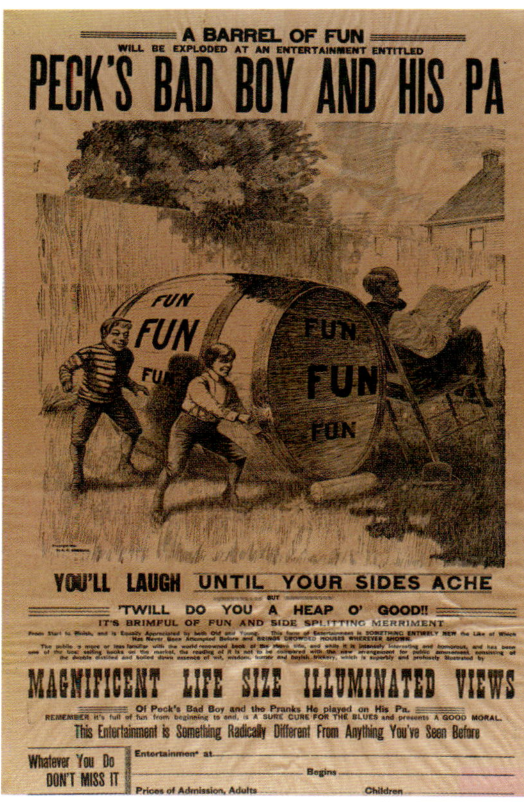

Fig. 10.29 Large 2' x 3' broadside for *Peck's Bad Boy*.

wonder if the art form would continue. Edison had built a new studio to create more elaborate, longer films. During the first six months of 1901 he produced 60 films; 60% of which were acted stories. They began to incorporate traditional magic lantern story-telling techniques: *close-ups*, dissolves, effect dissolves, a smoothly-executed pan shot. While Edwin Porter, Edison's film-maker, may not have looked directly to the lantern as the model of these techniques, he was certainly familiar with the lantern and what it could do, and was soon doing similar things.

Lantern Slides and Movies Combined, *Peck's Bad Boy*

Could the lantern and the movies be combined? That was an obvious question which was answered in 1902 when The Chicago Projecting Company catalog offered a new kind of comic fare, a mixture of lantern slides and movies that were explicitly designed to complement each other in telling a single story. "It's a BRAND NEW IDEA, but it's what people want, and is MAKING A BIG HIT", the catalog brayed.

The subject matter was *Peck's Bad Boy and His Pa*, first published by George W. Peck as newspaper columns in 1883 and then developed into books and plays (and lantern shows) as part of long series of similar titles (Fig. 10.29). Peck's books were among the most popular in the nineteenth century. The "Bad Boy" got himself into innumerable scrapes, played nasty tricks on his father and everyone else, and was generally a scamp (Fig.10 30). Each book was composed of short stories, which meant that each episode was brief and self-contained – perfect fodder for the lantern, and for the movies in their infancy.

The slides were made from life models and sold in sets of 52 or 72, with about six slides allocated to each story. The lantern set was presented in the catalog as "the **backbone and foundation** of the business". (Bold emphasis in the original.) It could be supplemented with the movies, "especially adapted to the 'Bad Boy' set, showing incidents that are not included in the stereopticon views". The set included ten movies, from 28 to 50 feet in length, "which would make a delightful diversion between the eleven [slide] chapters ... as they are full of action and strictly in keeping with the sentiment of the story, and add much value to the production".

Here then was a new form of amusement that the catalog called neither "Magic lantern Show" nor "Movies", but simply "Entertainment". It was not an ad-hoc mix of the two by a showman like Dibble; it was a pre-planned and pre-packaged artistic continuity of the two forms of screen experience. The lantern took the lead, providing "Fun and slide-splitting merriment", combining slides in full color and a droll script drawn from Peck's text. The movies provided the "action" – usually a simple practical joke.[41]

Perhaps the *Peck's Bad Boy* combo would be the future. Some must have thought so. But the movies were gathering steam on their own.

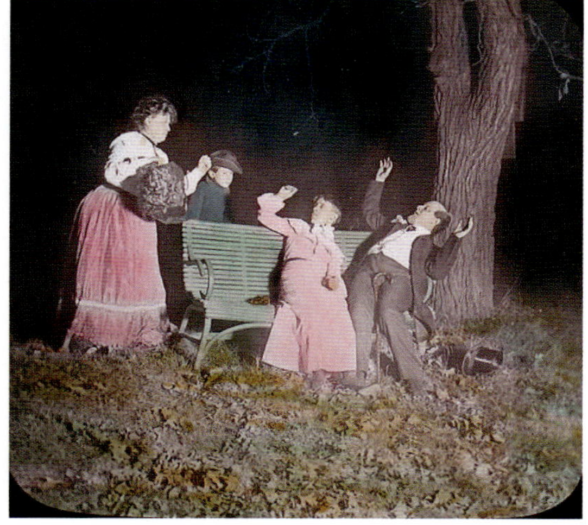

Fig. 10.30 Slide for *Peck's Bad Boy.* In the slide, the Bad Boy, rear, has just shown Ma how Pa is cheating on her.

1904 to 1909 The Movies Emerge

The period 1904 to 1909 saw the movies finally, after eight years, come into their own, and begin to develop as the dominant art form of the twentieth century. During this same period, not surprisingly, the lantern industry struggled. But the exact nature of that struggle is not what you might expect. Lantern lectures, according to *American Amateur Photographer*, were "waning in popularity… . The 'Man in the Street' is pretty clear as to one cause at least … the more attractive cinematograph.[42] But despite the general decline of the lantern, the growth of the cinema, and the wider changes occurring around Briggs and Beale during this period, their business seems at first to have been holding steady, and perhaps even prospering. In 1905 Briggs expanded the Economic Catalog from 24 pages to 28. Beale's output looks typical. Literature, though not quite so high a percentage as the preceding period, is still the lead category, closely followed by Religion. The Literature category, as we might expect by now, contains a mixture of Parlor Poetry like *Little Breeches* – a dramatic parlor poem in which a prairie farmer loses his little son in a snowstorm. (Fig. 10.31) – and "songs that never grow old", such as *Old Black Joe* and *Auld Lang Syne*.

But a new addition appears in the Literature category, one we have not seen since the very earliest years of Beale work on *How Jones Became a Mason*. This addition is the Comic Sketch format – not individual slides or dissolving sets of two slides, but 8–12 slide sets of fast paced, highly-visual, dramatic stories with no script, like *Mrs. Casey and the Billy Goat*. The 1904–06 period introduces three – *Uncle Rastus and His Mule*, *Paddy and the Pig*, and *Mr. Spurt and His Auto* (Fig. 10.32). All three involve a man and a cantankerous animal, or, in Mr. Spurt's case, a cantankerous machine. All involve a man trying to manage a force that is stronger than he is.

Pop psychologists might claim that the "man" is Briggs and the "unmanageable force" is the movies. I wouldn't go that far, but it is probably fair to suggest that this sudden interest in the

Fig. 10.31 Beale's slide 5 for *Little Breeches* (1906), by John Hay.

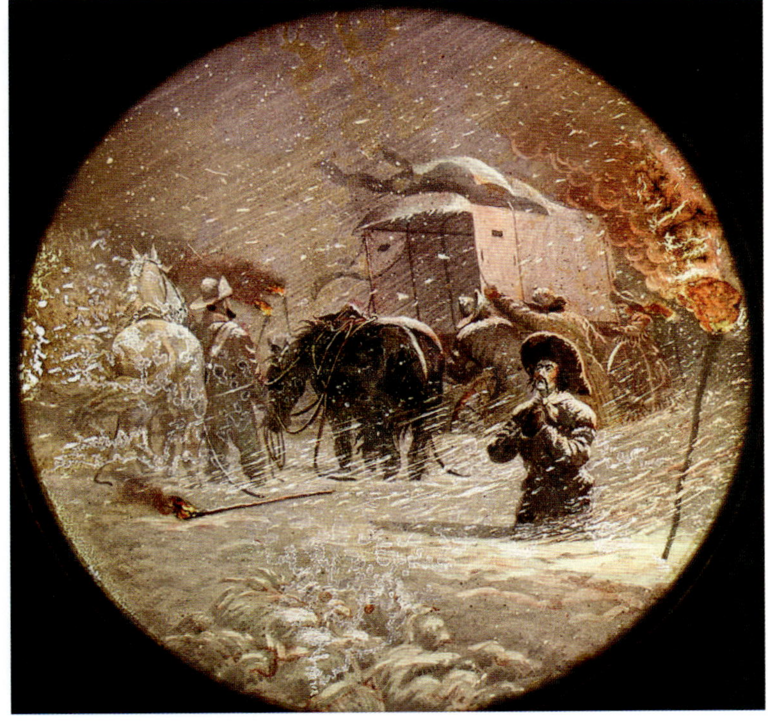

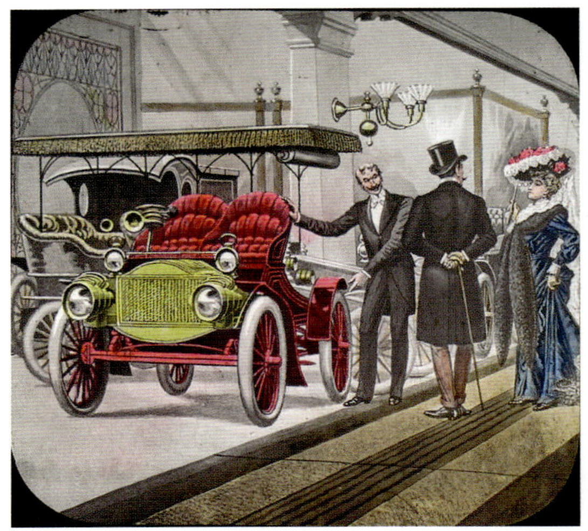

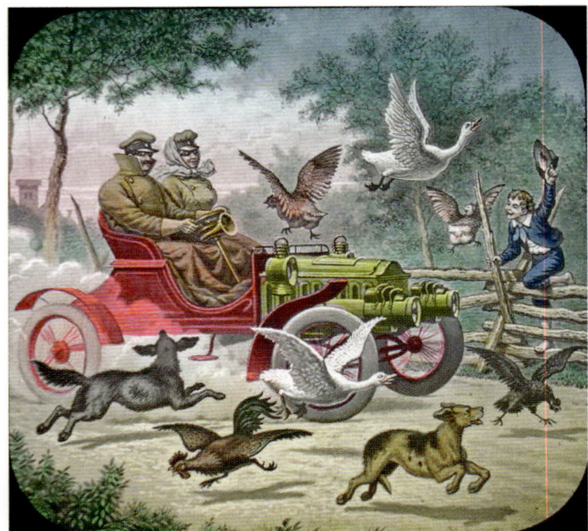

Fig. 10.32 Beale's slides 1 and 3 for *Mr. Spurt and His Auto* (1906) pokes fun at the pretensions of the auto class. The car itself, with headlight eyes, becomes a character.

Comic Sketch – hardly in line with Briggs's vision – is related to the movies' success. Much of that success, after all, was based on comic sketches – a visual joke with no verbal accompaniment, like Edison's *Happy Holligan Surprised*. The Comic Sketch sets also seem designed to have the slides changed every few seconds. Both *Uncle Rastus* and *Paddy* follow the action with a series of shifting "camera angles", much as we saw in *Mrs. Casey and the Billy Goat*. Comic Sketches are, in short, about as close to a movie as the magic lantern could come.

Another accommodation to the movies that Briggs makes in this period is creating more Motto slides. Beale had created some of these in the in the earliest days of his career. They were the *cover shots* used to begin and end lantern shows, and to make transitions between sections. The mottos done in 1903–06, which I have labeled "Movie Mottos", broaden the range with season-specific mottos (e.g. a "Good Night" accompanied by a witch). But they also include some that seem clearly designed to be used as part of movie programming, like "Frog Intermission" – essential to cover the time between movie reels.

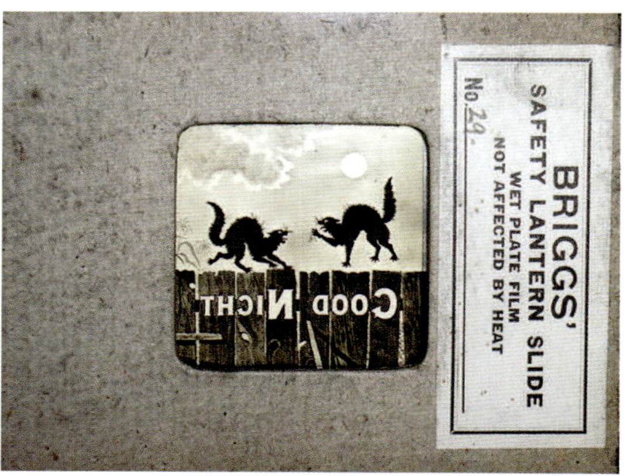

Fig. 10.33 Beale's "Cats on Fence" Announcement slide made into a Briggs Safety slide. It adapts a traditional Beale image to a new format.

In addition, Briggs created a new kind of "Safety Slide" in 1910 designed to stand the heat of the combined movie projector and lantern (Fig. 10.33). These were 3-1/4" x 4" slides containing a small glass (or perhaps mica) panel edged in heavy cardboard and framed in metal. The small piece of glass or mica, combined with the flexible cardboard frame, was intended to keep the slide from cracking. Red or green print on the glass proclaimed movie-related mottos like "Complete Change of Program Every Day" and "One Minute. Intermission While Changing Reels".

With these two kinds of Motto slides Briggs was obviously trying to adapt to the movies, treating it as an opportunity rather than a threat. By itself the production of Motto slides was certainly not a very lucrative strategy. But it may have been part of a larger plan that Briggs thought had more potential. One part of that plan was to exploit the opportunity for greater distribution – using the new catalogs that had emerged for movies as an additional way to sell slides.

The second strategy was to sell slides to the movies themselves.

The Movies Use Beale

It behooved Briggs to be thinking about collaborating with the movie producers; they were picking up steam. By early 1903 the copyright issue had been clearly enough settled so that producers could feel that they owned their work. Vitagraph was regularly making films that were five minutes long – long enough to tell a real story – and making some as long as 20 minutes. Film size was becoming standardized to 35mm. New types of intermittent mechanism reduced flicker. And most important of all, the country's leading film-maker, Edwin Porter, was in charge of Edison's new studio, and creating a new kind of story film that made greater use of lantern effects like dissolves and pans.

It was with Porter that Briggs may have seen collaborative opportunities, for in 1903 Porter used lantern slides themselves, this time in *Uncle Tom's Cabin* – a movie based on Harriet Beecher Stowe's famous polemic against slavery. The film closely followed a typical stage version of Stowe's novel, using existing sets, actors and an emphasis on dancing slaves. The movie was a smash success.

But the "Tableau" that formed the grand finale of this ground-breaking movie was not a moving picture at all. It was almost entirely composed of lantern slides, and drew on their narrative power to capture in just 35 seconds the tragedy of slavery. Three of the four images were by Beale (Fig. 10.34). George Kleine, a major distributor of lantern slides and movies, heralded the movie as "the most elaborate effort at telling a story in moving pictures yet attempted".[43] Yet paradoxically, Porter chose lantern slides – Beale's slides – to create that moving picture's powerful climax.

Whether Porter obtained permission from Briggs to use the Beale images in his film is doubtful. Stealing images was the order of the day in the movies. Nonetheless, the use of Beale's picture as the grand finale of the most successful movie to yet appear must certainly have given Briggs ideas. Perhaps he could use the rest of his vast repertoire of images in similar "Tableaus". He explored the idea later, and even entered into a contract to sell his images to Keystone-Brady, a movie company. Probably earlier explorations occurred as well. If so, nothing much came of such efforts. The "Tableau" idea continued to be used in movies, but not in a way that would create a market for slides.[44]

The Movies Adopt Some Lantern Stories

As the movies turned away from actualities and toward storytelling, they needed stories that would work on screen. Briggs, of course, had been consciously building such a repertoire. They were carried in many of the same catalogs that were also promoting the early movies – Kleine, Harbach, etc. So it might seem natural that movie producers would turn to the Briggs/Beale repertoire for ideas on which stories to choose, and how to present them. But there is little evidence of that. Of the 2,228 films that the movie database IMDb lists as American productions from 1890 through 1900, only 6 have any relation to Beale's subjects if we combine the multiple iterations of *Rip Van Winkle* and the various *Fire* titles.[45] If we take a broader range, 1890–1910, of the 8,506 films IMDb

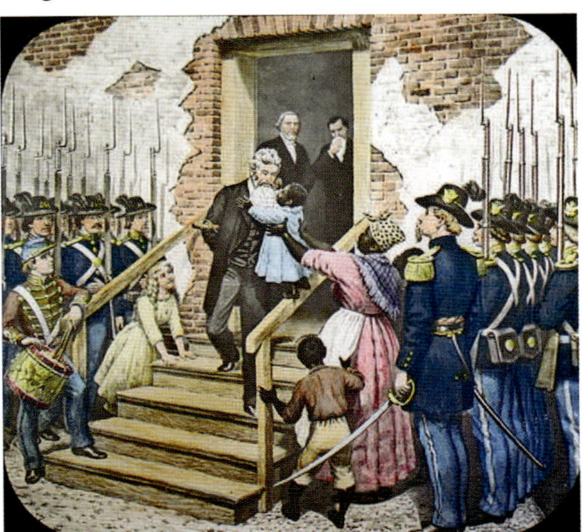

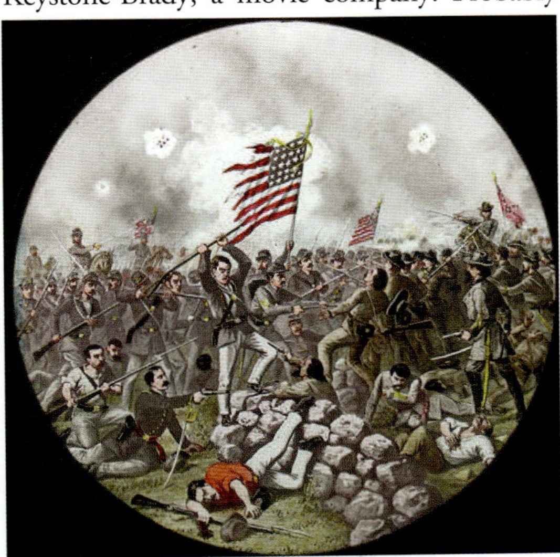

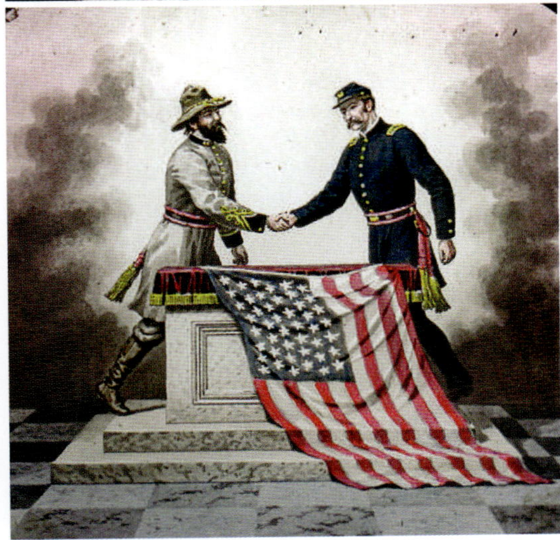

Fig. 10.34 Beale images that formed the final emblematic "Tableau" in Porter's movie of *Uncle Tom's Cabin:* Top right, "John Brown on the way to Execution". Bottom left, "Battle of Gettysburg", from the *Civil War* group. Right, slide 22, "The Blue and the Gray" from the *Patriotic Sons of America*.

lists as American productions only 37 have a title similar to Beale's, again combining multiple subject iterations. Furthermore, none of the existing images for these 37 films show evidence of directors having studied Beale's work to pick up ideas for costuming, blocking, story pacing, etc.[46]

Other than Porter's use of Beale's images in *Uncle Tom's Cabin* then, little indicates that his work directly influenced the early makers of movies, either in story content or style.

The Movies Find Their Own Stories

Much of the audience for movies was urban and working class. They wanted something racier than the classics, or the melodramatic little Parlor Poetry stories that formed the heart of the Beale/Briggs repertoire.

Porter gave it to them in one of the first mythic Westerns, the 1903 film, *The Great Train Robbery* (Fig. 10.35), a fourteen-scene, ten-minute film based on a play of the same name. The movie depended on the fact that audiences knew from dime novels and newspapers how such robberies were accomplished. A gang of robbers highjacks a train, escapes with the passengers' valuables, is hunted down and killed. The details of the robbery are meticulously presented; much of the movie is shot outdoors; many of the actors are amateurs who behave naturally. The film dissolves smoothly from scene to scene, contains some rudimentary parallel editing, uses a matte shot of a train passing outside a window, and employs *pan* shots to keep the action in frame. A separate shot of the gang leader firing "point blank at each individual in the audience" is a close-up that could be used at either the beginning or the end of the movie. All of the above were traditional magic lantern screen techniques, but here they were effectively integrated into the film medium in order to produce a clear, fast-paced, dramatic, and bloody story.

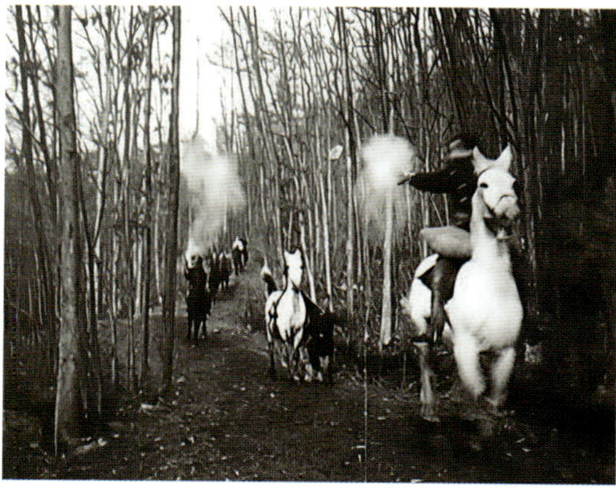

Fig. 10.35 Scene from *The Great Train Robbery*. Action scenes like this made the film a success. *Wikimedia Commons.*

The response was immediate and unprecedented. Theaters everywhere were showing *The Great Train Robbery*. Within a few months, Lubin had created his own, almost identical version. Kleine, now claiming to be the largest lantern and movie dealer in the country, devoted a six-page illustrated spread to *The Great Train Robbery* in his 1904 catalog, calling it "absolutely superior to any other moving picture film ever made. Kleine attributed its success to its "photographic excellence", its "matchless" story, its "continuous action", and its "sequence" of scenes leading to a "climax". He urged his customers to invest in longer story films like *The Great Train Robbery*, saying that though it was much longer (and hence more expensive) than most of his offerings, its popularity warranted the expense, and that its sales "have exceeded not only in feet, but in actual number of films those of any other subject, short or long, we have offered for sale".[47] The movies had finally found a story-telling approach that worked – artistically, and commercially. Other examples were sure to follow, and did, with a vengeance.

The lantern no longer looked like the entertainment medium of the future. The signs were everywhere. Kleine had changed the name of his catalog from *Stereopticons, Sciopticons, Magic lanterns and Views* (1894) to *Moving Picture Machines, Stereopticons, Magic Lanterns, Accessories, and Stereopticon Views* (1903). Harbach's 1903+/– catalog had made a similar change, and added a remarkable cover picture of a mermaid operating a combined movie projector and stereopticon.

The Movies Find a Home

Besides a good story the movies needed one other element to become successful, a new type of venue. They were now being shown in most of the vaudeville houses, but only as one portion of the program. Storefront theaters, charging 10–25 cents, had been tried from the earliest days of movies, but had never been very successful. The venues for movies seemed saturated.

Until 1905. In that year a successful vaudeville operator and real estate speculator, Harry Davis of Pittsburgh, was looking for a way to expand outside of his existing theaters in order to

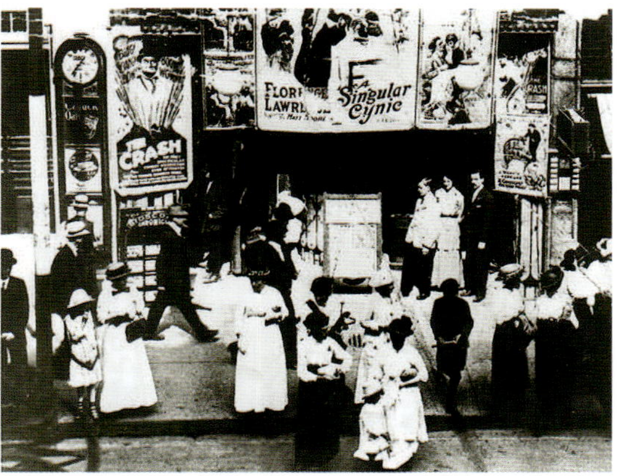

Fig. 10.36 People mill outside a nickelodeon in Canada about 1910. *Wikimedia Commons.*

counter competition. Pittsburgh was booming, and working people had a little change in their pockets. Davis decided to open a small, 200-seat, well-appointed theater, turn over the patrons every 20 minutes, keep it open all day, and – of critical importance – charge only a nickel. He emphasized this last point by calling his new theater the "Nickelodeon", and opened with *The Great Train Robbery* (Fig. 10.36).[48]

The idea caught hold. And Davis, real estate magnate and owner of empty storefronts all over town, was in a position to expand rapidly. In two years, by 1907, Davis himself owned fifteen nickelodeons in Pittsburgh; copycat entrepreneurs brought the city's total to forty-two. The idea was also spreading rapidly to other cities, driven both by Davis, and by his competitors. Individually, the nickelodeons were not impressive; cumulatively, they were a juggernaut. No longer were movies shown, like lantern shows, by traveling exhibitors who presented the same material again and again in constantly changing venues. Now the movies had a home, a permanent home, and people went there to see a constantly changing program, they "went to the movies".[49]

To Briggs, the spread of nickelodeons must have seemed like a cancer.

1907–1909
The Nickelodeons Explode in Numbers – Beale is Laid Off –

The significance of the years 1907–1909 for Beale and Briggs can be summarized in a simple comparison.

In 1905, Davis opened his first movie theater in Philadelphia. Three years later, in 1908, 200 nickelodeons were operating in the city.

They surrounded and overwhelmed what had once been the proud center of the magic lantern industry. Nationwide, the "nickelodeon idea" had grown to 8,000. And it wasn't just the small storefront movie theaters that were booming, either. In Philadelphia, Lubin opened a 1,000-seat theater, turning over thirty-five shows a day. (Think of it: up to 35,000 customers a day in one theater!) In Maine and New Hampshire, Keith transformed theaters of 1,250 and 1,700 seats from vaudeville to the movies, and renamed them both the "Nickel". The same kind of thing was happening everywhere.

The cumulative audience for those illustrated song slides was now huge, driven by thousands of small movie theaters, each seating 100–200 people, hosting 12–20 seatings a day. Add to that the movie "palaces" of a thousand seats or more, also filling multiple times a day. The demand for slides was insatiable. Sets were created for over 4,000 illustrated songs. A guestimate of the cumulative yearly national audience? Perhaps as large as a billion.

Briggs struggled with this new competition, which was compounded by the fact that a new financial panic hit in October of 1907. As he had in the previous panic, Briggs emphasized the Secret Societies, creating new sets for the Masons, the Oddfellows, and Knights of the Mystic Chain. He brought out a wave of new parables for the Religious market. He tried beating the movies at their own comedy game with two additional Comic Sketches. But he was only treading water.

Briggs Reacts to the Movies

Why didn't Briggs enter the field of the movies itself, just as his Philadelphia colleague Lubin did? He had the chops. He was a leader in the industry. He had bought out the Langenheims, had weathered the Panic of 1893 and had opened up new slide businesses with the Sunday Schools and the Secret Societies. Why didn't he do more than make "Safety Slides"?

While no contemporary evidence of Briggs's response to the movies explains his stance, later in life he did talk about his reactions:

> I said they would never amount to anything, and they didn't amount to anything until they started showing pretty women in them and telling stories. Before that, no one cared much about them. Of course, we told stories with magic lanterns, but not about beautiful women.[50]

The first thing that is striking about this remark is how succinctly Briggs sums up his position, and the factors that were to prove him wrong. He was right that the movies didn't amount to much until they started telling stories. And he was also right that they really took off when those stories concentrated on beautiful women. But what is even more revealing is the reason that Briggs gives for his lack of interest:

> The pictures flickered so, ... they were too imperfect. That killed them for me. They were not as sharp and clear as lantern slides.

It's easy to understand why Briggs would have reacted so negatively to early film. The news reports on the first movies complained repeatedly about the "flicker" – hence the nickname we still use today, "the flicks". The popularity of the Briggs lantern slides was anchored in the elaborate detail of Beale's images, and the high quality of their reproduction and coloring. How could a picture be popular, how could it even be intelligible, if it jumped all over the screen? And in fact the movies were not as "sharp and clear" as lantern slides. That is suggested by Fig. 10.37, the large image at the start of this chapter. It depicts in vivid detail and color an actual historical incident – the Indian attack on Schenectady when the gates were left open one night, defended only by a snowman. Film movies may have caught up with the drama, but not with the power and clarity of such slides. When we perform a modern magic lantern show in connection with a film movie (before digital), as we sometimes do, people frequently comment on how much "sharper and clearer" the antique lantern images are than the modern movie. The reason is quite simple: The slide being projected is about four times the size of movie film, so the image is about four times as sharp, and our projector is much closer to the screen. When Briggs looked at those fuzzy black-and-white movie images, chattering around on screen so fast it made his eyes swim, he must have shaken his head with disgust.

We can image other factors at work as well. By 1897, Briggs was 51 and reasonably successful. He may not have felt like charging into a new and highly risky business. Further, when we think of the vision Briggs had been pursuing – bringing such classics as *The Raven, Pilgrim's Progress*, and *Robinson Crusoe* to the screen – and think of the vision Sig Lubin was at first pursuing – the dancing midgets, the splits, the horsey hanky-panky – the contrast is striking. In addition, Briggs and Beale came from the old-line WASP culture that had retreated to the suburbs of Germantown. Lubin was a Jewish immigrant who ran his shop downtown amid the swarming masses. If Lubin was the sort who made movies, then Briggs may well have felt that it was not the business for him.

He would have been wrong of course. Improving movie technology gradually decreased the flicker. Action and good story telling and beautiful women compensated for the fuzzy images. Even Lubin was soon demonstrating that the movies could produce respectable "art" like *The Holy City* and *Uncle Tom's Cabin*. And WASPs, led by Edison, in fact dominated the early days of film, not Jews. But for a dozen years after the birth of the movies, it was not at all clear that Briggs was wrong. Then came 1908–09, and that explosion of nickelodeons.

Beale Is Let Go

Briggs certainly appreciated the talent of Beale. But Briggs was under severe financial strain. The stress began to show in his correspondence with Beale. For years Briggs and Beale had apparently had a fairly fluid financial arrangement, the exact nature of which is difficult to determine. It sounds as if Briggs guaranteed Beale a certain minimal monthly income. They then agreed on a price for each design depending on complexity, and Beale worked off the guarantee, or was paid extra if he produced above that level. But as Briggs's financial situation tightened, his letters from 1908 to the Fall of 1909 plainly reflected his growing difficulties.

> Dec. 18, 1908 – [Because of] both the hard times and poor business I feel that this [$20] is all I can possibly afford to advance and after this will send you a check when the drawings are received. Business has been half usual since last July – and money hard to get. I propose to keep

> you at work as long as I can raise the funds to do so, but if I continue to pay for what you send me it is all that I can do... .[51]

Apparently, Briggs had to insist on this "pay-as-you-go" arrangement, for eight months later he wrote again:

> August 20, 1909 – Money is very hard to get. At [the] present time we are not selling slides enough to pay running expenses and it is all I can do to raise money to keep you going and not to advance on work not done".[52]

In early September, Briggs told Beale that he no longer had a full-time job. Beale reported this layoff in several job-hunting letters, this one to Mr. Preston of The Preston Company, a Philadelphia manufacturer of calendars and advertising novelties:

> October 25, 1909 – But now, this September, [Mr. Briggs] writes [that] the moving pictures are cutting into his sales so much that I may do other work beside his. Therefore, I would be pleased to receive from you suggestions or orders for sketches of calendars, fans, and advertising novelties ... .[53]

The Briggs letter that Beale mentions, now lost, changed the working relationship between the two men that had existed since 1892. After 17 years of full-time magic lantern work, Beale was back to free-lancing – and not much of that.

Beale received a pleasant reply from his inquiry to the Preston Company, went to see them on November 5, and may have obtained a little work. He also wrote to several other companies, including his old employer, Harper and Brothers, and the well-known Philadelphia photographer, William Rau, who wrote back with a lead for religious illustration.[54] But such tidbits could not replace the steady income he had made as a magic lantern artist.

It was on October 29 that Beale decided on a broader job search, made up a job-hunting list (Fig. 10.38), and keyed it to the walking map shown at the end of Chapter 1.

He was as thorough and detailed in this job search as he was in creating his designs. He began with 164 different businesses, among them Quaker City Stained Glass, The Art Print Shop, The Baltimore Badge and Novelty Co., and C. H. Graves Magic Lantern Slides – a company so obscure that I have never seen it mentioned elsewhere. Beale winnowed his list

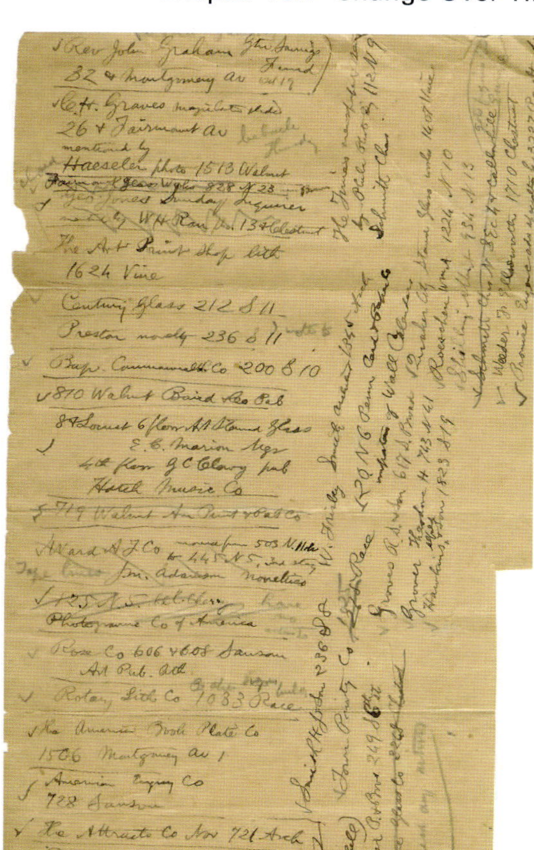

Rev John Graham
82 & Montgomery av
C.H. Graves magic lantern slides
26 & Fairmount av
mentioned by
Haeseler photo 1513 Walnut
The Art Print Shop lith
1624 Vine
Century Glass 212 S 11
Preston novelty 236 S 11
810 Walnut
E. C. Marion Mgr
Hatch Music Co
Photogravure Co of America
Rotary Lith Co 1033 Race
The American Book Plate Co
1506 Montgomery av
728 Sansom
The Attracto Co
Baltimore Badge & Novelty
974 Drexel

Fig. 10.38 Portion of Beale's final list of job possibilities.

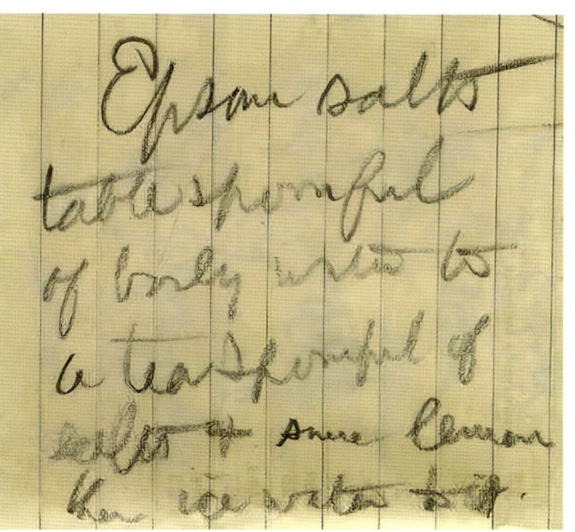

Epsom salts
table spoonful
of boiling water to
a teaspoonful of
salts

Fig. 10.39 Beale's recipe for an Epson Salt footbath. He was not used to the walking that job-hunting entailed.

down to the 28 most-likely prospects (including Graves); laid them out on his map; and, at age 68, set off to visit them. He may well have pounded the pavement on other treks as well, since he prepared two other numbered lists. Certainly, his feet hurt by the time he was done. Along with the job-prospect lists was found a recipe for a footbath, a combination of Epsom salts, lemon juice, and ice water (Fig. 10.39). It was a recipe that marked the end of Beale's magic lantern career – the demise of 250 years of magic lantern entertainment – the painful footfalls of a dying era.

Chapter Eleven

A Sad Ending – A Surprise Ending

Fig. 11.3 Beale's "Vessel Landing Immigrants [at Castle Garden, New York, City]" created in 1917 for the *Jr. Order of American Mechanics*, a fraternal society. Discussion on p. 265.

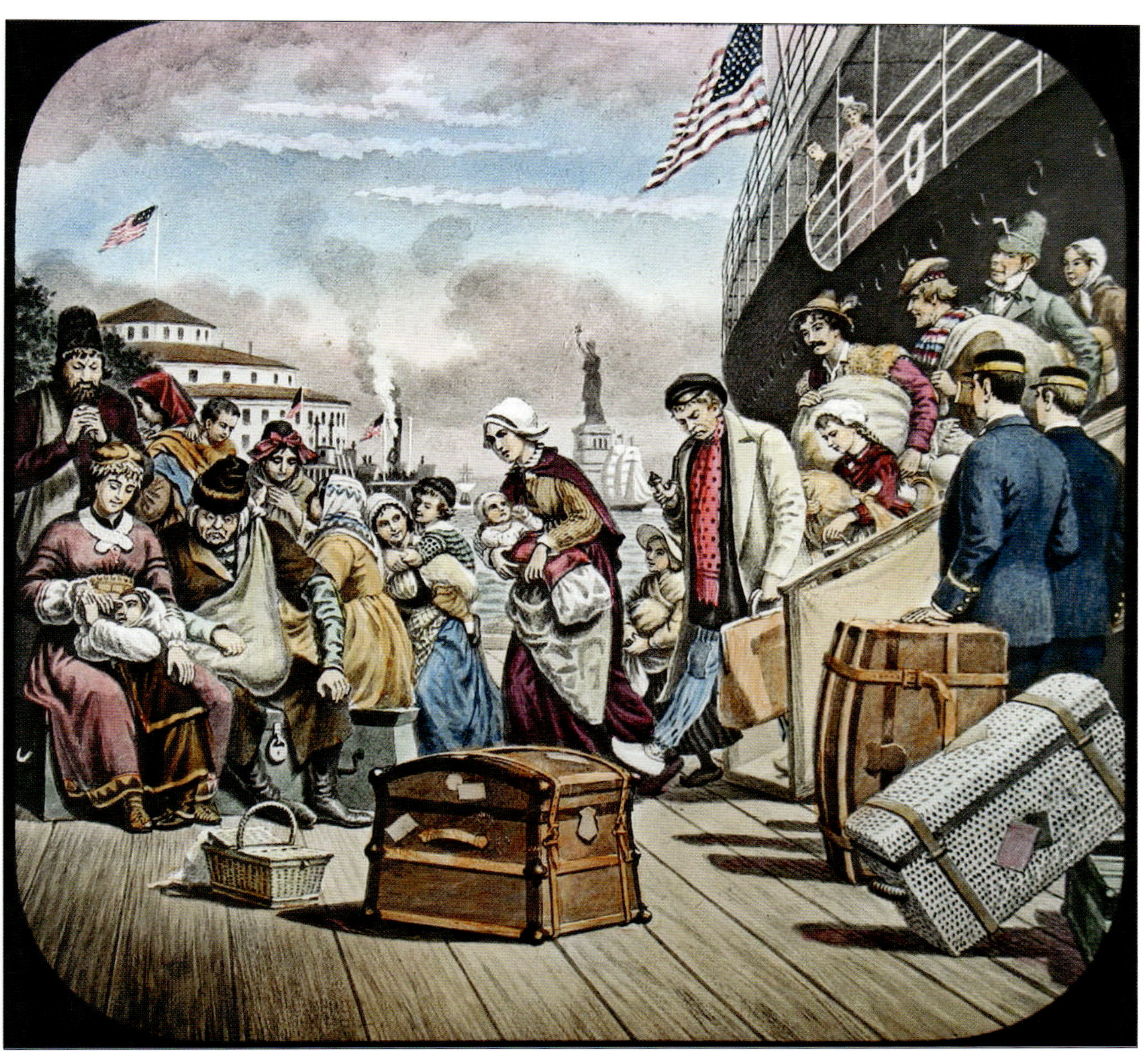

After the heyday of the magic lantern, and its rapid decline in 1907–1909, Beale continued to create slide paintings, albeit at a much-reduced pace. Sadly, the great project on which he and Briggs had been engaged would soon be over, and in time Beale himself would pass from the scene. But that ending was only the beginning of new manifestations of Beale's work, some of which were as bizarre and surprising as anything ever created for a magic lantern phantasmagoria.

A Sad Ending

The final years of Beale's slide image production – 1910–1917 – were a turbulent time in the nation. Ten percent of the country's population were immigrants who had arrived since 1900, eight and a half million foreign people that America needed to integrate into its society. A revolution also shook the arts. In 1913 the Armory Show in New York introduced modern art to America, and turned the traditional art conception such as Beale's on its head (Fig. 11.1). World War I began in 1914, drawing Americans into a horrific morass of trench warfare, followed by a flu epidemic in 1918 that killed 20 million worldwide, a half–million of them in the U. S. The combination of these traumas drained from the national psyche the ebullient and confident 19th century sensibility that Beale had captured so well.

Despite the world-wide chaos, or perhaps partly because of it, the magic lantern's competitor, the movies, continued to explode in popularity. By 1912, in a country of 95 million, attendance had reached five million a day. D. W. Griffith had directed his first movie back in 1908; his controversial classic, *Birth of a Nation*, came only seven years later, in 1915. Hollywood became the center of the movie industry. Max Sennet's Keystone Cops were making the chase a movie staple; Charlie Chaplin's waddle expressed the naïve hope of the common man in the face of turmoil; Pauline's perils kept them coming back for more. The movies became the dominant expression of American culture. By 1916 the small nickelodeons were mostly gone, replaced by larger theaters and the 2,000-seat "picture palaces".

In the midst of these turbulent times and the movies' ascendency, and after having been let go by Briggs, Beale continued to look for work. He was not very successful. The extant letters are all rejections, and the art in the catalogs of prospective clients is very different from Beale's own style. In Beale's effects were only a few ads

Fig. 11.1 Marchel Duchamp's "Nude Descending a Staircase at the 1913 Armory Show in New York. *Wikipedia Commons.*

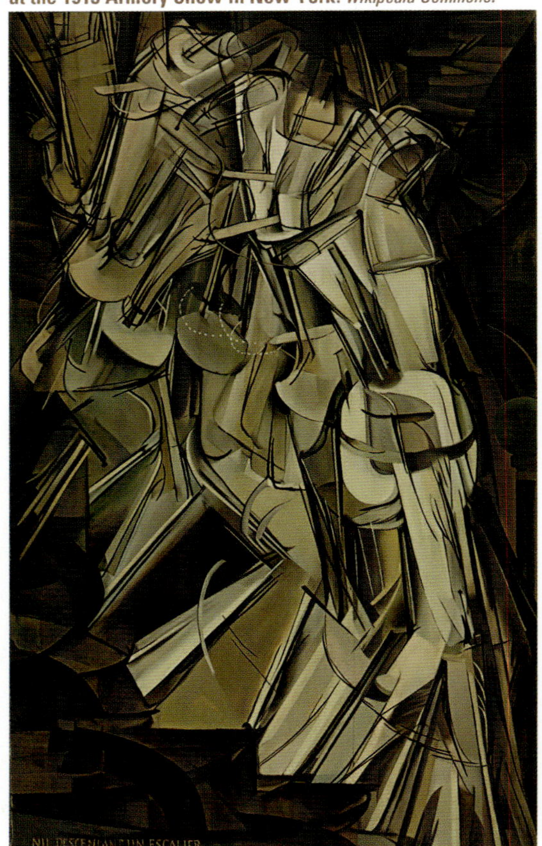

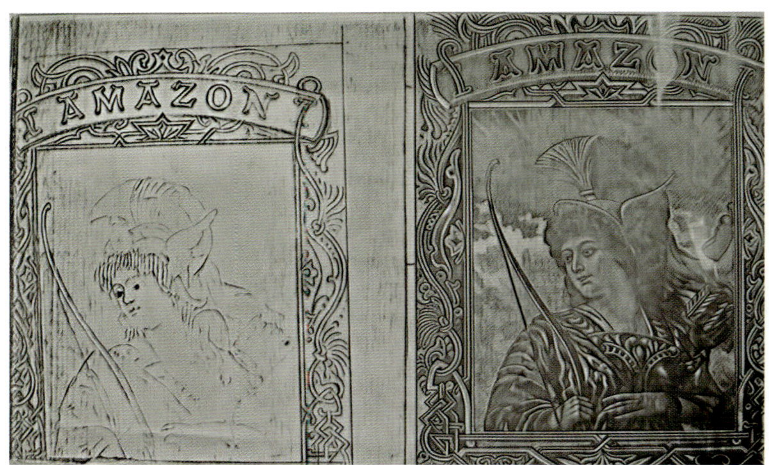

Fig. 11.2 Copy of Beale sketch for cigar advertising. His style fit well with the "classical" image of this company.

that he may have done in this period – for "Amazon" and "Calipso" cigars, and for "Syrup of Figs, Nature's Pleasant Laxative" (Fig. 11.2). He also did a little perspective drawing for his architect brother.[1] Briggs may have surmised his financial difficulties. A month after having let Beale go, he wrote him concerning some Religious slide work that was still on-going, and then added thoughtfully:

> November 22, 1909. Now I hope you are finding work that pays you much better than my work used to and if your time is all taken up with profitable work I shall be glad – but in case you should at any future time have any vacancies between jobs, and if you are willing to make some comic subjects with half the usual amount of work – for $5.00 each – please let me know and I will send you a few rough sketches which [I] thought might be worked up to make a laugh. If you are busy then no matter.[2]

Beale did in fact continue to work for Briggs on a much-reduced scale. These "rough sketches" were probably for *Mr. Timorous* which Beale mentions in a draft letter of November 29. In future commissions for Beale, Briggs found other ways to employ Beale part-time, while still saving money. To create *Othello*, and *Hamlet*, he went back to "matching out" existing engravings for many of the scenes, so that, as he had written Beale about *Othello* on Aug. 20, 1909, they "should not need as much time as when you design and make [a] drawing". Left unsaid was the implication that if the drawings did not require as much time, they should not require the usual price.

During this part-time denouement of eight years Beale produced 179 slides, about 22 a year, or about a quarter of his output during full-time work. Some of it, like the immigration scene of Fig. 11.3, the introductory image for this chapter, was as good as anything he had ever produced – a sweeping vision, full of story-telling detail, dramatically organized. Most, however, were not so polished. Perhaps it was a question of time. Briggs seems to have decided that if the movies were making a success of projected stories, he would redouble his efforts in that direction. But the emphasis in many cases was on keeping costs down. Briggs asked Beale to do another "comic stor[y] at half the usual cost" – perhaps *Bridget's Dream*. He added another matched-out set, *The Legend of Sleepy Hollow*, by having Beale paint over the line drawings of Beale's old idol, F. O. C. Darley. Sets of Shakespeare, mostly copies of Moritz Retzsch's outline drawings, were designed for schools. Beale's only opera, *Carmen*, seems to suggest a similar attempt to appeal to the education market.[3]

Briggs could also appeal to the children's market by reproducing existing images in the "Gem" slide format, a strategy he had first used in 1890. About the time that the traditional slide market was collapsing, inexpensive black-and-white Gem slides with three or four images on each slide, proliferated in advertisements for children and "exhibitors with small capital". The Amusement Supply Co.'s 1908 catalog, for instance, contained 554 Gem 3-image slides. But only about 30 of these were by Beale, and most of them had been available for years. Perhaps the profit margins were too low for Briggs to bother producing more. In 1912, Briggs also provided slides for the Edison Home Kinetoscope, Edison's home movie machine. These were in a tiny form of 1-1/8" x 4" containing ten pictures the size of home movie frames, in double rows of five each, the bottoms of the pictures touching so that the slide could be flipped to access the additional five images (Fig. 11.4).[4]

Non-entertainment markets, where the movies were not competition, and the profit margins more substantial, were also an obvious port in the storm. Briggs had Beale create more Religious and Secret Society slides, but together these

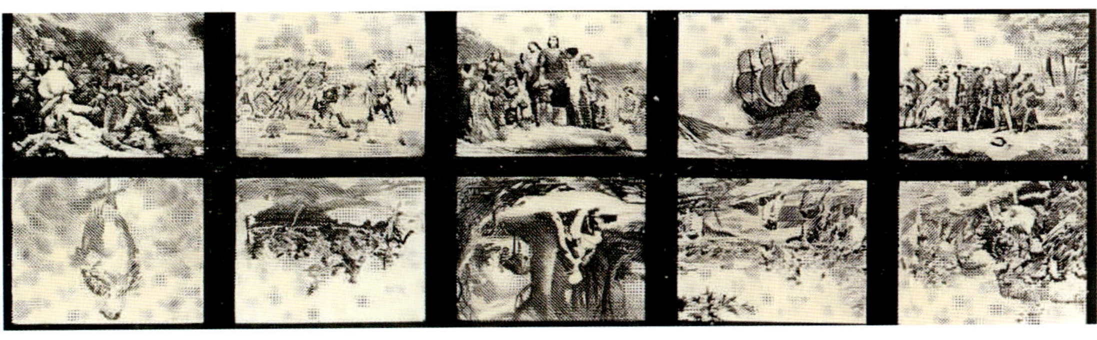

Fig. 11.4 Edison Home Kinetoscope Slide. "The Mayflower at Sea", second from the right at the top, is by Beale, as is the image on the far top left.

did not equal the emphasis on Literary subjects. Broadening out to do book illustration for the first time, Briggs sold the rights to some of his Religious slides to the Stebbins Publishing Company, which created two books heavily illustrated with Beale images.[5]

Finally, Briggs may have thought that World War I, like the Spanish-American War, would provide opportunities, even if the movies had now taken over the role of visual newspaper. *The Man Without a Country*, produced in 1917, and Beale's last set, ought to have found a very responsive audience after the First World War, but it does not seem to have sold well.

One last hurrah for Beale's work, and a grand one at that, occurred in 1913. The International Bible Students Association, better known today as the Jehovah's Witnesses, launched a massive religious education show called the *Photodrama of Creation* (Fig. 11.5). The *Photodrama* was a three-part, eight-hour combination of lantern slides, music, movies, and synchronized spoken recordings. About ten percent of the slides used were Beale's. Some were modified to fit Jehovah's Witness theology. The Witnesses were convinced that the world was going to end in 1914, and felt it essential to do everything they could to take their message to as many people as possible before then. One hundred teams of operators worked full-time for over a year presenting the *Photodrama* worldwide. Between nine and eleven million people saw the production. Thus, the paradox: In the final years of Beale's lantern work, when magic lantern shows were in rapid and terminal decline, his art reached its largest audience ever for a single show.[6]

Beale's Last Days

Beale lived the rest of his life in genteel poverty, cared for by relatives. His numerous nieces and nephews remembered him as a quiet man, sketching to the last, eager to encourage the artistic tradition of his family. Emily, his sister, had designated three hundred and fifty dollars to cover his funeral expenses and to erect a substantial monument over his grave at Mt. Moriah Cemetery in Philadelphia. He died at age 84 of arteriosclerosis in his home on February 26, 1926, outliving all but two of his 10 brothers and sisters. When we first visited Beale's gravesite in Mt. Moriah Cemetery, we had to cut our way through thick trees, vines and briars to see it. Volunteers have now cleared the underbrush. The marker is located in section 42, on top of a knoll, just outside of the very grand and centrally located "Masonic Circle" (Fig. 11.6).[7]

The Decline of the C. W. Briggs Co.

Though Beale's magic lantern work declined dramatically in 1909 and ceased in 1917, the magic lantern industry itself was by no means dead. Writing in 1914, *The Photo-Miniature,* a photographic magazine written in England but widely read in America, claimed that the industry was never in "so flourishing a condition":

Fig. 11.5 Left, Beale slide, "Hell with Motto", for *The Knights of Malta,* a Secret Society. Right, a modification of the image made for *The Photodrama of Creation.*

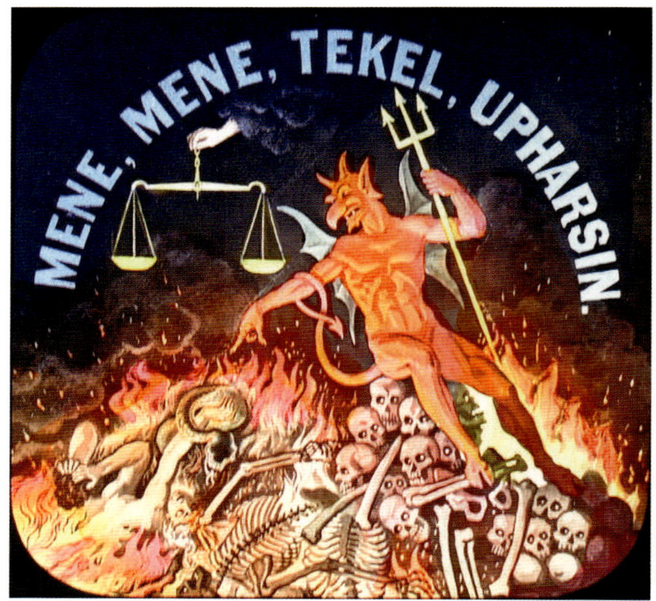

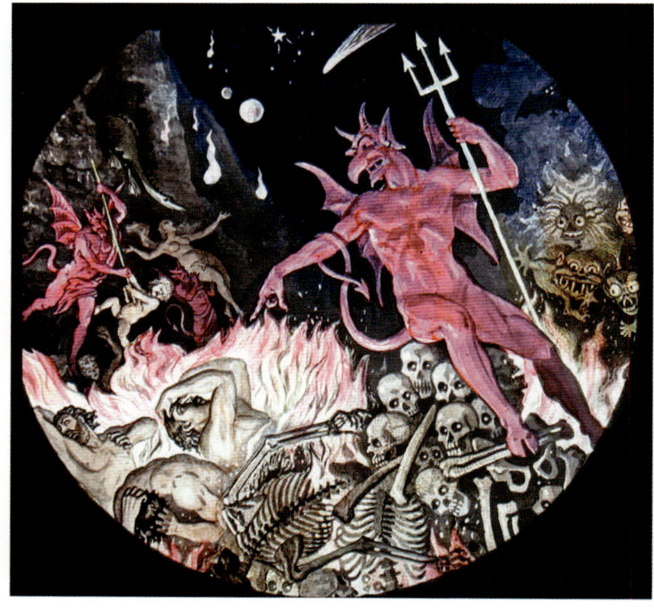

> Thousands of lanterns are made today where hundreds sufficed to meet the requirements of a few years ago. Behind every lantern there are thousands of slides in active use. And behind these are millions of lantern-slides in the making, or reserved by institutions or manufacturers, awaiting the call to service.[8]

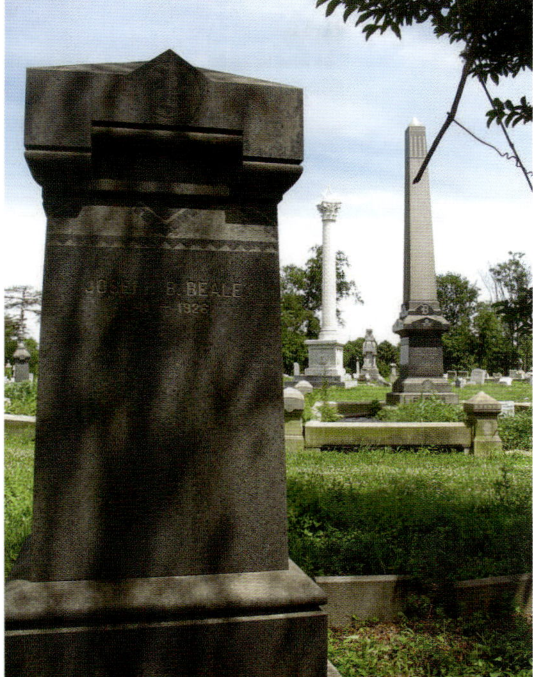

Fig. 11.6 Beale gravestone at Mt. Moriah Cemetery in Philadelphia, just outside of the "Masonic Circle", containing the huge monuments visible in the background.

Unfortunately for Briggs, those millions of lantern images that *The Photo-Miniature* described were largely photographic slides. The artist-illustrated segment of the market continued to decline. In 1918 Briggs turned over day-to-day operation of his business to his partners, his son L. Warren Briggs, and his nephew, Casper Briggs Carpenter, who struggled to keep the company going. By 1923 they were producing only 40,000 slides a year; and only 12,000 a decade later. Many of the Beale images were distributed in the new "Featherweight" format manufactured by the Victor Animatograph Company of Davenport, Iowa, then the largest lantern-slide distributor in the country (Fig. 11.7). The "Featherweights" used a single piece of glass with a heavy emulsion, framed in cardboard. They were much lighter than the old wood-framed slides or the all-glass Economy slides, but the coloring was often poor compared to earlier versions.[9] They were one of the transitions into the later audio-visual world of small 35mm slides and film strips. These filmstrips became a convenient, low-cost, and flexible means of showing Beale's images, often used by missionaries (Fig, 11.8).

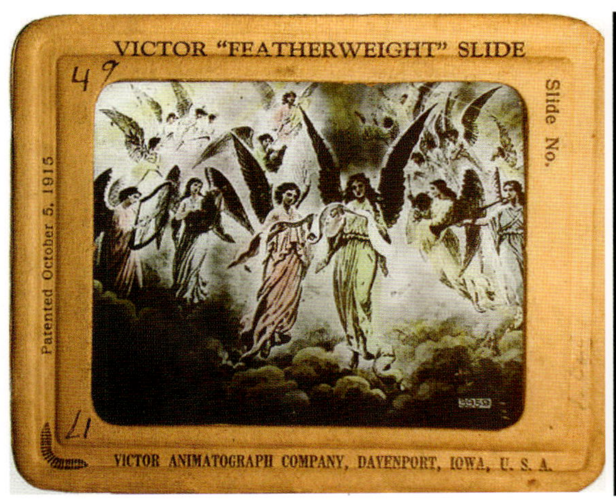

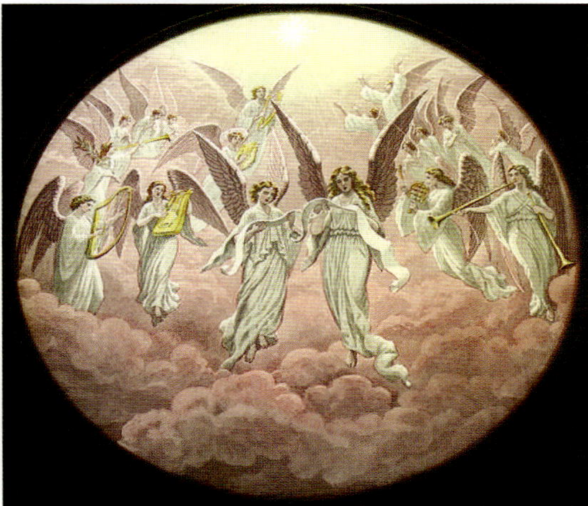

Fig. 11.7 A Victor "Featherweight" slide of Beale's slide 8 of *The Holy City*, and a standard version of the same image.

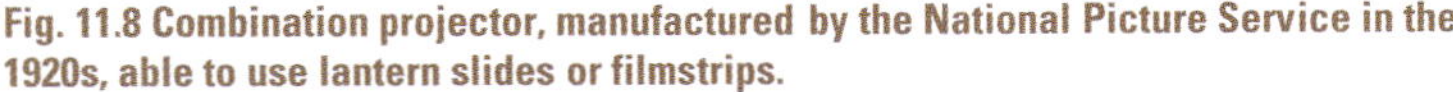

Fig. 11.8 Combination projector, manufactured by the National Picture Service in the 1920s, able to use lantern slides or filmstrips.

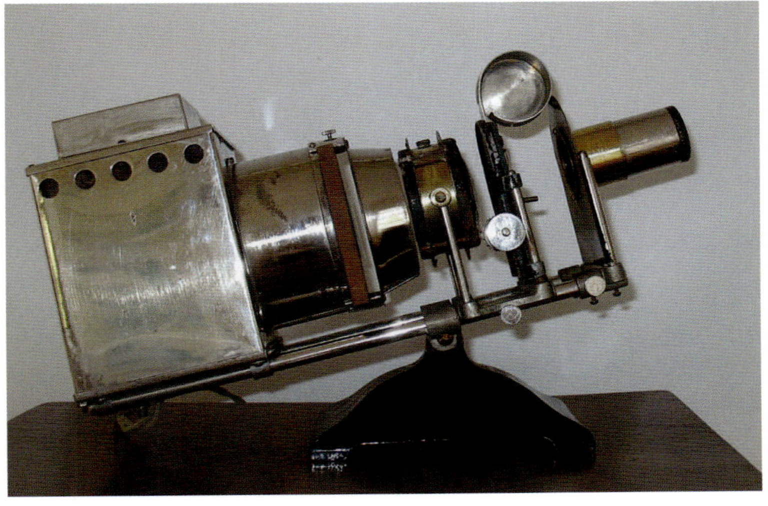

In 1925, the Briggs company made attempts to use its inventory of still images in the movies through the Brayco Films division of Keystone Brayco, Inc., a manufacturer of projectors and films. Unfortunately, this effort went nowhere.[10] In 1929 Briggs wrote his partners that

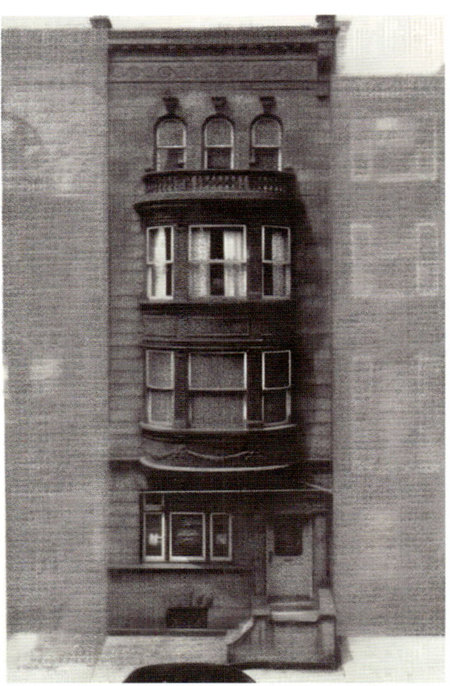

Fig. 11.9 The American Museum of Photography in Philadelphia.

he was willing to "accept the unavoidable" and sell off the business for whatever they could get. At the time of the sale, Briggs had 12,000 negatives; and 30,000 completed slides. Luckily for those interested in the magic lantern, the buyer (for $6,000 in 1930, about $120,000 in 2025 dollars) was Louis W. Sipley. Sipley ran the firm (sometimes calling it "BriggsCo") in a greatly reduced fashion, selling 35mm slides and filmstrips to schools and religious groups, both under the "Briggs" names, and through a much larger audio-visual firm, The Society for Visual Education.[11]

None of Sipley's efforts to market the Briggs material were very successful. In 1940 he closed the company, and opened The American Museum of Photography, the first museum of photography in the country, and the first to display Beale's slides (Fig.11.9).

A Surprise Ending, "The Discovery"

The Briggs business may have closed, but, surprisingly enough, Beale's work was to find a new life. Sometimes that life flourished under false pretenses, sometimes it was unacknowledged, sometimes it changed formats entirely. But in one way or another Beale's influence would grow steadily in the 20th and 21st century. I'll track that growth here by the generations of new audiences who enjoyed Beale's work, divided (very roughly) into four groups. First, the First Generation:

Fig. 11.10 Arthur Colen, in 1962. He is looking at a copy of one of Beale's design paintings, some of which he colored.

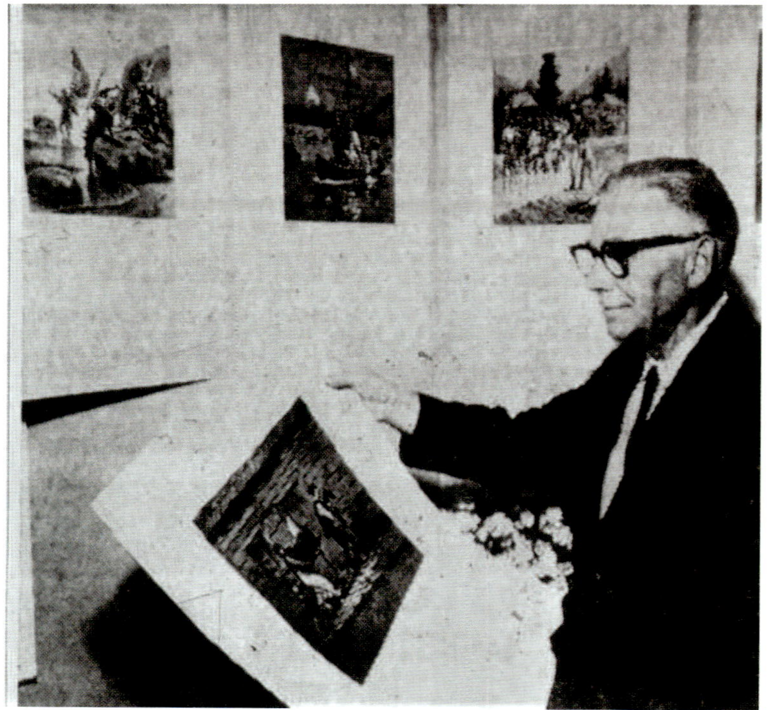

The Dissemination of Beales's Images, First Generation, 1935–1940s

When Briggs sold his company, he kept most of Beale's paintings stored in a trunk in his attic. In 1935, recognizing that the lantern business was finished, he tried to sell a few of Beale's pictures of Abraham Lincoln to Arthur W. Colen, owner of the Modern Galleries in Philadelphia (Fig. 11.10). Colen would turn out to be an important and controversial figure in the dissemination of Beale's work. He was a large, good-looking man, who, when he was making money, tooled around Philadelphia in a chauffeur-driven Cadillac. He had started out as a window-dresser for Philadelphia's downtown department stores, and then became a very successful interior designer. A good sculptor and painter himself, he could repair old masters, and paint portraits. He was of Jewish heritage, but also an avowed atheist, and would consequently have little interest in Beale's religious art. His gallery was an up-scale one, carrying some name artists, and catering to the wealthy. Personally, he was not as proper as his gallery, openly keeping a mistress while married. His son characterized him as "creative" and "entrepreneurial", but also an "egomaniac", who was "insensitive to others" and "constantly getting into fights with people".[12] The events of Colen's involvement with Beale's art substantiate that assessment.

Colen, the dealer, was sure he had a "find" in the Beale paintings, and persuaded Briggs to sell him the largest and best portion of his collection. At the same time Colen obtained – presumably from the Beale family – Beale's diary, some family photographs, and Beale's own copies of his slides. Then he set about promoting his discovery.

Colen apparently felt he faced three significant obstacles to successfully marketing Beale's images.

First was the age of the paintings. In 1935 some of them were only 20 years old, and almost all were less than 50 – the commonly agreed-upon minimum for an "antique" in those days. So Colen backdated the start of Beale's work, claiming that he began painting for Briggs in 1874, six years before he actually began freelancing. He also claimed that Beale stopped in 1900, 17 years before the date of his last work.

The second problem Colen faced was provenance. As we have seen, the paintings were the result of a highly collaborative process between Beale and Briggs, but Colen wanted to "discover" a single unrecognized artist, so he completely obliterated Briggs' role, never even mentioning him by name.

And finally, although Colen knew perfectly well that Beale's work was for the magic lantern, having talked extensively with Briggs, he seems to have felt that the lantern and its art were too passé a technology to be appealing. To solve this problem – quite incredibly – he simply changed the purpose for which the paintings had been prepared.

In August of 1935 *Time* magazine broke Colen's misleading version of the Beale story in a two-page spread that was both carried in the magazine itself and syndicated to newspapers nationally:

> From the Modern Galleries in Philadelphia last week went forth an offer to sell one of the strangest collections of drawings yet unearthed in the realm of Americana … . [The pictures depicted] a breathtaking medley of scenes and events … . Sentimental though most of the subjects were, the draftsmanship in each picture was remarkably good. And not a single one had ever seen the light of print or public exhibition … .
>
> A hard worker, particularly in his later years, Artist Beale seemed to have a more regular income than his infrequently published drawings would indicate. Only last week did newshawks ferret out where it came from.
>
> Beale's … hitherto unknown drawings reached the Modern Galleries through a retired manufacturer of lantern slides whose name the gallery proprietor last week staunchly refused to reveal. In 1874 the slide-maker had gone quietly to Joseph Boggs Beale and asked him to do a set of drawings to illustrate *Pilgrim's Progress*. They were a great success with Epworth Leagues and Sunday Schools. Soon the slide-maker asked for other drawings, in black & white, to illustrate books that he one day hoped to publish. From 1880 to 1900 methodical Joseph Boggs Beale produced drawings, always in the same technique, always in the same size, and the slide-maker always bought them for around $17.50 each. This private deal gave Artist Beale a regular income of between $35 and $40 a week.
>
> Altogether there were] 1,676 pictures that Joseph Boggs Beale hoped one day to see published.[13]

Every Week Magazine picked up the story in October and ran it the nation's newspapers, under the banner, "How Fame Came After Death for the Artist Nobody Knew" (Fig. 11.11):

> During his lifetime there was one side of Beale that no one knew about: that is, no one except one other man. That side was Beale's great desire to drop his hack work, of which he was ashamed, and see the drawings of which he was really fond in published form and on public view.
>
> The one other person who knew of this ambition of Beale's is the man in whose cellar the drawings have recently been brought to light.
>
> This man who employed Beale prefers to remain anonymous, but is willing to allow Arthur W. Colen, manager of the Modern Galleries in Philadelphia, which is now in possession of the collection, to tell how the relationship between him and Beale came about.

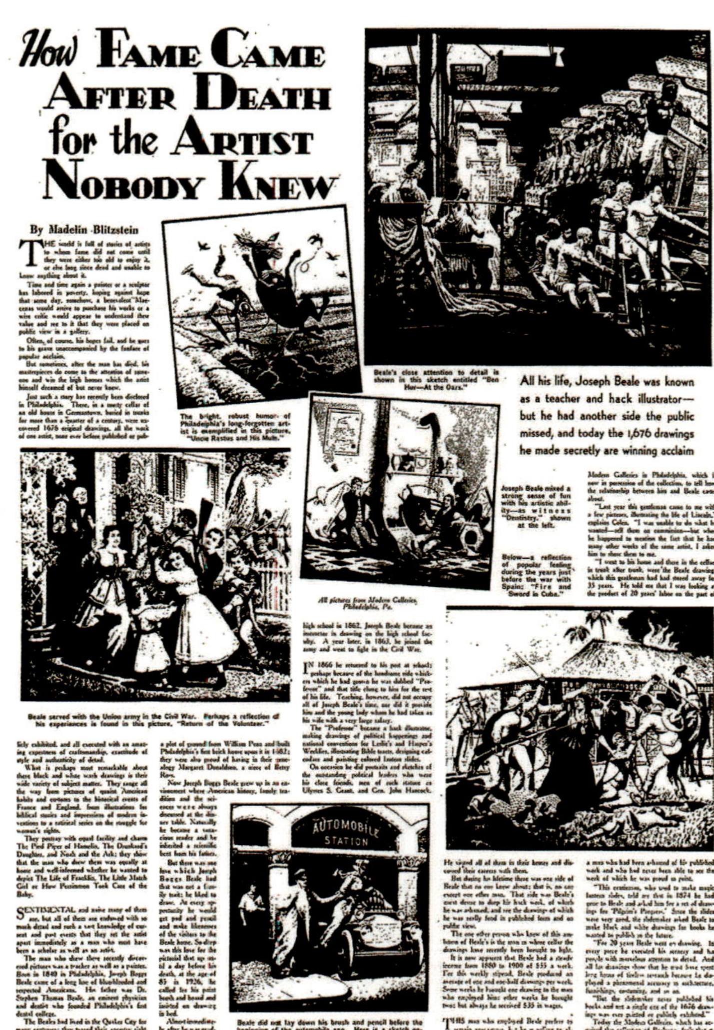

How Fame Came After Death for the Artist Nobody Knew

By Madelin Blitzstein

All his life, Joseph Beale was known as a teacher and hack illustrator—but he had another side the public missed, and today the 1,676 drawings he made secretly are winning acclaim

The bright, robust humor of Philadelphia's long-forgotten artist is exemplified in this picture, "Uncle Rastus and His Mule."

Beale's close attention to detail is shown in this sketch entitled "Ben Hur—At the Oars."

Joseph Beale mixed a strong sense of fun with his artistic ability—as witness "Dentistry," shown at the left.

Below—a reflection of popular feeling during the years just before the war with Spain: "Fire and Sword in Cuba."

All pictures from Modern Galleries, Philadelphia, Pa.

Beale served with the Union army in the Civil War. Perhaps a reflection of his experiences is found in this picture, "Return of the Volunteer."

Beale did not lay down his brush and pencil before the beginning of the automobile age. Here is a sketch entitled "The First Auto."

Fig. 11.11 An Oct. 13, 1935 nationally syndicated newspaper story in *Every Week* magazine.

"Last year this gentleman came to me with a few pictures ... . I went to his home and there in the cellar in trunk after trunk were the Beale drawings, which this gentleman had stored away for 35 years. He told me that I was looking at the product of 20 year's labor on the part of a man who had been ashamed of his public work and who had never been able to see the work of which he was proud in print ... .

"The slidemaker [had] asked Beale to make black and white drawings for books he wanted to publish in the future. For 20 years Beale went on drawing. In every piece he executed his scenery and his people with marvelous attention to detail ... .

"But the slidemaker never published the books and not a single one of the 1676 drawings was ever printed or publicly exhibited".[14]

What a story! It wasn't true, but so what? The response to it was immediate. In April 1936, the prestigious new Whitney Museum of American Art in New York purchased 13 Beale paintings and organized an exhibition of 76 Beale drawings at the Museum, together with paintings of David Blythe. The Beale collection was described in a catalog introduced by Colen (Fig. 11.12).[15] In his introduction Colen backdated some of the drawings even further than he had previously – to 1861. He took pains to correct the "erroneous report" that the paintings had been found in a cellar, not an attic, but continued to say nothing about the fact that they were magic lantern illustrations.

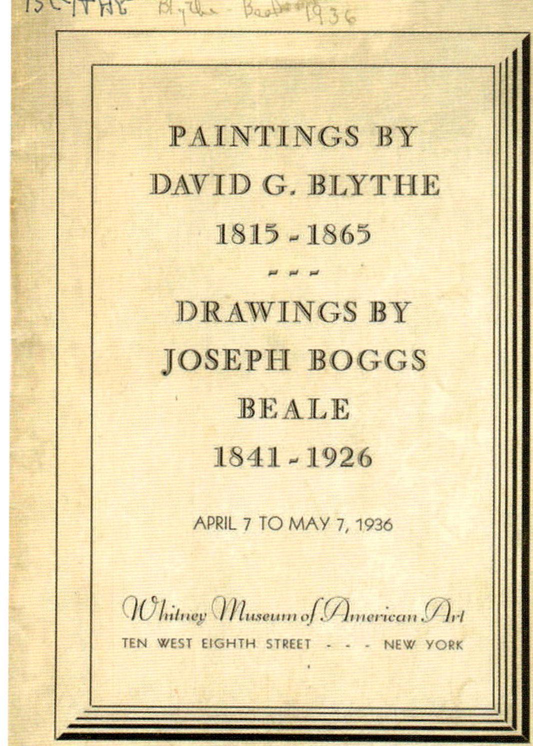

Fig. 11.12 Illustrated catalog of the Beale Exhibit at the Whitney Museum of American Art.

Critical response to the exhibit was generally good, remarking especially on Beale's detailed presentation, but the fact that the critics did not know they were looking at magic lantern narrative art understandably confused them. Edward Alden Jewell of the *New York Times* called Beale a "straightforward illustrator ... taking infinite pains and leaving naught to guesswork", and thought the series "remarkable". An unnamed critic at *Art News* thought *The Raven* series was "hilarious" with its "histrionic ranting and mourning", but critic Peter Banks, writing for the same publication, wrote that, "If Beale is not ashamed to 'tell stories' and display sentiment ... I can admit to enjoying it". And in fact, the "histrionic ranting" critic ended his assessment on a somewhat similar note. Though he did not know the drawings were for screen narration, he was perceptive enough to conclude by saying that Beale "fills his work with animation, no matter what the subject, and has a love of the dramatic as well as the melodramatic".[16]

One set of pictures, *Bridget's Dream,* received special comment because it was so unusual (Fig. 11.13). The story, which may have been based on a dream of Briggs and on his preliminary sketches, begins and ends with a typical realistic Beale drawing of an Irish maid (Bridget) ironing clothes in a kitchen.[17] But when Bridget falls asleep, the clothes become animated, and a screwball comedy ensues. In our shows I perform "Mr. Shurtz's" pursuit of "Miss Robe" at a break-neck pace. The dream characters flash across the screen, *loosely framed* and painted in white, on a totally black background in *high contrast.* Ironically, it was this 150-year-old phantasmagoria art style that the critics thought most inventive, one commenting that it was only in this set that Beale "approximate[d] to cleverness", and another that it was in the "clothes-line grotesques on black ground wherein Beale's imagination achieved its furthest flight".[18]

For a while Colen succeeded in hiding the magic lantern source of Beale's paintings, even in Philadelphia. Dorothy Grafly, a Philadelphia art critic, described the Whitney show in the *Philadelphia Record* under the headline "Gotham Hails 'New Cruickshank'", and derided Philadelphia's museums for refusing to show Beale's work, quoting their mealy-mouthed excuses in full – using tidbits no doubt supplied by Colen. *Art Digest* gave national play to the "new Cruickshank" label and belittled the philistine attitude in Philadelphia.[19] Colen mounted a show at his own gallery, which received good reviews from the *Philadelphia Inquirer*'s critic, who concluded by saying, "Truly comprehensive thematic material and all of it so delightfully human and at times so humorous as to engage the prolonged concern of the beholder".[20]

But of course, the Philadelphia museums were refusing to display Beale for good reasons. No matter what the merits of his art, it was certainly not what Colen represented it to be. The true story was already emerging among the art cognoscenti of Philadelphia, presumably to Dorothy Grafly's embarrassment. In December 1936, Louis Sipley, who had become a friend and admirer of Briggs after purchasing the Briggs' company, attacked Colen in *Pennsylvania Arts and Sciences.* His critique was not so much that Colen had obscured the purpose of the paintings, as that he had not mentioned the role of Briggs – who Sipley felt deserved his share of credit for the paintings.[21]

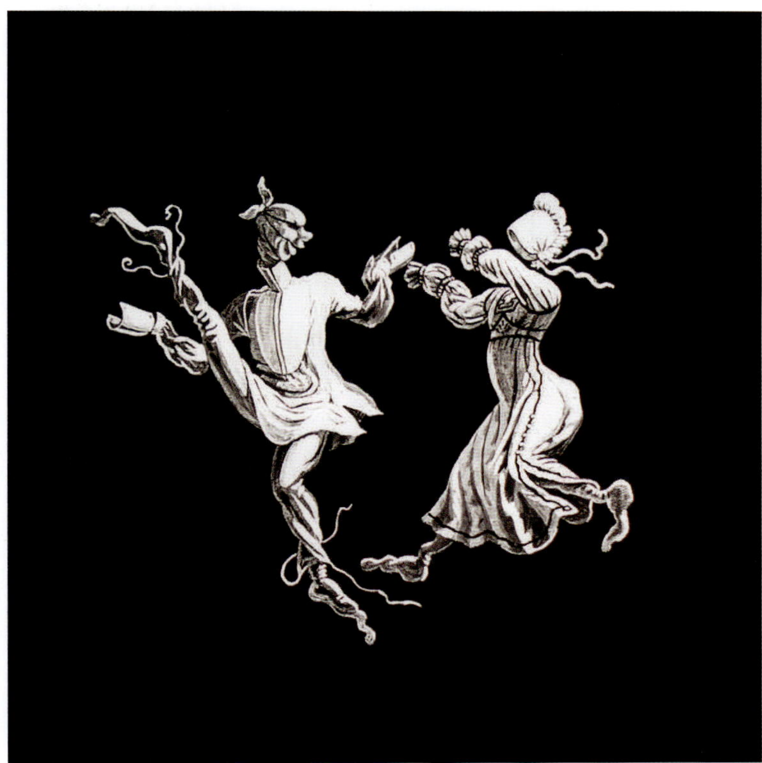

Fig. 11.13 Beale's slide 3 of *Bridget's Dream.* Mr. Shurtz dances with Miss Robe.

The feud between Colen and Sipley heated up when Colen wrote Sipley a letter in 1937 claiming that, "we have definite and exclusive rights to all publication [of the paintings], and under no circumstances will we tolerate any improper and unlawful use of such rights by unauthorized persons". Sipley had been publishing Beale's pictures printed from the negatives he obtained when he bought the business from Briggs. He wrote back a stinging reply:

> We are in receipt of your letter of the 10th Inst. which we find very interesting. During the many years in which our firm has been in business we have had the experience of seeing our own pictures reproduced by unauthorized individuals and organizations but never before [have we] had anyone instruct us what we were permitted to do with our own designs.[22]

Sipley then obtained a statement from Briggs to the effect that in selling the paintings to Colen, "no rights or privileges were transferred to the said Arthur W. Colen which would conflict or interfere with the ... sale by the C. W. Briggs Company of photographic reproductions ... of such drawings by Joseph Boggs Beale". That seemed to put a cap on the dispute; no further public record of it exists.

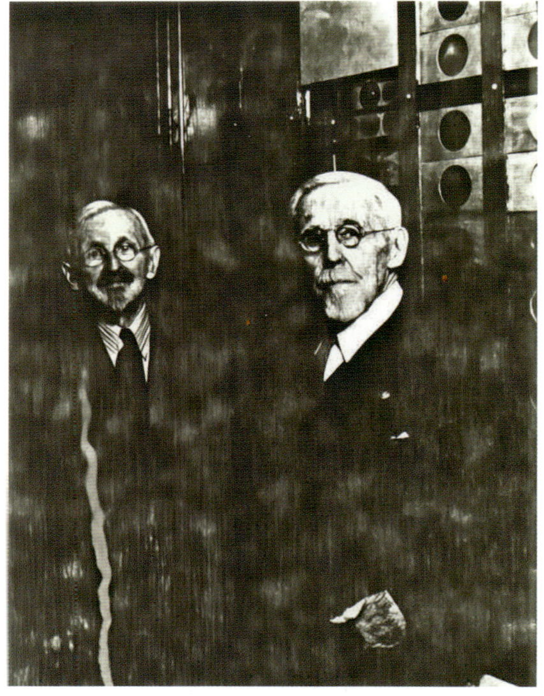

Fig. 11.14 C. W. Briggs (left) and William Jackson, the famous photographer, before the "slide wall" at the American Museum of Photography.

When Sipley had created The American Museum of Photography after closing his BriggsCo business, it was the first photographic museum in the country, and for many years it was the only one.[23] Because Colen had bought the best of the Beale drawings and had obtained Beale's own slides, they were not available to Sipley. But the BriggsCo collection contained thousands of other slide copies of Beale's images, the negatives from which they were made, and related financial records. Briggs donated to the Museum about 700 paintings Colen had not bought, including many Beale over-paintings. Of course, Sipley devoted a large section of the Museum to the magic lantern, including an illuminated "slide wall" that contained a number of Beale's slides (Fig. 11.14). For the next 30 years he continued to build the Museum's collection, and to write about it and Beale in the Museum's publication, *Pennsylvania Arts and Science.* All of the American Museum of Photography collection was sold at the time of Sipley's death in 1971 to the 3M Company, and then given in 1977 to the George Eastman House International Museum of Photography and Film (now the George Eastman Museum) in Rochester, New York, where it remains.[24]

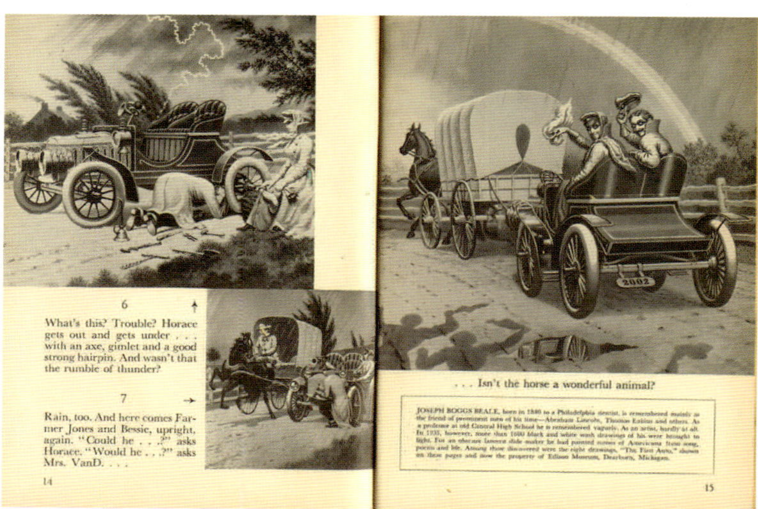

6

What's this? Trouble? Horace gets out and gets under . . . with an axe, gimlet and a good strong hairpin. And wasn't that the rumble of thunder?

7

Rain, too. And here comes Farmer Jones and Bessie, upright, again. "Could he . . .?" asks Horace. "Would he . . .?" asks Mrs. VanD. . . .

14

. . . Isn't the horse a wonderful animal?

JOSEPH BOGGS BEALE, born in 1840 to a Philadelphia dentist, is remembered mainly as the friend of prominent men of his time—Abraham Lincoln, Thomas Edison and others. As a professor at old Central High School he is remembered vaguely. As an artist, hardly at all. In 1935, however, more than 1600 black and white wash drawings of his were brought to light. For an obscure lantern slide maker he had painted scenes of Americana from song, poems and life. Among those discovered were the eight drawings, "The First Auto," shown on these pages and now the property of Edison Museum, Dearborn, Michigan.

15

Fig. 11.15 "Golden Jubilee Issue" of *The Ford Times,* featuring Beale's *Mr. Spurt and his Auto,* published by The Ford Motor Company to celebrate its Fiftieth Anniversary in 1953.

Toward the end of his life, Briggs received belated recognition with a Distinguished Service Award from The Pennsylvania Arts and Sciences Society. Its president (Louis Sipley) said that Briggs once held a "corner on [the] entertaining and educational aspects of photography".[25] On July 10, 1943, Briggs died at age 95. His Associated Press obituary, which ran nationally, described him as "the dean of American photographers who helped establish the motion picture industry but had little faith films would amount to anything". It ended with a totally incorrect description of his production of slip slides for various sets such as *Father, Dear Father*, and *Ten Nights in a Barroom* – sets which Beale had produced for him as standard (non-slip) slides. Beale and his art were not mentioned.[26]

On the 100th birthday of Briggs' wife, a few years after the death of Briggs himself, the mayor of Philadelphia sent her a congratulatory message, concluding – with considerable grace, "Perhaps the magic lantern shows your husband invented had something to do with the magic of your long and happy life".[27]

Beale's own lantern images – both the paintings and the slides – also survived, and in some unlikely ways. Even though Colen's "unknown" book paintings had been revealed in 1936 to be very public lantern-slide illustrations, and even though he had lost the exclusive right to publish some of them in 1937, Colen seems not to have been unduly deterred. The public was already beginning to look upon the magic lantern with nostalgia, and did not at all mind the fact that Beale had been painting for that medium. The Whitney Museum show gave the Beale collection a stamp of legitimacy, which Colen promoted to the hilt. He placed 14 designs about transportation at the Edison Institute, now the Henry Ford Museum (Fig. 11.15); and eight designs for *Swanee Ribber* at The Stephen Foster Memorial. Then, in January, 1940, The Atwater Kent Museum in Phila-

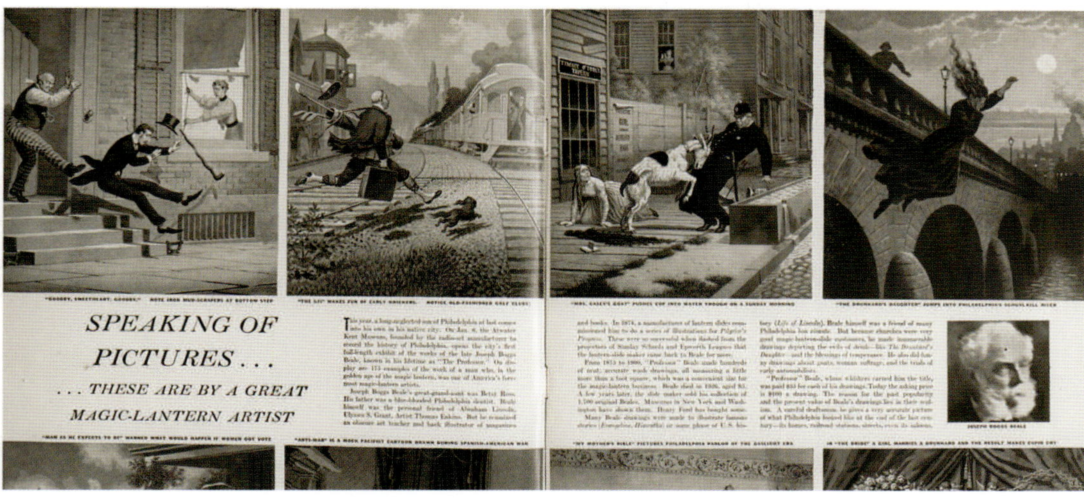

SPEAKING OF PICTURES . . .

. . . THESE ARE BY A GREAT MAGIC-LANTERN ARTIST

Fig. 11.16 Display in January 8, 1940 issue of *Life* magazine. *Life's* coverage brought national prominence to the Beale exhibit at Philadelphia's Atwater Kent Museum.

delphia finally gave Beale a home-town show, displaying drawings and calling them what they were, "magic lantern slide paintings". *Life* magazine gave the show national attention with a three-page spread of his pictures, calling Beale a "great magic-lantern artist" (Fig. 11.16).[28]

Through The American Federation of Arts, Colen arranged for a traveling exhibition of 50 Beale's painting to tour American museums. Most of these museums were small, and reactions were mixed, primarily because Colen again obscured the magic lantern origin of these images, and provided no context for them. Critics were understandably mystified, one suggesting a guessing game to figure out what the pictures were about. The same critic said that the drawings were "not masterpieces, but as illustrations they comprise one of the most interesting exhibitions which

Fig. 11.17 Two of *The Register* and *Tribune Syndicate*'s 1938 "roto" inserts for the Sunday papers. Such full-page display were syndicated in newspapers across the country.

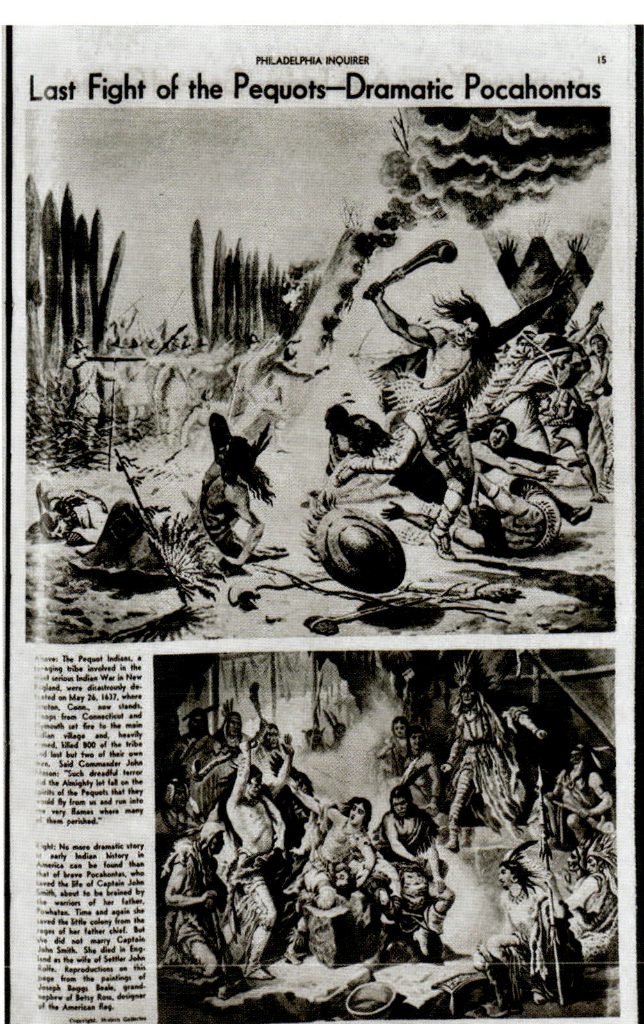

PHILADELPHIA INQUIRER 15

Last Fight of the Pequots—Dramatic Pocahontas

Above: The Pequot Indians, a foraging tribe involved in the most serious Indian War in New England, were disastrously defeated on May 26, 1637, where Groton, Conn., now stands. Troops from Connecticut and Plymouth set fire to the main Indian village and, heavily armed, killed 800 of the tribe and lost but two of their own men. Said Commander John Mason: "Such dreadful terror did the Almighty let fall on the spirits of the Pequots that they would fly from us and run into the very flames where many of them perished."

Right: No more dramatic story in early Indian history in America can be found than that of brave Pocahontas, who saved the life of Captain John Smith, about to be brained by the warriors of her father, Powhatan. Time and again she saved the little colony from the rages of her father chief. But she did not marry Captain John Smith. She died in England as the wife of Settler John Rolfe. Reproductions on this page from the paintings of Joseph Boggs Beale, grand-nephew of Betsy Ross, designer of the American flag.

Copyright, Modern Galleries

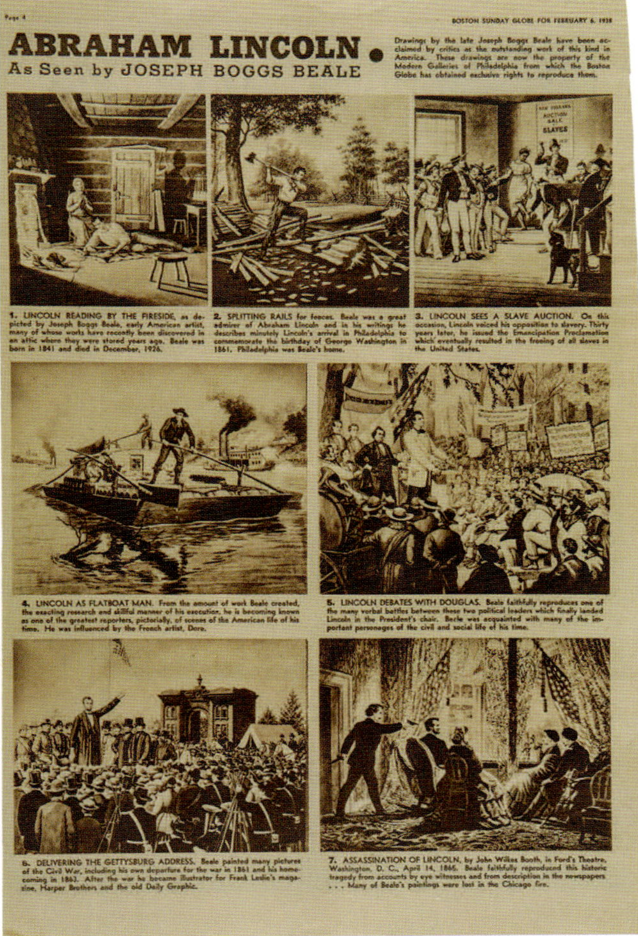

Page 4 BOSTON SUNDAY GLOBE FOR FEBRUARY 6, 1938

ABRAHAM LINCOLN • As Seen by JOSEPH BOGGS BEALE

Drawings by the late Joseph Boggs Beale have been acclaimed by critics as the outstanding work of this kind in America. These drawings are now the property of the Modern Galleries of Philadelphia from which the Boston Globe has obtained exclusive rights to reproduce them.

1. LINCOLN READING BY THE FIRESIDE, as depicted by Joseph Boggs Beale, early American artist, many of whose works have recently been discovered in an attic where they were stored years ago. Beale was born in 1841 and died in December, 1926.

2. SPLITTING RAILS for fences. Beale was a great admirer of Abraham Lincoln and in his writings he describes minutely Lincoln's arrival in Philadelphia to commemorate the birthday of George Washington in 1861. Philadelphia was Beale's home.

3. LINCOLN SEES A SLAVE AUCTION. On this occasion, Lincoln voiced his opposition to slavery. Thirty years later, he issued the Emancipation Proclamation which eventually resulted in the freeing of all slaves in the United States.

4. LINCOLN AS FLATBOAT MAN. From the amount of work Beale created, the exacting research and skillful manner of his execution, he is becoming known as one of the greatest reporters, pictorially, of scenes of the American life of his time. He was influenced by the French artist, Dore.

5. LINCOLN DEBATES WITH DOUGLAS. Beale faithfully reproduces one of the many verbal battles between these two political leaders which finally landed Lincoln in the President's chair. Beale was acquainted with many of the important personages of the civil and social life of his time.

6. DELIVERING THE GETTYSBURG ADDRESS. Beale painted many pictures of the Civil War, including his own departure for the war in 1861 and his homecoming in 1863. After the war he became illustrator for Frank Leslie's magazine, Harper Brothers and the old Daily Graphic.

7. ASSASSINATION OF LINCOLN, by John Wilkes Booth, in Ford's Theatre, Washington, D. C., April 14, 1865. Beale faithfully reproduced this historic tragedy from accounts by eye witnesses and from description in the newspapers . . . Many of Beale's paintings were lost in the Chicago fire.

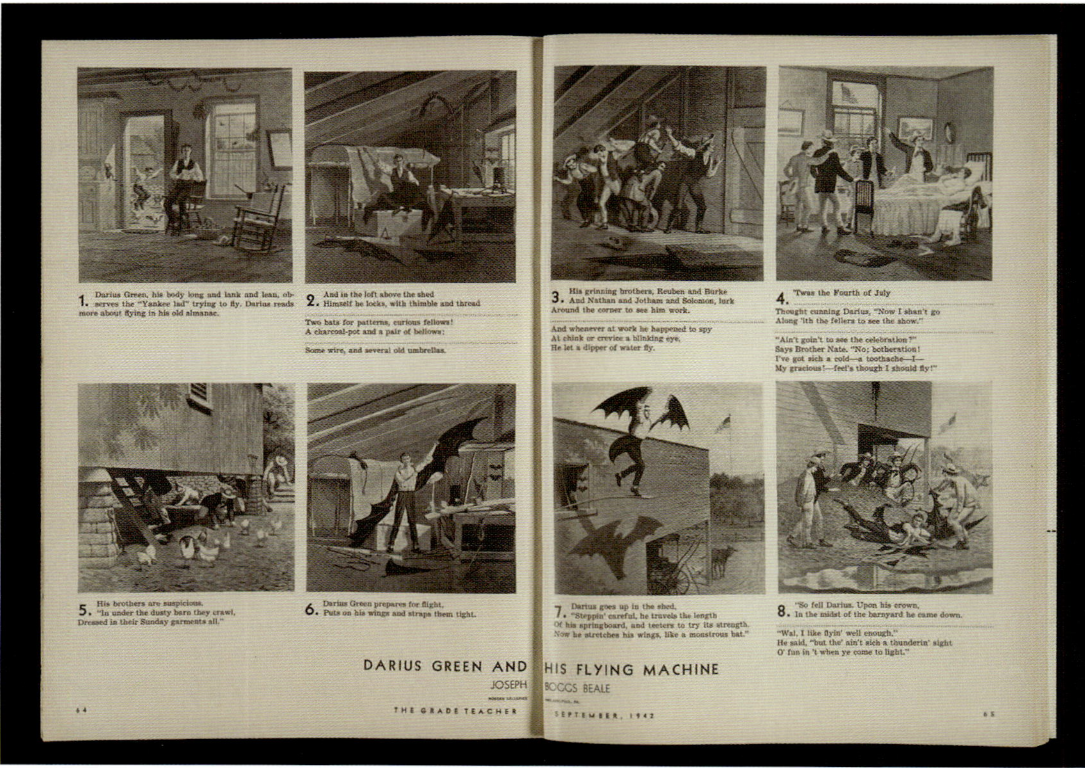

1. Darius Green, his body long and lank and lean, observes the "Yankee lad" trying to fly. Darius reads more about flying in his old almanac.

2. And in the loft above the shed
Himself he locks, with thimble and thread

Two bats for patterns, curious fellows!
A charcoal-pot and a pair of bellows;

Some wire, and several old umbrellas.

3. His grinning brothers, Reuben and Burke
And Nathan and Jotham and Solomon, lurk
Around the corner to see him work.

And whenever at work he happened to spy
At chink or crevice a blinking eye,
He let a dipper of water fly.

4. 'Twas the Fourth of July

Thought cunning Darius, "Now I shan't go
Along 'ith the fellers to see the show."

"Ain't goin't to see the celebration?"
Says Brother Nate. "No; botheration!
I've got sich a cold—a toothache—I—
My gracious!—feel's though I should fly!"

5. His brothers are suspicious.
"In under the dusty barn they crawl,
Dressed in their Sunday garments all."

6. Darius Green prepares for flight,
Puts on his wings and straps them tight.

7. Darius goes up in the shed,
"Steppin' careful, he travels the length
Of his springboard, and teeters to try its strength.
Now he stretches his wings, like a monstrous bat."

8. "So fell Darius. Upon his crown,
In the midst of the barnyard he came down.

"Wal, I like flyin' well enough,"
He said, "but the' ain't sich a thunderin' sight
O' fun in 't when ye come to light."

DARIUS GREEN AND HIS FLYING MACHINE

JOSEPH BOGGS BEALE

64 THE GRADE TEACHER

SEPTEMBER, 1942 65

Fig. 11.18 Beale's *Darius Green and His Flying Machine*, as it appeared in *The Grade Teacher*, September, 1942. Spreads like this were designed to be posted on the class bulletin board.

might be assembled, and form an important addition to 19th century Americana".[29]

Colen was on a roll. He put renewed effort into what we would now call the "merchandising" of Beale's images. In 1942 he wrote to the director of the Whitney Museum to report that a newspaper syndicate was featuring Beale's images nationally in a full-page inserts over 13 weeks (Fig. 11.17), that Columbia Records had developed a "History Speaks" series with Beale pictures on the record jackets, and that Beale's paintings were being used in a series of wallpaper murals.[30] Probably the most popular use of Beale's pictures on merchandise was a new 19-piece "Liberty" dinnerware service produced in both red and in blue for Woolworth's Department Stores by the Homer Laughlin Co. The blue version is rare, but the red version must have sold very well; multiple examples come up on eBay weekly.[31]

The Dissemination of Beale's Images, The Second Generation, 1940s–1970s

Colen devoted much of his energy in the '40s, '50s, and '60's to promoting Beale to a new generation, and succeeded in selling the rights to reproduce Beale's paintings to a number of other organizations, especially educational ones. For instance, *The Grade Teacher*, the leading professional magazine for elementary-school teachers, carried Beale's story-telling pictures as a regular monthly feature for six years, from 1939 to 1944, with spillovers into later years. Usually these were presented as a two-page spread of images to be pinned to the bulletin board and shared with the children, with captions drawn from the poems or songs. *Darius Green and His Flying Machine* (Fig. 11.18), that story about a boy's disastrous attempt to fly with his home-made wings, would have been particularly popular.

Based on the success of the *Grade Teacher* "picture stories", two sets of Beale's work were advertised in the magazine (and other magazines) in 1939 and following years, and were distributed to teachers free by the Fleer Corporation (Fig. 11.19). (Yes, the very same Fleer bubblegum company that went on to greater fame distributing baseball cards.) The largest of the Fleer promotional items, *Joseph Boggs Beale's American Pictorial History,* was a 9-1/2" x 11" portfolio containing 48 history pictures for bulletin board display. This portfolio was supplemented by classroom sets of 35 smaller (4" x 6-1/2") booklet versions, called *America My Country*, designed for students. The *Pictorial History* reached 10,000 teachers in its first two years, or about 350,000 students. By the time the promotion stopped more than a decade later in 1955, it must have reached several million.[32]

The enthusiastic response to Beale's pictures led to further distribution of his images in educational settings. Textbook companies often used Beale as a major source of their textbook illustrations. And a leading audio-visual publisher, The Society for Visual Education, Inc. (SVE) offered a 26-page catalog of 2" x 2" Beale slides, which also contained at least six 40-image filmstrips.[33]

The result of all this educational activity was that an entire new generation was raised on Beale's images. Since I was in elementary school in the 40's, my appreciation of Beale's work could well have started with those bulletin board pictures. I'd like to think that I was so enthralled that I helped our class collect 350 bubble gum wrappers so Miss Fay could get the entire Fleer portfolio of "Beale's Famous Pictures", and each of us kids could get one of the student booklets, but I don't think that's true. Miss Fay didn't approve of bubble gum.

Beale's work was not just reproduced in the school market. It was also widely distributed through magazines, newspapers, encyclopedias, and books, and later by television. For instance, the 1948 edition of *The World Book* contained 22 of Beale's illustrations[34]. What accounts for this dissemination, and for the fact that Beale's images are still often seen in the media today? The answer is that copies of his paintings and some slides were secured by the nation's leading stock photo house, The Bettmann Archive *and* by its chief competitors, Culver Pictures and Visual Education Services.

For many years Bettmann and its successors have been the leading supplier of archival pictures to publishers. (The firm was purchased in 1995 by Microsoft and hence Beale's pictures are now part of the digital age, marketed under the Corbis company name.) Otto Bettmann, the Bettmann Archive's originator, did not, as most supposed, have a massive collection of images. "In fact, the collection was highly compact and organized ... . Only the cream of the crop made it into the Bettmann Archive – all 'pictorial meat", as a visitor once remarked. In short, Bettmann was looking for pictures that told a story. Beale's style and content met his criteria beautifully, and he made copious use of Beale's images.[35]

Bettmann thus ensured that Beale's work would appear regularly in the media from the 1940's and '50s on. Even recently hardly a month goes by when I do not see one of his pictures reproduced in a magazine, newspaper, or on TV. However, such images are almost always identified by the archive's name. The artist, Beale, rarely receives credit, which is why he is almost unknown today, despite the publicity he received in the '30s and '40s, and the repeated use of his pictures in the public media since.

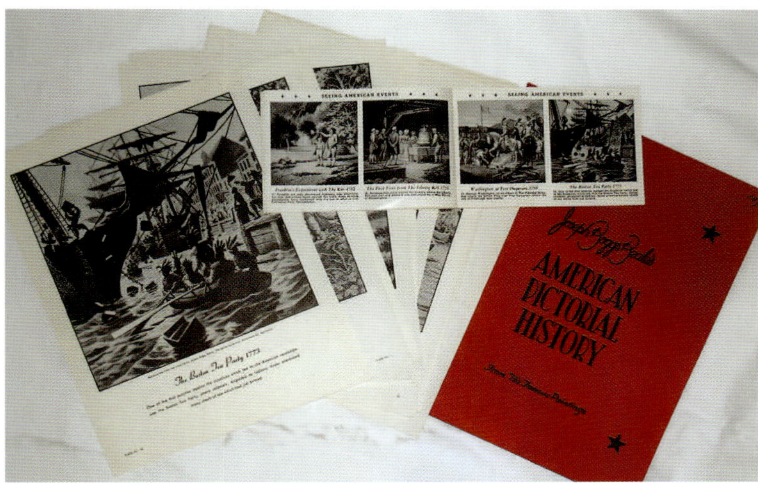

Fig. 11.19 ***The American Pictorial History*** **collection of Beale's Americana. These images were posted on tens of thousands of school bulletin boards.**

As the interest in Beale began to subside in the 1950s, Colen began to look for greener pastures. Exploiting his new connections in the art world and his prize dog – a boxer named "Boggs" no less – he struck up a relationship with fellow art collector and dog lover, Alfred Barnes. Barnes was a notoriously touchy and individualistic millionaire who had amassed one of the world's finest collections of Modernist and Impressionist art. Taking advantage of their dog-lovers fellowship, Colen wrote Barnes a letter in 1943, claiming that he was "flat broke" (a claim his son disputes), and telling Barnes that, "Boggs needs dog biscuits and I need something to eat too". He proposed that Barnes "help me make a living" by granting him "exclusively" the right to reproduce the Barnes paintings. Using a dog as a reference seems like a bizarre strategy, but Barnes was fiercely attached to dogs; he sometimes had one of his dogs "sign" his letters (Fig. 11.20). Perhaps because of the "Boggs" connection, Barnes agreed to hire Colen, and the two signed a contract that unfortunately was fraught with ambiguity.[36]

Colen must have been ecstatic; he was on his way to becoming a wealthy man again, with a connection in the highest realms of the art world. But almost immediately the pattern we have seen in his management of the Beale collection began to repeat itself. To announce his

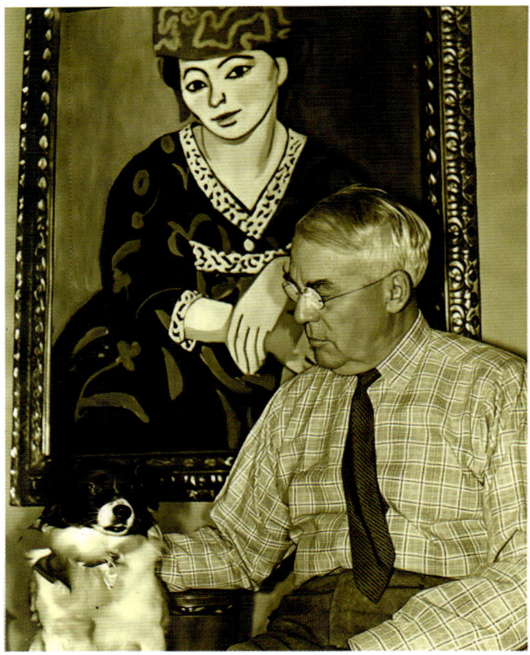

Fig. 11.20 Albert Barnes, the famous art collector, and his dog Fidèle seated before Matisse's *Red Madras Headdress*, one of the paintings in his collection.
Courtesy the Barnes Foundation.

new relationship with Barnes, Colen wanted to issue a press release, and sent it to Barnes for approval. Barnes immediately rejected it, calling it, "an amazing mixture of misstatements of fact, half-truths and tawdry publicity". The relationship rapidly deteriorated from there into controversy about the meaning of the contract, the tone and content of publicity, and the photography of the Barnes paintings. It ended three months later when Barnes wrote a letter challenging Colen to a "public showdown" based on the legal affidavits Barnes had collected, and concluding by saying, "my personal reply to the contents of [your] letter is – pooh! pooh!"[37]

It is interesting to speculate on what it might have meant to Beale's reputation if Colen had successfully developed the Barnes connection. Almost certainly it would have increased Colen's ability to sell and distribute the Beale images. But he had blown his big chance, and so he turned once again to his gallery and to interior decorating.

Then in 1953 or 1954 the husband of Colen's mistress found out about their relationship and went after Colen with a gun. Colen quickly sold off most of the Beale slides to a Philadelphia antique dealer, and decamped to Van Nuys, California with the paintings, where he again went into the home decorating business. He continued to try to find buyers for Beale paintings, and working with the Valley House Gallery of Dallas succeeded in placing a large collection with the American National Insurance Co. and elsewhere. He had difficulty, however, placing the religious paintings. (See sidebar.)[38]

And the magic lantern itself? What happened to it? Surprisingly, the lantern continued in use for many years after the Beale era, not for entertainment, but for illustrated lectures and

The Trouble with Angels

When Colen left for California, he took with him many Beale paintings, including 600 Religious images. But who, he must have asked himself any number of times, who would ever buy them? Then he had an inspiration: The Baptists!

He took the paintings to the national headquarters of the Baptists, and sure enough, great excitement ensued. The editors admired the conception of Beale's work, his story-telling power, the detail that anchored the viewer in the Biblical time. But then somebody said that they better consult their Art Director.

The Art Director came and looked through the paintings. He admired all the things that the editors had been talking about. Colen must have been salivating. But then the Art Director shook his head. "No", he said. "We can't use these".

"Why not?" the editors said. "They're terrific. Look at this. Look at that!"

The Art Director held up one of Beale's exultant angels. "Have you forgotten? Baptist angels don't have wings".

(And indeed, nowhere does the Bible say that angels have wings. But this incident occurred 50 years ago. Modern-day Baptists seem to have relaxed their strictures somewhat. It's very hard to show that an angel is an angel without angel wings.) See note 38.

This story retold by me, from *Memories and Images: The World of Donald Vogel and the Valley House Gallery*, by Donald Stanley Vogel.

other work-a-day applications. The large 3¼" x 4" slide format still provided that great detail, ideal for such diverse applications as art history classes and airplane identification in war. Some of the last uses? In 1962, a contractor to NASA was using the lantern to document its work on space suits (Fig. 11.21).[39] In 1965, the US Army published a catalog of 10,000 medical slides, many in the lantern-slide format, so we can guess that they were still being used for the next 10 or 20 years.[40] That would be a good 70 years after Beale received the letter laying him off, signaling the closing of the era when the magic lantern dominated the screen.

The Dissemination of Beale's Images, The Third Generation, 1970s–1990

In the 1970's, Colen, then in his eighties, decided to divest himself of the Beale collection. Working through the Valley House Gallery in Dallas, Texas, he sold 850 American history and literature paintings, together with some of the religious ones, to the American National Insurance Company. American National, which had its corporate headquarters in Galveston, Texas, used the Americana paintings to decorate the offices in its new skyscraper, and then gave about 130 of the New Testament religious paintings to Baylor University in Waco, Texas.[41]

For the nation's 1976 Bicentennial, American National decided to use its Beale collection to create a national patriotic celebration. A 1,000-person kickoff dinner launched a travelling exhibit of 65 Beale paintings to 12 different cities.[42] As opposed to the 1936–37 Arts Federation touring exhibit, which went mostly to small venues in small towns, this "Star Spangled History" tour went to large cities and significant venues. The exhibit itself was a polished multimedia affair, celebrating Beale's magic lantern context in the labels, in a continuous projection of color 35mm reproductions of his slides, and in a handsome illustrated catalog, *Star Spangled History*, curated by noted scholars (Fig. 11.22).[43]

Critical response to the exhibit was extensive but mixed, immersed as the critics were in the relativity and skepticism of Postmodernism – a time when the work of such contemporary illustrators as Norman Rockwell was disdained. Some of the critics simply called Beale's work

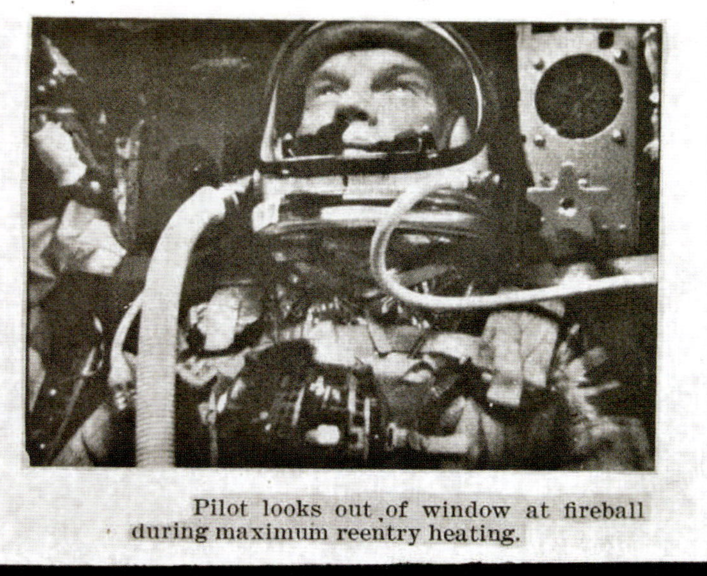

Fig. 11.21 Lantern slide of John Glenn, descending from the first orbit of earth on Feb. 20, 1962 as part of the Mercury MA-6 Mission.

Fig. 11.22 *The Star Spangled History* exhibit of Beale's work visited 12 cities. The president's wife, Lady-Bird Johnson, helped promote the tour.

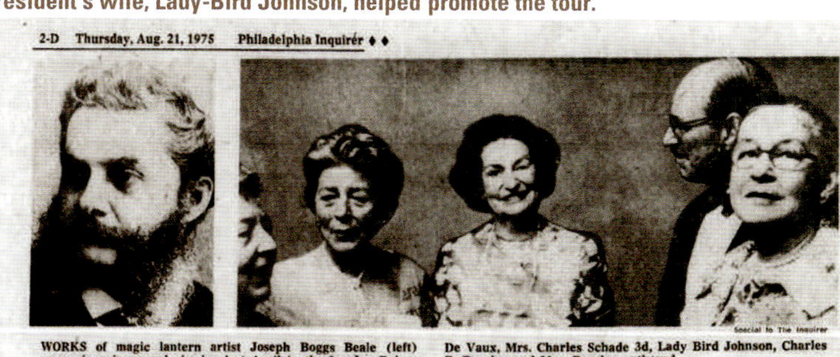

2-D Thursday, Aug. 21, 1975 Philadelphia Inquirer

Special to The Inquirer

WORKS of magic lantern artist Joseph Boggs Beale (left) were given inaugural viewing last April in the Lyndon Baines Johnson Library in Austin, Tex., where (from left) Mrs. Frank De Vaux, Mrs. Charles Schade 3d, Lady Bird Johnson, Charles B. Barclay and Mrs. Barclay gathered.

Beale Exhibition Opens Here Next Month

By RUTH SELTZER

Society

Joseph Boggs Beale is certainly not the most famous 19th-century American artist. He was born in Philadelphia in 1841 and died here in 1926. Now, almost a half-century after his death, Beale is on his way to becoming far better known than he was in his lifetime.

An exhibition of his wash drawings will open next month at the Historical Society of Pennsylvania. This show, titled "Star-Spangled History," will launch the fall-winter art season in this city.

On Tuesday, Sept. 16, the exhibition will open with a Bicentennial preview reception. **Mr. and Mrs. Charles B. Barclay**, the Philadelphia chairmen of the Beale show, will be hosting the invitational party to be held from 5 p.m. to 7 p.m.

Mrs. Barclay (nee Katharine Beale) is a grand-niece of Joseph Boggs Beale.

This past April, Mr. and Mrs. Barclay flew to Texas for the inaugural exhibition of the Joseph Boggs Beale Americana collection at the Lyndon Baines Johnson Library in Austin. With the Barclays traveled Mrs. Barclay's sisters, **Nancy Beale De Vaux (Mrs. Frank De Vaux)** of Blue Bell and **Marian Beale Schade (Mrs. Albert Schade 3d)** of Fort Washington.

Lady Bird Attended

Lady Bird Johnson attended the Boggs inaugural. In fact, she co-hosted the reception with the American Revolution Bicentennial Commission of Texas, the Bicentennial Association of Texas, and the American National Insurance Company.

Seventy of Joseph Beale's drawings were shown at the L. B. J. Library—the same ones that will be exhibited in Philadelphia before going on a coast-to-coast tour.

The 70 drawings are from the American National Insurance Company's corporate collection of more than 850 works of art by Beale.

Glendon E. Johnson, board chairman and president of the insurance company, selected the drawings for the Star-Spangled History show. The company, which is based in Galveston, acquired the Beale collection a few years ago from **Arthur Colen**, a former Philadelphian who now lives in Van Nuys, Calif. By the way, the insurance company's Glendon Johnson is not related to the Lyndon Johnson family.

Lived in Germantown

Joseph Boggs Beale lived in Germantown. His home still stands at the corner of Tulpehocken and Greene Streets — across the way from the Ebenezer Maxwell Mansion.

Beale was a magic lantern artist. He painted his watercolors in distinct black, white and gray washes so that they could be photographed to make the lantern slides. Many, many of his illustrations are patriotic. The American flag appears repeatedly.

It is appropriate that Beale's home city, Philadelphia, be the launching site for the nationwide tour. The exhibition here will be open to the public from Sept. 17 through Oct. 10 under the auspices of the Historical Society of Pennsylvania and the American National Insurance Company.

The tour will continue for 21 months. From Philadelphia, it will go to Boston, Chicago, Minneapolis, St. Louis, Denver, Albuquerque, Los Angeles, San Francisco, Dallas, Houston, Atlanta and New Haven, Conn. In the latter city, the Beale exhibition will be on display in the Sterling Library of Yale University during May and June, 1977.

Did Battle Sketches

Points of interest: Beale volunteered for service in the Civil War. He did battle sketches of the Gettysburg campaign for Frank Leslie's Weekly.

Beale, who attended the Pennsylvania Academy of the Fine Arts, was only 21 when he was elected professor of drawing and writing at Central High School in Philadelphia.

He was chosen over Thomas Eakins for the post. Eakins was 2½ years his junior.

Beale kept diaries from 1856 to 1862, that are now at the Historical Society of Pennsylvania. The artist's grand-niece, **Katharine Beale Barclay**, has read the diary. Mrs. Barclay has done considerable research into the life and times of her "Uncle Joe." Her cousin, **Dr. Donaldson Beale Cooper**, helped her with this. Dr. Cooper, who died a few months ago, was the artist's nephew. He lived in Haverford.

On Tuesday, we chatted with Mr. and Mrs. Barclay on the porch of the Merion Cricket Club. Said Mrs. Barclay, "I am so glad that Uncle Joe is finally getting national recognition."

David M. Robb Jr., a Philadelphian, has helped organize the Beale Americana exhibition. He is with the Kimball Art Museum in Fort Worth.

TITLED "Old Glory," this wash drawing by Joseph Boggs Beale will be in the exhibition of the artist's work at the Historical Society of Pennsylvania. The Beale show will open here in mid-September.

Look It Up Yourself In This Law Library

LIBRARY, From 1-D

elevator into the nalway on the 10th floor.

Lawyers from large and small law firms, student law clerks and people who have a passing, perhaps personal interest in the law, come daily to use the library's 200,000 volumes.

& Levy. "You don't feel like you've gone away."

The other day, for example, she was sharing a table with fellow law student Howard Trubman, who had just finished chatting with another classmate, Eileen Block. Both Trubman and Ms. Block are law clerks

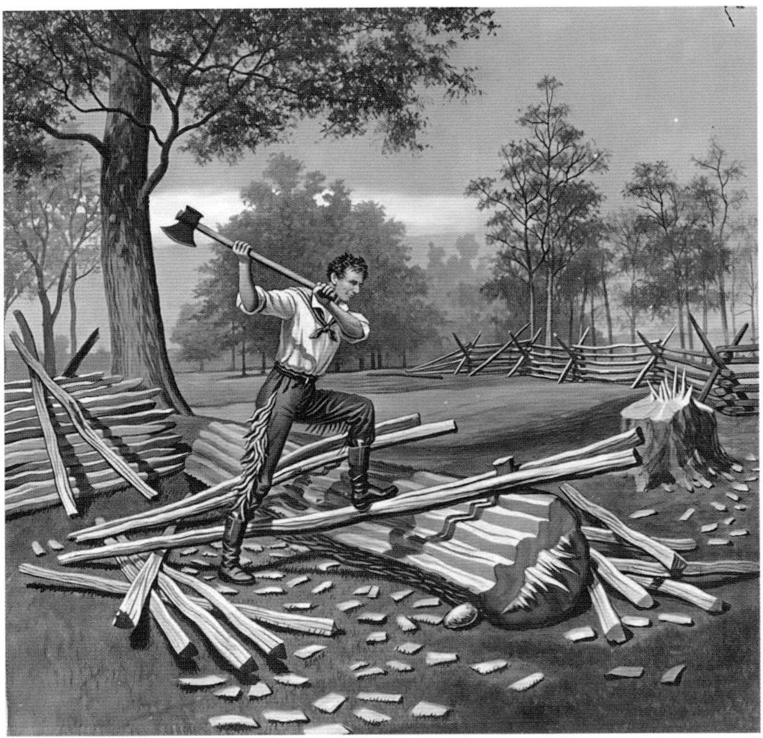

Fig. 11.23 Beale's "Lincoln Splitting Fence Rails" from *The Life of Lincoln*. It was one of Beale's pictures in the *Star Spangled History* exhibit.

"naïve". Others elaborated in more detail, most captured by Beale's art, despite themselves (Fig. 11.23).

> Beale, one of the last century's leading historical illustrators, attempted to present life as seen by the average American citizen of the time.[44]

> The ideas of the works are obvious and simple, as are the paintings. But they somehow are charming.[45]

> Perhaps the best that can be said [is that the images] are terribly naïve renderings of patriotic themes, perhaps well intentioned, but hopelessly lacking [in] either intellectual insight or emotional depth. At worst, they are pathetic examples of banal contrivance.[46]

> Beale's ... drawings ... [are] presented with such candor and simplicity, it is hard not to be excited by [them].[47]

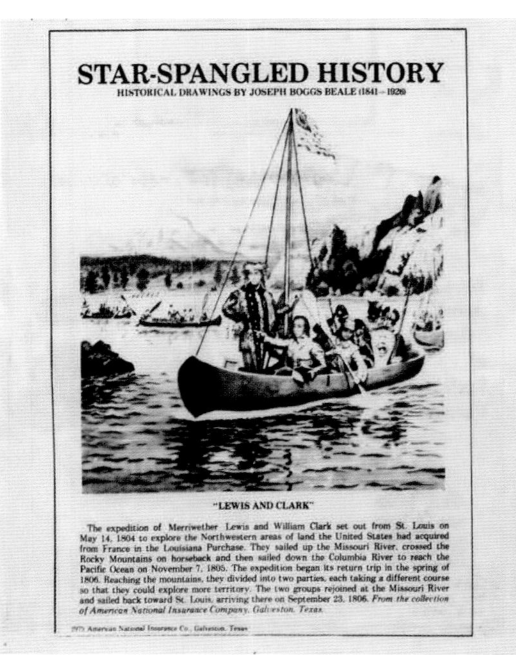

STAR-SPANGLED HISTORY

HISTORICAL DRAWINGS BY JOSEPH BOGGS BEALE (1841–1926)

"LEWIS AND CLARK"

The expedition of Merriwether Lewis and William Clark set out from St. Louis on May 14, 1804 to explore the Northwestern areas of land the United States had acquired from France in the Louisiana Purchase. They sailed up the Missouri River, crossed the Rocky Mountains on horseback and then sailed down the Columbia River to reach the Pacific Ocean on November 7, 1805. The expedition began its return trip in the spring of 1806. Reaching the mountains, they divided into two parties, each taking a different course so that they could explore more territory. The two groups rejoined at the Missouri River and sailed back toward St. Louis, arriving there on September 23, 1806. *From the collection of American National Insurance Company, Galveston, Texas.*

American National Insurance Co., Galveston, Texas

Fig. 11.24 Beale's "Arrival of Lewis and Clark" in the *Revolution* group, published in syndicated newspaper reproductions during the 1976 Bicentennial year.

The Philadelphia art critic Victoria Donohoe was the most prescient, especially considering the limited background information available. She was the only critic to explore the lantern context of Beale's work, including asking her 87-year-old uncle about her own family's home lantern shows. Writing under the headline "His Magical Drawings Brightened Many Nights", she assessed the screen qualities of Beale's art in a remarkably insightful manner:

> Each episode is rendered in great detail in grays and blacks with very pronounced white highlights for dramatic effects on gray charcoal paper. Dramatic incidents involving fire or explosions as well as clouds with silver linings and moonlight were sought out by the artist as particularly well-suited for lantern-slide portrayal... . Certain other watercolors show Beale making extensive early use of extended story-telling "scenarios" ... Beale was one of the few artists known to have created paintings for lantern-side presentation, which pushes him up front in the shift that popular culture was then making toward the projected image... . This exhibit confirms [his} role ... as a "pioneer" during a certain earlier period, rather than establishing his credentials as a full-fledged artist for all time.[48]

The Star Spangled History touring exhibit was supplemented by a series of 4" x 7" patriotic Beale pictures designed to be run weekly throughout the Bicentennial year in the newspapers across the nation (Fig. 11.24). They were produced by American National (with a discrete company credit at the bottom of the image caption) and offered free to newspapers. The pictures fit the moment, and were widely used. Once again, Beale's images were blanketing the country.

During the 1970s, Colen continued his efforts to place the rest of the Beale collection elsewhere. In 1973 he finally gave Beale's diary and some letters to the Historical Society of Pennsylvania, and sold the rest of the paintings to the Valley House Gallery in Dallas, Texas. Valley House in turn sold the religious pictures to The Biblical

Arts Center, a museum in Dallas. Unfortunately, The Biblical Arts Center caught fire in 2005, and all the Beale paintings and slides there were lost (Fig. 11.25).[49]

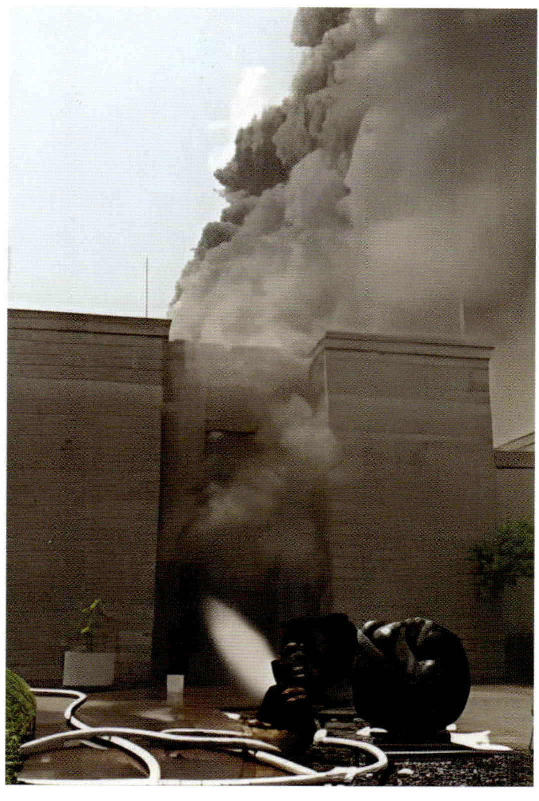

Fig. 11.25 June 27, 2005 fire at the Biblical Arts Center in Dallas. The fire destroyed 441 of Beale's paintings and about 100 Beale slides.
Donna McWilliam, Associated Press.

Beale's Slides Are Shown Again

Beale's paintings eventually found their ways to two dozen museums and to private collections.[50] But what of the slides that Beale purchased and that surrounded him in his attic studio? It seems almost certain that Colen obtained the set of Beale's personal slides when he purchased the diary from the Beale relatives in 1935. These particular slides, from which most of the reproductions in this book are made, have coloring of the best Briggs quality. Some are labeled in Beale's hand, and some carry his own comments about his artwork.

The existence of the slides must have been something of an embarrassment to Colen, given that he had first presented Beale's work as book illustrations.[51] Perhaps that is why almost nothing further was heard about them until 1954, when a woman named Katherine Leddick (Hill) received a strange letter from Philadelphia. Leddick ran The Liberty Eatery and Antique Emporium in Whitehall, New York, a hotel and antique shop perched precariously on the banks of the Champlain Canal. Often, after serving her guests dinner, she would break out an old magic lantern and give a spirited show using slides that she claimed came through the family of Alfred Stieglitz. Though a wonderful, vibrant performer she had little knowledge of lantern culture and knew nothing of Beale. Yet she obtained his personal collection of several thousand slides, and his personal magic lantern – in a most remarkable manner (Fig. 11.26):

Fig. 11.26 Katherine Leddick giving a show at the Liberty Eatery, dressed in her *American Revolution Show* outfit. She is using the lantern Beale bought in 1892.

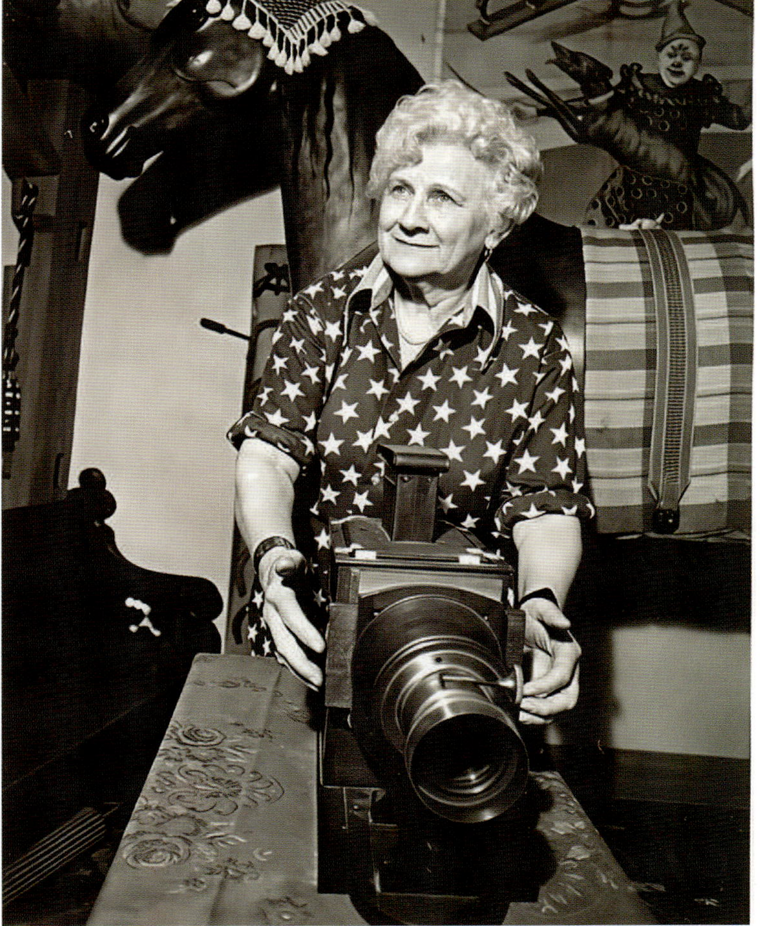

> While I was [giving my shows] ... an elderly gentlemen came night after night. He was chairman of the Board of Directors of the U.S. Vanadium Corporation. [In the Fall of 1954] I got a letter that said I was to go to Philadelphia to a certain address because there was something there for me. I thought it was a crank letter but ... [a friend] took me. Lilly Ostroff [an antique dealer] settled the estate and showed me all the Beale boxes. She had already sold a few to the Henry Ford Collection [The Edison Institute]. She said that a man came in, purchased the rest and wanted me to have them. I never knew for sure who bought them

> for me, but I assumed it was the man from Vanadium because he came back to watch ... [my] Beale shows, expressed great interest in them, and had them written up in the company newspaper.[52]

For the next 25 years Leddick used the Beale slides to give shows in the Liberty. With the Beale material to draw upon, her performances became increasingly popular, and she claimed that by passing the hat after her shows she was able to put her daughters through college. A deeply religious and patriotic woman, Leddick created a Beale Bible show called *The Torchbearers* that traced the growth of the Judo-Christian religious spirit, and a Beale American History show called *The American Revolution* that demonstrated how divine guidance governed the birth of America. *The American Revolution* attracted particular attention. Leddick and her relatives gave the show locally, and an automated version in 35mm format with recorded narration in English and French was shown daily at the 1967 World's Fair in Montreal. Leddick, who also gave a number of live performances at the Expo, claimed that a million people saw the 35 mm version, though this estimate may have been the product of her irrepressible enthusiasm.[53]

In 1979, after a performance of *The American Revolution* for the New York Historical Association, someone stole the show and some other slides from the Liberty. Leddick was heartbroken, and never gave another public performance. Well into her seventies at the time, she began looking for someone to purchase the collection, but refused offers from several museums because she wanted her performing legacy continued. In 1983 she sold her collection to me, with the understanding that I would once again perform Beale's unique work.

At that time, I was employed as Editor in Chief of *Weekly Reader*, the national children's newspaper. Giving magic lantern shows and collecting slides was a hobby. With the addition of the Beale Collection, the shows that my wife and I and a musician gave became more varied and sophisticated. Leddick came to see one performance, and was pleased to see Beale's work on screen again. Later, when she developed Alzheimer's, one of the few ways to connect with her was to put a slide in her hand. Then she would remember who I was, and who she had been.

The American Magic Lantern Theater, and the Lucas Museum – The Fourth Generation, 1990s to Present

As my wife and I became more familiar with the remarkable quality of the Beale collection, we became fascinated with the man and his art, and spent many vacations tracking down the information that has led to this book. Then in 1992 I decided that it was time for a career change, and that I would try to revive the lost tradition of professional lantern entertainment. I formed The American Magic Lantern Theater, the nation's only professional theater company recreating magic lantern shows. We developed ten different productions, each an hour-and-a half-long, most with a holiday theme such as *Halloween* or *Christmas*, each built around a core of Beale slide sets like *The Raven* or *Marley's Ghost*.

Today we continue to present the shows, with myself as showman, performing with a singer/pianist who sings solos, leads singalongs, and provides musical *underscoring* for the drama. We have traveled extensively throughout the country and occasionally abroad, giving more than 1,000 shows, playing in historic opera houses, modern theaters and cultural centers, museums and living history centers, festivals, fairs, and schools.[54] Audiences range from 100 to 3,000, from toddlers to Seniors. National Public Radio has called the shows "a living national treasure".[55] Once again Beale's work is being seen as it was meant to be seen, in color, projected on a screen before a live audience, supported with dramatic narration and music.

You might expect that Seniors would enjoy these shows – old folks who may even have played with toy magic lanterns as children and who are nostalgic for the good old days. You might even imagine that the post-WWII generation would be intrigued – those taught the classics of Longfellow and Poe, who were in high school before *Howdy Doody* mesmerized the first TV generation. But how about the children of today? How about those surrounded in the womb by the sounds of *Oprah*, those weaned on *Sesame Street*, teethed on Disney, fattened on *Star Wars*, matured on shoot-em-up video games?

As I mentioned in Chapter 1, it is the response of these Media-Age children to magic lantern shows that fascinates me (Fig. 11.27). Despite their upbringing in a world where images and colors and sounds swarm in two-second visuals and sound bites, where the content is often grotesque and violent, where interactivity is measured in milliseconds – despite all that, they can be transfixed by the screen language and subject content and audience involvement of the magic lantern patriarch. The old combination of Beale's cinematic technique, live music, and a narrative voice alone in the dark – the magic lantern art of a bygone era – can hold them spellbound, make them laugh, make them cry, and bring a roar of applause at the show's conclusion. Once again audiences are responding as Beale hoped they would.

And what happened to those hundreds of Beale designs decorating the American National Insurance Company's headquarters, and the thousands of Beale slides, magic lantern broadsides and other items jammed into my house? In 2010–12 American National decided to deaccession much of their Beale collection. Working with their curator, my wife and I succeeded in helping them place Beale designs in a number of museums, including major institutions such as Harvard University, The Henry Ransom Center at the University of Texas, and the Academy of Motion Picture Arts and Sciences. As a result, the distribution of Beale's work was increased substantially, and samples are now held by 25 different museums around the country. Our own 13,000 item collection – primarily "The Beale Collection" of Beale's designs, slides and related ephemera, plus "The Broadside Collection" of more general magic lantern material – together called the Borton Collection –all went to the new Lucas Museum of Narrative Art in Los Angeles, California, where it will provide an important and comprehensive resource for another generation of visitors and scholars.[56]

Summary and Conclusion

Beale worked as a lantern slide illustrator for about 35 years, from 1881 to 1917 – the heyday of American magic lantern art. He painted alone in his studio, producing an average of 110 pictures a year when he was working full-time. Beale was almost certainly the single largest creator of slides for the American magic lantern industry. By the end of his career, he had produced 2,085 images, used in 2,621 differently-

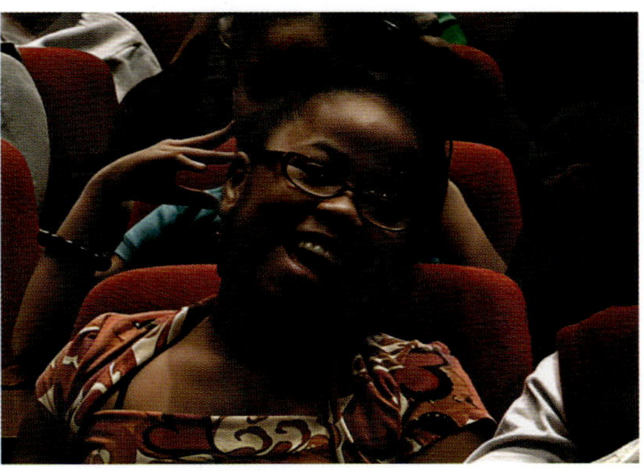

Fig. 11.27 Another picture from the video of those fifth graders enjoying a re-created magic lantern show.

named slides, about 10% of *all* the lantern slides on all subjects that were available to the public in the general slide catalogs. That work was concentrated by subject area. He produced about 25 percent of all slides offered in the subjects of Religion, History, and Literature, and about 50 percent of those offered in the Secret Society area. In total, Briggs sold an estimated 1.3 to 2.2 million Beale slides, used not once, but again and again. Certainly, over the years, those slides reached huge audiences of many millions.

Beale functioned on deadline in a workshop culture, under the artistic direction of C. W. Briggs, and sometimes in close artistic collaboration with him. That meant that some of his output was the re-working of other artists, or the re-working of Briggs sketches. About two-thirds of the time his work was original, some 1,400 images. Of those original paintings, he signed about half, but often he didn't sign a painting, even when it was clearly original, because he never expected it to be framed and hung on a wall. Though he was proud of his art, he understood that his drawings were production materials, the first step in a commercial illustration business that culminated in the screen images of magic lantern art.

Beale was content to remain anonymous, but his work demonstrates again and again that he was a talented illustrator. Though he was not an artist ahead of his time, like Thomas Eakins or Winslow Homer, he was abundantly *of* his times. He reflected those times back to an adolescent America hungry for a heroic image of itself. His meticulous style captured the salient details and energy of the life around him – an "American Cruikshank", as the Philadelphia art critic Dorthey Grafly called him. His strong sense of design allowed him to cram his images with visual information, yet produce striking, easily grasped compositions. His remarkable visual memory and his long commercial career gave him the ability to create – from his imagination alone – thousands of magic lantern images of variety and authenticity, despite their studio origins and rapid production. No wonder Briggs felt that, "We never had any work done by any artist which [was] so well done and so suitable in style for projection".[57]

To the critics reviewing Beale's black and white designs in the 1976 touring exhibit, fifty years after his death and in the midst of the craze for modern art, his work may have at first seemed "naïve". But his simplicity – that directness of intention and of conception – was in fact his strength. That is why, despite themselves, and despite images that were not color enlargements on screen, but small black-and-white production drawings, many of those very same critics ended their reviews by admitting that they were "charmed" or "excited" by Beale's work. He had, you may remember, what the nation's leading image-archivist of the 1960's, Otto Bettmann, called the ability to "get to the heart of the matter" – picturing not the" fat" or the "bone", but the "pictorial meat" of a story.[58] That ability to simplify drove his story-telling power. Copious detail sustained attention. Sophisticated narrative techniques immersed his audience in his stories.

Beale's narrative art used about 100 of the techniques found today in books on the "art of film" – employed again and again, in a clearly self-aware fashion. Beale did not originate most of these techniques, nor was he the only lantern artist who used them. But cinema historians increasingly point to Beale's work as critical to understanding how the movies emerged from magic lantern art. Charles Musser in his seminal *The Emergence of Cinema* discusses Beale's cinematic "perspective shifts" in *The Raven*, with succeeding slides "panning from right to left".[59] Discussing the same poem, Theodore Barber, in *Evenings of Wonder: A History of the Magic Lantern Show in America*, describes how Beale kept the background scene of several slides exactly the same while the character's position changed, which made "the protagonist actually seem to move in response to his visions".[60] Gary Rhodes, in *The Birth of American Horror Film*, describes the "continuity editing" of Beale's spooky stories.[61] Stan Walsh in *Chasing Rainbows: The Story of Classic Travel Adventure Cinema* describes how "two projectors converge on the screen to give the illusion of movement" in a Beale dissolve.[62] Terry Lindvall in *Sanctuary Cinema: Origins of the Christian Film Industry* describes how Beale's hymns "anticipated the cinematic technology of crosscuts, dissolves, and superimpositions".[63] And Fred Guida, in his book, *A Christmas Carol*, discusses all the screen versions of the Dickens's story – lantern, movie, TV – and describes how Beale's lantern-slide version created "through an implosion of words and images, a narrative, indeed a movie, ... in the mind of each individual viewer".[64]

Despite these connections between Beale's art and the movies, Beale was primarily, as the 1976 Philadelphia critic Victoria Donohoe said, a "pioneer" whose work entranced the people of his own time, rather than one whose work was adopted by the cinema settlers who followed him. He employed the traditional lantern techniques like the dissolve with great skill, and he developed a host of narrative techniques to attract attention, to hold attention, and to immerse his audience in his stories. Between 1881 and 1896 (the point at which the movies were introduced in New York), Beale was all but alone in the field, almost single-handedly creating American screen entertainment for the generation before the movies. But there is little evidence that either the Beale/Briggs choice of subject matter, or the wide range of Beale's art techniques directly influenced the movies. Beale was a master illustrator who shadowed forth our current Age of Media, but he did not mold the work of the early movie makers, or those who came to dominate the landscape of Hollywood (Fig. 11.28). He did, however, help to prepare the way for them, to mold a new visual culture. When the movies came to America, Beale had already trained audiences to appreciate an artistic experience that was entirely different from what they saw in art galleries or picture books. He had trained them that when the lights went out in an auditorium, they could expect wonders in the dark.

The impact of Beale's work, for his own period and for ours, lies not simply in his skill with narrative techniques, or the way he depicted the life and culture of his era. It is the way he combined the two. Because he was a creator of magic lantern art, his work was quite literally projected into the nation's darkened homes, churches, schools, theaters, and fraternal lodges.

It created a huge, colorful panorama that mesmerized his audiences. His pictures were ephemeral, gone from the screen in a minute or two, his name all but hidden. But his thousands of shimmering screen images were not simply shown once. They were shown again and again and again, imprinting Beale's vision on millions of American minds. His art spoke directly, devoid of revisionism, devoid of cynicism. It helped Americans of his time appreciate the most important aspects of their lives – the grandeur of their heroes and history, the meaning of their literature, the strength of their fraternal bonds, the source of their spirituality, the grit of their humor.

I think of Beale often as we dramatize his work during our touring magic lantern shows, sharing it as he intended it to be seen. I'm sure he would be pleased to hear that his slides are now admired as the American culmination of a tradition that reached back ten generations before his time. No doubt he would be delighted if he could see our modern audiences, now five generations after his death, forgetting their cell phones for a moment, staring in wide-eyed wonder at magic lantern art. Their response would make him proud of those years he worked for Briggs, painting away week after week, projecting his narrative vision into the dark, making stories come alive on screen.

And so, … we come to the end of Beale's story, and of mine. Thank you for your interest. It's time now for us both to say, "Adieu".

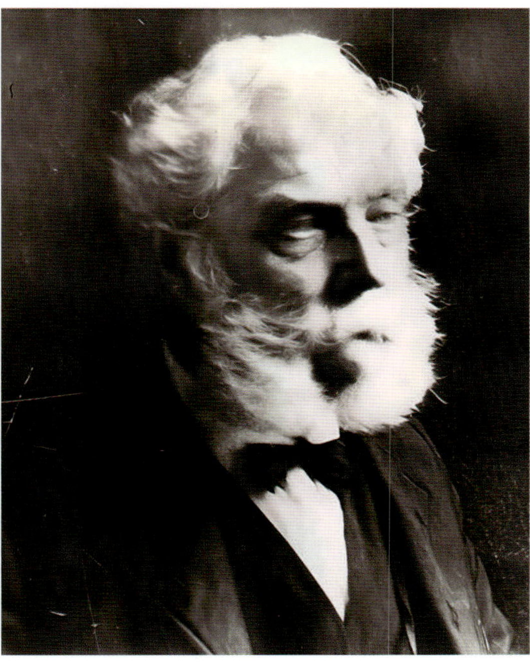

Fig. 11.28 Joseph Boggs Beale in his final years (1920–1926). He still sported the sideburns he had adopted during the Civil War.

Fig. 11.29 Beale's "Adieu" from the Motto's group, a slide that could be used in either magic lantern shows, or movies.

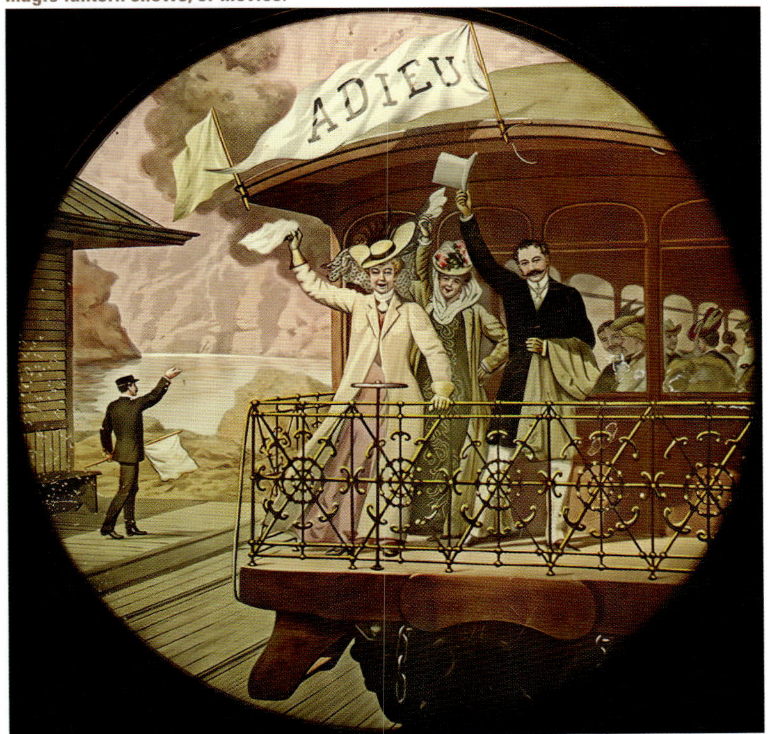

Endnotes

Abbreviations:
BC/LMNA, Borton Magic Lantern Collection at The Lucas Museum of Narrative Art, Los Angeles, CA.
CC/PHS, Colen Collection, Pennsylvania Historical Society, Philadelphia, PA.
SC/GEM, Sipley Collection, George Eastman Museum, formerly The George Eastman (House) International Museum of Photography and Film, Rochester, NY.
OMLJ, *The Optical Magic Lantern Journal*, published in England.

Chapter One. End of an Era - Start of a Passion

1. J. B. Beale to Harper and Brothers, Sept. 15, 1909, BC/LMNA. In this letter to Harper and Brothers, Beale reports that he got such a lay-off letter from C. W. Briggs, his employer. The letter itself has disappeared.

   And, right off the bat, a problem – how to spell "magic lantern projector" and similar compound uses of the term. In modern grammar, two words modifying a noun are hyphenated, i.e. "magic-lantern art". However, since Beale's audiences did not hyphenate "magic lantern show", I will not hyphenate "magic lantern" as a modifier, though I use the hyphenated convention in other cases, except for the name "Great Grandfather Carter".

2. Borton, "How Many Beale Slides Sold?", 3–24.
3. Editor, "Speaking of Pictures", 4–6.
4. Briggs and Beale probably used the term "designs" for Beale's production paintings because they were not the final artistic products, but the designs for them. I will adopt their term. Beale's magic lantern works were painted images on paper, but the technical description for them is "wash drawing", a confusing modern word used to designate paintings done in shades of one color on paper. Briggs and Beale also used the term "drawings" for Beale's work.
5. Borton, "How Many Beale Slides Sold?", 3–24.
6. Bronze Age: Robb, "Art (Pre)History"; General art history: Gombrich, *Story of Art*, 481–485; Hoopes, *American Narrative Painting*, 9–22; Casteras, *The Defining Moment;* Interative gaming: Meadows, *Pause and Effect.* (Art historian Paul Barolsky claims "There is No Such Thing as Narrative Art", but his sweeping claim is based on an analysis of a single Renaissance sculpture and makes no attempt to deal with the wide range of narrative art summarized here. Barolsky, "No Such Thing".)
7. Hoopes, *American Narrative Painting*; Eisner, *Comics and Sequential Art*; Nodelman, *Words About Pictures* (Picture books); Meisel, *Realizations: Narrative, Pictorial Arts* (Other art forms.) In my previous book about Beale, *Before the Movies*, written with my wife, Deborah (Borton, Borton, *Before the Movies*), I described Beale in the subtitle as "The Nation's First Great Screen Artist". To my mind, that's the same thing as saying, as I do here, that he was "The American Screen's First Great Narrative Artist", but in this book I want to emphasize the narrative techniques he uses to tell screen stories.
8. Cinema terms are widely used in college texts and academic books to define the art of the movies. See the most popular texts, Bordwell, Thompson, Smith, *Film Art*; Giannetti, *Understanding Movies*; Boggs, *The Art of Watching Film*; Moshansky, *A to Z Guide to Film Terms*; Brown, *How Films Tell Stories.* For cinema techniques used in early film see Gaudreault, Bedard, *Cinema 1900–1906.*

   Deac Rossell, among others, has argued about the dangers of *ex post facto* reasoning that looks at cinema history through the rear-view mirror of modern understanding. (Rossell, "Double Think", 26–31). Granted, a risk exists of missing something important in the 19th-century scene by using modern cinema terms. But using them is hardly *ex-post facto* reasoning since so many of the "cinema" techniques described by these terms come from other fields like the theater, art, and drama that in fact pre-date not only movies but magic lantern shows as well.

9. For a description of lantern techniques such as *phantasmagoria slides*, or *tank slides*, see Robinson, Herbert, Crangle, eds, *Encyclopaedia of Magic Lantern.*
10. Major collections: George Eastman Museum, Lucas Museum of Narrative Art. Other collections: Academy of Motion Picture Arts and Sciences, Baylor University, Bowdin College, Brandywine Museum of Art, Center for American Music, Drexel University, Duke University, Harvard University, Henry Ford Museum, Henry Ransom Center, Kent Museum of the Moving Image (England), Laval University (Canada), Museum of the Fine Arts (Boston), Museum of the Moving Image (New York), Munson Museum of Art, National Portrait Gallery (Smithsonian), Philadelphia Museum of Art, R. W. Norton Gallery, Rosenberg Library and Museum, San Diego University, Witte Museum, Wadsworth Atheneum Museum of Art, Whitney Museum of American Art.
11. This description of Great Grandfather Carter's shows is based on my father's stories of his childhood. His recollections were sometimes elaborated for effect. In this case they are collaborated by the notes of his fact-oriented sister, Faith Borton Weston.
12. If Beale produced about ten percent of the slides in the catalogs, why don't we see ten percent on eBay today? Twenty-five years ago, the percentage was much higher. I think many of the slides that were listed in catalogs have already been purchased. A large percentage of what is now available on eBay seems to have been produced by individuals, often amateurs.
13. Dugdale, "Preface" to *Magic Images.*
14. Dellmann, "Intermedial Performance Practices", 242.
15. Borton, Borton, *Before the Movies.*
16. In the scholarly publication of The Magic Lantern Society of the United States and Canada and elsewhere, I have described the scope of lantern shows in America, and the work of about 500 of the top American lantern showmen. See Borton, "How Many Lantern Shows?". See also Borton, "238 Eminent American 'Magic Lantern' Showmen: The Chautauqua Lecturers"; Borton, "The Professional Life of 'Magic Lantern' Illustrated Lecturers"; and Borton, "The Professional Life of 'Magic Lantern' Illustrated Lecturers, Part 2". The articles are available online at Academia.edu. See also the website, "The Museum of American Magic Lantern Shows", http://magiclanternmuseum.com.

Chapter Two. The Early Years, A Life of Imagery

1. Beale, *Diary.* Beale's garret and his panorama work are described in detail running from January 5, 1856 to March 14, 1857. Beale began the *Diary* on January 1, 1856, when he had just turned 15, and continued it on a daily basis, almost without interruption, for 1074 pages until July 26, 1865, when it stops abruptly. I have used the *Diary* so extensively that I do not cite dates for incidental items if the period is clear. Excerpts from the diary have been printed, with helpful notes in Wainwright, "Education". Available online at https://journals.psu.edu/pmhb/article/view/42995.
2. Oettermann, *The Panorama: History*, 10.
3. The panorama and other family entertainments are described in an undated memoir written by Beale's younger sister (Broome, "Memoir").
4. Editor's Table, *Ladies' Repository*, 319. Quoted in Huhtamo, *Illusions in Motion*, 158. The "Editor's Table" describes a "Storm at Sea" sequence in Uncle Edmund Beale's Cape Horn panorama.
5. *Two* of Beale's uncles, Edmund and George, were panorama showmen. Beale's involvement with his Uncle Edmund's panorama was at its most intense during the period when he was working on his own toy panorama (January 5, 1856 to May 1, 1856), but he continued to report on Edmund's successes for years. For the specifics about Edmund Beale's Arctic Show see Potter, *Arctic Spectacles*, 120–124, and Wamsley, "The Sublime", 194. For information on Edmund's panorama artist, George Heilge, see Groce and Wallace, *Dictionary of Artists*. For a comprehensive discussion of the panorama, see Huhtamo, *Illusions in Motion*.
6. Routhier, Avery, Hardiman, Jr., "Panorama's Progress", 94–101.
7. E. Beale, "His New Panorama".
8. Casper W. Briggs, *Ledger*, 3, 470–471. In 1890 Beale purchased the slides from designs that he had already produced. The evidence that he continued to do so is the 1700+ slides that dealer Arthur Colen obtained, presumably from the Beale family after Beale's death.
9. Beale, *Diary*. Beale gives his Walnut St. address on the opening page of his *Diary*, January 1, 1857. He mentions the move to Chestnut St. in a letter to his parents (Beale, "Letter to Parents", August 16, 1857).
10. Miller, *Betsy Ross*, 354–355, 359. Beale's possible reason for changing the setting of his Betsy Ross image to a more lavish room as seen in Fig. 2.9 was suggested by Miller in a phone conversation of the author. Part of Miller's evidence for Betsy Ross making the first flag is that she noticed that Beale, as a young man, had inked a star into his diary after visiting his aunt, the daughter of Betsy Ross, so he clearly thought – even at that early age – that she was the famous seamstress.
11. Genealogical information on the Beale family is drawn from American Historical Co., *Colonial Lineages*; and Collins, *Philadelphia*; and family records and genealogical charts graciously provided by Katherine Barclay of Wynwood, PA, a Beale family descendent.
12. The arrest and rape trial are covered by front-page articles in the *Philadelphia (PA) Bulletin* and *Philadelphia (PA) Public Ledger*, August 8, 1854 and October 25 to December 1, 1854; and by The *New York Times (NY)*, August 9, 1854, October 25, 1854, and December 1, 1854. The pardon is covered by back-page articles in all three publications, November 23, 1855. A detailed description of the trial, associated skullduggery, exculpatory testimonials, and character witnesses are presented in a booklet prepared in Dr. Beale's defense: Rood et. al., *Trial and Defense*. No mention of the trial or pardon appears in Beale's Diary, since both of these events occurred before he began writing.
13. *The Gettysburg Compiler*, Gettysburg, PA, December 3, 1855.
14. Beale, *Diary*, July 25, 1858. These Sunday activities are a bit above the norm for Beale, but not by much.
15. Beale, *Diary*, October 23, 1860. John B. Gough was a leading temperance lecturer. While Beale's attendance at such lectures was not habitual and he never mentions "taking the pledge", he was clearly a temperance advocate at this time. It is unlikely that he changed his mind in later life, in spite of the assertion by Arthur Colen (Beale's first collector and biographer) that Beale was a "bon vivant" (Colen, "Introduction"). That assertion was probably designed to make Beale more palatable to the post-prohibition America of the 1930's.
16. Beale's understanding of fraternal orders, like those listed here, was probably influenced by this early exposure to their parades. Later he was to create about 400 slide designs for fraternal rituals, particularly those of the Masons and the Knights of Pythias.
17. Beale, *Diary*, November 2, 1860. For more on the culture of parades in Philadelphia, see Davis, *Parades and Power*.
18. Beale, *Diary,* February 22, 1862. Beale described in some detail almost every Washington's Birthday celebration, but was particularly impressed with this one.
19. Beale, *Diary*, Nov. 8–20, 1864. Also, "Emancipation in Maryland: Celebration at the Headquarters of the Committee for Recruiting United States Colored Troops", *The Philadelphia (PA) Press*, Nov. 2, 1894, reprinted in *The Liberator*, Boston, MA, Nov. 11, 1864. Also "Emancipation in Maryland: Celebration at the Headquarters of the Committee for Recruiting United States Colored Troops", *Frank Leslie's Illustrated Newspaper*, Sept, 1, 1864. After the Philadelphia celebration, the transparency was taken down and moved to Nashville, Tennessee for a celebration there. "Removing Transparencies", *The Philadelphia (PA) Inquirer*, Nov. 28, 1864. My thanks to Kent Wells for finding some of these references.
20. For a discussion of a wide range of nineteenth-century theatrical entertainment, see Delgado, *Victorian Entertainment*.
21. Wells, "Stereopticon".
22. Beale, *Diary*, December 22, 1860. The photographic slides that impressed Beale used a process that had been discovered only eleven years before, by the Langenheim Brothers of Philadelphia, who later sold their business to C. W. Briggs, who in turn became Beale's employer. As Beale says, the photographs had originally been made for the stereoscope, a hand-held device which used two images side by side to give a 3-D effect. The "stereopticon", despite its name, used only a single image, and did not produce a 3-D effect. The advertisement and review quoted are from the December 21st and 28th issue of the *Philadelphia* (PA)*Bulletin*, respectively. Beale was encouraged to go to the show by his art teacher, Professor McNeil, who took a great interest in him, and gave him a complimentary ticket.
23. Beale's career as a student at Central is documented in his diary, while the curriculum he underwent is described in detail in Controllers of the Public Schools, *Annual Reports*, 1858–1862.
24. Peale, *Graphics.* Beale borrowed this book from school for home study (Beale, *Diary*, February 9, 1859), as well as Simon DeWitt's *Elements of Perspective* (August 25, 1862). Elizabeth Johns, "Drawing Instruction at Central High School" discusses the effect of the Central art education – particularly perspective drawing – on Beale's famous schoolmate Thomas Eakins, and, by implication, suggests its effect on Beale.
25. For a description of how the horizontorium perspective is created see Girling, *Stereoscopic Drawing*, 19-28. Beale's horizontorium has been lost, but I found this horizontoirum slide image in a set of architecture slides. It is a Philadelphia bank, and is a copy of the only known American print of a horizontorium, so it is probably the image Beale used as a model (Baker, *Horizontorium*).
26. Teale, "Stereoscopic Effects", 155–157.
27. One of Beale's slides, "The Eruption of Mt. Pelee" ("Destruction of St. Pierre, No. 2, People Fleeing") uses an unusual perspective device, one that could only be created with the magic lantern, a technique that might be called *thick glass perspective*. The distant volcano in the scene is painted on the opposite side of the glass from the rest of the picture, putting it slightly out of *focus* when projected. This gives the volcano the hazy *atmospheric perspective* that it would actually have if seen at a distance. The slide is the second in a dissolving set. The first is a distant view of the volcano, so this slide is in effect a "dissolving zoom".

28. Cinerama Exhibitors, *Seven Wonders*. In 1956, film artist Mario Larrinaga copied – without attribution – most of Beale's *Seven Wonders* perspective drawings to dramatize ancient sites in Lowell Thomas' CINERAMA movie production of *Seven Wonders of the World*.
29. The ivorytype, invented by Frederick Wenderoth in 1855, was a complex photographic process that produced a highly colored image with a "3-D" feel to it (Osterman, "Ivorytype").
30. For the course of study at the Academy see Bolger, *In This Academy*. Beale's study of the muscles using a "recent subject" began on January 16, 1861 (Beale, *Diary*). He also read books on the subject, like J. R. Smith's *The Key to the Art of Drawing the Human Figure* (Beale, *Diary*, May 3, 1862).
31. Letter of C. W. Briggs to J. B. Beale, November 30, 1910, BC/ LMNA. Briggs complains of Tholey's drawings and asks Beale to rework them.
32. Controller of Public Schools, *Report of Examiners*. The report provides a detailed description of the examination for Professor of Drawing, including all the questions, and the scores of the top three candidates. Beale was exultant with his new position, as is evident in his quoted comment, written on his first day of school as Professor, October 15, 1862 (Beale, *Diary*).
33. All inflation calculations are based on The Inflation Calculator, based on records of the U. S. Department of Labor. https://www.in2013dollars.com/
34. Beale, *Diary*. During his first year Beale comments regularly about his teaching activities: December 15, 1862; May 15, 1863; June 2, 1863. Milliette, "Art Annals" includes a section on Beale's career at Central and mentions that he was also teaching at the Polytechnic College and Crittenden's Commercial College in Philadelphia during the same period. An article from *The Daily Evening (PA) Bulletin*, March 1, 1866, pasted in Beale's diary on that date, indicates that he was also teaching one night a week at the Spring Garden Night School, apparently a charity institution. Busy!
35. Letters. Beale wrote long letters to his parents, from the war front, now in the Beale Papers, CC/HSP. He then re-wrote the information as journal entries. The quotation is from the Beale, *Diary*, July 13, 1863. A number of accounts of Beale's life indicate he submitted Civil War sketches to *Leslie's* and *Harper's* and that they were published. Beale does mention (June 20, 1863, *Diary*) sending a sketch to *Leslie's*, but never says that it was published. A letter from Beale's great niece, Elizabeth Vogel, to Arthur Colen (November 12, 1935) in CC/HSP takes the sketching story one step further and claims that Beale's Civil War pictures "were found on his person and he was held as a spy, but was released after a great deal of trouble". This is too good a story not to have been repeated if it were true; but even Colen never repeated it.
36. Beale, *Diary*, July 7 and 8, 1863.
37. Beale, *Diary*, December 12, 1864.
38. Beale, *Diary*. On February 4, 1863 Beale took the family children to see a magic lantern show in a church; on June 2, 1863 he attended a stereopticon lecture; on August 28, 1863 he attended another lantern show in church with the children; on March 31, 1864 he attended a stereopticon benefit at the High School for the Sanitary Fair; and on May 2, 1864 he attended a phantasmagoria benefit for the same cause.
39. Beale, *Diary,* October 15, 1863.
40. Beale, *Diary*, April 21, 1865. Professor Henry Morton began writing for *The Magic Lantern* in its third issue, November 1874.

Chapter Three. Training for Narrative Art

1. Beale, "Baseball Match", 733. Beale, "Burning of Union League", 604.
2. Unidentified newspaper article.
3. Beale's breakthrough to professional illustration and his later work at *Harper's* are described in a draft job-hunting letter to *Harper's*, 9/15/09, while his work for *Leslie's* is described in a similar letter to The Butternut Publishing Company, Jan. 1910, both in BC/LMNA. The circumstances surrounding Beale's departure from Central are a little mysterious. Certainly, given his success in the national papers, it makes sense that he left to launch a new career. But an untitled clipping from the September 12, 1866 *Philadelphia Daily Evening Bulletin*, pasted in the back of Beale's diary, carries this columnist's comment about Beale's departure: "We know of no satisfactory reason why Joseph B. Beale ... should have been removed", suggesting that he did not leave Central voluntarily. Perhaps this was simply a reportorial misunderstanding. It certainly seems highly unlikely that Beale had been "removed", as six months later he was awarded the Master of Arts degree from Central in recognition of his contributions there, a fact reported in a Feb. 14, 1867 clipping that Beale pasted right below the 1866 "know of no satisfactory reason" remark.
4. Adler, "Always Have Paris". Sellin, *Turning Point*, n36.
5. Lomas, "Philadelphia Sketch Club", 14. Sellin, *First Pose*, n36. Beale's entries in the Grand National Exhibition included "Grave Scene from Hamlet", and "Moonlight". (Falk, *Annual Exhibition Record*, 452.)
6. Marriage information is from Ancestry.com, though no certificate is cited. Beale, in letters to his nephew William Louis Taffard, on September 27, 1914, and in another letter, probably to the same nephew about the same time, spells her last name and that of the rest of the family as "Taffard" (BC/LMNA). The Ancestry source spells "Taffard" as "Taffer", though it does not cite any sources for that spelling. It appears from the combination of Ancestry.com and Beale's letters that Louise's father was Benjamin Toffart (spelling on Ancestry), born in France, and her mother Ann Newcomb Taffard (Beale attribution and spelling) and that Louise had, among a large number of siblings, a brother who died at Gettysburg, and another who was a drummer boy in Philadelphia (Beale letters). Louise was buried in Philanthropic Cemetery, now defunct, but "once the burial place for south Philadelphia aristocracy", according to findagrave.com, Her body was moved to Arlington Cemetery in Philadelphia when Philanthropic Cemetery was closed (Beale letters).
7. Adler, "Paris as Training Ground", 11–50.
8. Splitstone, "Our Sixtieth Birthday", 661. (Of *Leslie's* cartoon.)
9 Stern, *Life of Mrs. Frank Leslie*.
10. Davis, "How a Battle is Sketched", 661–668. Beale, "Grant Honore Wedding".
11. Lantern Society, Vice Chairman. "How I Became a Lanternist", 111.
12. Beale, draft letter to Harper Brothers, September 14, 1909 (?), **BC/LMNA**. I have not been able to locate this drawing.
13. Schoff, *Industrial Interests of Chicago*. The description of Beale's apartment building is from the text accompanying his illustration of it. (Beale, *"New Building*".) Beale also illustrated "the new office!" (Beale, "Offices of Baker and Co.") The comment about the "northern light" is from the printed text accompanying this illustration.
14. The story of the loss of Beale's work in the Chicago fire is mentioned in an unsigned 1935 memoir by an unidentified Beale cousin (Rupert?), now in The Historical Society of Pennsylvania. The story is also recounted in Arthur Colen's introduction to the Whitney Museum of American Art exhibit of Beale's work, but though Colen implies his source is a letter, this has not been found. He was probably referring to the memoir cited above. (Colen, "Introduction".)
15. The pictures of Beale and Louise were taken by Copelin Studios in Chicago.
16. A second, smaller Beale scrapbook was found in his attic. Leather-bound, it is embossed with a "J. B. Beale" on the cover. (BC/LMNA) Unfortunately, only 7 pages remain; fortunately, one of these has an ornate newspaper masthead that Beale designed, dated March 8, 1872. Beside it, Beale has written, "This is a page from my scrap book to show proofs of lettering I drew on the block. J. B. Beale". "Drawing on the block" means that Beale drew directly on the engraving block, rather than having his paper drawing transferred by others. The illustrations demonstrate Beale's skill at perspective in drawing

buildings of all sizes, his skill with ornate lettering for mastheads, and an ability, unseen elsewhere in his work, to render schematics.

17. A number of etchings with their preparatory sketches were found among Beale's effects after his death. (**BC/LMNA**) They demonstrate the wide range of activities Beale was called upon to illustrate.

18. Dahl, *Andersen-Illustrationer*. I am indebted to Mr. Dal, an expert on Andersen illustrators, for reviewing Beale's illustrations and assuring me that Beale appears to own no debt to any previous artist, though only his first image is signed.

19. The feathery forms on the left-hand side of the image are a deterioration in the image caused by dampness getting between the two pieces of glass. All of Beale's own slides were kept in damp conditions for many years at Katherine Leddick's hotel on the Champlain Canal, and unfortunately some show the results.

20. The lanternists did not use the modern names for the sound techniques described in the sidebar, but they did use the full range of effects used today: They used *diegetic sound* – sound coming from the *diegesis* of the story (the world of the story), like the conversation of characters. They used *external diegetic sound* coming from the story's environment (like an explosion); *internal diegetic sound* coming from the mind of one of the characters, and *off-screen sound*, like that of an approaching herald. They also used *non-diegetic* or *non-synchronous sound* like mood music (*sound over*), that was audible to the audience, but not to the characters in the story, and not directly related to the action on screen.

21. Beale surrounded himself with artwork that interested him. When a teenager he pasted over 100 large pictures from "pictorial papers" up on the walls of his room (Beale, *Diary*, August 13,1860). The intact scrapbook was an old checkbook of the Philadelphia Commercial Bank. Beale pasted his pictures over the unused checks. Based on internal evidence, he probably used the scrapbook in the 1860s and 70s.

22. Darley's lightness of line and energy gave these pictures a dynamism that Beale's more detailed and controlled renderings rarely matched. For that matter, Darley rarely matched it himself, one critic noting that Darley's early art reveals "a crude vitality often lacking in his later work". (Finlay, *The Art of F. O. C. Darley*, 15.)

23. Johannsen, *House of Beadle and Adams*. Online at https://www.ulib.niu.edu/badndp/bibindex.html accessed January 19, 2003. Huntzicker, "Picturing the News".

24. Prout, *Hints on Light and Shadow*.

25. As part of his search for employment, Beale prepared a list of books he had illustrated. (Letter to Harper and Bros., 9/15/1909?). In a similar letter to the Stafford Engraving Co., 1/25/10, he mentions that he has illustrated 50 books. (Both in BC/LMNA.) The illustration for most of these books was managed by Baker and Co. In many his signed illustrations are part of a group of images, some of which are signed by other artists. In addition to illustrating about a dozen books by Alan Pinkerton, Beale illustrated one that was to become a sociological classic, Charles Nordhoff's *Communistic Societies of the United States*, and one by E. P. W. Packard, the feminist. Beale's list appears in Borton, Borton, *Before the Movies*, 189.

26. Pinkerton , *The Molly Maguires*. Pinkerton makes a point of saying that the "sanguinary" (bloodthirsty) character of the illustrations is not the fault of the designer [i.e. the artist, Beale] but of the actions of the Mollie Maguires.

27. Perkins, "Notes on Lantern Slide Making", 88.

28. Bayley, *Modern Magic Lanterns*, 81.

29. Norton, *The Lantern and How to Use It*, 113. Expert, *The Lantern*, 50, 168.

30. Blitzer, *His Story*. Billy Blitzer, the cameraman of the famous early movie director D. W. Girffith, describes how he discovered the iris in his book as a way of fading out of a scene. But his "discovery", as he admits, was fairly trivial; he simply adapted an existing iris from an old still camera to his movie camera.

31. Similar attention-concentrating effect was often obtained with *masks* on the slide itself. The most common forms of masks were the circles, ovals, oblongs, squares, and "cushions" used to frame the image, and to hide undesired elements. But masks were also used for symbolic effect: a lover might appear on screen within a heart-shaped mask; or a religious subject within a cross.

32. Editor, *Photo-Miniature*, 463. (Living statuary and block-out mask); *Editor, Magic Lantern*, 1882. April–June. (Sidebar quotation); Landy, *The Magic Lantern*, 45. (Tinters); Editor, *Photo-Miniature*, "Untitled", 448–449. (Tints added in process of developing slide.)

33. Editorial, *The Vampire Etcher*.

34. Briggs discussed his conception of comic slides in a letter to Beale on 11/22/09 (BC/LMNA), suggesting that Beale work up a few of Briggs's sketches into slide designs "to make a laugh". The non-Beale "Before" and "After" smoking set was found with Beale's own copies of his slides, and is likely the reference for Beale's dissolving set with the wooden Indian.

35. Editor, *Magic Lantern*, "Flashed Effect", 46.

36. Robison, Herbert, Crangle, *Encyclopaedia of Magic Lantern*, 149. Solomon, *History of Animation*, 37.

37. Previous accounts of Beale's life (e.g. Robb, Robb, Roylance, *Star Spangled History*) indicate that Beale returned to Philadelphia and began working on *Pilgrim's Progress* for Briggs in 1874. This chronology is almost certainly wrong, and is probably the invention of Arthur Colen. For marketing reasons, he may have found it useful to say Beale began work for Briggs that early. It would have made the designs Colen was trying to sell seem more "antique". But the evidence is all against an 1874 date. Beale is listed as residing in various addresses in Chicago in the local Directories from 1871 to 1880.

If not the 1870s, when then did Beale return to Philadelphia? A chronology of the Briggs Company, published with Briggs's help, indicates that Beale began working for Briggs in 1880. (Sipley, *One Hundred Years*). Beale himself says 1881. (J. B. Beale, letter to nephew, William Louis Taffard, September 27, 1914 (BC/LMNA). The 1881 date is associated with the death of Beale's wife Louise on April 23, 1881. It seems most likely that Beale returned to Philadelphia to bury her there as she had requested, and once there, he stayed.

38. Beale may have created a mural for the Second Presbyterian Church, but the church was torn down when the congregation merged with the First Presbyterian in the mid-20th century.

39. At various times Beale lived at 39 Tulpehocken St., 72 Tulpehocken St., 72 East Washington Lane, and 43 Pastorius St., all in the Germantown section of Philadelphia. Briggs lived at 59 East High St., also in Germantown.

40. The shadow of Dr. Beale's trial for rape back in 1854 still fell over the Beale home. In 1892, just when Beale was starting full-time work with Briggs, William Rehfuss published what was to become a standard in the field of dental law. (Rehfuss, *Dental Jurisprudence*, pp. 87–97). It probably went unnoticed by the general public, but certainly not by the dental circles frequented by Stephen and Alonzo Beale, Joseph's dentist brothers, and certainly not by the wider Beale family. Rehfuss devoted 10 pages to the Beale trial itself, to a discussion of how rape might be imagined under ether. He mentions the eventual pardon of Dr. Beale, but the overall effect is to suggest that Dr. Beale may well have been guilty. In any case, to have the trial raised up again must have been profoundly upsetting to a family that thought this tragedy was buried 40 years in the past.

41. Beale's pictures of his family were found when his studio was cleared out, and are now in the BC/LMNA. The portrait of Beale was taken by the F. Gutekunst studio, of Philadelphia. Pictures of Pa and Ma, taken at the same studio in the same format, are dated on the back in pencil, April 23, 1886, so it is reasonable to think that Joseph's was taken the same year, if not the same day.

42. Rupert Beale, "Memoir". Rupert was Joseph Boggs Beale's nephew.

43. The "talks too much" incident is recounted by Beale in his diary, September 29, 1856, when Beale was 15. (He concludes the tale by saying simply, "Pa wrote the note".)

44. Miller, Fredric, Allen, *Still Philadelphia: A Photographic History*, 1890–1940.
45. Earle (?) B. Hart, Art Editor of *The Graphic*, letter to Beale, May 2, 1882. The letter thanks Beale for submitting a picture, and requests that Beale serve as a stringer. An undated *Graphic* press pass suggests that he did indeed serve in that capacity. Both in the CC/HSP.
46. Beale to Butternut Publishing Company, drafted on the back of a January 25, 1910 letter (BC/LMNA). This same letter is the source for the salary information mentioned above.
47. Macdonald, *Anatomy of Comics: Famous Originals of Narrative Art*, 21.

Chapter Four. The Power of Early Lantern Techniques

1. Robinson, Herbert, Crangle, *Encyclopaedia of Magic Lantern*. Rossell, *Laterna Magica/Magic Lantern*. Mannoni, *Great Art of Light and Shadow*. Barnes, *Optical Projection*. Barnes, "History of the Magic Lantern". Robinson, *Peep Show to Palace*. Rossell, *Living Pictures*; Lipton, *Cinema in Flux*. Rossell, *Birth of Cinema*.
2. Mannoni, *Great Art of Light and Shadow*, 28-45. Rossell, *Laterna Magica/Magic Lantern*, 19–27.
3. The quotation is translated from the caption of a Dutch 1781 engraving reprinted in Balzer, *Optical Amusements* on page 7.
4. *Boston Evening Post*, December 3, 1743. Originally held in the Judson Collection, The Magic Lantern Castle, San Antonio, TX. Current location unknown.
5. The standard taxonomy of slides is Barnes, "Classification of Magic Lantern Slides", 75–84.
6. A description of the "jiggle technique" is contained in a children's book reprinted by the Magic Lantern Society: Robin Ranger, *The Magic Lantern*, 51.
7. W. A. R., *OMLA*, "Reminiscences, First Lantern Show", 36–37.
8. Chairman, Vice, The Lantern Society, *OMLJ*, 1891, "How I Became a Lanternist", 111.
9. Norton, *The Lantern and How to Use It*, 112.
10. Lipton, *Cinema in Flux*, 6.
11. Toulet, *Birth of the Motion Picture*,17.
12. Editor, "Notes, Hatch", *OMLA*, 27.
13. Hasluck, "Cinematograph Management".
14. Unknown, "La Phantasmagorie", *La Feuille Villageoise*, 1793, 506–507. Quoted in Mannoni, 144.
15. Rhodes, *American Horror Film*, 72–75.
16. A projected ghost may have arrived in America even earlier, in 1796. Heard, *Phantasmagoria*, 179, 270–271.
17. Barber, "Phantasmagorical Wonders".
18. Barnouw, *Magician and Cinema*. See also, Barber, "Phantasmagorical Wonders", and Heard, *Phantasmagoria*.
19. Reyniere, *Le Courrier des Spectacles*.
20. Phantom, "How to Raise a Ghost", 23.
21. Beale's two dissolving zooms are *Destruction of St. Pierre* and *The Enchanted Grotto*.
22. Wilson, "New and Novel Effects", 2–3.
23. Wilson "Abide With Me", ("Flight of the Soul"). McIntosh, *Projection*
24. Hand, A Practiced. "The Magic Lantern", 137–139.
25. Moore, "Size or Realism",55–56.
26. Wilson, "How to Start a Show", 35.
27. Sabin, "Ally Sloper". See also, Petersen, *Comics, Manga, and Graphic Novels*, 90–93.
28. Aside from its family interest, this picture of our 1940s show is very unusual. It is the one of the very few photographs (rather than illustrations) of people watching an entertainment magic lantern show before modern hobbyists (or professionals) began re-creating shows.
29. Beale, *Diary*, October 15, 1863 and May 2, 1864.
30. Editor, "Lantern Explosion", 95. Welling, *Photography in America*, 209.
31. Wells, "Magic Lantern in Churches".
32. Broadside of Professor Boden's Grand Exhibition, 1870s, BC/LMNA.
33. Altogether, Beale created 168 effect dissolve slides, in 54 different sets or groups, or about 8 percent of his total slides. They appear in about 20 percent of his sets or groups. He also created 9 superimpositions.
34. Beale only used the *matte* technique for making dissolves about a half-dozen times that we are sure of: *The Moonshiners; Tramp, Tramp, Tramp; The Good Samaritan; Faust*; and *Marley's Ghost*.
35. Expert, An, *The Art of Projection*, 52. The Expert describes these techniques; the terms are my own.
36. Nicol, "Lecturing with the Lantern", 524.
37. Hand, A Practiced, "The Magic Lantern", 137–139.
38. For a fascinating explanation of how chromatropes achieve their effects, see Brown, "How Chromatropes Work", https://kieranbrowne.com/research/how-chromatropes-work/
39. Baum, *The Marvelous Land of Oz*,153.
40. Lipton, *Cinema in Flux*, 27 and xi.
41. Musser, *Before the Nickelodeon*, 186.
42. Lipton, *Cinema in Flux*, 51–53.
43. For a beautifully rendered video on "The Wheel of Life", produced by Museu del Cinema see https://youtu.be/-0bqmzLc9ZA/
44. According to Briggs, the "Dancing Skeleton" was developed by his employee, Stephan A. Morse. Letter from C. W. Briggs to Louis W. Sipley, May 22, 1938, SC/GEM. Nonetheless, Sipley, curator of the American Museum of Photography, continued to give Briggs credit for inventing it. See Louis Sipley, *American Museum of Photography*, 7. For a broader discussion see Brooker, Crangle, Gilbert, *The Magic Lantern Dancer*.
45. Quoted in Sipley, "W. & F. Langenheim".

46. Chairman, Vice, "How I Became a Lanternist", 111.
47. Kattelle, "The Marcy Sciopticon". The term, "sciopticon", became another of the many names for a magic lantern.
48. Robinson, "The Rise and Fall of the Triple Lantern".
49. Kember, Crangle, "Folk Like Us". 118–133,
50. Reader, "Clerical Lantern Work", 161.
51. For Bamforth speed record: Editor, *OMLJ*,"Prominent Men", 8. For "absurd" comment: Editor, "Notes", February, 1895.
52. Hrabalek, *Lanterna Magica Optisches Spielzeug.*
53. See Smith, "Aladdin", and W. F. Ryan, "Limelight".

Chapter Five. The Magic Lantern Sweeps America

1. Borton, Borton, "How Many Lantern Shows", 105–115.
2. Schaefer, "Illuminating the Devine", 296. Rossell has also concurred with this estimate. Rossell, *Chronology of Birth of Cinema*, 4.
3. McAllister, *Catalog of Stereopticons;* Borton and Borton, *Before the Movies*, 184–185. This is a list of 113 companies carrying Beale's slides, with the top fifteen starred.
4. McAllister, "Superb New Lantern Slides", advertisement in *National Geographic*, 1911.
5. Marcus, "Civil War Through Magic Lantern", 58–62.
6. The most thorough study of the American magic lantern is an unpublished thesis, Barber, "Evenings of Wonder". Barber has published several articles in the academic press based on this thesis.
7. Borton, "Professional Life", Parts 1 and 2.
8. McAllister, *Catalogue, 1892, 1900;* McIntosh, *Projection Apparatus*, 1913, 1916. Pages were counted "as a whole", so some roughness in the data exists when several categories overlap on the same page. "Secret Society" refers to slides used in the rituals of fraternal societies such as the Masons.
9. These vignettes are a selection from the on-line museum that I have curated, "The Museum of American Magic Lantern Shows", www.magiclantern-museum.org.
10. "Broadsides Wall", Slide, 1890s; "Wanted", Slip slide,1890s; "Post No Bills", Lever slide, 1890s; A. R. Robertson Hammer,1886; Bill Poster's Business Card, ca.1900.
11. "The Convention of Corpulency", Bunnell's Museum. 1880s; P. T. Barnum's "New & Greatest Show on Earth" (Advertising Receipt),1880s; "Fat Man", Slip slide, 1850s; "Stereopticon Advertising Receipt", see McAllister, *Catalogue of Stereopticons*, 1905. See also, Kember, *Marketing Modernity.*
12. Blum, "Lecture Flyer", pasted in Blum, *Old England and New England*, 1853; Slides, *Hamlet # 1, Merry Wives of Windsor # 8* by Beale, 1910, 1913.
13. "Stereopticon or Mirror of the Rebellion". Broadside, October 29 (1864); "Sheridan's Final Charge at Winchester". Slide, copyright permission of Faulkner and Allen, A. D. Handy Co. ca. 1886.
14. "Instructive & Amusing Exhibition". Broadside, Funk & Putnam. ca.1880; *Drunkard's Daughter* #5, 1882, slide by Beale.
15. "Lloyd's Round Trip Over Land and Sea". Broadside, 1870s; Slides: "Rock Climbing", 1880s; "Statue of Liberty", triple dissolve, 1890s.
16. "Free of Charge", Flyer, The Keystone View Co. 1893; "Quincy Market", Slide with Descriptive Card, Keystone View Co. 600 Set, ca. 1920. See also, Willis, "The Keystone 600", 231.
17. Quillay, "Pennsylvania Hospital for the Insane", 112-113. Also, Haller, Larsen, "Persuading Sanity". Illustration: "Should Prison Life Punish or Redeem?" *Illustrated London News*; Postcard, "Hospital, Middletown, Conn.", ca. 1920; Slip slide, "Man to Ass", ca.1890. See also Haller, Larson, "Persuading Sanity", 263.
18. "Lincoln Chautauqua", Poster, Lincoln Chautauqua Bureau, 1915; Postcards: "Auditorium of the Richmond Chautauqua", and "Chautauqua Train", ca.1900. See also Borton, "238 Eminent Chautauqua Showmen".
19. Fred G. Andrews, "Grand Magic Lantern Exhibition", Flyer, Dec. 26, 1884; "Laterna Magica" box for children's lantern and slides, ca. 1890; "Children's lantern Slide", ca. 1900; See also Hrabalek, *Laterna Magica* and Bak, "History of Toy Magic Lantern".
20. Stoddard, "Portrait", Print, ca.1890. "It Made Him Feel Dizzy", Newsprint Advertisement. ca.1890; "Stoddard, Madrid to Moscow", Ticket, ca. 1890. See Barber, "Roots of Travel Cinema".
21. "Burton Holmes, Himself", Promotional Pamphlet, 1918–19; "Burton Holmes", Photograph, 1907; Soule, promotional headshot, ca 1950. See also: Caldwell, *Burton Holmes Travelogues.*
22. Peck, "Story of the Conquest of Huascaran", Advertisement; Miss Annie S. Peck. Photograph. ca.1900; Hubbard, "Traveler and Explorer", Advertisement, *Talent*, 1906; "Labrador", 1900s, British slide.
23. "Illustrated Lectures by Katherine Gordon Breed", Pamphlet, 1898-99; Breed/Holmes, carriage photo: Caldwell, *Burton Holmes Travelogues*, 35; "Yellowstone Falls", Slide colored by Breed, ca.1900.
24. Hynes, *Negro Looking Up.*
25. Hazley, "Something New! Africa at your Door", Flyer, 1883; "Station to Liberia", Woodcut. "African women", Slide, 1920s.
26. "Devil's Kitchen", Broadside, 1920s; "Stereopticon Lectures at Colored Seventh Day Adventist Church", Flyer, 1929; Slides: "Prophet", Albert Prieger Co. 1920s; "Sunday School", 1920s.
27. "Terror of the West", *Puck*, 1882. "Sirs, thare is an article", Unidentified Letter, 1887. "Williams Family" photo, Martin, Fisher, "Willims Traveling Picture Show".
28. "Alaska, Klondike Gold Fields", Broadside, Sears Roebuck & Co. 1898; "Placer Mining", slide by the Keystone View Co., ca. 1900.
29. Brigham, "Illustrated Lectures", Advertisement, 1906; "Unkapupa the Critic", logo, *The Lyceumite.* 1906; "Grand Canyon from Grand View", Slide by F. J. Haynes, 1900s.
30. Harry Ellsworth Feicht, "Oberammergau", Brochure for Pike Opera House, 1890s; Slides: "1910 Oberammergau Cast", "Christ".
31. Flyer, "Coming Prophetic Events", 1894; "India her heritage and handicaps", Missionary handbook and sample page, 1920s; "Seven Headed Beast", Slide by Albert Prieger, 1920s.
32. Edward Curtis, "New Chest-Pegan", portrait, off-set lithographic plate, 1895–1918; Edward S. Curtis, "The Intimate Story of Indian Tribal Life", Program, 1911; Red Fox, "The Famous Blackfeet Interpreter of American Indian Music and Poetry", Flyer, ca.1915. See also The Curtis Legacy Foundation, https://www.curtislegacyfoundation.org/edward-curtis.

33. "Hiawatha's Departure", Inserted chromolithograph color ad, *The Lyceumite*, November 1903; Bowden portrait, advertisement, *The Lyceumite*, July, 1905; Bowden's original slide from "Hiawatha", 1903, courtesy of Valparaiso University Archives & Special Collections.
34. D. B. Nettz, "Coming Soon", Broadsides, 1900s; Slides: "*Life of Grant # 9, Ten Nights in a Bar Room # 8, Uncle Tom's Cabin # 3, all* by Joseph Boggs Beale. Dates respectively:1881–1893, 1882, 1887.
35. Calling card for Alexander Black. Images from Black, *Miss Jerry*. 59. See also Askari, "Photographed Tableaux", 194. Film Preservation Foundation, *Alexander Black*.
36. Mary Proctor, "Popular Lectures on Astronomy", Brochure, 1890s; Mary Proctor Letter, Oct. 4, [18]97; "Chautauqua Auditorium", *Frank Leslie's Illustrated Newsletter*, September 4, 1880; "Ring Nebula", Slide, 1959.
37. "Famous Outlaws" [Bonnie & Clyde]. Broadside, 1934; Slides: Photographic Slide of Clyde, courtesy of the website, "Bonnie & Clyde's Hideout", https://texashideout.tripod.com/bc.htm; Lantern Slide of robbery from *Drunkard's Career*, 1894.
38. "The Lights and Shadows of a Great City", Broadside. 1890s; Slides: "Typical Tough", "Bar Scene", 1890s.
39. Tracy, *Mississippi of Intemperance*, Broadside, 1880s. The quote and description are adapted from *Geographicus Rare Antique Maps* and other sources. https://www.geographicus.com/P/AntiqueMap/mississippiofintemperance-tracy-1882.
40. Top image "Madison Square, New York on Election Night", *The Brooklyn Daily Eagle*. 1891, November 4, cover, "Immense Crowds Eagerly Scan the Bulletins". 877; Bottom image and quotation: "Election Night in New York City", 1116; Second quote, bottom: "Election Night in New York City", 1122.
41. "Hunting Clothing, Andersonville Prison" by or after James Taylor, Slide, 1889: "The Boys of '61, or Four Years of Fighting", by Charls Coffin, Wikipedia Commons; This Evening Remember!! Heroes and Battlefields", Broadside, Chas. N. Thomas. 1890s; "Sutro Baths", Streetcar Poster, 1900.
42. "Cuba, The Maine, The Cuban War". Broadside, Sears Roebuck Co., 1900; Slides: "Maine Explosion", Beale. 1898; "Maine Sunk", photographic slide. 1898. Both slides by Sears Roebuck Co.
43. "Wonderful Animated Moving Picture Exhibition", Broadside, Sears Roebuck Co., 1900; "Announcement of Attractions", Booklet, Pond Agency, 1933–1934; "Triple Lantern", *Stereopticon Film Exchange Catalog*, 1899.
44. "European War, Wonderful Views in Natural Colors", Broadside, Novelty Slide Co. 1914; Slides: "French Infantry", "German Dirigible", Novelty Slide Co. 1914.
45. "Magic Lantern Showman", Tintype, 1870s; "Yosemite", Slide, 1890s.

Chapter Six. The Business Vision of Briggs, The Screen Art of Beale

1. Herbert, *Magic Lantern Inventions*, 7–70.
2. Information about Briggs is drawn from the following: "C. W. Briggs, Dean of Photographers"; "Movie Pioneer, 92", an unattributed article in the BC/LMNA; Laura Lee, "Granddaddy of Movies", 94, Didn't Think They'd Amount to Anything", *Philadelphia Bulletin*, March 19, 1941; and, Patterson, "Cinema Chrysalis", 11. All of these articles contain a great deal of misinformation, giving Briggs credit for the invention of slip slides, lever slides, the Ratcatcher, etc.
3. Sipley, "The Magic Lantern", 39–90. Sipley's contention (p. 42) that Briggs dominated the slide industry at this period is doubtful. The same article contains samples of the Briggs photos, and a reprint of an 1883 advertisement for the "Walk About" sets. On the front cover of the magazine is an advertisement for Briggs photo slides "made before 1883" but still available in 1939.
4. Booker, Crangle, Gilbert, *Magic Lantern Dancer*, 132–133.
5. Sipley, "Pictures of Briggs", 228–231. Sipley also says that the Briggs set of *The Bottle* is by Beale after Cruikshank, and gives a picture. (p. 231). This is almost certainly an error.
6. Bloxham, "Preparing Engravings for Lantern". The over-painting technique was used by Beale on several individual slides, and extensively in certain sets, where it was often combined with his own work, most notably in *Evangeline*, the Shakespeare plays, *Rip Van Winkle*, and *The Legend of Sleepy Hollow*. Since it is impossible to draw a line on the degree of originality, we have counted a work as "by Beale" if we can tell that he worked on it.
7. Sipley, "Celebration".
8. The "eyesore" comment is in Register, "Dissolving with Precision", 112–113. The "100 times" comment is Sipley, "Pictures of Briggs", 228.
9. Beale also did a little matching out, particularly in preparing sets like *Evangeline*, when he was also doing original designs. As long as Beale's contribution is clear, we have counted these images as part of his oeuvre.
10. The Maison de la Bonne Presse in France produced beautifully rendered illustrated slides, but not until 1896, well after Briggs and Beale began work.
11. Reader, "Clerical Lantern Work", 161.
12. Kember and Crangle, *Folk Like Us*.
13. See Borton, Borton, *Before the Movies*, 65–66 for a more complete discussion of Nisle and the other Briggs artists. Nisle's full name is unknown.
14. Sipley, "Pictures of Briggs", 228–231.
15. Schaefer, "Lantern and Religious Pedagogy", 283. See also Malan, "Gustave Dore: Lantern Slides", 1–7.
16. Briggs, *Ledger*, SC/GEM. The entry under Milligan's account, September 12, 1890, mentions a lantern for Beale. On October 1, 1890 Beale is transferred to the "Major Account" section, indicating that he is doing increasing work for Briggs.
17. The first credits for Beale images in the extant catalogs are in McAllister, *Catalogue of Stereopticons*, 1892, which suggests a more formal relationship beginning in that year.
18. Entries in the 1891 *Briggs Ledger* (8/18/1905, 12/18/1908, 8/20/1909) suggest that Beale was paid by the piece, depending on complexity, with perhaps a monthly retainer against which he worked. Arthur Colen, Beale's first collector, claimed he was paid $17.50 a painting or between $35–40 a week, about between about $1,230 and $1,400 in 2025 dollars. (Editor, "The Professor"). This assertion seems unlikely, given Beale's long history of employment at $50+ a week. Perhaps the $35 was a minimum, or perhaps it was a per -picture price. If Beale continued to average his previous $50 a week, or $2,500 for a 50-week year, that would be about $88,000 in 2025 dollars, roughly the average that a commercial artist makes today as reported by Salary.com.
19. The "wet collodion" process and ways to obtain the correct exposure were the subject of extensive discussion in the trade literature. See for instance, Chute, "Making Lantern Slides", 106; Beadle, "Lantern Slide Making", 37; Vulte, "Lantern Slides from Engravings", 319. *The Photo-Miniature* claimed that the wet collodion process was not superior in its ability to capture tonality, but was better for commercial purposes because the process was relatively inexpensive and produced consistent results, even from negatives of "very moderate quality". (*Photo-Miniature*, 1898, 452).
20. *New York Daily Tribune*, "Illustrated Lecturing: Pleasant and Lucrative Field Open to Women of Ability", July 3, 1909, 6. The numbers of photographers and colorists cited at Briggs are from "700 Old Pictures Found in Trunks", a newspaper article, publisher and date unknown, found in the SC/GEM.

21. Borton, "Outstanding Colorists", 3–23. Moens, "Luminous Colours of Magic Lantern", 30.
22. Editor, *The Photo-Miniature*, December 1899, 467.
23. Editor, "Spurious Colored Slides", 57. The author also reports that, "Mr. Briggs says said dealer has copied many of his slides – the more reason for rejecting them".
24. Sipley, "Philadelphia Presents", and "Pictures of Briggs". Also see Shepard, "Lantern Slide in Entertainment".
25. Gage and Gage, *Optic Projection*, 689.
26. A copy of the *Old Black Joe* letter of Beale to Briggs (11/22/05) discussing the coloring of slides is in the BC/LMNA. It was made from the original at SC/GEM; current whereabouts of the original is unknown. The SC/GEM contains a notebook of Beale's in which he provides color specifications for military uniforms. Extensive color notes and sketches for military, secret society, and flag slides are also in the SC/GEM collection.
27. Quoted in Toulet, *Birth of the Motion Picture*, 24.
28. Woodbury, "Various Colours on Lantern Plates", 5.
29. Borton, "How Many Beale Slides Sold? 14. The percentage of Beale images to the overall catalog slide offerings is based on a detailed examination of the 1910-1911 McIntosh Stereopticon Company catalog. These estimates are for the 1890–1908, the period for which I could find catalogs, not the full range of Beale's work with Briggs, 1881–1917.
30. Borton, "Professional Life, 1 & 2".
31. The McAllister catalog of 1897, for instance, lists Beale's name extensively along with those of other artists, but only in the "Bible" and in the "Artistic Gems" sections (which includes "Masterpieces of Prominent Artists").
32. Beale, Letter to C. W. Briggs, Dec. 8, 1909, in BC/LMNA.
33. Eight early 20" square designs appear to be original Beale work. He appears to have been experimenting with a larger format than the 13" square design he settled on.
34. Farrington, "Photography and Illustration", 118.
35. It is difficult to overstate the degree to which the criteria of tonality in lantern slides was *the* central technical quality stressed by photographic authorities. See for instance, Stieglitz, "Remarks on Lantern Slides", 204–206; Wilson, "Lantern Slides", 400; Editor, *American Amateur Photographer*, "Lantern Slides", 469; For the "tar and whitewash" comment see Bothamley, "Sunlight in Lantern Slides", 60.
36. The maximum range of brightness from a paper image was 1:40; from a projected transparency, 1:100. (Milner, *Making Lantern Slides*, 15–20.)
37. The compensating cover-glass method Stieglitz used was to overdevelop his lantern image, and reduce his values locally by means of an under-exposed negative image on the cover glass. By combining the two, he created a fuller range of tone. (Editor, *The Photo-Miniature*, 1898, 448–449.)
38. McCullough, *Americans in Paris*, 348.
39. Bothamley, "Sunlight in Lantern Slides", 63.
40. Editor, "*Photo-Miniature*, Editorial", 428–429.
41. Monod, "Theater to Film"; Vardac, *Stage to Screen*.
42. Editor, *American Amateur Photographer*, "Lantern Slides", 488.
43. The only exception to this description: Beale includes in this scene an illustration based on lines that occur much earlier in the poem – a description of the judge gazing into the "marble hearth's bright glow" where he watched "sweet Maud Muller hazel eyes" in the flickering fire.
44. Arthur Colen, who publicized Beale's work after his death, claimed that Beale's style was influenced by Dore, and cites letters as evidence. (Colen, "Introduction, Drawings by Beale", 23.) No doubt Beale was influenced by the most famous illustrator of his time; he had a leather-bound copy of Dore's *London: A Pilgrimage* among his effects when he died. But I have not found any Beale letter about Dore's influence, such as Colen claims, nor any comment in any other context. The similarity of style that Colen noted might well have come from the fact that Beale re-drew 26 of Dore's works, which were then re-attributed to Beale in the catalogs.
45. Beale, Seymour, "Line in Pictorial Photography", 175. (Seymour Beale, no relation to Joseph.)
46. Borton, "How Many Beale Slides Sold?", 7.

Chapter Seven. Beale's Narrative Techniques

1. Bettmann, *Portable Archive*, 3.
2. Farrington, "Photography and Illustration", 115–117. Farrington's examples are all photographic, but his point applies equally well to illustrated slides such as Beale's.
3. Casteras, *The Defining Moment*, 14.
4. Brown, *How Films Tell Stories*, 10.
5. Elsaesser, Buckland, *Studying American Film*, 80–88.
6. *Photographic Times* Editor, "Copyright", 295.
7. Wilson, "My Catalog", 79. The praise of Wilson's work appears in *The Magic Lantern* three years later, when he was backing out of his *vertically integrated* business – production, distribution, *exhibition* – to concentrate on exhibition alone (Wilson, "Editorial", 5).
8. Several of the examples in this chapter are from the period between the introduction of the movies in America (1896) and Beale's layoff because of competition from the movies (1909). That is because this chapter focuses on the working sketches and storyboards found in Beale's studio after his death, and most of that material is from the end of his magic-lantern career. As we shall see, Beale and Briggs certainly changed their *content* after the birth of the movies, but little evidence suggests that Beale, the *metteur en scene*, or "master of the scene", changed his *artistic approach*. The cinematic solutions we see him developing in these draft documents are also evident in many of the completed designs from his earlier work, though not necessarily in the work of the first few years.
9. Creating an "establishing view" in this case was more difficult than most because the first four lines of the poem place the children crying in bed, before switching to the living room scene. Beale chose (wisely I think) to ignore those first few lines.
10. Sometimes the finished designs did not represent the *final cut* or *release print*. The George Eastman Museum contains examples of designs that have been re-painted for other purposes, making the originals examples of *outtakes*.
11. Rosenbloom, "Slowing Down".
12. In the scene of Annie and Willie praying, the text mentions the mother's rocking chair. As we have discussed, it is removed in the scene of Father and Aunt

setting up the presents. But in the final two scenes, a new side chair appears. In slide 5 it is set beside the bed. In slide 6, the final scene, it is moved to the center of the image, where Father sits on it to cuddle his children.

13. Ebert, Siskel, *Future of Movies*, 261.
14. Fletcher, *Wonderworks: Science of Stories*, 17, 47.
15. Meisel, *Realizations: Narrative, Pictorial Art*, 30
16. Cohn, Magliano, "Visual Narrative Research".
17. Bordwell, *Narration in the Fiction Film*, 35-40.
18. Eisner, *Graphic Storytelling*, 135–139.
19. Brown, *Beyond the Lines*, 68–71.
20. "Baptist Church Entertains", *Mount Vernon [NY] Daily Argus*, October 19, 1900, 2.
21. Wilkinson, *Signs and Symbols.*
22. "Amusements", *(Philadelphia) Evening Star*, January 31, 1896, 10.
23. For a discussion of our lantern version of *Ben Hur*, see Willis, "Image between Stage and Screen", 237–246.
24. Griffith, *When Movies Were Young*, 66. First published by E. P. Dutton and Co., New York, in 1925.
25. Kember, Crangle, *Folk Like Us.*
26. Other examples are "Gloria in Excelsis" in the *Christmas* set when the angels arrive before the shepherds, and "Soldier's Return" from the *War in Cuba* set when the soldier, with his back to us, is welcomed home by his family. For a non-Beale example of lantern slides that work in this fashion see, Claggett, *"Immersive Media"*. The device is a common one in artistic practice. The most famous modern example is Andrew Wyeth's *Christina's World.*
27. Eisner, *Comics and Sequential Art*, 48.
28. Borton, Borton, *Before the Movies.*
29. The technique of off-screen shadows is used in *The Village Blacksmith, Mr. Spurtz and His Auto, Tenting on the Old Camp Ground, Story of the Blind Man, Unjust Judge, Spanish American War*, and *Damon and Pythias.*
30. Robinson, Herbert, Crangle, *Encyclopaedia of the Magic Lantern*, 91.
31. Armstrong, *Victorian Glassworks*, 295. Quoted in Mura Lyons, "The Dissolving View", in *Acts of Projection*, Drake University Press, 2024, 5.
32. Guida, *A Christmas Carol*, 60.
33. In addition to "The Enchanted Grotto", Beale created several other slides with similar mechanical movements: Slide 2 of *The Knights of Pythias, Third Rank, Pythagoras* with moving goblins, and the moving fire for "Abraham Preparing for the Sacrifice" in the *Abraham and Sarah* group. Beale also created 11 other "real motion" slides, particularly comic slides, by painting two slides in which the backgrounds were registered to remained constant, but the figures moved, as in "First Cigar" that we have already seen.
34. Other examples include *Knights of Pythias, First Rank; The Raven;* and *The Little Match Girl.*
35. Hepworth, *Book of the Lantern*, 275.
36. Glebas, *Directing the Story*, 47–49. In movie parlance, the storyboard contains many scenes. The beat board presents the entire movie in a few summary images that capture the main "beats" of the film.
37. Beale was following extremely detailed art directions for this set, probably from a clergyman. (Clergyman, *Good Shepherd* Art Directions, BC/LMNA.) That may have been typical for some religious slides. A letter (Beale to Charles Clark, September 27, 1909, BC/LMNA) suggests that because of the sensitivity of dealing with different religious beliefs, precise directions were often supplied for religious subjects, and that the sketches were reviewed by a clergyman for Biblical accuracy.
38. Beale is careful to maintain what cinematographers call the *screen direction* (the right-left axis of the scene itself) and the *axis of action*, the imaginary line that runs through the characters and defines right and left, so that the good shepherd does not suddenly switch from one side of the image to the other.
39. Barber, *Evenings of Wonder*, 499. Barber points out this process in Beale's work. Sets where a changing pace of slide treatment occur include the Shakespeare plays, *The Raven, Evangeline, Curfew Shall Not Ring Tonight, Visit of St. Nicholas*, and *Paddy* and *His Pig.*
40. The story of *Paddy and the Pig* was a common one in lantern slides, as it was in the general culture. Whether a particular lantern set was a direct ancestor of Beale's presentation is unknown. Wilhelm Busch's *Simon and His Pig* is similar, but this set does not feature Paddy's opening exaltation paired with the closing debacle that makes Beale's set so effective.
41. Beale also added an establishing shot to *Leap for Life* after it had been issued without one.
42. I've never been able to find the "Northern" version of *Dixie* that this set illustrates.
43. Elsaesser, Buckland, *Studying American Film*, 173. In a few other cases Beale characters look directly at the audience, but they are not story characters. Rather they are emblematic figures such as "Uncle Sam" waving hello, the woman gesturing for the audience to be quiet in "Silence", and the couple saying goodbye to us in "Adieu". In the scene from *Mr. Spurt and His Auto*, the characters are looking at the shadow people, and by extension at us, but not directly at us.
44. Interestingly, the Bible makes no mention of a child on the Ark.

Chapter Eight. Beale's On-Screen World: Part One – Literature (SEE cross refs)

1. This estimate of the number of Beale slides is slightly higher than our previous figure of 2,078 (Borton, Borton, *Before the Movies*, 41), because we have found some additional Beale images.
2. A *Set* is a collection of slides that was presented as a unit in the catalogs – *Pygmalion and Galatea*, for instance. The lanternist was expected to buy the entire set, since it was a cohesive piece. A *Group* is a set created by my wife and myself to break large catalog categories such as *The Bible* into smaller, more understandable sections. The lanternist might purchase all the slides in a group like *Noah's Ark*, or he might purchase just a few.
3. Borton, Borton, *Before the Movies.*
4. The totals of the different groups of slides add up to more than the 2,085 that Beale created. That is because some Beale images were used for more than one subject, especially in the Historical, Religious, and Secret Society groups. The percentages of Beale's work given are based on this "multiple use" total of 2,621. For the percentage of all literature offered in the magic lantern catalogs, see p. x.
5. Paul Revere's Ride, The Bridge, The Village Blacksmith, The Wreck of the Hesperus.
6. Dicksee, Gilbert (illustrators), *Evangeline.*

7. The instructions to Beale can be seen in the margin of *Evangeline*, negative #14 in SC/GEM.
8. Why is *A Christmas Carol* called *Marley's Ghost* in the magic lantern catalogs? Probably it was an effort, albeit a weak one, to avoid copyright infringement suits. See note 18.
9. See Borton, Borton, *Before the Movies*, n.29. Almost immediately after *Uncle Tom's Cabin's* publication in 1852, a lantern show of it appeared in New York, probably simply using the book's illustrations.
10. Pumphrey, "Robinso n Crusoe". See also, "Script for *Robinson Crusoe, First and Second Series*" in BC/LMNA.
11. A lantern script in the BC/LMNA is an example. It is called *Watermill Hollow*, author and publisher unknown, probably ca.1900, clearly English. This script has multiple numeric slide designations written into it in pencil and in three different colors of ink, indicating extensive juggling of slides.
12. The six Shakespeare plays have a total of 78 images, of which only ten are signed, and six of those are in *The Merchant of Venice.* With the exception of *Merchant,* Shakespeare doesn't seem to contain much that Beale was proud of.
13. In *Romeo and Juliet*, for instance, four of the 15 slides are devoted to *Act V, Scene 3,* the death scene. In *The Merchant of Venice,* four of the 12 slides treat *Act V, Scene 1,* Portia's appearance in court and Shylock's speech. In *The Merry Wives of Windsor,* five of the 12 slides concentrate on *Act V, Scene 4. See* Barber, *Evenings of Wonder*, 499.
14. Pollin, *Images of Poe's Work*. My thanks to Dr. Pollin for his comparison of Beale's images to those by other artists. Beale signed three of *The Raven* images; several bear some resemblance to those of Gustave Doré, but are not copied from him.
15. Musser, *Emergence of Cinema*, 33–36.
16. Bacon, *Manual of Gesture*, 133.
17. We know what the original four slides were because of an unusual catalog that shows pictures of each slide. See Briggs, *1893 Picture Catalog (1892-94 Blueprint Catalog)*. The single slide from which the four-slide set grew was probably that shown in Fig. 8.22.
18. In 1895, an English lantern slide maker, Riley Brothers, made a set of life-model slides for *Ben Hur*, and the author, Lew Wallace, and his representatives sued in the United States for copyright infringement. After several permutations the case eventually established the rights of an author to any media using his work. The Beale slides were offered in some catalogs as *Ben Hur*, and in others, who were perhaps worried about a suit, as *Jewish Life*. See *OMLJ* Editor, "Notes", 1896, 92; *OMLJ* Editor, "Correspondence", 1896, 135; and *OMLJ* Editor, "Wallace v. Riley Brothers", 1896, 166.
19. "Rastus" was a common and derogatory generic name for a Black man. Pairing Blacks with mules generally, and Uncle Rastus with a cantankerous mule in particular, were part of a common trope, and the likely source, in some form, for this story. See Blades, *Negro Poems*, 32, 85.

Chapter Nine. Beale's On-Screen World: Part Two – Religion, History, Secret Society

1. Holley, *Bible in Pictures*, vii.
2. "Pulpit Advertisements", *Christian Secretary*, October 11, 1839. Quoted in Wells, "Magic Lantern in Churches", 9.
3. Wells, "Magic Lantern in Churches", 10.
4. The New Testament "Miscellaneous" category contains several sets that are simply re-groupings of previous slides (*Bible Story, First Christmas*), and an unusual set, *The Photodrama*, that is also a re-grouping, but is so unique and fascinating that I'm going to hold off telling you about it until Chapter 11.
5. McIntosh, *Projection Apparatus, 1907,* "Tissot's Paintings", 162.
6. Marshall, Warner, *James Tissot*, 163–164. Another painter who was a "competitor" of Beale's in the Religious area was Heinrich Hofmann (1824–1911), a German whose 28-slide set of *The Life of Christ* was carried in both the McIntosh and McAllister's catalogs.
7. Because of the Tissot paintings' supposed "authenticity" and their fame – and perhaps because of their previous use on screen – Tissot's scenes were imitated by filmmakers, including the Pathe' brothers (*Passion,* 1912) and D. W. Griffith (*Intolerance,* 1916). More recently, according to Fandom, the makers of *The Raiders of the Lost Ark* modeled the ark of the tabernacle on Tissot's depiction. See https://indianajones.fandom.com/wiki/James_Tissot.
8. Choi, Younsun, "Historicizing Colonial Affect".
9. In Beale's original square design, and in the 20th century reproductions of it, two smaller Indians can be seen at top left, throwing tea overboard – increasing the sense that the stamp image is derived from Beale's. The two Indians have been cropped out in this version of the slide.
10. Even the title, "Spanish–American War" suggests its importance.
11. Schuyler, James, *Dictionary American Biography*.
12. Harbach, *Motion Picture Machines*, 3. Much the same spread appeared in the catalogs of the Chicago Projection Company and the Amusement Supply Co., suggesting that Briggs may have provided this material.
13. Smith, *A People's History*, 23.
14. *OMLJ* Editor, 1892, "Notes", 99.
15. Robinson, Herbert, Crangle, eds., *Magic Lantern Encyclopaedia*, 214.
16. Borton, Borton, *Before the Movies*.153–163 (Secret Society), 117–140 (Religious). The "E" and "F" slide designations used to make these dual-use calculations are explained on p. 90. My thanks to Kyna McClenaghan, whose questions sparked this comparison.
17. For a balanced history of the Masons and estimates of their size and influence in 1903, see Ridley, *The Freemasons*, 268–270. For a detailed description of the various other orders and their rituals, see Axelrod, *Encyclopedia of Secret Societies*. For a broader look at the social service aspects of these societies, see Beito, *Mutual Aid to the Welfare State*, 3. Beito says that, "a conservative estimate would be that one of three adult males was a [fraternal] member in 1920". This is the only estimate I have found of the total secret society membership for the 19th century and later periods. The author's phone interview (Oct. 28, 2010) with Don Grant, Supreme Secretary of the Supreme Lodge of The Knights of Pythias, was also very helpful in understanding how the lantern was used in lodge work.
18. Samples are included in the BC/LMNA.
19. The "Secret Societies" guarded their rituals well, and until recently it has been extremely difficult to learn exactly what happened in their meetings. Luckily, however, masses of material have now been placed online. See, Phoenixmasonry, "Knights of Pythias".
20. Borton, Borton, *Before the Movies*, 22–23.
21. Scottish Rite Masonic Museum & Library. The Museum now sponsors an extensive website focused on fraternal lantern slides, with a particular emphasis on slides by Beale. https://srmmlonlineexhibitions.omeka.net/exhibits/show/the-secret-society-lantern—ma/the-lantern-today
22. The "Artistic Gems" category was composed of slides "Photographed from Choice Engravings of the Masterpieces of Prominent Artists". By 1911 Beale accounts for 27 or 8% of the 342 slides offered (Mcintosh, *Projection Apparatus*, E 12).

23. The "Other" category contains several smaller groups. "Mottoes" were images supported by a title, like cherubs with "Good Night", for use in magic lantern shows. The "Announcements" were similar, but included slogans useful in the movies, like "Silence". "Skirt Dancing Effects" were slides specifically designed to be projected on the dress of a moving dancer. "Hymns with Limited Distribution" were Beale hymns in special formats sold by very small catalogs.

Chapter Ten. Change Over Time – 1881 to 1909

1. For a full list of Beale's slide sets by date, see Borton, Borton, *Before the Movies*, "Appendix 2".
2. A pre-Beale set of designs for *Ten Nights in a Bar Room* exists, and slides appear in an 1875-76 catalog. The existing "Beale" designs are a different set and are reported to be on Beale's grey paper. A set of *Ten Nights* exists as Beale Owned Slides, so he probably created them, reworking the previous images, which were perhaps copied from a book.
3. Barber, *Evenings of Wonder*, 498. Barber discusses Beale's changing vantage point in the *Leap for Life* set, which shows a decidedly looser sense of stage setting than most Beale work of this period. Given the nature of the story, it would hardly have been possible to draw it from a single vantage point. The poem was also called *The Main Truck*. The magic lantern name for *The Night Before Christmas* was *The Visit of St. Nicholas*.
4. Gusfield, *Symbolic Crusade*.
5. Interestingly, the signature is in script, not the block letters Beale used later, and is also off the projected circular image – perhaps another indication that Beale did not yet appreciate the fact that he was creating material to be projected in a circular form.
6. Interchange Editor, "American Lantern Interchange Slides", 115.
7. Ten Nights in a Bar Room may have been copied from an earlier source (see note 1), so this conception of the set may not have been Beale's. On the other hand, he did not change it.
8. Beale uses cutouts similar to those in *Pygmalion* in *The Good Samaritan* (1894) and *Raid on the Moonshiners* (1895). Other than that, he opts for greater variety in his presentations.
9. The British publication, *The Optical Magic Lantern Journal and Photographic Enlarger (OMLJ)*, covered the general field well, and reached a world-wide audience, including, to judge from the Letters to the Editor, many in America. But in the period when Beale was doing his free-lance work, *illustrated* slides were simply not the major focus of *OMLJ*, or of the lanternist's repertoire of the time—on either side of the Atlantic.
10. Beach, "Lantern Slide Making", 147. *Amateur Photographer* Editor, "Lantern Slides from Illustrations", 66.
11. Musser, *Emergence of Cinema*; Robinson, *Birth of American Film*; Rossell, *Chronology of Cinema*.
12. Rossell, *Chronology of Cinema*, 17.
13. The journalist's comment is quoted in Mozley, *Eadweard Muybridge*, "Introduction".
14. Muybridge's photographic images were physically manipulated and re-photographed to elongate them and make up for the fact that he did not use an intermittent shutter. They were then copied on glass by artists, probably the artists in Briggs studio, since they were there in Philadelphia, and certainly familiar with this kind of work. Herbert, *Eadweard Muybridge*. For a visual description of the process and its result see also: https://www.youtube.com/watch?v=a-sWjIKf2cA
15. *OMLJ* Editor, "Decadence of Lantern Lectures", 225. See similar complaints in other *OMLJ* 1894 issues: April, 75; September, 138 and 144; November, 181.
16. Barnes, "Lantern Slide Work", 56. For "slide fever", see *Amateur Photographer* Editor, "Lantern Slide Methods", 158.
17. Wells, "Magic Lantern in American Churches".
18. The Sunday School enrollments cited are for 1917, the nearest approximation to our period. See Rice, *The Sunday-School Movement.*
19. Beale prepared at least 22 Old Testament slides specifically for the Sunday School project. These designs, which were all at The Biblical Arts Center in Dallas, had unusual marginal notes in the format of, "1895 Third Quarter Lesson 6" and were all signed. All of these designs were lost in the 2005 Biblical Arts Center fire, but my wife and I saw them there before the fire, and kept copies of the curator's notes. Presumably the New Testament designs were marked in the same way, but they are at Baylor University and are framed, so the margins could not be examined.
20. Schaefer, "Illuminating the Divine", 296.
21. Casper W. Briggs to Beale, November 25, 1909 (BC/LMNA). In this letter, written shortly after Beale had been let go, Briggs reminds Beale of his previous work in creating "comic designs" at $5.00 each (half the usual rate), and offers some work under the same terms again.
22. *OMLJ* Editor, "Novel Improvements", 41, and *OMLJ* Editor, "Startling Optical Novelty", 44.
23. Lumsden, "Lantern Slides", 491. Stieglitz, "To Our Readers", 24.
24. Borton, Borton, "How Many Lantern Shows?", 115.
25. Eckhart, *King of the Movies*.
26. Collaboration between the lantern manufacturers and the Secret Societies is suggested by a note in the 1892 *McAllister* catalog: "The above list gives the views generally in demand, though other views can be made to order from any engravings or designs that may be furnished".
27. Dibble, *Pop Dibble*, 851. Original manuscript, quoted courtesy of Jack Judson, The Magic Lantern Castle. Now in the Erkki Huhtamo Collection.
28. "Immense Crowds", *New Haven (CT) Union*, May 2, 1899, 1. The event was also reported in *The New Haven Daily Palladium, The New Haven Morning News* (front page). and in *The New Haven Morning Journal and Courier*. Thanks to Erkki Huhtamo for these additional references. A color movie of the American flag was available at this time, so the reaction to the flag could have been to the movie rather than a slide, but since the reference is in the context of reactions to "colored pictures" it seems most likely that it was a reaction to a slide, and if so, it seems highly likely that it was a reaction to Beale's transcendent image, or some combination of a movie and this slide.
29. On Hart's agency: *OMLJ* Editor, "Lanternists: American Enterprise", 179–180. Example of the many articles promoting the cinema to lantern lecturers: Hughes, "The Cinematograph", 9–10. The demise of the cinematograph is lamented in: Showman, "Correct Presentation of Dioramic Effects", 153.
30. McAllister, "Economic Catalog".
31. Parkes, "Dearth in Lanterndom", 67.
32. Dibble, *Pop Dibble*, 881.
33. Beale did create three additional pictures specifically for *Quo Vadis*, which became part of a smaller 30-slide set sold by the Bubb lantern catalog in 1899–1904.
34. "President McKinley", *Chicago Record-Herald*, Sept. 14, 1901.
35. Dibble, *Pop Dibble*, 880.
36. Dibble, *Pop Dibble*, 863.

37. Kleine Optical Co., "Making of Illustrated Song Slides", 129.
38. Sears Roebuck, *Motion Picture Machines, Stereopticons*, 95.
39. Moore, Bond, *Stereopticons, Moving Picture Machines*, 212.
40. The negative "dupes" are in the BC/LMNA. A 1921 Moore Bond envelope protects one of the negatives, and dates the duping process.
41. Willis, "Lantern Work, C.1900". Willis describes a similar simultaneous production of movies and slides by Bamford and Co. in England, but the two media were not intended to be used together as they were in *Peck's Bad Boy*.
42. Nicol, "Lecturing with The Lantern", 521.
43. Quoted in Musser, *Before the Nickelodeon*, 244.
44. The Keystone-Brady contract is in the BC/LMNA.
45. IMDb, https://www.imdb.com/search/title/?ref_=fn_asr_tt The subjects are *Rip Van Winkle* (8 titles), *Fire* (8 titles), *The Sausage Machine, Faust and Marguerite, Why Curfew Did Not Ring Last Night, Santa Claus' Visit.*
46. Henkes, "Christmas Films, the Magic Lantern", 97-106. Henkes argues that Beale's slide version of *The Little Match Girl* directly influenced the 1914 British film, *The Little Match Girl*, but this seems unlikely. There is no evidence that Beale's work was known in England, and no obvious relationship exists between the movie's images and Beale's, except that they illustrate the same story.
47. Kleine Optical Co., *Complete Illustrated Catalog*, 30–36.
48. Bowers, *Nickelodeon Theaters*..
49. Ripley, "Romance and Joy"; Gaudreault, "Missing Link", 139.
50. "Granddaddy of the Movies, 94, Didn't Think They'd Amount to Anything", Laura Lee, *The (Philadelphia) Evening Bulletin*, March 19, 1941.
51. Casper W. Briggs to Joseph Boggs Beale, December 18, 1908, BC/LMNA.
52. Casper W. Briggs to Joseph Boggs Beale, August 20, 1909, BC/LMNA. Most of the letters from Briggs to Beale in this period have the same testy tone.
53. Joseph Boggs Beale, draft of letter to Preston Company, Philadelphia, October 25, 1909, BC/LMNA.
54. Joseph Boggs Beale, draft of letter to Harper and Brothers, Sept. 15, 1909, BC/LMNA. Beale reminds Harper of work he has done with them before and writes, with many alternative wordings, "Now he [Briggs] writes to me that his business is about half what it used to be; it may be that the moving pictures have something to do with this falling off. He sees no prospect that warrants him in getting up more new subjects/ no prospect that we can find demand enough to warrant our working together in the future as heretofore./ He will try to keep me going and ... suggest[s that] I can be looking around, that a man of my abilities should be in demand by Publishers who seem to be prosperous ... . Since you are the latest publisher to copyright my work, I respectfully ask, "Will you remember me, please, when you have a book to illustrate". Beale attached to the letter a long list of the books he had previously illustrated. (See Borton, Borton, "*Before the Movies*, "Appendix 7".)

Chapter Eleven. A Sad Ending – A Surprise Ending

1. Joseph Boggs Beale, copy of job-hunting letter to unspecified architectural firm, Feb. 3, 1910, mentions doing perspective drawings for his brother. The letter, cigar and laxative ads are all in the BC/LMNA.
2. Casper W. Briggs to Joseph Boggs Beale, Nov. 22, 1909, BC/LMNA.
3. Shepard, "Magic-Lantern Entertainment", 92.
4. Amusement Supply Co., *Amusement for Profit*, 333–338. On the "Kinetescope" (sic) slide: Sipley, "The Magic-Lantern".
5. Wilder, *Very First Christmas*, and Stebbins, *Bible Story in Pictures*.
6. Nelson, "Propaganda for God", 230-255. Also, Lindvall, *Sanctuary Cinema*. The estimate of the percentage of *The Photodrama* using Beale's work is based on the print version. (Russell, *Photodrama of Creation*.) In Fig. 11.5, right, of *The Photodrama* the Witnesses wanted to show what was *not* true – that God condemned the Patriarchs to Hell – so Beale added the figures at bottom left. I am pleased to credit my granddaughter, Rebecca Borton, age about 5 at the time, for the discovery of the revision "patch" pasted over the original painting to change the left Beale image in Fig. 11.5 into the one at right. Her sharp eyes and low angle of vision allowed her to spot what I had missed.
7. "Prof. Joseph B. Beale: Funeral of Noted Artist Will Be Held This Afternoon". *The Philadelphia Inquirer*, Feb. 28, 1926:19.
8. Tennant, *How to Make Lantern Slides*, 472.
9. The Victor Animatograph format (3-1/4" x 4") or the "Viopticon" format (2-1/4" x 2-1/4") were both made of glass, covered with a hard collodion sheet rather than a second glass plate, and then framed in cardboard, rather than wood. (Robinson, Herbert, Crangle, eds. *Magic Lantern Encyclopaedia*, 316.)
10. Agreement between C. W. Briggs Company and Keystone Brayco, Inc., February 11, 1925, at SC/GEM. This agreement was almost immediately weakened by a supplemental agreement on May 29, also at SC/GEM, a fact which suggests that the effort may have been so unsuccessful that it was discontinued by mutual consent.
11. Agreement of Sale between C. W. Briggs Co., and Louis Walton Sipley, May 26, 1930, SC/GEM. See also BriggsCo, "Educational Filmslides" in the same collection. This catalog features Beale's work, both in the graphics and in the listings. See also Society for Visual Education, *Catalog of Film Slides*, SC/GEM. Substantial portions of this catalog are labeled as coming from C. W. Briggs Co.
12. Author's phone interview with Paul Colen, son of Arthur Colen, May 25, 1998.
13. *Time,* "The Professor", 44–45. According to Sipley's widow, Alice Sipley, Louis Sipley tried to get *Time* to correct this story, but to no avail. Author interview with Alice Sipley, Nov. 28, 1986.
14. Blitzstein, "How Fame Came".
15. Colen, "Introduction, Drawings by Beale". The catalog lists 13 paintings as from the "Collection of the Whitney Museum of American Art". An article in a fine arts magazine confirms the Whitney purchase of Beale paintings. (*Art News*, "The Whitney Museum",19.) The Whitney currently has no record of the purchase.
16. *Art News*, "Blythe and Beale" 8. Peter Banks of *Art News* and Edward Alden Jewell of the *New York Times* are quoted in "What the Critics Say", a promotional brochure of Colen's Modern Galleries, held in the archives of The Pennsylvania Academy of the Fine Arts.
17. For the attribution of this story to Briggs, see Sipley, "Pictures of Casper Briggs", 231.
18. *Art News*, "Blythe, Beale Brought to Light", 8. The *Bridget's Dream* images are listed as owned by the Whitney Museum in the Exhibit catalog (Colen, "Introduction, Drawings by Beale"), but this may have been a mistake of Colen's – intentional or unintentional – as ownership eventually devolved to the Whitneys themselves. The paintings were sold in 1959 at an auction of some holdings of Cornelius Vanderbilt (Sonny) Whitney, and bought by a New York dealer, Joseph A. Heckel, for $1,430, about $17,000 in 2025 dollars. It was seen as one of the two major purchases of the auction. From there the

paintings went to the collection of Sir John Richardson, noted art historian and biographer of Pablo Picasso, who kept them until his death and probably saw this set as "early modernist". (Gerard, "Eleanor Goes Shopping", 5.) They are now in the BC/LMNA.

19. Dorothy Grafly, "Gotham Hails 'New Cruickshank'", *The Philadelphia Record,* April 6, 1936. The story gained national exposure in *Art Digest*, (Grafly, "Beale, Betsy Ross' Great-Grandnephew".) George Cruickshank (1792–1878) was a famous British illustrator who documented the life of his time.

20. C. H. Bonte, "Beale Interest Revived at Modern Galleries". *The Phildelphia Inquirer*, April 9, 1936: 18.

21. Sipley, "Pictures of Casper Briggs".

22. Arthur Colen's first letter to Lewis W. Sipley, a polite but pointed request for proof of copyright, was on April 14, 1936. It was followed a year later, on March l0, 1937, with the letter asserting legal right to the paintings. Sipley's caustic response was on March 12, 1937, and by March 15 he had secured the signed statement from Casper W. Briggs. All are in the SC/GEM.

23. Sipley, "First Museum of Photography".

24. The George Eastman Museum (GEM) collection includes 254 Beale "designs" and 916 non-Beale designs. Some of the Beale designs, probably the best of them, were given by Briggs to the Museum in a separate transaction from the original sale to Colen. They are described in an unidentified and undated news clipping entitled "700 Old Pictures Found in Trunks" that is in the Sipley Collection at GEM. The other designs may have been donated later. Many of the Beale designs in the GEM collection are actually overpainted engravings or matched-out engravings. It is probable that Colen rejected these images when he made his selection from Briggs, as they would have been difficult to sell as originals. See Vestal, "Louis Walton Sipley". quoted in Eastman Museum, *American Century of Photography*, 1978.

25. "Honors Inventor, 91, of Animated Movie Cartoons", *The Daily News (Sudbury, PA)*, March 11, 1938: 7.

26. "Briggs Dies: Helped Establish Film Industry", *The Evening Star (Washington)/Associated Press*, June 12, 1938: 9.

27. "Movie Pioneer's Widow is 100 Years Old", *Pennsylvania Daily News*, Feb. 3, 1967: 16.

28. Maurice Ritter, "Magic-Lantern Show of Plush and Bric-a-Brac Era Honors Philadelphia Artist", *Philadelphia Evening Bulletin*, Jan. 6, 1940; and *Life*, "A Great Magic-Lantern Artist". Colen's other museum placements are described in a promotional brochure for his Modern Galleries in the archives of The Pennsylvania Academy of the Fine Arts.

29. "At the Art Center", *Fitchburg Sentinel,* (Fitchburg, MA), July 2, 1936: 1; and "Exhibit Opens at Art Center", July 2, 1936: 1.

30. Arthur W. Colen to Juliana Force, Director of the Whitney Museum of American Art, December 29, 1942, Archives of the Whitney Museum. The newspaper rotogravure sections were printed as a full page, usallly in brown ink, usually featuring a single story, and syndicated nationally, for example, "Curfew Must Not Ring Tonight", *Syracuse (NY) Herald,* Jan. 30, 1936. The creation of "History Speaks", using Beale illustrations, was reported in the press, but I have not been able to find a copy featuring Beale images. ("Educational Series", *Wisconsin Jewish Chronicle*, 7.) Likewise, I have been unable to find wallpaper using Beale's images.

31. Jasper, *Homer Laughlin China*, 23; and Atterbury, Denker, and Balkin, *Twentieth-Century Ceramics*, 112.

32. Fleer Corporation, "10,000 Teachers Using Portfolio", 11. The portfolio was also distributed through other educational channels such as *American Childhood, The Instructor, The Catholic School Journal.* Colen was ever on the alert for an opportunity. He began offering for sale a competing portfolio of Beale pictures – fee payable to himself – in the same issues of *Grade Teacher* as the Fleer promotional free give-away. No record exists of what Fleer thought of this gambit, but not surprisingly, the effort appears to have failed, and Colen's son remembers stacks of unsold portfolios sitting around the gallery. Colen, "The Beale Portfolio", 63.

33. Society for Visual Education, *S. V. E. Kodachrome Slides.* Many of the Beale Owned Slides in the BC/LMNA collection have penciled "FS" numbering on them, presumably written by Colen, to indicate their FilmStrip placement.

34. Editors, *The World Book.*

35. Quote: Bettmann, *Bettmann the Picture Man*, 51, 79. See also, Bettmann, *The Bettmann Portable Archive.*

36. Dog Art Today, "Albert Barnes and Fidèle", 1. https://dreamdogsart.typepad.com/art/2010/11/albert-c-barnes-and-fid%C3%A8le.html Letters and contract from Arthur Colen to Alfred Barnes, 11.24.43 and 12.1.43, Archives of American Art.

37. Letters from Alfred Barnes to Arthur Colen, 1.12.44 and 3.1.44. Archives of American Art.

38. This story is retold by me, adapted from Vogel, *Memories and Images*, 200–202.

39. A Set of seven slides in the BC/LMNA, was probably prepared about 1962 by a NASA contractor, Hamilton Standard Co. My thanks to Richard Kline, formerly in the Office of The Chief Engineer, NASA, for helping me understand this rather remarkable artifact.

40. Armed Forces Institute of Pathology, *List of Educational Aides.*

41. For a more detailed description of the sale of Beale's paintings, see Borton, Borton, *Before the Movies*, 27–30.

42. "Beale Exhibit", *Galveston (TX) Daily News,* Feb. 29, 1976: 118.

43. Robb, Robb, and Roylance, *Star Spangled History.* The show opened in April at the Lyndon Baines Johnson Library in Austin, Texas with a reception hosted by Lady Bird Johnson. It then went on to Philadelphia, Minneapolis, St. Louis, Denver, Albuquerque, Los Angeles, San Francisco, Dallas, Houston, Atlanta, and New Haven. Records of the various transactions are in the archives of the American National Insurance Co. in Galveston, TX, and The Valley House Gallery of Dallas, TX.

44. "Museum Exhibit Celebrates America", *Hi-Desert Star* (Yucca Valley, CA), Aug. 25, 1976: 7.

45. Jennie Lusk, "Recalls America's Early Days", *Albuquerque (NM) Journal,* July 1, 1976: 29.

46. Burt Wasserman, "Sensitive Eye", *Courier-Post* (Camden, NJ), Oct. 4, 1976: 15.

47. Phillip A. Shreffler, "Star Spangled Art at Science Museum", *St. Louis (MO) Post Dispatch*, March 30, 1976: 32.

48. Victoria Donohoe, "His Magical Drawings Brightened Many Nights", *The Philadelphia Inquirer*, Sept. 28, 1975: 23.

49. The Biblical Arts Center in Dallas collection contained 441 Beale designs, most of the Old Testament, and 108 slides, most Beale-Owned. Luckily, before the fire, my wife and I obtained copies of the curator's detailed descriptions, so though the designs, the slides, and the original curator's notes were lost, we know what the designs and slides were and what they looked like.

50. Borton, Borton, *Before the Movies*, 27.

51. Colen made no explicit comment about owning the slides, probably because he was so invested in obscuring the fact that the Beale paintings were done for slide production. It is clear that Colen did own Beale's diary, family photos, etc., since he gave a collection consisting of the original diary and 29 other items to The Historical Society of Pennsylvania in 1973. (Colen Collection, Historical Society of Pennsylvania.) Presumably Colen would have obtained these items from the Beale family, not from Briggs, and it is likely that he obtained the slides at the same time, since Beale had purchased slides made from his designs and presumably kept them in his studio.

52. Leddick, "Notarized statement".

53. Hill, "'The Liberty' and Lantern Shows", 2–4.

54. In addition to The American Magic Lantern Theater touring group, AMLT helped establish a permanent Magic Lantern Theater at the Amish Experience tourist site and theater at Bird in Hand, near Lancaster, PA. For five years the theater operated a regular schedule of Christmas, Halloween, and Bible shows, all featuring Beale slides. It closed in 2021 due to the Covid pandemic.
55. Borton, Terry, interview with John Cech of National Public Radio, "Keeping the Lantern Lit". Oct. 10, 2002.
56. At the Lucas Museum of Narrative Art the Beale and Broadside collections are referred to as The Borton Magic Lantern Collection.
57. Beale to Harper and Brothers, publishers, September 15, 1909, BC/LMNA. In the letter Beale quotes the praise of Briggs while seeking work after his layoff from the Briggs firm. Because Briggs worked regularly with Harper and Brothers, and the reference could be easily checked, there is no reason to believe that Beale distorted or exaggerated Briggs's comment.
58. Bettmann, *Bettman, the Picture Man*, 51, 79.
59. Musser, *The Emergence of Cinema*, 36.
60. Barber, *Evenings of Wonder*, 501
61. Rhodes, *The Birth of American Horror Film*, 73–74.
62. Walsh, *Chasing Rainbows* (DVD).
63. Lindvall, *Sanctuary Cinema*, 48–49.
64. Guida, *A Christmas Carol*, 60.

Bibliography

Adler, Kathleen. "We'll Always Have Paris: Paris as Training Ground and Proving Ground." In *Americans in Paris: 1860–1900*, ed. Kathleen Adler, Erica E. Hirshler and H. Barbara Weinberg, 11–50. London: National Gallery Company, 2006.

Amateur Photographer Editor. "Lantern Slides from Book Illustrations". *American Amateur Photographer* 3, no. 2 (1891): 66.

— "Lantern Slide Methods". *American Amateur Photographer* 4, no. 3 (1892):158.

— "Lantern Slides from Book Illustrations". *American Amateur Photographer* 3, no. 2 (1891): 66.

— "Lantern Slides". *American Amateur Photographer* 10 (1898): 469.

— "Lantern Slides". *American Amateur Photographer* 12 (1900): 488.

American Historical Co. *Colonial and Revolutionary Lineages of America, Vol. 17.* New York: American Historical Co., 1953.

Amusement Supply Co. *Amusement for Profit.* Chicago: Amusement Supply Co., 1908.

Armed Forces Institute of Pathology. *List of Educational Aides.* Washington, DC: American Registry of Pathology, 1965.

Armstrong, Isobel. *Victorian Glassworlds: Glass Culture and the Imagination, 1830–1880.* London: Oxford University Press, 2008.

Askari, Kaveh. "Photographed Tableaux and Motion-Picture Aesthetics: Alexander Black's Picture Plays". In *Multimedia Histories: From the Magic Lantern to the Internet*, eds. James Lyons and John Plunkett, 194–208. Exeter, UK: University of Exeter Press, 2007.

Art News Editor. "Blythe and Beale Are Brought to Light". *Art News* 34, no. 29 (1936): 8.

—"The Whitney Museum". *Art News* 35, no. 37 (1937): 19.

Atterbury, Paul, Ellen Denker, and Maureen Balkin. *Twentieth-Century Ceramics: A Collector's Guide to British and North American Factory-Produced Ceramics.* New York: Sterling Publishing Co., 2006.

Axelrod, Alan. *The International Encyclopedia of Secret Societies and Fraternal Orders.* New York: Checkmark Books, 1997.

Bacon, A. *A Manual of Gesture, Embracing a Complete System of Notation, Together with the Principles of Interpretation, and Selections for Practice.* Chicago: J. C. Buckbee and Co., 1875.

Bak, Meredith A. "Ten Dollars Worth of Fun: The Obscured History of the Toy Magic Lantern and Early Children's Media Spectatorship". *Film History* (2015): 111–134.

Baker, J. J., after Mason, William. *Horizontorium, Philadelphia Bank, SW cor. Chestnut and Fourth Sts.* Philadelphia: Historical Society of Pennsylvania,1832.

Balzer, Richard. *Optical Amusements: Magic Lanterns and Other Transforming Images, A Catalog of Popular Entertainments.* Watertown, MA: Museum of Our National Heritage, 1987.

Barber, X. Theodore. "Phantasmagorical Wonders: The Magic-Lantern Ghost Show in Nineteenth-Century America". *Film History* 3 (1989): 73–86.

—"Evenings of Wonder: A History of the Magic Lantern Show in America". New York: New York University, unpublished Ph. D. dissertation, 1993.

—"The Roots of Travel Cinema: John L. Stoddard, L. Burton Holmes, and the Nineteenth-Century Illustrated Travel Lecture". *Film History* 5, no. 1 (1993): 68–84.

Barnes, Catherine Weed. "Lantern Slide Work". *American Amateur Photographer* 4, no. 2 (1892): 56.

Barnes, John. *Optical Projection: Barnes Museum of Cinematography, Catalogue of the Collection.* Saint Ives, Cornwall, UK: Barnes Museum of Cinematography, 1970.

—"The History of the Magic Lantern". In *Servants of Light*, edited by Dennis Crompton, Richard Franklin and Stephen Herbert. North Yorkshire, UK: The Magic Lantern Society, 1987.

—"The Classification of Magic Lantern Slides for Cataloguing and Documentation". In *Magic Images: The Art of Hand-Painted and Photographic Lantern Slides*, edited by Dennis Crompton, David Henry and Stephen Herbert, 75–84. London: The Magic Lantern Society, 1990.

Barnouw, Erik. *The Magician and the Cinema.* New York: Oxford University Press, 1891.

Barolsky, Paul. "There is no such thing as Narrative Art". *Arion, A Journal of Humanities and the Classics* Fall (2010): 49–62.

Baum, Frank L. *The Marvelous Land of Oz.* New York: Dover Publications, 1969.

Bayley, Child. *Modern Magic Lanterns: A Guide to The Management of the Optical Lantern, for the Use of Entertainers, Lecturers, Photographers, Teachers, and Others.* London: L. Upcott Gill, 1895.

Beach, F. C. "Lantern Slides and Lantern Slide Making". *American Amateur Photographer* 1, no. 4 (1889): 137.

Beadle, C. "Lantern Slide and Transparency Making". *Optical Magic Lantern Journal and Photographic Enlarger*, October (1890).

Beale, Edmund. "His New Panorama and Diorama of the Creation and Deluge". Newark, NJ: Promotional Card in BC/LMNA, 1851.

Beale, Joseph Boggs. "Diary". Philadelphia: (1856–1865). Colen Collection, Joseph Boggs Beale Papers, Historical

Society of Pennsylvania.

—"Letter to Parents". Aug. 16, 1857. Arthur Colen Collection, Joseph Boggs Beale Papers, Historical Society of Pennsylvania.

—"Base-Ball Match Between The 'Athletics,' of Philadelphia, and The 'Atlantics' of Brooklyn, Played at Philadelphia, October, 30, 1865." *Harper's Weekly* 9. Nov. 18 (1865): 733.

—"Burning of the Union League in Philadelphia." *Harper's Weekly* Sept. 22 (1866): 604.

—"New Building". *The Land Owner* Jan. (1872).

—"Offices of Baker and Co." *The Land Owner* Feb. (1873).

—"Grant-Honore Wedding." *Frank Leslie's Weekly* Nov. 7 (1874).

—"Notebook". (1800–1890). Rochester, NY: George Eastman Museum, Colen Collection, Box 8.

—"48 Historical Pictures". *The Catholic School Journal* 41, no. 1 (1941): 3.

—"48 Historical Pictures". *American Childhood* 41, no. 1 (1955): 2.

—"48 Historical Pictures". *The Instructor* 3, (1955).

Beale, Rupert. "Memoir." Arthur Colen Collection, Joseph Boggs Beale Papers, The Historical Society of Pennsylvania. n.d.

Beale, Seymour. "Influence of Mass and Line in Pictorial Photography". *American Amateur Photographer* 9, no. 4 (1897): 175.

Beito, David. *From Mutual Aid to Welfare State: Fraternal Societies and Social Services, 1890–1967.* Chapel Hill, NC: University of North Carolina Press, 2000.

Bettmann, Otto L. *The Bettmann Portable Archive.* New York: Picture House Press, 1966.

—*Bettmann the Picture Man.* Gainesville, FL: University Press of Florida, 1992.

Black, Alexander. *Miss Jerry.* New York: Charles Scribner's Sons, 1893.

Blades, W. C. *Negro Poems, Melodies, Plantation Pieces, Camp Meeting Songs, Etc.* Boston: The Gorham Press, 1922(?). Accessed 9.2.22. https://www.forgottenbooks.com/en/download/NegroPoemsMelodiesPlantationPiecesCampMeetingSongsEtc_10235153.pd.

Blitzer, Billy. *Billy Blitzer, His Story.* New York: Farrar, Straus and Giroux, 1973.

Blitzstein, Madeline. "How Fame Came After Death for the Artist Nobody Knew". *Every Week Magazine* Oct. 13, 1935. Syndicated nationally.

Bloxham, W. "New Method of Preparing Engravings for the Lantern". *Optical Magic Lantern Journal and Photographic Enlarger* May (1890): 92.

Blum, Alfred. "Lecture (Shakespeare)". In *Old England and New England*, by Alfred Blum. London, 1853.

Boggs, Joseph M. and Dennus W. Petrie. *The Art of Watching Films.* New York: McGraw Hill Co., 2008.

Bolger, Doreen. *In This Academy.* Philadelphia: The Academy of Fine Arts, 1976.

Bonte, C. H. "Beale Interest Revived at Modern Galleries". *The Philadelphia Inquirer*, April 9, 1936: 18.

Booker, Jeremy, Richard Crangle, and Martin Gilbert. *The Magic Lantern Dancer: The Choreutoscope and Its Place in the History of the Moving Image.* London: The Magic Lantern Society, 2023.

Bordwell, David and Kristin Thompson. *Film Art, An Introduction, Fifth Edition.* New York: McGraw Hill Co., 1997.

Borton, Terry and Deborah Borton. "How Many American Lantern Shows in a Year?" In *Realms of Light: Uses and Perceptions of the Magic Lantern from the 17th to the 21st Century*, eds. Richard Crangle, Mervyn Heard and Ine van Dooren. 105–115. London: The Magic Lantern Society, 2005.

—*Before the Movies: American Magic-Lantern Entertainment and the Nation's First Great Screen Artist, Joseph Boggs Beale.* New Barnet, Herts, UK: John Libbey Publishing Ltd., 2014.

—"238 Eminent Magic-Lantern Showmen: The Chautauqua Lecturers". *The Magic Lantern Gazette, A Journal of Research* 25, no. 1 (2013): 3–34.

—"Outstanding Colorists of American Magic Lantern Slides". *The Magic Lantern Gazette: A Journal of Research* 26, no. 1 (2014) 3–24.

—"The Professional Life of Magic Lantern Illustrated Lecturers: Part 1". *The Magic Lantern Gazette: A Journal of Research* 27, no. 1 (2015): 3–35.

—"The Professional Life of Magic Lantern Illustrated Lecturers, Part 2". *The Magic Lantern Gazette, A Journal of Research* 27, nos. 2–3 (2015): 3–39.

—"Tips on Giving Magic Lantern Shows, Nos. 1–10". *The Magic Lantern Gazette.* (2020–2022).

—"How Many Beale Slides Were Sold in America?" *Magic Lantern Gazette Research Issue* 35, no. 4, July (2025).

Bothamley, C. H. "Sunlight in Lantern Slides". *American Amateur Photographer* 2 (1898): 6.

Bowers, David Q. *Nickelodeon Theaters and Their Music.* New York: Vestal Press, 1986.

Briggs, Casper W. *Ledger, C. W. Briggs Company Records, 1890.* Rochester, NY: Sipley Collection, George Eastman Museum.

—*Picture [Blueprint] Catalog, 1893.* Philadelphia: C. W. Briggs Co., Sipley Collection, George Eastman Museum.

BriggsCo. *Educational Filmslides for Use with Standard 35mm Still Projection Apparatus.* Philadelphia: BriggsCo., 1930?.

Brigham, Nat. "The Brigham Illustrated Lectures, Perfect Projection Effects" (Advertisement). *The Lyceumite*, March, 1906.

Brooker, Jeremy, Richard Crangle, and Martin Gilbert. *The Magic Lantern Dancer: The Choreutoscope and Its Place in the History of the Moving Image.* London: The Magic Lantern Society, 2023.

Brooklyn Daily Eagle, The. "Immense Crowds Eagerly Scan the Bulletins". Cover, Nov. 4: 1891.

Broome, Clara S. Beale. n.d. "Memoir". *Joseph Boggs Beale.* Arthur Colen Collection, Joseph Boggs Beale Papers, Historical Society of Pennsylvania.

Brown, Joshua. *Beyond the Lines: Pictorial Reporting, Everyday Life and the Crisis of Guilded Age America.* Berkeley: University of California Press, 2002.

Brown, Kieran. *"How Chromatropes Work".* 2019. Accessed June 20, 2024. https://kieranbrowne.com/research/how-chromatropes-work.

Brown, Larry A. *How Films Tell Stories: The Narratology of Cinema.* Nashville, TN: Creative Arts Press, 2018.

Caldwell, Genoa. *Burton Holmes Travelogues: The Greatest Traveler of His Time, 1892–1952.* Koln, Germany: Taschen, 2006.

Casteras, Susan P. *The Defining Moment: Victorian Narrative Paintings from the FORBES Magazine Collection.* Charlotte, NC: Mint Museum of Art, 1999.

Chairman, Vice. Magic Lantern Society. "How I Became a Lanternist". *Optical Magic Lantern Journal* (1891): 111.

Choi, Younsun. *Historicizing Colonial Affect in Curriculum: Shaping the Ideal Man through Visuality.* Draft Ph. D. thesis, University of Wisconsin. n. d. Personal communication by email, 11.25.24.

Chute, R. J. "Making Lantern Slides". *The Magic Lantern* Sept. (1875).

Cinerama Exhibitors. "The Lowell Thomas Production of Seven Wonders of the World, as seen through the modern wonder of CINERAMA". London: Cinerama, 1956.

Claggett, Shalyn. "Immersive Media: Communal Identity and the Victorian Magic Lantern Show", *Nineteenth-Century Contexts* (2024). Accessed 4.15.23. doi:10.1080/08905495.2024.2299128.

Cohn, Neil, and Joseph P. Magliano. "Editor's Introduction and Review: Visual Narrative Research: An Emerging Field in Cognitive Science". *Topics in Cognitive Science* 12, no. 1 (2019). Accessed March 20, 2024. doi:https://doi.org/10.1111/tops.12473.

Colen, Arthur. "Introduction" in *Paintings by David Blythe; Drawings by Joseph Boggs Beale.* New York: Whitney Museum of American Art, 1936.

—"The Beale Portfolio". *The Grade Teacher.* Nov. 1941.

Collins, Herman, ed. *Philadelphia: A Story of Progress, Vol. 4.* New York: Lewis Historical Publishing Co., 1941.

Controllers of the Public Schools. *Annual Report.* Philadelphia: Philadelphia Board of Education [Pedagogical Library], 1858–1862.

Controllers of the Public Schools. *Report of Examiners.* Phildelphia: Philadelphia Board of Education [Pedagogical Library], 1862.

Dahl, Erik. *Udenlandske H. C. Andersen-illlustrationer: 100 billeder fra 1838 til 1968.* Copenhagen: Danish Typographers Assoc., 1969.

Davis, Susan. *Parades and Power: Street Theater in Nineteenth-Century Philadelphia.* Philadelphia: Temple University Press, 1986.

Davis, Theodore R. "How a Battle is Sketched." *St. Nicholas* 16 (1889): 661–68.

Delgado, Alan. *Victorian Entertainment.* New York: American Heritage Press, 1971.

Dellmann, Sarah. "Getting to Know the Dutch: Magic Lantern Slides as Traces of Intermedial Performance Practices". In *Performing New Media: 1890–1915*, Kaveh Askari, Scott Curtis, Frank Gray, Louis Pelletier, Tami Williams and Joshua Yumibe, eds. New Barnet, Herts, UK: John Libbey Publishing, Ltd., 2014.

Dibble, John Pierce. "Pop Dibble: 'Daddy of Them All', His Seventy Years Recollections of Picture Shows and Other Things, A Hodge-Podge of Memory", 1920?. Manuscript now in Huhtamo Collection.

Dicksee, F., Gilbert, J. (illustrators). In Longfellow's *Evangeline.* London: Petter and Galpin (Cassell), 1882.

Dugdale, Tony. "Preface". In *Magic Images: The Art of Hand-Painted and Photographic Lantern Slides*, Dennis Crompton, David Henry and Stephen Herbert, eds. London: The Magic Lantern Society, 1990.

Ebert, Roger, and Gene Siskel. *The Future of Movies.* Kansas City: Andrews and McMeel, 1991.

Eckhart, Joseph P. *The King of the Movies: Film Pioneer Siegmund Lubin.* Philadelphia: Fairleigh Dickinson University Press, 1997.

Editor. "Albert Barnes and Fidele". *Dog Art Today* Nov. 9. 2010. Accessed June 25, 2020. https://dreamdog-sart.typepad.com/art/2010/11/albert-c-barnes-and-fid%C3%A8le.html.

Editor. "Educational Series", *Wisconsin Jewish Chronicle*, June 26, 1942: 7.

Editor's Table. *Ladies' Repository*, Aug. 1851.

Editors. *The World Book.* Chicago: Field Enterprises, 1938.

Eisner, Will. *Comics and Sequential Art: Principles and Practices from the Legendary Cartoonist.* New York: W. W. Norton and Co., 2008.

—*Graphic Storytelling and Visual Narrative.* New York: W. W. Norton and Co., 2008.

Elsaesser, Thomas and Warren Buckland, *Studying Contempory American Film: A Guide to Movie Analysis.* New York: Oxford University Press, 2002.

Expert, An. *The Art of Projection and Complete Magic Lantern Manual.* London: E. A. Beckett, 1893.

Falk, Peter Hastings, ed. *The Annual Exhibition Record of the Pennsylvania Academy of the Fine Arts, 1807–1870.* Madison, CT: Sound View Press, 1988.

Farrington, W. D. "Photography and Illustration". *International Annual of Anthony's Photographic Bulletin* 8: (1896): 115–118.

Finlay, Nancy. *Inventing the American Past: The Art of F. O. C. Darley.* New York: New York Public Library, 1999.

Fleer Corporation. "Over 10,000 Teachers Are Using the Free Beale Portfolio No. 1". *The Grade Teacher.* Sept. 1941.

Fletcher, Angus. *Wonderworks: Literary Invention and the Science of Stories.* New York: Simon and Schuster, 2021.

Franck, Harry A. "Your stop in China takes you back 1000 years" (Advertisement). *The Literary Digest* May 12 (1929).

Frank Leslie's Weekly. "Station to Liberia at the Mount Olive Baptist Chapel" (Illustration). April 29 (1880).

Gage, Simon, and Henry Gage. *Optic Projection: Principles, Installation and Use of the Magic Lantern, Projection Microscope, Reflecting Lantern (and) Moving Picture Machine.* Ithaca, NY: Comstock Publishing Co., 1914.

Gaudreault, Andre, and Yves Bedard. *Cinema, 1900–1906.* Brussels: Federation Internationale des Archives du Film, 1982.

Gaudreault, Andre. "1904–1905: Movies and Chasing the Missing Link". In *American Cinema: 1899–1909.* Piscataway, NJ: Rutgers University Press, 2009.

Geil, William Edgar. "The Man of the Hour". *Talent* July (1906).

George Eastman Museum. *An American Century of Photography, 1840–1940: Selections from the Sipley/3M Collection,*

May 19–October 1, 1978. Rochester, NY: George Eastman Museum, 1978.

Giannetti, Louis. *Understanding Movies.* Upper Saddle River, N. J.: Pearson Education, Inc. (Prentice Hall), 2008.

Girling, Arthur N. *Stereoscopic Drawing: A Theory of 3-D Vision and its Application to Stereoscopic Drawing.* London: Reel Three-D Enterprises, 1990.

Glebas, Francis. *Directing the Story: Professional Storytelling and Storyboarding Techniques for Live Action and Animation.* Burlington, MA: Focal Press, 2009.

Gombrich, Ernst H. *The Story of Art.* London: Phaidon Press Ltd., 1995.

Grafly, Dorothy. "Solemn, Satirical Blythe; Beale, Betsy Ross' Great-Grandnephew". *The Art Digest* April 15, 1936.

Grant, Don, *Supreme Secretary, Supreme Lodge of the Knights of Pythias,* Morton, PA. Author's phone interview. Oct. 28, 2010.

Graphic, The. "General William Booth Lecturing". Jan. 3 cover (1891).

Griffith, Mrs. D. W. *When the Movies Were Young.* New York: Dover Publications, 1969.

Groce, George, and David Wallace. *The New York Historical Society's Dictionary of Artists in America, 1564–1860.* New Haven, CT: Yale University Press, 1957.

Guida, Fred. *A Christmas Carol and Its Adaptations: A Critical Examination of Dickens's Story and Its Production on Screen and Television.* Jefferson, NC: McFarland & Co., 2000.

Gusfield, Joseph. *Symbolic Crusade: Status Politics and the American Temperance Movement.* Urbana: University of Illinois Press, 1963.

Haller, Beth, and Robin Larson. "Persuading Sanity: Magic Lantern Images and the Nineteenth-Century Moral Treatment in America". *Journal of American Culture* Sept. (2005): 263.

Hand, A Practiced. *The Magic Lantern: Its Construction and Management.* London: Ward, Lock & Co., 1888.

Harbach & Co. *Motion Picture Machines, Magic Lanterns, Films, Slides.* Philadelphia: Harbach & Co., ca. 1903.

Harper's Weekly. "Madison Square, New York on Election Night". Nov. 17 (1881): 877.

—"Election Night in New York City". Nov. 14 (1896): 1116.

Hasluck, Paul. "Cinematograph Management". In *The Optical Lantern and Accessories: How to Make and Manage Them,* Philadelphia: David McKay, 1903.

Heard, Mervyn. *Phantasmagoria: The Secret Life of the Magic Lantern.* Hastings, UK: The Projection Box, 2006.

Henkes, Caroline. "Early Christmas Films in the Tradition of the Magic Lantern". In *Screen Culture and the Social Question, 1880–1914,* by Ludwig Vogel-Bienek and Richard Crangle, eds. 97–106. New Barnet, Hertz, UK: John Libbey Publishing Ltd., 2014.

Hepworth, T. C. *The Book of the Lantern: A Practical Guide to the Working of the Optical or Magic Lantern.* London: Hazell, Watson and Viney, Ltd., 1894.

Herbert, Stephen. *Magic Lantern Inventions: 75 US Patents: 1864–1904* (CD). East Sussex, UK: The Projection Box. 2002.

—*Eadweard Muybridge: The Kingston Museum Bequest.* Hastings, UK: The Projection Box, 2004.

Hill, Katherine Leddick. "'The Liberty and Lantern Shows". *Magic Lantern Bulletin* 4, no. 2 (1982): 2–4.

Holley, J. E. *The Bible in Pictures, Old Testament.* Los Angeles: National Pictures Service, Inc., 1926.

Hoopes, Donelson F. "American Narrative Painting". In *American Narrative Painting,* Nancy Wall Moore and Donelson F. Hoopes, eds. Los Angeles, CA: Los Angeles Museum of Art with Praeger Publishing, 1974.

Hrabalek, Ernst. *Lanterna Magica Optisches Spielzeug.* Munich: Keysersche Verlagsbuchhandlung, 1985.

Hubbard, Leonidas. "Mrs. Leonidas Hubbard, Jr., Traveler and Explorer". *Talent* Dec. (1906).

Hughes, W. C. "A Little Information about the Cinematograph". *Optical Magic Lantern Journal and Photographic Enlarger* 9 (1898): 9–10.

Huhtamo, Erkki. *Illusions in Motion: Media Archaeology of the Moving Panorama and Related Spectacles.* Cambridge: MIT Press, 2013.

Huntzicker, William. "Picturing the News: Frank Leslie and the Origins of American Pictorial Journalism." *1995 Symposium on the Antebellum Press, The Civil War, and Free Expression.* Chattanooga: University of Tennesee, 1995. http://cecasun.utc.edu/commdept/conference/98conf/Huntzicker.html.

Hynes, W. G. *Negro Looking Up.* Self Published, 1920?.

Illustrated London News. "Should Prison Life Punish or Redeem?" Feb. 25, 1922.

IMDb. *Advanced Title Search, Movies, By Year, American, 1990–2023.* Accessed May 24, 2023. https://www.imdb.com/search/title/?ref_=fn_asr_tt.

Interchange Editor. 1898. "The American Lantern Interchange Slides: The Hamilton Camera Club". *American Amateur Photographer* 10 no. 3 (1898): 115.

Jasper, Joanne. 1993. *The Collector's Encyclopedia of Homer Laughlin China.* Paducah, KY: Collector Books, 1993.

Johns, Elizabeth. "Drawing Instruction at Central High School and Its Impact on Thomas Eakins". *Winterthur Portfolio,* 15, no. 2 (*1980*).

Johnsen, Albert. 1950. *The House of Beadle and Adams and Its Dime and Nickel Novel: The Story of a Vanished Literature, Vol. 1.* Norman, OK: University of Oklahoma, 1950. https://www.ulib.niu.edu/badndp/bibindex.html .

Jones, Christopher P. *Great Paintings That Tell Stories.* Wilmington, DE: Thinksheet Publishers, 2023.

Kattelle, Alan. "The Marcy Sciopticon: An Improved Magic Lantern by a New England Inventor". *The New England Journal of Photographic History* 92 (1993): 7–10.

Kember, Joe. *Marketing Modernity: Victorian Popular Shows and Early Cinema.* Exeter, UK: Exeter University Press, 2009.

Kember, J. and Crangle, R. "Folk Like Us: Emotional Movement from the Screen and the Platform in British Life Model Lantern Slide Sets 1880–1910". *Fonseca: Journal of Communication,* 12 (2018): 118–133. Accessed Oct. 5, 2022. https://ore.exeter.ac.uk/repository/bitstream/handle/10871/36346/Kember%2c%20Folk%20Like%20Us.pdf?sequence=1&isAllowed=y.

Kleine Optical Co. *Complete Illustrated Catalog of Moving Picture Machines, Stereopticons, Slides, Films.* Chicago: Kleine

Optical Co., 1904 and 1905.

Kobayashi, Genjiro. "Utsushi-e". Princeton, NJ: Chou University Publishing (?), 1975.

Landy, L. H. *The Magic Lantern and Its Applications.* New York: E. & H. T. Anthony & Co., 1886.

Leddick (Hill), Katherine. "Notarized Statement on Source of Beale Slides", Oct. 26, 1983, BC/LMNA.

Lee, Laura. "Granddaddy of Movies, 94, Didn't Think They'd Amount to Anything". *Philadelphia Bulletin*, March 19, 1941.

Life Editor. "Speaking of Pictures...These Are By A Great Magic Lantern Artist". *Life* Jan. 8, 1940.

Lindvall, Terry. *Sanctuary Cinema: Origins of the Christian Film Industry.* New York: New York University Press, 2007.

Lipton, Lenny. *The Cinema in Flux: The Evolution of Motion Picture Technology from the Magic Lantern to the Digital Era.* New York: Springer, 2021.

Lomas, Sidney. "Seventy-Five Years of the Philadelphia Sketch Club." Philadelphia: Archives of Philadelphia Sketch Club. n. d. 13.

Lumsden, George. "Lantern Slides". *American Amateur Photographer* 9, (1897): 491.

Lyceumite & Talent. "Cartoon of Agents". June (1907).

Lyons, Maura. "Intermedial Magic Lantern Projections and Wartime Anxiety". In *Reckoning with Trauma: Intermedial Visual Culture and the Civil War.* De Moines, IA: Drake University, 2024. unpublished.

Macdonald, Damien. *Anatomy of Comics: Famous Originals of Narrative Art.* Paris: Flammarion, 2022.

Magic Lantern Editor. "Flashed Effect". *The Magic Lantern* June (1878).

—"Beware of Spurious Colored Slides". *The Magic Lantern* Sept. (1881): 57.

—*The Magic Lantern* 8, (1882): 4–6.

—"Living Statuary". *The Magic Lantern,* (1899).

—"Notes". *The Magic Lantern* 1 Feb. (1895).

Malan, Dan. 2002. "Gustave Dore: Magic Lantern Slides". *The Magic Lantern Gazette* 14, no. 2 (2002): 1–7.

—*Poe's The Raven: Ultimate Art Reference Book.* St. Louis, MO: MCE Publishing Co., 2021.

Mannoni, Laurent. *The Great Art of Light and Shadow: Archaeology of the Cinema.* Exeter, UK: University of Exeter, 2000.

Marcus, Robert. "Before the Movies, Americans Viewed the Civil War Through the Magic Lantern". *Military Images* Summer (2020).

Marshall, Nancy Rose, and Malcom Warner. *James Tissot: Victorian Life/Modern Love.* New Haven: Yale University Press, 1999.

Martin, Lynn, and Jackie Williams Fisher. "Williams Family Traveling Picture Show, 1901–1904". Presentation at the convention of *The Magic Lantern Society.* Tacoma, WA, Summer, 2003: 61.

McAllister, T. H. *Catalogue of Stereopticons, Dissolving View Apparatus and Magic Lanterns, with Extensive Lists of Views for Illustration of All Subject of Popular Interest.* New York: T. H. McAllister, Manufacturing Optician, 1880–1917.

—"The Economic Catalog". *Catalogue of Stereopticons, Dissolving Views, Apparatus, Magic Lanterns, with Extensive Lists of Views for Illustration of All Subject of Popular Interest.* New York: T. H. McAllister, Manufacturing Optician, 1900.

McCullough, David. *The Greater Journey: Americans in Paris.* New York: Simon and Schuster, 2011.

McIntosh Stereopticon. *Magic Lantern Slides, Projection Apparatus.* Chicago: McIntosh Stereopticon Co., 1897?.

Meadows, Mark Stephen. *Pause & Effect: The Art of Interactive Narrative.* Indianapolis, IN: New Riders, 2023.

Meisel, Martin. *Realizations: Narrative, Pictorial, and Theatrical Arts in Nineteenth-Century England.* Princeton, NJ: Princeton Unversity Press, 1983.

Miller, Fredric M., Morris J. Vogel, and Allen David, eds. *Still Philadelphia: A Photograpic History, 1890–1940.* Philadelphia: Temple Univrsity Press, 1983.

Miller, Marla. *Betsy Ross and the Making of America.* New York: Henry Holt and Co., 2010.

Milliette, Earl B. "Art Annals of the Central High School". *The Barnwell Bulletin* (The Barnwell Foundation), 1943.

Milner, C. Douglas. *Making Lantern Slides and Filmstrips.* London: The Focal Press, 1953.

Moens, Bart G. "Luminous Colours of the Magic Lantern: Shedding Light on the Palette of Life Model Slides". *Tijdschrift voor theater* (Academia.edu) (2019):13–39.

Monod, Paul. "The Magic Lantern from Theater to Film". Middlebury, Vt: Middlebury College Zoom presentation. Accessed 11.15.22.

Moore, Bond & Co. *Stereopticons, Lantern Slides, Moving Picture Machines.* Chicago: Moore, Bond & Co., 1907.

Moore, Duncan. "Size or Realism". *Optical Magic Lantern Journal* (1894): 55–56.

Morgan, J. A. *"Uncle Tom's Cabin" and Visual Literacy.* Columbia and London: University of Missouri Press, 2007. Accessed 10.3.22, from https://www.google.com/books/edition/_/IIZST4X2UIAC?hl=en&gbpv=1&pg=PR3&dq=Hammatt+Billings

Moshansky, Tim. *A to Z Guide to Film Terms.* Vancouver, B. C.: First Wave Publishing, 2007.

Mozley, Anita Ventura. "Introduction". In *Eadweard Muybridge: Muybridge's Complete Human and Animal Locomotion: All 781 Plates from the 1887 Animal Locomotion, Vol. 1.* New York: Dover Publications, 1979.

Musser, Charles. *The Emergence of Cinema: The American Screen to 1907, Volume 1.* Berkeley: University of California Press, 1990.

—*Before the Nickelodeon: Edwin S. Porter and the Edison Manufacturing Company.* Berkeley: University of California Press, 1991.

—*Politicking and Emergent Media.* Oakland: University of California Press, 2019.

Nelson, Richard Alan. "Propaganda for God: Pastor Charles Taze Russell and the Multi-Media Photo-Drama of Creation". In *Une Invention du Diable? Cinéma des Premiers Temps et Religion*, by Roland Cosandey, Andre Gaudreault and Tom Gunning, eds. 230–255. Lausanne: Editions Pavot, 1992.

New York State Archive. "Division of Visual Instruction, instructional lantern slides". *New York State Archive.* Accessed June 7, 2023. https://digitalcollections.archives.nysed.gov/index.php/Detail/collections/4243.

Nicol, John. "Lecturing with the Lantern". *American Amateur Photographer* 15, no. 12 (1904): 521.

Nodelman, Perry. *Words About Pictures: The Narrative Art of Children's Picture Books.* Athens, GA: University of Georgia Press, 1988.

Norton, C. Goodwin. *The Lantern and How to Use It.* London: Hazell, Watson and Viney, Ltd., 1893.

Oettermann, Stephan. *The Panorama: History of a Mass Medium.* New York: Zone Books, 1987.

OMLJ Editor. "Lecturers and Lanternists: American Enterprise". *Optical Magic Lantern Journal and Photographic Enlarger* 18, (1897): 179–180.

—"A Startling Optical Novelty; Photoramic and Phono-Photoramic Effects". *Optical Magic Lantern Journal and Photographic Enlarger* November 15 (1889): 44.

—"Notes (Hatch Slide Holders)". *Optical Magic Lantern Journal and Photographic Enlarger* 1 (1889).

—"Notes, Novel Improvements". *Optical Magic Lantern Journal and Photographic Enlarger* November 15 (1889): 41.

—"Notes". *Optical MagicLantern Journal and Photographic Enlarger* (1892): 99.

—"Notes". *The Optical Magic Lantern Journal and Photographic Enlarger* Nov. (1893).

—"The Decadence of Lantern Lectures and Its Cause". *Optical Magic Lantern Journal and Photographic Enlarger* (1894): 225.

—"Notes". (absurd comment) *Optical Magic Lantern Journal and Photographic Enlarger* 6 (1895): 17.

— "Correspondence". *Optical Magic Lantern Journal and Photographic Enlarger* Aug. (1896).

— "Notes". *Optical Magic Lantern Journal* June, (1896).

—Wallace and Others vs. Riley Brothers". *Optical Magic Lantern Journal and Photographic Enlarger* Oct. (1896).

—"Prominent Men in the Lantern World, New Series, No. 1: Mr. James Bamforth of Holmfirth, Yorkshire". *Optical Magic Lantern Journal and Photographic Enlarger* 13 (1902): 8.

Osterman, Mark. "Ivorytype". In *The Focal Encyclopedia of Photography: Digital Imaging, Theory and Applications, History, and Science*, Michael R. Peres, ed, Waltham, MA: Focal Press, 2007.

Parkes, James. "Dearth in Lanterndom". *Optical Magic Lantern Journal and Photographic Enlarger* 12, (1901): 67.

Patterson, Marie Louise. "Cinema Chrysalis". *Arts in Philadelphia*, June–July (1939): 11.

Peale, Rembrant. *Graphics: The Art of Accurate Delineation, A System of School Exercises.* Philadelphia: E. C. Biddle, 1850.

Peck, Annie S. "Story of the Conquest of Huascaran". *Bulletin of the Brooklyn Institute* (1909).

Perkins, T. "Notes on Lantern Slide-Making." *The Optical Magic Lantern Journal and Photographic Enlarger* May (1895).

Petersen, Robert S. *Comics, Manga, and Graphic Novels: A History of Graphic Narratives.* Santa Barbara, CA: Praeger, 2011.

Phantom, A Mere. *The Magic Lantern: How to Buy and How to Use It; Also, How to Raise a Ghost.* London: Houlston and Wright, 1870s?.

Philadelphia Photographer Editor. "Lantern Explosion". *Philadelphia Photographer* (1870): 95.

Phoenixmasonry Museum. "Knights of Pythias Ritual". *The Phoenixmasonry Masonic Museum and Library.* Accessed 5.28.23. http://www.phoenixmasonry.org/masonicmuseum/fraternalism/knights_of_pythias.htm.

Photo-Miniature Editor. "Untitled." *The Photo-Miniature: A Magazine of Photographic Informaton* (1898): 448–452. 460, 463.

—"Lantern Slides". *The Photo Miniature: A Monthly Magazine of Photographic Information* Dec. (1899): 458.

—"Editorial". *The Photo-Miniature: A Magazine of Photographic Information* (1899): 428–429.

—"Living Statuary". *Photo-Miniature: A Magazine of Photographic Information* (1899): 463.

—"Untitled". *Photo-Miniature: A Magazine of Photographic Information* Dec. (1899): 467.

—"Untitled". *Photo-Miniature: A Magazine of Photographic Information* Dec. (1900).

Photographic Times Editor. "Copyright". *Photographic Times-Bulletin*, July (1901): 295.

Pinkerton, Allan. *The Molly Maguires and the Detectives.* New York: G. W. Carleton Co., 1877.

Pollin, B. R. *Images of Poe's Work: A Comprehensive Descriptive Catalogue of Illustrations.* New York: Greenwood Press, 1989.

Potter, Russell. *Arctic Spectacles: The Frozen North in Visual Culture, 1818–1875.* Seattle: University of Washington Press, 1997.

Prout, Samuel. *Hints on Light and Shadow, Composition, etc.: As Applicable to Landscape Painting.* London: Ackerman, 1838.

Puck. "The Terror of the West". April 22 (1882).

Pumphrey, Alfred. "Robinson Crusoe". In *Lantern Readings, Original and Selected, To Accompany Sets of Photographic Transparencies, Vol. 1.* Birmingham, England: Alfred Pumphrey, n.d.

Quillay, Angelique. "The Collection of Magic Lantern Slides from the Pennsylvania Hospital for the Insane". In *A Million Pictures: Magic Lantern Slides in the History of Learning*, Sarah Dellmann and Frank Kessler, eds. New Barnet, Herts, UK: John Libbey Publishing Ltd., 2020.

R., W. A. "Reminiscences of my First Lantern Show". *Optical Magic Lantern Journal and Photographic Enlarger* (1890): 36–37.

Ranger, Robin. *The Magic Lantern.* New York: The Sunday School Union, 1862. Reprinted by The Magic Lantern Society.

Reader, A Cambridge. "My Clerical Lantern Work". *Optical Magic Lantern Journal and Photographic Enlarger*, Oct. (1895): 161.

Register. "Registration: or the Art of Dissolving with Precision". *Optical Magic Lantern Journal and Photographic Enlarger* (1891): 112–113.

Rehfuss, William. *A Treatise on Dental Jurisprudence for Dentists and Laywers.* Philadelphia: The Wilmington Dental Mfg. Co., 1892.

Reyniere, Grimond de la. "Untitled". *Le Courrier des Spectacles.* Feb. (1800). Quoted in Mannoni, 162.

Rhodes, Garry D. *The Birth of the American Horror Film.* Edinburgh: Edinburgh University Press, 2018.

Rice, Edwin. *The Sunday-School Movement, 1780–1917, and the American Sunday-School Union, 1817–1917.* Philadelphia: The American Sunday-School Union, 1917.

Ridely, James. *The Freemasons: A History of the World's Most Powerful Secret Society.* New York: Arcade Publishing, 1999.

Ripley, John W. "Romance and Joy, Tears and Heartache, and All for a Nickel". *Smithsonian,* March, 1982, 76–83.

Robb, Frances Osborn, David M. Robb, and Dale Roylance. *Star Spangled History: Drawings by Joseph Boggs Beale, Magic Lantern Artist, 1841–1926.* Galveston, TX: American National Insurance Co., 1976.

Robb, John. "Art (Pre)History: Ritual, Narrative and Visual Culture in Neolithic and Bronze Age Europe". *Journal of Archaeological Method and Theory, 2020.* Accessed March 8, 2024 on Academia.edu.

Robinson, David, Stephen Herbert, and Richard Crangle, eds. *Encyclopaedia of the Magic Lantern.* London: The Magic Lantern Society, 2001.

Robinson, David. "The Rise and Fall of the Triple Lantern". In *Servants of Light: The Book of the Lantern*, Dennis Crompton, Richard Franklin and Stephen Herbert, eds. 34. London: The Magic Lantern Society, 1997.

—*From Peep Show to Palace: The Birth of American Film.* New York: Columbia University Press, 1996.

Rood, A, et. al. *Trial and Conviction of Dr. Stephen T. Beale.* Philadelphia:T. K. Collins. 1855.

Rosenbloom, Stephanie. "The Art of Slowing Down in a Museum", *New York Times, Oct. 10, 2014.* Accessed 7.8.21. https://www.nytimes.com/2014/10/12/travel/the-art-of-slowing-down-in-a-museum.html.

Rossell, Deac, *Laterna Magica*Magic Lantern.* Vol. 1. Stuttgart: Fusslin Verlag, 2008.

— *Living Pictures: The Origins of the Movies.* Albany: State University of New York, 1998.

— "Double Think: The Cinema and Magic Lantern Culture". In *Celebrating the Centenary of Cinema: 1985*, edited by John Fullerton, 26–31, New Barnet, Herts, UK: John Libbey Publishing Ltd., 1998.

— *Chronology of the Birth of Cinema 1833–1896.* New Barnet, Herts, UK: John Libbey Publishing Ltd., 2022.

Routhier, Jessica Skwire, Kevin J. Avery, and Thomas Hardiman, Jr., eds, "The Panorama's Progress: A History of Kyle and Dallas's Moving Panorama of Pilgrim's Progress". In *The Painters' Panorma: Narrative Art and Faith in the Moving Panorama of Pilgrim's Progress*, by Jessica Skwire Routhier. Lebanon, NH: University Press of New England, 2015.

Russell, Charles Taze. *Photodrama of Creation: Science, History, Philosophy, Springing from the Hand of God.* Clawson, MI: International Bible Students Association, 1914.

Ryan, W. F. "Limelight on Eastern Europe: The Great Dissolving Views at the Royal Polytechnic". In *The New Magic Lantern Journal: The Ten Year Book.* London: The Magic Lantern Society, 1986.

Sabin, Roger. "Ally Sloper: The First Comics Superstar?" *Image [&] Narrative: Online Magazine of the Visual Narrative*, 7 ed. n.d. Accessed 1 13, 2023. www.imageandnarrative.be.

Schaefer, Susan C. "Illuminating the Devine: The Magic Lantern and Religious Pedagogy in the USA, ca. 1870–1920". *Material Religion* (2007). doi:10.1080/17432200.2017.1308176.

Schoff, S. S. *The Industrial Interests of Chicago.* Chicago: Knight & Leonard Book Printers, 1873.

Schuyler, Robert, and Edward James. *Dictionary of American Biography, Supplement Two.* New York: Charles Scribner and Sons, 1958.

Scottish Rite Masonic Museum & Library. "Illuminating Brotherhood: Magic Lanterns and Slides from the Collection". Lexington, MA, 2005. https://srmmlonlineexhibitions.omeka.net/exhibits/show/the-secret-society-lantern—ma /introduction-1.

Sears Roebuck. *Motion Picture Machines and Stereopticons.* Chicago: Sears Roebuck & Co., 1907.

Seldon, Charles M. *In His Steps: What Would Jesus Do?* New York: Street and Smith, 1896.

Sellin, David. *The First Pose: 1876: Turning Point in American Art—Howard Roberts, Thomas Eakins, and a Century of Philadelphia Nudes.* New York: W. W. Norton & Co., 1976.

Shepard, Elizabeth. "The Magic Lantern Slide in Entertainment and Education, 1860–1920". *History of Photography* April–June, 1987.

Showman, The. 1899. "The Correct Presentation of Dioramic Effects". *Optical Magic Lantern Journal and Photographic Enlarger* 10, (1899): 153.

Sipley, Louis Walton. "The Pictures of C. W. Briggs". *Pennsylvania Arts and Sciences* Dec. (1936): 228–231.

—"Philadelphia Presents". *Pannsylvania Arts and Sciences* (1936).

—"W. & F. Langenheim, Photographers". *Pennsylvania Arts and Sciences* Christmas (1937): 28.

—"The Magic Lantern". *Pennsylvania Arts and Sciences*, Fall (1939).

—*In Celebration of One Hundred Years of the C. W. Briggs Company of Philadelphia in the Business of Photography.* Philadelphia: The American Museum of Photography, 1939.

—*The American Museum of Photography.* Philadelphia: American Museum of Photography, 1940.

—"The First Museum of Photography". *Pennsylvania Arts and Sciences* (1941).

Smith, Lester. "Aladdin". In *The New Magic Lantern Journal: The Ten Year Book.* London: The Magic Lantern Society, 1986.

Smith, Page. *A People's History of the Post-Reconstruction Era: The Rise of Industrial America.* New York: McGraw Hill Book Co., 1984.

Society for Visual Education. "S.V.E. Kodachrome Slides". *AV Guide.* (1942).

—*Combined Catalog of Film Slides.* Chicago: Society for Visual Education, 1930s?.

Solomon, Charles. *Enchanted Drawings: The History of Animation.* New York: Random House, 1994.

Splitstone, F. J. "Our Sixtieth Birthday." *Leslie's Illustrated Weekly Newspaper* Dec. 15 (1915): 661.

Stebbins, Charles M. *The Bible Story in Pictures (Parts One and Two).* Kansas City: The Stebbins Publishing Co., 1914.

Stern, Madeline. *Purple Passage: The Life of Mrs. Frank Leslie.* Oklahoma City: University of Oklahoma Press, 1953.

Stieglitz, Alfred. "To Our Readers". *American Amateur Photographer* 7, no. 1 (1895): 24.

—"Some Remarks on Lantern Slides". *Optical Magic Lantern Journal and Photographic Enlarger* 8 (1897): 204–206.

Tapia, John E. *Circuit Chautauqua: From Rural Education to Popular Entertainment in Early Twentieth Century America.* Jefferson, NC: McFarlnd & Co., 1997.

Teale, Oscar S. "Stereoscopic Effects with the Optical Lantern". *Optical Magic Lantern Journal* 2, no. 29 (1891).

Tennant, John. 1914. "How to Make Lantern Slides". *Photo-Miniature* 12, no. 130 (1914): 472.

The Vampire Etcher, Editor, "Editorial". *The Vampire Etcher* 1, (1880): 1.

Time Editor. "The Professor". *Time* Aug. 19, (1935): 44–45.

Toulet, Emmanuelle. *Birth of the Motion Picture.* New York: Harry N. Abrams, Inc., 1995.

Unknown. "La Phantasmagoria". *La Feuille Villageoise* Feb 28, 1793. (Quoted in Mannoni, 506–7.)

Vestal, David. "Louis Walton Sipley". *Camera* 6, (1978): 30–41.

Vogel, Donald Stanley. *Memories and Images: The World of Donald Vogel and Valley House Gallery.* Dallas: University of North Texas Press, 2000.

Vulte, H. T. "Lantern Slides from Line Drawings or Engravings" in *The International Annual of Anthony's Photographic Bulletin* 5, 1892.

Wainwright, Nicholas B. "Education of an Artist: The Diary of Joseph Boggs Beale, 1856–1862." *The Pennsylvania Magazine of History and Biography* 97, no. 4, Oct. 1973.

Walsh, Stan. *Chasing Rainbows: The Story of Classic Travel Adventure Cinema* DVD. 2009?

Wamsley, Douglas. "The Sublime Yet Awful Grandeur: The Arctic Panoramas of Elisha Kent Kane". *The Polar Record* 35 (1999).

Wasserman, Burt. "Sensitive Eye". *Courier-Post (Camden, NJ),* Oct. 4, 1976: 15.

Welling, William. *Photography in America: The Formative Years, 1839–1900.* New York: Thomas Y. Crowell Co., 1978.

Wells, Kent. "The Stereopticon Men: On the Road with John Fallon's Stereopticon, 1860–1870". *The Magic Lantern Gazette, Research Edition* 23 no. 3 (2011): 2–35.

—"The Magic Lantern in American Churches Before 1860". *The Magic Lantern Gazette, Research Edition* 27, no. 4 (2015): 3–33.

Wilder, Charlotte. *The Story of the Very First Christmas.* Kansas City: The Stebbins Publishing Co., 1915.

Wilkie, Edmund H. "Optical and Mechanical Effects for the Lantern". *Optical Magic Lantern Journal and Photographic Enlarger* 9, (1898): 128–130.

Wilkinson, Kathleen. *Signs and Symbols: An Illustrated Guide To Their Origins and Meanings.* London: Dorling Kindersley, Ltd., 2008.

Willis, Artemis. "The Lantern Image between Stage and Screen." In *The Image in Early Cinema*, Scott Curtis, Philippe Gauthier, Tom Gunning and Joshua Yumibe, eds. 237–246. Bloomington: University of Indiana Press, 2018.

—"The Keystone 600 Version 2.0: Archival, Pedagogical and Creative Approaches to an Educational Lecture Series". In *A Million Pictures: Magic Lantern Slides in the History of Learning*, Sarah Dellmann and Frank Kessler, eds. New Barnet, Herts, UK: John Libbey Publishing Ltd., 2020.

—"Lantern Work, C. 1900". Presentation at Domitor Conference, 2020.

Wilson, Edward. "How To Start a Show". *The Magic Lantern* Nov. (1874): 35.

—"New and Novel Dissolving Effects". *The Magic Lantern* Jan. (1878): 2–3.

—"Abide With Me [Flight of the Soul]". *The Magic Lantern* Aug.–Sept. (1881): 37.

—"My Catalog". *The Magic Lantern* Oct.–Dec. (1882).

—"Editorial". *The Magic Lantern* Jan. (1885).

Wilson, Martin. "Lantern Slides". *American Amateur Photographer* 9, (1900): 400.

Winship, M. "The Greatest Book of Its Kind: A Publishing History of Uncle Tom's Cabin". The Amercan Antiquarian, (2002): 309–333. Accessed 10.3.22 from https://www.americanantiquarian.org/proceedings/44525181

Woodbury, Walter. "To Obtain Various Colours on Lantern Plates". *Optical Magic Lantern Journal and Photographic Enlarger* 5, Jan. (1893).

Index

Note: Items pertaining to Beale's life are listed under "Beale". Other items are listed separately. Types of lantern shows are listed under "magic lantern". Only Beale Sets or Groups that are discussed or pictured in the text are indexed, all in *italic*. For a list of all Sets or Groups see pp. 206–297 and 230–231. "Cinematic techniques" used by the magic lantern and the movies are in *italic* as they are in the text; "magic-lantern techniques" not usually employed by cinema are in ***italic bold***, as in the text. Not all instances of techniques are indexed.

M/N/O/P